ROM
ES

S. M. EISENSTEIN
Towards a Theory of Montage

S. M. EISENSTEIN

Selected Works

VOLUME II

Towards a Theory of Montage

Edited by

MICHAEL GLENNY AND RICHARD TAYLOR

Translated by

MICHAEL GLENNY

BFI PUBLISHING
London

S. M. Eisenstein
SELECTED WORKS
General Editor: Richard Taylor
Consultant Editor: Naum Kleiman
Volume II: Towards a Theory of Montage
Edited by Michael Glenny and Richard Taylor

First published in 1991 by the
British Film Institute
21 Stephen Street
London W1P 1PL

British Library Cataloguing in Publication Data
Eizenshtein, Sergei *1898–1948*
Selected works Vol. 2. Towards a Theory of Montage
1. Soviet Union. Cinema films
I. Title   II. Glenny, Michael   II. Taylor, Richard *1946*
III. British Film Institute
791.43
ISBN 0-85170-211-2

Typeset by Discript, London
Printed in Great Britain by
St Edmundsbury Press
Bury St Edmunds, Suffolk

*This volume
is dedicated to the memory of
Jay Leyda (1910–88)
who first saw the ray of light
in the realm of darkness*

Contents

General Editor's Preface

Sergei Eisenstein is by general consent the most important single figure in the history of cinema. His contribution to the practice of film-making is universally acknowledged and his films, from *The Strike* to *Ivan the Terrible*, are well known, if not always as widely shown as we might assume. But the bulk of Eisenstein's theoretical writings has remained largely inaccessible and, despite the invaluable efforts of Jay Leyda in particular, the English-speaking world has only a partial acquaintance with the ideas that underlay his films.

It is the primary purpose of this edition to make available the most important of Eisenstein's writings in a comprehensive and scholarly, but nevertheless accessible form to the English-speaking reader for the first time. The nature of those writings has posed considerable editorial problems for the organisation of the volumes in the series. We have opted wherever possible for a chronological approach: the ultimate justification is quite simply that this is the order in which Eisenstein himself wrote and therefore the order that enables the reader most easily to trace the development of his ideas. The first and third volumes in this edition therefore follow Eisenstein's career from his first published article in November 1922 to his death in February 1948. The documents have been chosen not merely to record the development of his aesthetic ideas but also to illuminate the context in which that development occurred.

Sometimes the sheer amount of material has rendered a chronological approach unsustainable, as in this volume, *Towards a Theory of Montage*: here understanding is better served by grouping Eisenstein's sometimes fragmentary and often unfinished writings on montage from the 1930s and 1940s together in one large volume. It has nevertheless proved necessary to exclude some material, as explained in the Note on Sources.

It is the aim of this edition to make Eisenstein and his ideas more accessible to the English-speaking reader. If the organisation of the volumes or the quality of the translations or the annotation obstructs that purpose, then we shall not only have failed in our duty to the reader, we shall have failed in our responsibility towards Eisenstein.

RICHARD TAYLOR
Swansea, Wales
July 1991

Michael Glenny: An Appreciation

Michael Glenny began work on the Eisenstein papers that were eventually to form the backbone of this volume in 1975 when he was a National Endowment of the Humanities Fellow at the University of Southern Illinois at Carbondale. He died in Moscow on 1 August 1990 a few days after the translations were completed.

Nobody has done more to bring to the English-speaking reader the enormous variety and complexity of twentieth-century Russian cultural life. Michael's translations have brought to life the otherwise linguistically incarc-erated ideas of people as different as Isaak Babel and Marina Tsvetayeva, Vladimir Nabokov and Mikhail Bulgakov, Alexander Solzhenitsyn and Boris Yeltsin. He had the unique ability to translate Russian texts in a way that made them read and sound as though they had originally been written in English. His acute and musical ear was complemented by a working knowl-edge of a dozen languages and both these factors made him the perfect translator for a man of the depth and breadth of Sergei Eisenstein.

Michael bore his gifts lightly: his professionalism was leavened by a heightened sense of the absurd, his conversation peppered with an extraor-dinarily infectious laugh. Yet he, more than anyone, exemplified the notion that translation is not merely a skill, or even a craft, but an *art*. He felt very strongly that translation was a creative activity and an undervalued one, and he gave vent to this feeling on a number of occasions. One of his more restrained statements on the subject was his contribution to the *Times Literary Supplement* symposium in October 1983 to mark the twenty-fifth anniversary of the Translator's Association. There, and elsewhere, he argued that the relationship between the translator and the original author was similar to that between a musician and a composer, or an actor and a playwright. It is a useful analogy, because it emphasises that the nature of the relationship is symbiotic, rather than parasitic, as some would argue.

There is however one essential difference between the performing artist and the translator. The musician or actor appears before the public, even in a sound recording or a radio performance. He or she is highly, and in the present day increasingly, *visible*. His or her performance is compared minutely, sometimes agonisingly, with that of others, both for its inherent virtues and for its fidelity to the original, whatever that might be. The tragedy of the translator is that his or her success is crowned with *invisibility*: the reader only notices a translation when it is a bad one, when the translation interferes with the process of communication between the original author and the public. It is as if we might notice a musician only when he plays out of tune, or an actress when she fluffs her lines.

It would be no exaggeration to say that, in dealing with the enormous range and complexity of Eisenstein's thought, Michael's talents as translator were at their most invisible. In the piece I have already mentioned, he wrote:

> Yet there is such a thing as a special translating talent, motivated by an urge to communicate between cultures; it is essential for the health of civilization. Where would we be without the labours of those paladins of translation, the anonymous Jacobean divines who gave us the Authorized Version of the Bible?

There could be no better or more lasting memorial to Michael Glenny than for the reader of this volume to ask where he or she would be without the labours of this particular paladin of translation.

Michael could justifiably borrow the epigraph from Pushkin's poem: *Exegi monumentum.*

RICHARD TAYLOR

Note on Sources

The contents of this second volume of Eisenstein's *Selected Works* were left at the time of his death largely in draft form. That is why we have given the volume the somewhat tentative title, *Towards a Theory of Montage*.

In the early 1930s Eisenstein had written the first volume of his work on 'Direction' (*Rezhissura*), entitled 'Mise en scène', but had no time to start the second volume, 'Mise en cadre', before he began filming the ill-fated *Bezhin Meadow* in 1935. Only ' "Eh!" On the Purity of Film Language' was published in May 1934 (see vol. 1, pp. 285–94).

After the filming of *Bezhin Meadow* was stopped on official orders in March 1937 and Eisenstein was forced to publish a self-critical article, 'The Mistakes of *Bezhin Meadow*', he returned to his notes on montage. The manuscript from the draft introduction to 'Unity in the Image' was written between April and November 1937 in Kislovodsk and Pyatigorsk, two spa towns close together in the Caucasus, where Eisenstein spent the summer and autumn of that year. The content is based on the lectures he had given at VGIK, the Film Institute in Moscow where he had become Professor of Direction in January 1937. But Eisenstein did not avail himself of the stenographic records of his lectures that were kept at the Institute, relying instead on his memory. There are two possible explanations for this: on the one hand, they were quite simply too heavy for him to carry; on the other, he left rather suddenly for the Caucasus, almost certainly at the suggestion of the writer Isaak Babel, because his life was in danger after what he himself called 'the catastrophe of *Bezhin Meadow*'.

In Kislovodsk Eisenstein began to write this material out for the first time as a text rather than a course of lectures and the themes covered in Part One, 'Montage in Single Set-Up Cinema', are essentially those that he would have tackled in 'Mise en cadre'. 'Unity in the Image' was finished just before he began work on his next film *Alexander Nevsky*, at which point he broke off writing 'Montage'. The true position of 'Tolstoy: *Anna Karenina* – the Races' is not known, so it has been placed where it seems to fit most closely. It could have been followed by 'Stanislavsky and Loyola' but we chose to exclude this on grounds of both the length of the volume overall and the fragmented state of this particular part of the manuscript. 'El Greco and Cinema', first written in September 1937 as part of 'Montage 1937', was moved by Eisenstein in 1939 to form part of his book on 'Direction'.

Once *Alexander Nevsky* was completed in the autumn of 1938, Eisenstein constituted 'Montage 1938' (originally subtitled 'Horizontal Montage') from notes and fragments of the materials for 'Montage 1937', which explains why there is some repetition. It was first published in January 1939 in the journal *Iskusstvo kino*. In 1939 he began 'Montage 1939', which became 'Vertical Montage', was finished in 1940 and first published, again in *Iskusstvo kino*, in two parts in September 1940 and January 1941. What began life as 'Montage 1940' and was written in that year was revised to become part of *Nonindifferent Nature* entitled 'Once Again on the Structure of Things' and contributed also to his writings on colour.

The order in this volume has been established by the team of Soviet scholars working under the guidance of the Consultant Editor, Naum Kleiman, the Director of the Central Film Museum, and is based on the Eisenstein collections of TsGALI, the Central State Archive for Literature and the Arts, in Moscow.

R. T.

Eisenstein on Montage
Geoffrey Nowell-Smith

There is nothing mystical about montage. Montage is the ordinary word for film editing in French and in Russian (*montazh*), Italian (*montaggio*) and Spanish (*montaje*). It is a word with strong practical and even industrial overtones. *Chaine de montage* is the French phrase for a factory assembly line, and the same association between splicing together bits of film and other forms of construction exists in English where the word assembly is used by film-makers to denote the stage when the footage for a film is put together in playing order prior to the actual cut. Montage and assemblage are also terms used in art practice to describe ways in which materials from different sources are put together to produce an object.

The idea of film-making as construction and montage as the putting together of parts of a machine (a machine for signifying, rather as Le Corbusier conceived of houses as machines for living in) had a strong appeal in modernist circles in the early years of the Russian Revolution. It can be found in some of Eisenstein's early writings on film aesthetics and can be plausibly held to underlie his editing and mode of film construction in *The Strike* and *The Battleship Potemkin* (1925). But by the early 1930s such ideas were dangerous heresy and people who espoused them and put them into practice were being forced to recant or desist or face the penalties of disgrace. Eisenstein's mentor, the great Vsevolod Meyerhold, was among the disgraced, and Eisenstein himself was in deep trouble early in 1937 after the denunciation of his film *Bezhin Meadow*. His return to the subject of montage in the essays that comprise this volume was therefore a matter of more than academic interest. Would he stand by his earlier beliefs, would he recant, or would he surprise the world by having something new and different to say?

There is an element of recantation in the montage essays, symbolised by some embarrassingly sycophantic remarks about Stanislavsky and a corre-sponding silence about Meyerhold; there are also passages of stout defence of his earlier positions; but most of what he writes in these essays is entirely original and represents a deeply thought reworking of all his ideas – not just those on montage as such, but on cinema in general, and indeed on art as a whole.

While the most obvious pressure on Eisenstein to change his ideas came from the political sphere, a more profound reason was aesthetic. The coming of synchronised sound to the cinema had fundamentally changed the limits of what cinema could be, opening up many new avenues but closing down others. Although sound as such could be counted an addition to the range of cinematic possibilities, synchronised dialogue should rather be reckoned a constraint – or so many film-makers thought, Eisenstein included.* Dialogue functioned as a restriction not only on the variety of things that could be done with the image but also on the potential of the soundtrack itself, subordinating it to the requirements of a type of dramaturgy that film-makers had hoped to be able to turn their backs on. Early technology imposed severe limits on how dialogue could be recorded, so that once the principle of synchronised dialogue was accepted its enactment had to be on extremely conventional lines. But accepted the principle had to be; once the dialogue film had caught on there was no opposing its rise to dominance as the only cinematic mode audiences would accept.

Strange though it may seem at first, the coming of sound to the cinema worldwide and the imposition of socialist realism in the Soviet Union are related events. Both represent a similar turn away from modernism and a turn towards (or a rejoining with) a humanist notion of realism that modernism had repudiated. By restoring voice to the actor's persona the dialogue film reasserted human integration; by giving primacy to the exchange of words between characters it put focus on individual human attributes. These effects, demanded of the sound film throughout the world, fit perfectly with the demands of socialist realism for a new conception of the hero and its associated humanist rhetoric. The combination was lethal. The sound film, developed throughout the world as dialogue film, becomes in the Soviet context the favoured vehicle for the populism and pseudo-humanism of Stalinist ideology.

Eisenstein saw this. But there was nothing he could do about it. Both the dialogue film and socialist realism had to be lived with. After a desperate period in the early and mid-30s when he attempted not to live with them, his response in practice comes in 1938, with the triumph of *Alexander Nevsky*, and in theory in 1937–40, with his essays on montage. The basic strategy of the essays is that of counter-offensive. Rather than see the concept of montage limited to that of a special case of film editing, he argues that montage as he had himself conceived it in his earliest writings on the subject is in fact a special case of montage in general, which is a principle to be found underlying artistic construction of all kinds. Within this enlarged concept of montage, which he had already begun to elaborate in 1928–29,† he is then able to include not only the pieties that he was obliged to subscribe to but many aspects of artistic practice that he had come to believe in and respect.

*See his 'Statement on Sound' (co-signed by Vsevolod Pudovkin and Grigori Alexandrov), on pp. 113–14 of Volume I of this edition.
†See in particular the articles 'Perspectives' and 'The Dramaturgy of Film Form' (Vol. I, pp. 151–60 and 161–80) for an early and rather rough-hewn formulation of the 'enlarged' concept.

Eisenstein's original concept of montage was that meaning in the cinema was not inherent in any filmed object but was created by the collision of two signifying elements, one coming after the other and, through the juxtaposition, defining the sense to be given to the whole. The obvious vehicle for such a form of meaning-construction is the shot, which within the conception needs to be a relatively simple element. But what if it is not simple? What if it contains within itself juxtapositions of different elements, whether contained within the composition or produced by camera movement or movement within the frame? And what about the juxtapositions created by the coincidence or collision of sound and image in the synchronised film? Does this undermine the concept of montage, or provide a case for its extension?

In the 1937–40 essays, Eisenstein divides montage into three types: montage in single set-up cinema; montage in multiple set-up cinema; and sound-film montage. The second of these corresponds roughly with the concept of montage he had developed in the silent period, since it covers the effects that are produced by the sequential movement from one set-up to the next. Both the first and the third, however, deal – at least in principle – with the montage of simultaneous elements, in cinema and in art generally. The argument rambles somewhat (with the exception of the last two, these essays were never revised for publication in his lifetime), but the central line of it is clear: montage exists not only in time but in space, and not only in the object but, crucially, in the perception of it. Montage as a principle is not limited to cinema: it is found in literature, in theatre, in music, in painting, even in architecture. But it is in cinema that it finds its highest expression. Not only that, but it is through montage that cinema becomes the first art form successfully to transcend the dichotomy posed by Lessing in his *Laocoön* between the sphere of painting, which is spatial, and that of poetry, which is temporal. These propositions are illustrated by a wide and eclectic range of examples, from Homer to nineteenth-century Russian realist painting. In the Athenian Acropolis Eisenstein finds an example of the disposition of masses in space which can only be grasped in its ensemble through a montage effect. In a portrait of the actress Maria Yermolova by Valentin Serov, he finds a two-dimensional static object which only yields up its secrets when reconceived as a series of views akin to a progression of shots in cinema. From an analysis of the rhythm and imagery of a poem by Pushkin, he shows how cinematic montage can realise what in poetry can only be imagined.

What these examples do not address, however, is the problem of how representation relates to reality. This was a question Eisenstein knew he could not evade but for which it was very difficult for him to find an answer that would satisfy both himself and his detractors. The answer he proposes is at first sight familiar and orthodox enough, and is based on a distinction between two levels at which representational works of art can operate: 'depiction' (*izobrazhenie*) and 'image' (*obraz*). The problem for the artist is how to get beyond depiction and organise the material before him into images which are not only aesthetically satisfying but also succeed in crystallising within them the truth of the object represented. This distinction is suspiciously similar to that made by the Marxist aesthetician György Lukács between description and narration and to analogous distinctions made by other Marxist writers of the period, all aimed at separating a superficial level of verisimilitude from a deeper level of actual truth. Most of these Marxist writers, however, Lukács included, regard truth as already given in History, so that the artist's job is limited to finding a means of joining up what is easily seen and depicted or described with the deeper level of truth revealed by history (and Marxist interpreters thereof).

Eisenstein's distinction between 'depiction' and 'image' is far less historicist and far more properly aesthetic. It is also heuristic in the sense that the finding of a new image creates a new form of knowledge rather than merely replicating something already known. Part of the function of the image, undoubtedly, is to capture 'reality' in the most condensed and effective manner possible – meaning by reality the facts of history that pre-exist the work of art and provide the artist with material. But this aspect of conforming to already given truth is the one which interests Eisenstein the least. Or rather, what interests him is not this truth-bearing function but the fact that in order to achieve it in a work of art you have to proceed in an imagistic way, that you have to produce images which are by their nature metaphorical rather than literal. If history is determining on the shape to be taken by a work of art it is not because it tells the artist what is true (and must therefore be portrayed as such) but because it constrains the artist in his or her choice of metaphor. Colour, for example, as a mere property of the physical world, has no meaning except in so far as it can be used as metaphor, and what this metaphor can be is not pregiven by the nature of colours themselves but arises out of a complex cultural process through which values are assigned to different colours and colour-words in different contexts.

Eisenstein's notion of the image could thus be defined as standing midway between Marxism and Symbolism – Marxist in its recognition of the social determination of meaning, Symbolist in its insistence on the image as vehicle of artistic expression. Also partly derived from Symbolism, but interpreted in a Marxist and materialist way, is his fundamental intuition that image, metaphor and montage are at bottom the same thing: that images are created when the terms of a metaphor are articulated through montage; that a metaphor which does not give rise to an image is a dead metaphor and an image that has no metaphoric weight is not an image at all; and that montage achieves its destiny only when it escapes from the metonymic linkage of object to object and achieves the metaphoric association, through the image, of object and idea. In this sense, for Eisenstein there is something mystical in montage after all.

On the Story of 'Montage 1937'
Naum Kleiman

The reader who is not very familiar with the details of Eisenstein's life will probably be surprised at some of the rhetorical passages to be found in the pages that frame his work *Montage*, a work which bears an eloquent date – 1937.

How could a man who was both clever (one of the cleverest of his generation, according to the evidence of his contemporaries) and honest (even his enemies never doubted that) write these lines in the Foreword in the very year that the Stalinist terror culminated?

> The twenty years of our victorious Revolution – an event of unprecedented scope – have proved the greatness of the slogan 'All is for man's sake' as a stimulus to unheard-of triumphs'?!

Surely he must have known about the unparalleled repressions and the unheard-of human sacrifices in that anniversary year?

How dare an acknowledged art theorist maintain in the concluding section that the synthesis of the arts was organic specifically to the coming epoch, because it 'reflected the full-blooded joy of contemporary man' and contrasted with the 'anatomical atlas' of the aesthetics of, for instance, architectural modernism? And the man who made this statement was supposedly proud of his acquaintance with none other than Le Corbusier himself?!

Nevertheless these and similar phrases reflected a genuine tragedy: the personal, biographical tragedy of Eisenstein, the tragedy of the 20s avantgarde, the tragedy of Russian public consciousness at that time.

First of all, Eisenstein did not just know of the repressions by hearsay – he himself had become a victim of them at the beginning of the year, although fortunately this had not ended in his arrest, shooting, or transportation to the camps. The price he paid for this was his 'baby', his film *Bezhin Meadow*, which had been taken out of production on the eve of its completion, publicly disgraced and physically destroyed. The director nearly shared the same fate: indeed it was to this end that the whole campaign against the film, unleashed by the head of Soviet cinema, Boris Shumyatsky, was directed. A period of 'witch-hunts' always requires people who can be accused of 'disorganisation', of 'decadence' and of 'straying from the true path', especially if they are ready to accuse you of the same thing. Eisenstein was particularly suited to the role of scapegoat: he was too independent, too ironic and, in many people's opinion, excessively learned, and, on top of all that, he was constantly filming things that did not quite correspond to what those people in high places who issued the 'orders' considered worthwhile. Hence he filmed *Bezhin Meadow* not as a poem about a 'young hero of our time' exposing his kulak father, but as a tragedy of patricide and filicide against the background of the rapid reordering of the countryside, of society, and of religious beliefs. . . .

In the spring of 1937, after a series of screenings of the incomplete and unedited footage of *Bezhin Meadow*, accompanied by discussion (i.e. condemnation) of it, after the enforced repentance of the article 'The Mistakes of *Bezhin Meadow*', written literally under the threat of arrest, which his former friend Grigori Alexandrov had openly hinted at to him, Eisenstein suffered a psychological crisis. One day (according to the reminiscences of Pera Atasheva that she shared with me in 1964) Sergei Mikhailovich did not leave his room for either breakfast or lunch. It was a sign of severe depression when he 'didn't shave and didn't eat'. After repeated requests that he should at least say something, Eisenstein suddenly called out from behind the door that, if he did come out, it would only be so that he himself could go and tell 'them' once and for all exactly what he thought of them, and then – come what may. Pera was terrified and decided to telephone Isaak Babel, whose stock with Eisenstein as a wise and experienced adviser was particularly high. Eisenstein let Babel into his bedroom immediately. It seemed to Pera as if they talked for an eternity. All of a sudden they came out together and Eisenstein asked Pera to do him a favour: to deliver a letter that he would now write. Shortly afterwards he handed her an envelope on which he had written this address: J. V. Stalin, The Kremlin, Moscow.

This letter from the disgraced director to the omnipotent dictator is probably preserved in the Kremlin archives, which are still closed to cinema historians. Only the draft is known to us and in it we can decipher individual phrases like: 'I am asking not for privilege, but for trust', 'I feel I have within me the strength to make many more *Potemkins*'. . . In the draft there is no trace of repentance for his film 'mistake'. We cannot exclude the possibility that Babel participated in the writing of this absolutely crucial text, a simple request for a favour which should in no way be represented as a grovelling entreaty for forgiveness. Pera immediately took the typed envelope to Red Square and put it in the special post-box for the 'royal personage' which was situated, if I am not mistaken, not far from the Saviour's (Spasskaya) Tower.

However the letter was still no guarantee against arrest. It is probable that it was that very same wise and experienced Babel who, although he was unable to save himself, advised Eisenstein to leave Moscow straight away. There was, of course, no question of adopting a conspiratorial life-style: under Stalin's régime this was quite simply impossible, even for a prominent artist. Sometimes, however, the people for whom the NKVD came in the night were saved by the simple fact that they were not at home. It was always possible that the executioners would move on 'in accordance with the plan' to their next victims the following night. In any event Eisenstein tried to leave as soon as possible for a sanatorium in the Northern Caucasus, in the city of Kislovodsk. It was here, away from film production and far from 'criticism' that he began the book that he had announced as a sequel to his textbook on direction before he started filming *Bezhin Meadow* in 1934 (see his note on the subject in ' "Eh!" On the Purity of Film Language'). The first pages – the 'Foreword' – were, as was usual for him, done in a rush and were confined to rough notes on his chosen theme. But Eisenstein really threw himself into it and in twenty or thirty days he had filled as many pages. We cannot discount the possibility that this kind of feverish activity while his heart was recovering was a form of salvation from dark thoughts. . . .

When Yelena Sokolovskaya, the head of the Mosfilm studio, wrote and informed Eisenstein on 18 May that she was trying to secure a script by Pyotr Pavlenko about Alexander Nevsky for him, he began to suspect that his letter had had an effect. This was confirmed after his return to Moscow when his arch-enemy Boris Shumyatsky offered him a choice of patriotic heroes as the subject for a film: either the merchant Minin and Prince Pozharsky, who had led the struggle against the Polish intervention in 1612, or Prince Alexander Nevsky, who had beaten the Germans in 1242. Behind this proposal, of course, lay an instruction from the Leader himself, who had 'entrusted' Eisenstein with one more production. This is not the place to examine the way in which the director used this trust to re-work a one-dimensional agitational script by a semi-official writer into a film fresco about a prince who had been canonised by the church and who was at the same time Eisenstein's 'family saint' through his mother's line, the Konetskies. But even the preparation for the film could not tear him away from the book that he had begun: he carried on working on it until deep into the autumn.

Pera Atasheva recalled that for Eisenstein 1937 was, above all else, a year of financial problems. Eisenstein had not completed a single film since *The General Line* in 1929 and this meant that he did not receive a director's fee. Following the accusations against *Bezhin Meadow* for 'Formalism and mysticism', he was driven out of the Institute of Cinematography (VGIK), and this meant that he was deprived of his professorial salary. The advance for *Nevsky* went on the most pressing needs. The book *Montage* might provide another advance, if Goskinoizdat agreed to take it. In order to make sure that the cinema publishing house took the manuscript for consideration, certain rituals had to be observed. The crudest and most essential of these rituals was the direct glorification of the 'genial leader of the peoples'. As far as possible Eisenstein tried to avoid this. There were other methods: citing the classics of Marxism, for example, or authorities recognised by the state. That is probably the origin of the 'Foreword' based on an aphorism of the state writer, Maxim Gorky, 'All is in man – all is for man's sake!'

We should not however suppose – or so it seems to me – that this was nothing more than political camouflage. Or that it was merely a polemical attack on the critics who had long ago accused Eisenstein of 'inhumanity' because he made historical film frescoes rather than psychological dramas. Behind the Gorky quotation were some very serious ideas about how the 'human scale' in cinema could consist not only in the appearance of a character on the screen but in the actual construction, the structure of a work. In fact, this is what his text-book on direction had been about – and *Montage* was supposed to constitute its second part. These very ideas reflected the crisis of the Constructivist illusions of the 20s, which had sought to base structural laws above all on non-subjective and, generally speaking, on non-human principles: on material, on mechanism, on non-personal history... Eisenstein's concepts of the late 20s and 30s ('inner monologue' or the 'organicity of art', for instance) broke with the mechanicism of his early declarations. For this reason both the 'Foreword' and some of the vulgar formulations in the last chapter (written rather obviously for the censor) deal with very serious matters. It is important in this context to catch the nuances: in a period dominated by pseudo-Classicism Eisenstein admits that he liked Le Corbusier and Gropius. He does not argue against these 'pillars of Formalism' but against their imitators... Nowadays these nuances can only be discerned by a historian: in those days phrases like that sounded almost like a challenge.

However the real challenge was *Montage* as a whole. It cannot be included in the aesthetics of Socialist Realism, which was then advancing on a broad front: there are no declarations about *narodnost'* and *partiinost'* in this book, no invocations of the 'truth of life', which would supposedly preserve a work by its expressiveness and its effectiveness. Had it been published at the end of the 30s, it could not have avoided accusations of Formalism. And no quotations or formulations, naïvely framing Eisenstein's theoretical text, would have saved it.

Moscow
August 1990

Foreword

'All is in man – all is for man's sake!'

It is not by chance that I preface this study with the immortal words of Maxim Gorky (from his '*Man*').

In its unique, historic scope, our victorious twenty-year-old revolution has proved the greatness of the watchword 'All is for man's sake!' as a stimulus to unprecedented achievements. Those same twenty years have also shown how much art and culture have been enriched by a slogan which, instead of 'art for art's sake' or 'culture for culture's sake', proclaims 'all is for man's sake': socialism for man's sake, culture for man's sake, art for man's sake.

No less profound is the affirmation that 'all is in man'. In him and from him; only in him and from him; from the individual human being and from the human collective – the people: only in them and from them is it possible to derive unending inspiration.

Writers, poets and artists come and go, but the people, that great collective being, remains. And only someone who is of the people, with the people and amid the people can contribute to that great, immortal cause – the people's cause. The great cause of humankind. The great cause of man.

I am regarded as one of the most 'inhuman' of artists. The description of the human being has never been either the central or the most fundamental concern of my works. In my basic cast of mind I have always been more preoccupied with *movement* – mass movements, social movements, dramatic movement – and my creative interest has always been more keenly directed towards *movement itself*, towards the actions and deeds as such, rather than towards *the person* performing them.

For that reason, the experience of my seventeen years of artistic endeavour has been expressed less in the image of man in art than in the image of the [concept underlying] the work itself. But that by no means implies that the slogan 'all is in man' is alien to me. On the contrary – the more profoundly one analyses the topic of this study, the more insistently one is made aware of the degree to which 'all is in man', and that not a single element in the genuinely living image of a work can possibly arise or flourish unless it derives from man and from the human condition.

If in my work I have, perhaps, been somewhat remiss in my treatment of the image of the human individual (although perhaps not in my depiction of the human collective), then may this study of the human element and of man in the image of a work of art serve at least in part to make good that omission. For the fundamental, all-pervading and most profound theme of this study is man himself, not only in the subject-matter and plot of a work of art, but in its very structure and its total image, or to be more precise – in that stage of the creative process in which the underlying idea and theme of the work themselves become the means of exerting an artistic impact on the perceptions [of the audience].

'*Meine Tendenz ist die Verkörperung der Ideen*' ['My inclination is towards the embodiment of ideas'] said Goethe. That definition expresses the entire significance of form in art, and it embraces even stylistic extremes, from symbolism and allegory to banal chatter about ideas or the clumsy retailing of a story in blunt, pedestrian language. I shall examine the underlying principles of how form serves to avoid falling into such excesses, by studying the progression: the shot – montage – sound montage. And through this and other topics, into which a deeper study of particular matters and details may lead us, there will always run, like a red thread, the fact that for all the experience, all the power, all the strength of a work's expressive imagery – as well as for all the skill that goes into its construction (with which we are here chiefly concerned), provided that this skill is directed towards creating a work of art *for man* – the fundamental, principal and nourishing source of inspiration will be derived from three things: from Man; from Man; and from Man.

'All is in man – all is for man's sake!'

17 November 1937
On the 20th Anniversary of the October Revolution.

1 Draft of 'Introduction'

Only the fool does not change, for time brings him
no development and experiences do not exist for him.

Pushkin

The epigraph from Pushkin has not been chosen at random. We are to make
a survey of the development of montage – a survey in the good German
tradition, to include both retrospect [*Rückblick*] and prospect [*Ausblick*], which
will give a résumé of the course taken by montage so far and indicate the
directions in which it is going. Even more important is to locate and define
our present-day understanding of this shifting concept. Much will be unexpected when compared with yesterday. We shall emphasise this unexpectedness, though not forgetting that our developing comprehension has advanced
in a succession of qualitative leaps from what it was yesterday or the day
before yesterday. Indeed, a real understanding of the nature of montage as
one of the constituent disciplines of film-making can nowadays only proceed
from an exact knowledge of its prior development.

The days are long past when montage practically usurped sovereign rights
in the realm of cinematic expression; but the many people who nowadays
want to 'bury' montage with whoops of joy are also in the wrong.[1] They think
because there is less cutting of the picture in sound cinema that montage is
dead, but they forget that what they are burying is an outworn phase whose
characteristics were inseparable from silent cinema.

Others want to go on living in the new phase without the trouble of
reexamining the intellectual baggage of the past, even though they may have
carefully removed from it any unwanted excesses.

Most of us give it no thought at all and simply ignore this powerful
component of film composition. This happens largely because we have not
fully succeeded in identifying the place and function of montage, in particular
the *new aspect* which it has assumed in the *new conditions* of the sound film.

At first glance, it is indeed extremely difficult to identify. *De prime abord*
it would seem that in the history of montage to date we have a completed
'triad'. There was the shot (the single set-up). It was broken into fragments
by montage. The fragments were put together again into a unity within the
shot. Internally, however, matters are more complicated: most sound scenes
are shot from a single set-up, and this would seem on the face of it to be a
regression – which in many cases it is.

The object of this work is to examine the propositions set out below.

A truly realistic work of art, deriving from the fundamental tenets of realism, must contain as an indissoluble whole *both* the representation of a phenomenon *and* its image; by 'image' is meant a generalised statement about the essence of the particular phenomenon. They are inextricably linked by their presence, their appearance and the way they merge with one another.

In film, this *second* characteristic has been lost.

Our task is to establish how this element of generalisation has been realised in the three phases of film history: the single set-up, the multiple set-up and the sound film.

In single set-up cinema by plastic composition.

In multiple set-up cinema by montage composition.

In sound cinema by musical composition.

At the same time this proposition discloses a new way of looking at the question of montage. The 'sources' of montage are in plastic composition; the 'future' of montage lies in musical composition; the factors of consistency in all three stages are the same.

This proposition enables us to trace the distinctive way in which montage has been modified, as represented by its three qualitatively different aspects, conforming to the three phases of cinema's development.

In the first or plastic mode of structuring film, the 'role' of montage is played by a combination of the compositional generalisation *about* the image and the image itself: a purposeful 'fusion' of compositional elements together with a generalised 'contour' of the image.

In the second stage, montage plays the generalising role; here 'generalising' [*obobshchenie*] means the attitude taken towards a phenomenon based on the experience (which is, in its way, class-mediated) of a series of corresponding phenomena.

In sound film the role of montage lies basically in the internal synchronisation of sound and picture.

In the first period, the pictures are not a representational image but derive from the unity of the ideational image, i.e. they interrelate in the same way as do the elements of generalised plastic composition, and this is only fully attainable in colour film.

The latter consideration raises the issue of sound film as a synthetic art form.

At the end, we shall consider the notion that living man, his consciousness and activity, is not only the basis of what is expressed in the content of a film, but that man is also reflected in the exigencies of form and the structural laws of a work of art, of its generalised image.[2]

In the following passages, and in the specific ways in which particular problems are solved, solutions to the montage problem at the successive stages of cinema's development will be adduced. If they have still not been reduced to a generalised, final form (even if only final as of today!) – which is what I am trying to do now – in practical terms this, nevertheless, in no way diminishes the meaning and value of having learned them and made use of them *in particular areas* within the field as a whole. Besides, any real mastery of what has to be done and any progress are only possible on the basis of a firm grasp of what has already been done in the past.

Strictly speaking, of course, this book is not about montage. Within the limits of the author's powers and abilities, it is basically attempting to show, in one particular aspect of the work of art (the methods of its composition), how to disclose simultaneously the representational factor and the generalised image, and how both must form an indissoluble unity and must interpenetrate one another.

The book demonstrates this in one small sector of a specifically cinematic problem within the multiplicity of problems to be found in film-making, namely in the matter of montage and in the problem which is inseparably linked with it – the shot. Since, however, montage has not been written about at all, or at any rate not in such painstaking detail, this book is – this time speaking quite strictly – about montage.

Its subject, indeed, makes this a much-needed work, since while it naturally does not exhaust the problem and does not even attempt to examine all its aspects, in my view this book nevertheless poses the most essential of all problems in the field of audiovisual film composition, namely the question of representation and image: a problem which in itself far transcends both montage and cinematography as a whole.

It is particularly important to pose this question at the present time,[3] for not only has cinema lost the experience and mastery gained in its silent phase, but the stage of most of the allied arts is now such that they are practically unable to offer cinema any help in this connection. Herein also lies the reason why, for my models and illustrative digressions, I shall be obliged to draw much more upon examples taken from the history of literature and the arts than upon contemporary sources, since the features characteristic of my subject matter have largely disappeared. I shall not embark on criticism or analysis of this state of affairs in itself, but it is, in fact, this situation that has chiefly motivated me in writing this book.

Such, therefore, are the considerations which have made me delve more deeply into the nature of the phenomenon on which I have based my research.

Finally, and in the same line of thought, this inoffensive 'academic treatise', devoted to one very limited problem within one particular branch of the arts, actually touches upon a very large, general question. And, in its own way, the 'treatise' itself, for all its inoffensiveness, is therefore highly polemical.

'My regular readers' may find this work surprising in its abundance of quotations from Stanislavsky's 'Method'.[4]

It is fairly well known that in all the seventeen years of my research work in art, parallel to my creative career I have almost always dealt with precisely that area which Stanislavsky's 'Method' leaves untouched, or which, at any rate, he does not subject to theoretical analysis or illuminate as he does the art of acting.

I am dealing with the compositional and structural imperatives that govern a work of art, and their separate elements, together with questions of form in general (not to mention questions of *film* form). Thus, in the book which Stanislavsky has devoted to a detailed exposition of his 'Method' (at least in its earlier, English, edition entitled *An Actor Prepares*,[5] which I have to hand), there are literally only two lines dealing with the question of form. This is not mere chance, but a conscious act of choice in selecting the field to which the author of the 'Method' directed his main attention. . . .

But that is not all. It is equally well known, furthermore, that my development as an artist and the growth of my creative abilities have not only taken place in a different field, but have taken quite a different *direction* (or, as people used to say, are 'on another front') from that pursued by the theatre headed by Stanislavsky.[6]

Thus we overlapped neither in the direction we took nor in our areas of enquiry. These areas have described, as it were, concentric circles: in the one the centre of attention is *man in action*, while in the other it is *the action of structuring a work of art*, in which man is considered as one, the leading one, of several factors (though not always!). Besides, our areas of interest were on the one hand *acting* in the *theatre*, and on the other, *cinematic composition*.

It is, therefore, all the more interesting to observe the great degree to which the premises (and the approach) formulating the rules for my field of activity invariably, step by step, echo similar premises in Stanislavsky's 'Method' approach to acting.

In the final analysis, this should cause no surprise, since both sets of premises stem equally from a single, common source: the only true, authentic source of art in all its forms and variants.

The source is . . . but then everyone knows the source of Stanislavsky's 'Method'. The fact that it is also the ultimate source which nourishes the creation of form, and of film form in particular and more than any other – this we shall attempt to show in the course of this work when we reach the question of sound film as the model of a synthetic art form.[7]

As for the wealth of quotations which I allow myself to scatter throughout my research material, there are two reasons for this. First, the material which I have to examine comes from somewhat varied and specialised fields, so it is better to treat it in the terms devised for it by specialists. Second, the 'montagiste' character of my stylistic manner in the cinema may be to blame: minimum distortion of the units from which the montage image is constituted. But it is also important to present the material with maximum objectivity, and as far as possible without tendentious bias in favour of the preconceived principles which I am expounding. What could be more objective than to juxtapose the observations of different authors who have no connection whatsoever with the general line of my argument or with the basic topic –

montage – which occupies the centre of our attention? Just as in film shots, where I am basically trying to use camera angles and lighting to outline and emphasise those elements in the shot that work towards what I want, so in this matter, too, I shall try to minimise my incursions into the nature of phenomena which are not within my immediate competence, preferring instead, wherever possible, to let the experts speak for themselves. In such cases, I shall limit myself to compositional editing. In its overall scope, this method should lend added conviction to the total picture. For what attracts me, above all, is not the originality but the universality of the propositions which I shall examine. For the rest, I hold to the view expressed by a certain old Frenchman: 'It is only those who have no hope themselves of being cited who cite nobody' (Gabriel Nandé).

Part One
Montage in Single Set-Up Cinema

2 Montage 1937

In the days when it was making its most serious explorations into composition, cinematography shifted its centre of gravity almost entirely to problems of 'ensemble', in particular to the 'ensemble' of a complete work and of its *montage*, devoting considerably less attention to resolving the problems of *shot composition* – a detached house, as it were, in 'Montage Street'.

While some may find it trivial, this analogy goes much deeper than mere external resemblance. That a shot can be 'noisy' (or as we would put it, cluttered), its elements 'incorrectly laid out': that this produces a corresponding degree of 'discomfort', in this instance to the eye of the spectator (even though he may not complain but simply walk out of the film dissatisfied, or less satisfied than he might have been), is equally true for cinema as a whole. There are many instances where failure along these lines has a marked effect, if not on the spectator's working efficiency, then at least on the clarity and ease of his perception and on the emotional depth at which he experiences and grasps the theme of the work. Imprecise composition invariably results in an over-expenditure of psychic energy in perception and robs the spectator of allround depth in perceiving the thought and underlying ideas of a work. That is to say, because it affects the expenditure of psychic energy, it also indirectly affects that same working efficiency mentioned above.

Seen in this light, composition is far from being something 'trivial'. Within a work of art, it is one of the aspects of concern for man: a concern for clarity and precision, for fullness of perception combined with a maximum economy of perceptual effort.*

As to the problems of shot composition, once the progressional link between shot and montage had been established (see my article 'Beyond the Shot', 1929),[8] matters were limited to saying that the experience gained in the art of montage might, in suitably adapted form, also be applied to the culture of the shot. Whereas some directors have done a great deal of practical research on montage in many films, practically no special exploratory work has been done in the area of the shot. This does not mean, of course, that no work at all has been done on the shot! The concept of montage composition is inseparable from shot composition: one cannot exist without the other. But

---

*It is surely noteworthy that the Sanskrit word to denote 'magnificent, beautiful' (in the French sense of *admirable*) is *darsaniya*, which literally means 'easy to look at'. [The latter phrase in English in the original.]

while much research and compositional inventiveness have been devoted to montage, the question of how the shot looked was somehow 'self-evidently' incorporated into that broader category and no one gave it any thought.

Theoretical ideas in cinema, in those far-off days when they were struggling to emerge, were chiefly concerned with the question of montage. The problem of the shot as such was hardly ever raised. Montage was something more tangible. The required sharpness of rhythmic perception was the same, but the means of production and of analysis were more accessible: a pair of scissors and a ruler. The permutations were easier: transposition, re-editing, lengthening and shortening. The aesthetics were measurable by rule of thumb, the key to the sequence's overtonal resonance derived from the molecular unit.[9] The process of building up this resonance relates entirely to its final point, i.e. to those features which sum up the sequence. Its inherent laws are located 'upward' from the establishing shot. The 'downward' process – towards the nature of the shot's composition – is not undertaken. In 'The Middle of Three' and in my speech to the [1935] conference,[10] I tried to throw some light on the psycho-social origins of the fact that at that stage juxtaposition played a more significant role than the introduction of creative intent into the juxtaposed elements.

It should be added that this was the period of the first youthful flowering of cinema's exploratory efforts. And in such periods, as Engels pointed out, people are mainly interested in connections and movement as such, less attention being devoted to *what* it is that moves. . . .[11] One way or another, the two situations coincide. On the one hand we have the problems of montage, which have been examined in considerable detail; the question of the shot, on the other hand, is a less happy one, though it has not been wholly ignored. In my article 'Beyond the Shot', I succeeded in establishing two propositions which are, I think, highly relevant to a 'biography' of the shot. The first proposition concerned the shot as a whole and its reciprocal links with montage. The incompatibility of contrasting the shot with montage was exploded. And for the first time it was definitively stated that montage is a stage derived from the shot; in other words, that the conflict of compositional elements within the frame is, as it were, a cell, a nucleus of montage which obeys the law of fission as the tension of that conflict rises. Montage is the leap made by internal shot composition into a new quality. Hence the developmental link between them, as in a single genetic progression of development. Hence the conclusion was drawn that the entire set of rules, proceeding to the right and upwards from the 'leap' into the methods of montage may, with suitable qualitative adjustment, be pursued to the left and downwards, towards the problems of shot composition.

All interest was concentrated on montage. As to the shot, the way was obvious: 'anyone who wanted to' could investigate the appropriate structural laws relating to the shot. Since then (six years!) no one has been found who did want to. Another proposition, fundamental to any analysis, was established and that is as follows: given that as a basis for analysis of the structural laws of montage there is a meeting – or collision – of shots (but whose spectrum can also include a *lack* of collision; instead, one shot can 'overflow' into another), then as the starting-point for defining the compositional laws [of the shot] we should posit an encounter between the object represented and an event, together with the angle from which it is viewed, and the frame which cuts it off from its surroundings. I also proposed to go into the methodological details, and to draw from them specific conclusions about the ways and means of internal shot composition. No one wanted to. It is always easier to raise a polemical howl than to do the concrete work of analysis. It was easier to wail about the 'undue priority' given to montage and about 'ignoring the content of the shot' than to see that the question concerned the compositional laws of that content in montage; that the analysis was not dealing with the compositional exposition of this internal shot content, but outlining ways in which this might be done. People preferred to wail about the disregard for content in general; and people who want to do *this* can always be found.

One way or another, since no one is working on these matters, we must undertake to examine the problems of shot composition. We certainly do not propose to cover the entire matter here, but we should like to touch on certain extremely important elements of this problem. Trusting that people will not bark at me for being 'one-sided', I shall treat the question narrowly and . . . from one side. When one is jabbing with a scalpel at the cornea of the eye, one may permit oneself the luxury of not having to discuss the heels at the same time. Their turn will come: we will examine questions of composition from other angles, too. For the time being, we shall limit ourselves to those which constitute the material for the two proposed essays.

The question of how to compose a shot has not been posed arbitrarily. The significance of the shot has increased lately. The blade of our attention will probe '*what* it is that moves', *what* things are juxtaposed. Nowadays people sometimes talk more about the shot (or they should talk; more often they mumble about it) than about the juxtaposing of shots in montage. Hence the importance of the composition of the shot's content is increasing colossally. I repeat: we shall deal with the question of the *composition* of that content, the composition of the visible part of content, in terms of its (for the audience) most effective cognitive form.

There was, by the way, one film which brought this very problem of the shot into the foreground and which, at the compositional level, relegated montage to a purely auxiliary, narrative function. The historical fate of this film surpassed all expectations in this respect: its existence took the form of a chaotic jumble of shots, lacking any integration by the author's compositional sense, or even the author's ideas, but simply spliced together by some anonymous incompetent following the strict order of events, confining itself, in essence, to ensuring that an actor simply stayed alive until the plot killed him and that the hero's corpse did not appear until he had been trampled to death by horses' hooves. I am talking about *Que viva México!*, and I would stress here that of the special problems which it posed (any work of art worthy of the name invariably does raise questions of form,★ in addition to political, thematic, philosophical and narrative problems), questions of shot composition were among the most important.[12]

The sad fate of this picture deprived us of the chance of completing and absorbing all the practical experience we had gained, and of interpreting it theoretically. (Thus, for example, the picture was intended to make some most interesting searches into the use of national style – in this case Mexican – and the problem of utilising folklore in cinema, not to mention certain minor and more specialised topics, such as landscape in cinema, and so on.)

Nevertheless, to have shot 250,000 feet of film, in which director and cameraman deliberately set out to make a special study of shot composition, cannot have failed to yield a certain amount of experience in composing shots.

My comparison of [. . .] the shot to a detached house or a separate apartment was not fortuitous, for the shot is the basic home, the fundamental scene of action by the principal master of the picture – the living man in the form of the actor. The concentration of attention on the actor's performance, the specific conditions of sound film, and the present-day view of montage in sound cinema (which will be dealt with thoroughly and in more detail below), resulting in a great increase in the average length of the single shot, have all forced us to give the problem of shot composition much more serious attention than before. Otherwise, there is a serious risk that instead of composing film shots we shall drift into the photographic reproduction of ordinary painting, or follow the bad example of provincial actors' stage groupings (examples of both frequently appear on our screen and in the West).

But by examining certain fundamental problems of the composition of the film shot, we shall also fulfil the first part of our self-appointed task: we shall gain some insight into the question of montage under the conditions of single set-up cinematography.

That period of cinematography,[13] now so distant from us and so primitive, did not leave us any contributions to the theoretical study of composition. However, by examining the proposed aspects of shot composition, we shall not only establish retrospectively the premises for the structural laws of montage at its rudimentary stage, but we shall simultaneously examine one of the most topical of problems: the plastic composition of the individual montage shot.

For the individual montage shot is also, in essence, single set-up cinematography, in which, as distinct from single set-up cinematography as *a stage of development*, its 'load' does not derive from the entire content of the film as a whole but only from a certain fragment of the plot.

Let us begin our examination with the simplest possible instance: a

---

★In the majority of recent films, the main problems of cinematic form are the acquisition of film-acting technique and the creation of a human image on the screen.

motionless object, shot from one set-up.

In this case, there is no need for us to summon up our great and undoubted knowledge of cinematography; we need simply to study the object as a plastic phenomenon, and, in the first instance, to study those of its features about which a knowledge of painting tells us too little.

For years now, we have been stressing the link between theatre and cinema, as between two stages of development. . . .

So, when we need to analyse or throw light on some aspect of cinema, it is always methodologically advisable to remember that link, and to begin the analysis with an appropriate example from the theatre, gradually proceeding to a new stage of the same phenomenon in that new phase of theatre which is cinema. . . .

That is how we shall proceed here, too, since it will be methodologically correct to begin with the more obvious in order to progress to the more complex. . . .

We are, then, discussing the encounter between an object and (a) the angle from which it is observed and (b) the frame which picks it out of its surroundings. Both are essentially the same: the second is an encounter with the edges of the frame, the first with the inclination of the plane of the frame. (The depiction of depth – the specific 'handwriting' of the lens – we shall for the time being leave aside; it belongs to the next stage of analysis.) The first we customarily refer to as the camera-angle [*rakurs*], the second – framing [*obrez*].

On the stage you can go out by the door. In life, too. In cinema, though, there is another means of exit. What is more, you can find it anywhere, even when there are no doors: you can move out of the frame. The same applies to any other indicative action, for cinema's means of expression are the result of expanding the expressive potential of objects and phenomena in real life, or in real life as organised in theatrical terms. The *mise en cadre* is a leap from the *mise en scène*. It is, as it were, a 'second-stage' *mise en scène*, when the *mise en scène* of changing camera positions is superimposed upon the broken lines of the *mise en scène's* displacement in space.

If *mise en cadre* is the 'offspring' of *mise en scène*, then what, it would be interesting to know, is the parentage of shot framing?

The shot, as we have said, is a stage of montage. Obviously it is the 'offspring' of whatever is the equivalent stage of montage relative to *mise en scène*.

But what – in the narrowest sense – is *mise en scène*? *Mise en scène* (including all the phases of its deployment: gesture, mime, intonation) is, as it were, a graphic projection of the character of the action. And when applied to the unit of action in particular, it is the spatial calligraphy of the unit. It is like handwriting on paper, or a characteristic footprint impressed as a person walks on a sandy path, in all its completeness and its simultaneous incompleteness. With good reason, the art of theatrical production is not limited to *mise en scène*, just as film is not confined to montage. For character manifests itself in action (and in a particular form of action – in the human image). A particular semblance of action is movement. We judge action from movement (from voice and words too). The imprint of action is the *mise en scène*. We shall seek to define shot composition along this line of approach: the line of character. And we shall begin with the character of a man. By this route it will be easier to approach the depiction of a landscape and the nature of an enacted event.

Based on the available social and individual data, the character of a dramatic personage is created by the selection of only one *particular* set of characteristics and elements of action and behaviour out of all the *possible* sets. Character presupposes the isolation of a certain set of features and elements: an organic set. Also the contrasting of its shared class features with a different, particular set of class attitudes, and the contrasting of its purely individual features with another, personal set of features.

One way or another, selection takes place. A cutting-off from the rest. Let us change 'off' for 'around', and this will define the next functional stage in individuation. Framing. This will be the part played by the shot in the delineation of character: a spatial frame which defines a character by a summation of the features which distinguish (or separate) it as an individual from the swarm of others. This does not mean that if, for instance, it is characteristic of a man to keep his hands out of sight, the camera should obligingly cut off his hands with the edge of the frame; on the contrary, the shot should aim to show the figure in just such a way as to make the hiding of the hands clearly stand out as a concealment and not as an absence. When a human figure is shown in black, the white hands are characteristic. The shot should not try to eliminate them. If, however, in a well-defined characterisation the figure's headgear happens to be irrelevant, then it can simply be guillotined by the edge of the frame. And so on. We are here at the lowest level of shot composition, the anecdotal level of selecting naturalistic detail. Are the hands needed in the shot or not? Should there be an umbrella or not? But very soon this becomes inadequate.

We shall now make use of the organic link between theatre and cinema for a full elucidation of our present topic.

Let us begin with the problem of *mise en scène* or rather with one particular aspect of that problem, a special aspect but one that is, in my view, of the greatest importance in the aesthetics of *mise en scène*. It is a question which has received almost no attention; furthermore, if it is important in *mise en scène*, then the role that it plays in the aesthetics of its offspring – *mise en cadre* – is many times more important.

Let us take a concrete example.

Let us suppose that we are in the theatre and that we have to plan the scene of Vautrin's arrest in the dramatisation of Balzac's *Père Goriot*.[14] Or, to be more precise: the moment during Vautrin's arrest when he utters his accusatory speech. I shall here avoid *all* the problems of *mise en scène* except the one which happens to be immediately relevant to our purposes. I set this

Fig. 2.1

task as an exercise during one of my lectures at GIK [State Institute of Cinematography].[15] The first solution proposed by the student who was called to the blackboard is shown in Fig. 2.1. With the typical impetuosity of youth, this young man could only envisage this highly temperamental scene by making Vautrin leap up on to the table! Dumbfounded by what he has to say, the other characters have crowded around the table from which Vautrin lashes them with his barbed remarks.

Was this solution correct? If we approach it from a purely naturalistic standpoint, the solution contains nothing particularly disturbing. The leap on to the table might raise some doubt, but even that is perfectly acceptable if we allow for a high degree of rage and temperament. And even if it arouses suspicions on grounds of verisimilitude, we can pull the table out from under Vautrin and still keep the general disposition of the *mise en scène*: Vautrin in the centre, with those he is accusing around him.

Is it really satisfactory? I repeat: from a naturalistic viewpoint it is all right. People are perfectly capable of grouping themselves in this way. Vautrin might well move among them like this; approach them; accuse them.

Yet there is something wrong with this arrangement. And the collective instinct of the audience, as I now recall, immediately opposed this solution, even before offering any specific counter-proposals.

Whereas on a naturalistic level it was quite acceptable, on *some other level* it was obviously *not* acceptable. There was a very definite feeling that: 1) there was some other level, and 2) that level was not *immediately* determined by

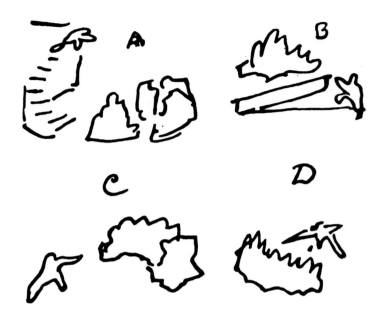

Fig. 2.2

naturalistic considerations, or limited to them. We purposely did not define in advance what that level was, but gave free rein to the counter-proposals. Depending on temperament, these solutions took various forms (see Fig. 2.2). Some chased him up a staircase, from whence he thundered. Others sent him down into the orchestra. The third and fourth versions, less adventurously, confined themselves to counterposing Vautrin to the group of Mme Vauquer's lodgers, disposed in a variety of positions. Again there were arguments. But whereas in the first instance, for all its probability in naturalistic terms, the plan was somehow felt to be 'impossible' for some other reason, this factor was absent from all the other solutions. We argued about details, but we agreed that all the latter solutions had something in common and that this common factor was somehow expressively correct. What was it?

Obviously A, B, C and D can all be reduced to a single common scheme. In each case Vautrin is positioned to the right, to the left, above or below, but in all the examples one condition has been observed: Vautrin is not placed in the centre of the group, as in the first instance (see Fig. 2.3), but *has been moved outside it*. Moreover, he has been sharply *counterposed* to that group. Evidently the difference in impression lay *precisely* in this, since from a purely naturalistic viewpoint all the combinations were possible in absolutely equal measure.

What is this second level, on which, if – and only if – it is brought into

Fig. 2.3   *Fig. 2.4*

play, even a naturalistically quite satisfactory solution begins to be expressively convincing? What words did we use to define the new set of dispositions as distinct from the first? We said that Vautrin had been *moved out*, or let us say *thrown out* of the group of Mme Vauquer's lodgers. And we said that he had not only been moved out but also *counterposed* to that group. Literally, spatially, directionally, graphically. But what has taken place dramatically and psychologically in this scene?

A few moments earlier, before the police appeared, Vautrin was Monsieur Vautrin, the richest and most respected man *among* Mme Vauquer's lodgers. He was flesh of the flesh and blood of the blood of that 'respectable' society to which all the unattractive inhabitants of that house also belonged.

The police appear. The mask is torn off (or rather the wig!). Vautrin is exposed: he is Jacques Collin, an escaped convict. He has been *driven out* of the *circle* of respectable people. In the last minutes before he is led away by the gendarmes, he tears himself away from them and hurls a challenge at the society which has driven him out. He accuses it. At this moment Mme Vauquer's lodgers – this little group of people – represents the whole of bourgeois society. Vautrin opposes it with all his courage and strength. He alone is *counterposed* to that society and fights it. It is no better than he, a criminal. It is full of equally villainous people, and so on and so forth.

That is to say, if we scrutinise the psychological and dramatic outline of the action, we discover that it is expressed, as it turns out, in exactly the same words. The only difference will be that these words will not be applied in the literal but in the metaphorical sense.

Thus the linear movement and spatial disposition of the *mise en scène* turns out to be a 'converted' metaphor. In translating the connotation of the psychological content of the scene into *mise en scène*, the process of staging has, as it were, brought about a reversal from the metaphorical to the nonmetaphorical, primary, initial sense.

I say 'reversal', because it is well known – indeed the very meaning of the word 'metaphorical' (Greek: μετα–φορ = to carry over) constantly reminds us of it – that metaphorical connotations figured at an earlier stage as simple, straightforward physical actions ('I am *drawn* to you', 'I *grovel* before you', etc., etc.).

From this observation we can establish a law with which we are already familiar, i.e. that to be expressive, a *mise en scène* must fulfil two conditions.

It must not contradict people's normal, accepted behaviour.

But that is not sufficient.

In its structure it must also be a graphic scheme of what in its metaphorical reading defines the psychological content of the scene and the interaction of the characters.

We said 'a scheme'. Scheme contains a double meaning. Its more general sense relates to the concept of paucity, impoverishment, incompleteness. In essence, this is the understanding of 'scheme' in the sense of 'schematic'. But scheme also has another meaning, namely in the sense of a graphic representation of the most generalised conception of a phenomenon. It is in this sense that we shall use the term 'scheme'. If we look at Fig. 2.2 (showing the A, B, C, D versions of the Vautrin scene) without knowing what it is about, one thing is absolutely plain: a certain unit is counterposed to a certain mass (or group of units). What is more, the unit is identical and *common* to all four cases A, B, C and D; i.e. the scheme has captured the fundamental relationship, beyond all the particular representational and concrete meanings of its separate elements. In other words, it has shown that the generalisation is so great that it becomes what we call an abstraction.

If it permeates and spatially disposes specific characters – the actual participants in an action which has, or can have, this very abstraction as its scheme – then the picture acquires total conviction and expressiveness.

We may formulate the following proposition as the essential condition for a *mise en scène*: the *mise en scène* must act as a graphic generalisation of the content of the action.

When this occurs, conviction and expressiveness emerge, because only when they do will the construct be truly realistic, showing both the everyday behaviour of a particular group of people in a particular dramatic situation and, simultaneously, these same relationships reduced to their most generalised form.

Strictly speaking, only when both these conditions are observed (leaving aside all secondary and specific attendant factors) can we speak of the realistic composition of the *mise en scène*, or indeed of its composition *in general*!

What was it that was unsatisfactory about the first, erroneous solution of this scene? It was that the naturalistic elements of the action were arranged according to a compositional scheme which did *not* correspond to the shape of the internal relationship between the characters. Indeed, it was arranged according to a scheme whose generalisation very clearly expressed a quite different type of relationship between the individual and the group. Forget about the situation and look at the scheme (Figs 2.3 and 2.4). For all its abstraction, it will nevertheless suggest to you a very definite set of possible relationships – but the relationship required in setting the test is most certainly not among them. You can read it in several ways: as a benevolent father blessing his obedient children, or as a group of people hurling themselves at a criminal from all sides, but by no means as a closed group opposing an individual or vice versa.

It is perhaps worthwhile noting that just as *mise en scène* is not limited to the horizontal plane of the floor, so its 'metaphor' may equally be read vertically as well.

It is intriguing to note that in the incorrect solution, a *part* of it – the vertical plane, as it happens – contained an element of correctness: a man can be removed from a group in a vertical direction, upwards. The dominating nature of Vautrin was obviously the feeling which made the student put him up on the table. But these good intentions were cancelled out by the false resolution of the horizontal plane, in which the group of people 'embraces' Vautrin!

I like to regard every phenomenon as some kind of intermediate stage, as a sort of 'today', with its 'yesterday' and its 'tomorrow'; as something within a sequence, having its 'before' and its 'after', i.e. its preceding and subsequent stages. Certain 'throwback' features lead to a leap backwards into the preceding stage, while the line of maximal forward deployment leads to a leap into the following stage: modified, the general laws proceed dialectically from stage to stage, acquiring new readings and new meanings, but retaining their common, fundamental premisses.

Let us trace the correctness of our propositions in terms of two such 'neighbouring' stages of *mise en scène*.

I have always believed and taught that gesture (and, at a further stage, intonation) is *mise en scène* 'concentrated in the person', and vice versa – *mise en scène* is gesture that 'explodes' into spatial sequence. This correlation is repeated in the latest phase of theatre, i.e. in cinema: there we say that a shot 'explodes' into a sequence of montage shots. And vice versa, that a montage progression concentrates itself, exerts a retroactive effect on the compositional handwriting of the shot. On the other hand, we have just recalled the fact that *mise en cadre* is *mise en scène* at a higher stage of development.[16]

So let us take our proposition about the second, metaphorical or generalising, imperative to which a structure must submit in order to be 'read' fully, and let us test it in two 'neighbouring' phases: in gesture and in shot composition. For it is quite obvious that the graphic composition of the shot is 'the eye taking a walk' across the plane of the screen, i.e. a *mise en scène* of the eye, transferred from the horizontal plane of the stage to the vertical plane of the cinema screen. Gesture and its derivatives are not the direct subject of our analysis, so we shall pass over this area fairly quickly, without going into it too deeply and dealing only with those elements of this discipline which are of immediate interest to us and which relate directly to the subject of the present study.

Shot composition is, however, one of the fundamental, prerequisite links in our theme: here we shall have to go into considerably more detail, here we shall see that in applying the laws inherent in this newly discovered field, we shall find countless examples which reaffirm and recall earlier epochs of our cultural heritage.

So to return to the two elements in gesture and in particular to the second: the inner generalising element.

Let the reader summon up before his mind's eye a series of the most varied expressions – of figure, gesture and face – all on the same subject. Let it be, for example, the expression of aversion. Slight aversion and absolute aversion. From a grimace to nausea. Physical aversion and moral aversion. Aversion at different ages and aversion in the most widely varying circumstances. Let the reader imagine these expressions occurring before him in actual reality. Let him mentally experience and physically act out such diverse instances of aversion.

The variety of expression is legion.

This whole legion can, however, be reduced to a common denominator. Its multiplicity is a set of variants on one basic scheme, which will permeate all instances and varieties. Moreover, any movement that is not linked to this backbone, or does not correspond to this scheme, will *never* be read as aversion.

What is this common denominator?

An advantage of studying the design of film sets is that it can be presented graphically, that is why I always begin with it.

The ground-rules are of the same kind in other areas of our subject, but then one has to have recourse to verbal description, which is always less clear and vivid.

Let us try to extract from the variety of individual manifestations at least a description of what is essential to aversion, and which will be present in all the separate instances of aversion. Here we are much more fortunately placed than we might have supposed. The decisive common factor, which is equally characteristic of all particular cases will be . . . aversion (from the Latin: *a-vertere* = to turn away). And indeed, however many single examples of aversion we may adduce, they will always contain this basic motor characteristic.

While it will vary in scope and clarity, in all instances the essence of the movement will consist of *turning away*, of a-version from the object which evokes this attitude. This movement completely embodies the meaning, the essential content of the emotion we feel towards a repulsive phenomenon, a phenomenon causing aversion.

What does this show? That the term itself, converted from its figurative, metaphorical meaning *back* into the physical movement which was the prototype of the corresponding psychological attitude – restored, in fact, to its primary motor sense – turns out to contain the exact formula or scheme that is characteristic in equal measure of all *particular* shades of meaning, and of which it also serves as a *general* designation. Is it only the mighty and powerful Russian language which is so fortunate in this respect? Of course not. This is a purely semantic phenomenon, and inevitably occurs to an equal extent in other languages too. The language of a Frenchman, an Englishman or a German will render him the same service: *a-version*, a-version, *Ab-scheu*.

But perhaps it applies only to aversion? Of course not. Take 'bootlicking', take 'overbearing', or take 'overcome' with grief. In every case the signification of the word, i.e. the generalised concept for a variety of particular instances, will contain the exact compositional scheme of that fundamental, generalising, figurative and characteristic element without which the particular movement or pose will *never* be construed in the sense that is contained in its signification.

Of course, the method of *finding* this or that attitude or gesture will never proceed by this means. Finding them will always be a process resulting from keenly experienced perceptions and emotions of the appropriate kind. When the perception is totally authentic, it will give rise to an image that is faithful to it in both the particular reading and the generality. But . . . we cannot rely on everyone being capable, everywhere and at all times, of such totality of expressive skill.

Not all actors possess such a subtly flexible expressive technique as that demanded by A.N. Ostrovsky:

> In order to become the complete actor it is necessary to acquire such freedom of gesture and intonation that, on receiving a certain inner impulse, instantly, without hesitation, the appropriate gesture, the appropriate tone of voice will follow like a pure reflex. That is true stage art.[17]

For very, very many actors this transformational process is a thorny and difficult one, and in ninety-nine cases out of a hundred the actor will need the corrective eyes and instincts of the director; and apart from possessing an equally acute *instinct*, the director must also be *intellectually* aware of the process.

As we see, the picture is absolutely identical to the one that we analysed in the case of *mise en scène*.

Having thus confirmed in another field the correctness of our views on *mise en scène*, let us now turn to our fundamental theme: to single set-up cinematography, or to the graphic composition of a montage sequence, or simply to the composition of a shot. Let us forget for a while everything that we have been talking about so far, and let us get a spontaneous impression

Fig. 2.5

from the two accompanying drawings, which are sketches representing a barricade (Figs 2.5 and 2.6).

It is obvious that in figurative terms and in the amount of naturalistic detail they contain, both pictures are absolutely identical. But it is equally

Fig. 2.6

obvious that when asked which of the two sketches is more *expressive* of a barricade, anyone seeing them will choose No. 2 rather than No. 1. Why is this so?

In a naturalistic, objective, figurative sense they are identical.

Wherein lies the difference between them? The difference is in the compositional placing of those figurative elements.

What does this compositional difference consist of? The difference is in the fact that one of the pictures (the second) as distinct from the other (the first) does not confine itself to the mere representation of a barricade, but is so constructed that in addition it also incorporates an image of the essential significance of a barricade: struggle.

Its compositional elements are so disposed that each one is read as a metaphor, and the sum total of all of them is read as an image of struggle, i.e. as a generalised image of the inner content of what is depicted in the sketch. Indeed:

1. If we take the plane of the houses and the plane of the barricade, we see that in Fig. 2.5 they are simply juxtaposed. In Fig. 2.6 the plane of the barricade *cuts into* the wall of the houses.
2. If we look at the line of the base of the barricade, we shall see that in Fig. 2.6 (unlike Fig. 2.5) this line *cuts into* the roadway.
3. If we follow the line of the upper edge of the barricade in Fig. 2.6 we see that this is shown as a jagged line, which seems to evoke the phases of a struggle: each peak of the spiky contour is a point of conflict in the changing fortunes of two opposing sides. This jagged line can be shown as in Fig. 2.7.

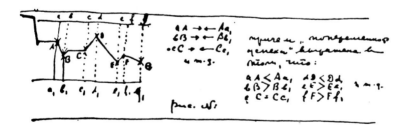

Fig. 2.7

4. The banner cuts into the sky at a characteristically acute angle.
5. Finally, in Fig. 2.6 the ultimate in metaphor is attained in the placing of the shop sign with its stylised pretzel. Here, what is normally seen above us has been brought downward: the pretzel sign has been placed level with the foot of the barricade, in this case not by showing the baker's shop sign as lying physically beneath the barricade but by purely *compositional* means. The distinction between these two examples lies in the fact that in the first sketch

the shop sign cannot be interpreted on any other than a naturalistic level, whereas the subtextual meaning of the second pretzel sign reads not as 'a sign thrown down' but as 'an overthrow': that which was above is now below. And we are made to adopt this metaphorical reading by the fact that the removal of the sign has been brought about not physically but compositionally, i.e. by the viewpoint from which the event is observed.

If we summarise all these elements we see that in Fig. 2.6 we have three instances of one thing *cutting into* another: plane into plane (1); line into plane (2); angle into plane (4); we have a jagged line looking like the seismographic record of a *struggle*; finally we have the elements of a landscape so disposed as to prompt us to think of the overthrow of the established order.

Thus in all its features Fig. 2.6 literally expresses the idea and image of a struggle:

1. at its simplest, by objective *depictive* means: the sketch depicts a barricade.
2. by objective *imaginative* means: the elements are compositionally so disposed as to give the impression of overthrow. In this, by overturning various objects the composition repeats the depictive aspect, in which things are also tipped over or overturned on the barricade (keep this in mind, for we shall return to it again).
3. by the greatest possible generalisation: the clash of planes, of planes and lines, of lines and planes.
4. finally, in the linear character of the basic outline, which reads like the record of the whole process of struggle.

What is more, all these features interpenetrate one another and in no way upset the naturalistic, depictive integrity of the phenomenon as such. (It employs no broken shapes, no Cubist 'deformities', no multiple perspectives and so on.)

Obviously the same notion should with equal logic also pervade the lighting and colour scheme. Over and above the correct naturalistic disposition of colour and highlights, the lighting scheme should also evoke in suitable fashion the metaphor of struggle.

When referring to this example in future, of the many possible variants we shall confine ourselves to citing its simplest, most straightforward significance, namely that if a grouping of objects aims to depict a barricade, then their disposition should be such that their overall contours indicate an *intrinsic, generalised image of what a barricade implies*: struggle.

Without this fully realised perception of the barricade, a Barricade with a capital B will not come into being.

It is fitting to mention at this point that any sketch would be equally incomplete if it were to eliminate the depictive element and confine itself to a mere generalised image. The result would be a sketch which might represent . . . anything you like (see Fig. 2.8).

You may find any number of pronouncements on this subject by great

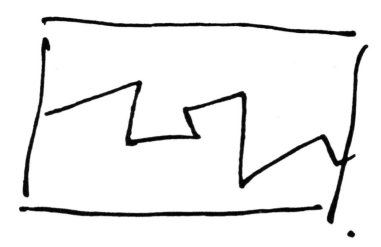

Fig. 2.8

artists. Right now we are celebrating the anniversary of the great Realist sculptor Mark Antokolsky.[18] On this occasion therefore, let us quote his words: 'There are two extremes which are bad in art: one is to reduce art to abstraction, the other is blindly to subordinate oneself to nature.' (I quote from his remark in an article by E. Levi in *Izvestiya*, 5 July 1937.)

I believe that it is in the existence of these two elements – the *specific* instance of depiction and the *generalising* image which pervades it – that the implacability and the all-devouring force of artistic composition resides.

It is precisely this factor which plays such a tremendous role in the art of shot composition.

It is odd that painters have been aware of this from time immemorial, whereas artists of the shot have devoted no attention to it, even though they have sometimes realised it intuitively (and in some films often and fully). This is all the more remarkable since in the concept of *montage* and *sound montage* this apparently purely graphic feature plays a tremendous part. And this is because it is the application to composition of one very broad general rule, a rule which, with good reason, is a fundamental constituent of what we understand by realism in the broadest sense.

We shall see what painting has to say about this, and take a look at how it applies to related fields. Later we shall observe how, in the transition to multiple set-up cinema, this element is metamorphosed into a new quality, and achieves the *apogee* of generalisation in the sound film.

Let us turn in the first instance to painting, and for greater clarity begin by choosing from the huge variety of possible examples those in which two conditions are most forcibly expressed. These are, first: painting in which line plays a great part; and second: painting in which generalisation is an especially strong element and at times of such importance that the artist is prepared to sacrifice the representational aspect.

Art of the first kind is to be found in Asia. Lawrence Binyon, for instance, in his *Painting in the Far East* (London, 1923), has this to say about it: 'The painting of Asia is throughout its main tradition an art of line.'[19]

The Hindu teachers of aesthetics are never tired of reminding us of this: 'The same is implied by Indian authorities when they remind us that it is the line (*rekhā*) that interests the master, while the public cares most about colour.'[20]

N.B. This statement should not be vulgarised: the divergence in interests between artist and public must be understood in its proper sense. What appeals immediately to the perception is colour, in this case standing for representation. Secondary, and in 'mediated' form, is line, which here stands for revelation of the generalised image, in the sense in which we have been discussing it above.

The second condition – the emphasis on generalisation – we shall, of course, find above all in Chinese painting, which shows most fully the tendency to abstract from a phenomenon its generalised, essential reality, freeing it from whatever is transitory and impermanent.

This is particularly characteristic of the 'southern' or so-called 'literary' school of painting. This type of landscape painting was introduced by Wang Wei in the middle period of the T'ang dynasty (618–907 AD) and its salient points are described by Chiang Yee in The Chinese Eye:

> The painters of the 'literary' school do not study a landscape tree by tree and stone by stone, and fill in every detail as it appears to them, with brush and ink; certainly they may have been familiar with the scene for months and years, without seeing anything in it to perpetuate: suddenly they may glance at the same water and rocks in a moment when the spirit is awake, and become conscious of having looked at naked 'reality', free from the Shadow of Life. In that moment they will take up the brush and paint the 'bones', as it were, of this Real Form; small details are unnecessary.[21]

Here we encounter the word 'bones'. This linear skeleton, whose function is to embody the 'Real Form', the 'generalised essence of the phenomenon', is that same skeleton of which we spoke when analysing the example of the barricade. [. . . .]

It is particularly interesting to note that this linear skeleton is also simultaneously the basic means of expressing the artist's emotional handwriting [*roscherk*] – his 'brushstroke', the record of his movements. This is absolutely right, because a *generalisation about an object*, as distinct from the *object itself*, '*an und für sich*', is a separate entity related to the artist's individual consciousness and is an expression of his attitudes towards and judgments about the object in question: a self-expression mediated, as it were, through the author's consciousness and reflecting the context of social relationships in which the artist's personality has been formed.

Line may also be the repository of this generalising factor in genres which are by no means as emphatically linear as Asian art. Let us take an example from western painting in which dense colouring predominates. In this the 'contour line' is created in a unique and special way, but its function is the same. Here, for instance, is what Fritz Burger writes in his book *Cézanne und Hodler*:

> Delacroix . . . and Cézanne in their picture depict space, but without ever losing sight of the unifying, imaginary, boundary-defining element of the strokes of paint. These are contours without autonomous material existence. Cézanne borrowed this too from Delacroix. . . .
>
> Daumier was also aware of how to use this painted contour; it was the instrument on which he played his wild, passionate cadenzas, like a virtuoso striking light out of the darkness with his fists. . . . His wild contours – some light and some dark, which define and enliven everything – link every part of the picture to a common denominator. But he is not concerned with its mimetic effect, its figurative function, the formal structure of the picture: for Daumier the contour is gesture, never a representational motif. It is here, above all, that he differs from Cézanne, whose contours are colour, which partakes of the rich interplay of the total colour-scheme. . . .
>
> But this contour is never given a dominant status, an independent existence or a special function. It is everywhere and nowhere, the silent servant of the whole; it is the 'draughtsmanship' of his pictures, which otherwise we will look for in vain.[22]

It is obvious that the roles of depiction and *image* (generalisation) in painting are easily interchangeable. Generalisation may speak through the colours spread over a representational drawing, or in a complex system of linear composition, or it may be a motif running through the coloured background which has a primarily representational function. Finally, when they (i.e. colour and line) merge with each other, they may, by a process of inner equilibration, perform both functions simultaneously.

It was Cézanne who spoke with particular clarity of this unity: a unity not only of content in both areas (to which, in the interests of clarity, we have *deliberately* ascribed *separate* functions of depiction and generalisation), but also a unity in the process of conception and artistic creation; for Cézanne, 'painting and drawing were, in his own words, one and the same thing: "Drawing and colouring are in no way separate . . . one draws, and the more the colours harmonise, the more precise becomes the drawing. . . ."[23]

I think that after all that has been said there can be no doubt that we are not making a 'mechanical' break between the representation and the image! As in the matter of content, so too in the potential sequence of priority in these functions, we have observed their absolute unity in the process of creation.

The quotation from Cézanne is especially relevant to cinematic composition, for it is there that the process of the figurative disposition of the concrete elements of reality is truly inseparable from the simultaneous compositional structuring by their outlines of the frame's inner contours.

Here one may mention yet another example of the unity between drawing as gesture and the power of colour as the basis of representation. I am speaking of Van Gogh. It is a mistake to take the crazy, wriggling outline of what he is depicting as *drawing* in our sense of the word. Drawing and contour in our sense burst out of these limitations and surge into the heart of the colour background itself, solidified by means not only of a new dimension but of a new expressive environment and material: *by the movement of the brushstrokes*, which simultaneously both create and define the picture's areas of colour.

To complete the picture fully we still need to point out that the depiction and the image (the generalised content of that depiction) are also *historically* phased; i.e. that generalising by way of depiction is something which grows and develops gradually. Imagistic generalisation physically grows out of simple depiction. The process which takes place in our creative consciousness every time we make a composition required for its development a whole period in the history of art.

Here is a rare and vivid example, which illustrates our proposition and is an instance of such a 'transitional' type, in which the imagistic design is still governed by the objective, representative character of that image.

Let us first of all make one point clear.

What we have just been tracing and illustrating in sketch form as 'representation plus a generalisation about the inner essence of what is represented' (in interpreting it in graphic terms) is, as it were, a reflected *image* of the process which occurs both in any individual consciousness and in the history of man's progress towards forming generalised concepts out of individual phenomena. There are stages when only particular cases exist and there is as yet no generalised concept. Then come stages of development when, parallel to the awareness of a great number of particular cases, there also emerges the concept of a phenomenon that is common to them all. (One 'permeates' the other.) Finally, historical periods occur in which that generalisation – the 'idea' – begins to exist philosophically as the sole essential factor, which swallows up the particular, the 'random', the transitory, even though it is the latter which actually lends flesh and blood and concrete objectivity to this 'idea' of the phenomenon. These systems of consciousness, principles and stages of development in various phases of the history of art are perceived by us as different styles, primarily of course as the three basic principles: naturalistic, realistic and stylised, these being the basic three principles which correspond to the fundamental stages in the development of perceptual consciousness. Each segment of history passes through these phases, just as each new social structure passes through similar phases as it takes its turn at the helm of history and is appropriately reflected in the consciousness of the people and the images they create.

The arts pass through these phases as though cyclically echoing history, each time in a unique way but invariably stylistically.

Fig. 2.9

The 'moment' that interests us here represents a stage in the formation of consciousness when the generalising concept has not yet wholly managed to 'separate itself' from the objectification of a particular instance; a stage in which, for instance, the generalised concept of 'carrying' still cannot separate itself from depiction of the more familiar idea of 'a carrier'. It is precisely this process that has been captured in a certain very curious and extremely ancient Hindu miniature (see Fig. 2.9).

We must assume that in this case the generalising outline of the composition does not represent some dynamic, overall scheme, as do the sketches of Vautrin's arrest or of the barricade, but retains some elements of semi-abstract representation.

And this applies, with the utmost clarity, to our miniature.

The miniature depicts a bevy of heavenly maidens carrying the god Vishnu from one place to another.[24] The maidens are shown carrying the figure of a seated man. The action is very accurately depicted. But the artist was not satisfied with mere representation. He wants to convey fully the idea of the girls carrying Vishnu. What have we done in the instances we have been considering? Apart from objective depiction we have also forced the compositional elements – in particular the contour – to reiterate the content,

31

but in a maximally generalised form. We have taken generalisation beyond the limits of immediate depiction and into the compositional arrangement of the subject depicted.

Our Hindu proceeds in the same way, but he does not confine himself to what would have been done at a later stage of development. He does not transpose the 'idea' of someone carrying someone else into the interplay or relative disposition of masses, or into the pattern of tensions in and around the contours; nor is the expressive articulation of space echoed in the actions of the figures. He proceeds differently. He knows that the carrying of royalty is associated with being seated on an elephant, that on solemn occasions Indian rajahs and high officials move among the people on elephants. The idea of ceremonial transportation is indissolubly linked in his mind with an elephant, i.e. with the creature which transports a rajah on ceremonial occasions. Here, however, the divinity is not being carried by an elephant, but by girls! What is he to do? How is he to combine a depiction of girls carrying with the 'image of carrying' – an elephant?

Our master has found the solution! Look at the *contour* into which the maidens, in their flowing diaphanous garments, have been grouped: all these figures and details have been arranged into a contour which corresponds to the outline, the silhouette of . . . an elephant! This astonishing example, unique of its kind, shows graphically how generalisation develops from requirements that are firmly depictive in nature, and how even in this still impure form it assumes a compositional function.

At one point in our analysis we referred not merely to *carrying* but to the *carrying of royalty*. I believe the example in question can be interpreted in two ways: as a case of straightforward, primary metaphorical meaning – something which, in essence, every word is – and as a case of metaphorical description. That is to say, the contour of the elephant may be interpreted as a wish to depict the supreme form of transportation together with the *idea* of transportation as such. Or it may be interpreted as a wish to express the idea of *royal* transportation. Both cases can be supported by argument. Restricting ourselves to the second case, we simply broaden the horizon of our speculations. We must stress once again that the 'generalisation' we are discussing is an artistic type of generalisation, i.e. a generalisation that is tendentiously and emotionally coloured. Any kind of generalisation applied compositionally to an artistic representation gives it a resonance that is in the tonality which we wish to impart to the phenomenon depicted. It derives from our social relationship to that phenomenon. At this point we may also widen the scope of our example of the barricade. While the image of struggle was an essential element revealed by its contour, that is by no means all that the contour should tell us. The characteristics of the barricade, read as concrete object, will, apart from this *general idea* of the barricade, always also include the particular *image of the idea* peculiar to the situation in which that barricade figures. *Carrying* was the *idea*; the carrying of *royalty* was the image; the 'metaphor' of the elephant was the means.

The *zigzag* of the barricade's outline corresponded to the idea of struggle contained in the representation of the barricade.

However, a barricade may be, for example, 'victorious', 'unassailable', 'smashed'. Each one of these readings will have its particular shape, and essential to each will be its own figurative 'elephant', even if it does not figure within the composition in quite so complete a form. For there is no other way.

And no one will ever be able to sketch the outline of a 'smashed' barricade that is different from an 'unassailable' barricade unless he can: 1) *first of all* envisage a characteristic picture of the 'smashedness' [*razdavlënnost'*] of something; and 2) in suitable fashion 'separate' from all the individual instances the characteristic features of 'smashedness' as distinct from 'unassailability'; and finally, 3) gather the necessary realistic details of his material – in this instance the objects comprising the barricade, the road, the walls of the houses, the shop sign* – into a composition according to a scheme whose generalising effect is to express precisely that content as distinct from all other possible ones.

I believe only one more thing remains to be dealt with in this matter: to 'disentangle' two interlocked concepts – image and metaphor. It is quite obvious that we have here a three-stage link (as in the case: single frame, shot, montage). I refer to: word, metaphor, image. Every figurative word is a metaphor, though deprived of the keen edge of its primary usage.

In such words our awareness of the transference has been lost: they are the lifeless end-products of processes of transference that took place at some time in the past. A metaphor – an effective metaphor – is an example of the creation of figurative meaning, of participation in the act of forming a new figurative sense. Hence the need for novelty in its formation. A hackneyed metaphor does not fulfil this condition. A fresh metaphor, however, involves participation in a unique process of the following kind: an exchange of qualities between a pair, to one of which a certain quality properly belongs and to the other of which that quality, normally not associated with it, is unexpectedly transferred from somewhere else. Here we have the rudiments of the process which comes to its full flowering in the image. Perception of the object is not only immediate and direct, but is extended beyond the bounds of the signs and tokens that normally delimit that object. Perception thus occurs in two dimensions. It was precisely with this in mind that Diderot said of the metaphor:

What do you understand by these felicitous expressions . . . ? I would reply that they are those which are proper to one sense – to touch, for instance – and which are at the same time metaphoric to another sense,

---

*Obviously in another instance the same idea of 'smashedness' could relate to the composition of the pose in which you might want to show a man struck down by the blows of fate. Compositionally, the graphic approach and method remain the same.

such as the eyes. From this derives a double illumination for the person addressed: the true, direct light of the expression itself and the reflected light of the metaphor.[25]

Finally, the image, which in my view is constituted as a generalisation, as an aggregation of separate metaphors into a single whole: this is again not a process of formation; it is an end-product, but an end-product which, as it were, contains a swarm of *potential* dynamic (metaphoric) features that are ready to explode. It is the sort of immobility that is not inaction but the acme of dynamism. It is potentially dynamic in the sense that its separate constituents flicker like summer lightning, each one capable of turning into a single lightning-flash of metaphor. I feel compelled to use these meteorological terms because at this moment I have before me as I write precisely the image of a thunderstorm. It is that of Peter the Great in Pushkin's poem 'Poltava', where he is likened to 'the thunder of God'. The complex image of 'Peter-thunderstorm' is just such a composite generalisation, not in its separate signs and tokens but in their various metaphors, in all those *unwritten* 'flashes' of his glance, the 'thunder' of his voice, 'outbursts' of movement, 'hurricane' of emotions, etc., which surge through the generalising image without being named or specifically registered. (We have already encountered this in the example of the barricade where the *image of struggle* – not a *verbal* image, as here – also grew out of the aggregate of separate metaphors in the compositional arrangement of the scene.)

The next step in this sequence would be still greater generalisation, verging on abstraction, in which 'the thunder of God' would appear purged of any representational aspect, merely as a schematic thunderstorm and tempest. Abstraction is nothing to be afraid of. In our case it would entail, for instance, the transposition of Peter's actions into poetic *rhythm* and the *sound* of thunder, with the thunderstorm figuring in verbal description: a system of thunderous rolls in sound, of sharp outbursts and explosions in the rhythm of the phrasing and the clash of phrase on phrase. This would give the same impression of storm and thunder, conveyed by their most purely generalised characteristics: thunder and lightning clashing (in this case the clash of verbal masses – the phrases); lightning in the zigzag of the changing length of line and the pointing of phrases; thunder in the alliterative rumble of consonants. We may confidently say 'gives' instead of 'would give'. When writing in this vein, complete mastery depends on the poet's ability to maintain a single figurative idea simultaneously in all the different expressive 'strata': 'leftward' in the direction of word and metaphor, and 'rightward' in the direction of maximal generalisation in metre, rhythm and texture of sound.

> Out of the tent
> Comes Peter. His eyes
> Are shining . . .
> In movement swift,

He is magnificent.
He is the thunder of God itself.[26]

We have dealt very thoroughly with the question of graphic composition. We have examined instances where its means were line and colour. We have included an instance where its means were words and sounds. We have devoted so much attention to these matters that we are already being haunted by the phantoms and ghosts of countless . . . Firses, threatening us with their bony fingers: 'But you've forgotten the man?!'[27]

Dear Firses! We have not forgotten man at all. At this point we want to talk about man. It is here that he is most essential.

Obviously, there should be total harmony on the screen: harmony of dramatic situation, of human character, of the graphic structure of the screen image and the tonal structure of the sound.

The determining principle, the key to this harmony, is naturally the hero of the production: man.

What we have been observing of human activity in the graphic arts is merely a reflection in artistic categories of the fundamentals of man's expressive behaviour in general.

Our interest here, however, is not so much a picture of man's consciousness as the way it is manifested in human expressiveness. We have already touched on the dual nature of gesture in the conditions of its perception and interpretation. Let us only say in passing that within the gesture of a man talking about something, in the imagery formed by such a gesture there is to be found precisely the same inextricably linked two-dimensionality: the figuration of an event and the expression of an attitude towards that event. It cannot be otherwise, for it is clear that any graphic work of art is the embodiment *not in oneself* as in gesture but *on canvas** of these two *mutually interpenetrating elements of the content* of every gesture.

Descartes wrote of the physical two-dimensionality of reaction.

Nowadays we would also describe this 'duality' of potential reaction as a most interesting example of the simultaneous duality of reaction that is 'in contradiction': an immediate reaction and a mediated reaction – that is to say one which responds immediately to the event, and another which reacts on the basis of wisdom acquired through experience, i.e. of certain generalised data gained from the practice of immediate reaction. The picture of man's *physical behaviour* is completely identical to what we have been dealing with so far.

Even more interesting is another classic on the nature of expressiveness. It is by the man who first fully posed the question of the inherent dualism of the *psychological content* of gesture. I have in mind that most interesting thinker of the late 18th century, almost totally forgotten throughout the 19th century,

---

*It would be equally valid to say in an orchestra or in verbal material.

and now enjoying a sensational 'renaissance' in all the most recent studies and research on *human expressiveness*.

This is Johann Jacob Engel.[28]

People generally like to make a 'figurative' connection between mimicry and physiognomy. A person's physiognomy generalises, as it were, those mimetic features which are most peculiar to him. His habitual movements seem to be frozen in the permanent *character mask* of his face, his persona (the same applies to the overall mimetic aspect of the figure as a whole).

When it comes to the artificial re-creation of such a persona, the actor must depict on his own body (as a Chinese artist does on silk) the same duality within a single mimetic display: the persona (a generalisation about the person, his character) and the mimetic expression which passes across it (the particular instance of the emotion experienced by that character), e.g. a 'miserly' person is 'sensually' inclined, a 'suspicious' man is 'playfully' inclined, an 'introspective' person is 'startled', and so on.

It is quite obvious that in such cases the appearance of the physiognomy is again built on the laws of the reversed metaphor. In this respect we could repeat everything that has been said about 'Vautrin's arrest', 'aversion' or the 'sketch of the barricade'. Let us limit ourselves to just one example. A great master of this subject was Lev Tolstoy.

It is no wonder that Marietta Shaginyan, for instance, remarks with such enthusiasm and so perceptively about the features with which Tolstoy endows Katyusha Maslova:

> . . . and in addition to all this, there is her squint – a terrible characteristic, but a stroke of genius on Tolstoy's part – which combines the motif of 'come hither' with a simultaneous sense of 'impunity' on the part of the man who seduces Katyusha; a squinting, unfocused* look lowers one's sense of responsibility when face to face with such a person, because it somehow deflects one from direct contact with them.[29]

We can also observe these same elements in dialogue, which is the next stage of gesture: they occur in both the *delivery* and the *construction* of dialogue, the basis of whose structure must always contain either the intonation of its true content or the intonation (and the words) with which that true meaning is concealed ('Words are given us to conceal our thoughts', as Talleyrand said);[30] but one way or another, the *intonation* must be there.

A most expressive example of such ambiguity can be a conversation between lovers, in which the generalised element – the exchange of feelings – may be couched, and usually is couched, in the most absurd verbal material, which nevertheless manages to convey the full depth of the relationship.

Relevant here is an anecdote about Stendhal, who wanted to test the

---

*'Unfocusing' would be more accurate.

faithfulness of one of his countless mistresses. By means of a bribe, he succeeded in concealing himself in a room where his mistress was to meet her paramour. But such was the absurdity of the lovers' conversation that Stendhal burst out laughing and revealed his presence; he forgave his mistress and parted from her, it seems, after conceding her to the other man.

A brilliant literary example on the same theme is the famous dialogue between Pugachov and the innkeeper in Pushkin's *The Captain's Daughter*. This is one of the most perfect examples of the use of veiled allusion, in which the concealed meaning of a verbal exchange is conveyed by vague, oblique wording. Curiously enough, it is not the fact itself (the mutiny of Cossack troops at Yaitsk in 1772) which turns out to contain the greater breadth of connotation, but the folk sayings – so indeterminate that they forfeit any precise delineation of meaning – which coalesce into an overall, allusive description of the mutiny. This example is interesting as a case of 'exchange of function' between the two elements in our analysis: yet another confirmation of the unity of these two aspects, of how they arise from one another (the Indian elephant) and of how one mutates into another (the exchange of function, as in the present example).

But here is the example itself:

'Where is the driver?' I asked Savelyich.

'Here, your honour,' a voice answered me from above. I looked up at the bunk over the stove, and saw a black beard and two glittering eyes. . . . I handed him up a cup of tea; he tasted it and grimaced. 'Do me a favour, your honour, and order me a glass of wine. . . .'

The host took a measure and a glass out of the sideboard, went over to him, looked him in the face and said:

'Aha! So you're back in these parts again! Where have you sprung from?'

My driver winked meaningfully and answered with a proverb: 'Flew into a garden and pecked at the hemp; grandma threw a stone and missed me. What about your people?'

'What about our people!' replied the host, keeping up the allusive exchange. 'They started to ring the bells for vespers, but the priest's wife wouldn't let them: the priest was away on a visit, she said, and the devil's in the churchyard!'

'Quiet, old man,' countered my tramp. 'There'll be rain, so there'll be mushrooms; and when there are mushrooms someone'll come along with a basket. And now (here he winked again) hide your axe behind your back: the forester's a-coming. Your honour! Here's to your health!'

So saying, he took his glass, crossed himself and drank it in one gulp. Then he bowed to me and returned to his bunk.

At the time I could understand nothing of this thieves' cant; but later I guessed that they had been talking about the business of the Cossack troops at Yaitsk, who had then only just been pacified after the mutiny of 1772.[31]

Taking one example after another, we have analysed the stages at which meaningful gesture turned into meaningful intonation, and at which meaningful intonation consolidated into something more tangible: a word. It remains to demonstrate how this dual process can advance to the next stage of objectification, namely to turning an object into a metaphor. In contrast to the example where the imperial eagle is torn down from the chemist's shop sign, let us provide an example where the metaphorical nature of the object is displayed with such tactful *unobtrusiveness* and *non-literalism* that it does not slide into facile allegory. I have in mind the funeral of the Duke in Feuchtwanger's *Jew Süss*:

> The interment was conducted with unusual solemnity and splendour: the interminable procession of mourners' carriages, the torch-bearers, the ceremonial mourning attire of the princes, nobles, officials and servitors; the troops marching past for hours on end, the tolling of bells, the funeral orations, the singing of church choirs, the artillery salutes in honour of the departed. . . . But the huge stately coffin, over which the lamentations were pronounced, the bells were rung, the cannon-shots boomed out and the chorales were sung, was empty. While his widow had been engaged in dispute with the duke-regent, the body of the deceased duke Karl-Alexander – despite the skill of the doctors who embalmed him – had grown so decayed and had begun to exude such an evil-smelling stench that long before the solemn funeral he had to be secretly interred in the new vault at Ludwigsburg.[32]

It would be difficult to convey less obtrusively, with such justified descriptive realism and without apparent 'ulterior motive', the idea of just what an 'empty vessel' the duke had been all his life!

This example has, in fact, brought us to the point at which generalisation goes further than in the preceding instances: it is not limited to a perceptual function, but actually formulates a value judgment.

And here, in our examination of judgment and generalisation, we pass beyond the immediate confines of the subject we have been discussing and on to the next one. What is it?

Let us again make use of an analogy from painting. To illustrate this point, I have selected a comment on the technique of painting taken from Gauguin's remarks on 'Les Fauves' (c. 1905):

> To render the same sensation the line was modified . . . at the risk of denying the truthfulness of appearances as they are recorded by the retina during our everyday existence; at the risk of sacrificing the accuracy of the measurements, they sought to discover, beneath the fleshy envelope,

the internal structure of individuals and to bring out what in their character approached a general conception of life.[33]

Here is an example of a similar process of dual generalisation that applies purely to painting: from chance elements in the outward appearance of separate individuals to derive the generalising images that are inherent in them, and from a generalisation of these images to derive in turn a concrete, generalised perception of life as such, of Life with a capital L.

Thus we see that whenever we undertake a searching examination of some manifestation of reality, we invariably proceed, through a series of ever deepening levels, to ever greater generalisations. The *content* of those generalisations can be extremely varied.

Gauguin, a fugitive from urban culture, a sort of eccentric nineteenth-century Jean-Jacques [Rousseau], in reverting to a primitive stage of mankind, envisaged as the ultimate generalisation a certain pantheistic ideal of life as such.[34] The Chinese seek the ultimate metaphysical immutability of the world within each particle of it. As participants in the final and decisive struggle of class forces for the liberation of mankind and for a classless society, we [in the Soviet Union] chiefly perceive phenomena as the embodiment of that struggle and of the social conflicts that gave rise to it. Naturally, therefore, generalisations of that particular kind predominate in the ultimate conclusions to be drawn from our [Soviet] works of art.

I think we may safely say that while being concerned with artistic forms and structures, we have at the same time delved into the work of art to the point of its graphic and philosophical unity.

To return to the graphic material, let us again recall our Indian elephant and juxtapose it with an example from another art which also deals with the concept of carrying. If the elephant, for all its clumsiness (indeed, largely thanks to that clumsiness), clearly revealed in its configuration the *mechanism* of the metaphor, being an example of composition wavering between metaphor and image, then this next example already comes close to unifying the image with the generalising idea. I have in mind the Greek statues of Atlas and of the caryatids from the Erechtheum.[35] Both are called upon to support the heavy cornices of porticoes. Greek architecture is astounding, indeed unsurpassed, in that each of its elements *not only fulfils* this or that structural *function* but simultaneously expresses the *idea* of that function architecturally. Here the idea of 'support' is incorporated into the primary image, the same image which produces the concept of support that is inherent in Man-as-supporter. The idea is embodied into the specific object from which, by generalisation, it first arose. Passing beyond the 'elephant' metaphor, the figures of Atlas and the caryatids of the Erechtheum provide us with a most remarkable image, disclosed in the unity between the idea and its originator and bearer, who is made to embody the idea in his or her own image. Thus it was that we gradually expanded the *particular* depiction of a barricade into the metaphorical zigzag of single *particular* images and thence into the generalised idea of struggle as such, Struggle with a capital S, which lies behind all of them.

It is an interesting fact that one may have recourse to exactly the same property of artistic forms that we are now investigating so pedantically, if one wishes *visually* (figuratively) to illustrate a philosophical generalisation through a simple phenomenon. Søren Kierkegaard does it, for instance, when he wants to make an especially vivid presentation of the specific nature of Socratic teaching:

> There is an engraving that portrays the grave of Napoleon. Two large trees overshadow the grave. There is nothing else to be seen in the picture, and the immediate spectator will see no more. Between these two trees, however, is an empty space, and as the eye traces out its contour Napoleon himself suddenly appears out of the nothingness, and now it is impossible to make him disappear. The eye that has once seen him now always sees him with anxious necessity. It is the same with Socrates' replies. As one sees the trees, so one hears his discourse; as the trees are trees, so his words mean exactly what they sound like. There is not a single syllable to give any hint of another interpretation, just as there is not a single brush stroke to suggest Napoleon. Yet it is this empty space, this nothingness, that conceals what is most important.[36]

Why should we not read this quotation in reverse? Why should we not say what we have deduced above, namely that in its final generalisation a graphic composition is metamorphosed into a philosophical conception of the given phenomenon?

We have followed this process in painting through various epochs and cultures. Passing beyond the confines of painting, we have noted its metaphorical function in human gesture and expressive movement.

Let us once again go beyond the confines of painting, this time in order to show that this highest form of generalisation can equally well occur elsewhere than in painting.

What if it applies to the smallest constituent elements of a work of art, to gesture on stage and to the graphic composition of a film shot? If so, then it is equally applicable to the conception of a work as a whole, be it in the theatre or cinema.

In the theatre this corresponds to what the inventor of the 'Method', Stanislavsky, called the 'super-objective'. By methods of inference and of gradual, deepening generalisation, it entirely echoes – where a *play* is concerned – what we have been expounding with regard to painting, to the film shot and to gesture.

Suppose we are producing Griboyedov's *Woe from Too Much Wit* and we decide that the main purpose of the play can be described by the words 'I wish to strive for Sophy'. There is a great deal in the plot that would confirm that definition. The drawback would be that in handling the play from that angle the theme of social denunciation would appear to have only an episodic, accidental value. But you can describe the super-objective in the terms of 'I wish to struggle, not for Sophy but for my country!' Then Chatski's ardent love of his country and his people will move into the foreground.

At the same time the indictment of society theme will become more prominent, giving the whole play a deeper inner significance. You can deepen its meaning still further if you use: 'I wish to struggle for freedom' as the main theme. In that set-up the hero's accusations become more severe and the whole play loses the personal, individual tone it had when the theme was connected with Sophy; it is no longer even national in scope, but broadly human, and universal in its implications.

In my own experience I have had some even more vivid proofs of the importance of choosing the right name for the super-theme. One instance was when I was playing *Le Malade imaginaire* of Molière. Our first approach was elementary and we chose the theme 'I wish to be sick'. But the more effort I put into it and the more successful I was, the more evident it became that we were turning a jolly, satisfying comedy into a pathological tragedy. We soon saw the error of our ways and changed to: 'I wish to be thought sick'. Then the whole comic side came to the fore and the ground was prepared to show up the way in which the charlatans of the medical world exploited the stupid Argan, which was what Molière meant to do.

In Goldoni's *La locandiera* we made the mistake of using 'I wish to be a misogynist', and we found that the play refused to yield either humour or action. It was only when I discovered that the hero really loved women and wished only to be accounted a misogynist that I changed to 'I wish to do my courting on the sly' and immediately the play came to life.

In this last instance the problem concerned my part rather than the whole play. However, it was only after prolonged work, when we realized that the Mistress of the Inn was really the Mistress of our Lives, or, in other words, *Woman*, that the whole inner essence of the play became evident.

Often we do not come to a conclusion about this main theme until we have put on a play. Sometimes the public helps us to understand its true definition.

The main theme must be firmly fixed in an actor's mind throughout the performance. It gave birth to the writing of the play. It should also be the fountain-head of the actor's artistic creation.[37]

From the sound of the Italian title *La locandiera* I cannot help recalling the Spanish words *la soldadera*. *La soldadera* was an episode in the Mexican civil war which was prepared but not shot for the film *Que viva México!*.[38]

And it is appropriate to recall it here not only because of the verbal consonance: it is an example of something on the same theme but in cinema, where the scope of the material is much wider and richer than in theatre; as we shall see, though, the same principles apply to both art forms.

A *soldadera* is a soldier's woman-friend. His wife. His companion in peacetime and on campaign. An army of soldiers is preceded by an army of soldiers' wives. During the revolutionary period, Mexico had neither a quartermaster's service, nor military hospitals, nor front-line medical posts. The feeding and nursing of the wounded was the responsibility of the soldiers' wives, the *soldaderas*. In a cloud of dust raised by the trotting gait typical of Mexican women, a swarm of *soldaderas* moved ahead of the army. It occupied villages, collected supplies, baked and cooked the simple Mexican dishes in order to greet the troops with a hot meal and a few tortillas as they marched into the villages. The *soldadera* scoured the deserted battlefield, searching among the corpses for the wounded body of her soldier-companion, side by side with whom she frequently fought, in order to carry him away on her own shoulders, or bury him and make a cross of coloured stones on his grave, after which she would become the wife of another soldier.

There is a curious characteristic of these remarkable women. With uncomplaining obedience they changed from soldier to soldier, sharing with each the hardships of the campaign, caring for him, nursing him, or burying him when he fell in battle. Even more curiously, the *soldadera* moved not only from soldier to soldier but from army to army, often switching between hostile armies which had just destroyed each other. There is something symbolic and profoundly human in this image of a woman standing above the armed strife which was tearing her country apart. She somehow embodies the great idea that the Mexican people is fundamentally united, for all its fifty-two different ethnic groups; that the fighting and internecine warfare, into which the separate parts of that unified nation are forced by political adventurers, by generals seeking power, by the Catholic Church and by foreign capitalists, is basically profoundly alien to the people itself, which pays with its blood for the interests and advantage of others. It was from this idea that *the figure of the soldadera Pancha (Francesca) grew into the personified image of rebellious Mexico*, torn by civil war and clashing political forces, a Mexico being passed, like Pancha, from hand to hand and flung back and forth between Federalists (the forces of the dictator Porfirio Diaz), Villistas (the forces of Pancho Villa), Zapatistas (the forces of Emiliano Zapata), Carranzistas (the forces of Venustiano Carranza) and so on and so forth, in order to end the film at that shining moment of short-lived national unification of Mexico when Pancha rides in triumph into Mexico City along with the united forces of north and south – of Zapata and Villa. It was the happy moment of Mexico's progressive, national unification, from which the civil war might have begun to develop into a socialist revolution. But this unity started to disintegrate almost at once; following a series of betrayals, treachery and renewed ordeals, it sullied itself in the mire of the narrow nationalism and reactionary chauvinism that replaced it.

At the moment of its conception, the image of Pancha the *soldadera* glittered before my inward eye in all its colourful visual brilliance and with all its powerful generalising significance. (As I now recall, this happened to me in a car on the way from Mexico City to the pyramids of San Juan Teotihuacan.) And I could have started to make it a reality! Although fate decided otherwise, that at least is the story of how the image of Pancha the *soldadera* evolved, even though she never did rise to the height of a generalised statement about 'the eternal female', as did her similar-sounding Italian sister, *La locandiera*.

A true daughter of the revolutionary masses of the Mexican people, she was called upon to embody no less than the image of her heroic, fighting country. We should not, however, forget that *Soldadera* was only one episode within the epic conception of *Que viva México!*.

The conception of the film as a whole was meant to represent an even broader generalisation.

It was constructed like a necklace, like the bright, striped colouring of the *serape*, or Mexican cloak, or like a sequence of short novellas. (In the form in which the film is now being screened it represents just one of these novellas, blown up out of all proportion and illegally expanded into a complete film on its own.[39])

This chain of novellas was held together by a set of linking ideas, proceeding in a historically based sequence, but not so much by chronological epochs as by geographical zones. For the culture of Mexico of any one epoch from the vertical column of history seems to be like a fan spread across the surface of the land. Various parts of Mexico have retained the cultural and social features which characterised the country as a whole at certain stages of its historical development. When you travel from Yucatan to tropical Tehuantepec, from the tropics to the central plateau, to the civil war battlefields in the north or to the completely modern Mexico City, you seem not to be travelling in space but in time. The structure, the look, the culture and customs of these various parts of the federation seem to belong to prehistoric times, to the pre-Colombian era, to the age of Cortés,[40] to the period of Spanish feudal rule, to the years of the struggle for independence.

Thus was the film conceived: in the form of a sequence of small episodes which would traverse these gradations of history, episodes which themselves grew naturally out of the visual features and the mores of different parts of the country. Three couples moved across the three central episodes. A boy and a girl: two creatures living almost like biological 'particles' of a carefree tropical paradise before the discoveries of Columbus and the conquests of Cortés (whose stamp still lies on sleepy Tehuantepec). Then a couple who were the victims of inhuman exploitation by Spanish landowners and the Catholic Church. Finally, a man and a woman as comrades in arms, a *soldadera* and a soldier in the battles of the revolution for a free, united Mexico (the story of Pancha).

As we see, throughout the film as a whole, throughout the depiction of

Mexico at various decisive stages of its history and culture, at a second level there was traced the theme of relationships between man and woman – from the almost animal-like cohabitation of the tropics, through the struggle for the right freely to possess one another (in the fight against the feudal *jus primae noctis*), to the joint struggle, side by side, for the full possession of life as a whole (by participating in the liberation movement).

The picture, however, had a third – the most generalised – level: the theme of life and death, or rather of victory over death.

The theme of death ran through the film at three points: in the prologue; in the culmination of the action; and in the epilogue. It also expressed the idea of social immortality as opposed to biological mortality, the thought that genuine immortality, i.e. existence beyond the limits of the allotted span of one physical life, is only possible in the unbroken chain of collective social creativity down the generations, in striving devotedly to achieve a single, socialist ideal of society.

The film began with an image of total servitude to the idea of death – the biological and physical end of man. Its background and leitmotiv was the cult of death: a funeral rite amid the dead ruins of memorials to the past: the central theme of all the most ancient religions of Mexico.

This was succeeded by the affirmation of life in all its biological plenitude, the animal-like thirst for life and fecundity of the languid and voluptuous tropics.

Into this lushness, exploitation and the Church irrupted 'with cross and sword': the strokes of the landlord's whip and the self-flagellation of Catholic ascetics before the Madonna; St Francis with the emblem of death, a skull; a bull, harried to death in the bull-ring, burning like gold in the sun; the brutal reprisal of the *haciendado*,[41] whose horses' hooves smashed the skulls of peons buried up to their necks in the ground for having dared to rebel against the regime, the second triumph of death in Mexico; the Catholic Church's preaching of mortification of the flesh and the mortification of flesh by the slaveowning Spanish landlords.

The revolt against this, the struggle for an affirmation of life at the social level, the civil war as a continuation of the struggle in which Sebastian died beneath the hooves of his *haciendado*'s horse, a struggle now gripping the whole of Mexico: this is the episode of Pancha the *soldadera*, with the ending as described above.

In the incomplete version of the film, that is to say the rough cut before editing, the ending expressed the same thought but in a different form. That ending was built up out of exactly the same material, wholly derived from folklore, national rituals and popular festivals, as is the film as a whole.

The ending was envisaged as a generalised representation of an *avasallada*,[42] into which merges a figurative picture of Mexico, represented by all its peoples and costumes, in mourning for the tragic death of Sebastian and his comrades, interpreted so as to develop into an image of the entire oppressed class of Mexico. (Just as in the following episode Pancha the *soldadera* represented Mexico as a whole.)

The idea of the social conquest of death as the continuation of the struggle by a *whole* class after the death of one of its individual members was embodied in the generalised and socially reinterpreted episode of the 'Day of the Dead' as it is celebrated annually, according to Mexican custom, on 2 November.

What is this Mexican *avasallada*, to which we gave the function of overcoming death?

It invests with irony that magnificent contempt for suffering and death which every Mexican feels. From ancient times – starting with the famous remark of the Emperor Cuauhtemoc,[43] who groaned to one of his courtiers, 'Don't groan – I am not lying on a bed of roses either', when the Spanish *conquistadores* were roasting them on gridirons in order to discover where some treasure was hidden; through the endless years of civil war, which effectively never ceased but only flared up and died down again – the Mexican has grown so accustomed to scenes of death and suffering that all fear of them seems to have been tempered out of him.

An ironic attitude to death completely pervades the second, life-affirming, half of the festival known as the 'Day of the Dead'. The first half is given over to remembering the dead, to praying for them, to their invisible presence among the living: a table is set for them, food is placed for them on the tombstones amid a forest of candles that burn all night in a place such as the mountainside cemetery of Ameca-Meca or on the shore of Lake Patsucaro in the state of Michoacán. Then as dawn breaks, life begins to come into its own: to the living, life. Echoing the amusing words of the café sign opposite the main entrance to the famous Père Lachaise cemetery in Paris: 'Au repos des vivants' [For the Repose of the Living], life claims its rights. Food and drink are consumed, fireworks are lit (in broad daylight!) alternating with that traditional expression of joy – pistol shooting, carousels whirl around, stalls and puppet shows do a roaring trade, and on top of gravestones in the cemetery, amid the burnt stubs of candles and crêpe-festooned portraits of the deceased brought from home, men and women strive to ensure that the human race shall not die out. All forms of food and amusement on that day bear the emblem of death: pitchers shaped like skulls, sweetmeats shaped like skulls. Especially big ones – the size of a child's head – are made of sugar, decorated with coloured patterns, and with the name of the dear departed picked out on the forehead. Chocolate coffins come complete with sugar cadavers. And by the end of the day all these have found their way into the tummies of the little bronzed children, who from the tenderest age are accustomed to associate skulls with sweets, not with the grim Franciscan motto which adorns the skull and crossbones: 'Thou I was – me thou shalt become'. In the last shot of the film one of these chubby little boys breaks open a sugar skull, bigger than his own head, and gobbles down the pieces in delight! But there are not only sweets: a sea of toys shaped like skeletons, skulls and little coffins floods the market-stalls which fill the *alamedas* [town squares] on those days. Broadsheets and leaflets with scurrilous ditties, political pamphlets (in the form of epitaphs on live politicians, assumed to have 'passed on') and the unique engravings of the incomparable Posada,[44] all on the same ironic theme of death, are handed round and read by adults and children who, as they dance, cover their faces with masks . . . of death. They wear emblems of death in their buttonholes, but with a political slant: a skull in a top hat, a skull in the broad-brimmed sombrero of a *haciendado*; a skull in a matador's cap with a plait of hair down the back of its bony neck; a skull under a minister's tricorn hat, a fireman's helmet, a gendarme's uniform cap. A skull under a general's kepi and a skull in a bishop's mitre.

Thus Mexico celebrates victory over death, and scorn for death, in the name of an all-conquering life force.

It was natural to use this as the ending after the mourning for the murdered victims, to give it a social interpretation in that context, and finally to tie it all together in the strange, picturesque scene of the finale. But the people who cut up *Que viva México!* (what they did cannot be called montage) were, of course, totally unaware of the overall meaning of the footage that was shot for the 'Day of the Dead'. They even failed to add this material to the episode of Sebastian; instead, they ignored all its suggestive quality as image, reduced it to mere ethnographic 'illustration' . . . and made it into a separate short film about the Mexican way of celebrating the 'Day of the Dead'!

I mention this here because it contains an exact, ironic equivalent of the topic with which we began this section: the example of the barricade, in which 'the idea emerged through the depiction'.

See what a *tour de force* results from the method of illuminating the one through the other!

The social context of the skulls, the living face and the death-mask, the real skulls (the emblems of St Francis), and finally a very amusing leaflet illustrated by one of Posada's engravings: all these merged in my mind into the following image. Posada's pamphlet (entitled 'Calavera de Don Folias y el negrito', or 'The skull of Don Folias and the negro boy') showed a skeleton among a group of other skeletons, but with the skull . . . of a negro. And of course in just the same way that negroes themselves depict angels for instance, the negro's skull was black in Posada's engraving!

I think it was this that prompted the solution of the carnival-of-death scene, which I set to the music of the rumba in the finale. It was the falling away of the persona (the face) within the essential substance (the skull), while maintaining the same outward features – in this case, the features of death – that determined this.

People are dancing in death-masks. Here are all racial groups, all levels and classes of society, workers, peons, men and women, and, as though by chance, members of the ruling classes dressed in exactly the same costumes that they wore when they appeared during the various earlier episodes of the film: the daughter of the hacienda owner, the *haciendado* himself, the general. This, however, extends beyond the fictitious characters. For instance, there is a character with the star and ribbon of an order wearing a top hat above a cardboard death-mask; as though by chance, it so happened that the President of the Republic was filmed in just this attire for one of the film's final scenes. There is a character in a mitre and episcopal robes; as though by coincidence, the real Papal Legate (who had agreed to pose for the 'Spanish' episode of the film) happened to have been filmed in exactly this costume. At the height of the carnival, the white cardboard death-masks slip down from the faces to show the cheerfully grinning features of peons, workers, children, proletarians. But then the masks also slip away from the faces of the bishop, the President, the landowner and his daughter, whose horse trampled the peon Sebastian to death with its hooves. Behind their masks there are no smiling faces, indeed there are no faces at all: in place of the masks are real bony skulls.

The death-masks of the carnival *avasallada* are an ironic grimace made at extinction and death, just as a brutal reprisal is only a momentary delay in the relentless advance of the proletarian class towards life. And the same *avasallada* mask conceals for a while the dead countenance of a class which, though still capering in the dance, is already condemned to death; nay more, it is a class without a future, a dead class.

Thus were the film's characters brought together in the finale and thus was vengeance wrought for the murder of the peon Sebastian.

Ironic in form, tragic in content.

And all to the music of the rumba. . . .

It is doubtless unwise for anyone who is not a Mexican to laugh at death. Whoever dares to mock her is punished by the terrible goddess of death.

Her reward to me was the death of that scene and the death of the entire film.

But even if I never managed to realise fully my conception of death, in the film as a whole I paid the homage due to her!

To venture into this kind of 'super-generalisation' always entails a certain risk. If taken too far, it inevitably lapses into metaphysics and mysticism. We have a classic example of this brand of super-generalisation in Gogol's *The Government Inspector*. Fortunately, it does not show up in any tampering with the classic, realistic text of the comedy itself, for the simple reason that it arose many years after the play was written; even then it did not take the form of a reworking, alteration or distortion of the basic script but consisted only of the author's 'commentaries', made during the period in which he suffered an acute psychological disintegration and a propensity for mysticism. I refer to a certain passage in *The Dénouement of 'The Government Inspector'*,[45] where Gogol 'generalises' the little town of *The Government Inspector* into 'The City of the Spirit', the gendarme of the final scene into a symbol of 'Divine Retribution', and the tsar on earth into an image of the 'King of Heaven'. This result is inevitable whenever an author, carried away by the urge to generalise, loses touch with concrete reality and generalisation in its social – that is, primary, fundamental and decisive – form, whether at a *realistic* or a *philosophical* level. (There is an element of self-criticism in this statement. If

I successfully avoided this danger in the conception of *Que viva México!*, it was in this very area that I went wrong in *Bezhin Meadow*.[46])

In the previous examples we have, I think, traced and demonstrated with absolute clarity that the inherent law which we revealed by comparing two representations of a barricade applies *in toto* to the system of constructing the image that must pervade a figurative representation, from the composition of the shot to the conception of the film as a whole; or rather, from the conception of the piece as a whole and penetrating the composition and formal structure of the work down to its smallest details, the individual scenes and individual shots.

In addition to describing the results of a gradual expansion of the levels and scope of generalisation, I should like to mention a brief instance of the way in which a similar process can 'unfold' before our eyes.

This is an example of how, from a simple contour line, from a simple 'record' (though admittedly one which describes a great historic event!) we may deduce ever more profound levels of generalisation. I stress the word deduce, because in the example cited we are dealing with one-half of the creative process: with the origin and development of a conception, with the germ of a project that needs to be given form. The second half of the process will be the question of what is to be the *solution* of that project so that *at all levels* there will be a fusion of both the fact itself and the generalisation that we want to impart to this fact.

If we are to limit ourselves to a brief greeting to the *heroes* of the event in question – which is the reason it was chosen in the first place! – then this task itself is essentially also the solution, which only requires a suitable choice of words and their arrangement in a syntactical and rhythmic sequence. If, however, it is to be the subject matter of a literary or cinematic poem, then this fact will to an equal extent determine the compositional structuring of the material and the scope of the whole work.

You open the newspaper one day in June 1937. Before you have had time to read anything, your glance is riveted by something unusual: you are amazed by the unfamiliar way in which a map has been printed. You are used to seeing the route from the USSR across Europe to the USA in the horizontal, yet here is a map cutting vertically down the page of the newspaper. San Francisco is not to the left of Moscow across the Atlantic Ocean and not to the right across the Pacific. San Francisco is placed vertically above Moscow, and they are joined by a thick black line as straight as an arrow crossing the Arctic. It is the track of the historic, unprecedented flight of Heroes of the Soviet Union Chkalov, Baidukov and Belyakov. Several weeks previously, we were surprised by a similar track shown on the map, but in that case the line stopped at the Pole, marking the realisation of the dream of the conqueror of the North Pole, Hero of the Soviet Union Vodopyanov.[47]

The usually horizontal map of a conventional flight path has been changed for a vertical transpolar flight map.

In your mind, you connect the horizontal and the vertical with the action of rising from the horizontal into the vertical: something has risen, stood up. The map has 'reared up': this is the first image which accompanies the action.

But 'rearing up' is a temporary state: the association is an incorrect one!

You take it further in the direction indicated: what was standing on four legs (the horizontal) has risen up on to two legs (the vertical). While this represents a temporary process within the brain of a single horse, the quadruped in general, to which the horse belongs, has done the same thing as a *species*. And permanently.

Despite Kant (who proved that the four-footed posture was the normal state for man), the animal, as it climbed up the evolutionary ladder, straightened out its spine and stood up on two legs in the vertical position. The depiction of phylogenesis inevitably summons up an autogenetic image. Using less complicated words, Goethe has this to say about it: 'Even if the world progresses generally (! – S. M. E.), youth will always begin at the beginning, and the epochs of the world's cultivation will be repeated in the individual.'[48]

Also related to this topic is the riddle of the sphinx about the four-legged youth and the two-legged adult. The three-legged old man is irrelevant, because the picture of the first two already serves as an adequate image to typify the progress of any phenomenon from the stage of youth to its full-grown state.

Despite its direction, the vertical line of the flight from the USSR to the USA draws a horizontal line under the sum total of a whole epoch of the infancy of aviation, and as it enters on a new stage of its history (the Soviet period), world aviation starts out with 'head held proudly high', having for the first time 'straightened up to its full height' like a man walking in pride.

But man, as opposed to animals, cannot help being shocked by something else that disturbs you as you read the same page of the same newspaper: the destruction of Bilbao, and the image, which only a moment ago was firmly lodged in the rarefied sphere of generalisation, descends and merges indissolubly with the political reality of the present day, and you add to the previous paragraph: '. . . like *socialist* man walking in pride, unlike the beastly, animal-like – "horizontal"! – raids of the Fascist bombers and fighters, destroying flocks of defenceless women and children'.[49]

But let us return again to our example of the barricade, and this time from another angle. Our example of the barricade is particularly rich and many-sided. It is also a most striking example, because its very *subject matter* is *struggle, conflict*. Hence the graphic clarity of the compositional *calligraphy* in the outline of the barricade, which looks like a seismographic trace of the ups and downs of the struggle. Hence, too, the vividness in the *grouping and relative positioning of details* in the street, which are transposed not only physically but compositionally – in this case entirely by the choice of the angle of vision and the set-up: the shop sign has not only been *physically* torn down from the shop (sign A) and thrown *under the feet of the people advancing* on the barricade, but the same shop sign (in this case shop sign B, the pretzel) has equally been cast downwards *to the foot of the frame* – but compositionally, by a change in set-up.[50] And by purely compositional means it also conveys the idea that what was up is now down, and that what was below has now been raised up; i.e. there is the 'feel' of something having been *overturned within the subject matter of the scene*, arising from a perception of the purely visual displacement of elements in the composition, i.e. in the formal structure.

In our example, despite the fact that the theme of the scene is conflict or struggle, the two levels of its expression – both its visual representation and the generalised image of the inner content of what is depicted – are not in conflict *between themselves*. By its *own* means, each level expressed *the same idea*: both the figurative and the compositional graphics (the outlined movement) and the grouping of details emphasised by the choice of set-up (the 'feel' of something having been overturned, due to a disturbance of the usual placing of objects within a normal setting): all these elements work together *in one direction*.

But equally often these levels *conflict* with one another, and work in *opposite directions*. This occurs in those instances where the *visual representation* – the *outward appearance* of the phenomenon – *does not correspond* to that true, generalised image of the subject's *inner content* which the author sees in it. This is a relative factor, and is dictated by the author's attitude or standpoint in relation to the phenomenon depicted. In it there is, of course, an element of arbitrariness, although only up to a certain point, because the author's attitude is historically determined by his social allegiance. This factor, therefore, is a function of the author's attitude and his treatment of the subject matter; both these factors reflect the (relatively) arbitrary way in which the phenomenon is refracted in his consciousness or in the bias that he applies in the interest of the class to which he belongs or which he supports.

Only if the author belongs to the proletarian class or projects the viewpoint of that class on to the subject matter will his treatment not be an *arbitrary refraction* of the event but a *true revelation* of that event or phenomenon. For only that class possesses the immutable weapon of Marxism-Leninism, which is capable of tearing away every mask and of laying bare the very essence of a phenomenon beneath whatever 'appearances' it may assume; this will be so, however unexpected or paradoxical the structuring of the subject matter may seem at times to be.

This may affect the treatment (conception) of the work as a whole: for instance, in the treatment of a historical event where the structuring, in aiming to reveal the *inner content* (meaning, essence) of the phenomenon, may result in something which is in direct opposition to the documentary record, which gives only a factual version of the event.

The results of achieving *inner truth* may seem at first sight to contradict the visible, 'physical' facts of a historical event. Take, for instance, the historical interpretation of the Paris Commune: outwardly the Commune was 'crushed' by the boots of the men of Versailles, while simultaneously, in its historic *significance*, the Commune was one of the most brilliant victories on the road to the dictatorship of the proletariat.

Nor would I be far wrong in presuming that it was this very image of the Commune – victorious in its defeat – which the script-writer and the director of *The Battleship Potemkin* had in their mind's eye and inspired them to 'distort' the story of their film in a similar way.[51] We all know the sad fate which met the mutinous battleship in real life, its tragic finale at Constanţa. We are also aware of the enormous and positive political significance of that mutiny in the fleet, even though it was suppressed. Apart from all the other means used to attain the desired result, it was in the treatment – namely in the handling of the historic sequence of events, breaking them off at their *culmination* (when the *Potemkin* sails unharmed through the admiral's squadron) instead of pursuing them to their *factual end* (the disarming at Constanţa) – that the emotional impact of the event as a great victory was achieved, i.e. its inherent historical meaning was revealed.

Let us mention another similar example, a situation in which a conflict arising out of inconsistency between factual truth and artistic truth is also resolved in favour of the artistic image at the cost of divergence from factual accuracy. The example, from the same film, is largely emotional in its effect and comes from the scene before the one where the sailors refuse to shoot their comrades, who are covered with a tarpaulin. At naval executions by firing squad no one was ever, on any occasion, covered by anything – not on the *Potemkin*, or on any other vessel of the tsarist navy. A tarpaulin actually was used at such executions, but unrolled and spread out – to prevent the blood of the victims from staining the deck. . . . Seizing upon the somewhat imprecise description given by an eyewitness of the actual scene, I interpreted the handling of the tarpaulin in my own way: I made them cover the condemned men with this simulacrum of a shroud. (The preparation for this association is given in the preceding shot, in which the rolled-up tarpaulin, looking like a swathed corpse, is carried across by the petty officers in charge of the execution.) The image of this 'shroud', separating the condemned sailors from their comrades, from the sunlight and from life as a whole, proved to be so powerfully expressive that it completely convinced the audience, who never for a moment doubted the authenticity of this method of execution as compared with any other. Incidentally, I never heard any objections even from people well-informed in these matters – ex-sailors of the tsarist navy, now staunch crewmen of the Red Fleet: for them, too, the effect of this image was more significant and decisive than a documentarily accurate but artistically meaningless factual account of the procedure.

Exactly the same happens, can happen (and should happen!) in all the elements of the picture down to its smallest fragment, i.e. the single shot, where the same processes occur and are developed. Here too, wherever necessary, exactly the same conflicts (collisions) take place between the representation of an object or a phenomenon and its generalised image, the aim of which is to disclose its true inner meaning. In the unity of that collision is born the true meaning and form of the event or phenomenon, not only in its natural 'being' but also in its full social significance. We should not, of course, forget that this also includes the case – e.g. the barricade referred to above – where the contradiction between the particular and the generalised aspect of the phenomenon is removed; when the one, showing through the other, leads directly and undeviatingly onward to an intensification of the expressive process. In this instance, the only tension of contradiction that remains is in the area of interaction between the different dimensions in which the same thought is expressed. Might one, perhaps, compare this to the tension *within* a chord, as distinct from the tension set up by the interaction of two musical themes?

There are numerous, vivid examples of intra-shot treatment.

First and foremost there are, of course, countless examples of 'degradation', 'debasement' and 'elevation' achieved by changing the set-up. The crudest examples of this reduced the process to shooting the object 'from above' or 'from below': an amusing attitude to the set-up which had a certain currency around the years 1926 or 1927.

Further developments came with the more sophisticated forms of shot composition, which set out to achieve effects that were in the nature of metaphor, i.e.: 'Tractors advance into the fields like tanks into battle'; 'The dawn mist spreads itself across the bay like a mourning garment' (no matter that the garment is white; the important point here is the rhythm of the graphic image. Incidentally, in China white is the colour of mourning!); 'The ears of grain, like hostile bayonets, stand facing the saboteur preparing to set fire to the crop.'[52]

And so on and so on, in all gradations from fusion to concordance, from disparity to contradiction, but, one way or another, always in a form that embodies a relationship to the object represented. In an adjacent area – literature – the greatest master of interpretation through the *form of exposition* or *description* of the object depicted (especially when it came to debunking) was Tolstoy. Not a single instance of insincere or undeserved praise ever escaped his sarcastic unmasking, whether it be the image of the young 'L'Aiglon' ['Eaglet'], whose portrait is brought to Napoleon before the battle of Borodino: 'It was a portrait, painted in brilliant colours by Gérard, of the child of Napoleon and the daughter of the Austrian Emperor, the little boy whom everyone for some unknown reason called the King of Rome.'[53] Or the theatrical heroism of the Polish uhlans who, at the crossing of the Niemen, chose to swim the river in front of Napoleon instead of using the ford:

Some of the horses were drowned, some, too, of the men; the others struggled to swim across, some in the saddle, others clinging to their horses' manes. They tried to swim straight across, and although there was a ford half a verst away, they were proud to be swimming and drowning in the river before the eyes of that man sitting on the log and not even looking at what they were doing. . . .

Forty Uhlans were drowned in the river. . . . The majority struggled back to the bank from which they had started. The colonel, with several of his men, swam across the river and with difficulty clambered up the other bank. But as soon as they clambered out in drenched and streaming clothes they shouted 'Vive l'Empereur!' looking ecstatically at the place where Napoleon had stood, though he was no longer there, and at that moment thought themselves happy.[54]

[. . .] By one means or another, never descending to a deliberate *distortion of the veracity of the event depicted*, merely by a choice of the separate *features* which he employs for the *defining outline** of the subject matter as a whole, Tolstoy ruthlessly and precisely conveys his disapproval of the depicted fact, *the viewpoint from which he regards the fact* and an awareness of the *significance of the event* from his viewpoint. The method, as we see, is absolutely identical.

Looking ahead, we may also say that his method is identical with what we will encounter in the next stages of development of cinema, when we shall move forward from the immobility of single set-up cinematography.

For it is now obvious that without distorting the coronation of the reigning princeling, for instance, or the ultra-pathetic speech of the Menshevik, they can by means of montage be made to *dance a waltz* together, thus revealing the ludicrous part they play in the narrative. In exactly the same way, by the appropriate use of context and montage the pounding of the ship's engines can be presented as the anxious heartbeat of the crew of the mutinous battleship in expectation of the encounter with the admiral's squadron (*Potemkin*).

And looking even further ahead, let us also mention music which can, *when integrated into the narrative*, reinterpret the first two scenes in 'burlesque' terms and increase the tension of the third episode even more completely and with far greater ease than can montage alone.[55]

Let us remember this link: generalised contour† – montage – music. We shall be returning to that trio: it will help us towards a correct understanding of the interrelation and roles of these separate elements in the sound cinema.

In our account of the foregoing proposition we have introduced into cinematic practice a further concept of contradiction, another form of conflict. Actually, this concept should have been placed at the head of the list of

---

*For example his use of purely physical features and not the dynastic elements in the description of the portrait of the King of Rome; the 'difficulty' with which they – the colonel and several of his men – '*clambered up*' on to the bank, instead of some phrase such as 'their heroic struggle with the watery element'. Admittedly they looked 'ecstatically', but they were looking at an empty place, where 'he was no longer', and so on.

†Let me recall that the *generalised contour* of the object represented and its image-making role are far from being the only aspects in which that generalising, image-making role is embodied in that representation. It can equally successfully be embodied in the gradations of light, and later of colour; or in the interrelation of objects in space, the expression on an actor's face, etc., etc. For ease of descriptive definition and for maximum clarity of reproduction in a book, I have selected this particular graphic example. But this by no means implies that it is the principal, sole, exhaustive or all-embracing example.

'conflicts' which we drew up once long ago, when we classified them mainly by their outward attributes.

What we have expounded here is, of course, the highest form of conflict, which discloses the *inner*, emotionally mediated visual dynamics of a film sequence. As such, the dynamics derive even more immediately – wholly and directly – not only from the content, but from an unremittingly responsible attitude towards the content. Being derivatives of the same premises, the remaining types of graphic conflict, too, are indissolubly linked but, because of their remoteness, their greater abstractness, it is less easy to perceive them as being in the same close and direct connection as in our case of the tension *between the depiction and the image of the subject matter.* When, however, an excessive stress on the theme intrudes itself upon these dual elements, there is always the risk of a leap into schematised linear and tonal symbolism. Evil begins to be depicted on the screen with a black palette, good with white.*

[. . .] Let us briefly recall the types of conflict that we have classified in various articles and elsewhere: linear, volume, conflict of spatial levels, lighting conflict, and so on; these were the simplest examples. More complicated-sounding were the designations of the other types, which represented each and every cinematic discipline reduced to a single 'terminology of conflict'. This was not done as a mere piece of word-play, but with the aim of reducing all the various specialist areas of cinematography to a single common method: an opportunity to study them in relation to one another, i.e. to utilise our accumulated experience in the study of any one branch in order to study the others.

These definitions of conflict sounded unfamiliar, but the definitions themselves suggested a path by which to approach the deciphering of the inner aesthetics of these areas of cinema. Thus we came to speak of lighting as a conflict or collision between a flow of light (i.e. a cone of light) and a resistant object: the problem of lighting; of a collision between the visual flow (i.e. of a cone of sight through the lens) and the same object: the problem of camera angle, connected with the angle of inclination between object and camera.

The clumsiness of these formulations was at least redeemed by the fact that from such a definition alone it was evident that the compositional laws of such remote areas as foreshortening and lighting can both be formulated

---

*Used tactfully and in moderation this can sometimes function excellently as an expressive factor; for instance, the white-grey-black tonal palette of the cinema was well used in its time, for its associative value, by Ernst Lubitsch, who in his film adaptation of *Lady Windermere's Fan* apportioned this colour-scale to his various characters (the 'innocent' May McAvoy was white, a 'neutral' character was grey, while the villain was 'black' in looks, costume and lighting treatment).

But this method is fraught with danger: in *Becky Sharp*, for instance, the sudden use in a brief shot of people running in *red* cloaks, when panic set in at the advance of Napoleon, only looked naïve. This conscious 'insert' ruined the texture of something which could have been remarkable if allowed to arise naturally from the action.[56]

and deduced from a single set of premisses.

The following pair of examples was typical: (i) the conflict between an object and its appearance; and (ii) the conflict between a flowing process and its own duration.

On closer examination these proved to be due to: (i) the distorting role (and optical peculiarities in general) of the various lenses in their rendering of space and the degree of softness or hardness of their 'handwriting' in the rendering of the picture; and (ii) the speeding up or slowing down of the shooting speed compared to the normal camera speed.

The culminating conflict was the audiovisual counterpoint, which was largely discussed in terms of theoretical adumbration of its potential.

Only after passing through the whole gamut of the film-makers' practical experience has this terminology acquired a wholly concrete objectivity.

Unfortunately, it is equally true that in the overwhelming majority of films, the application of this branch of cinematic theory is totally lacking.

All the more reason, therefore, to develop this question as fully as possible, which is the purpose of the third section of our study of montage. To do so, however, is only possible on the basis of a detailed analysis of the previous stages of montage, and this we are undertaking in the two sections which precede it.

As for the concept of conflict itself, in the present work we will limit ourselves to remarking on its existence, but we will nowhere embark on an analysis of the inner nature of the phenomenon of conflict and of contradictions within form as such. A no less painstaking separate analysis will be devoted to this problem.

Here we will confine ourselves to describing the existence of conflict, while in later sections we will engage in an analysis of the inner laws of the dynamics of conflict, the laws of how it progresses through contradiction.

The most important part of that analysis will be to show clearly that experience and cognition, culture and artistic skill, the very nature and multiplicity of the forms and areas of application of conflict are all drawn from the one, single and determining source, which is the same one that is applicable to montage in the broadest sense of the word. We shall disclose it in an analysis of montage when we come to dwell on it at the end of the present work.

Just as here we are discussing the problem by stages (frame – shot – montage – audiovisual counterpoint), so also in the later sections we shall proceed by stages: physical movement (expressive movement) – spiritual movement (emotion) – movement of the mind (image and character) – movement of the action (drama). All this will constitute an attempt to establish how each of them and all of them together embody a reflection of social conflict and movement occurring within the contradictions of reality as a whole.[. . . .][57]

To the enumeration of all the aspects of conflict in the article 'Beyond the Shot' (1929)[58] – where we first formulated both the organic evolutionary

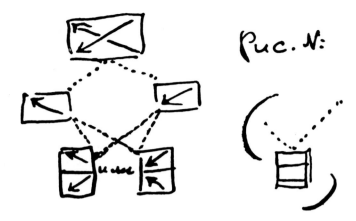

Fig. 2.10

link between the shot and montage (montage as a leap – the montage leap! – out of the shot into a new quality of *inter-shot* conflict that occurs after the *intra-shot* conflict, the montage sequence as an exploded montage 'cell'), and in other writings on the same subject – we invariably added the proviso that each conflict may explode along the line of each 'wing' of the conflict into two (or more) parallel but independent sequences. In the terms of that article, this was easy to visualise and imagine. For instance, two intersecting movements within the shot would, as the tension increased, obviously break apart into two shots, of which each would contain one of these two movements (see Fig. 2.10), and so on.

At what point does the tension explode and the leap occur into a new quality along the line of the new form of conflict which we have added to the series?

The single shot will explode into a chain of shots. But given a truly compositionally correct structuring of the sequence of that chain, the graphic continuity not only of depiction but of *composition of the image* will retain its compositional integrity but with the added achievement that the compositional outline of the individual segment will either progress by permeation through the whole series of segments, remaining unchanged through the various 'segmentary plots' (only perhaps allowing itself some play on scale and repetition – the crudest option; see Fig. 2.11, 'The Eskimo and the Yurts'), or will establish its own interplay of metamorphoses throughout the succession of segments: either in the form of consistently changing delineation of the compositional outline from shot to shot; or in the consistent interrelation between long shot and foreground as they alternate; or in the disintegration of a large, solid shape into a series of smaller shapes which echo the large one in outline and movement; and by reintegrating these small shapes into the new agglomeration of an analogous large shape, but one which now suggests a different narrative or semantic signification. I know of only one example of analysis of a similar kind, and that is one that I did several years ago on a small fragment of *Potemkin*.[59] It is striking in that it illustrates a basic situation from several angles simultaneously: linear; spatial levels; the number of figures in a shot; interrelation of scales, and so on. And all done on the firm basis of its function of embodying in images the advancement of the meaning of the theme.[. . . .][60]

If this describes the route by which we trace the immediate progress of the specific graphic composition of the shot, stranger still is its explosion into a new quality, not only as the *application* of a method, but also as the *principle* underlying that method!

Its continuation along that path will take place in the new stage of cinema, that of 'montage' cinema; it will not only be a movement whereby the contour changes continuously through a chain of segments but it will be much more: a line, made up of single points, from which in successive shots the camera will look at the filmed phenomenon while selecting and collating the montage segments in which this phenomenon presents itself; in other words, in terms of that unique form of *mise en scène* which the camera creates through the phenomenon, pausing at various parts and details of the *mise en scène* while simultaneously moving closer in or moving back from them (the interplay of changing scale).

This method can be used for documentarily informative or dispassionate narrative; it can also, however, be interpretative and it can also be emotional. Hence it can be not only uniquely rhythmic but uniquely imaginative in the tendentious, purposeful way that it generalises the phenomenon which it is shooting!

However, the transition into this area of

Fig. 2.11

study has imperceptibly caused the subject matter of this chapter to explode into the content of the next chapter, just as, historically, the era of single set-up cinematography exploded into the era of multiple set-up cinematography. We shall now turn our attention to that era, beginning with an exposition of the premisses which underlay what is vulgarly called the stage of 'montage cinema'.

3 Montage and Architecture

In cinema the word 'path' is not used by chance. Nowadays it means the imaginary path followed by the eye and the varying perceptions of an object that depend on how it appears to the eye. Nowadays it may also mean the path followed by the mind across a multiplicity of phenomena, far apart in time and space, gathered in a certain sequence into a single meaningful concept; diverse impressions passing in front of an immobile spectator.

In the past, however, the opposite was the case: the spectator moved through a series of carefully disposed phenomena which he absorbed in order with his visual sense.

This tradition has been preserved in children's drawings. Not only has the movement of the eye been given back to the action of the child himself moving in space, but the picture itself appears as the path along which a number of aspects of the subject are revealed sequentially.

This is a typical child's drawing.[61] We cannot see it as a representation of a pond with trees along the bank until we understand its internal dynamics. The trees are not depicted from one viewpoint, as adults would show them in a picture or in a single frame of film. Here the drawing depicts a series of trees as they are revealed along the path that the observer follows between them. If the line A–B represents the path taken by the observer, then at any given point in the sequence 1–9 each separate tree is disposed entirely 'reasonably': a frontal view of the tree in question is represented at each corresponding point on the path.

Exactly similar are the surviving drawings of old Russian buildings, such as, for instance, the fifteenth-century (?) palace of Kolomenskoye, in which there is an identical combination of 'plan' and 'elevation'.[62] For here the path is a movement across the *plan*, while the frontal views of the buildings are shown in *elevation*, seen from specific points on the plan.

This can be seen even more vividly in the example shown here of an Egyptian painting, representing a pond with trees and buildings around it, depicted according to exactly the same principle.[63]

It is curious that in the period of artistic decadence at the turn of the 20th century (which reflected the decadence of bourgeois society), in a period marked by every form of regression in the arts (for further comment on this see below), there occurred a curious 'renaissance' of a similar kind of archaism. We may interpret it as something like a shriek uttered by painting as a premonition of its metamorphosis into cinematography. In Fig. 3.1 is shown

Fig. 3.1

the plan for a series of paintings by David Burlyuk.[64] In a slightly different mode, he is pursuing the same aim as Delaunay, who distorted the Eiffel Tower by dislocating its structural elements.[65]

It is also curious that in this final stage before its transition to cinematography, painting turns its depiction *inwards*, whereas the same aspiration at the dawn of drawing and painting presented objects through *extroversion*. That *introversion*, of course, contains a profound sense of retreat 'into oneself', of regression 'away from' reality, unlike the second instance, which is characterised by looking outwards into the surrounding reality, into an expansive widening of horizons.

Painting has remained incapable of fixing the total representation of a phenomenon in its full visual multi-dimensionality. (There have been countless attempts to do this.) Only the film camera has solved the problem of doing this on a flat surface, but its undoubted ancestor in this capability is . . . architecture. The Greeks have left us the most perfect examples of shot design, change of shot and shot length (i.e. the duration of a particular impression). Victor Hugo called the medieval cathedrals 'books in stone' (see *Notre Dame de Paris*). The Acropolis of Athens could just as well be called the perfect example of one of the most ancient films.

I shall here quote in full from Choisy's *History of Architecture*.[66] I shall not alter a single comma, and I would only ask you to look at it with the eye of a film-maker: it is hard to imagine a montage sequence for an architectural ensemble more subtly composed, shot by shot, than the one which our legs create by walking among the buildings of the Acropolis (see Fig. 3.2).

The Acropolis is a cliff, isolated on all sides, whose summit is dedicated to the worship of the national deities. At point 'T' was the mark made by Poseidon's trident, while near to it grew the olive tree sacred to Athene.

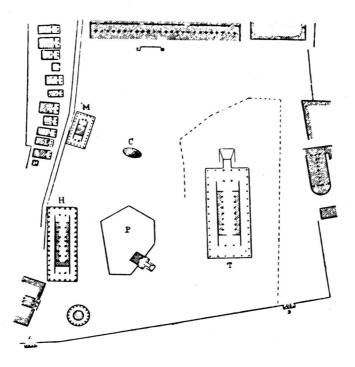

Fig. 3.2

In immediate proximity to this sacred spot a temple was built to both gods.

The site being empty after a fire, it was therefore possible to build a new sanctuary on the very spot indicated by legend. The temple was moved to point 'S' and given the name of Erechtheum.

The highest point, 'P', was the site in this and another era (i.e. the time of the Pisistratidae and after the Persian War) of the great temple of Athene – the Parthenon.

Between the Parthenon and the entrance to the Acropolis was disposed a series of smaller temples, evidently relating to both the ancient and the new Acropolis. . . . In this same space the colossal statue of Athene Promachos (The Warrior) was erected in the 5th century BC.

The Propylaea (M) formed the frontal façade of the Acropolis (in both the old and the new layout). . . .

The two layouts differed only in detail. The first, however, was a collection of buildings of various epochs, whereas the second was laid out to a single plan and adapted to the site, which had been cleared as

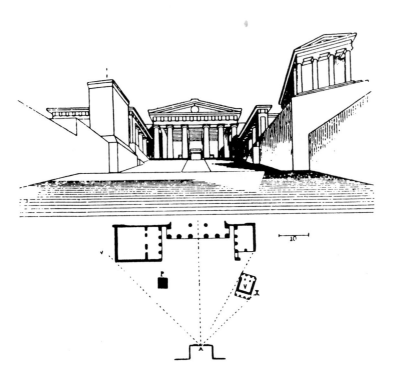

Fig. 3.3

the result of a fire. The apparent asymmetry of this new Acropolis is only
a means of lending picturesqueness to this group of buildings, which have
been laid out with more art than any others. . . .

[This] becomes clear from the series of panoramas which unfolded
before visitors to the Acropolis in the 5th century BC:

View of the Propylaea: the general idea of the plan of the Propylaea
can be seen in Fig. 3.3.

We see the symmetrical central block and two noticeably different wings
– the right one broader and the left-hand one less so. . . .

At first sight nothing could be more uneven than this plan, but in
fact it constitutes a completely balanced whole, in which the general
symmetry of the masses is accompanied by a subtle diversity in the
details. . . . The optical symmetry is impeccable. . . .

First view of the square; Athene Promachos: passing by the Propylaea,
the spectator's eye embraces the Parthenon, the Erechtheum and Athene
Promachos (Fig. 3.4).

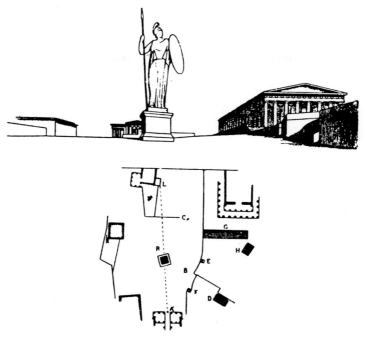

Fig. 3.4

In the foreground there towers the statue of Athene Promachos; the Erechtheum and the Parthenon are in the background, so that the whole of this first panorama is subordinated to the statue, which is its central point and creates an impression of unity. The Parthenon only acquires its significance when the visitor loses sight of this gigantic piece of sculpture.

The Parthenon and its oblique perspectives (Fig. 3.5): to modern thinking, the Parthenon – the great temple of the Acropolis – should be placed opposite the main entrance, but the Greeks reasoned quite differently. The cliff of the Acropolis has an uneven surface, and the Greeks, without altering its natural relief, placed the main temple on the highest point at the edge of the cliff, facing the city.

Placed thus, the Parthenon first of all faces the spectator obliquely. The ancients generally preferred oblique views: they are more picturesque, whereas a frontal view of the façade is more majestic.* Each of them is allotted a specific role. An oblique view is the general rule, while a view *en face* is a calculated exception (Fig. 3.6).

---

*This can often be tested in film shots that are not taken 'head-on' but from an angle or on the diagonal.

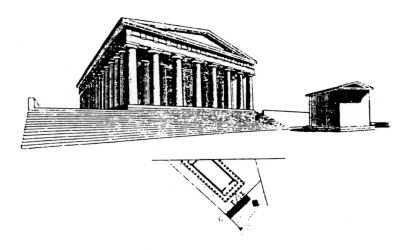

Fig. 3.5

The central body of the Propylaeum is presented *en face*, just as we head straight for the *pronaos* of the Parthenon, crossing the square of the Acropolis. With the exception of the two examples given, where this effect is deliberately calculated, all the other structures present themselves at an angle – as does the temple of Athene Ergane (H), when the spectator reaches its precinct at point E. . . .

After the first panorama from the Erechtheum, let us continue our way across the Acropolis. At point B the Parthenon is still the only structure in our field of vision, but if we move on to point C, it will be so close to us that we shall be unable to encompass its shape; at that moment the Erechtheum becomes the centre of the panorama. It is

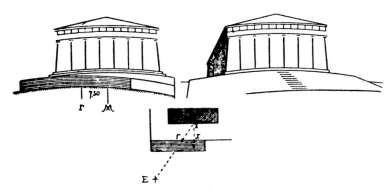

Fig. 3.6

precisely from this point that it offers us one of its most graceful silhouettes (Fig. 3.7).

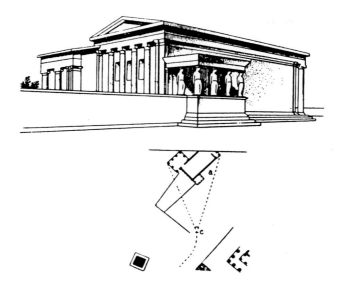

Fig. 3.7

The bare wall (a) is enlivened by the Porch of the Caryatids, which stand out from it as though against a background specially created for them.

Thus three pictures have passed before us, corresponding to the three chief points – A1, B and C – on Fig. 3.4.

At each one of them only one architectural monument was dominant: at Point C – the Erechtheum; at Point B – the Parthenon; and at Point A1 – Athene Promachos. This one, principal motif ensures the clarity of the impression and the unity of the picture.

How responsibly and with what careful thought this has been done is witnessed by the following supplementary comment by Choisy:

Erechtheum and Athene Promachos. Let us return to the starting-point (Fig. 3.4), i.e. to point A1, at which our whole attention was concentrated on Athene Promachos. The Erechtheum with its caryatids is in the background. One might fear that the graceful caryatids would appear crushed by force of contrast with the gigantic statue of the goddess; to prevent this, the architect sited the base of the statue in such a way that it shut out the view of the Porch of the Caryatids – line A1–K – which only revealed itself to the eye of the spectator when he was so close to the colossus that he could no longer see all of it, and therefore a comparison only became possible in memory.

Further, Choisy sums up as follows:

> If we now recall the series of pictures that the Acropolis has given us, we shall see that they are all without exception calculated on the first impression that they make. Our recollections invariably take us back to first impressions, and the Greeks strove above all to make it a favourable one.
>
> Both wings of the Propylaea balance out (Fig. 3.3) at the exact moment when the general view of the building opens out in front of us.
>
> The disappearance of the caryatids when looking at Athene Promachos (Fig. 3.4) is also calculated on the first impression.
>
> As for the Parthenon, the fullest view of its façade with its asymmetrical flight of steps is revealed to the spectator when he passes through the precinct around the temple of Athene Ergane.
>
> This creation of a favourable first impression was evidently the constant concern of Greek architects.

The calculation on a film shot effect is obvious, for there, too, the effect of the first impression from each new, emerging shot is enormous. Equally strong, however, is the calculation on a montage effect, i.e. the sequential juxtaposition of those shots.

Let us, in fact, draw up the general compositional schemes of these four successive 'picturesque shots' (Fig. 3.8).

It is hard to imagine a stricter, more elegant and triumphant construct than this sequence.

Shots (a) and (b) are equal in symmetry and at the same time the

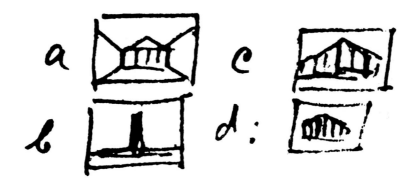

Fig. 3.8

opposites of each other in spatial extent. Shots (c) and (d) are in mirror symmetry, and function, as it were, as enlargements of the right-hand and left-hand wings of shot (a), then reforming again into a single, balanced mass. The sculptural motif (b) is repeated through shot (c), by the group of sculpture (d) and so on and so on.

It would further be of particular interest to analyse the length of time in which each of these pictures was presented to the spectator. We will not go into the details of this here, only remarking that the length of these montage sequences is entirely in step with the rhythm of the building itself: the distance from point to point is long, and the time taken to move from one to the other is of a length in keeping with solemnity.

In the 'montage plan' of the Athenian Acropolis we find, of course, the same unsurpassed artistry as in other monuments of antiquity.

From a somewhat different aspect or point of view (and, of course, a different quality and scope!) we can find other elements of montage in Christian (Catholic) cathedrals.

This occurs in one version of what is invariably found in any church: the so-called 'Stations of the Cross', i.e. the twelve sculptural groups representing the twelve stopping-places which legend ascribes to the procession to Golgotha. The twelve 'stations' are placed at a certain distance from each other, usually around the outer ambulatory of the cathedral. That is how I saw them in Chartres Cathedral and a number of others. But in places of pilgrimage, especially those of mass pilgrimage, they may also be placed outside the cathedral. I had occasion to see this type of disposition in Mexico, in the pilgrimage centre of Amecameca. As with the majority of Catholic churches in Mexico, this church had been built on the site of an ancient pagan temple. The wise colonisers and missionaries did this so that the new faith should not lose the popularity of an already familiar spot and so as to use the well-trodden paths of pilgrimage to other gods for its own, Catholic, purposes. Therefore this church, like many others, was sited on a high pyramid-shaped hill. The hill was pyramid shaped for the simple reason that it is nothing other than a genuine, but crumbling and overgrown pyramid, created artificially as prescribed for the construction of places of worship in the era of paganism. A winding road was laid out around this fairly steep hill, and it is along this road that the 'twelve stations' are placed, the ultimate destination ('Golgotha') being the church at the top. From 'station' to 'station' the road ascends a certain number of metres. The business of climbing that distance is particularly impressive because it is the custom to go from 'station' to 'station' and on up to the very top *on one's knees*. The emotional reaction from stopping-place to stopping-place thereby increases with the pilgrims' ever-increasing physical exhaustion. At another place of pilgrimage (Los Remedios, near Mexico City) this is done not only kneeling but 'blind' – with the eyes blindfolded. The blindfold is only removed (symbolising 'spiritual insight') at the very top.

Having thus turned our attention to Catholicism, via the pilgrims of

Amecameca and Chartres Cathedral, I cannot help recalling another example of a montage structure which is in the centre of the Catholic religion, in Rome, at its very heart: St Peter's, and in the very heart of that cathedral, under the famous canopy with its 11½-metre-high columns that tower above the high altar of the cathedral, the altar at which the Pope alone may celebrate Mass and then only on the most solemn occasions.

I refer to the eight representations in relief of the coat of arms of the Barberini Pope, Urban VIII, which adorn the two outer sides of the four plinths of those gigantic columns that support the canopy. The canopy, the columns and the decoration of the plinths with coats of arms form one of the most spectacular compositions of that great master, Bernini, and were erected in 1633 during the pontificate of Urban VIII and in his honour.

These eight identical coats of arms, apparently devoid of significance, are in reality not only not identical but far from devoid of significance.

These eight coats of arms are eight shots, eight montage sequences, of a whole montage scenario. Identical in their general design, they differ in their component details and taken together they represent a whole drama that unfolds step by step. Both the subject matter of the drama, which closely concerned Urban VIII, and the location of its depiction within the holy of holies of Catholicism, of which he was the head, fully justify its description as *satira marmorea tremenda*, 'a tremendous satire in marble', as it was called by one of the authors who has described the canopy, the plinths of its columns and the drama narrated in the eight coats of arms that adorn those plinths.

What is happening on them?

It has been described by several scholars:

1. Fraschetti: *Vida de Bernini*
2. Gaetano Dossi: *El Baldaquino de San Pedro*
3. Prof. G.E. Curatolo, Professor Libre de Obstetricía y Ginecología en la Real Universidad de Roma: *El Arte de Juno Lucina en Roma. Historia de la Obstetricia desde sus origenes hasta el siglo XX, con documentos ineditos* (Rome, 1901) (I only know the full title in Spanish). Also in the following article:
4. Dr Noury in *Chronique Médicale* (Paris, 1903)
5. In the book by Dr G.J. Witkowski, *L'Art profane de l'église, ses licences symboliques, satiriques et fantaisistes* (Paris, 1908)
6. And finally, the voluminous work by Guillermo Dellhora, *La Iglesia Católica ante la Critica en el Pensamiento y en el Arte* (Mexico City, 1929)

N.B. All the above-quoted authors also refer to much earlier descriptions. Each one describes the same thing, although each from his own point of view and with a completely different purpose.

The first two try to play down the whole story. The third – Professor Curatolo – writes with the aim of demonstrating the state of seventeenth-century knowledge of *gynaecology*!

Dr Noury, in his 1903 article, writes from a medical standpoint and G.J.

Witkowski, in his 1908 pamphlet, attacks the Roman Church – an attack, it must be said, that shows more interest in shocking stories and mockery than in more serious matters, although the author does possess a certain degree of genuine anti-religious free thought.

Finally there is Dellhora, for whom this matter is the culmination of his whole book, which is wholly devoted to the anti-clerical and anti-religious struggle of modern, intellectually based atheism. Writing in *Le Monde* of 17 May 1930, Henri Barbusse wrote as follows:

> In this work Dellhora has brought together a large quantity of written and iconographical documents against clericalism in Mexico, in Latin America in general and all over the rest of the world. He supplies the reader with a complete arsenal against the Catholic religion. . . .
>
> This anti-clerical struggle, which should be conducted everywhere . . . is particularly necessary in Spanish-speaking countries. No one can deny that the progress of the Spanish people has been checked by the fact that the Catholic religion has planted itself especially deeply in Spanish soil. In Spanish America there have been deeds of fanaticism and obscurantism that recall the Middle Ages. In Mexico in 1926 we saw black-clad hordes, tools of the priests, bathing the country in blood to cries of 'Long live Christ the King!', and there are no crimes that these fanatics have not committed, fanatics who at one time numbered 30,000 and who raged over the country for three years. That is why Guillaume Dellhora's courageous, avenging work is of particular value in those regions where the tragic wave of clericalism has not yet subsided. One must rejoice at the great success which this work has had in Latin America and specially in Mexico. . . . (In June 1929 sales amounted to 2,000 copies, in September 6,400, in December 10,300.)*

I think the reader's curiosity will have been sufficiently aroused by all these preliminaries, so I will therefore proceed to describe the montage drama of eight sequences (shots), which the caustically ironic stone-carver Bernini engraved in the eight coats of arms on the four plinths of the magnificent columns that support the canopy in St Peter's, Rome, over the altar that surmounts the tomb of the saint.

The dimensions, design and disposition of all the coats of arms are identical (see Fig. 3.9). They display three bees, the heraldic device of the Barberini family to which Pope Urban VIII belonged. Above the shield, in the conventional decorative curlicues around it, is a woman's head. Beneath the coat of arms is a no less conventional piece of ornamentation, whose

---

*The topic in Dellhora's book that interests us is set out with a wealth of detail and supplied with an exhaustive quantity of photographs and drawings. We recommend this book to readers who are interested in such details, which we can only recall here in very abbreviated form.

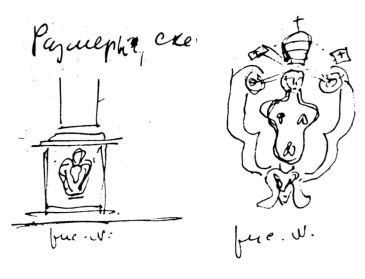

Fig. 3.9   Fig. 3.10

swirling strands form themselves into the head of a satyr. The whole is surmounted by a papal tiara ('the triple crown'), placed over a huge pair of crossed keys ('the keys of St Peter') (see Fig. 3.10).

Such is the general layout of all eight coats of arms.

Thus far they are all identical and in no way remarkable. If, however, we start to examine them more carefully, we shall see that, starting with the left-hand front plinth, the expression on the face of the female head above each shield changes sharply from shield to shield. From being calm and contented it passes through all the stages of pain and terror until above the eighth coat of arms it returns to an expression of tranquillity (although with a slightly different cast of character). But that is not all: above the sixth shield in the sequence the woman's head suddenly disappears and is replaced by a no less traditional Renaissance ornament: a child's head (*putto*) with wings. Over the seventh and eighth shields the woman's head returns with new and different facial expressions. The mask of a satyr on the lower part of the shield also undergoes a marked deformation. On the shield proper the same also occurs with the three bees of the Barberini family. Here (Fig. 3.11) is a plan of the canopy, showing the layout of the coats of arms on the plinths of the columns. The distance along the line (a) is approximately six metres. Furthermore, the deformation that occurs on the surface of the shield itself is the most curious of all. Flat at first, beginning with the second shield its lower part starts to bulge outwards, until with the sixth shield it 'subsides' and remains flat on the last two shields. . . . What can this mean?! In the literal sense, what sort of an allegory is this?

For an explanation, let us turn to any one of the authors listed above.

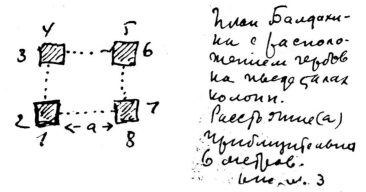

Fig. 3.11

We shall see that the first two, while not denying the fact itself, try to brush it aside with the querulous remark: '. . . These decorations, taken in conjunction with the coat of arms, could cause some people to weave fantasies and create mysterious allusions. . . .'

What in fact are those 'allusions', which are far from being mysterious but were intentional and evident?

What do these eight shields represent 'taken in conjunction'?

The answer is given by, among others, Witkowski. These eight shields are pictures

which express, through the physiognomy of a woman, the various stages of childbirth. She relaxes as the womb releases its burden.

The shield is topped by a life-sized woman's head, above which are the pontifical crossed keys surmounted by the tiara.

At each crisis in the labour, the expression of the face changes. The scene begins on the face of the left-hand front plinth; the woman's face begins to contract; on the second and following plinths the features pass through a series of increasingly violent convulsions. Simultaneously, the hair becomes increasingly dishevelled; the eyes, which at first express a bearable degree of suffering, take on a haggard look; the mouth, closed at first, opens, then screams with piercing realism; Zola must have been unaware of this archaeological curiosity, otherwise he would not have failed to make use of it in his *Rome*. It would have been at least piquant to see the master of literary naturalism in the presence of such a shrieking example of artistic naturalism.

Calmness returns for a moment in between the pains, but the face still remains in pain, as though numbed, stupefied – then the pains come back with greater intensity, the features contract again, she looks terrifying. . . .

Finally comes the delivery: the belly subsides and the mother's head disappears, to give way to a cherubic baby's head with curly hair, smiling beneath the unchanging pontifical insignia. . . .

But that is not all. Below the papal shield, which the artist has sculpted in the shape of the torso of a pregnant woman, there is the head of a satyr, whose lower part represents the external female genital organs, the anatomical details of which are quite complete and which undergo changes that occur throughout the stages of labour.

(Witkowski, L'Art profane, vol. I, pp. 255–6)

At this point let us break off Witkowski's over-extensive description of the lower part of the ornament and, instead of his ribald comments, let us rather turn to the words of Professor E. Curatolo, which deal with the astounding pictorial accuracy of the entire picture – which can perhaps only be appreciated in all its subtleties by the experienced eye of a *gynaecologist!* This is also his explanation for the fact that the whole story is little known among the wider public.

The title will perhaps arouse the admiration of those who, despite knowing the great masterpieces of the 17th century with which Rome is adorned, are ignorant of one of its most original creations, revealed by the ingenious artist to those who have some knowledge of the science of obstetrics.

There are few indeed who know this original creation by Bernini that is to be found in the basilica of the Vatican. Many people, including some of the most distinguished lovers of architecture and the fine arts, are ignorant of it, in part because it is an insignificant detail of a great work of art – the canopy of St Peter's – and in part because its conception cannot be fully understood except by obstetricians.

(Curatolo, El Arte)

The same anatomical precision is confirmed by the drawings of the head of the satyr that Dellhora reproduces.

What is it all about? Whence came the idea for this monumental piece of mockery, placed under the Pope's very nose in the holy of holies of Catholicism in Rome, which contains an obvious attack on the Barberini Pope, executed alongside the eight coats of arms of his family? And what is the 'secret' behind this marble representation of a woman giving birth in eight montage sequences at the base of the canopy of the high altar of St Peter's, Rome?

The zealous defenders of Catholicism, of course, have immediately to hand an explanatory interpretation of this 'symbol'. One such version is put forward by Witkowski: it came to him immediately after the first publication of these observations in France in 1903. The pen, indeed, is barely capable of copying these lines. Such is the saccharine emotion with which they are written that the ink positively runs and smudges the paper:

Compare the papacy to a woman who, in great pain, is giving birth to souls for God; for a pope, as for the rest of the Church, it is sometimes a pregnancy and a birth that are truly painful. What disappointments, what opposition, what struggles, what suffering do the pope and the Church not endure in order to bring into the world children of Grace, in accordance with holy writ! . . .

The Church is a mother – a sacred metaphor which She ceaselessly affirms; why, therefore, should it be any surprise that the artist should have personified Her as a woman, and that he should have clothed Her in the pontifical insignia, since the pope incarnates and personifies Her on earth?

(Witkowski, *L'Art profane*, p. 262)

Popular legend, however, has preserved a quite different account of this story. Here it is, as it was recorded by Dr P. Noury of Rouen, quoting the words of Lamberto Lelli:

While Urban was commissioning the canopy from the great architect [Bernini], it happened that a nephew of the pope, probably Taddeo – later to be a cardinal, a generalissimo of the Church and Prince of the Palatine – fell in love with a sister of one of Bernini's pupils and made her pregnant.

As a result of this family misfortune, the girl's brother could think of no other solution than to implore his master to intercede with the pope and to save the situation by a marriage.

Bernini, confident and sincere, believing that among the children of Christ differences of social class ought not to prevail, went to the pope to ask for justice.

Urban not only rejected the request; he scolded the artist for his gross presumption: 'How, Bernini,' said he, 'could you entertain such an idea? The pope's nephew marry the sister of a stonemason! Not only must you never mention it again, but this woman must be prevented from importuning my nephew.'

Indignant, his conscience affronted, the artist returned to his work, and when he witnessed the pain of the unhappy mother and heard the whimpering of the new-born infant, he swore this solemn oath: 'The pope refuses to recognise his own flesh and blood – the son of a member of his family! Very well. For the rest of his life, around the altar at which he says Mass, in the midst of the church from whence goes forth the word of Christ, he shall have the innocent victims forever beneath his eyes: the mother and the child, nay the very act of their martyrdom.'

Se non è vero, è ben trovato [it may not be true, but it's a good story], one might say about this colourful anecdote. There is, however, one more detail that may serve to put the finishing touch to its satirical accuracy and

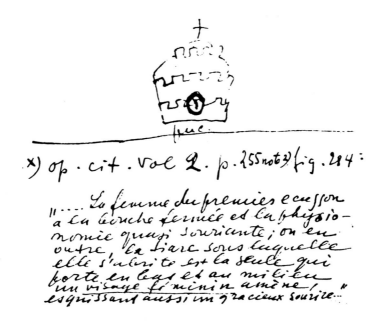

Fig. 3.12

verisimilitude. Professor Curatolo writes:

> But there is more. A minute examination has shown us that in the papal
> tiara on the first of the sculptures, which begins the sequence mimicking
> a woman in labour, there is a small baby's face (which should not be
> confused with the large face carved in relief on the sixth shield) and which
> does not figure in any other of the seven tiaras.

This baby's head, placed as indicated in Fig. 3.12, is not interpreted by
Professor Curatolo and is mistakenly seen by Witkowski as a miniature version
of the woman's head.* It might be read as something like a chapter heading
or an introductory epigraph about the birth of a new scion of the family that
was crowned with the papal tiara.

Dellhora prefers a more gracious interpretation:

> The explanation is logical and provides an interpretation of the satire
> itself.
>
>   After sculpting the last shield, which in place of the mother's head
> bears the head of the new-born infant, Bernini reproduced this in

---

*'The woman of the first shield has her mouth closed and is almost smiling; furthermore,
the tiara above her is the only one which bears in the middle of it a female face which is
also displaying a gracious smile.'

miniature, placing it above the papal tiara, in precisely the place where a being born of the Barberini family should find its logical placement.

The pope – on behalf of his nephew – had repudiated the offspring of his family, and the great sculptor, assuming the role of minister of justice and of morality, positioned the bastard's head above the papal tiara, exactly where it deserved to be.

(Dellhora, *La Iglesia Católica*, p. 357)

Whether these different interpretations of the story of this baby are true or not, the fact remains that the anecdote is entirely in keeping with the characters of those historical personages which the story ascribes to them.

It corresponds absolutely to the character of Urban VIII and the Barberini family. A popular saying, immortalised by the words of Pasquino, has nailed them for ever: *Quod non fecerunt barbari, fecerunt Barberini* ['What the barbarians did not do, the Barberinis did'].

It is from Pasquino that we derive the word *pasquinade*, meaning a satirical quip or epigram. It may be of some interest to remind readers of his particular brand of popular satire and mockery, which persisted throughout the years of papal tyranny, and was the most venomous satirical voice to be raised in protest against it.

Who was Pasquino? More correctly, who were Pasquino and Marforio, who were responsible for the majority of the satirical quips aimed at the papacy? In the book *Pasquino et Marforio, les bouches de marbre de Rome, traduits et publiés pour la première fois par Marie Laffont* (Paris, 1877), we read the following description of Pasquino, given by Castelvetro in his *Ragione d'alcune cose*. The facts about Pasquino date from the 16th century:

'When I was a boy,' said an old man of Ferrara, the wise and learned Tibaldeo, 'there lived a tailor of some renown named Master Pasquino. His shop was situated in the Parione district. He made clothes for a large number of the city's artisans – and not only them, but he and his apprentices also clothed the Pope, the cardinals and other prelates and monsignori of the Apostolic Curia. These men scorned his barbed witticisms and, such was their disdain for the common people, would have felt it beneath their dignity to show that they were wounded by them. This lofty tolerance only served as an encouragement. If anyone dared to coin a malicious phrase criticising the way of life or the doings of some powerful man, to protect himself from the consequences of his temerity he would shelter behind the scurrilous reputation of Pasquino and his apprentices and attribute the epigram to them. Gradually it became the custom to make Pasquino responsible for everything bad that was said about the ecclesiastics and courtiers of Rome.

'Now it happened that after his death, while digging up a street in Parione in order to repair it, the workmen obstructed the public footpath by placing up against the tailor's shop an antique marble statue of a gladiator, partly mutilated. On seeing it there, the common people gave it the name of Master Pasquino, and continued to ascribe to the statue any malicious remarks or lampoons to which the authors could have only admitted at their peril. Assured of impunity, Pasquino became henceforth the historic censor and scourge of the Popes.'

(Laffont, *Pasquino et Marforio*, p. 7)

Marie Laffont adds a few more details which are not essential for our purposes. Quoting Fioravanti and Martinelli's *Roma ricercata*, she describes the origin of 'Marforio', the other *bouche de marbre* [mouth of marble]: it was a statue found under the ruins of the ancient Forum of Mars – *Martis forum*, or in distorted form *Mars fori*, whence Marforio.

From the moment that the statue nicknamed Pasquino was placed at the corner of the Palazzo Orsini, it became a sort of newspaper:

The *Capi Rioni* or district officials made use of the statue's position in the centre of the city and on a much-frequented route by allowing it to be used by the bill-posters. They began by sticking municipal notices and regulations on its plinth; in time, the church authorities took to using it to display banns of marriage, papal bulls and indulgences, which provoked malcontents to affix to it, furtively and by night, their protests and satires.

No sooner was the fiction that personified Pasquino accepted than it was extended to Marforio. They made him his cousin, his intimate friend and interlocutor, and these two mutilated statues, sad yet eloquent symbols of Freedom and of Rome, would talk and answer one another, and their immortal dialogues were the perpetual scourge of evil and of arbitrary rule. . . . Thanks to them, we now know what the inhabitants of that unfortunate city really thought – a city which, in expiation of twelve centuries of glory and triumph, was gagged for five hundred years by the stifling hands of police spies and executioners. . . .

Most of those satires and lampoons were anonymous. It would have been too dangerous to admit to their authorship, but in the powerful inspiration that animates them, in their abundant verve and in the finesse of their subtle irony – at once piquant, biting and mocking – we can recognise the ancient spirit and genius of Rome.

(Ibid., pp. 12–14)

Moreri, in his *Grand dictionnaire historique ou le mélange curieux de l'histoire sacrée et profane* (1759), expresses his amazement: 'it is surprising that in a city where the authorities know so well how to shut men's mouths, they have not yet found the secret of forcing a piece of marble to be silent.'

There were, however, attempts to do so: M.A. Gazeau, in his book *Les Bouffons* (Paris, 1882), shows a picture of the statue of Pasquino in Rome (p. 181) but he claims that its original was not a tailor but a shoemaker, and writes about attempts that were made to stop the 'marble mouth':

> Several popes tried without success to suppress the unbridled scurrilousness of these satires, which at times degenerated into defamatory libels. Among others, Adrian VI (1522–3), who was strongly attacked for a parsimony that verged on avarice, resolved to have the statue removed and thrown into the Tiber. He was dissuaded only when it was pointed out to him that Pasquino would not be made dumb by drowning, but would make himself heard even more loudly than the frogs in the Pontine marshes. Adrian VI had the good sense not to put his plan into effect.

This was the same Pope Adrian whom the Romans hated so much that on the day after his death crowds of the populace gathered outside the house of his greatest enemy and adorned its entrance with the inscription: 'To the liberator of the Roman people'.

Apart from those that we have mentioned, Pasquino's attacks on Pope Urban VIII were extremely numerous; Laffont cites a whole series of them. The targets were the Pope, his family and especially his nephews. Thus he proposed that Don Taddeo, the culprit in the 'affair' depicted on the plinths of the canopy, should be castrated: 'Castrate Francesco, Antonio and Don Taddeo' is to be found in the pamphlet *Il grosso e idioto Pasquino*. In another pamphlet, entitled *Pasquino's Answer to the Beggar who asked him for Alms*, he scourged the avarice of the Pope:

> *Ohimè! Io no ho quattrino*
> *Tutto 'l mio è da Barberino!*
> [Alas, I have not a farthing;
> Barberino has everything I possess!]

The bees, the heraldic emblem of the Barberini family, are attacked in a rhyme pamphlet *Pasquino e le api* [Pasquino and the bees]:

> To the Pope and to his nephews, who go by the name of those bees that they bear on their coat of arms:
> *Pasquino*: Oh Bees, whom heaven has sent down upon the soil of Rome to gather nectar to your hearts' content, show me now your wax and let me taste the sweet honey that you have made.
> *The Bees*: How greedy you are! Barbarous war and the blood that you have shed on the earth for our sake – those shall be your wax and your honey.

If Pasquino himself was an out-and-out anti-papist, his name was, however, used by the Catholics themselves for their own pamphleteering purposes. There are, for example, some no less biting pamphlets written by Catholics attacking the Calvinists, collected under the following general title:

Passevent Parisien respondant à Pasquin Romain. De la vie de ceux qui sont allez demeurer à Genève et se disent vivre selon la réformation de l'évangile: faict en forme de Dialogue (Paris, 1556). These were written in the form of dialogues between Pasquino and Passevent, attacking the Calvinists in every possible way and 'Les gros paillardz de leur Eglise, comme Calvin, Favel et Viret.'

Bernini was equally uninhibited in the scope and extent of his ideas and in the means of putting them into effect. On the one hand the boldness of his satire, and on the other the central feature of St Peter's, into which he was not afraid to plunge the arrow of his sarcasm, both are typical of the man. We have only to recall how, in the guise of portraying the mystic ecstasy of St Teresa (again in the holy of holies of a church, in this case Santa Maria delle Vittorie*), he created an image of the orgasmic rapture of the great hysteric that is unsurpassed in its realism. This was a malicious joke, aimed at the Pope, who nine years later (by a decree of 15 March 1642), under a resolution of the Council of Trent, issued an instruction *urbi et orbi* 'to banish from every Christian house all images that are obscene, lascivious and immodest'. For all the friendship that existed between these two brigands, the statue of St Teresa was entirely in character with the one – Bernini – who was also a great artist. We should not forget that the two were together responsible for the vandalistic plundering of 'a hundred and eighty-six thousand, three hundred and ninety-three pounds of bronze' (Larousse, *Grand dictionnaire universel*) from the portico of the Roman Pantheon. 'Urban stripped Flavian bare to clothe Peter' was the ubiquitous Pasquino's jocular comment. It was perhaps in 'compensation' for this that Bernini, aided and abetted by Urban, disfigured the Pantheon of Agrippa with two Renaissance campaniles, or bell-towers. Whichever way one considers it, they thoroughly deserved their nickname of 'Bernini's asses' ears'. Later, artistic good taste prevailed, and these two 'dovecotes' no longer exist, having been demolished; but in 1725 they were still in place, as can be seen in albums of architectural drawings made in that year. History, however, has fixed a much worse pair of asses' ears on the head of Urban VIII: the twin vices of obscurantism and repression. Mankind will never forget 1633, the year the canopy over the high altar in St Peter's was built. For the year of its construction was one of the most shameful moments in the history of Rome and the papacy: in that same year – on 22 June 1633 – there took place the enforced, public recantation of the 'prisoner of the Inquisition', Galileo Galilei, at which he was made to renounce the 'heretical teachings of Copernicus'!

It is natural that the question should arise: how was it that no one noticed Bernini's malicious practical joke? How was it that for many, many years Pope Urban VIII celebrated the liturgy while beneath his very nose was this marble lampoon directed against the whole Barberini clan? Again, legend has

---

*The façade of this church was decorated at the expense of Cardinal Scipione Borghese in exchange for a statue of a hermaphrodite, which was found in the nearby gardens of a Carmelite monastery and which adorned a gallery of its courtyard.

preserved a reference to the fact that certain rumours and suspicions may have arisen. It is in this connection that the Pope is said to have questioned Bernini about the decoration of the plinths; P. Noury writes of it thus:

> When Pope Urban VIII asked him to explain his work, Bernini replied ambiguously: 'It concerns your family.' The Pope assumed that the artist was alluding to the coat of arms of the Barberini family, but in the artist's mind that phrase had a different meaning.

The coats of arms remained untouched.

The extent to which this 'hint' remained undetected, thus preserving the ornamental coats of arms undamaged, is confirmed by eyewitnesses; Dr H. Vigouroux, for instance, told Dr Witkowski of a letter he had received on this subject from his brother, the Abbé Vigouroux, in Rome:

> The drawings published by the *Chronique médicale* are quite exact, but one must be a physician in order to see what he [the correspondent] saw in those escutcheons. I have often noticed them, because they are placed immediately adjoining the tomb of St Peter and St Paul, only a metre or so above ground level, and everyone can see them; but it is certain that no one suspects anything unless he has been forewarned. When I went there, men and women were leaning against these escutcheons, to hear the Mass that was being said nearby, and they saw nothing more in them than someone or other's coat of arms.
>
> (Witkowski, *L'Art profane*, p. 262)

How these 'men and women' behaved, who had noticed nothing until the Roman magazine *L'Asino* (famous for its anti-clerical caricatures), seized upon the material published in the *Chronique médicale* and opened their eyes to those ill-fated shields, we may gather from a few of the headlines printed in that weekly magazine during the year 1903:

> Consequences of Revelations on Significance of the Bernini Sculptures . . .
> Incredible Influx of Curious Visitors from all over the World in Irreverent Pilgrimage to the Cathedral of St Peter . . .
> The Prime Basilica of Christianity Turned into a Theatre of Comic and Grotesque Scenes . . .
> Demonstrations, Tumults, Violence . . .
> The Holy Temple in a State of Siege . . .
> Measures Taken by the Vatican . . .
> The Roman Curia Intends to Cover Bernini's Carved Escutcheons . . .

and so on.

If we want to find the solution to the riddle of why this hurricane, these tumults, were not unleashed earlier, and why the secret of Bernini's satire in all its fullness was not revealed sooner, we shall seek the answer in vain from the popes, from St Peter, from doctors Noury and Witkowski; nor shall we find it beneath the canopy or the boards, with which, apparently, the Roman Curia never did cover up the ill-starred escutcheons of the Barberini family.

The answer to the riddle lies entirely in the fact that the full picture, the true 'image' of this montage statement only *emerges* in the sequential juxta-position of its constituent 'frames'. Each shield in itself means nothing. Viewed in isolation, each one is dumb. But in the joint combination of all eight of them, and taken together with the tomb of St Peter and the basilica as a whole, they ring out across the centuries as a devastating pamphlet against the plunderers and brigands concealed beneath the papal tiara.

In themselves, the pictures, the phases, the elements of the whole are innocent and indecipherable. The blow is struck only when the elements are juxtaposed into a sequential image. The placing of the shields – or rather their 'displacing' – around the four plinths, at right angles and at six metres' distance from each other, together with the need to walk round the whole vast quadrilateral of the canopy and to begin from one particular corner (the left-hand front pillar): these are the factors that make up the cunning separation of the eight montage sequences. Such is the method by which, in the very heart of Catholicism, a most venomous satire on its triple-crowned head has managed to remain in encoded form for centuries.

The separation of its elements is the best means of concealing an image that emerges, or should emerge, from their sequential juxtaposition.

Here I cannot help recalling an analogous instance. Admittedly it is to be found at the other end of the continent, almost three hundred years later, and in a totally different class context. In one thing, however, it resembles the foregoing: both there and here it was a means of avoiding the vigilance of the censorship, a censorship no less corrosive than that of the tsarist government in 1905. In both cases the method of pulling the wool over the censor's eyes was the same. In both cases the principle was the dissociated display of images that only acquired significance through the montage technique of sequential juxtaposition. In this instance the medium was not carved marble and was not intended to last for centuries; it was printer's ink on the pages of a satirical magazine, one of those which, like the clouds of arrows of a light advance-guard, were showered down upon the enemy, accompanying a great popular upsurge, the first wave of the movement that was to overthrow autocracy.

I am describing this from memory, on the basis of memoirs that I read somewhere, written by an old journalist who was active in 1905 when it was strictly forbidden to make any reference to such events as the dispersal of a crowd by armed force. How, then, could such a scene be conveyed in a magazine? A way round the ban was found: two unrelated pictures were drawn, either in the form of an initial illuminated letter or a pictorial endpiece to an article. One – a purely cinematographic frame! – showed the legs of a rank of soldiers marching in step; another, a confused mass of civilian legs in disorderly retreat. The pictures were shown to the censor separately, and he saw no objection to passing these vignettes, each of little significance and in any case 'harmless' in themselves, which were, furthermore, shown to him on different days. On the pages of the magazine, however, they were placed in such a way that they merged into a single image, the dispersal of a crowd, which instantly sprang to life. The censor had been circumvented. The hint went home. The issue of the magazine was confiscated after its appearance, but too late. The name of the censor was Savenkov; the magazine was called *Zritel'* [The Spectator].

Shebuyev's magazine *Pulemët* [The Machine-Gun] introduced 'montage' of this kind as an integral part of its make-up. Over many issues, the front and back covers played the role of such montage shots. The meaning of what they depicted and their full graphic significance were largely revealed by the juxtaposition of the first and last pages.

The cover of issue No. 3 showed 'a Russian sailor' with the caption: 'Russia's freedom was born on the sea'. The back cover had the caption: 'The God-fearing warriors', and showed a galloping detachment of maddened Cossacks. The juxtaposition of the two spoke for itself. The cover of No. 4 showed Father Gapon, with a crowd of typically Russian faces behind him. The caption was: 'Follow me!' On the back cover there was the same caption: 'Follow me!', but the picture above it showed a crowd of injured people limping away from a demonstration . . . and so on.

Zritel' also used 'montages' of a kind that were more complex in the mental juxtaposition linking them. One drawing, for instance, showed twenty-five dark figures, among whom it was fairly easy to identify Nicholas II, Alexander III, several grand dukes, Father John of Kronstadt and a number of ministers. The caption read: '25 Silhouettes', followed by a multiplication sign, then the figure '4'. The censorship passed the drawing, having failed to notice that it was a cryptogram: the twenty-five black figures multiplied by four made a hundred black figures, a 'Black Hundred'. The expression 'Black Hundred' thereafter passed into general use, although it was strictly forbidden to use it in print.[67]

Where architectural interiors are concerned, one might adduce more 'direct' examples, taken from other pages in the history of architecture, such as the system of rising vaults in Hagia Sophia, which reveal their scope and magnificence step by step, or the interplay of arcades and vaulting in Chartres Cathedral, whose calculated magic of sequential montage I have myself admired more than once.

The examples not only link montage technique with architecture; they vividly underline the even closer, more immediate link within montage between *mise en cadre* and *mise en scène*. This is one of the corner-stones without which not only can there be no understanding of either sphere, but still less can there be any planned, consistent teaching of the art of montage.

4 Yermolova

The subject for discussion is Valentin Serov's portrait of Yermolova in the Tretyakov Gallery.[68]

Many were those who experienced the quite special feeling of *exaltation* and *inspiration* that gripped the spectator when watching the original of this portrait.

The portrait shows an extremely sparing use of colour. It is almost chilling in the severity of its pose; it is almost crude in its disposition of masses; it is devoid of background and 'stage props'. A single vertical black figure stands against the grey background of a wall and a mirror. This cuts the figure at the waist and reflects a piece of the opposite wall and ceiling of the empty room in which the actress has been painted.

Yet, in contemplating this canvas, one is seized by something of the same emotion which the personality of the great actress must have evoked on the stage.

There have been, of course, malicious tongues which denied there was anything in any way remarkable about this portrait.

One such, for instance, was the late Ivan A. Aksionov, who grumbled about it: 'Nothing special. She always used to act with her stomach stuck out. And in Serov's portrait she is standing with her stomach thrust forward.'[69] Here, no doubt, Aksionov's odd 'non-acceptance' of the actress herself (whom he disliked) has become fused with his attitude towards the way Serov recreated her image with such exactitude.

I never saw Yermolova on stage, and I only know about her acting from the descriptions and very detailed accounts of those who saw her, but my impressions of Yermolova, gained from the 'data' of the Serov portrait, are similar to the enthusiasm with which Stanislavsky wrote about her:

> Maria Nikolayevna Yermolova represents a whole epoch of the Russian theatre, and for our generation she was a symbol of womanliness, beauty, strength, emotional power, genuine simplicity and modesty. Her gifts were unique. She had a power of insight amounting to genius, an inspired temperament, great nervous sensitivity, inexhaustible spiritual depths. . . . To every part that she played, Yermolova always gave a particular image that was unlike the preceding one and unlike that of any other actor.
>
> The roles which Yermolova created live on in the memory with an

independent existence, despite the fact that they were all compounded of the same organic material, of her single spiritual personality.

. . . All her movements, her words, her actions, even if they were misjudged or mistaken, were suffused with fire from within, with an emotion that could be warm and gentle or fiery and thrilling. . . .Wise in the ways of the female heart, more than anyone else she had the ability to reveal and display *das ewig Weibliche*.[70]

Something resembling this feeling overcame me when I stood in front of this portrait at the exhibition of Serov's work at the Tretyakov Gallery in 1935. For a long time I reflected on how, with an almost total absence of a painter's usual external effects – and Serov possessed a considerable arsenal of effects – he had achieved such a remarkable inner power of *inspired exaltation* in painting the figure.

I think I have solved this mystery. This *unusual* effect has been achieved through the application of truly unusual means of compositional expression. Furthermore, the means used here are such that in essence they have already outdistanced that stage of painting to which the picture itself still belongs.

To my mind, every truly great work of art is *always* distinguished by this characteristic: it contains, as part and parcel of the artist's *method*, elements of what in the next phase of development of that particular art form will become the *principles* and *methods* of a new stage in the forward progress of that art.

In the given instance this is especially interesting, because these *unusual* compositional factors not only lie beyond the limits of the methods of painting used in Serov's era, but *altogether beyond the limits of painting as it is narrowly understood*, at least from the viewpoint of those who do not regard the pictorial medium of cinema – its dynamic use of light and montage to make pictures – as a contemporary form of painting. There actually are such eccentrics who obstinately refuse to understand this and are totally unable to accept cinema – that miracle of pictorial potential – as part of the mainstream of the development and history of painting. This seems to me profoundly unjust: the difference of 'technology' is irrelevant. After all, the hospitable edifice of the history of painting embraces such technically diverse media as, say, etching and . . . the mosaics of Ravenna!

As for the fundamental and decisive factor, that is to say *artistic thinking*, then the 'gap' between Picasso and the cinematographer is significantly narrower than that between Paul Signac and the Wanderers [*Peredvizhniki*].[71] And as for the classification of photography as a 'mechanical' art, allegedly devoid of the direct, living touch of the creative 'act', I must say that the subtle structuring of a shot, the refined nuances of lighting and the strict calculation of tonal values found in the work of our best cameramen have long been capable of competing on equal terms with the best examples of the art of the past!

Let us, however, return to the portrait of Yermolova.

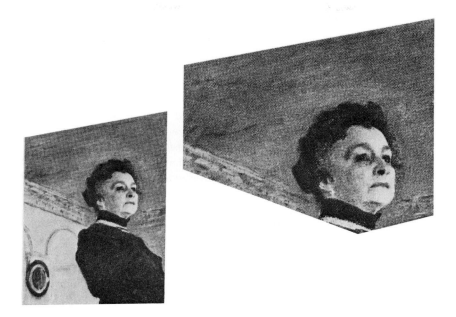

V.A. Serov: *Portrait of M.N. Yermolova*

It was not by chance that I referred to the mirror as cutting the figure. To my mind, in that 'cut' and in the montage-like juxtaposition of the results of that cut there lies the fundamental secret of the effect of this portrait.

I have written and spoken many times about montage as being not so much the sequence of segments as their *simultaneity*: in the consciousness of the perceiver, segment is piled on segment, and their incongruences of colour, lighting, outline, scale, movement, etc., are what gives that sense of dynamic thrust and impulse which generates a sense of movement, ranging from the perception of purely *physical movement* to the most complex forms of *intraconceptual movement* when we are dealing with a montage that juxtaposes metaphors, images or concepts.

Therefore we should in no way be confused by the following reflections, which concern the *simultaneous conjoint presence* on one canvas of elements which are, in essence, *the successive phases of a whole process*.

Nor should we be puzzled by the fact that the various elements are simultaneously seen both as separate *independent units* and as *inseparable parts of a single whole* (or as separate groups within that whole).

Moreover, as we shall see below, the very fact of that unity of *simultaneity* and *sequence* proves to be a unique means of producing an absolutely specific effect.

But let us get down to business.

I said that the frame of the mirror 'cuts' the figure. The figure is cut not only by the frame of the mirror; it is also cut by the line of the skirting-board, i.e. the line at which the floor meets the wall, and it is cut by the broken line of the cornice, that is to say the line, reflected in the mirror, at which the wall meets the ceiling.

Strictly speaking, these lines do not cut the figure: they go as far as her outline and politely break off; only by mentally extending them do we slice across the figure at various levels, thereby separating from each other the lower part of the dress, the bust and the head.

Let us extend these lines in fact, and 'cut' the portrait into sections (see illustration).

When this is done, the straight lines which figure *as objects* in the picture (as do the frame of the mirror and the lines of juncture between floor and wall, wall and ceiling) function simultaneously, as it were, as the *edges* of individual film shots. Admittedly unlike the standard edges of film frames, they have irregular outlines but they nevertheless fulfil to perfection the basic functions of film shots.

The outline traced by the first line surrounds the figure as a whole; this is a 'full-length shot'.

The second line gives us the 'figure from the knees upward'.

The third, 'waist-length'.

And finally the fourth gives us a typical 'close-up'.

For purposes of greater clarity, let us go a little further and physically cut the picture up into a set of four shots. We will place them side by side and check out the features (apart from the difference of scale) which distinguish them. To do so, let us separate these 'cut-outs' of the figure and study each one individually as an independent shot.

What, in general, distinguishes one shot from another, apart from the scale and the edges of the frame?

Above all, of course, the placing of the set-up.

Let us examine our 'shots' in sequence, from the viewpoint of . . . the setup.

From which point, if one may so express it, was frame No. 1 – 'full-length' – shot?

We see that in it the floor is not shown as just a narrow strip, but as a large, flat, dark grey surface, on which the hem of the dress is disposed around the figure as a broad black mass: the figure has clearly been shot *from above*.

Shot No. 2. 'Figure from the knees upward.' As it now appears in the cutout, the figure has been placed *parallel* to the wall on which the mirror is fastened. As for the set-up, this frame would have been shot *head-on*.

Shot No. 3. When this part of the picture is detached from the rest, we see the upper half of Yermolova's figure against a background of a certain spatial depth: when cut out with this particular framing, that space is no longer perceptible as being a reflection in the mirror. The depth provided by the mirror functions as the depth of an actual spatial background.

This is a typical and well-known case in film-making practice, when a relative impression of space is produced by means of simply altering the frame. But much more important in this instance is the fact that, due to the relative positioning of the figure, the walls and the ceiling, the figure in this 'shot' no longer appears to have been shot head-on: it has clearly been shot slightly *from below* (the ceiling can be seen overhanging the space above it).

Shot No. 4. The face is seen in close-up against a horizontal plane, which we know as the ceiling.

When is this kind of result produced in a shot?

Only, of course, when it is shot emphatically *from below*.

Thus we see that all four of the theoretical 'shots' of our sequence differ from each other not only in the *scale* of what they depict but in the *displacement* of the set-up (the points from which the object is viewed). Furthermore, this movement of the set-up strictly duplicates the process of gradual enlargement towards a close-up: as the object increases in size, the set-up moves consistently from an *overhead* set-up (A) to a *head-on* shot (B), thence to a set-up that is *partly below* (C), and the shooting finishes *from below* at the lowest possible point (D) (see Fig. 4.1).

If we now imagine shots 1, 2, 3 and 4 connected in a montage sequence, then it transpires that the eye has described a complete arc of 180 degrees. The figure has been shot in sequence from four different viewpoints, and the combination of these four points gives a sense of movement.

But *whose* movement?

We have already seen some instances of a combination of various phases

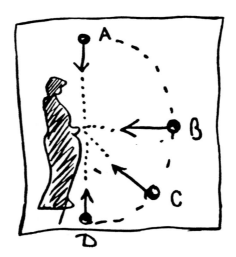

Fig. 4.1

of movement in which the eye traverses the *object* of the shots in one single movement. We may take as an example the montage of the three marble lions in a sequence of poses on the steps of Alupka Castle. Combined by montage, they give the illusion of a *single lion leaping to its feet.*[72]

Here we seem to have a similar case.

In this instance, however, is the effect of motion *of the figure itself* produced because its four sequential positions are perceived as four succeeding phases of movement, thereby resulting in the illusion of a continuous movement by the figure as a whole? This is the source of the dynamism to be found, for example, in the figures of Daumier and Tintoretto,[73] where the separate parts of a figure are disposed in accordance with the various phases of a single, continuous process of movement; the eye, as it travels over these separate phases of 'distributed' movement, involuntarily performs the leap from one phase to another and perceives this sequence of impulses as uninterrupted movement.

Exactly the same means are employed to create the basic effect of dynamism in cinematography, where the only difference is that the projector shows to the spectator, in sequence and in the successive phases, not just separate parts of the figure but the figure as a whole.

It is interesting to note that in order to convey movement *expressively*, the film-maker is not content to use this basic effect of cinematic dynamism alone; to transmit movement in a way that is gripping and expressive, the cinema has recourse to something similar to the method of . . . Daumier and Tintoretto. In this case – in montage editing – the cinema reverts to showing dynamics through the separate parts of a figure. The question, however, remains: is this the case in the portrait of Yermolova or not?

The answer, of course, is a categorical negative!

Because what has here been fixed on canvas is not a series of four successive positions of an object but four successive positions of *the eye of the observer*. Therefore these four points are not a function of *the behaviour of the object* (as with the aroused lion and Daumier's lively figures) but are a characteristic of *the behaviour of the spectator*. And this behaviour reveals itself in a movement from a viewpoint that is 'above' to one that is 'below' the figure, as though moving to a point . . . 'at the feet' of the great actress!

But the behaviour of the spectator can also be defined as the *attitude of the spectator*; or rather, it is the attitude imposed upon the spectator by the artist and it derives entirely from the attitude to the subject of the artist himself.

It is this – the artist's attitude – which obliges him to have recourse to the particular graphic structure which most fully expresses that attitude.

I think that if a line is capable in some way of expressing a thought and an attitude towards something (which it does here), the line of the viewpoint along the arc ABCD entirely corresponds to the idea of 'admiration' which one involuntarily feels when looking at the portrait of Yermolova.

But that is not all.

This basic 'tendency' in the overall composition of the portrait is reinforced by two more powerful means of influencing the spectator.

These are the spatial structuring and the use of colour (or rather the use of light), which also modulate in a downward arc along with the movement towards close-up and the shift of the 'set-up' from 'shot' to 'shot'.

A constant *expansion of space* takes place in the progression through shots 1, 2, 3 and 4.

No. 2 presses closely up against the wall with the mirror.

No. 3 is projected against the apparent depth of the room reflected in the mirror.

No. 4 stands out against a background of immense, boundless space.

Thus from shot to shot the ever-enlarging image of Yermolova herself dominates an ever-expanding space.

But at the same time the shots become progressively brighter.

No. 1 is completely dominated by the black mass of the dress.

In No. 2 the black part of the figure ceases to function independently, but instead tends to lead the eye towards the brighter area of the face.

In No. 3 the remaining areas of black now only cast shadows on the bright face.

In No. 4 the main part of the frame is wholly taken up with the face, which seems to glow from within.

This increase in the intensity of lighting from shot to shot, merging into a single uninterrupted process, is perceived as a *gradual brightening*, an *increasing illumination* and *animation* of the actress's face, which gradually advances out of the dim background of the picture.

Unlike the movement of the set-up, however, these two characteristics do not relate to any action by the spectator but to the apparent behaviour of the subject portrayed: thanks to them, Yermolova seems illuminated by a growing inner fire and by the light of inspiration, and that inspiration seems to radiate on to the ever-growing number of her enthusiastic admirers.

Thus a reciprocal interplay is set up between the *admiration of the enthusiastic spectator* in front of the picture and the *inspired actress* on the canvas – in exactly the same way that the auditorium and the stage once merged as both were captivated by the magic of her acting. It is interesting that by his compositional method Serov expresses graphically almost *literally* the very same things that Stanislavsky says about Yermolova in words (I take the liberty of stressing those words which relate directly to our analysis): 'in each part that she played, M.N. Yermolova always conveyed a *special* spiritual image, which was unlike the previous one and unlike any other.'[74]

The chosen method of composition is undoubtedly 'special' and 'unlike any other'. The montage principle of composition used here is profoundly original and individual.

(Just what a disaster can result from failing to use a 'special' approach to the solution of a similar problem in painting we shall see from another example, also from the area of portraiture, which will be illustrated below.)

'The roles created by Yermolova live on in the memory *with an independent existence*, despite the fact that they were all *created from the same organic material*, from her *single spiritual personality*.'

It would be hard to find a more exact graphic equivalent of what has been said here than the way in which Serov has broken up the picture, as we have seen, into four parts that are autonomous yet which simultaneously continue to exist as a single, indivisible, organic whole!

Taken separately, these 'levels' are like the 'roles' which live on 'with an independent existence', while taken together they constitute the single organic whole of the 'full-length shot', i.e. 'her single spiritual personality'.

'All her movements, words, actions . . . were suffused with fire from within by an emotion that could be warm and gentle or fiery and thrilling.'

This is the same feeling that is conveyed with such perfection by the gradual lightening that occurs from level to level, on which we remarked above.

'For our generation . . . Yermolova was a symbol of . . . *strength, emotional power*, genuine *simplicity* and *modesty*.'

There is 'simplicity' and 'modesty' in the 'conventional', unpretentious painterly means that are used in the picture with such astonishing restraint, both in the pose of the actress and in the colour resolution of the portrait itself.

There is 'strength' in the enlarging of the face from level to level.

And finally, *emotional power* is conveyed as the *unity of opposites* within the compositional principle.

Like the *unity of the consecutive and the simultaneous*.

Like the *simultaneity* of the existence of the picture both as a *single whole* and as a *system of successively enlarging shots*, into which the picture breaks down and from which the picture is again reconstituted into a whole.

I am profoundly convinced that the compositional principle which we have analysed was not, of course, 'consciously' selected but arose for Serov purely intuitively. In no way, however, does this lessen the force of the strict logic of what he did in the composition of this portrait.

We are well aware of how long and agonisingly Serov struggled over the composition of his portraits; how much time he spent on ensuring that the visual solution of the *psychological* task which he set himself in the portrait should *wholly* correspond to the image that suggested itself to him at the meeting, or rather the 'confrontation', with the sitter.

I quote at random from his letters.

'You know, I think, that for me each portrait is like living through an illness' (1887, to his wife).

'This evening I shall try and sketch the princess (Yusupova – S.M.E.) in pastels and charcoal. I think I know how to do her, yet – I don't know; with painting you can never predict anything beforehand' (1903).

'And then if I concentrate on one thing – even if it's just Girshman's nose – I find I'm stuck up a blind alley' (1910).

'Well now, it seems that I have finished my paintings, although as always I could keep working on them, I suppose, for an eternity, or at least for half an eternity' (1903).

And above all there is the invariable, the principal, the fundamental theme: *'The chief thing is – how to capture the character of the sitter.'*

In this painful movement towards the fixing on canvas of the image floating dazzlingly and tantalisingly before the artist's eyes, the creative impulse gives rise to those amazingly complex and unyielding structures which later astonish us with their inevitability and immutability. [. . .][75]

Let us, however, return once more to the purely compositional aspect of the picture, whose effect has been to give us such a remarkably vital impression of the great Yermolova, and we shall find an astounding link with our initial example of the barricade. For there, too, two qualities emerged simultaneously: the depiction of a barricade together with a certain outline which revealed the essential, overall meaning of the barricade as an element in a struggle. By forcing the eye to follow its zigzags, the particular shape of that jagged line conveyed a *sense of conflict*. The feeling that it aroused was imprinted on our consciousness as the perception of a *struggle*. Every variation of the zigzag line AB from the straight line CD can be perceived as a thrust exerted on it from opposing sides, which with alternating success strike it at points d, d1, d2, d3, d4, d5 along the straight line and displace it towards points c, c1, c2, c3, c4, c5 (see Fig. 4.2). The 'alternation of success' may be seen from the adjoining column, which can be interpreted as a chart of the struggle between two forces.

Both sets of quantities are perceived simultaneously, and the result is the depiction of a barricade that is steeped in a feeling of struggle (not to be found to the same degree in a picture of a barricade which has not been treated in like manner).

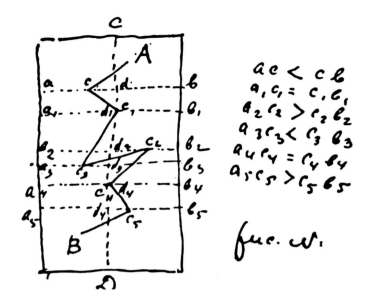

Fig. 4.2

In the portrait of Yermolova we have exactly the same thing – with the difference, of course, that the expressive message and the content of the drawing are not the same and the expressive aim is different. The variation between the two is not, however, limited to this.

The line CD is not actually drawn as such, nor even suggested, but is a line made up of a series of imaginary points that the eye follows as it moves; moreover, the plane of this imaginary line does not coincide with the plane of the picture, but is perpendicular to it (see Fig. 4.1 above). Yet at the same time the line also derives from a more profound perception of the subject matter than the mere visual registration of its outward appearance. This deeper perception is inextricably linked with a more profound interpretation of the picture: its *meaning* is made up of a detailed apprehension of the subject plus our individual attitude to it. For a scrap-dealer the barricade is by no means an image of struggle but is a collection of second-hand goods suitable for resale (a bed, armchairs, shop signs, barrels and so on), while for a tourist it represents a heap of potential souvenirs!

We see in the portrait a complete repetition of the same multi-level construct noted above.

There is one level which I have purposely not mentioned, although I have by no means forgotten it. I shall not analyse it, because it does not form part of the subject matter of this study; even so, it can do no harm to mention it. I refer, of course, to the most elementary positioning of the model – not *on the canvas* (with which we are mainly concerned) but *in front of the canvas*. I have in mind the model's *real-life behaviour*, and since this is inevitably motionless, I mean the *pose* of the model. In the case of cinema this would include the actor's behaviour, mime, gesture and voice. We shall not deal with this theme here, but it should at least be stressed once more that the entire visual composition of the actor's screen existence should be in complete harmony with this factor. Each of these aspects derives inseparably from the other and, taken together, they both derive from the idea, theme and content of the screenplay. Almost exactly the same comment, in almost exactly the same words, is applicable to the pose of the painter's model. The pose must equally be a total, generalising image of the multiplicity of positions and movements that are characteristic of the sitter. We know that in this respect, too, Serov was meticulous and took as much trouble in placing his sitter in front of the easel as he did in positioning the portrait on the canvas. See how much careful thought has gone into the poses of the Gruzenbergs, Miss Gershelman or Lamanova. Or look at the pose of Yermolova herself. In the pose, of course, as in everything else about the picture there should also be a second level of generalisation, above and beyond any generalisation at the everyday, realistic level. I refer to the metaphor of pose and gesture (on which we have cited quotations from Engels and Gratiolet about people in action or actors), or rather the image – for example 'the image of the hero', 'the image of the leader', 'the image of the owner' or 'the image of the traitor' – which through the choice of pose and the use of the painter's medium should emerge from the straightforward anatomical depiction of the sitter.

Here, I think, lies the watershed between two different types of realists such as Serov and Repin.[76]

Repin stops at the point of realistic generalisation. Here he is truly great: how vividly the 'actors' in the scene of *Pushkin at the Examination* generalise their roles. A generalising image of wider import, however, is beyond his powers. If he attempts one, the result is either allegory (what spaciousness) achieved by the *setting* of the scene, or else such appalling paintings as his version of the 'inspired' Tolstoy (that full-length portrait of Tolstoy in which he is shown with arms slightly outspread and a face shining from within with a pink glow, like one of those paper lanterns used to illuminate a summer garden-party).

I have in mind Repin's portrait of Lev Tolstoy known by the title, *Tolstoy Renouncing Worldly Life*. It was painted in 1912 for the Moscow Society of Art and Literature. In it Repin set himself a task similar to that undertaken by Serov in his portrait of Yermolova. The portrait was an attempt to show the inner translucence, the other-worldly light shining within a great writer who has achieved the highest degree of spirituality.

We have observed the complex but consistent path followed by Serov in order to achieve his desired result by purely compositional and painterly means. Nor should we forget how Serov went to the extremes of 'asceticism' in his use of pictorial effects by omitting even the slightest gesture by Yermolova: everything is intended to concentrate the picture's effect on the great actress's inner spiritual resources ('Her unfathomable spiritual depths',

I.E. Repin: *Tolstoy Renouncing Worldly Life*

in the words of Stanislavsky). We have demonstrated above how consistently the sense of 'inward illumination' and 'inner light' were achieved in her portrait.

This is not Repin's method: he goes for it 'head-on', in a direct 'plain man's' fashion.

Whereas Serov – painting an *actress*, of all people – removed from his canvas everything theatrical, everything connected with the stage (up to and including such eloquent means of expression as gesture), not only does Repin above all emphasise gesture but *exaggerated* gesture – in other words, the pose. And who is his subject? One of the sternest of moralists and castigators of everything faked and theatrical, to say nothing of the merely false (one has only to recall Tolstoy's Savonarola-like intolerance of even Shakespeare). Yet here, with the artist trying so hard to be 'monumental', the great sage (so often drawn by Repin himself in his plain yet truly monumental everyday simplicity) suddenly becomes a 'saintly' little old man with his arms inanely stretched out at his sides!

Even worse, however, is the fact that Repin tries to convey the idea of 'inward illumination' equally simplistically, with head-on literalism. As a result, instead of the head of a great sage we have something like a Chinese lantern, with the simulacrum of a literal, physical source of light inside it, a source of light whose pink glow shines through a pink-tinted face!

One cannot help recalling the words of Chekhov . . .

The beer was served. Gvozdikov sat down, lined up all six bottles in front of him and, with a loving glance at them, started to drink. After three glasses he felt as though a lamp had been lit inside his chest and another inside his head: he had such a feeling of warmth, brightness and wellbeing. . . .

After the second bottle he felt that the light in his head had been put out and it was growing dark.[77]

And this portrait was painted seven years after Serov had achieved such a brilliant solution of an analogous problem!

The error of Repin's method lies in his wanting to convey the *generalised* theme, i.e. a theme extending beyond the limits of simple depiction, by purely *depictive* means. The result is a work of appalling falsity. We have seen that an aim which 'transcends' mere depiction – a generalisation *about* what is depicted – should employ means which transcend the artist's normal methods. We have seen this in the very primitive example of the barricade, where the expressive character of the compositional outline is utilised. We have seen this in equal degree in a perfect example: the portrait of Yermolova. Reread once more the passage which describes how this 'apotheosis' of the actress is realised, in particular the means whereby Serov achieves the sense of inner illumination of the face, as distinct from Repin's portrait of Tolstoy, where it has been attempted by crassly literal pictorial means, by a flat, empty picture of the old man's head, lit from within as though by 'the light of thought'.

Our reaction to this approach can only, of course, be one of bewilderment. Compare it with the mastery by which something no less elusive – the sense of a ballerina's 'airiness' – is conveyed in [Serov's] portrait of Anna Pavlova merely by draughtsmanship and the use of background, for she is not depicted in flight when the quality of lightness would be conveyed by the pose itself. The same comments apply to pre-screen composition (in this respect the screen is, after all, only the more sophisticated brother of the painter's expanse of stretched canvas).

Here, too, *Yermolova* is equally perfect.

Let us repeat: what makes her portrait so expressive is the fact that we have before us in this picture the *simultaneous unity* of monumental *immobility* and a whole gamut of *dynamic movement*: the 'zoom' effect of ever-increasing close-ups; the growing movement of space and light; the shifting viewpoint in relation to the subject.

This combination of contradictions within a unity also contributes to producing that thrill which grips us whenever we are fortunate enough to live through a direct experience of the dialectical process. It is also interesting to observe that the effect has been achieved without a departure from realistic depiction, which, despite everything, retains its representational integrity. [. . .][78]

Let us return to *Yermolova* one last time and to that imaginary line joining up each successive viewpoint; this 'all-round observation' of the subject, which we remarked in the portrait of Yermolova is *exactly* what happens when we progress byond the limitations of single set-up cinematography! It is a precise illustration of how in montage the elements into which an event is broken up are reassembled into the montage image of that event. To describe this complex dual process, in 1933 I invented the term *mise en cadre* (in all respects analogous to the concept of *mise en scène*).[79]

We shall return to this subject when we move on to the next section. . . .

There only remains to draw one further generalising conclusion from the total phenomenon which we have investigated in such detail with all the examples given in the first section, and which stood out with particular force in the case of the portrait of Yermolova.

The simultaneity with which the construct exists at two levels – in the *whole* and in the *parts* – is the precise analogue of a fundamental characteristic of human perception in general, which has the ability to comprehend a phenomenon in two ways: *as a whole* and *in its details*; *immediately* and *in mediated form*; *complexly* and *differentially*. The terms we use depend on the area we choose to examine, but this peculiarity of human perception is to be found in equal degree in all aspects of man's activity and thought and it invariably permeates them. . . . At various periods of mankind's development, these two characteristics of perception have been distinct or separated from each other. Engels discussed this exhaustively in *Anti-Dühring*. Only when man reaches the appropriate age in his personal existence, in the existence of his species (social development), and in the existence of his society (the stage of dialectical philosophy which characterises mankind in its maturity) does this separation merge into the unity of a new quality. The one-sidedness of the *child's* synthesising mode of thought becomes the *adult's* analytical thinking, having acquired the differential principle. In the same way the mind of *man at the dawn of culture* evolves into the *mind of man in the epoch of a developed culture*; similarly, philosophy develops from *primeval chaos* into *materialistic dialectics*.

The curious feature about this process, of course, is the following: synthesising perception is, of course, the lower stage of perception (*vide* Engels), whereas differential perception is a step forward (*vide* ditto). Observation which is capable of *generalising* is, of course, the highest type of all. (It figures in science as the *generalised concept*, in art as the *generalised image*, belonging in equal degree to the highest category of man's intellectual activity; provided, of course, that one is either consciously or intuitively directed towards the progressive development or advancement of social conditions, to the degree and in the direction permitted by the social epoch.)

Here a contradiction seems to arise: the highest stage – the generalised image – seems *in visual terms* to coincide with the most primitive type of synthesising perception. But this is only an apparent contradiction. In reality we have in this instance that very same 'apparent reversion to the older stage' which Lenin mentions in discussing the dialectics of phenomena. The fact is that generalisation is *a true synthesis*, i.e. simultaneously a synthesising (immediate) and a differential (mediated) perception of the event (and a perception *about* the event).

A generalisation from which the purely representational element has been removed would be a bare, non-objective abstraction dangling in mid-air. Such would be a third version of our barricade, so generalised as to be deprived not of the compositional outline (as distinct from the first version), but of the actual picture, and retaining only the 'image-expressing' zigzag line of its contour. All the 'pictorial' and 'expressive' qualities would instantly evaporate from the sketch, while the zigzag itself might not be interpreted as a barricade but as . . . *anything you like*: as a graph of the rise and fall of prices, or as a seismographic trace of subterranean tremors, and so on and so forth (see Fig. 4.3). It would be open to all these interpretations until the abstraction reverted (as in our case) to the representation of some concrete, objective subject matter.*

In a sketch that contains the full complement of elements, its main, fundamental characteristic is clear, namely that the effectiveness of our chosen examples rests on the fact that each element in them appeals to its own

---

*Here it is tempting to suggest a link with the Constructivists,[80] but the congruence would be incomplete and ineffective. The Constructivists aestheticised the physical structure of materials into a central theme of their work, to a greater degree than our examples of psychologically expressive structuring of a phenomenon.

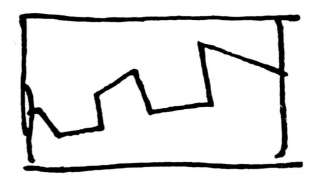

Fig. 4.3

particular part of our perception and that the combination of them appeals to the totality of our synthesising consciousness, drawing the spectator 'from head to foot' into its effect.

It is this characteristic of human perception, of course, which determines both the fact of the structure and the existence of precisely this kind of structure in any truly complete and perfect human artefact.

In this drawing *the nature of the artefact is a reflection of the characteristics of human consciousness – of Man – within its formal structure alone.* This will be *as much reflected in the form of the artefact* as the reflection of Man is the prime condition of a vital and meaningful *content of the artefact.*

Having noted this we should not forget it while dealing with the immediate problems of montage, because we shall return again to the principle we have just enunciated.

Post Scriptum

I don't like Repin. That, however, has nothing to do with my analysis of the method that made his portrait of Tolstoy such a disaster. In judging it so unfavourably I am in the company of Igor Grabar, a fervent admirer of Repin's painting. Although he does not analyse the reasons for the ugliness of this particular work by Repin, he does not mince words in his criticism of it. In a chapter significantly entitled 'Downhill', Grabar writes: 'But worst of all, it must be said, is the portrait commissioned in 1912 by the Moscow Society of Art and Literature, and which was entitled by the artist *Tolstoy Renouncing Worldly Life*'.[81]

I think this quotation disposes of any accusation that I am prejudiced in my criticism of this portrait:

We now come to a most essential factor in Repin's work, *his lack of imagination* – not only in *The Zaporozhians* and *St Nicholas of M . . . ,* but in all Repin's work in general. Lack of imagination need not be a drawback for an artist; it is sufficient to say that neither Velázquez, Frans Hals or Holbein had it. But they, with very rare exceptions, never tackled themes which were outside the range of their talents or beyond their ability; Repin, unfortunately, was attracted to just such themes: *Sofia, The Zaporozhians, St Nicholas*; later *Get Thee Behind Me, Satan*, and others. For topics such as these required the gigantic imagination of such an artist as Surikov. . . .

Three of Repin's characteristics determined the entire content of his painting – a lack of imagination, a passion for problems of expression, and a longing to depict complex processes of human action, movement and thought, chiefly as seen through their physical manifestations.[82]

Let us allow ourselves to take the *literal* meaning of that missing trait: 'imagination'. I believe that it should least of all be interpreted in the sense of 'invention' or 'fantasy'. It has two main connotations: 1) an entering into the image of what is depicted, and 2) a transposition 'into image' of what you are depicting. Hence, the portraits of Repin are really, if anything, an 'atlas' (Grabar somewhere calls *The Zaporozhians* an 'atlas of laughter') of types and prototypes, features great and small taken from nature as though to compile a textbook for an actor who might wish to play them (that is why on my bookshelves monographs on Repin are to be found among the books that are of use to actors, not among the books on painting at all!), whereas Serov's portraits are like a gallery of uniquely *personified* images of living people, acted out by the artist. Later, when discussing El Greco, we shall again come across the case of the artist as actor, putting his own role-playing into his works.[83] But in this matter El Greco will not be in the same class as Serov, who was a master of absolute self-personification in the image he created, whereas El Greco transposes 'into himself' all the multiplicity of his subjects and models. It is to this second point, i.e. Serov's ability (and his method) not only to depict but to 'imagine' what he depicts, that the whole of this section on the Yermolova portrait is devoted. Comparing Serov to Repin only serves to consolidate our position, and it is further confirmed by the characteristic, mentioned by Grabar, of Repin's lack of imagination. [. . . .][84]

I would not like to leave the subject of Repin without having defined more precisely what I mean about the nature of his art. No one will deny that the realistic figures which he *depicts* are typical. But the point is that his work as a painter is limited to representative depiction. Repin does not typify his subjects by simultaneously depicting the man and generalising his features into an image. Repin does something different: he copies from nature the features of people he has found who happen to be typical. Typicality is thus not achieved by artistic means but through the features of a model, conscien- tiously recorded by the painter. It is in this sense that the expression 'a well-set scene' was appropriate when we used it with reference to *Pushkin at the*

Examination, but apart from qualifying Repin as a skilful stage director we might also call him a good entrepreneur in the skill of type-casting his actors.

For the film-maker, it would be difficult to find a more exciting description of type-casting than that relating to another realist artist: Surikov, in particular the case of the mathematics teacher who turned out to be the perfect 'image' for Menshikov.[85] Surikov, however, differs from Repin in that he uses a large number of purely painterly means to create the image of a man and the image of the scene in which he is placed. The sense of 'enclosure' comes out with special force in one particular scene, which is also thematically linked with imprisonment or enclosure. And this theme in itself brings us back again to Menshikov, this time not to his physical prototype but to the picture of his exile in Beryozova.

Descriptions of dead bodies being transported over long distances usually create a very powerful impression: those coffins enclosed one inside the other

V.I. Surikov, *Menshikov at Beryozova*

– an oak coffin, then a lead coffin, a covering over the oak, a covering over the lead – as in the engravings of Napoleon in his coffin after the shipment of his body from the island of St Helena; the body seems outlined by the heavy, quadruple contour of the coffins, from the inside one to the plain outer box surrounding the inner layers. I don't know whether the image of Napoleon on St Helena was hovering in front of Surikov's mind's eye when he was painting his picture, but whenever I look at *Menshikov at Beryozova* I involuntarily think of the prisoner of St Helena, whose wings have also been inexorably clipped by the walls of the tiny cottage, by the fence of the little surrounding garden, by the unyielding contours of the island itself and the vast watery space around it, to say nothing of the English guardships patrolling the coast: such are the images of Bonaparte alive (if such an existence can be called living) or of the dead Bonaparte encased in the fourfold outline of his coffins! And that, to me at least, is how Menshikov appears, with his passionate, unbending nature, as though buried alive and fettered by his Beryozova exile in four coffins which clasp him one after another in their embrace – with only the slight difference that his coffins are not physically real but are a metaphorical effect achieved by means of the 'concentric' rectangles of the composition which squeeze each other inwards.

In the centre of the composition is his tightly clenched fist, an image of the will-power by which he restrains his urge to hurl himself pointlessly into the fray. The fist is 'gripped' by the huddled group of his family, pressing closely in upon him for compositional reasons. The rough-hewn log walls of the cottage clasp the group in their turn. The dim light of a winter's day shines through the window, so that we sense that the cottage, too, is in the grip of frost, even before our eye is allowed to come to rest on the pitiless rim of the frame, which encloses the picture as a whole, reminding us of the famous prisoner in the reign of Louis XI, who for years was kept in an iron cage which allowed him neither to stand up nor so much as to straighten his back. With Surikov, this feeling stretches past the edges of his canvas and extends beyond this picture to others; *Menshikov* stands at the centre of a whole cycle, which includes *Boyarina Morozova* and *The Morning of the Execution of the Streltsy*, as distinct from another cycle linked by thematic unity – *The Capture of the Snowbound Town*, *The Conquest of Siberia* and *Suvorov Crossing the Alps*.

We shall find nothing analogous to this with Repin. In his pictures, typicality is achieved by other means; we have attempted to point out exactly what these means are. The typical as a simultaneous demonstration of both a phenomenon and a conclusion (generalisation) drawn from that phenomenon; the typical, fully realised so as to embrace both objective representation and generalised image: this is not within Repin's powers. And that, perhaps, is the reason why he is so strong as a purely representational painter and why he is so popular with those who are looking for realistic depiction above all. Here, too, perhaps is the secret of the diametrically opposite effect made by the two exhibitions, both held in the Tretyakov Gallery – one in 1934, the other in 1935 – the first showing Repin, the second Serov. The general impression produced by each exhibition as a whole repeated in reverse the effect of comparing the separate, individual works. Each one of Serov's pictures, in its typicality and in its unexcelled ability to express character, surpasses Repin. The ensemble of the Repin exhibition – as a comprehensive, all-embracing 'portrait of the epoch' – far outdoes Serov's incomparable gallery of faces, through each *separate* one of which there speaks the whole epoch. Why is this? I think it is precisely because a generalisation within a picture, i.e. the element which goes beyond the limits of representation, is inaccessible to Repin; that everything he depicts, whether it is a pure tone or a pure colour, is taken directly from nature. He never succeeds in mediating a generalising statement on canvas. Only in the multitude (the unrestrained abundance of Repin's paintings sanctions the use of this archaism to indicate their quantity!) of the total collection can there emerge a generalisation, of whose features each separate picture is no more than a single *stroke*. With Serov nothing like this occurs: each portrait, each picture by Serov is its own world, capable of containing an idea in all its dimensions. *The Rape of Europa* alongside *The Girshmans, Lamanova* alongside *Peter* [the Great] remain autonomous worlds that do not merge with each other; whereas [Repin's] *The Church Procession* has much in common with his *Ivan the Terrible*, and nothing prevents *St Nicholas of Myra* from combining with the portrait of Rubinstein and *The Archdeacon* to form a general physiognomy of the period. This applies to Repin's entire *opus*.

Interestingly enough, the same thing occurs with the cycles of paintings within his total *œuvre*. His cycles are not of the Surikov type, that is to say they are not unified by linking images. With Repin, the cycles are formed by unity of subject matter. Most interesting in this regard is the case of one of Repin's last works, in which a cycle is made up of separate paintings intended to form part of one joint picture. These exist both as a cycle of several portraits and as the large work containing them all. Amazingly, whereas the collection of individual paintings produces the most striking impression, the picture which incorporates them all leaves us quite cold. Wherein lies the secret? In the fact that the work which unites them in one is a mere *collection*, a mere process of sticking them into one common *picture*, and is not a *generalisation* into a single whole. Let me reveal that I am referring to Repin's picture *The State Council*, which is shown to the spectator in two forms – both as a completed picture and as a collection of superb portrait sketches, the studies that were made in preparation for the big picture.

The effect of the big picture is to leave us more than indifferent (not only because of the theme!) but basically because of its qualities of artistic composition – or rather because of its total lack of them. A glance at the great variety of the individual studies conveys an astounding effect, so strong, in fact, that I still recall the impression which they made on me the first time I saw them, and that was a long time ago, before the war, at the exhibition on the Field of Mars in Petersburg where they had their first public showing. Readers may make their own judgments on my age and the distance in time! I saw these sketches for the second time at the Repin exhibition of 1934, but this time alongside the completed picture. I tested my recollection of it, and was not only convinced that it was right but I think I also defined the secret of why the two forms of the work made such differing impressions. The fact is that when the spectator runs his eye over the individual portraits, he forms a generalised image: that of the collective face of the State Council, which comes across so clearly through the features of its members that there also emerges the face of the regime of which they are the supreme executives. Nothing of the sort comes out of the group picture itself. The figures and features are transplanted into it from the separate portraits in exactly the same way that spectators are seated in an auditorium – according to the numbering of their tickets – only here they are disposed according to rank, i.e. on grounds dictated by governmental statutes and decrees and not by artistic criteria at all.

Why is it that in the big picture the faces do not merge into a collective image? It is because in a picture that generalising aspect and image have to be given by the artist himself. If he fails to provide it, the spectator is disorientated, and in order for him to assemble the elements of the picture into his own overall conception or generalising image, he must take the finished picture apart, break it up into fragments and then consciously reassemble them; in other words he must do a 'home-made' version of . . . the preparatory sketches, in which the artist's *strictly pictorial* mode of combining them – which goes no further than spacing out the individual figures! – at least does not disturb his own imaginative combination of his figures! The conclusion to be drawn is that the combination of the *separate portraits* on *pictorial* grounds not only fails to provide any new generalising, interpretative element but even deprives them of that expressive force which, in each separate portrait, derived from the spectator's need to perceive each one mentally in a *montage-like* relationship with all the others. It is this compositional montage – this process of grasping the whole in a single action and simultaneously subordinating it to a rhythm which would define and generalise the theme of that action – that Repin the artist has failed to do. Please do not think that I am making some kind of 'leftist', anti-realist demand: accusations of the kind I have made above cannot be made against the densely peopled canvases of Surikov (*Boyarina Morozova*), of Alexander Ivanov (*Christ Appearing to the Multitude*),[86] or of Leonardo da Vinci (*The Last Supper*). It is significant that *Christ Appearing to the Multitude*, which is also on view to the public as both a collection of individual heads and as a complete picture, *in no way* produces the effect that we have observed in the case of Repin. With Ivanov the individual heads are separate and are simply interpreted as disconnected portraits (one of the surprising features being that the head of Christ is copied from the [same artist's] head of Apollo). Yet the true power of a dynamic image emerges when these same heads, in the implacable hands of the painter, force the spectator to perceive an expressive image in the unique compositional structure with which he has linked them all. The whole scope of Ivanov's mastery of composition stands out with particular clarity in his sketches illustrating the scriptures, in which there are some quite unforgettable pictures such as *The Stoning* [of the woman taken in adultery] and others. The fact remains that with Repin the generalising factor is not to be found within one picture but in the combination of a number of pictures, a process which the artist himself fails to carry out when putting them on to one canvas. Either the resulting picture does not work at all (as with The State Council) or the outcome is what happened in the portrait of Tolstoy.

A.A. Ivanov, *Christ Appearing to the Multitude*, detail

Clearly I am not alone in reacting to *The State Council* in the way described above. N. Radlov, for instance, writing on a quite different topic, namely Repin's painting technique, has this to say when referring to 'the group of works in which . . . the nature of Repin's talent stands out most plainly and obviously. These are', in Radlov's opinion, 'Repin's studies for *The State Council*'. He goes on to say:

> In both the ends and the means of pictorial representation this work entirely reflects Repin's talent and strength. These are a series of characteristic [portraits], seized rapidly and immediately, as was demanded by the shortness of the sittings, and therefore devoid of any attempt at typification or drawing theoretical conclusions. The method used here by the artist is one of simplified tonal distinctions without any attempts at expressive colouring or sophisticated draughtsmanship.[87]

Thus Repin's 'talent and strength' lie in the graphic 'immediacy' of what he records. His drawings, free of 'typification' and 'theoretical conclusions', i.e. of generalisation by artistic means, best correspond to his 'talent and strength'. The other characteristics mentioned – the *simplified* tonality, the lack of pretensions to expressing colouring, and the *unsophisticated* draughtsmanship – all mean that the studies not only create a generalised image by virtue of their *function*, but that on *structural and technical* grounds they are typical 'montage' fragments.

What has been written in this and subsequent chapters, incidentally, lies completely outside the scope of Part One, and for a full clarification of this passage it would do no harm to reread it alongside the explanations which I shall be giving in Part Two, where I shall refer to the way in which the montage image is created. The comments made in this passage serve as additional illustration to Part Two itself.

Here let us conclude our analysis of Repin with a final thought. A generalised image of Tolstoy, worthy of the methods used by Serov, which Repin failed to create in the portrait we have analysed, nevertheless does exist in Repin's *œuvre*. But where? It is to be found in the generalising image and representation of Tolstoy which emerges from the loving, heartfelt sketches and pictures in which Repin has purely graphically caught the great old man at a number of separate moments. In these innumerable works Repin managed to fix pictorially one *single* characteristic of Tolstoy at a time, catching *one* feature in each picture or sketch. The graphic artist can ask no more.

Part Two
Montage in Multiple Set-Up Cinema

5 Laocoön

The period of multiple set-up cinema is now commonly called the period of 'montage cinema'.[88] This is vulgar in phrasing and simply incorrect in substance: *all* cinema is montage cinema, for the simple reason that the most fundamental cinematic phenomenon – the fact that the picture moves – is a montage phenomenon. What does this phenomenon of the moving photographic image consist of?

A series of still photographs of different stages of a single movement are taken. The result is a succession of what are called 'frames'.

Connecting them up with one another in montage by passing the film *at a certain speed* through a projector reduces them to a single process which our perception interprets as movement.

This could be called the stage of micro-montage, for the laws governing this phenomenon are the same as for montage, and the combination of montage segments which allows the perception of movement of a higher intensity (montage aimed at increasing the 'tempo') or of a higher order (the achievement of an inner dynamic by means of skilful *mise en cadre*) is a repetition of the same phenomenon at a higher stage of development. One can even talk of *macro-montage*; by this is meant neither the compositional assembly of *a shot* (micro-montage as the combining of single cells [i.e. frames]) nor the assembly of several *shots* (montage as the combining of montage units), but a compositional combining of separate *scenes*, of whole *parts* of a complete work.

Thus montage pervades all 'levels' of film-making, beginning with the basic cinematic phenomenon, through 'montage proper' and up to the compositional totality of the film as a whole.

So far we have not treated the question of the shot as a montage sequence of frames. Now we perceive even the still shot as a montage process, as the first link in a continuous chain of montage that extends throughout the entire work.

So far, too, we have examined the shot only as a graphic unit, differing in no way from the medium of painting. Compositionally speaking, we have been able to treat both the still and the moving shot identically, because in the first case we were dealing with a *fixed contour* and in the second case with the *record of a movement*. In the purely graphic sense there was *in principle* no compositional difference between them. Now we must take a quick look at that unitary shot as a *montage complex* and examine how there are embedded in it the rudiments of the process which unfolds in all its completeness in the second stage of the montage form.

Let us, as always, begin with its 'ancestors'. When discussing the graphic composition of the shot we found its forebears in painting. [. . . .] It may be asked whether the 'basic cinematic phenomenon' has its ancestors in the stages which precede it, i.e. whether other art forms contain the unusual situation where two objects, motionless in appearance, when caught by the artist in two successive phases of movement and juxtaposed, produce a qualitatively new phenomenon, namely that they merge into an apparent perception of the process of movement?

Undoubtedly, yes. Naturally the first examples that come to mind are Futurist drawings of 'eight-legged' people with the legs drawn in eight different phases of movement,[89] but it is worth remarking that in such instances no perception of movement arises from them: this purely experimental, logical game is intended simply to 'reveal the method', thereby destroying the 'flimsy deception' which might create an illusion if it were executed more subtly (for examples of this, see below). Apart from that, the method, like the majority of 'isms', is no more than a regression to certain stages of the past, when art went through similar stages in its progressive striving to master reality and not run away from it. Thus in certain very early miniatures (11th–12th centuries) we can find exactly the same phenomenon. The artist is not yet able to catch the dynamic of movement in the dynamic of his drawing. So what does he do? He divides the movement into two phases, sometimes into three, and endows one figure with the succession of attitudes through which the movement passes. The picture conveys 'a movement of the hand' by showing the hand in two positions. In this connection, I have long wondered whether perhaps the many-armed Hindu gods are not, in fact, meant to be conveying sequential movement through the depiction of a number of arms. In antiquity Lucian put forward a similar 'debunking' explanation of Proteus, whose 'versatility' and capacity to change appearance and personality he interpreted as no more than the skill of the actor, with its ability to metamorphose into a multiplicity of parts.[90] The 'stopped-action' picture of a phase of motion, which makes that fragment of movement appear motionless, long predates photography; to seize a 'fragment' of movement in momentary immobility mankind did not have to wait for the invention of the camera with shutter-speeds of a twenty-fifth, a hundredth or a thousandth of a second.

We need only recall Tolstoy's description of a running horse at night by the light of flashes of lightning.[91]

Perception of phases and the breakdown of movement into phases developed from a great number of observations of a similar type. At first the representation of movement used a similar jerky, 'chopped-up' method, in which the integrity of form and literal reality of depiction were destroyed, but the method itself – of depicting sequential phases for conveying a sense of movement – is firmly entrenched in those paintings which particularly surprise us by showing apparent movement while simultaneously retaining the integrity of the object, person or phenomenon depicted. Such qualities are possessed in equal degree, for instance, by the lithographs of Daumier and the ceilings of Tintoretto.[92] The 'trick' of the unusual mobility of their figures is purely cinematic. Unlike the miniatures of the Middle Ages, however, they do not give the temporally sequential phases of the movement to one limb depicted several times but spread these phases consecutively over different parts of the body. Thus the foot is in position A, the knee is already in stage A + a, the torso in stage A + 2a, the neck in A + 3a, the raised arm in A + 4a, the head in A + 5a, and so on. By the law of *pars pro toto*, from the position of the foot you mentally extrapolate the attitude which the entire figure should be taking up at that moment. The same applies to the knee, the neck and the head, so that in effect the figure drawn in this way is interpreted as if it were six successive 'frames' of the same figure in the various sequential phases of the movement. The fact that they are serially juxtaposed to each other forces the spectator to interpret them as 'movement' in exactly the same way that this occurs in cinema.

This takes place in equal degree in works by Daumier and by Tintoretto.

The masterly skill of both artists lies in the fact that despite the difference between the stages of movement in the various limbs, they contrive to retain an overall impression of the *wholeness* of the total figure. A 'break-up' of the figure occurs very rarely, and I have purposely selected from the total *œuvre* of Daumier's lithographs one rare example in which a 'breakup' of this kind does occur.[93] It is particularly vivid, and it will make it easier to examine and decipher those examples where the integrity of the figure has been preserved. The abruptness of the gallant gentleman's turning movement is conveyed by a very sharp disjuncture of its phases, in which, on the one hand, his torso and head are in their real positions, and, on the other, his arm as far as the elbow has retained the position which preceded that abrupt turning movement. It is quite obvious that in this picture his arm is 'anatomically' broken at the elbow. Despite the fragmented look of the successful examples – and their number is enormous – one of the great aids to achieving an effect of visual integrity is Daumier's technique of drawing: the ragged, sketch-like character of the line, which is 'rounded out' into fully drawn, completed forms only at certain points. Tintoretto achieves the same result by the use of his own, purely painterly means. This being the method for the artistic representation of a 'self-contained' movement – i.e. gesture – it is also the logical tradition for depicting the sequential nature of big, complex series of actions.

For this, the history of art teems with examples. Within one and the same medieval miniature the Prodigal Son leaves his father's house, gives himself up to riotous living, then, right alongside, there he is eating out of the pigs' trough, and in the corner opposite to the start of the series he is returning to the paternal embrace. A classic example is that of Memling,[94] who lays out the entire city of Jerusalem in one painting and depicts simultaneously, step by step, in one little street and one little house after another, all the successive

H. Daumier, *Ratapoil Offers His Arm to the Republic*

phases of the events of Holy Week. Here a threefold tradition is made manifest: 1) architectural, as described above; 2) ecclesiastical, in which the twelve stages of Christ's Passion or the Stations of the Cross were (and still are) recalled by a procession around the cathedral, each one being a reminder of the successive phases of the Passion as suffered by Christ; 3) theatrical, since the medieval stage represented a whole city with the various scenes of action, passing from Hell to Heaven on either side of the city, through which the plot could move both simultaneously and successively.

The development from this primitive conception to more realistic forms follows a path that is an exact analogy of what we have observed in Daumier and Tintoretto: the phases of the scene are deployed between groups of participants who are, in essence, depicting the successive stages of a single act. A classic example of this is Watteau's *L'Embarquement pour Cythère*, as it has been described and analysed by Rodin.[95]

Antoine Watteau, *L'Embarquement pour Cythère*

It is typical of the sculptor that he employs a similar method. Sculpture, indeed, uses it even more widely than does painting. The 'sketchiness' of incompletely delineated forms is less common in sculpture although, as it happens, Rodin, in his statue of Balzac (which might have been sculpted from lines drawn by Daumier), follows Daumier's method completely. The torso, head and details are all in different phases: this gives such colossal dynamism to a monument which – thanks entirely to the Popular Front government – has survived all intrigues and has finally been erected in a square. The restless modelling of what seem like unfinished shapes causes all the phases to merge into a single graphic whole. Michelangelo does likewise. Beneath his anatomical deformities and hypertrophy of the forms of the human body lies concealed the same method. The apparent movement of irritated disgust shown by Moses at the worshippers of the golden calf, stemming from his seemingly immobile pose, has been creatively interpreted by . . . Freud.

In a little study, which has nothing to do with psychoanalysis and is limited to an examination of the interrelation between the turning of the torso, the position of the beard and the hand grasping it, Freud attempts by deduction to recreate the movement which gave rise to this interrelation and to interpret it psychologically. [. . . .][96]

It is interesting to note that the same dynamics are present in Serov's portrait of Gorky. This has come about because in his portrait of Gorky, Serov was reproducing a compositional scheme taken from . . . a madonna by Michelangelo in Florence.

Apart from Rodin's *The Burghers of Calais*, a sculpture in which the whole gamut of an *inward movement – the emotion of sorrow –* is expressed through each in turn of the figures in this sculptured group, there is an analogy to the simultaneous movement of *L'Embarquement pour Cythère* to be found in a very ancient piece of sculpture: the statue of Laocoön. This provides a perfect example, both in the phase of external movement – the attack by the two snakes – and in the phase of the mounting intensity of suffering, expressed through the gradations of behaviour of the figures. The most curious aspect of the Laocoön group, however, is the head of the central figure, and the strangest feature about that head is that the *keenness* of its expression of human suffering is achieved through the illusion of *mobility*, an illusion attained by depicting wrinkles of pain that *cannot* occur *simultaneously*. The features of the face distorted by pain are shown in two different phases of a physically impossible facial expression. We owe this observation to Duchenne,* famous for his experiments in the electrical stimulation of separate muscles.[97]

He it was who discovered that the simultaneous contraction of all the facial muscles of Laocoön is physically impossible. In his book, alongside a reproduction of the head of the Greek *Laocoön,* he showed the head of an anatomically 'corrected' Laocoön, i.e. Laocoön with his features distorted in a manner that is anatomically possible. And with what result? In the 'anatomically feasible' version of Laocoön there is not a fraction of that dynamic effect of suffering, achieved by the cinematic method, which has made *Laocoön* immortal through the centuries!

We shall not dwell on any examples from literature, except to point out

---

*It is to his work on the study of the individual activity of each single muscle that we owe a maxim that describes a fundamental characteristic of expressive [affective] movement: 'L'action musculaire isolée n'est pas dans la nature' [isolated muscular action does not exist in nature] (1858).

V.A. Serov, *Portrait of Maxim Gorky*

that there, too, we may find examples of juxtaposition of the phases of an action instead of the depiction of a process. Naturally such examples must be sought in early literature. Here we shall limit ourselves to two instances: one Japanese *tanka* (a short verse-form), and three lines from the 'The Lay of Igor's Host'. They are as follows:

> The butterfly is flying.
> The butterfly has gone to sleep.

and

> Igor sleeps.
> Igor wakes.
> Igor in his mind
> Surveys the field.[98]

Undoubtedly the lapidary power of the second example and the feeling of ephemeral transience of the flight of a butterfly, both sharing an equal degree of freshness and immediacy, are achieved by the same method.

Here it is pertinent to remark that it is characteristic not only of the phases of a movement to merge in our minds into one movement, that it is also typical not only of separate expressions of sorrow to fuse into a general impression of grief (a 'symphony of sorrow'), but that it is characteristic of series of linked fragments to combine perceptually into a single phenomenon. As an example I shall limit myself to citing one very odd, curious ancestor of montage. It stems from the inventive mind of John Phoenix, an American humorist of the mid-19th century,[99] and is taken from a parody of a sensational newspaper report, published in his comic magazine, the *Phoenix Pictorial*, in 1855.

Made up of a row of traditional printer's blocks – i.e. standard images – this extremely funny juxtaposed sequence may rightly be regarded as both an ancestor and a parody of cinematic montage, which was only born many, many decades later!

If we accept *The Great Train Robbery*[100] as the ancestor of all motion pictures, then Phoenix's parodic train crash can certainly be numbered among the forebears of film montage!

In the use of this technique, cinema is, in its potential, merely a technically more complete device. It is therefore quite natural that its scope is correspondingly so much greater: from the application of the very first principle of cinema film, via the normal functions of montage (of which more below), including the more eccentric aspects of montage, and up to those cases where cinema, exploiting our tendency to 'unify' skilfully presented fragments into an image or a concept, actually presents them to the spectator's perception (Fig. 5.1). Here let us recall the lions from *The Battleship Potemkin*, where three different lions that had been sculpted into three different poses were unified by montage into one lion 'leaping up'; or the 'parade of gods' in *October*, in which a

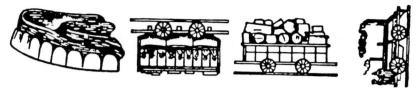

Fig. 5.1

succession of gods descended from a splendid baroque Christ through all kinds of divine images down to a wooden Chukchi idol.[101] Edited by montage into a series, they were interpreted as a unique and ironic way of debunking the image of God and hence the very concept of God. Many years later this idea was revived in an amusing passage of a book by Jean Cocteau, devoted to another divinity: Paris fashions. This passage stresses yet again how our mind or our eye characteristically fuses a skilfully selected series or succession of elements into one movement:

> Someone should make a [speeded-up] film of the slowly passing epochs and the successive waves of fashion. Thus it would be fascinating to see, at speed, dresses lengthen, shorten, and lengthen again; to see sleeves puff out, deflate, puff out again; to see hats shrink and curl up, crinkle, flatten, sprout feathers and shed them; to see bosoms expand and shrink, flaunt themselves and hide in shame; to see waists shift their position between the breasts and the knees, the movement of thighs and buttocks, stomachs protruding and retreating, hemlines narrowing and foaming out again in ruffles, underwear vanishing and reappearing, cheeks hollowing and puffing out, paling, reddening and turning pale once more; to see hair lengthening, disappearing, growing long again, pulled out into strands, then curling, puffing up and collapsing, twisting and untwisting, cramming itself with combs and pins, dropping them and putting them back again; shoes which bare the heels or cover them up, undershirts worn beneath prickly wool, silk conquering wool, wool conquering silk, floating tulle, heavyweight velvet, glinting sequins, pleated satin, furs sliding over dresses and around necks, going up, down and around with the same mad mobility as the beasts from which they were flayed.[102]

Thus we can see that the *principle of cinema* is not something which dropped upon mankind from the heavens, but it is something that has grown out of the very depths of human culture. It seems to us that this cinematic *principle* is growing and developing within the cinema itself; and that since all forms of cinema are determined by the nature of the society which creates them, it is in the highest form of social organisation – ours – that we are moving towards the fullest understanding of the aesthetics of this art form, that is to say towards a level of comprehension where all its many and varied achievements contribute to an ever-clearer image of the principles which underlie it. In this it reflects the essence of our system, in which society is constructed on the premiss of being the most perfect generalisation of that small primary unit from which it is built up: the human being. Our system is a society that is humane to the utmost degree, the genuine and only possible form of human society, permeated as it is by the image of man, for whom the system was created. In aesthetics, I think, this is principally reflected in the fact that in the most advanced achievements of any art form, the principles of that art form maximally approach the first principles of all art. Men with the foresight of genius may have been able to run ahead of their times and against the social structures which were fated to give birth to a system such as ours, but their genius-like insights were inevitably distorted and blurred by being reflected in the consciousness typical of a system to which they were knowingly antagonistic, but which their minds could not help reflecting.

Such, I believe, was the case of Scriabin[103] in the art of music. What we are describing in this study as one sequence in the art form of cinema – namely the progression: frame–shot–montage–sound film – exactly echoes what Scriabin's conception did for music. But, whereas in his case it was a single insight which became embodied in the individual manner and style of one artist of genius, in our case, I believe, it is not a question of one single style or trend; it is the outcome of a collectively attainable understanding of the principles of an entire branch of culture, or rather of a whole tendency within one art form: cinema. This precise definition is necessary lest I am once again pelted with stones for ignoring other tendencies that are inextricably linked with it, and from which is woven the complete fabric of a work of cinematic art. For in each constituent part of a film production we find reflected in the whole the principle of its smallest component (in appropriate qualitative form), just as in the completed work we see that cinema as a whole is – not only visually but in its compositional totality, i.e. in its form – a reflection of the same thing, namely man.

But here is the passage on Scriabin which I have in mind:

The basic characteristic of the harmonic material with which Scriabin operates is its 'ultra-chromatic character'. . . . In the structure of these harmonies Scriabin intuitively perceived a reflection of the structure of sound in general, as being a complex of simultaneously sounding tones which constitute the parts of a single acoustic whole. Sometimes these are harmonic organisms, made up on the principle of the structure of a simple 'musical' sound which, as we know, contains a number of additional sounds or upper overtones, which are, as it were, the actual realisation of these overtones. Sometimes they are a reflection and an intuitive recreation of those incomparably more complex sonorities which we perceive in the timbres of bells or other sounding bodies. . . .

This link between its structure and the structure of timbres, this method intuitively perceived by Scriabin of recreating harmonic complexes 'in the image and likeness' of timbres, creates a bridge between two concepts which have acoustically long since merged into one – between the sound-complexes merged into the single impression of 'sound-timbre' and the sound-complexes that are merged in the concept of harmony.[104]

This difference also inevitably occurs in whatever is taken as the primary cell of the 'prototype' of the structure of a work of art.

It is characteristic of Scriabin that he has taken 'the structure of sound *in general*' (see above) as this basic factor, i.e. he has taken an element of nature as such and not an element of nature that has first been assimilated by consciousness. When we say that in the fundamental structures of film aesthetics there is retained the unique nature of the cinematic phenomenon – the creation of motion out of the collision of two motionless forms – we are not dealing with natural, physical movement but with something that has to do with the way our perceptions work. This is not only the primary phenomenon of cinematic technique; it is above all a primary phenomenon of the human mind's capacity to create images.

For strictly speaking what occurs in this case is not movement; instead, our consciousness displays its ability to bring together *two separate phenomena* into a *generalised image*: to merge two *motionless* phases into an *image of movement*.

Any other interpretation of the basic phenomenon of cinema (and the corresponding conclusions to be drawn from it) would not only be factually incorrect but would furthermore be purely Impressionist. The dominance of the retina of the eye, i.e. of the *pictorial imprint*, over the brain centres, i.e. over the *reflected image*, was an example of that trend. It was precisely on the issue of this argument that the Impressionists were defeated by Cubism, which historically superseded them. Cubism (despite the considerable faults of its excessively one-sided approach) appreciated this position absolutely correctly, even though it conveyed it in forms that were more expressive of decadence than of a 'reunifying' art. Here, incidentally, Cubism was also to blame because its medium of expression – static painting – was not capable of carrying out the task which it was called upon to fulfil. To level this accusation at Gleizes and Metzinger[105] would almost be like reproaching Leonardo da Vinci for fooling around with birds instead of using an advanced model of the Antonov-25 for his experiments in the theory of flight! But here is what these two authors have to say about Impressionism. (I quote from G.V. Shaposhnikov's brochure on neo-Classicism, *The Aesthetics of Number and Dividers*, so titled in paraphrase of the subheading of a book by Gino Severini, *From Cubism to Classicism: The Aesthetics of Dividers and Number*, Moscow, 1926.[106])

First, however, let us cite a brief remark on Impressionism:

Impressionism . . . strives to ensure that a work of art be permeated by

the momentary impression, in all its freshness and purity. The Impressionists reject all received ideas based on prior observation, i.e. everything
not acquired through an immediate, individual visual impression. The
Impressionists do not allow visual impressions to be corrected on the
basis of experience or recollection, since to do so would be to lose the
authenticity of the impression and with it the truth; thus the outcome
would be some blurred compromise midway between true observation
and mental interpretation. The artist who paints an eye, a vase, a house
or a tree rather than the impression of light and colour emitted by these
objects is prone, in the Impressionists' view, to a similar delusion. He is
thinking instead of seeing. Impressionism regards this kind of thinking as
the artist's gravest sin.

Here now is the Cubists' critique of Impressionism:

In their polemics with the Impressionists, the Cubists pointed out to them
that they were slaves to all the worst visual conventions, that they did not
even suspect that the visible world only becomes the real world thanks
to the action of thought, and that the objects which strike us most forcibly
are not always those of the richest visual content. Merely in order to
justify the predominance of the retinal membrane over the reason (*vide!*
– S.E.), the Impressionists proclaim that intellectual abilities are incompatible with artistic sensitivity. The Cubists affirm that to recognise
forms we need, apart from the visual function and the ability to move,
to bring to the task a certain degree of intellectual development, since to
recognise forms is to test them against a previously existent idea.

Let us now examine the essence of these two positions.

To think is, of course, above all to generalise, and the familiar credo of
Impressionism, which we have recalled above, is an extreme example of the
hegemony of pictorialism finally 'swallowing up' the generalising 'image', to
revert to the terminology which we have adopted for this study.

What 'way out' was there for an Impressionist who wanted, nevertheless,
to give a total image of a phenomenon and not simply a representation of a
single impression of it? Obviously there could only be one way: to record a
series of impressions of the subject. And the forerunners of Impressionism –
the Japanese – adopted just such a practice: to mention the most popular
examples we need only recall Hokusai's *One Hundred Views of Fuji* and the
Thirty-six Views of Fuji by . . . the same artist. The overall impression derived
from these gives a complete mental image of Mt Fuji.[107]

If the Impressionists made a mistake in their relentless insistence on
uniqueness, then the Cubists who criticised them were equally mistaken in their
stress on the quality of *summation* existing within a single canvas. Delaunay's
famous *Eiffel Tower* is really 'One hundred views of the Eiffel Tower' crammed
into a single picture of it![108] As we shall see, *when engaged in revealing this*

problem no one single trend in painting was capable of solving it. (I stress 'when engaged in revealing this problem', because hundreds of instances of an integrated synthesis of generalising typicality, mobility of figures or graphic depiction are to be found in classic works of art prior to the 19th century which were quite unconcerned with revealing these particular problems, while isolating and detaching other, separate problems from the integrated expressive, and above all ideational, content of the totality of the picture.) A way out and a solution for both of them would have been to create a dynamic fusion of a series, moving past the spectator, of those hundred views of the Eiffel Tower or Fujiyama. But that is precisely what lies beyond the scope of painting; that is the missing link which would enable it to progress towards a successful solution to this problem. (On a different tack, namely the attempt to convey movement by phases, another 'revelatory' trend in art – Futurism – can also claim certain achievements, even though it is a trend which came to nothing, due to the impossibility of accomplishing this task within the framework of the art of painting. Neo-Classicism is, in fact, a reaction against this, in its consistent refusal to tackle problems that lie outside the scope of painting. Hence the neo-Classicists' predilection for 'forms of monumental, stable composition' which gives them the right to repeat this line from Baudelaire: 'I hate movement which disturbs the lines'.[109]) But it is precisely this ability which is the starting-point for the next art form after the qualitative leap from painting: namely, the cinema, in its unity of shot and montage.

It is curious to note here that in this sense the *principle of cinema* is no more than a reflection, transferred to film-stock, footage, frame and projection speed, of an inevitable and absolutely basic psychological process that is common to each individual consciousness from its first steps in the absorption of reality. I refer to what is called eidetics.[110]

Reality exists for us as a *series* of foreshortenings and images. Without eidetics we would never be able to reduce all those 'split-second photographs' of the separate aspects of phenomena into a single image. [. . . .]

Hence, too, the difference in practical consequences between the distinctive features of Scriabin's method in music and the method to be followed in cinema. It is not only the contrast between an *individual style* in the former instance and the *aesthetic premisses* of cinematic form in the latter. It lies also in the fact that cinema is called upon to function within human limits, within a human module, within the limits of the human mind and emotions, without going, as Scriabin does, beyond the bounds of man. By this I do not mean into the realms of humanity in general but into the cosmos, into super-sensuality and super-consciousness, where it inevitably borders on mysticism and solipsism. Thus an almost imperceptible difference in the definition of the initial premisses, when developed, leads on to programmes and systems that are polar opposites.

Let us take a closer look at the 'nucleus' of a cinematic production as we now understand it. How is it characterised? Quite clearly, two functions are present in it. One of them involves visual depiction, the other involves an attitude to what is depicted, or rather to a succession of pictures in a montage sequence. The first lies entirely in the film, the second in the perception of the spectator. The first produces a series of still photographs, the second establishes an image of movement that persists throughout that series. That this is indeed what happens is confirmed by the simplest demands of the perceptual process, without which there can be no perception of normal movement. A dog, a cat, a lynx or a deer can move in front of us at any tempo or rhythm; we will always interpret their activity as actual movement. But the cine-camera only has to deviate from the speed of twenty-four frames per second for our perception of the true image of the movement to be destroyed: it can break down into phases – animation impulses – which even the magic of time cannot reconstitute into a single process; or, by suppressing our awareness of the intervals between frames, it can go to the other extreme and cease to be interpretable as movement. (Imagine a super-rapid camera of fantastic speed shooting an arm being slowly raised through ten centimetres!)

In such instances it is not the event itself that is distorted but the treatment of that event by the speed of the apparatus, as a result of which our mind interprets it as another image of the event. Where visual depiction is concerned this assertion might be disputed: slowed-down movement can be interpreted as 'normal (i.e. a normal image of the movement), but placed in abnormal conditions'; the very term 'slowed-down' presumes the existence in our mind of a normative tempo from which the movement has deviated. That is why speeded-up movements on the screen (in a newsreel, for instance) are *funny*. But for the same reason they are *not funny* when they occur, for example, in some episode of *heightened activity* in a crowd scene, i.e. where the visual distortion of plain reality is *imaginatively* more in keeping with the theme than straightforward, literal depiction would be. (We all know how much more convincing a cavalry charge can be if the shots are filmed more slowly, and consequently the horses gallop across the screen at a faster speed.)

It is interesting that with sound the same factor of tempo has a much more decisive effect on the metamorphosis of the image. Everyone knows that slowing down or speeding up the projected sound produces a phenomenon that is not analogous to accelerating or retarding the visual picture. The spoken words are not pronounced slower or faster; they become *higher* or *lower* in pitch. This alters the image of the event to a significantly more marked degree than in the case of the picture.

To our perception, a tenor slithering down into a bass voice is a much greater distortion of the image than is a jump projected in slow motion. The slowed-down movement of the jump is interpreted as a jump *in different conditions* of projection . . . whereas a bass instead of a tenor is interpreted as *another voice*! Nor should we think that this distortion of the image is purely *subjective*, i.e. occurring only in the perceptual process of our mind. The tempo *objectively* restructures the *image* of the event, even though elements of the depiction remain unchanged (in a case where the projection speed is altered).

It is, however, obvious that as soon as a deviation of tempo is made from the sole possible norm in which the psychological phenomenon of cinematic movement can occur in our mind, then the phenomenon of that movement breaks down.

Thus two frames, placed in juxtaposition, perform two functions: that of visual depiction as such and of a generalisation of that depiction into an image of movement. This happens in the first stage of cinema, which we are here describing. At this point it is not registered by our consciousness. It is 'swallowed', and there is no effort that can be made, in conditions of normal projection, to force ourselves to interpret this process discreetly. The first condition of the two functions is also retained in the second step in film montage, i.e. when we are no longer dealing with two frames making up a shot, but with two (and more) shots that go to make up a montage movement.

Galloping hooves, the rushing head of a horse, a horse's rump disappearing into the distance. Those are three pictures. Only when they are combined in the mind does there arise a visual *sensation* of a galloping horse. It is interesting that for the 'average spectator', as they say, these shots are also merged into one. For a non-professional to 'see' a scene as a series of montage segments is almost impossible and requires special training. I myself remember what exertions it cost me, at the start of my career in cinema, to learn to see on the screen a scene, let us say, in which Douglas Fairbanks puts out a cigarette; to see it not as a single action but professionally, i.e. in all three of its montage segments: 1) medium shot – takes cigarette out of mouth; 2) close-up – hand extinguishes cigarette on ashtray; and 3) knee-level shot – having dropped the cigarette-butt, Douglas walks away from table! Here, with relatively little effort, it is possible to differentiate between both functions: we can interpret the three consecutive pictures . . . consecutively, and we can perceive the total image of the event. Interestingly enough, there is in this instance no difference in principle from what we are saying about Daumier's 'manner'. By the law of *pars pro toto*, every close-up conveys the idea of the complete action. Essentially, too, the three fragments of the galloping horse mentioned above (hooves, head, rump) repeat, as it were, in a higher qualitative category, what would be shown by three consecutive frames depicting three consecutive phases of a galloping horse seen in full shot. But a similar qualitative heightening also occurs in the intensity of perception: there is an increased intensity of psychological exertion due to the fact that this is not a case of three different poses of the horse fusing into a single movement, but three different *images of equine movement* evoked by three different shots and merging into a single *image of a galloping horse*. Here the time factor is decisive; not only the tempo within the edited sequence but the length of the sequence: both play a decisive part. Time in this case is not 'fateful' but is time which is *relatively* under our control. The phenomenon of montage segments merging into an image of movement has to take place within certain limits. And here, too, it is as if the frames were under a microscope!

In the third phase we have an even more extreme situation. If we take as an example John Phoenix's *Terrible Railroad Disaster* (Fig. 5.1),[111] transferred into film shots – the false teeth in close-up, the overturned passenger car, the up-ended locomotive – we shall see that here is what may be termed a reversed extreme: this is a case which demands a *certain* effort of the mind to reduce these elements into one and to perceive the image not merely by direct visual sensation, as was the case with the galloping horse, but to perceive from these three fragments the total image of a catastrophe. 'Tempo' plays practically no part here. The breakdown into the two processes is almost more evident than their fusion into one! Quite obviously this will continue as the matter proceeds further. Each separate one of the montage scenes of the episodes of a battle is an *image of fighting*, but as a *depiction* of one part of the total battle they will, when juxtaposed, give a generalised idea, a generalised image of battle. Through the pictorial elements there will arise before the spectator a great perception which depiction alone cannot convey: namely, a generalised image, a concept, a generalisation. When carried by its content beyond the limits of depicting an event on to the level of a generalised perception and concept of the event, both in the means of its presentation to the spectator and in the means of the art form itself, it also steps outside the bounds of its original dimension.

We have spoken of this as applied to graphic composition. What was its outcome there? There it led away beyond the limits of depiction to the superstructural, expressive, spatial-compositional 'disposition of objects depicted' (or colour, or spaces and so on) in any degree of generalisation of the metaphor (see the story of the pretzel-shaped shop sign)[112] and to a graphically generalised *scheme of content* which pervades their compositional outline. This, which is not limited to intra-shot 'depiction', also leads on to the purposeful compositional 'juxtaposition' of these shots – i.e. the montage segments – in time.

To contrast the spatial nature of the first instance with the temporal nature of the second is pointless, for in a picture spatial disposition which is not aimed at inducing a certain sequence of perception has nothing to do with composition. On the other hand, sequential montage which does not simultaneously create a sense of a spatial environment is equally far from being what can be called composition in film. (This is also true for those cases where a montage composition has no topographical unity.)

Is the cinema without precedents in this respect?

Of course not; and so, less as a means of confirming this assertion than of providing additional clarification of the idea, let us examine the same phenomenon, but in the form that it takes in a drawing. We shall naturally look for an example first and foremost among works of graphic art in which violent themes and bold ideas are forcibly expressed, for it is there that we will find the phenomenon most fully and vividly presented. It is in works of conscious ideological purpose that the framework of method shows through most clearly, just as it is easier to see the shape and interplay of muscles when the body is tensed for vigorous exertion than when it is in a state of rest. The

M. Dobuzhinsky, *October Idyll*

method is best discerned in the artistic treatment of aggression and violent action. We will find an example of this in the first number of the magazine *Zhupel* [The Bugbear] for the year 1905, one of the splendid examples of militant satire of that time: Dobuzhinsky's *October Idyll*, which unmasks all the treachery and mendacity of the 'Manifesto of October 17th'.[113]

Let us try to recreate the process by which we perceive the drawing, and the creation of the dramatic image to which the picture itself serves as an epilogue. In their different ways, thousands of people have come and are still coming to experience the emotional effect of this drawing. I make no claims for the universal or absolute validity of the sequence which I describe below, but in recounting it I shall keep roughly to the sequence in which, for me, the image of the event is built up out of the clues we are given.

1. First of all the eye is riveted to the pool of blood in the centre of the drawing.
2. In following its outline, the eye stumbles on the doll. Doll and pavement. Why? The eye gropes about on the pavement in search of an explanation. It is abruptly drawn to the rubber galosh in the bottom right-hand corner. Alongside it is a pair of spectacles.
3. In its search for a key the eye attempts to encompass the whole picture. The galosh and the pool of blood force it to follow the line between them. This is a diagonal, running from lower right to upper left. The eye moves along the diagonal. It comes to the window. In the window is a bullet hole.
4. Interest sharpens. The eye glances past the sheets of white paper stuck to the wall and the poor box, which seem as yet to have nothing to do with the 'clues to the crime', and at this point these details are simply taken for what they are. Following the bloodstains, our glance stops at the fire hydrant. By purely graphic means the hydrant and the tree then lead the eye past the corner of the house. It rests on the far side of the street. And on the [tsarist] tricolour flags. The street is empty.
5. The eye sees the deserted street and the tsarist flags. The year being 1905, this is, as it were, the 'negative' of the street, and the mind immediately makes up the missing 'positive': the crowded street and . . . the red flags.
6. From that moment the pool of blood becomes an image of the dispersal of a demonstration. The doll, the galosh and the spectacles are an image of the extremities in the age range of the crowd which was so mercilessly dispersed: they tell of children and old people, between whom we mentally imagine adults, youths, women. The bullet hole in the window is an image of the peaceful, innocent nature of the demonstration, whose participants believed in the 'freedoms' promised by the manifesto. It is an echo of the gunning down of the peaceful demonstration on 9 January.[114] The pool of blood is an image of a firing-squad.
7. Suddenly we interpret the sheets of white paper, chiefly by their shape: a cross. The typical outline of a memorial headstone over a grave. (A clue to this interpretation is the similar small white cross over the poor box. This, I think, is its basic compositional significance, apart from the obvious thematic

associations of a church collecting box in this particular context.)

8. If we look carefully at the 'gravestone', it is seen to bear the wording of the notorious manifesto. *The words* are the outward appearance of the manifesto: the granting of freedoms. The cruciform *shape* of the sheets of paper is its real essence: the graveyard of freedom, a cross placed over the 'insane dreams'.

9. The street is filled with a moving mass of people. We see the dispersal of the demonstration. We see the reprisals. We see old men and children. We see the peaceful onlookers, driven away from the windows by bullets as the incident – which the bourgeois newspapers used to call 'street disorders' – reaches its climax. The scene fades into a long shot of the idyll as we now see it [in the drawing]. And like the gravestone of those hard-won freedoms, the scene moves towards the camera, just as the horror of the reactionary repression which followed the notoriously misleading manifesto moves into our minds and our memories.

Thus step by step, detail by detail, image after image is created. The images people the frame of the picture. The images move into action. The images interact and give rise to a new, overall, generalising image. And what we have experienced in the picture is not what it *depicts* but the clash of the images which the artist has been able to evoke within our imagination, intellect and emotions by his skilful choice of details.

As we have seen, his method differs in no way from the manner in which images are created in the mind and emotions of the film viewer.

The imaginary path followed by the eye (and I do not think this is too far from the truth) is a montage sequence.

The details would be in close-up.

They would be held in the footage.

The emergence of the images and their interaction constitute the same process that occurs in cinematic perception, which we have analysed above.

How characteristic of Dobuzhinsky this method was, we may find in a symposium entitled *Masters of Modern Graphics and Engraving*:

It has been said on more than one occasion that Dobuzhinsky was above all an artist who recorded the city. . . . Especially in his later works there is a striving to convey architectural forms or groupings of such forms *per se*. In the final analysis, however, our artist still finds it more important to convey the life which flows through and around these wooden or stonebuilt human dwellings. What we see are not ordinary architectural landscapes but rather pictures of 'the soul of the city', its inner existence. This is always so, whether Dobuzhinsky, in keeping with a general interest in the past, is depicting a decaying little Russian town of the 1830s or fantasising about the gigantic structures of the future, where, against a background of endless walls, the tentacles of monstrous machines intertwine. In all these – buildings, machines, people, animals – the minutest details of everyday life are perceived as an organic whole, unified, not by their outward forms, but by the associations created by these forms. The quality of the spectator's artistic experience is determined largely by the images, recollections and moods connected with the objects shown in the painting or the drawing. Thus 'characteristic details' acquire an enormous significance, not by piling them up but by their felicitous juxtaposition. . . . Of course, when treating his basic theme of 'The City' Dobuzhinsky does not always tell a story; he is always, though, *illustrating poetic images* (italics *not* mine – S.M.E.) which are present in his mind rather than reproducing what his visual experience has given him.[115]

That final assertion is not quite correct. It would correspond more to what, according to Shklovsky, Khodasevich once set out to do: to illustrate the descriptive digressions and not the events which occur in Pushkin's works.[116]

Dobuzhinsky needs to be described with greater precision. His visual experience, which is far removed from immediacy and is saturated with literary and historical reminiscences, generates images in his mind. With his superb skill, Dobuzhinsky knows exactly which real-life details will express an image, so that two or three such details will conjure up in the spectator's mind an image which is the same one, though individually modified, that the artist saw with his inward eye. We shall give below some examples of a similar kind drawn from literature. For the moment, as a means of transition to those examples, let us recall, reformulate and define our fundamental premises:

1. The montage segment (especially a close-up) is a part (*pars*).
2. By the law of *pars pro toto*, that *part* stimulates the mind to complete the construction of *a certain whole*.
3. This applies to any detail and to any separate fragment.
4. Thus the montage combination of a series of segments is *not* interpreted by the mind as a certain sequence of *details*, but as a certain sequence of whole scenes – and scenes, moreover, that are not depicted but arise within the mind in image form. For *pars pro toto* is also a means of compelling the mind to generate the image of an event without depicting the event itself.
5. Between themselves, the montage segments reproduce the very same process that occurs between the individual frames within each segment.

In that process, movement comes from the juxtaposition of a series of pictures. From a collision between pictures of two consecutive phases of a movement there arises the *image* of a movement (a movement which, in actual fact, *is not depicted* but is conveyed by two still pictures). In the transition from combining frames to combining shots, the phenomenon and the method remain the same (while nevertheless advancing to the next qualitative stage). In the montage segment, *pars* (the part) evokes an image of *toto* (the whole). Thus in the mind this fragment has already become an image of a complete picture, thence of a series of imagined pictures. And each imagined picture enters into the same relationship with the next one as the literal picture in one frame does with the literal picture in the neighbouring frame: they both generate an image.

The difference between the two, however, is *enormous*. For the frame is actually depicted. It is the product of an alien will, which is imposed upon the spectator by the director and/or the cameraman.

In the montage segment, on the other hand – in our *pars* – the depiction of the whole is *imagined*, i.e. on the basis of a given *pars* it is a *toto* that each individual spectator has, *in his own way*, seen, and has in his own way created. It is quite obvious that the degree of intensity with which *such an image is experienced* is far greater than a *depiction* that is created and executed by someone else. In the former case, the spectator's entire creative, imaginative faculty will be involved.

Below we will analyse in detail how emotion and suffering should *correctly* be generated in an *actor*, by studying Stanislavsky's system. We shall also demonstrate that the montage principle underlies this system too, having meanwhile discovered that the montage principle is an essential factor in the *creative perception* of an event; i.e. it is the correct means of generating emotion and sympathetic feeling in the *spectator*. It is the montage nature of this method that puts an 'equals' sign between the technique by which the finest school of acting generates an emotional response within the actor and the technique of generating an emotional response within the spectator.

In our case, the unifying 'outline' which gives a generalised (I would even say a maximally generalised) scheme – the ultimate metaphorical interpretation of content and theme – will be the '*mise en scène*' provided by a change of viewpoint on the events. In the example of the Yermolova portrait we have already established a link between graphic composition and montage composition. We have seen that every sort of *mise en scène* can be of a dual nature: pictorial and metaphorical. So far we have dealt only with objects and how they are shown: we have not yet touched upon such matters as order, duration or sequence. We have hitherto considered only subject matter or objects *per se*. We have not yet mentioned montage form; we therefore have the right to say that so far we have discussed only the pictorial shot and pictorial montage, even though pictorial montage is more correctly termed narrative or storytelling: a story, too, is the depiction of an event, only it is set out sequentially.

We have seen that even pictorial (narrative) montage is a necessary condition of generalisation in relation to the shot, while also being an element of another dimension. The very nature of montage, of course, should provide the potential scope within it for even greater generalisations. And in fact only from the moment at which that occurs can one begin to talk of the problem of montage form, that is say of the image-structure of montage.

Let us take a very striking and memorable example from *The Battleship Potemkin*: the shooting on the Odessa Steps. In its time, this scene engraved itself upon the mind and emotions of audiences almost throughout the entire world, but *not* because it showed at length, in circumstantial detail and with unsurpassed bloodthirstiness the soldiers firing on a crowd that was in a revolutionary mood. This scene owes its memorable effect neither to the details of the *mise en scène* nor to the way in which the camera moved through the thick of the crowd under fire. If we examine the mountains of writing on the film in all languages and about that scene in particular, we shall see that the power of the scene lay in the generalising perception of an *oppressive regime* that emerges in its full stature from a single incident in which one rank of soldiers shoots at five hundred people running and tumbling down one long flight of steps in one seaport city. The perception that arose from the depiction of this scene extends far outside the limits of the scene itself, and in the means of its realisation not only goes beyond the limits of mere depiction and beyond the limits of the separate shots, but also beyond the narrative function of montage, as it obligingly shows the spectator first one little corner of the drama, then another, then suddenly overwhelms him with a long shot that reveals the whole scale of the bloody massacre on the steps. The sense of generalisation, the image of a clumsy, deadening, oppressive regime, emerges from expressive means that are of a no less generalised nature, and which take over the 'aiming' function of a depiction of the event. A generalisation which surpasses the bounds of depiction is bound to have recourse to means that are out of the ordinary. Even such a realistic theatre as the Moscow Art Theatre could not fail to sense the need to step outside the limits of naturalistic depiction when it wanted to embody the full generalising significance of the aphorism which in *The Government Inspector* Gogol puts into the mouth of the mayor: 'Who are you laughing at? You're laughing at yourselves!'[117] In seeking to extend the meaning of this remark *beyond* the group of characters surrounding the mayor, the theatre could not simply have it spoken within the confines of the stage-set. In the realistic Art Theatre, the actor Moskvin,[118] in order to speak this line, steps *outside the limits of the action*: he puts one foot on the prompter's box and hurls the words into the auditorium!!!

What is it in our example that achieves this effect of lifting the generalisation beyond the bounds of mere depiction? Or rather, which one of the complex of expressive means used in our example carries out the function of this ultimate, maximal generalisation?*

It is not the narrative by montage, but the *rhythm* of the montage, for of course the rhythm of the scene is the final, ultimate generalisation to which the theme can be subjected while retaining the vital link with the event yet simultaneously extending far beyond it; not breaking its texture but raising it to the utmost limits of specific generalisation (i.e. without drifting off into 'cosmic abstractions').

The rhythm is a maximally generalised depiction of a *process* within the subject matter, a graph of the changing phases of contradictions within its unity.

---

*Without making a 'leap' into the 'cosmos'.

We have already touched on this *en passant* in the previous section, when we established that the linear contour had two separate functions: to generalise the depiction and to give the rhythm which indicates the relation of the depiction to the generalised element.

If the '*mise en scène*', on which the montage segments are threaded, was the emergent line of a contour in a new quality, as it were, then the rhythms of both one and the other serve in equal and identical degrees as the ultimate in the imaginative generalisation of the idea that is embodied in the depiction. For that very line – in one case a 'contour', in the other 'the route taken by the montage segments' – is the final stage of generalisation achieved through the juxtaposition of shots.

In juxtaposing the shots, the line is traced by the predetermined route of the spectator's perception. The line is simply a track of that route. In both instances three possible stages are inherent: the line can be purely pictorial, giving the characteristic outline of an object; it can be semi-pictorial and at the same time metaphorical, just as the pretzel-shaped shop sign, 'cast down to the dust' by a compositional metaphor, is metaphorical; and the line can be a 'pure' expression of the *dynamics* of the subject matter, through the rhythm of its articulation.

The progression goes from *metaphor* (i.e. the *pictorial function* of juxtaposition) to the *rhythm* of juxtaposition (i.e. to *generalisation*). The rhythm of the juxtaposition of elements is the fundamental means whereby the generalisation will express itself – both in line and in physical composition – much more fully than by using metaphor as the connecting link, for metaphor is always surreptitiously trying to slide into allegory or to sprawl over into a symbol!

I took the example of the 'Odessa Steps', an example from long ago. I could have taken another, more recent example, and one which has undoubted associations with the 'Odessa Steps'. And with good reason: this is not only a case of continuity, but the one is, as it were, an answer to the other. Just like the two old songs, one called 'By the Hearth' and the other, 'Forget about the Hearth'.[119] Both examples show the soulless machine of tsarist power, in each case behaving in the same way; the only difference is that in the first instance it is doing the shooting, while in the second it is being shot at. In the first case it is the destroyer; in the second it is destroyed. I am referring to the episode of the 'psychological attack' from the film *Chapayev*, directed by the brothers Vasiliev.[120] The example, of course, may not seem entirely appropriate. *Chapayev* is a sound film, and we know the 'psychological attack' in sound. What could apparently be simpler than to go to the silent version? When we do so, a most remarkable fact is revealed: in the silent version, the *generalising force of the image* of the advancing White troops in the 'psychological attack' and their defeat *does not work*. It fails to work because the rhythm of the montage does not raise that scene to a level where it expresses a generalised idea, as it does, for instance, in the 'Odessa Steps' sequence. We would be acting like some comic schoolmaster, some old-fashioned pedant, if on the strength of this we were to condemn or belittle the achievements of the Vasiliev brothers. We would be like the ridiculous Beckmesser in Wagner's *The Mastersingers*, who pedantically criticised isolated errors of composition while ignoring the scope of the work as a whole. But what is the point at issue? It is that, when all due allowances are made, only a blind man could fail to see that visually even the sound version of the 'psychological attack' has been edited less than competently, so much so that in the silent version not only is there no generalisation but the proper tempo and suspense are not created either. Even in the sound version there is not an adequate build-up of tension to the culminating shout of: 'Go on – shoot!'

The answer, of course, is ready to hand: 'Gavrik saved the day!' By this I mean the *inexorable rhythm of the music* which Gavril Popov wrote to that scene.[121] Even after that exclamatory phrase has been purged of any element of vulgar insult to the creative powers of the two directors, it nevertheless expresses the true essence of what happened in this case.

For the rhythmic function of creating the generalising image, which in the best examples of 'montage cinema' should be performed by montage, has in this instance been taken away from montage and transferred to sound; it has been handed over to the composer and his world of sound. The 'fault' of the directors in failing to edit the visual picture in the proper way has here been redeemed by the fact that they have entered the realm of the sound film, which permits – and in many respects demands – the removal of the generalising function not merely beyond the confines of the shot into montage, but past the bounds of montage and . . . into sound. This will be discussed below. (To say this, however, does not absolve the directors of their failure to seize such a brilliant opportunity to realise that audiovisual counterpoint of which the present author has been dreaming since 1928, and whose realisation was destroyed in the catastrophe of *Bezhin Meadow*.[122])

Thus in exactly the same way that a combination of motionless cells produces an image of movement, so from a combination of fragmentary pictures the rhythm of their montage juxtaposition is the source of the nuance of generalisation that is created by the director, *the image that his creative will adds to the event*, or rather the will of that social collective whose channel of expression he is.*

In my article 'Beyond the Shot' (1928–9)[123] I wrote about the fundamental significance of the 'act of montage' as being above all a tendentious and socially purposive act, the reconstitution of images of reality in the interests of transforming and refashioning reality itself. (On the strength of that article, certain naïve eccentrics decided that I allegedly 'ignored' intra-shot content, despite the fact that in the very same article the first attempts were made to define the single law which governs all elements of cinema, in other words

---

*Let us not forget that a montage sequence is also internally structured according to the same rules, being in no way a 'thing unto itself' but an element of a single, overall conception.

the same topic which, more detailed and extended in treatment, forms the subject matter of the present study.)

There occurs in art (as in everything else) a phenomenon that is characteristic of all behaviour, only raised to a higher level of intensity and set in the context of creative purpose: human nature is incapable of total objectivity in communicating an event, especially one which in any way affects us emotionally. Each person's perception has its own way of redistributing the emphasis and stress when giving an account of an event (selecting its own 'close-ups', which are different from anyone else's), to the point where it discards whole elements of the event, whole links in the chain of a process. One need only compare the testimony of several witnesses to one and the same event to be convinced that selecting the shots of a filmed event and editing them by montage will make a picture of that event which is not only unique and different from others but will often even contradict them! Hence that common expression, 'He lies like an eyewitness', which is the basis of an entertaining story, 'The Crime of Captain Gahagan', included in *The Paradoxes of Mr Pond*, a posthumous collection of the short stories of G.K. Chesterton (London, 1937).

A man is accused of a crime because in one evening he gave three women three completely different accounts of where he planned to spend his time. Mr Pond is able to establish the man's innocence by proving that his alibi was valid because in fact he told exactly the same story to all three women. Each woman, however, had extracted from his statement her own, as we would say, 'montage conception'; and those three different versions were determined by which part of his statement had affected each of the three women emotionally.

How wrong it is, though, to go to extremes in overemphasising *individual attitude* in art, and reduce everything to this *alone* in cases where it is not merely a phenomenon of psychological behaviour but a precondition of artistic creativity! [. . . .][124]

Here we are about to put our finger on the fundamental nerve: why did the system of montage thinking emerge and develop in connection with cinema?

I wrote about this at the very start of my career as a film-maker, in an attempt to sort out this phenomenon in my own mind. I had already made tentative efforts to do so when I was still working in the theatre (for this, see my article 'The Middle of Three', published in the tenth anniversary issue of *Sovetskoe kino*, 1935). I also spoke about it in great detail in my lecture at Yale University, USA (summer, 1930).[125]

Wherein lies this secret? Where is that vital nerve?

The essence of the matter is that in cinema we are not dealing with *an event*, but with *the image* of an event. If an event is shot from one viewpoint, the result will always be a *depiction* of that event, and not a *perception* of the event capable of making the viewer experience it sympathetically.

In theatre, for example, despite its conventionality and relativity, a physically real event actually unfolds in front of the spectator. The actors are actual people, not shadows; the voices, though actors' voices, claim to be those of the characters that are being personified; their actions are genuine actions.

Not so in cinema: here there is no physical reality, only the grey shadow of its reflection. Therefore in order to make good the *absence* of the principal factor – the live, immediate contact between the person in the auditorium and the person on stage – we have to find ways and means other than those used in theatre.

For the fact is that an event which is shot 'theatrically' turns out to be a hopeless failure on the screen. Though you may take a film camera and give an ideal performance of a scene in front of it, this simply does not work. (This failure is, of course, relative and *comparable in intensity* to how it appears when acted 'live', and not to the actors' reflections on the screen.) Let us say the scene is of a murder. Shot head-on in 'long shot', it would produce about 25 per cent of the effect that it produced on stage. Why is this so?

Let us try and present it in another way. Let us break it down into close-up and medium shot, and into the whole conventional series of shots of 'hands gripping throat', 'eyes starting from their sockets', 'fingers drawing a knife from a belt', 'anger in one pair of eyes', 'fear in another pair of eyes', and so on and so forth. 'Cunningly' edited, skilfully set in the appropriate tempo, graphically put together, these shots *as a whole* can produce exactly the same 100 per cent effect as that produced on stage, and most certainly not produced by the stage version shot from one viewpoint in long shot.

Where lies the difference? As long ago as 1924 I wrote that it is pointless for cinema to attempt to reproduce the theatre, and that it must overcome its limitations in this respect by using the means that are proper to cinema.[126]

A fight filmed from a single viewpoint in long shot will always remain the *depiction* of a fight and will never be the *perception* of a fight, i.e. something with which we feel immediately involved in the same way that we feel involved in a fight between two live people, genuinely (even though intentionally) fighting before our eyes. So what *is* the difference between this and a fight consisting of a number of fragments which *also* depict a fight, though not as a whole but in parts?!

It is that these separate fragments function not as depiction but as *stimuli that provoke associations*. The convention of their *partialness* is particularly conducive to this, because it forces our imagination to add to them and thereby activates to an unusual degree the spectator's emotions and intellect. As a result, the spectator is *not* subjected to a series of fragments of actions and events, but to a swarm of real events and actions evoked in his imagination and his emotions by the use of skilfully chosen suggestive details.

As the event itself progresses, you are drawn into its sequence, its unfolding, its coming-into-being – unlike your ready-made perception of a scene in long shot, which *presents itself* instead of unfolding before us as an evolving process.

In its simplest form this can, for example, be vividly shown by the insertion of, shall we say, two types of 'lead-in' into the action, and by the difference between them. Let us suppose that we have the scene which precedes our fight: a lead-in episode, in which the fight is still only an argument. The scene of the argument can be introduced in two ways: either in long shot or by way of montage. In the first instance you show it all in long shot: two men arguing, trying to wrench a parcel out of each other's grasp. In this case everything is *given*; you are immediately able to perceive the full picture of the argument as such. You see the depiction of an argument. It is a different matter if the argument is introduced to our perception by montage: 1) the parcel; 2) hands holding the parcel; 3) a second pair of hands grasp it; 4) first man; 5) second man; 6) two pairs of hands, each trying to wrench the parcel from the other; 7) two men, each wrenching the parcel from the other; 8) a general view of the room and the two men arguing over the parcel; and that is all.

In this version you are wholly involved in the development of the entire scene, and the eighth fragment adds up to a total statement of what you experienced, as it evolved, in the seven preceding fragments. In them, the complete image of the scene was built up: the act of dispute and the *appearance of the disputants*, who are unknown until the moment when, in the third fragment, you are already aware that *someone* wants to pull something away from *someone else*, and so on.

You are *not seeing the depiction of an argument*: the *image of an argument* is evoked within you; you participate in the process of the image of an argument coming into being, and thereby you are drawn into it as though you were a third participant in the evolving dispute. (This example is particularly vivid because in this case the coming-into-being of the action coincides with the actual start of the action. But any fragment of any action is just as much an illustration of its coming-into-being, even when the fragment is an intermediate and not an initial link in the chain.)

You will say: but the theatre version is in long shot, isn't it? Surely theatre gives the same overall perception of the whole scene as in long shot? In theatre, too, you grasp the fact that two people are fighting, yet the fight does not 'come into being' before your eyes in the way that is achieved by the cunning methods of cinema?! How is it, then, that a fight, which does not show you the process of its coming-into-being *nevertheless* 'works', especially since the *reality of a fight* in theatre is still only a *relative* reality which cannot be compared with a *genuine* fight in real life?

To that I reply: there are fights and fights. There is the fight which is planned and rehearsed, in which the chosen scenario unfolds move by move and action by action just as it was planned; and yet that fight will be as lifeless, ineffective, unconvincing and emotionally unexciting as the depiction of a fight in 'long shot' on the screen. On the other hand there is the fight in which every phase 'arises' before the spectator's eyes. While being equally strictly outlined in accordance with a compositional plan, it nevertheless is created, brought to life, as the active expression of an emotional logic deriving from the aims which the actors set themselves in their progression from phase to phase of the action as predetermined by the plot. In spite of the painted backdrops, false beards and faces smeared with make-up, *that* sort of fight, dialogue, argument or declaration of love will be sympathetically experienced as a real and genuine process. Its effect will be distinctive to the same extent that the effect of the *montage-structured* fight differs from the fight shot from one set-up in long shot. The art of montage in film-making *is not an analogy with but is exactly the same thing* as an actor's playing on stage; provided that the actor is not playing something ready-made but if, instead, his playing is a *process* within which, step by step, emotions are brought into being that are in true accord with the circumstances.

Herein lies the relevance of Stanislavsky's advice to the effect that the actor must, when playing, recreate a process and not act out the results of a process. He expresses it as follows:

> The mistake most actors make is that they think about the result instead of about the action that must prepare it. By avoiding action and aiming straight at the result you get a forced product which can lead to nothing but ham acting.[127]

Scriabin too sets himself this objective: 'What he sought was not a description of the act, not a representation of the act but *the act itself.*'[128]

Scriabin achieves this objective better than anyone else. Nay, more: in his work the very act of creativity can be perceived through the act of bringing the work of art into being.

> Scriabin is attracted by the *dynamic of the creative* process and its embodiment in art. In this respect he is reminiscent of Rodin, who daringly attempted to convey in sculpture not merely the movement of forms *but their very genesis.* In *Sadko* Rimsky-Korsakov shows us an image of the artist performing existing works or improvising, and we see the same thing in Liszt's *Orpheus*, but no one except Scriabin reveals to the listener the very *laboratory of musical creativity.* When we listen to him we are initiated into the agonies of artistic creation; this can be said of the 'Divine Poem' and the 'Poem of Ecstasy'.[129]

And the same thing can be perceived in montage, the method of an art form within which both Stanislavsky and Scriabin were destined to merge in synthesis, an art form which, in ways achieved by no other, unites man in action with the music of active form and reveals him both visually and aurally.

Using the actor as an example, we have shown the place of montage in the craft of acting, and not only in its outward manifestations where it is visible in the counterpoint of the expressive use of stage space, movement and diction, which grow out of a single emotion and reveal that emotion to the spectator, infecting him and involving him with it.

In this connection I have always furiously opposed those who maintain that the 'close-up' was invented by film-makers and that therefore the alteration of the dimensions of the picture and the play between these dimensions only emerged with the coming of cinema. Anyone who believes this either understands nothing of the art of theatrical composition or has never so much as set eyes on a stage set composed with even minimal competence!

Close-up, the shifting of emphasis between foreground and background, and the use of changes of level and dimension – not as an arbitrary game but as a compositional device for embodying the director's intention – are wholly and firmly entrenched in the theatre, and every theatre director, unless he is incompetent, knows about this and exploits it. Admittedly he does so less completely, at the same time more subtly but less consciously than does the film director, because he is not obliged to 'make up his frame', i.e. to put into the frame only what is necessary for the given phase of the sequence. The selection of only what is needed for a particular moment is, however, equally essential for constructing a scene on stage. True, the theatre director lacks the ability physically to exclude the inessentials, whereas in film this is made possible by the edge of the frame; nor is he able to enlarge the essentials to the extent that is possible with close-up. This, however, only means that he must use all the more finesse in deploying the specific means of *mise en scène* in order with equal precision to thrust everything else beyond the limits of the spectator's perception and to direct his attention now to one person, now to another, now to one group, now to another, now to two people looking at each other, first simultaneously, and then separately and consecutively, now to all 250 people in a crowd scene as though to a single whole, now to concentrate on the look conveyed by the eyes and eyebrows of the protagonist as he stands against the background of those 250 people.★

In this sense cinema is only a technically more advanced and well-equipped art form. The best 'preparatory school' for learning montage construction is theatre. But examples for study are even to be found far outside the scope of both: in literature, for example. Indeed, the aspiring film director could derive enormous benefit from studying the change of levels, the interplay of details in close-up, the glimpses of the behaviour of heroes and episodic characters, the type-casting and crowd scenes in long shot that unfold on the grandiose canvas of the Battle of Borodino in Tolstoy's *War and Peace*.

The point here, of course, is to be found neither in the specific nature of cinema nor in specifics at all, but in the fact that the picking out by montage

---

★In recent decades some directors, unskilled in the art of *mise en scène*, have begun to have recourse to a repulsive 'intermediate' form, namely to the beam of a spotlight, which obligingly picks out the necessary figures in a group at the required moment, the edge of the spot replacing the edge of the frame. The art of *mise en scène* lies, however, in picking out the necessary 'focus' of the spectator's attention with equal sharpness but without skulking behind such artistically dubious methods.

of particular groups of material and their juxtaposition in deliberate combinations is the foundation of every conscious, volitional attitude to reality.

A good touchstone of this ability, without which no creative activity is possible (using the word 'creative' in a much broader sense than the merely artistic), was the test which I introduced into the examinations at VGIK from 1932 onward.[130]

The examinee was shown a painting, usually with a highly dramatic narrative content, and therefore more often than not selected from the works of the Wanderers.[131] The test was to cut it up, i.e. to break it down into parts and details and to list them in an ordered sequence, so that taken together they could be read as a certain form of compositional treatment for the picture's subject matter. For instance, Repin's *The Church Procession* was taken and the student was asked to break it down and compose a montage sequence for such themes as: 'Rule by Truncheon' or 'The Russia of the Poor and the Russia of the Rich', or for a less concrete theme such as 'Heat', in the same way that Repin's *The Zaporozhian Cossacks' Reply to the Sultan* was used to illustrate the theme of 'Mounting Laughter'. More complicated tests involved the transcription of the theme, emotion and rhythm of a scene on to an appropriate montage sheet which reproduced them in dramatic form (*Menshikov at Beryozova, The Boyarina Morozova, The Morning of the Execution of the Streltsy*).[132]

With equal success one might use a series of large canvases or engravings by Hogarth, Watteau, Greuze or Delacroix and the 'dramatic' compositions of Ingres. [. . . .][133] At the moment, however, this is not the topic under discussion. Our topic is that we should also examine the application of the montage principle – a factor which might seem to be 'purely' cinematic in the narrowest sense – to one highly sensitive area of the activity of the leading person in cinema: the actor. And not only as displayed in its outward manifestations of ensemble and solo acting, where it is obvious, but also in the area where its application is hardly suspected, namely within the very 'holy of holies' of the actor's creativity: that mystery, thanks to which – by means that may be arbitrary or may be controlled and purposive – the actor achieves the display of lively emotion and genuine feeling which cannot be 'produced to order' and which can only be evoked; which are as spontaneous as the harmony created from a combination of melodies, which are as 'super-objective' as the rhythmic generalising image that is brought to life by a combination of specific, realistic, illustrative shots in montage.

It is noteworthy that the method of the creative act in stage acting depends quite as much on montage as it does in the cinema.

We will show this with examples from the acting technique devised by Stanislavsky, which is still the most complete and detailed teaching on this subject, and one whose practical application has proved it to be the method which comes closest to realism.

What is the aim which every acting system sets out to achieve? The aim is, through emotion, to evoke a stage experience which will convey the full truth of the author's intention. It is what corresponds to a generalised *perception* in contrast to a *depiction*, as we analysed them when giving examples of graphic composition and montage in film. Indeed, the best theatre schools most strongly and specifically condemn the *depiction* of the emotion, when what is required is that the emotion be *perceived* and *experienced*. Here too, however, just as we showed in the example concerning graphic composition, it is entirely inappropriate to go to the sort of extremes in which *the experience of the stage emotion* would be deprived of its natural *mode of expression*, namely a visible picture of feelings that are being experienced.

What is the method governing the primary, fundamental, principal factor with which the actor must be *imbued* as part of the creative process of acting? It transpires that this method is completely identical with the function of montage in film-making, where the aim is also to take elements of one dimension and from them to bring to life an event within a new, different, higher dimension, and what is more a dimension which cannot be shown by direct portrayal. An example of this in film is our perception of 'the regime' through the behaviour of the soldiers firing and the Cossacks trampling people underfoot.

For the actor in theatre it consists in creating live emotion, a genuine feeling of artistic truth out of an artificial and conventionalised text of prescribed words; out of painted backdrops; out of actors in funny clothes, their faces smeared with paint. The method, in fact, is the same and proceeds in the same way that we proceed in cinema, where, if the result is not to be a mere 'representation' but a total sympathetic experience, it will derive not from the separate, depictive shot-fragments but from the total, genuine involvement that comes from a synthesis of the emotions evoked by skilfully chosen suggestive details.

The process of 'drawing out' that undepictable, unreproducible yet real state into which the actor 'comes' is exactly similar. Indeed, in theatre the objective itself is absolutely identical with that for which we are aiming in film. In cinema, using an artificial combination of several metres of celluloid ribbon, coated with an exposed emulsion of silver bromide on which flickers a depiction of the grey shadows of events, we have to create something which will stimulate the spectators' emotions and make them live and feel what the author is trying to convey.

In theatre, in surroundings made up of painted canvas, the uneven boards of the stage, and the smell of paint and dust, the task is to make *the actor believe in the reality of his imagined, theatrical emotions and the total truth of his feelings* in order to fulfil the author's intention; and thereby to move the spectator, a spectator who can be moved *by these means alone.*

In both cases, out of *unreal objects* we have to create *a real emotional experience*: in the one instance directly for the spectator, in the other through the actor, in order by the same means to activate the emotions of that same spectator.

In both art forms the basis of the method is the same.

Where film is concerned we have already demonstrated this.

It remains to produce the evidence to show that in principle, and therefore in practice, the methods of attaining the same thing on stage by what is acknowledged to be the best system of achieving the truth of theatrical emotion, i.e. the Stanislavsky system, are exactly the same. The fundamental watchword of the system expresses how, from a combination of artificially, consciously and arbitrarily created circumstances, results are produced which transcend them in quality and dimension: 'Let me remind you of our cardinal principle: Through conscious means we reach the subconscious.'★[134]

The system 'enables us to realise one of the most important precepts of our approach to art: *to stimulate the actor's subconscious creativity through conscious psycho-technique*'.[135]

This applies to the principles of the system in general, and to all areas of its creative application, beginning with the most elevated.

Inspiration

My 'System' will never manufacture inspiration. It can only prepare a favourable ground for it.

If I were you, I would give up chasing this phantom, inspiration. Leave it to that miraculous fairy, nature, and devote yourself to what lies within the realm of human conscious control.[136]

The fundamental objective of our psycho-technique is to put us in a creative state in which our subconscious will function naturally.[137]

But never try for a direct approach to inspiration for its own sake.[138]

Put your thought on what arouses your inner motive forces, what makes for your inner creative mood. Think of your super-objective and the through line of action that leads to it. In short, have in your mind everything that can be consciously controlled and that will lead you to the subconscious.[139]

Have you noticed that each time this truth and your belief in it is born, involuntarily, the subconscious steps in and nature begins to function? So when your conscious psycho-technique is carried to its fullest extent the ground is prepared for nature's subconscious process.[140]

This also applies to the auxiliary disciplines of the system.

★I have no intention here of entering into any evaluation, whether critical or approving, of the thesis as such, or of discussing the question of the 'subconscious' as such or as it is understood in the Stanislavsky system. My interest here is to pursue, from another angle, its analogies with the method that is fundamental to montage, namely the juxtaposition of concrete, controllable, specific constants in order to evoke the existence of an 'intangible', e.g. a perception of movement from two still photographic frames or two montage pieces, just as in theatre genuine emotion is generated through the juxtaposition of a series of fictitious circumstances.

Emotional memory

When you are choosing some bit of action leave feeling and spiritual content alone. Never seek to be jealous, or to make love, or to suffer, for its own sake. *All such feelings are the result of something that has gone before. Of the thing that goes before you should think as hard as you can. As for the result, it will produce itself.*[141]

Given circumstances

. . . *If* gives the push to dormant imagination, whereas the *given circumstances* build the basis for *if* itself. And they both, together and separately, help to create an inner stimulus.[142]

You will find that 'sincere emotions', or 'feelings that seem true' will spontaneously grow in you.

However, when you use this third principle of acting, forget about your feelings, because they are largely of subconscious origin, and not subject to direct command. Direct all of your attention to the 'given circumstances'.[143]

And the necessary emotion will emerge and apply itself.

Nor should we forget that the same thing also occurs in the basic technique of planning and building up the actions for a given part. I refer to the method of 'breakdown into pieces', a breakdown that must, of course, be inseparable from an overview of the whole.

Finally, there is the theory of the 'pervading action', whose function [in the actor's creation of a role] is the same as our 'embracing contour' in a picture, or the 'montage sequence of shots', or, finally, the progression of the action itself through a chain of episodes. Here the analogy is closer, the identity [between stage and film] less surprising and unexpected.

This identity is, of course, most interesting where it concerns the specifics of the inner working of an actor's creativity, the most intimate ways of creating the soul of a character, his emotional states and how they are experienced. It is here that we find a total congruence between the methods.

At a certain point in his book, Stanislavsky introduces the reader to this aim too: 'It is now that we confront the logical consequences of our elusive, invisible . . . inner feelings . . . We can begin to think about the next and even more important step, which is the *creation of the human soul* in the part.'[144]

For the sake of variety and vividness, our next illustration of this theme will not be an aphorism but the description of an appropriate exercise, devised by Stanislavsky himself. In this *étude*, a cashier is sitting at home totting up money with which he, as an official, is entrusted. His wife suddenly calls him into the next room. While he is out, his wife's brother, an idiot and a hunchback, throws the money into the fire. The cashier returns; he sees what has happened, hurls himself in fury at the hunchback and kills him in the struggle. Hearing a cry, the wife runs in. While this happens, the baby drowns in the bath. The cashier falls into despair. It is an ultra-melodramatic example such as this that brings out most clearly the method of piling up separate fragments, elements and ideas which relate to the objective: a method devised to evoke the proper emotions and hence the proper actions. It also demonstrates, through the process of juxtaposing them, how to arouse the same proper emotion, the direct approach to which is prohibited by the system 'Never seek to be jealous, or to make love, or to suffer, for its own sake'.

In the following quotation I will tabulate and number all those elements in the Stanislavsky system which are juxtaposed in sequence for the same reasons and with the same objective as they would be in film.

The Director had me go over the scene with the money. As I was counting it I happened to look at Vanya, my wife's hunchback brother, and for the first time I asked myself: why is he for ever hanging around me? At this point I felt I could not go on until I had clarified my relations with this brother-in-law of mine.

This is what I, with the Director's help, concocted as a basis for the relationship: the beauty and health of my wife had been bought at the price of the deformity of this, her twin brother. At their birth an emergency operation had to be performed and the boy's life was jeopardized to save the mother and her baby girl. They all survived, but the boy became a half-wit and hunchback. This shadow has always lain on the family and made itself felt. This invention quite changed my attitude towards the unfortunate moron.

I was filled with a sincere feeling of tenderness for him and even some remorse for the past.[145]

Kostya, who is the first-person narrator of the book, has thus traversed three stages.

He needed to establish a relationship, to generate certain human emotions felt by his wife for her brother, something that he was incapable of achieving directly, immediately, 'to order'. So he has recourse to collating a series of fragments from which to constitute a relationship (the sort of fragments from which any relationship between two people is built up in real life).

In his mind and feelings he ran through these fragments (of which four have been enumerated above), and in so doing he evoked a genuine human feeling towards his wife's brother: the same feeling which, had he tried to produce it 'to order', could only have emerged mechanically, 'illustratively', as though it were 'a depiction of emotion' and not an *emotion* itself.

The authenticity of this emotion prompts the creation of another complete scene between Kostya and the hunchback: 'A wholly new scene was created; it was lively, warm and gay. There was an instant response to it from the audience.'[146]

In other words, the proper emotion gave rise to a little scene which in turn produced the right *image* required to communicate the relationship between the cashier and his wife's brother (at this point the effect corresponds wholly, in outcome as well as in method, to the effect of montage in cinema).

However, to continue:

Then came the moment to go into the next room. To whom? To my wife? Who is she? And there was another question to be solved. I could not go on until I knew all about this person to whom I am supposed to be married. My story about her was extremely sentimental. Nevertheless I really felt that if the circumstances had been what I imagined them to be, then his wife and child would have been infinitely dear to me.[147]

The same thing. And finally:

To go back to my desk and papers became understandable and necessary. I was, after all, working for my wife, for my son, and for the hunchback!

Once I had become aware of my own past, the burning of the public money acquired quite another significance. I now only had to say to myself: 'What would you have done if all this had happened in reality?' for my heart at once to start beating faster from distress. My immediate future, as it bore down upon me, seemed so terrible. . . .

Having put all the facts in place, the next thing was to understand what they were leading to, what lay ahead of me, what incriminating evidence threatened me.

First of all there was my large, pleasant apartment. It suggested that I was living beyond my means, which had led to embezzlement.

The total lack of money in the cash-box and the documents that would have exonerated me half burnt; my idiot brother-in-law dead, and not a single witness to my innocence; my son drowned, which suggested preparations for an escape, in which a babe in arms and a hunchback cretin would have seriously hindered me. . . .

The death of my son involves not only me but my wife in the crime. What is more, the killing of her brother will inevitably complicate our personal relations. . . . One must acknowledge the brilliance of Tortsov's method. But I realised that its success was based on the effect of that magic 'if' and on the given circumstances. They brought about the shift within me.[148]

I am horror-struck at the prospect of my future; public opinion will brand me not only as a thief, but also as a murderer of my own brother-in-law. Moreover, I shall be looked upon as an infanticide! No one can restore me in the eyes of the public. Nor do I even know what my wife will think of me after my having killed her brother.[149]

From the last example, the whole story clearly falls into place. Each one of these five scenes is, as it were, a generalising, figurative, emotional *deduction* from an absolutely distinct montage group made up of the particular, emotionally experienced elements of a situation. The whole sequence of them is, as it were, a little film made up of five montage episodes which flash momentarily through the mind and emotions of the actor.

That is to say, the logic of the method also continues to function within the episodes. Let us take number 4. It is clearly made up of a number of little scenes, such as the unfortunate cashier being turned away from houses where he was once a familiar visitor; his being refused a job; how even the intervention of sympathetic patrons cannot help him, and so on. Here it is particularly characteristic – and this I would add from *personal experience* – that the form in which such situations pass through our consciousness is entirely *similar to the characteristic nature of close-ups* in cinema, namely in the effectiveness of the unspoken *hint*. Each one of these little subsidiary scenes is seen only from one angle, showing only one sharply characteristic feature. If any of these fragments is allowed to last too long (using too much footage of film), attention would lapse and the whole would disintegrate, instead of there being – as happens with individual frames and fragmentary close-ups – a gathering together, a unifying and merging of these separate elements into a single whole.

Now, as I write down the *components* of piece number 4* as they occur to me, I see each one of them as follows: first I see a hunched figure, creeping furtively down the steps from the doorway which bears the name of a firm, but I see neither the people who turned him away nor the scene of him being turned away. Then, by contrast, I see a married couple haughtily turning aside; on this occasion the cashier is not in the picture. (He is instead merged with myself, which does not prevent me from either seeing 'myself as the cashier' in my mind's eye, or from merely sensing him 'in myself': in the imagination, as in a dream, it can happen that one contrives to be simultaneously both observer and observed!) Or I see only the sad face and the evasive look in the eyes of the unfortunate patron (for some reason with index finger raised). Or it may be a sudden vision of a wet shoe-sole with a hole in it, which has come away from a shoe and which clumsy fingers, blue with cold, are trying to mend . . . and so on and so forth. There will be a difference, of course – although not a fundamental one – in the fact that a part of all this will not be manifest to me by visual means, but by the shuddering and hunching of my own shoulders in place of the total scene of being refused a job; by rapid, jerky breathing instead of the whole picture of running downstairs; by the rush of blood to the cheeks instead of the scene of humiliation on meeting former acquaintances, etc., etc.

---

*Or rather the *factors*, for the result that we get is not a sum but . . . a product, in both the 'artistic' and the mathematical meaning of that term, which is that the resulting product is *higher* in *degree* and *dimension* than each of its constituent parts. '2a' is of the same degree and dimension as 'a', whereas 'a^2' is different.

It is not part of my intention to expound either Stanislavsky's system as a whole or the separate components of its discipline. I have only allowed myself to make so many quotations from it in order to demonstrate the existence in quite a different branch of the performing arts of basic principles and tenets similar to those which we have already established as pertaining to montage. (I would add that the book itself, *An Actor Prepares*, contains no all-embracing formulations of this principle.)

Thus we see a complete congruence in the basic method whereby the *main element* in cinema and in stage acting is created directly (an element which cannot be created artificially).

In this connection we can say that we have hereby established not only a unity of method between shot and montage, between montage and sound film montage (which we will discuss in detail later), but a further most important area of unity of method: the unity of method in all areas of film-making with the method which gives life to the fundamental nucleus of the film's content, man, in the person of the actor at work.

If the system is an organic whole in itself, then we may assume that, when subjected to qualitative change, it will in principle also continue to proceed by the same method and according to the same logic through the compositional and structural elements, and that *there too* it will continue, through the method, to reflect the basic feature of the primary phenomenon.

This phenomenon is completely identical with the primary phenomenon of cinema.

There, *movement* is created out of two motionless cells.

Here, a *movement* of the soul, i.e. emotion (from the Latin root *motio* = movement), is created out of the performance of a series of incidents.

In cinema the movement is not actual, but is *an image of movement.*

On the stage, too, the feeling is not actual, but is a *special* way of feeling the truth, a feeling of theatrical truth. In Stanislavsky's book, many pages are devoted to distinguishing it from the truth of real life. I think that there is just one distinction and it is obvious. In our own words, let us say of it that *theatrical emotion is not genuine emotion but an image* of *genuine emotion*, just as the people walking about on stage are not genuinely King Lear, Macbeth or Othello but images of Othello, Macbeth or King Lear. In both cases the image, with all its non-immediate and non-objective reality, yet with the whole gamut of its *generalising force*, extends far beyond the bounds and dimensions of merely specific depiction.

The basic cinematic phenomenon was repeated, but more richly, in the cinema's first steps in compositional form, in its first steps and in the very principle of composition: montage.

A complete event was broken down into pieces, pieces which were not autonomous but with the intention that these pieces should play a certain role, by a specially chosen way of combining them in a progression that is determined by them.

Where the stage actor is concerned, this corresponds to the phase of his preparatory work on the part. This phase, in a new quality and newly enriched, totally reproduces the basic phenomenon of the outward appearance of genuine theatrical feeling.

The role is broken down into pieces. The pieces are determined by the objectives. The pieces are combined in a sequence related to the pervading action, which is built up by the successive pieces achieving their objectives.

The dead printed text of the play has fallen apart in order to be born again as a unity as it is creatively experienced in the actor's emotions.

The dead single-take long shot has fallen apart into montage pieces in order that they may be brought together again into new unity by a vital reliving of the event in emotions and sensations.

It is almost the image of the seed-grain which must first die – fall apart – in order to be reborn as a new, living plant!

The principle, at all events, is not only one which, as we have seen, embraces every aspect of a work of cinematic art: the actor, the role, the shot, montage, the film as a whole; but one which also embraces other arts beyond the bounds of cinema; a principle which even has significant scope beyond the limits of art itself. . . .[150]

First, however, let us show that this principle governs not only cinema and theatre (the Stanislavsky system was created for theatre, and as an achievement of theatre belongs in the general area of the cinematic disciplines; here, for the first time, we are examining it as a single whole along with cinema terminology and the methods of film-making). It is also used as a literary method, with varying degrees of consistency, and hence with varying degrees of vividness.

So for a start let us take an example of extreme and startling clarity.

We shall also seek examples of it in works of great intensity, works of exaltation.

We shall find it in its purest form in one of the greatest exponents of exaltation in literature: Walt Whitman.[151]

Let us approach it in a practical, workmanlike fashion, without white gloves. Whitman wants to sing a paean to America, the America of the pioneers. He wishes to hymn his country through the emblem of the pioneers' first working tool, the axe. He does so in his 'Song of the Broad-Ax'. But an axe is an axe. An emblematic axe is an emblematic axe. He needs to make an Axe with a capital A, an emblematic Axe, out of an axe with a small a, out of a real axe. How does Whitman set about it? Like a true montage artist. Taking as his 'long shot' the *real, physical axe*, he splits it up into a multitude of 'montage fragments' of *what an axe can do*, what can be done with an axe, giving rise to the endless enumeration of a cunningly juxtaposed succession of items which brings to life a whole sea of associations. They are strung out along the powerful rhythm of the embodiment of an idea. In the perception of the reader this endless series is reassembled into a unity; but what emerges is not the axe-as-object, a merely pictorial rendering, but a new quality of axe, the Axe-as-emblem, the Axe-as-image, encompassing in its generalising sweep the image of the young American democracy, whose thousands of axes created the state by laying a path for its power through the dense, impenetrable forests of North America.*

Here are a few passages from the 'Song of the Broad-Ax' which provide especially vivid illustrations of the method used in the poem, of Whitman's method, and of the use of the 'montage' method in art as a whole.

> The shapes arise! Shapes of the using of axes anyhow, and the users and all that neighbors them. . . .[152]

This is his structural method; as for the examples he cites, some of them are simply lists of objects that are made by using an axe, while others are whole situations surrounding the things that are created with the help of an axe. (Sometimes the participation of the axe is extremely remote, involving no more than the feeling of the raw material of fabrication, lumber!)

> The ax leaps!
> The solid forest gives fluid utterances,
> They tumble forth, they rise and form,
> Hut, tent, landing, survey,
> Flail, plough, pick, crowbar, spade,
> Shingle, rail, prop, wainscot, jamb, lath, panel, gable,
> Citadel, ceiling, saloon, academy, organ, exhibition-house, library,
> Cornice, trellis, pilaster, balcony, window, turret, porch,
> Hoe, rake, pitchfork, pencil, wagon, staff, saw, jack-plane, mallet, wedge, rounce,
> Chair, tub, hoop, table, wicket, vane, sash, floor,
> Work-box, chest, string'd instrument, boat, frame, and what not,
> Capitols of States, and capitol of the nation of States,
> Long stately rows in avenues, hospitals for orphans or for the poor or sick,
> Manhattan steamboats and clippers taking the measure of all seas.
>
> The shapes arise!
> The shapes measur'd, saw'd, jack'd, join'd, stain'd,
> The coffin-shape for the dead to lie within in his shroud,
> The shape got out in posts, in the bedstead posts, in the posts of the bride's bed,

---

*First, it must be remembered that for Whitman and his era, American democracy really seemed the most democratic democracy on earth, at least in its proclaimed ideals.

Second, that Whitman still saw his America as the America founded on the ideals of emancipation from the colonial rule of European powers – England, France, Holland – and as the America that had escaped from foreign domination, which obscured from his view the fact that those same pioneers were simultaneously acting as colonisers and enslavers, first of redskins, then of the blacks, later of the workers of their own nation, and later still of whole nations beyond the frontiers of America.

The shape of the little trough, the shape of the rockers beneath, the shape
    of the babe's cradle,
The shape of the floor-planks, the floor-planks for dancer's feet,
The shape of the planks of the family home, the home of the friendly
    parents and children,
The shape of the roof of the home of the happy young man and woman,
    the roof over the well-married young man and woman,
The roof over the supper joyously cook'd by the chaste wife, and joyously
    eaten by the chaste husband, content after his day's work.

The shapes arise!
The shape of the prisoner's place in the court-room, and of him or her
    seated in the place.
The shape of the liquor-bar lean'd against by the young rum-drinker and
    the old rum-drinker,
The shape of the shamed and angry stairs trod by sneaking footsteps,
The shape of the sly settee, and the adulterous unwholesome couple,
The shape of the gambling-board with its devilish winnings and losings,
The shape of the step-ladder for the convicted and sentenced murderer,
    the murderer with haggard face and pinion'd arms,
The sheriff at hand with his deputies, the silent and white-lipp'd crowd,
    the dangling of the rope.

In addition to the overall method, a most striking feature in certain
passages is the way that a 'close-up' is used to stand for a whole scene – in
other words, our familiar principle of *pars pro toto* ('the . . . white-lipp'd
crowd', 'the dangling of the rope', 'the gambling-board', 'the sly settee', 'the
shamed and angry stairs', 'the liquor-bar', 'the planks', 'the little trough', 'the
rockers', 'the cradle').

    Whenever one of the objects constituting the general image of the poem
also needs to be raised beyond the limits of mere depiction, the poet applies
the same to that object as a separate component:

The shapes arise!
Shapes of doors giving many exits and entrances,
The door passing the dissever'd friend flush'd and in haste,
The door that admits good news and bad news,
The door whence the son left home confident and puff'd up,
The door he enter'd again from a long and scandalous absence, diseas'd,
    broken down, without innocence, without means.

The method, as we can see, is the same for the poem as a whole and for
its separate parts.
    While the method is found with particular vividness in the poetry of Walt
Whitman, this does not mean that it is peculiar to him or used by him alone.

For those who would like to deny the existence of this method outside the works of this unfamiliar and unusual poet (even though they may not regard him as the 'idiotic apostle of the new democratic religion', as Ilya Repin called him[153]), we can provide an analogous example from a source that is his polar opposite. It is taken from the work of a writer whom the average philistine does not regard as at all 'suspicious'. In this case the method does not stand out in such hypertrophied form, but the author nevertheless has recourse to it to convey heightened emotion, and this antipode to Whitman is none other than our own . . . Ostrovsky. Here is a passage of his verse-drama *Koz'ma Minin the One-Armed* (1862), taken from Minin's monologue in Act II, Scene 2, in which he decides to embark on his feat of valour; I have stressed the appropriate lines:

> There on the banks the specks of firelight gleam.
> Their toil forgetting, the haulers of the barges
> Prepare their humble meal. Now they begin to sing. No, not joy
> Inspires their song but servitude,
> Leaden servitude and ceaseless toil,
> Ruinous war, charred villages,
> Wrecked houses and nights without a roof.
> Oh sing! Sing louder! *Gather up*
> *The sea of endless tears by Mother Russia shed:*
> *The tears of Novgorod, the tears of Pskov,*
> *Tears from the river Oka and the Klyazma,*
> *Tears from the Don and from the Moscow river,*
> *Tears from the Volkhov and the broad-banked Kama.*
> Let him all flow into a single song
> To break my heart, to burn my soul with fire
> And steel my feeble spirit to this deed.[154]

As I hardly think it is worth piling up any more such examples, we shall limit ourselves to these two representatives of widely differing literary traditions.

It may be pertinent to recall *en passant* that in Soviet cinema there have been at least three examples (twice in subtitles and once in dialogue) in which Ostrovsky's motif is echoed, where the concept of 'all Russia' is conjured up by reciting all the provinces into which tsarist Russia was *fragmented,* and again by listing all the capitals of the national republics from which the Soviet Union is constituted. Twice this was done for emotional effect: in *The End of St Petersburg*[155] by the repeated listing of soldiers – the Russian people at war – by their home provinces: the men of Vyatka, the men from Pskov, and so on; and at the end of *Aerograd,*[156] where the air squadrons of the various Soviet nationalities are enumerated, all merging into a single image of the mighty all-Union air force. . . . The same method was also used ironically in *The Youth of Maxim,*[157] when the [tsarist] colonel of gendarmerie announces to

Maxim, on the latter's release from prison, that he is free to go and live wherever he likes except for 'the provinces of St Petersburg, Moscow, Tver, Orenburg, Ryazan, Kazan', and so on and so on, listing all the non-Siberian provinces of Russia, and thereby creating in the mind of the spectator, and of Maxim himself, an image of the entire Russian Empire, in which, with the exception of the regions of Siberia, Maxim is forbidden to reside.

In conclusion let us cite one further example from life: an example of how an 'image of storm' is set up in the mind of the spectator out of a skilfully composed sequence of pictures related to storm.

This time the creator of the montage sequence is none other than . . . Leonardo da Vinci.[158]

For the reader with little sensitivity to the evocation of an *image* in his mind, the reader whose temperament is rather that of an accountant than an artist, the reader from whom details add up to an *account* of an object rather than give rise to an *image* of the object or event – that reader may quite naturally ask: what has montage to do with all this? Where are the 'key' details? The quotation is an example of nothing more than da Vinci's typically conscientious habit of making 'inventories' of details. It is simply a list, a catalogue of minutiae, a collection of samples. Of course, an accusation of this nature can obviously be made if one starts from the premiss that the reader himself lacks the ability to synthesise details into an *image*, as has been suggested above; it cannot, however, be denied that *not every* 'enumeration' or listing is capable of evoking a generalising image, that not all details are equally significant and that in consequence it is not just any random mixture of medium shots and close-ups whose content adds up to a true montage sequence. It is equally obvious that the basic characteristic of a montage sequence is its suggestiveness, i.e. it has features that are capable of evoking a sense of the totality of a conception. We have already remarked on this factor in an earlier passage. Here we may add to this some remarks on the limits within which it can achieve this effect.

Those who are seeking ready-made formulas and recipes in my work will be disappointed. The characteristic feature of a montage sequence must of course satisfy two demands and one preliminary condition. The montage detail must be, as it were, an essential abstract of that part of the event or phenomenon which it represents: it must be the very flesh and blood of its real nature; in other words, a typical detail. Furthermore, the fragment (or rather, the detail) must also be sufficiently unexpected and unusual to rivet our attention and stimulate our imagination, while at the same time not being so unexpected and unusual as to disturb our normal conception of that phenomenon. For example, the oversized close-ups which were once fashionable disturbed our conception of a face, thanks to eyes, lips and nose of dimensions that gave it so unexpected an appearance that the very perception of a face as such was lost, and at moments when precisely that was needed as a component of the montage set ('you can't see the face for the eyes'). The same also applies to the choice of a characteristic detail of an event.

I myself fell into this trap more than once. Perhaps the most striking example from my own experience occurred, I remember, in the film *The Old and the New*.[159] To illustrate the argument of the first part of the film, the subject of which was the greed for property typical of the old peasantry, particularly evident in the way that comparatively large farms were split up among members of a family into a series of small, economically useless farms, I needed some particularly impressive scenes of property being divided. They had to be as striking as possible, but at the same time 'taken wholly from life'. It would have been impossible to invent scenes that were clearer than those which we found in the actual life and customs of Penza province. There, when property is divided up, the peasant cottages are simply *sawn in half*. They do not dismantle the framework and leave the pieces whole; every single beam is cut in two. The property owner's principle of 'equal shares' is interpreted *literally*, in total disregard for the economic idiocy of this attitude. Like it or not, it is a fact, a 'super-factual' fact, and at the same time what a vivid, unfamiliar image! But after we had shot this episode, it did not occur to us in our quest for vividness to notice that this scene and this image were *so* remote from the patterns of thought familiar to us (as remote as the atavism of the practice itself is from our age!) that they diverged from 'typicality' completely and simply could not be structured into the image we required. From being an episode which by means of montage would merge with others into an image of the property-owning instinct carried to the point of total absurdity, it became an independent scene. Furthermore, it even became an episode which people perceived as inauthentic. Some were suspicious of its real-life verisimilitude; this completely destroyed its meaning and interest, which rested precisely on it being factual. The reaction of others was worse still: they thought the scene was a made-up allegory. Indeed, what else could they think, being unable to conceive of such a primitive custom still being practised these days!

If we look at Leonardo's 'catalogue' from this standpoint, we shall see that it is not a mere 'list of terms' at all, but a remarkable selection of elements so chosen that when combined together they evoke a grandiose image of a flood.

His details are striking in their unexpectedness, yet at the same time they remain probable, possible and convincing (e.g. the bloated corpses of animals, floating and bumping into each other). Trivial things, i.e. normal obvious details, have been so strikingly and expressively 'seized by the camera' that one's imagination is riveted to them as though they were the most unusual objects (such as those animals and people who have remained alive). The situation is the same in cinema, where it is equally true that whereas trivial subjects may be vitalised by artistic means (for instance by the composition of the shot), when the phenomenon itself is unusual, then unfamiliar means of treating it should be played down. Besides, I find that even compositionally da Vinci's fragments are very cleverly put together, and that they are not merely a 'copy-book text' for a painting but a unique, autonomous dramatic poem. It contains, for instance, the complete *gamut of sound* for a flood, which offers very little *immediate* inspiration to a painter, but whose emotional function happens to be colossally stimulating. And with what finesse he directs the overall shift of accentuation within the total picture, now veering off into sound, now plunging back again into depiction, as the orchestration of the audiovisual counterpoint is subtly built up. It is a vivid lesson not only to young painters, but also, I suggest, to more than one hardened old film director!

The qualitative difference between material suitable as detail and capable of evoking a generalising image, and details which lack that ability, is most essential. It is very slight, but the difference is very much one of principle.

Notice for instance how generously Stanislavsky, within *his* sphere and in pursuit of *his* objective, heaps up separate montage fragments which *are conducive to the evocation* of a generalising perception of, for example, 'maternal love'.[160]

Notice, on the other hand, how severe and pedantic he is in picking out and rejecting anything which qualitatively, *by the very nature* of its wording, is either devoid of indicative function or is endowed with indicative functions which point in the direction of other aims, other regions. Here we should remark in passing that the part of speech whose specific nature points towards what he needs – towards human action and human emotions – is the *verb*. [. . . .][161] Notice with what insistence he rejects everything which is not by its nature a verb or even semi-verbal. Because of the essence of the montage fragment, the essence of the characteristics which we require of a montage fragment, he is right in this and is right to proceed from the montage method as a whole, for the actor has to evoke the conception of motherhood *as a whole*.

Stanislavsky does not allow him to play 'motherhood'. This is nothing new to us: it is the very heart of the system and we have explained it above. What is interesting here is how it is done in practice: *motherhood* as a generalisation, as an image, blends itself together in our minds as a result of innumerable specific deeds and acts of motherhood. These separate acts that are characteristic of a mother, her behaviour or attitude towards her child, are as much montage fragments of a single generalising image of *motherhood* for the actor (who is in the foreground in theatre) as for the spectator (who is in the foreground in cinema), and to exactly the same degree as the images of galloping combine into the image of a galloping horse.

In its fragments, the *noun* 'motherhood' must be manifested in *verb* form, in nouns which are, as it were, in a phase of becoming.* As we shall see yet again, the method is all-embracing.

---

*Just as in another sphere and in its specific conditions, the verb is created from a process of juxtaposition of two results: initial and final – as for example the cinematic phenomenon, as we have described it, arises from two adjacent cells. Or as in the morphology of the Chinese ideogram conveying the concept of the *action* 'to eavesdrop', which is created out of a clash between two objects (nouns): a *picture* of a 'door' and a *picture* of an 'ear'.[162]

The fine qualitative distinction between the characteristics which we have adduced and enumerated by their capacity to generalise into an image was known, too, in more ancient times. It was described and very subtly analysed by Lessing in *Laocoön*:

> These descriptions of material bodies, [normally] excluded from poetry, can indeed be used wherever there is no question of imagery, wherever the author appeals only to his readers' reason and employs only clear and, as far as possible, whole concepts; not only the prose writer but also the dogmatic poet (for where he dogmatises, there is he no longer a poet) can use them with great advantage. Thus, for example, does Virgil in his *Georgics* describe the cow most suitable for breeding: 'The best-formed cow is grim-looking, her head ugly, her neck thick, with dewlaps that hang right down from chin to legs; her long flank too will have no end to it; all things large about her, even her feet; and under crumpled horns are shaggy ears. Well content would I be if she were marked with white spots, or rebellious against the yoke, and sometimes dangerous with her horn; more like a bull in face, her whole frame tall, with a tail that sweeps her footprints as she goes. . . .'
>
> Or a handsome colt: 'He carries his neck high; his head is shapely; short is his belly and his back full-fleshed; his gallant breast ripples with brawny sinews.'
>
> For who does not see that the poet was here more concerned with an account of the parts than with the whole? He wishes to enumerate for us the points of a fine colt or a good cow, so that we, when we have seen several of such beasts, may be able to judge of the quality of the one or the other; but whether all these characteristics can lend into a lively picture, or not, was probably a matter of indifference to him.[163]

This quotation provides us in general with a good 'montage' transition to Lessing's *Laocoön*, in which a considerable number of pages are devoted to the subject which interests us. Furthermore, it seems to me that the *Laocoön* itself lies wholly within the area of our theme. For it is obvious that the fundamental subject of his discourse is not so much the conflict between two art forms – painting and poetry – as the conflict between two methods. Indeed, between precisely the two methods that we have been discussing above: the method of depiction, as a method dealing in data and results, and the method of images, as a method concerned with becoming, with process. In Lessing's work, painting and poetry rather represent two *instances*, of which in one art form one method is predominant, and in the other, another method. And, despite Lessing's stern disclaimer, both methods have their part to play in each art form. I repeat that in both separate art forms each method has only a primary and immediately obvious prevalence.

I believe that this strict separation into incompatible opposites is explained by the fact that in Lessing's day neither Edison nor Lumière[164] had yet supplied him with that most perfect apparatus for research and assessment of the aesthetic principles of art: the cinematograph.

'Thus it will always be: the sequence of time is the preserve of the poet, while space belongs to the painter', writes Lessing (Chapter XVIII).

His discussion does not embrace that perfect art which was able to synthesise *both* these principles into a new quality: cinema. Consequently he sees each art form separately, only from the standpoint of its own internal laws, and not from the summit of the joint achievement of both, where within each one, together with its own specific features, there are illuminated the rudiments of the opposing features – not as something alien to it but as the potential data for the next synthesising step.

Thus Lessing observes in painting exactly the same phenomenon which we have dealt with when discussing the rudiments of cinema. Since, however, he saw no prospect of passing beyond the limitations of painting and of merging the two principles in a new art form which came into being more than a hundred years later, Lessing . . . condemns the phenomenon:

> To show two different moments of time in one picture, as does Fr Mazzuoli when he depicts both the rape of the Sabine women and their husbands' reconciliation with their relatives, or Titian when he paints the whole story of the prodigal son (his debauched life, his misery and his repentance), is for the painter to trespass on the territory of the poet – something of which good taste can never approve.
>
> To recount to the reader a succession of parts or things which in nature must all be observed at once if they are to add up to a whole in the attempt to give the reader a picture of the whole, is for the poet to trespass on the territory of the painter – and in doing so to waste much imaginative effort in vain.
>
> (Chapter XVIII)

As we see, Lessing is severe and passes stern judgment.

He might not have done so. After all, he had before him that same *Embarquement pour Cythère*[165] which suggested to Rodin the possibility of introducing dramatic sequentiality into sculpture, a medium in which he had no compunction in producing two *Rapes of Europa* worthy of Fr Mazzuoli, as we have already mentioned above. Or is Lessing's neglect of *L'Embarquement* explicable by the fact that Watteau's patron was the same de Caylus against whom the polemical force of *Laocoön* was directed?[166]

The fact is that no picture is *graphically* a picture unless the artist has observed in it the precondition which Lessing posits as essential for a picture in poetry: '*whereby elements that are temporally coexistent are transformed into a process of sequential evolution.*' We have seen that even in the theatre, where action and the real sequence of actions is at the centre of everything, this condition must be observed, otherwise the essentially dynamic medium of theatre will turn out to be static and lifeless, just as a picture is dead in the one case and full of life in the other. While renouncing such examples of painting as Mazzuoli and Titian, it is quite unnecessary to resort to the Futurists or Cubists, who at the cost of destroying form achieve an effect of form that is *in process of becoming*, unlike the *dead existence* of form in, say, academic painting (or the effect of colour produced by the scattering of blobs of pure tone in the *reductio ad absurdum* of the Pointillistes' method),[167] and justify Lessing by the fact that all this occurred somewhat after his time. For between these two extremes lies the inexhaustible expanse of *normal* composition. Composition itself, at its mature stage of development, assumes the function of conducting the action, without the need for sequential depiction of the stages of an event but by incorporating in their compositional resolution that intersection of past and future which Lessing himself in his subtle analyses detects in painting. Incidentally, that role of composition, whereby it expresses abstractly an earlier phase, in which the concepts of *progression* and *action* have not yet been separated from the depiction of the human figure as 'walking' and 'acting', was much less known in the 18th century. In those days they were much less clearly aware that, in painting, composition is largely a method of totally predetermining the *mise en scène* for the eye of the spectator, i.e. laying out a prearranged, sequential path along which the eye must travel to perceive all the elements that have to be absorbed if they are to *cohere* into the totality of the picture. For a striking example of this one only has to consider, for instance, the 'spiral' *mise en scène* in the composition of Ivanov's *Christ Appearing to the Multitude*,[168] to say nothing of all the tortuous patterns, both *sequential* and *stimultaneous*, to which the eye of the spectator is subjected 'in the hands' of such a virtuoso as Serov.

It is, of course, in this comprehension and perception of the *unity* of simultaneity and sequentiality that the root of the problem lies, both in its comprehension and in its concrete application. When we come to audiovisual unity we shall no longer encounter this problem in the same way.

Nevertheless I would still like to read through *Laocoön* from our viewpoint: as a comparison not so much of art forms as of methods, and I believe Lessing himself provides us with every ground for doing so.

Even after he has allotted the methods to their different art forms, he still leaves a loophole for a rapprochement between these opposites.

> But just as two friendly neighbours may not allow each other to make unseemly intrusion into the inner regions of their respective properties but may nonetheless allow that on their outermost common borders a certain mutual indulgence prevail, which shall peacefully tolerate any minor incursions necessarily made by one into the territory of the other: thus too should painting and poetry behave towards each other.
>
> (Chapter XVIII)

What is more, Lessing himself establishes the point at which the art forms may merge and fuse with one another, when they approach a single *perfect* method of recounting an event in the *process of occurrence*.

It is not, however, my intention that either the poet or the painter should derive justification from my previous comparison of the two friendly neighbours. A mere simile neither proves nor justifies anything. But this it must justify: as when in a painting the two different moments are so close together in time that they can, without straining our credulity, count as one; so when in a poem the numerous expressions describing various features and characteristics follow each other in such pressing and rapid succession that we seem to be hearing them all at once.

(Chapter XVIII)

The most direct indication that the *Laocoön* may be interpreted in this way is, of course, given by Lessing in the last paragraph of his introduction to it:

It should be noted that by the term 'painting' I refer to the visual arts in general; nor do I deny that in using the term 'poetry' I should also take some account of the other arts in which figurative depiction plays a large part.

(Introduction)

This generalisation is almost an admission that the matter at issue is that of depiction and image within the artistic method as a whole.

Even without that confirmation [by Lessing] it is clear that his argument is essentially concerned with this, with obvious and forceful emphasis on the method of the *coming-into-being of an image* as distinct from *static, representational depiction*.

The significance of this in political terms is provided by the following extract from the preface to the Russian translation of *Laocoön* published in 1933.

At first sight the fundamental theme of *Laocoön* is to define the boundary between poetry and painting, or, more precisely, between the arts that are figurative and spatial and the arts that exist in the dimension of time. . . . But in actual fact the point at issue is the dividing line between two diametrically opposed views of art: the aristocratic, courtly attitude comes into conflict with the bourgeois-democratic attitude.

Historically speaking, our views on the matter now represent a further, third stage in the essential evolution of this question. Lessing's opponents with whom he is arguing – the English antiquarian Spence; the leading figure of English classicism, Alexander Pope; and the critic and art-patron de Caylus – are basically defending the same thing:

Their fundamental position is that the laws of poetry are the same as those which govern painting and sculpture. The primary obligation of the poet is to strive for sculptural and pictorial effect, for precise description of all features of the material form of objects and phenomena.

(I quote again from the Russian preface.)

In other words, they are defending the primacy of static pictoriality, extending it even into dynamic art forms, i.e. those which are organically opposed to it. Lessing divides the issue into two methods, localised in the art forms of which they are most characteristic; he thereby removes from poetry the enslaving function of depiction and stresses the principle of dynamic coming-into-being, without admitting it beyond the confines of poetry and leaving only a 'loophole' through which the two art forms might be united by a single dynamic method.

Finally, on the basis of our experience in cinema, it is now our turn to say that we wish to understand the problem itself more broadly: as a comparison of the possibilities inherent in the two methods – the method of depiction and the method of making images – on the premiss that both are feasible *in any art form*; that the second is predominant; that the point at issue is their unity; that each should be given its due and highly respected place; and that, finally, in any art form the usurpation of all functions by the other leads to bankruptcy and failure.*

Lessing's proclamation of the method of dynamic 'becoming' in poetry is, of course, a historically familiar example of art anticipating a principle which was fated to be formulated almost simultaneously in philosophy. For both categories embody in equal degree the reflection in consciousness of the relationship of class forces, their struggle and the consequent emergence of a picture of social structures. The perception of this by art, however, can precede its formulation in philosophical terms. Such, it seems to me, is the significance of Lessing's battle for the principle of coming-into-being, alongside that of Hegel, who gave the principle of coming-into-being an all-embracing philosophical significance and put an end to the 'a priori data' of metaphysics.

The final and conclusive proof that *Laocoön* deals with the same problems as those that concern us here is, of course, the subtlety with which the essay examines Homer's methods from entirely the same standpoint that we have adopted in our enquiries. No doubt we would not have dwelt on Lessing's work in such detail, had not one of our aims been to demonstrate the similarity between the methods of montage and this ancient, seminal epic that dates from the very infancy of mankind. It would be difficult to find a better

---

*For example, in the case of an actor who may be ideal in arousing and embodying emotions according to the Stanislavsky system, but is devoid of depicting ability, i.e. the ability to experience emotion beyond its external manifestation. Or, on the other hand, our first drawing of a barricade.

exposition of this than that given by Lessing.

There are three occasions when, in his approach to Homer and to the subject that interests us, Lessing forces the attentive reader concerned with montage to pay particular attention to him. In Chapter III we read:

> We can judge Timomachus' other work, depicting the infuriated Ajax, from Philostratus' report. He does not show Ajax at the time when he is rampaging among the flocks and herds, killing and trussing bulls and sheep instead of people. Instead, the artist wisely chose the moment when Ajax is sitting down exhausted by his frenzy and contemplating suicide. And Ajax is presented to the spectator in all his fury – not because he is seen raging before our eyes but because the clear traces of that fury are apparent in his whole demeanour: the full force of his recent rampage is clearly reflected in his utter despair and shame; *we can see the storm that has just passed from the debris and corpses* strewn all around him.* (The italics are mine. S.M.E.)

Ajax's fury is not *portrayed*; his rampaging is *suggested*. The debris strewn about is the means of achieving this: these details suggest to us the deeds that make up the 'total image' of what the demented Ajax has done.

In Chapter IV we may observe the same method of juxtaposing Philoctetes' various torments, which go to make up Sophocles' image of the inhuman sufferings to which Philoctetes was subjected.

All this is still somewhat peripheral to our subject; one remark in Chapter VI, however, makes us jump because of the pure montage-like quality of the ideas put forward. As is well known, Lessing proves that Virgil's description of Laocoön preceded the sculptural composition and that the sculptors followed the poet in creating the group, not the other way round. Lessing expounds his thoughts at length and recalls Sadolet's description of the same scene in the completed statue. He then says,

> These lines were written by Sadolet; had they been written by Virgil, they would have been more picturesque and, of course, they would have been better than those he actually wrote if he had had the image before him to work on his imagination. 'Twice their scaly bodies entwined the priest's waist and twice / His throat, their slender necks looming up above him.'

Of course, these features in Virgil's description satisfy our imagination too, but on condition that the imagination is not so arrested by them as to carry them to the point of absolute clarity and with the further proviso that we will *visualise Laocoön and the snakes by turns* without

---

*This example of evoking the perception of a process by showing the details of its effects, while being apparently diametrically opposite in appearance, is identical in principle, and is something that may be classed with the examples I gave in connection with the principle governing Stanislavsky's use of verbs.

conjuring up a vivid picture of the group as a whole. When Virgil's depiction is apprehended as a whole it ceases to please us and seems extremely unpictorial.[169]

There is no need to go on. We can already see an exact congruence with the concept of montage as we have demonstrated it, in the contrast of the overall *depiction* of the fight with the *alternating* consecutive images of the fighters.

But there is better still to come. Lessing is absolutely brilliant in Chapter XVI, where, discussing Homer's method, he writes that it was Homer himself who put him on the track and led him to all his ensuing conclusions. Here we see the mark of the essentially laconic character of the 'montage sequence'.★ Here is the verb-like quality of the action instead of a description of its outcome. Here, too, is the remarkable device of how to achieve the effect of something *coming into being* instead of merely providing us with a *fait accompli*.

I find that Homer does not depict anything other than sequential actions and all other people and objects are only described in so far as they form part of the action and, even when they do, usually with no more than a single stroke. . . .†

A ship for him is either a black ship or a fast ship or at most a well-found many-oared black ship. Homer does not go into any further detail in describing the ship. By contrast, the voyage itself, the departure, the landfall are the object of detailed depiction, for which, if a painter wished to transfer them on to canvas, he would need five, six or even more paintings.

In other words, the ship is not depicted in detail but we are presented with an image of the ship through its various actions (sailing, departure, landfall). This portrayal, once again, is not conveyed as a datum but as a generalising image derived from 'five, six or more separate pictures'. That is to say, literally five or six montage sequences for the image of the ship sailing on the waves, five or six for its departure, five or six for its landfall. In the end, we have the image of the ship, though nowhere is it portrayed as such. Now try to deny the identity of this method with the film techniques described above!

But the most interesting thing is still to come. Here is a description of how Homer set himself the task of creating an image and the way in which

---

★It also coincides both with the montage build-up of a jumping horse and with the verb forms in the Stanislavsky system.

†At the time when the so-called 'montage cinema' was flourishing, we ourselves wrote that the uniqueness of a montage sequence, in the sense of its having just one element of significance, was one of the most important features of its value. Here the case is identical, in so far as objects are used only to the extent that they fit perfectly into the action.

he accomplished it by montage with the means at his disposal:

> If special circumstances occasionally oblige Homer to draw our attention
> at greater length to some material object, the result is not *a picture which
> an artist would be able to reproduce* with his brush. On the contrary, with
> the help of countless devices he manages to *fragment the depiction of this
> object into a number of moments, each of them presenting the object in a new
> light*, whereas a painter has to wait for the last of these moments before
> he can show *in completed form* what we have seen *emerging* in the poet's
> words.★

Thus, for example, if Homer wants to show us Juno's chariot, he makes
Hebe put the chariot together before our eyes. We see the wheels, the axles,
the bodywork, the shafts and the harness, not in their assembled state but as
Hebe is putting them together. The poet *even* describes the wheels in several
stages; he *draws our attention consecutively* to the eight copper spokes, the
golden rims, the brass tyres, the silver hubs, *and to each part separately.*† It
could be said that since there is more than one wheel, as much extra time is
spent on describing them as would be needed in reality to assemble all the
wheels, compared with the time needed to assemble one wheel.★★

If Homer wants to describe how Agamemnon was dressed, he makes the
king put on one article of clothing after another – the soft tunic, the wide
robe, the beautiful sandals, and the sword. Only when he is fully dressed
does he pick up the sceptre. We visualise his clothing as the poet depicts
the *process* of dressing. Somebody else might describe his dress down to
the last little pleat but, in that case, we would see no action.

I would add: nor would we experience any effect upon us.

★Here it must be clearly borne in mind exactly what we have been talking about, which
concerns expanding our conception of the problem beyond a particular art form into
questions of method. Thus the painter and the poet in this instance are not representatives
of different art forms but of different methods: of static, lifeless depiction on the one hand
and, on the other, of the live, dynamic process of building up an image.

†That is to say there are literally four consecutive shots of the wheels, shots in which each
one emphasises compositionally some aspect that is decisive for the particular shot: i.e. the
characteristics, in turn, of the spokes, the rim, the tyres or the hubs.

★★This last thought is more of a frivolous joke than a profound reflection. I do think, though,
that the important point here is not the length of 'footage' that would be needed for 'all four
wheels'. It is something different: the reason why so many montage sequences are used to
draw our attention to the wheels is that in the image of a *chariot* [*kolesnitsa*] that is being
formed in our mind's eye, it is precisely the *wheels* [*kolesa*] which play the most essential
part! Therefore it is both in the amount of 'footage' and, more importantly, by virtue of the
method whereby they are not 'depicted' but the image of them is 'built up' that they merit
this 'special treatment'.

What does Homer do when he wants to give a clearer and fuller picture of the sceptre, which here is simply called 'his father's immortal sceptre', in the same way as a similar one elsewhere is merely called 'a sceptre studded with golden nails'? Does he describe for us the wood itself or the carved head of the sceptre in addition to the golden nails? No. He would do that if his description were intended for heraldic purposes or so that another identical sceptre might be made from his description. I am sure that many modern poets would provide just such a precise description of the king's dress in the simple-minded conviction that they have indeed succeeded in creating a vivid portrayal if an artist were able to paint a picture of it based on their words.* But what is it to Homer whether and to what extent he surpasses the painter? So he tells us the *story* of the sceptre instead of depicting it. At first we see it in Vulcan's smithy, then glittering in Jupiter's hands; later it is shown as a symbol of Mercury's qualities, after which it serves as a commander's baton in the hands of warlike Pelops and as a shepherd's crook in those of peace-loving Atreus and so on. . . .

In this way I finally come to know this sceptre better than if the poet had put it before my eyes or if Vulcan himself had handed it to me.

Thus, as we see, an almost physical, material perception of the object is achieved.

I now regard the history of the sceptre as a masterly artistic device that enables the poet to draw our attention to a particular object without entering into a tedious description of its parts. . . .

Likewise, when Achilles swears on his sceptre to avenge Agamemnon's insult, Homer gives us the history of that sceptre as well. We see it at the very outset, still green on the mountainside, then being lopped off the trunk, stripped of its leaves, smoothed and made fit for its task – to serve the leaders of a people as a symbol of their god-given rank.

But the most interesting part comes at the end of the description of these two sceptres. Here Lessing touches on the most remarkable feature of montage, namely that montage is not only the means of *recreating the image* of an object or phenomenon *in general,* as it is in 'unretouched' nature. Fundamentally, only montage is capable of producing a *purposeful image*: not of recreating but of creating for a specific purpose the *required image* of the object or phenomenon. In this sense it is not accidental that the sceptres are shown in the process of being made and both are shown undergoing *identical* processes; this serves the purpose of throwing into sharper relief the differences

---

*How true this is of the cinematic 'portraitists' of our own day, who have their own antecedents just as the 'poets of the cinema' have theirs!

in the making of the two. This is not accidental either. Agamemnon's dress, after all, is not shown in the process of *being made*, beginning with lush grass and the flocks grazing on it, the weaving of the wool from a fine fleece, etc., but in the process of *his putting on his clothes*. Lessing explains why such montage sequences of actions in relation to the sceptres were chosen and why analogous series of identical actions were performed upon them.

> In these two descriptions Homer did not, of course, intend to describe two sceptres differing in material and form; he made use of this excellent opportunity for a vivid demonstration of the difference in the two kinds of authority symbolised by the two sceptres; one the work of Vulcan, the other cut from a mountainside tree by an unknown hand; one the ancient heirloom of a noble dynasty, the other made for any casual passer-by; one wielded by the monarch of many islands and the whole of Argos, the other belonging to an ordinary Greek, one man among many others charged with maintaining the law. This was precisely the distance separating Agamemnon from Achilles, a distance Achilles himself could not gainsay, however much he may have been blinded by anger.

These last words of Lessing's complete the circle begun here with the example of the barricades where the 'encompassing outline', which in the ensuing stage became a 'montage sequence', was also called upon to find its own breaks, its compositional juxtapositions or the rhythm of the montage series in aiming at the image we wish to *attribute* to an event and by which we want to *represent* that event.

It is also interesting to note that Lessing derives the method itself from the one and only reliable field of knowledge, that of human behaviour and perception.

> How do we achieve a clear understanding of any object in space? First, we examine each component separately, then the connection between these parts and finally the whole. Our senses perform these varying operations with such astonishing speed that for us they all merge into one and this speed is, without question, essential for our conception of the whole, which is none other than the end result of the perception of the separate parts and their inter-relation.

We, too, did something analogous earlier on, when, in considering the basic nature of film, we took the starting-point of cinema aesthetics to be the psychological phenomenon of creating an image, as being the conscious *human* content of this primary cell of 'the technical marvel' of cinematography.

In considering those of Homer's images that Lessing deals with, we are willy-nilly reminded of the quotations from Whitman given above. His 'tone' is the grandchild of the description of Achilles' shield, in the decorations of which the entire world was reflected. The general method is obvious here, although there is also a difference. Apart from the fact that Whitman to the utmost degree reveals the method itself, the difference lies elsewhere: it is determined by a difference of historical epochs, and with it a corresponding difference not only in content but in the way of thinking. Whitman scatters fragments of reality right and left by the handful, fragments of nature, of himself, of the globe, of the universe, and they form themselves of their own accord into his gigantic, elemental images. This stage in the evolution of method was not yet available to Homer. It is thus characteristic of him that the processes whereby images emerge, and are developed and created* are inseparable from the creator and from the action by which that emergence and that development are achieved. This was the only available method, for until the ability to abstract was able to separate these processes from the primal situation, the process was not yet separable from the creator. Hence each object and event to be imbued with dynamism is shown either through the process of its making (the sceptre), or gradual enrobement (Agamemnon) or its assembly (Juno's chariot). The *principle* of assembling [*sborka*] is also indicated here by depicting the putting together. Whitman, however, is free of this hampering necessity. He often does use it, but only by the exercise of free creative choice, by a conscious decision of his imagination, as a stylistic requirement of some compositional task that he has set himself.

Such are the methods used at different stages of the power and vitality of epic poetry. Let us see, however, whether something similar is not to be found at other of its stages and in different kinds of genre and form.

After the poetry of straining torsos and sinews that is found in both the subject matter and in the forms of Homer and Whitman, let us look at the fragile constructs of poets who are the very antithesis of them. Let us take an example a long way from their cosmic scope and thunderous rhythms, and turn to those who, shunning such titanic visions of the world and its struggles, put their ear to the tiny nuances of personal feeling in the calm lyricism of the sonnet. In other words, let us see what happens to our method when applied to artists who are the very opposite of Homer and Whitman: to the Symbolists and their leader, Mallarmé.[170] Let us begin with his own words: 'Nommer un objet, c'est supprimer les trois quarts de la jouissance d'un poème.' [To name an object is to spoil three-quarters of the enjoyment of a poem.]

I believe these words say the same thing. Not to name things in a poem but to make the image emerge out of the poem: therein lies the power of poetry's effect on us.

Not to 'muddy the waters' by explicitly naming things is a method of

---

*'The poet shows us the gradual creation of that which the painter can only present in its finished state. . . .' What a splendid term 'creation' [*obrazovanie*] is; one is tempted to read it as 'the formation of an image' [*stanovlenie obraza*]. The German language appears to have come to a similar conclusion: *Entstehung–Bildung – das sich bildende Gebilde*. (Cf. Lessing's comments.)

giving the reader that shower of clues which conjures up for him the desired generalised image.

That is how we must understand Georges Bonneau's remark about Mallarmé: 'Art does not consist of suggesting to others what one feels oneself but of creating for them incentives to their own powers of suggestion.'[171]

This proposition tallies with two other concepts: first, the question of montage, how we understand it and how it has its place in the Stanislavsky system; second, the phenomenon of lability (instability; proneness to change) which we saw in the example from Chinese speech and Chinese concepts and in the extract from *The Captain's Daughter*, where it was introduced purposely.[172]

This twofold congruity is entirely right and proper. What is more, our quotation from Mallarmé unites the two concepts like the links of a single chain. The Chinese example is one of a prior status quo elevated into a rigid system – a stage of development artificially frozen at a given point long after it had ceased to correspond to the current stage of development. This is the kind of *ne plus ultra* of conservatism to be found in Chinese culture. There we find complete lability of words and concepts, certainly well beyond the usual norm. A degree of lability is, however, characteristic of any word, even at the level of complete consciousness, and even more in the case of not just a word but an image, the interpretation, i.e. the reading, of which allows a far greater lability (see above, for examples of the 'white horse' in montage).

What does Mallarmé do? As a Symbolist, he is inevitably regressive and one-sided in method. On the one hand, he takes it as axiomatic that every element of a verbal depiction is read and 'felt' differently by each perceiver. In this he is a 'Chinese'; he is also blatantly asocial in denying the similarity of image perception by people of the same social background or class. This makes him excessively individualistic, with the result that he avoids insisting on any image as definitive. Yet at the same time it is just this that spurs him on to arrange his indicative fragments in such a way that the resulting generalising image approaches what he sees and senses himself. Mallarmé is not at all aimless; he is in his own way a consistent 'constructor of a way of life'; the trouble is that the form and structure of the world he builds is at variance with the real world around him, from which he retreats into 'other' worlds, worlds of the senses but which lack concrete objectivity. No one will deny that this is what he does. See, for example, the comments in Benedikt Lifshits' translated anthology, *French Lyric Poets of the 19th and 20th Centuries*:

> Not a single French poet before or since Mallarmé was as all-embracing and absolute in pursuit of the 'transformation' of reality and in the construction of 'another' reality. All the symbolic images in Mallarmé's poetry, as in such poems as 'The Swan', 'The Faun', 'Hérodiade', 'The Windows', etc., need to be decoded as ideas for realising an imaginary world that the poet found within himself and which was susceptible to proof of being the uniquely authentic reality.[173]

By the means that he adopted to construct the image of his world, Mallarmé cannot help aligning himself with both the underlying principles and the practical techniques of the montage method. It is specifically a case of 'alignment' rather than complete attachment. Apart from anything else, in order to attain that, he has to pass through the pre-image stage of affect, which attracts him, i.e. his urge to express diffuse nuances of feeling rather than the clear perception of an image. In this he is again 'Chinese'. This makes him deal not with *fragments that evoke images but with mini-fragments, capable of eliciting only vague sensory perceptions.* Quoting Mallarmé's celebrated sonnet, 'The Swan' ('Le Cygne'), Bonneau describes his perception of the poem as follows: 'A synthesis, a swan; a harmony resulting from the juxtaposition not of words but of syllables; such is the scheme of the poem. Do not interpret; in the clear light of commonplace logic, the pure symbol would fade away.'[174]

That is to say that the image arises from juxtaposition, just as we have described it in connection with cinematography. Such an image is rightly called a harmony, because it arises as harmony does from melody (see above). But this image is *sensuously indeterminate*, because the elements from which it is compounded are not graphic, are not words evoking images, but only aural stimuli, syllables, i.e. elements that in this case are much closer to music than to specific concepts. The 'mechanism' of the method, however, is the same.

Strange as it may seem, something similar can occur in cinematography, and it is not by mere chance that we have cited Mallarmé. Anyone using montage knows what a treasure so-called 'smeared frames' and smeared sequences are for the film-maker, i.e. those frames where there is blurred movement that does not register clearly on the film. This occurs when the movement is too fast, and in the time of exposure allocated to a single frame the film does not capture a 'momentary snapshot' of that movement; but instead, the movement itself has time to go through several consecutive phases during that exposure. This results in the same 'blur' on the frame or sequence of frames as occurs in a still photograph when a car in motion or a horse at the gallop are photographed at an insufficiently fast shutter speed.* Why then are these blurred frames and sequences so valuable and when do they have a place in montage?

Everyone knows from practical experience that the demand for blurred frames and sequences arises when it is necessary to give the viewer the *sense* of speed rather than just the image of a fast-moving object. Short montage sequences consisting of blurred frames are then linked by smeared frames. A selection of sequences of blurred movements in such a case becomes very

---

*This happens in film mainly when a sudden movement occurs in close proximity to the lens. The speed of movement in relation to the distance to the lens grows in proportion to the square of the distance, i.e. the photographic effect does not correspond with the direct impression of the 'naked' eye. 'Blurring' can easily be avoided even then by changing the length of the exposure, the lighting and the aperture. Carelessness on the part of the cameraman, the conditions under which filming takes place and, sometimes, special instructions from the director for montage purposes lead to the image being blurred.

valuable in itself. Compositionally, this demand arises when the situation and the action are themselves already quite clear, so that the narrative function of montage can be abandoned and the technique can be used for creating pure sensation. We know all about the chase, who is doing the chasing and who is fleeing from whom. We have seen the pursuer. All that is left to do is to make the spectator *feel the chase* as vividly as possible. This is where the editing of short sequences comes into the technique of montage, making it possible to indicate by a mere hint in the whirlwind tempo of the action what is happening, how it is happening and where it is happening. This is where the blurred frames come into their own: by giving a sense of the movement of an object rather than of the object itself. It is precisely here that we see both the similarity to Mallarmé's approach and the difference. The similarity stems from the fact that in film, too, we are dealing with sensation only. Bonneau's words are equally appropriate here: 'Do not interpret; in the clear light of commonplace logic the pure symbol would fade away.' Here, as there, there is no image, only a blurred smear. The difference is that we permit this blurred brushstroke and introduce it at a given moment of our generalising depiction: it is a brushstroke that works for us as a stage in the depictive process. Mallarmé's whole structure consists of similar blurred, non-concrete, elusive images. In a glossary of montage, a blurred frame could be defined as a montage syllable.

There are instances when the role of blurring may not apply to the actual depiction of an object or to its *photographic treatment* but to certain means of treating the object *in front of the lens.* Such means could be dense smoke that obscures the picture, a spray of water or rain sweeping past a person, a sandstorm or a cloud of dust smothering him. The method of treatment remains the same. We assemble a montage sequence 'through smoke', 'from smoke into smoke', 'from wind into wind' or 'out of the spray into spray'. Here a photographic blur extends, as it were, into a blur acted out by the objects themselves in front of the camera. But the method is still the same.

As regards Mallarmé in general, his tendency to employ montage techniques of composition is much greater than we have just indicated. This is further confirmation that our analysis of his method is correct. The anthology of French lyric poets quoted above has the following to say on this point:

> Mallarmé wrote very little and published even less. Nevertheless, his influence was enormous. Mallarmé's syntactical, grammatical and even purely typographical experiments – he attached great importance to the typographical layout of his works – in many ways anticipated the ideas of the Cubists and Futurists.

As can be seen, Mallarmé paid tribute to the 'montage' aspects of his poetry by devoting a great deal of attention to them.

The imagery of Walt Whitman and the above comments on Mallarmé's concern with typesetting as montage, an experiment which influenced the Futurists, inevitably call to mind our greatest contemporary poet – Mayakovsky – and his treatment of the line in poetry. In discussing montage, we have up to now paid most attention to the process of purposefully selecting and juxtaposing those montage elements that are apparently random, in order that they may become a class-determined phenomenon presented in class terms. When I have to analyse the principles and technique of film editing in special detail, I like to quote a short stanza by Mayakovsky. Its relevance, by and large, lies in its approximation to the monosemantic character of the shot and in that part of its signification that is achieved by separating the essential from the 'generality' and in the necessary disposition of the sentences by cutting them up into 'shots', sometimes consisting of just one word.

> The void. Fly, you,
> Cutting into the stars. . . .[175]

This is a brilliant example of the classic spacing-out into three 'montage segments' of one action, that of someone bursting into a particular environment. 1) The environment – the void (possibly with a vast expanse of stars throwing the emptiness of the rest of the void into even greater contrast); 2) 'The flier'; and finally, 3) 'The flier' cutting into 'the environment'.

Prose, too, has a certain similarity to the technique of montage; it constructs 'its own world' based on impressions of the real world rather than trying to capture and reflect it in 'short sequences'. This is not so much the 'page montage' of Andrei Bely, but above all the well-known 'short line' used by Doroshevich primarily to give a precise, tangible picture of what he is writing about.[176] It reads like a montage scenario, and the drumrolls of his sentences beat out a picture of his subject matter with extraordinary perceptual realism, almost without recourse to metaphor or imagery but using only sharply caught details of objective reality or by 'spotlighting' their most unambiguous characteristics. I always recommend both these authors to beginners in the art of montage as 'literary training' to develop appropriate modes of thinking and the ability to see things in montage terms – to see what is primary and what is secondary, what is typical and what is atypical, what is of particular and what of general significance, all those phenomena, in fact, which the beginner will have to show and reveal in cinematic terms.

But from whence does this method of dismemberment and reassembly derive, this method to which we have been devoting so much attention? Where does it come from and where are its roots?

Taking 'The Song of the Broad-Ax' as an example, Whitman is singing about an object *outside himself.*

Yet by using the same method, he is also singing *about himself.*

The same fragmentation takes place, though here the subject matter is a man, and in its application to man the name of the method no longer sounds like a metaphor but seems to designate the actual manipulation of a human being.

Let us look closely at the terminology. Let us be like the Germans, about whom Lessing wrote in his *Laocoön*:

Better than any other people, we have the ability to draw whatever conclusions we like from this or that interpretation of a word. Baumgarten admitted that he owed the majority of the examples in his [work on] aesthetics to Gessner's lexicon.

Let us try, however, to give the method an interpretation that is not arbitrary. Instead, let us listen through it to the voice of its most ancient ancestors: a voice that comes from an era in history when a metaphorical meaning was not yet metaphorical.

Balzac wrote rapturously in *Louis Lambert*:

Is it not thus with every verb? All of them are imbued with a vital force which they derive from the soul and which they restore to it through the mysterious, miraculous process of action and reaction between speech and thought. Is it not like a lover who draws as much love from his mistress' lips as he bestows upon them?[177]

Riding on the back of this metaphorical term, let us now make an equally miraculous voyage deep into the history of art.

'The dismemberment of an axe': the phrase sounds like delirious raving – or a metaphor. Let us reject the notion of delirium and examine it as a metaphorical expression. And there is good reason for doing so, since within this phrase there are clearly echoes of a situation in the distant past that really was connected with dismemberment and with limbs torn apart in order that they might be reunited in some superior new quality: something 'divine and transfigured', in contrast to what is earthly and transitory. But what springs immediately to mind as soon as we have coined an image such as this? We are at once reminded of the myths and mysteries of Dionysus, of Dionysus being torn to pieces and the pieces being reconstituted in the transfigured Dionysus. Here we are at the very threshold of the art of theatre which in time was to become the art of cinema, that threshold at which religious ritual gradually turned into art, at which the straightforward *cult act* gradually turned into *symbolic ritual*, then to metamorphose into an *artistic image*.

More ancient than the legend of the dismembered and reconstituted god, very ancient indeed is the primal social act which is reflected partly in legend, partly in ritual.

The unity of the tribe, its fusion into a single entity, was achieved by the ritual murder of the tribal chief at a certain stage of his reign and the eating of his flesh by the tribe.[178] The oneness of his body was transformed into the unity of the tribe. His body unified the tribe. Unity, apart from the physical unity of a human body, was as yet unimaginable and did not exist as a concept. Understandably enough, tribal chiefs gradually tried to abolish this somewhat uncomfortable ceremony. The sacrifice of the actual chief of the tribe began to be replaced by the sacrifice of a 'dummy' or 'surrogate' chief. Thus the Aztecs of Mexico would choose a slave who was treated with royal honours for a year, and who, when that term had expired, was sacrificed instead of the king, in the role of the 'effigy' of the king. The earliest versions of Dionysus exemplified this situation in their own way. Tribal chief–ancestor–totemic animal–god: these all form part of a single series. At the earliest stage, the *tribal chief* was physically torn apart. The later myth poeticised the same thing in the tragedy of a *god*, a tragedy represented later still in the several variants of the Dionysus myth. In its earliest forms this centred on the totemic animal: the culmination of the rite consisted in the crowd tearing a bull to pieces – the symbol of the tribe's common ancestor – and when they then ate it the unity, not of the bull but of the whole tribe, was re-established through its communal participation in the rite of unification. This stage of belief persists to this day, though divided into two elements. Though its form has been modified, the act itself has been retained, despite the loss of its cult aspect. The cult element has, however, also been retained, though transformed into purely symbolic ritual divorced from the presence and associations of a bull. The first of these elements is none other than the bullfight. Its cult origins are complex and multilinear. Apart from the aspect we are writing about, many other strands are woven into it. What interests us now is the fact that here we have an instance of the survival of the erstwhile practice of killing the totemic animal. 'But . . . what about eating it?' you will ask, referring to that part of the procedure that strikes you as most surprising. Believe it or not, this has survived too! I have taken part in it myself. Admittedly it is no longer seen as a ritual but as a tradition, in accordance with which the *aficionados* devour steaks from the bulls just killed in the *corrida* in a little restaurant opposite the bullring. This occurs equally in Spain, Mexico and South America – everywhere, in fact, where bullfighting is still practised. The function of 'communing' is, of course, absent here, but that separated function is to be found not far away, almost around the corner, or at least no further away than . . . the nearest Catholic church, and it is practised with particular zeal in those same regions of Mexico, South America or Spain, at any rate in those parts of the latter country which Franco is drowning in blood.[179] We have used the ecclesiastical term 'communing' [*priobshchenie*] with good reason; 'communing' is another way of saying 'taking communion' [*prichastie*]. Both words retain the concept of merging with something that is 'common' [to a social or religious 'community'], of being a participant in it. Both words serve to define the central 'sacrament' of the Christian churches. First, ordinary bread and ordinary wine are 'miraculously' assumed to become flesh and blood. Then these fragments of the single body of Christ are given to the faithful to consume, thereby accomplishing the mysterious unification of the Church as a whole and its unity with its founder. We should not forget the persistent frequency with which the term 'Body of the Church' is used, nor should we forget that the Christian Church was the first religion to postulate the supranational unity of all mankind. We may recall what Engels wrote about this:

Christianity struck a chord that was bound to echo in countless hearts. To all complaints about the wickedness of the times and the general material and moral distress, Christian consciousness of sin answered: It is so and cannot be otherwise. Thou art to blame, ye are all to blame for the corruption of the world, thine and your own internal corruption! And where was the man who could deny it? Mea culpa! The admission of each one's share in the responsibility for the general unhappiness was irrefutable and was made the precondition for the spiritual salvation which Christianity at the same time announced. And this spiritual salvation was so instituted that it could be easily understood by members of every old religious community. The idea of atonement to placate the offended deity was current in all the old religions; how could the idea of the self-sacrifice of the mediator atoning once [and] for all for the sins of humanity not easily find ground there? Christianity, therefore, clearly expressed the universal feeling that men themselves are guilty of the general corruption as the consciousness of sin of each one; at the same time it provided, in the death-sacrifice of his judge, a form of the universally longed-for internal salvation from the corrupt world, the consolation of consciousness; it thus proved its capacity to become a world religion and, indeed, a religion which suited the world as it then was.[180]

The device used to manipulate belief in this ecumenical unity 'in the spirit' is the practice of communion, the ritual for achieving 'unity in Christ'.

Interestingly enough, it is in these same lands of pre-republican Spain, Mexico and South America that those separated elements of an erstwhile cultic unity are constantly striving to come together again. It is the practice in those regions, for instance, to hold *corridas in honour of the Virgin*, and particularly splendid bullfights take place on the days of important Church festivals. I personally witnessed that splendour during the quatercentenary of Our Lady of Guadalupe in Mexico City in 1930.

Later forms of the Dionysiac cult dispensed with this crude, primal form of the ritual. The actions became symbolic and figurative. The fate of Dionysus (which was similar to that of youth-gods of other cults and other countries) and the games which enacted that fate were gradually formalised, and from being a collective act became a performance. Tragedy was born. At first its subject matter was limited almost wholly to the theme of the god; the seasonal and fertility elements of these symbolic plays are fairly well known, and there is no point in dwelling on them here. When describing montage earlier in these pages, we had recourse to the parable of the grain of wheat which must disintegrate and die in order to rise again as a living plant. In this, the wheat repeats the cycle of myriads of other plants, indeed, of the whole of nature, which dies in winter in order to burst into life again in spring. Here we have another component of the image of the death and resurrection of the *daemon* or god, a component that derives from the same principle. Let us trace the historical course of that fundamental image which concerns us in this study. At first, as we have mentioned, both the subject matter and the structure of tragedy, newly metamorphosed into this form from the practices of the Dionysiac cult, still dealt with that theme. Then the story-line gradually ebbed away to be replaced by a new one although in the most archaic tragedies it was still retained, not in the representation of the action but in the underlying structure. Winterstein has this to say about it:

In a chapter of Harrison's book *Themis*, Gilbert Murray attempted to trace the derivation of the formal elements in a large number of Attic tragedies from the ancient liturgical drama of the death and rebirth of the '*Eniautos-daemon*'; according to him, within the structure of this sacred ritual it was a case of other personages and events having taken the place of the god or demi-god [*daemon*] and his story. The content of the sacred 'action' or 'plot' was said to consist invariably of the following elements:

1. An *agon* or struggle of the year against its enemy, of light against darkness, of summer against winter. (The *agon* later becomes a verbal duel, e.g. Ajax, Medea.)

2. A *pathos* [suffering] of the year–*daemon*, usually a ritual or sacrificial death, in which *Adonis* or *Attis* is killed by the taboo animal; the *Pharmakos* is stoned to death; *Osiris, Dionysus, Pentheus* or *Hippolytus* are torn to pieces (*sparagmos*).

3. A *messenger*. The reason for this element is easy to see, since the *pathos* seldom or never actually takes place before the eyes of the audience. . . .

4. A *threnos* or lament for the dead. . . .

5 and 6. An *anagnorisis* – discovery and recognition – of the dead and mutilated *daemon*, which is followed by his resurrection from the grave and his apotheosis or epiphany. . . . This naturally goes hand in hand with a *peripeteia* or change from pain to joy. . . .

These ritual elements constitute, as it were, the skeleton of the tragedy. (Placing the tragedy in spring was psychologically necessary due to its origin in ritual.) Basing his thesis on the dramas of the three great Attic tragedians [Sophocles, Euripides and Aeschylus], Murray shows that in almost all their works the rigid liturgical structure underpins the lively, dynamic body of an imaginative work of art, even though, understandably enough, the constituent parts have been occasionally mixed together and conflated. The strict sequence has been most faithfully retained in those plays whose hero is identical with the ancient *sacer ludus* (Dionysus and Hippolytus, also Orestes).[181]

Subsequently, this development went even further: we are now no longer dealing with a *narrative account* of a dismembered *daemon* undergoing his 'epiphany', or even with the *structure* of the consecutive peripeteias in his story (which form the basis of a different plot-line) but with a *principle*, which has absorbed the basic characteristics of the narrative and reassembled them in a form that gives it a new quality.

This, *as a principle*, permeates the structure of all possible kinds of artistic composition.

In the course of its progress, the principle oscillates between being directly figurative and moving away as far as possible from figurative representation in the direction of pure principle. This does not only involve a simple forward development in a straight line; it can also include unexpected reversals and regressions.

The principle itself can be subject to a threefold form of internal modification.

Most amusing of all are examples of unmediated 'physicality', without which the unity of a work of art cannot be constructed.

Let us take three examples of 'regression'. They relate to the 16th and 17th centuries, and belong, of course, to that sphere which bases its success on the implantation and cultivation of the regressive aspects of human psychology, namely religion.

A little book entitled *Curiosités théologiques par un bibliophile* (Paris, Garnier, pp. 335–9) gives the following curious examples:

Dévotes salutations aux membres sacrés de la glorieuse Vierge Marie par le Révérend Père J.H., Capucin (Paris, 1678). 'Ce livret ne se compose que d'une demi-feuille in-16. Un littérateur bien connu et amateur fervent des livres rares, Charles Modier, l'a signalé. . . .'

No less amusing is another example from the same passage:

Le Livre de la toute belle sans pair qui est la Vierge Marie (Paris, 1520) contains some bizarre chapters, to judge by their headings: 'Méditation dévote du nez de la Vierge Marie. Comme le sacré ventre de la Vierge est la fontaine de la vie. Méditation aux cuisses qui sont force et espérance. De l'office de l'oreille. Méditation aux épaules . . .' [. . . .]

Instead of piling up examples of this kind, we would do better to consider another form of application of the principle.

Whereas in earliest times the unity of the *body* was the principle that consolidated social unity, so the *name* of a body may similarly function as a consolidating principle. Indeed, we know of a period when the name was equivalent to the body and the signifier to the signified object.

A very ancient form of word combination, the acrostic, may serve as a most vivid example of this.

Let us begin with the acrostic which invariably figures on the title-page of the collected works of Gogol; this, as far as is known, is his first surviving work and dates from the time of his schooldays at Nezhin:

> *S*uch is the image of an impious life
> *P*rone to frighten every monk,
> *I*ntractable inmate of a monastery,
> *R*ightly unfrocked for his sin,

In which lies the cause of his
*D*isgrace and shame.
*O*h reader, have patience, for his
*N*ame lies in the first letters of each line.[182]

A footnote indicates that this was . . . written about one of Gogol's schoolfellows, Borozdin, whom Gogol persecuted with jibes, calling him 'Spiridon, the unfrocked monk' because of his very short haircut. In the evening of 12 December (St Spiridon's day [in the Orthodox calendar]) he displayed a banner that he had made himself, which showed the devil cropping a dervish's hair and bearing the above acrostic. [. . .]

An acrostic (from the Greek *akros* = 'extremity, outer end' and *stichos* = 'verse') is the name given to a set of verses, the first or last letters of whose lines, when read in sequence, form either one word or several words that make a certain sense. . . . Acrostics originate in remotest antiquity. [. . . .] According to Cicero, Ennius composed acrostics, but this detestable form of poetry was not accorded any honour until the first centuries of the Christian era, i.e. a period of decadence. It is indeed to this era that the synopses which preface the twenty comedies of Plautus belong. These synopses consist of as many lines as there are letters in the title of each play and each line begins with a letter of that title. The synopses are generally attributed to Priscian, a sixth-century grammarian. Here is an example from the *Casina*:

*C*onservam uxorem conservi duo expetunt,
*A*lium senex adlegat, alium filius.
*S*ors adjurat senem; verum decipitur dolis.
*I*ta ei subpicitur pro puella servulus
*N*equam, qui dominum muleat atque villicum.
*A*dolescens ducit civem Casinam cognitam.

(Two slaves of the same master woo a young woman slave on behalf, respectively, of the old master and his son. Fate favours the old man, but he is duped by a trick. A brutal slave, who beats his master and the master's tenant, is substituted for the young woman. The son marries her and soon afterwards she is made free.)

We know of no examples in our demotic tongue from the Middle Ages, but they abound from the Renaissance onwards. Here is an acrostic in praise of Paris, composed by Gromet:

*P*aisible domaine,
*A*moureux vergier,
*R*epos sans danger,
*I*ustice certaine,
*S*cience haultaine,
    C'est Paris entier.

The celebrated macaronic poet Teofilo Folengo concealed the name of his mistress, Girolama Dieda, in an acrostic *canzone*, and Clément Marot did the same for his mistress in a *rondeau. . . .*[183]

In a chapter of his *Amenities of Literature* entitled 'First Sources of Modern History', [Isaac] D'Israeli makes mention of 'Ralph or Ranulph Higden, author of the *Polychronicon*, an encyclopaedic summary of human knowledge as it stood in the 14th century', which 'was no more, as was realised later, than a paraphrase of the *Polycratica temporum* by another monk by the name of Roger.' Even so: 'The initial letters of each chapter combine into a sentence which states that Ralph, a monk of Chester, is the author of the work.'[184]

Finally, let us cite an ultra-modern example. More than any other form of literature, detective fiction has echoes of certain ancient patterns and systems in its methods and in the ways that it creates its effects. Below, we give another example in a different connection. One of these days I intend to devote a special little treatise to the explanation of these characteristics of the detective novel. The example I am about to quote is only a game, but it is significant that it was precisely an acrostic that was chosen for this kind of game. It is taken from the table of chapter headings in one novel from a collection of detective stories by one of the best writers in that genre, Ellery Queen: *The Greek Coffin Mystery*.

1.	*T*omb	22.	*B*ottom
2.	*H*unt	23.	*Y*arns
3.	*E*nigma	24.	*E*xhibit
4.	*G*ossip	25.	*L*eftover
5.	*R*emains	26.	*L*ight
6.	*E*xhumation	27.	*E*xchange
7.	*E*vidence	28.	*R*equisition
8.	*K*illed	29.	*Y*ield
9.	*C*hronicles	30.	*Q*uiz
10.	*O*men	31.	*U*pshot
11.	*F*oresight	32.	*E*lleryana
12.	*F*acts	33.	*E*ye-opener
13.	*I*nquiries	34.	*N*ucleus[185]
14.	*N*ote		
15.	*M*aple		
16.	*Y*east		
17.	*S*tigma		
18.	*T*estament		
19.	*E*xpose		
20.	*R*eckoning		
21.	*Y*earbook		

Here, it would seem, we are coming close to an unexpected realm: we know that modern games and sporting contests had a cult origin in times past, and in keeping with that origin they are linked with archaic forms of symbolism. Interestingly enough, ball games such as tennis, cricket, basketball, etc., were known to the Mayan civilisation of Yucatan, while in other regions, such as ancient Persia, they symbolised the world passing back and forth between the hands of Ormuzd and the hands of Ariman, i.e. swinging between the principles of good and evil. Not only that: the ball also symbolised the alternation of night and day, because during a game one of its halves is inevitably illuminated by the sun while the other is in shadow.

Other games are even more interesting, since they do not represent 'cosmic' concepts but are connected with the origins and development of human consciousness. In the popular children's game of charades, one side silently acts out a scenario, and then asks the other side to guess what it is and to state *in words* the content of the mime. Obviously this is a game which perpetuates the memory of a transition from kinetic to verbal speech. Even more likely, it reproduces the stage when that transition was in the process of being established. It is curious that [in the Russian version of this game] the person who has to do the guessing is called 'the king'; this derives from the fact that riddles of this kind were posed by priests to kings about to conduct a sacrifice, and the riddles themselves consisted of a game which required the ability to perceive the conceptual content within an imagistic form. In other words, it was always a game played between an old and a new conception of natural phenomena and of reality, in exactly the same way that the game of charades treats the question of the mimetic and the verbal expression of the same thought. When analysing the nature of detective fiction, I cited detailed examples of the setting, conditions and content of similar games in the Vedic culture of India.

Now let us consider games that directly concern our present study. Here we must note that the 'Osiris principle' has also survived in a number of games which continue to entertain us to this day. There is a game, for instance, in which you take a line of poetry and break it up into as many separate words as there are players – minus one. Each word is given to a player, who has to concoct a new sentence in which he 'hides' the word he has been given. Then the player who was left out of the word distribution is invited to listen to the newly devised sentences, which contain the hidden 'members' of the line of verse that was broken up into single words. He must then spot those words, camouflaged in the new sentences, and reassemble them into the original line of poetry.

We may mention in passing that this category of games also includes that great modern pastime of idle minds, the crossword puzzle. Does not the same principle apply? And is not a girl who spends an evening solving a crossword acting just like Isis, searching out separate word-limbs and putting those scattered word-limbs together in order to constitute a 'body' out of words, the letters or syllables of which were scattered among the word-limbs of the clues?

The American game of 'anagrams' also belongs in this category: indeed it is even closer to montage as we understand it, because it allows one not only to disentangle the jumbled-up letters but also to create from them arbitrary verbal combinations and images.

Our category also includes all the innumerable forms of 'patience' (we shall not forget that in the past cards were used for 'magical' purposes, a practice that survives to this day in 'fortune-telling' with cards). All types of patience can, after all, be reduced to the process of breaking up a fixed sequence of cards ('shuffling') and then reassembling them *by highly entertaining, formalised methods* into a particular, predetermined combination.

Finally, there are instances in which a person's name or an emblem serves directly, by the shape of its outline, as the unifying factor for a group of people, symbolising through that emblem or name the unity of millions of sub-groups. One only has to recall our sporting events at which hundreds of gymnasts lay their young bodies down on the asphalt of Red Square or when dozens of aircraft flying in formation trace the initial letters of our beloved country in the sky or the name of the man who is dearest to us.

Something that is directly relevant to our category is the intriguing instance of so-called *vers figurés*. Here the montage form, as a form involving duration in time, coincides with a form of composition by outline, i.e. the 'frame' form. In other words, duration is not expressed in time but in space: the method is for the successive lines of varying length to form a column, the outline of which delineates something, usually allegorical, that illustrates the theme of the poem or simply the object that the poem is describing.

> *Vers figurés*, that is to say poems laid out in the shape of material objects, were invented by Simmias of Rhodes, who, according to Vossius, lived in the reign of Ptolemy Lagidus around 324 BC.
>
> Apart from 'The Wings', 'The Egg' and 'The Axe' written by this poet, antiquity has also bequeathed to us the two 'Altars' by Dosiadas; 'The Syrinx' by Theocritus; 'The Altar', 'The Syrinx' and 'The Organ' by Porphyrius. . . .
>
> Simmias' 'The Wings' are each made up of six 'feathers' or six choriambic verses which gradually diminish in metre and consequently in length according to their position in the 'wing', until the last one contains only three syllables. Simmias intended the subject of his poem to correspond in some degree to its form. In it he speaks of a *winged god*. . . .

Even more entertaining is the composition of his poem 'The Egg', since in this case not only is the shape delineated but also a predetermined *path of movement around its graphic form*, or if you like, a path determined through a *succession of montage sequences (which, in this particular instance, amounts to the same thing)*.

In this paradoxical example we have the fusion in a *physical* unity of what we have defined as belonging to the fundamental unity of its qualitative variables: *outline* in the frame and the *path* that runs through montage sequences.

[In] 'The Egg' . . . each end is formed by short lines becoming progressively longer as they approach the middle. These verses are in different metres, and the poet, who spared himself no trouble, has chosen metres that are the most awkward and the least commonplace. But that is not all: read straight through from top to bottom it it absurd, unintelligible, an enigma without a clue. In order to make some sort of sense of it, one must go from the first verse to the last, from the second to the penultimate, from the third to the antepenultimate and so on until the two verses in the middle. . . . The disposition of the verses decides their subject matter. The poet is presenting his readers with a Dorian nightingale's egg . . . which Mercury took from under his mother's wings to give it to mankind. Thus the twenty-two verses of this bizarre composition express this clear and ingenious allusion.

'The Organ', the best poem by Publius Optatianus Porphyrius, who lived under the Emperor Constantine, is made up of three parts placed one above the other. . . . The shape of this poem is of some interest, because it exactly represents that of the ancient water-powered organ.

Curious, too, is the remark made in this connection by Ludovic Lalanne, from whose work we have taken most of our examples:[186] 'In contrast to the Greeks, who engaged in these trivialities in the period when their literature was flourishing, the Latin poets only indulged in them during their era of decadence.'

I do not think Lalanne is justified in adopting such a censorious tone ('trivialities'). I believe, with good reason, that examples of the kind are indeed to be found among the Greeks in their periods of greatest brilliance and among the Romans during their decline.

Odd though it may seem to us today, a stage of such bizarre 'inventions' in the development of literature is entirely logical. It is quite as logical in that development as is the example of the Indian elephant to which we have referred above. The principles underlying these compositions reflected the remarkable thought patterns that are to be found at the stages when a culture is moving towards ultimate awareness of the proper places for such concepts as theme, content, form, framework, progression and other elements which subsequently become the normal, accepted constituents of works of art. It is equally natural that this should manifest itself among Roman writers in a period of decadence, i.e. of regression. There it was a sign of a downward slide from the level of perfection which mankind had attained in art and poetry and a regression to an 'infantile' stage. The 'childishness' of *children's* behaviour is normal and charming. Childishness in *adult* behaviour is absurd (although it can often be no less charming in our perception of an individual;

much of the charm of Paul Robeson, for instance, is due precisely to this).

The last word in this argument belongs to Rabelais. Rabelais found the only appropriate place for this phenomenon in both developed and developing literature. That place is in punning humour. One of the most ironic passages in *Pantagruel* concerns the higher wisdom of wine, '*dans la Dive Bouteille*'. Panurge's prayers addressed to 'the divine bottle' are laid out in the shape of a *bottle*, and two chapters later one finds a *glass* made up in the same way.[187] In fact, there are actually examples of this form combined with . . . an acrostic! A *tour de force* of this kind was composed in the 9th century:

> In the 9th century Rabau-Maur, who was first Abbot of Fulda and later Bishop of Mainz, his native town, wrote in Latin a *Treatise on Praising the Cross* in two books (Pforzheim, 1501; in-folio). This work, which for a long time enjoyed an enormous reputation, is a collection of four-sided acrostics of thirty-five verses, each verse having thirty-five letters and making up mystic forms of the cross.
>
> . . . The same century provides a poem inserted into the *History of Blois* by Jean Bernier, which is a worthy rival of Rabau's work. It is in praise of Guillaume, Count of Blois, and the first and last letters of each line make up the following:
>
> *Te virtute crucis soter, Guillelme, coronat.*
>
> Moreover the same line is repeated in such a way as to form a cross in the centre.

Another form of poetic curiosity, the so-called 'cento', is even closer to montage. Its basis is an interesting method of assembling and juxtaposing literary fragments from various sources with the aim of lending a new meaning to the resulting compilation. The remarkable films made by Esfir Shub are essentially 'ciné-centos'; in her work, the use of this aspect of the potentialities of montage is displayed in its purest form. Sequences from newsreels shot in the context of *one* set of events – indeed, within one ideological system – are totally transformed, in both senses of the word, by new juxtapositions and combinations with other fragments of *other* events and stories. (Particularly striking is her use of tsarist newsreels in *The Fall of the Romanov Dynasty*.[188])

It is curious that here, too, as in so many instances, methods that in other art forms would be no more than freakish or overdone kitsch are completely acceptable in the cinematic stage of their development. Indeed, more than that: it is precisely such elements that in cinema turn out to constitute the bedrock of its technique. (Compare examples from Memling's method; the stage at Donau-Eschingen; 'mobility' in the work of Daumier, Rodin or Watteau; the cento, etc.)

It certainly seems as though all art forms *in their extreme manifestations*, i.e. where they attempt to expand the limits of their potential and their material, invariably end up by trying to appropriate the rudiments of the art of the future: the art of cinema. And that when they attempt this, things which in those other art forms can only be done successfully by outstanding talents and geniuses, in cinema are found to be the basic principles of its methods!

Here is an example taken from antiquity:

Cento (from the Latin *cento*, a patchwork garment made from scraps): a work compiled from verses or prose extracts drawn from one or several authors.

The most famous is the Nuptial Song by Ausonius (310–394 AD), in which the poet, challenged by the Emperor Valentinian, succeeded in making Virgil's chaste muse obscene. This is how he described his own work:

'It is', he wrote in a dedicatory letter to Paulus:

'a pure feat of memory: I gathered together a lot of disconnected scraps and made a whole out of these fragments. . . . A little work in which I have made a coherent narrative from cut-out pieces, a whole made up of discrepant parts, a burlesque constructed from serious ideas, and which though using the property of others is yet my own. . . . One cuts out these rags at all the caesuras allowed by heroic verse. . . .'

. . . In the same period that Ausonius was writing, Proba Falconia, wife of the Praetorian Prefect Anicius, composed a history of the Old and New Testaments, which, published together with the works of Ausonius (Venice, 1472; in-folio), was subsequently reprinted many times. Here are several verses, purporting to describe how God forbids Adam and Eve to touch the forbidden fruit (A stands for the *Aeneid*, G for the *Georgics*):

A 2/712   Vos, famuli, quae dicam animis advertiste vestris:
A 2/21   Est in conspectu/ramis felicibus arbos.   G 2/81
A 7/692   Quam neque fas igni cuiquam nec sternere ferro,
A 7/608   Religione sacrae/nunquam concessa moveri   A 3/700
A 11/591 Hac quicumque sacrum/decerpserit arbore foetus.   A6/141
A 11/849 Moret luet merita/nec me sententia vertit.   A 1/241

A 2/712   Ye servants, heed what I say.
A 2/21   There lies in sight/A tree with joyous boughs   G 2/81
A 7/692   Whom none may lay low with fire or steel.
A 7/608   By religious awe/
          Fate forbade that she ever be disturbed   A 3/700
A 11/591 That her sacred limbs/
          Hath plucked from the tree . . . the fruitage   A 6/141
A 11/849 Shall pay the debt of death/
          Lest the thought turn me.   A 1/241.[189]

Before becoming one of the components of cinematic technique, the 'cento method' went through one further stage. We might call it the stage of the 'pictorial cento'. This variant appeared, and was enthusiastically taken up as a fashion, in the 18th century. The craze was known as *découpage* or cutting-out. This is what the *Dictionnaire de l'ameublement et de la décoration depuis le XIIIe siècle jusqu'à nos jours* [Dictionary of Furnishing and Decoration from the 13th Century to the Present Day] has to say about it:

> In the 18th century . . . a kind of 'cutting-out' made its appearance; it deserves to be recorded because it has its place among the strangest crazes that gripped our forebears. This is how the newspapers of the time announced the sudden onset of the passion for 'cut-outs': 'Embroidery and crochet-work are out of fashion' – writes the *Mercure de France* of December 1727 – 'knitting-needles and shuttles have been abandoned, nothing but "cutting-out" will do nowadays; it is applied to every kind of furnishings that lend themselves to it – fire-screens, draught-screens, hangings, ceilings, the interiors of carriages and sedan chairs – it is put everywhere. This fashion has driven up the prices of prints and engravings to extraordinary levels, and as there are not many dealers who sell them and colour them, their shops are never empty. As soon as a gentleman enters a lady's house he is given a print, he takes his scissors from his pocket and cuts it out. A skill at cutting-out is a new kind of accomplishment. This is how it is done. You take an engraving or a coloured print; from it you cut out flowers, animals, trees, bouquets or some other object or figure, depending on the composition that you wish to make. . . . When you have cut out enough pieces needed to compose the desired subject, you take the object you intend to decorate. . . .'

Here one may include the parallel tradition of those masters of *découpage* who were not merely playing at it in amateurish fashion but were using it as a specific medium of artistic expression, such as Max Ernst (e.g. his collection entitled *La Femme: 100 têtes*), or those who used this technique in fighting for their political convictions (e.g. the photomontages of John Heartfield and Rodchenko; see illustrations).[190]

Even so, the most striking example of the genre precedes even eighteenth-century *découpage*. It resembles *découpage*, in that it combines two separate elements in one picture, but it is even more reminiscent of pure montage, possessing all its characteristics except one: consecutiveness.

This is a seventeenth-century illustration to the life of St John of the Cross (see illustration). At first sight the picture is merely puzzling, especially the incomprehensible foreshortening (which relates to no pictorial tradition) in the right-hand half of the picture. On closer inspection, however, we see that the picture consists in essence of two 'montage sequences', one a general view and the other a close-up of the cross. In the 'general view' the saint is looking at the cross (in the left-hand corner), whereas in the close-up the cross is shown precisely at the angle from which the monk sees it when looking at it from above and to the left of it. That is the explanation of the incomprehensible foreshortening of the crucifixion! It is, I think, an example quite unique of its kind, both for its period and for its thinking in 'montage terms'.

Having considered the above examples from the 16th, 17th and 18th centuries, let us return to the next step taken by the 'Osiris method'.

I do not know how literature is taught in schools nowadays. In my day, the textbooks by Nezelyonov and Savodnik were invariably used for the study of the Russian classics. They made us compile descriptions of such figures as Famusov, Chatsky, Chichikov or Akaki Akakievich[191] *from the clues to their character traits to be found scattered throughout the book in question.* Ever since my schooldays, thanks to that method of teaching, I remember thinking of a writer's work as being something like a game of 'hunt-the-thimble': an author surreptitiously creates a person made up of many, many traits, and then cuts

Max Ernst, *La Femme: 100 têtes*

Decipher the Latin text in the picture (probably a pun on St John *of the Cross*) [marginal note by S.M.E.]

him up into little bits and scatters them around, hidden among descriptions of landscapes – simply in order to make life more difficult for schoolchildren! Even though the 'Savodnik method' is liable in large degree to instil a regrettably mechanistic notion of a writer's work, and though certain authors do indeed tackle their craft in just such a crassly mechanical fashion (*Nomina sunt odiosa!* [No names, no pack drill]), on the other hand it cannot be denied that the 'Osiris method' is undoubtedly at work here too. If you provide an 'official questionnaire' type of character sketch of a personage before the beginning of a novel, you relieve the reader of the need to 'collate' his impressions of your hero's character; but you will exclude him from the process whereby the picture of the character is built up in the course of the novel, and you will never achieve that fullness of empathy with him that you will produce by using the other method. This, of course, has nothing to do with the business of editing or the mechanics of cutting – *as is the case in montage!* – but it concerns the carefully planned route chosen to *reveal*, facet by facet, the fully rounded picture of a character, along which the author guides you.

In literature, however, we also find examples of the *physical* assembly of a person or an event out of 'fragments'. What is more, there is a whole genre of literature in which this is not merely one method but is . . . the basic content of the plot, underlying a multiplicity of sub-plots. This is the second time that we have had occasion to mention . . . the detective novel. In it, a picture of the crime takes shape through the gradual accumulation of information, and the identity of the criminal is revealed by the piling up of hints and clues. 'Dionysus' pure and simple. And is not this 'Dionysian' intensity one of the secrets that make detective novels so 'gripping' and why one 'can't put them down'?! Just leaf through any volume of Sherlock Holmes. . . .[192]

Matters become even more interesting when we come to the third form which this principle can take. So far we have observed it in the variants that derive from the unity of a *physical body* and we have pursued others based on a *name*. The third aspect is *via the body as a process*: the process of birth, growth, development, decline and death – in other words, where the unifying factor in a work of art is the biographical curve of the fate of a human being. Let us remind ourselves that one of the most ancient forms of literature is the *hagiography*, or – if we extend hagiography beyond the individual to an account of a community or a society – the *chronicle*. In these there is as yet no distinction between narrative and compositional elements. Let us take an example where both composition and content deliberately converge on the latter and are thereby artificially made to coincide fully with each other: a person's life is not only the content of the work but also determines the shape in which it is put together, or, if you like, the other way round: not only does a person's life clearly articulate the shape of the work (just as years and the sequence of events naturally articulate annals and chronicles, be they [Alexei Tolstoy's historical satire] *Gostomysl'* or Holinshed's *Chronicles*), but the stages of his life also constitute its content and plot, as in Leonid Andreyev's *Life of* *a Man.* More interesting than this, though, are more complicated examples of which the most important is now enjoying a colossal success in both its forms. I refer to the great current fashion for published diaries, memoirs, collections of letters and correspondence, not only of outstanding historical personalities but also of quite ordinary rank-and-file people. With these one must also include the genre of so-called *biographies romanisées* or fictionalised biographies, which in the past decade have provided an abundant harvest of books.*

Nor should we forget that the contemporary Soviet cinema has scored some of its greatest triumphs with just such fictionalised biographies. Think of *Chapayev*, *The Baltic Deputy* (Timiryazev's portrayal of Polezhayev), *Peter the First*, *Suvorov* and *Alexander Nevsky*.[193] The same has been true in America too, with such films as for example *Pasteur* and *Viva Villa!*[194] We have already mentioned this genre as being one which in literature tends, through certain processes involving a loss of the work's *image-creating structure*, to become simply a chain of facts. But that chain of facts can also be regarded as the source and the starting-point from which the work moves upwards and onwards towards an integral image-creating quality, assembling the chain of bare facts into a generalised image of the events and the biography into a generalised image of the central character. The historically objective individual personage is replaced, through art, by a generalised type. The chronicle of events is qualitatively enhanced to become a network of dramatic conflicts that are the essence of tragedy.

This is perhaps similar to the process that takes place within the artistic creativity of an individual dramatist, especially if his work is wide enough in scope. So it is in Shakespeare's works, particularly in his earlier chronicle plays, i.e. his *biographies romanisées*, and in the universalised tragedies of the period of his maturity when his genius was in full flower. Shakespeare is shown at his best in equal degree by both genres, which are either modelled on a body in action and maturation in the 'chronological' mode of biography and chronicle, or on a body emerging and assembling itself into a dynamic portrayal of character (on the 'Osiris' model).

Aksionov has written graphically about this shift of genre in general and not specifically with reference to Shakespeare. He dwells in detail on the way that all or most of the kings managed to be vindicated or whitewashed, and in doing so he shows how the only king whom the English chroniclers were permitted to depict as a monster was the last of the Plantagenets, who had to

---

*To this genre must undoubtedly be added such currently popular compilations as *The Living Pushkin* and *Gogol to the Life* by Veresayev, or *Pushkin Recollected by his Contemporaries*. One may say of these that the impressions of a writer, scattered here and there among the impressions left to us by his associates, have been reassembled by the skilful hand of a montage-editor into a life-like portrait. Note once again how *the intensity and vitality of perception* conveyed by this lively, dynamic image, which *emerges* out of fragments, in many ways surpasses the '*constructed*' depiction of a writer to be found in any conventional biography.

be overthrown in order that the new (Tudor) dynasty might come to the throne.

> where such a character [as Richard III] was concerned, writers could be uninhibited, and they could depart from historical accuracy – not towards whitewashing his character but towards blackening it as much as possible. . . . The right to do this was widely used, and the character of Richard III was progressively vilified with every new account of his reign, until he was transformed into a completely unhistorical villain. In revenge for such injustice, it would seem, this stage figure so far outgrew the confines of the theatre that it smothered any remaining historical elements and turned a mere chronicle play into true historical drama. This king's final crime was to destroy the historical chronicle as a traditional form of stage villainy. But for such an analysis of the human personality to have been conducted within the limitations of dramatised history, it was necessary to create such a potential interest in the human personality in general as could not possibly have been found in the early days, when chronicle texts were simply transferred into the prosaic dialogue of the first versions of this genre. . . .
>
> For this [i.e. a greatly increased concern with the nature of human personality] to have happened, a new social system had to come into being, a system which created a new epoch. In it, the question of the nature of the human personality was posed anew with a fullness and scope unequalled since antiquity (when, of course, it had been expressed in the particular terms of its historical context).
>
> Just such an epoch, which raised the question of personality to heights of unprecedented importance, did come into being: this was the era of the Renaissance, and personality stands at the centre of attention in the work of Shakespeare and the whole Pleiad of his contemporaries. In Shakespeare's work the human personality stands at the centre of the composition, the centre of the project.[195]

For Shakespeare, however, the solution to the problem of the human personality was different from that put forward by Marlowe and his coevals: 'the personality was to be valued, but not in the way that Marlowe thought of it. The personality only becomes valuable when it is harmoniously structured. The doctrine of the harmony of the personality is fundamental to all Shakespeare's works' (Aksionov).

This fact alone leads us to suspect that, since the human personality occupied the centre of his attention as a creative artist, Shakespeare's working methods are bound to include the 'method of Dionysus and Osiris' interpreted and applied in his own unique way. When this supposition is put to the test, the results exceed even our boldest assumptions. Furthermore, they confront us in a wholly new area that we have hitherto not touched upon in the examples so far cited. This justifies turning our attention to Shakespeare in greater detail and enables us to crown our chain of examples with the most vivid and striking manifestation of our subject matter.

But first we should say a few words on montage in Shakespeare's works in general. Here we must say at once that in this technique he is an absolute master. He is equally strong in the art of montage when it is a question of handling his dramatic primary sources, which in terms of montage reworking – 're-montage' – are in many cases his own works; Aksionov states as much when giving detailed analyses of specific examples of this. Here it should be noted that 're-montage' is profoundly ideological, tendentious and meant to ensure that in its 're-scripted' and 're-montaged' form the material, which in itself had no connection with Shakespeare's ideals, would be made to serve his ideas and in particular the most fundamental of them: the harmony of the personality and its clash with the discord that rules in the surrounding environment.

> He accomplished this task by means of his incomparably skilful reworking of the material that came to hand. Whatever it might have been, he always made it serve to illustrate that theme and, using the material of his predecessors he created new and original works, which only in the terminology of modern literary scholarship can be called a fourth redaction of an age-old text.
>
> (Aksionov)

As for the basic methods of montage, in particular the montage of short episodes, Shakespeare had, of course, mastered them to absolute perfection. One only need recall the composition of the short, separate, episodes of battle in the last acts of *Macbeth* or *Richard III* and his astounding skill in creating from these tiny fragments of human conflict such powerful images of the totality of a battle.

Many of the other Elizabethans, incidentally, were skilled in this art. I think that an unsurpassed example of the contrapuntal montage of fragmentary scenes, in which several plot-lines are pursued simultaneously and whose totality adds up to a marvellous generalised image – an image of the dizzy whirl of a fairground – is Ben Jonson's structuring of *Bartholomew Fair*. Besides, Webster even used such a dubious film-maker's device as the purely cinematic technique of the flashback. Let us recall the remarkable scene from his play *The White Devil*, in which the Conjuror shows Duke Brachiano by a 'flashback' a dumb show of the scene of his wife's murder (Act II, Scene 2):

CONJUROR   Pray sit down.
            Put on this nightcap, sir, 'tis charmed – and now
            I'll show you by my strong commanding art
            The circumstance that breaks your duchess' heart.

A DUMB SHOW

Enter suspiciously JULIO *and another: they draw a
curtain where* BRACHIANO'S *picture is; they put on
spectacles of glass, which cover their eyes and
noses, and then burn perfumes afore the picture,
and wash the lips of the picture; that done,
quenching the fire, and putting off their spectacles,
they depart laughing.*

    Enter ISABELLA *in her night-gown, as to bedward,
with lights; after her* COUNT LODOVICO, GIOVANNI,
*and others waiting on her: she kneels down as to
prayers, then draws the curtain of the picture,
does three reverences to it, and kisses it thrice; she
faints and will not suffer them to come near it; dies;
sorrow expressed in* GIOVANNI, *and in*
COUNT LODOVICO.

    She is conveyed out solemnly.

BRACHIANO   Excellent! Then she's dead.

CONJUROR   She's poisoned.
By the fumed picture. 'Twas her custom nightly,
Before she went to bed, to go and visit
Your picture, and to feed her eyes and lips
On the dead shadow: Doctor Julio,
Observing this, infects it with an oil,
And other poisoned stuff, which presently
Did suffocate her spirits. . . .[196]

Then follows a technically similar scene depicting another murder.

Let us, however, return to Shakespeare. The truly interesting examples are still to come.

In 1935 Caroline Spurgeon published her book *Shakespeare's Imagery and What It Tells Us*. As its title indicates, this book is devoted to a detailed analysis of the verbal structure of those images which Shakespeare uses in his plays. Here we shall use this valuable work of research to throw light on the very essence of several of his dramas; in particular, we shall look to see whether there is to be found within Shakespeare's imagery that same motif of the human body torn to pieces and made whole again, which we have been pursuing through all the multiplicity of compositional techniques. At first it was simultaneously both a depiction and a structural principle; later it suffered relapses, the emphasis was shifted from the body to the processes of physical movement, etc., etc. Hitherto we have always examined it at the level of the major compositional elements. Let us now study this method at the level of the internal structure of the very fabric of imagery, and for this we shall now turn to Shakespeare to see whether he can provide us with some examples.

Where his overall compositional structure is concerned, Shakespeare applies the *principle* of the unity of the whole and its parts to such an exalted degree that we would search in vain among his works for any glaringly *obvious* examples in this area. With Shakespeare, everything is so harmoniously integrated on a human scale – as opposed to a superhuman scale, as is the case, for instance, with Walt Whitman, where it is precisely this which enables the structural ligatures of his technique to be laid bare. Shakespeare, however, enriches us in equally vivid fashion when we come to examine this new field of application of the same principles.

For the very fact that in Shakespeare's works the human personality lies at the core of his fundamental theme and is his central preoccupation makes us assume that this basic idea will 'demand' to be given expression in images associated with the human body. This motif must occur as the pervasive, *central* theme of all his writing, if every individual theme within his tragedies undergoes the treatment described in her book by Caroline Spurgeon. We are, in fact, prepared for this in advance, because it is the general thesis of her work: 'In the tragedies [this imagery] is closely connected with the central theme, which it supplements and illuminates, sometimes with extraordinary force, as in *Hamlet* and *King Lear*, or with rare beauty, as in *Romeo and Juliet* and *Antony and Cleopatra*.'[197]

In describing the way in which Shakespeare 'materialises' his themes in concrete, tangible images, she writes thus: 'When we trace out in detail this series of images we recognise that it is a good example of Shakespeare's peculiar habit of seeing emotional or mental situations throughout a play in repeatedly recurring physical pictures.'[198]

But our expectations are actually surpassed by the examples of this kind that we encounter in the text itself. The human body turns out to be treated on an equal level with two of nature's other kingdoms – flora and fauna – which are generally regarded as more popular areas from which to draw images and metaphors.

In this respect Shakespeare proves to be the first among his contemporaries not only in the quantity but also in the quality of those images of the human body and its parts with which his works are filled. He presents us with the body in various aspects: first, the body as such; second, 'the body as process' or the body in action. But whereas in the composition of a whole major class of his plays – the history plays – we find what we have called 'the body in action', i.e. in plays whose composition consists of a movement through the biography [of their central characters], this image of 'the body as process' is just as frequent, but in them he introduces in equal, proportionate degree the full scope of movement itself: what we find here are *not elements of the biographical progression of the body* but elements of *the body's physical movements in general*. (Nowhere so far have we cited this variant of the basic bodily archetype; we have been saving it for our study of Shakespeare, where it is more abundantly present than anywhere else!)

The third type of treatment of the body is the very frequently used method of 'personification' of phenomena through human imagery. It is quite clear that all three types belong to the same category of ever more subtle application of one and the same method, which moves further and further away from the immediate application of the principles that we have been discussing. Here are the results of Caroline Spurgeon's analysis of this range of imagery:

> Indeed, pictures drawn from the body and bodily action form the largest single section of all Shakespeare's images . . . and this apart from his very large number of 'personifications', which two groups it is difficult always clearly to separate. Certain types of bodily image belong to the common stock of Elizabethan imagery, especially parts of the body: face, eye, tongue, etc.; and particular actions, such as bearing a burden on the back, falling from a height, treading a path, climbing, swimming and so on. (This is also of more general interest because it emphasises the charac-teristic that interests us in image depiction even beyond the confines of Shakespeare – E.) But even allowing for these, the proportion of Shakespeare's body images to the whole is considerably larger than that of any of the other dramatists examined. Ben Jonson comes nearest to him as regards number, but it is significant that in the five plays of his examined there is no image of swift bodily action, save two of dancing, neither of which conveys any feeling of lightness or of quick movement. No one of the other dramatists approaches Shakespeare in the number and vividness of his images drawn from quick, nimble action, such as jumping, leaping, diving, running, sliding, climbing and dancing.[199]

Here, I think, we might say that in the structuring of his images Shakespeare has also progressed beyond the stage of phasal perception, beyond the aesthetics of phase, and into the region of compositional dynamics which flows from the relationship *between* phases, from the combination of phases, from phases which converge into an image of movement, from the interrelation of montage sequences, in fact. In his imagery there is a transition from *the assembly and disposition of random extremities* to a different model: the assembly and disposition of the same extremities but in conditions of *sequentially changing* positions in the context not of a body that is torn apart *in itself* but of a body that is breaking up the static configuration of its parts as it moves from phase to phase of a movement. The transfer of this to a sequence of visual images is not merely one of the methods of film-making: it is the fundamental phenomenon of cinema itself!

There is something else remarkable in Shakespeare's works, namely that the two next most frequently used sources of his imagery – flora and fauna – are also chosen from, as it were, a human aspect, 'interpreted in human terms', as though they were categories which preceded that natural kingdom which evolved into man. It is in this 'Darwinian' mode that Bradley in his *Shakespearian Tragedy*[200] (quoted by Spurgeon on p. 342) perceives them when, discussing *King Lear,* he characterises the abundance of animal metaphors in that tragedy as 'humanity . . . reeling back into the beast'. If perhaps in slightly less bloodthirsty terms, but no less consistently and frequently, Shakespeare (as Spurgeon points out) uses metaphors and images drawn from plants:

> Just as Bacon seems continually to see and reflect on human nature in terms of light and shade, so Shakespeare visualises human beings as plants and trees – choked with weeds, or well pruned and trained and bearing ripe fruit, sweet-smelling as roses or noxious as a weed. . . . Shakespeare, in the mouth of Iago, reflects that our bodies are gardens and our wills the gardeners, so that whatever is planted or sown in our own natures entirely depends on the power and authority of our wills.[201]

Such examples are numerous but what is interesting in them is the special viewpoint from which Shakespeare is *particularly attracted* to the vegetable kingdom:

> Shakespeare is particularly interested in the processes of growth and decay, and, as he expresses it in the fifteenth sonnet ('When I consider everything that grows'), in the likeness between men and plants in coming painfully and with many struggles and checks to perfection, to stay there but for a moment and then begin to decay.[202]

Thus even within his favourite image of *movement* there is also . . . movement, for what else is growth but the movement of movement itself?! But what is interesting here is something else. As we have seen, Shakespeare gives due weight to each phase of the development and variations of both structural elements and imagery in the technique of his craft: those elements which, in the primitive, initial stages of Dionysian tragedy were a physical depiction *through the body and the changes to which it was subjected* of an image of natural life as a whole. But the creative richness that is in Shakespeare's imagery goes even deeper than the 'Dionysian' model, deeper than that prototype of 'form as structure', deeper than that 'structural law': Shakespeare actually merges with what was the prototype in nature of the Dionysus-figure, the prototype for which the legend of the tragedy of Dionysus was a means of materialising the image through the physical material provided by his body.

For is not Dionysus himself a metaphor for the change and progression of the seasons on the one hand, and as such is he not a divinity of the vegetable kingdom with its inevitable alternation of growth and decay? Is he not the spirit of those cereals, of which the seed has to die in order to be resurrected and to burgeon again as a plant? And with this are closely linked age-old images in animal form: that is to say, the third most abundant source of Shakespeare's imagery.

However we may explain it, the fact remains that in peasant folklore the corn-spirit is very commonly conceived and represented in animal form. May not this fact explain the relation in which certain animals stood to the ancient deities of vegetation, Dionysus, Demeter, Adonis, Attis and Osiris . . . ?[203]

In three of Shakespeare's plays it is noteworthy that the human body appears as a recurrent image. Furthermore the body, especially in two of them and less so – for perfectly good reasons – in the third, appears in the imagery as quite as suffering and tormented as we have seen it to be in the subject matter of the myths of Dionysus and Osiris! The three plays are *King Lear*, *King John* and *Henry VIII*. Nor is it by chance that this subject should be so prominent in the imagery and metaphors of precisely these plays.

The balanced, harmonious body of the state is a projection [*Auswuchs*] of the harmony that should pertain in the human body. Whereas in his creative thought as an artist Shakespeare had already progressed beyond being restricted to depiction without the possibility of thinking in abstractions, in his model of the ideal polity he still sees the state as an organisation founded on resemblance to a human being – not yet in principle, but in form and likeness.

The image of the state, borrowed from Plutarch, which he presents in *Coriolanus*, is probably connected with Shakespeare's own ideal conceptions of the state:

Coriolanus, however, has a central symbol, and a very definite one, but it is significant that this has not been born out of the creator's feeling of the tragedy; it has just been taken over by him wholesale, with much else, from North's *Plutarch*.

It is the old tale, with which the play opens, expounded by Menenius, of the rebellion of the various members of the body, the citizens, against the belly, the senate, which they accuse of being idle while they do all the work, and the belly's answer, somewhat developed by Shakespeare, that, on the contrary, it is the 'storehouse and the shop of the whole body', sending out, through rivers of blood, sustenance to all. . . .

The king, statesman, soldier, horse and trumpeter are compared to the head, eye and heart, arm, leg and tongue, and Menenius laughingly taunts one of the basest of the citizens with being the great toe of the rebellion. The people are the hands, the tribunes are the 'tongues o' the common mouth', or they are the mouths themselves, as when Coriolanus, turning on them, asks: 'You being their mouths, why rule you not their teeth?'[204]

And herein lies the key to the reason why three plays that could otherwise never be classified in a single group – and which furthermore are set in widely different historical periods – are linked, thanks to recurrent imagery, under a common thematic denominator: the unity and harmony of the state in the likeness of the harmony of the well-balanced human being. (In *Richard III* the recurrent image is the garden, because the dominant theme is one of genealogy; hence also images of heraldry and allegories based on 'Plantagenet' that are close to heraldry.[205])

Thus we have revealed in Shakespeare each and every variant of the 'montage approach' and 'montage thinking', from the most atavistic examples (the 'Osiris principle' in his imagery) to the most sophisticated aspects of compositional montage, e.g. in the battle scenes in *Macbeth* and *Richard III*.

It only remains to say one last thing: if Shakespeare has such mastery of all the forms that derive from the *Urphänomen* of cinema, i.e. of all those specific compositional devices that we have enumerated, then is he not equally inclined towards the very *Urphänomen* itself?

What can that cinematic *Urphänomen* be . . . outside cinema? For an author who is not a film-maker, what can its attraction be when he is working within his own, non-cinematic art form?

The main attraction will, of course, be the essential content of that phenomenon: *movement*. And more precisely: not so much movement as such but the *image of movement* (in the sense in which we have been discussing it hitherto). If we were to be utterly pedantic, we could say that perception of the phenomenon of any movement consists in the continual break-up of a certain static form and the *reordering* of the fragments of *that* static form into a *new* form. If in phase 'A' there was a certain relationship between the head, the trunk and the limbs, and in phase 'B' their mutual relationship was different, then in the interval 'A–B' a process took place whereby the previous state 'A' was broken up and a new state 'B' was collated. We must imagine the span of 'A–B' as infinitely changing, and then, by taking this to its extreme, we arrive at the fact that each phase is a process of assembling the new state, in exactly the same way that every moment of the present is a transition of something that is past into a particular future. In film, the chromatic nature of this modulation of one phase into another undergoes what is no more than tempering (like a sound when it is fixed, unalterably, by the keys of a piano, as distinct from the voices of a stringed instrument which are capable of *glissando*). In this, it in no way forfeits its similarity with the perception of non-cinematographic movement. Perception is intermittent, but here it is the role of the obturator or interrupter to remove from our perception the *non-significant* elements of the progression of a movement from phase to phase, i.e. it disregards those transitional stages of displacement between one perceptible phase and another which do not contribute to assembling the elements into a defined *readable image* (it is *readable* because it is an *image*). The *undefined* imageless stages between two reasonable combinations are not 'read' and only exist as though non-existent in the mind of the perceiver!

So once again it is the image that decides everything! And the image of movement must be the centre of attention for any writer in whose mind there burns the *Urphänomen* of film, or rather the preconditions (which are, as we have seen, comprehensive in their scope) that underlie the principle of that *Urphänomen*, and for which cinematic form in all its ramifications is only the most coherent and naked variant.

And so it is in Shakespeare's works. It is also characteristic that he demonstrates particular skill and inspiration not just in the *depiction* of movement but also in the *image* of movement – above all of inner *psychological* movement in his plots and themes – his command of the *image of movement* is equally wide, indeed boundless. The area in which he applies the *image of movement* is paramount. We have already noted this characteristic of Shakespeare, as an aspect of his characters' inner motivation to act, when we were talking about the dynamics of his use of the verb in metaphor. We are now also beginning to see the same phenomenon and the same examples from another angle, namely in the series of techniques which, at various moments in history, derive from a single premiss and are given expressive form, from the perceptible symbols of the Phoenix and of Osiris right up to the abstract philosophical concept of the dialectical interaction of unity and multiplicity, and which in artistic terms are most tangible in what we have called the *Urphänomen des Films*, with all its consequences that affect the entire theory and practice of cinema. It is no coincidence that cinema has flourished most in the country where [Marx's] principle of base and superstructure, in its clearest and most consistent form, underlies the social and political structure enshrined in the historic document of the Soviet constitution.[206]

'[The] most perfect of all the works to be achieved by the art of man [is] the construction of true political freedom.'[207]

I shall end my study by taking a look at the man I consider to be the last bourgeois writer. I think he stands at the pinnacle of what it is possible for bourgeois literature to attain, specifically as bourgeois literature, i.e. reflecting all the inherent contradictions of its class and displaying a clear picture of the inevitability of that class's destruction, though not in the form of explicit awareness and still less as a conscious tendency, but as an unintended aura that arises of its own accord from this writer's work.

Such is the image of the bourgeoisie that emerges, at the beginning of its era of class predominance, from the vast fabric of Balzac's novels, in which the author condemns the bourgeoisie almost without being aware of it and with no revolutionary intent whatsoever.

Such, too, is the image of it, compressed into a single novel, in its last days, when it only remains for the bourgeoisie either to be crushed under the heel of the victorious proletariat in a world revolution, or to take a leap into its new persona: the fascist beast, as the logical, barefaced culmination of all its inherent features, hitherto obligingly masked by Social-Democratic liberalism.

I regard James Joyce's *Ulysses* as this ultimate work.[208] It is the final peak attained by bourgeois literature. In the above paragraphs I have described exactly how I understand this: bourgeois literature in the sense that its aim is not to destroy the bourgeoisie, either wholly (if it were, then we would simply be dealing with proletarian literature) or partially, an aim which emerges with particular force from the works of those writers of the bourgeoisie who thereby rise above its limitations and thus retain their creative vitality, are reborn and flourish anew, according to the degree to which they align themselves with those forces that are summoned by history to destroy not only the bourgeois class but class as such, the proletariat.

Ulysses is perhaps the most terrible image of the inevitable collapse, the inner frustration and the total hopelessness of man's spiritual nature under capitalism, if indeed one can even talk of a 'spiritual nature' in the exalted sense of that expression as being at all applicable to Leopold Bloom.

Nowhere in *Ulysses* does this appear as a conscious, intended theme; nowhere, I would even say, does the author seem to be aware of this state of affairs.* The picture that Joyce paints remains epically conscientious and epically dispassionate; the author never joins battle and only, perhaps, consoles himself with the illusion that it is possible to fly up and away beyond the confines of this world and then only for certain superhuman individuals, which every author seems to be in his own eyes: it is surely no coincidence that Joyce's self-portrait in the novel has been given the name of a 'flying man', Daedalus!

From every point of view – in its power, in its boldness, in its scope and in its integrity – *Ulysses* is undoubtedly the last monument of the bourgeois epic. As such, it has affinities with the first monumental creation of European literature: Homer. This is stressed in the work itself, in which, as we know, the narrative sequence and imagery of Homer's *Odyssey* have been ironically taken as the compositional basis for a story that describes a few days in the life of an insurance agent.

At a 'final point' such as this, it is natural that a resemblance to the very first link in the chain should be particularly marked. And no other work of literature between Joyce's *Ulysses* and the earliest myths of antiquity have so completely embodied the 'Dionysus and Osiris principle' that we have been examining.

To begin with, the whole novel is in essence . . . one man, and its entire content is a picture of everything that happens, that passes through a man or passes a man through itself in the course of a few days. The interweaving of a recital of events with the interior monologue of the person who passes through these events, and with those, his passing through which the main character experiences as an event: that is what *Ulysses* consists of in terms of plot and thematic material. To an ever greater degree – but not *beyond the limits* of what is accessible to the reading and perception of literature – the same occurs in Joyce's novel *Work in Progress*, whose *nocturnal* subconscious

---

*The best proof of this, I think, is provided by Joyce's next book after *Ulysses* entitled *Work in Progress*, an example of as powerful an image of the decay and decadence of tomorrow's bourgeois literature as *Ulysses* was the culminating point of its recent past, its yesterday.

is the equivalent of the *daytime* consciousness of *Ulysses*. In this later work, the framework of the novel coincides with the hollow bony sphere of the human cranial cavity, while its content is that mishmash cooked up in the kitchen of the subconscious and which passes through a person's mind when they are dozing or asleep.

A novel which is thematically the absolute equivalent of a human being must take as its perfect compositional exemplar the human body. And indeed *Ulysses* blatantly gives the name of a dismembered part of the body to each chapter. These random parts of the body – whether limbs or innards – are not only a device for articulating the novel into a unity modelled on the human body: they make for thematic unity by symbolising the subject matter and the image of the chapter to which they correspond.

But that is not all. The principle of a body dismembered into chapters is the model for all the other unities that have been broken up and scattered among the constituent parts of the novel, and when the chapters are collected together they reassemble these too.

In temporal terms the twenty-four hours have been broken up and scattered, then assembled into a unit of time: the day.

In spatial terms, the city has been carved up into 'decent' and 'indecent' streets, cemeteries and maternity hospitals, restaurants and newspaper offices, libraries and brothels, which are then brought into a general image of the capital of Ireland: Dublin.

In terms of the 'three kingdoms' of nature, there is a spectrum which is broken down by chapters into the primary colours, each one of which dominates a chapter. There are metals and minerals, each one assigned to a particular chapter. The same is done in terms of human labour and the arts: a chapter for painting, a chapter for language, a chapter for music and so on, each one embodying in its structure the laws of that form of art to which it is devoted. Particularly noteworthy is the chapter on language, which is written with the use of every kind of linguistic structure, from the most ancient literary techniques to the most ultra-modern forms of prose: a chapter through which, in the language itself, there passes the very concept of the birth of language. The subtlety of Joyce's skill as a writer is displayed in the fact that he even uses this technique in the chapter which is also *thematically* devoted to birth: *its* action takes place in a maternity home waiting for the outcome of a birth. (I think this is an absolutely unique, unsurpassed example of the dramatic fusion of imagery and form with its exposition in writing!)

Finally, the whole range of literary forms and genres themselves, which together make up the term 'Literature', is also distributed over separate chapters. One is written in the form of a catechism – in questions and answers – another on the model of newspaper reports with screaming headlines (this is the chapter the action of which takes place in a newspaper office). A third is in dramatic form. Another is the chapter mentioned above on the development of language; yet another is in the famous last chapter in the form of a stream of consciousness without punctuation marks or division into sentences, and so on and so on. All this is, as it were, a miniature encyclopaedia of all the forms and genres of literary composition, which arise from the complex of chapters that go to make up the image of 'Literature'.

Here we have only touched upon the principal and most glaringly obvious elements contained in *Ulysses*, in order to demonstrate as vividly as possible how the last descendant of the literary technique of a certain class – *Ulysses* – stretches out a hand to Dionysus, the prototype of that technique. Furthermore it is characteristic that for all its finesse in form and language, in social terms *Ulysses* is, of course, almost as archaic as Dionysus. Whereas in its composition the entire work is a brilliant example of the principle of dynamic impulsion and growth, in the most essential element of all – in the book's *conception of society* – what we see is precisely stasis, immobility and acceptance of the status quo. There is something profoundly appropriate in this dichotomy, as an image of destruction, as a reflection of the dead, inert hopelessness of the bourgeois social structure, which, in giving birth to the revolutionary force and dynamism of the proletariat, itself remains static, immobile, frustrated, lifeless.

Mention of Joyce's *Ulysses* invariably calls to mind the names of two other authors and one tendency. The names with good reason; the tendency – not so. The two names are those of Balzac and Zola, and the association is justified in terms of the artistic principle that is the object of our study.[209] With Joyce it is the chapters, with the other two it is their novels that form themselves into a single body; on the one hand, the body of an individual human being; on the other, the bodies of a family and a class. I refer in particular to Zola's *Histoire naturelle et sociale d'une famille sous l'Empire* (an anthropological counterpart to the *Histoire naturelle* of Geoffroy de Saint-Hilaire). On the one hand a body; on the other, the anatomical atlas of a class (Balzac) or a genealogical tree (Zola).

Zola's contribution, of course, goes further than the widely branching tree of the Rougon family. His method, to which he remains faithful throughout his many novels (and thus differs from Balzac), is planned in advance as an organism unified through children, grandchildren, great-grand-children and all other forms of family relationship, and is also maintained in his single novels that do not form part of this cycle (if one considers that this theme of the family tree is also central to one of his novels, *Docteur Pascal*); all his other novels are constructed on the principle of a single generalising image for each given novel. This is so well known that we shall merely limit ourselves to recalling the fact, especially since it does not, perhaps, normally come to mind when considering that series of phenomena that we are now demonstrating.

Thus in each novel we have not only a specifically defined locale: a provincial town or a Parisian market; a working-class environment or the world of the *cocottes*; striking miners; or a railway junction. But in each case the descriptive elements, closely linked with the unfolding of the plot, are such that they merge into the creation of a single colossal generalisation – whether it be in the image of the Magasin des Modes or the image of the Earth, or the image of the Strike, or of War, or of the Stock Exchange – in such a way that finally all the novels build up into an unforgettable image of Paris.

The method is one to which he remains true for the whole series, or rather for the whole collective organism of his novels, a method which, as we see, is also maintained in creating the image that dominates each separate novel; he also keeps to it in unfolding the theme which develops between the leading characters within individual novels. It is here that he distributes those varieties and nuances of one or another narrative technique depicting the personalities and actions of his characters, a method that also serves to gather into a generalising image of such themes as lust for life (*La Joie de vivre*), or the image of artistic creativity (*L'Œuvre*), the image of fertility (*Fécondité*), the image of political intrigue, either at court (*Son Excellence Eugène Rougon*) or on a worldwide scale – such as the 'octopus' of Catholicism as the dominant image created by the acolytes around the papal throne in his novel *Rome*. The separate features of the generalised image are so skilfully distributed through-out the cast of characters in each single novel, and so subtle and precise is his writing in depicting each bearer of these features as a living, plausible human being, that, since the characters are endowed with such frankness, these features do not prevent individual features from merging into a unified generalisation of an individual exhibiting all those characteristics, bringing together all the specific variants.

Such is the case with the two authors who are by tradition inseparably linked with Joyce.

The trend, however, that is invariably and with unjustifiable insistence immediately evoked whenever Joyce is mentioned is Surrealism, that most vivid reflection of the ultimate disintegration of bourgeois culture.

As an example of disintegration, it should stand in direct opposition to the method that we are studying here.

Surrealism, in its method, is the reverse of what we are describing and investigating. Everywhere we have been pursuing a single characteristic in the whole range of 'montage' elements, wherever, however and by what means they were represented in all the possible areas of our observations. Everywhere their fundamental, defining feature was their potential urge to combine, to join into a whole; and if wholeness broke up into fragments, then it was in order to be not only reassembled but assembled anew into a more perfect whole imagined by the human mind, a new, transformed, exemplary whole.

The method of Surrealism is completely different. Its 'automatic writing', a type of purposeless meditation, is diametrically opposed in its aim to what we have been describing. The purpose of Surrealism is aimed at dispersing unity and wholeness, at dissolving unity and wholeness. One feels impelled to give a 'graphic' interpretation to the fact that the first Surrealist manifesto in 1924 was published together with André Breton's novel *Le Poisson soluble*, 'The melting fish'! Fish or no fish, the fact is that the meat of the Surrealist method consists in letting a fact spread out into associations *without* the intention of combining the associations objectively and methodically so that they contribute to the assembly and emergence of a new image. It could not have been otherwise, because if the associations were combined into a new image, the result would be common-or-garden realism. Instead, 'Surrealism' lays claim to 'super-realism'; yet in fact it goes far down the road to 'sub-realism' (*sousréalisme*), lowering art into the realms of the subconscious, the automatic, the meaningless and the asocial.

A striking and irrefutable contrast between Joyce's intelligent mastery of his craft and the 'automatic' techniques of the Surrealists is to be found in the emphatic words of Stefan Zweig taken from his relatively little-known article entitled 'Comments on *Ulysses*'.[210] Zweig contrasts Joyce, not to the *epigoni* of the Surrealist tradition but to its founder Arthur Rimbaud, author of *Illuminations* and *Une Saison aux enfers* [A Season in Hell], in which he preaches 'le dérèglement de tous les sens' [the deregulation of all the senses]: 'so it is a chaos, but not one muzzily dreamed up by Rimbaud's drunken brain, smothered in the fumes of alcohol and wrapped in demonic gloom, but conceived by a bitingly witty, ironically cynical intellectual and boldly and purposefully orchestrated.'

It is interesting that even *The Battleship Potemkin* grew up in the Balzac-Zola tradition. It would seem that only the actual vicissitudes suffered by the ship served to compose and articulate the action of the film. It is indeed a fact that it represents a point at which narrative and structure merge again; they are no longer seen as *two* functions, but intertwine with one another. It is, however, precisely in works of this kind that the structure – growing out of the same principles used in the narrative, to which they may be more appropriate – needs to be put together with extreme skill.

The 'trick' in the composition of *Potemkin* lies in the fact that through the chronological progression of events there is 'sensed' – and, in places, purposely revealed – a very specific, cunning and effective 'skeleton' to the work: the five-act skeleton used in the very best classical tradition of tragedy. Disregarding, however, this use of structural rhythm (in the sense in which we touched on it earlier), *Potemkin* calls to mind an example of a literary work which includes a description of *The Battleship Potemkin* and which actually absorbed this film into its stylistic and compositional methods. I am referring to Lion Feuchtwanger's novel *Success*.[211]

This is what Feuchtwanger himself wrote about it: '*The Battleship Potemkin* . . . had a great deal of influence on my subsequent work: it revealed to me the technical means used in film-making and the possibility of transferring them into the art of epic prose.'[212]

But how did the novel embody precisely those principles that we are now discussing?

The novel is composed on two levels, just as *Potemkin* is. On the one hand the narrative is conducted entirely in the mode of chronological progression. It is, step by step, 'the biography of a province' ('Die Geschichte einer Provinz', as the author himself describes it in his foreword). Within that, it is also the final part of the biography of one man, Martin Krüger, and the sequence of actions undertaken by another man, Johann Krein, who is planning to save him; all of this occurs in the initial stages of the biography of a certain repellent 'social' movement and of the politicians leading it (the early, Munich, period of nascent National Socialism). The central portion of the novel seems simply to consist of a chain of linked encounters in the picaresque manner of *Gil Blas* or *L'Histoire comique de Francion*,[213] in which Johann Krein seeks meetings and acquaintanceships with people capable of helping him in his purpose. But the novel does not degenerate into a set of episodes of the kind that typifies the examples that I have quoted. Why not? Because it is simultaneously built on that very firm 'skeleton': the concept of the dismembered body which throughout the narrative is steadily engaged in assembling its scattered constituent parts into a whole.

Feuchtwanger does not treat this concept with such a degree of abstraction as to make it provide the rhythm of the book. (cf. the rhythmic construction of *The Battleship Potemkin*): this, too, is a technique which is capable of welding a work into a whole, if one starts out from certain fundamental assumptions about method and about the relationship between theme and form. Feuchtwanger's skeleton is objectified, and this gives it a direct affinity with . . . Walt Whitman and with . . . Bach. (People have also written about the similarities between the composition of *Potemkin* and the works of Bach.) The fact is that Feuchtwanger called his novel *Success* with a purpose: he gave it that title with the same 'methodological' justification with which Whitman called his long poem 'The Song of the Broad-Ax'. Feuchtwanger has fragmented the concept of *Success* into every possible shade of meaning of the word, up to and including its opposites, even up to the unity of those opposites.

The success of the book's mission, which coincides with the death of the prisoner, Krüger, lies, as it were, in the negative resolution of its thematic content; for it is the failure of his mission which results in success for Krein's ideas and provides a positive ending to the novel. And with that thought we may successfully move on to the concluding reflections of this section.

It is precisely through the application of *the same guiding principles* to both the cell and the total organism of a film as a whole (despite the fact that the completed film is made up from those cells) that I see the divergence from any 'atomistic' method of reading what happens in the 'body' of the film. In this, our conception is just as far removed from the atomism of antiquity as it is from its more recent manifestation in the 18th century, in the so-called era of the Enlightenment.

The men of the Enlightenment regard all forms of links in nature, in society or in art as something derived from the aggregate of initially independent, homogeneous elements. The doctrine of the French materialists that defines thought as the sum of individual sense impressions;

Locke's and Rousseau's teaching about social intercourse as the result of a contract between initially independent individuals; Hume's and Berkeley's doctrine of the laws of art as the resultant of a large number of individual aesthetic tastes: all these proceed from one and the same atomistic premiss, from the bourgeois individual with his personal interests as the primary foundation of all social bonds.[214]

Our approach is completely different, and that is because our premiss – the type of social structure that we have – is also completely different.

For us, a film is not the sum of its basic cell units, nor is it the sum of its larger units, its montage sequences. In our view, a film consists of a combination of more complex formative elements. As we see it, the single cells do not simply add up to the phenomenon of movement. We consider that these single 'cells' do not simply go to make a sum, but combine to achieve a new quality, the quality of the image of movement. In this phase of a single physical phenomenon, these two points of view are above all speculative considerations and are merely two ways of 'interpreting' what we see before us as a datum. (However you 'read the process', the picture on the screen is moving!) That interpretation, however, acquires an enormous significance of principle when we progress from the phenomenon of the cell units to the question of understanding montage sequences. Here, we now have the preconditions for a conscious treatment of the material. Here, theoretical premises are inseparable from practice, from training, from the system and the purposive tendency of film as a creative art. As we understand it, here, at the second stage of putting a film together, the same guiding principle is maintained; and an episode is not simply formed as the sum of its montage sequences but emerges in the process of the interaction between sequences as the generalising image of them.

In my article 'Beyond the Shot',[215] written as long ago as 1929, I was already groping for this formulation, but my interpretation of it was still excessively mechanistic. I had not yet reached the point of reading the process of interaction between sequences in terms of 'image'. I was still at the stage of considering the dynamic effect that arises from the collision of two adjacent montage sequences. Even in those days I was already fiercely attacking other interpretations of this phenomenon, in particular that of Kuleshov who maintained that, 'If one has an idea-phrase, a fragment of the story, a link in the entire dramatic chain, then this idea is expressed, laid out in shot-signs, like bricks.'[216] Incidentally, I am amazed at the way in which, despite my polemical ardour, I restrained myself from reading his term 'laid out' as a colloquial synonym for 'castrated'![217] For castration is exactly what happens with the method of laying out or revealing thought by means of montage sequences, whereby the thoughts are called upon to be born and emerge out of the juxtaposition of sequences!

I think the concept of pictorial conflict, which I dwelt on at excessive length, was above all a reflection of the picture evoked by the workings of our social organism, a picture of conflict. Nowadays, in expanding that concept we not only reflect on the actions of our present-day social organism, in which the struggle is increasing, but on the fact that the struggle is daily flaring up more and more. We do not forget about that struggle, but this 'final and decisive battle'[218] does not prevent us from looking into the very depths of the structure of our social system, and from analysing and setting it to rights in such a historically important act as the drafting and acceptance of the Soviet Constitution in 1936.

The intensification of our research into problems of the nature and structure of our art form is, I think, a direct reflection of this historic stage. The very conception of it, in my view, reflects the social system that has replaced bourgeois society and its underlying assumptions, assumptions which determined the attitudes that we call 'atomistic'.

Perhaps it is not out of place to recall here that other sciences, physics for example, have also moved away from atomistic concepts, having run up against the fact that physical laws which were correct when applied to single units and bodies turn out to be not always applicable to what were previously regarded as sums of units or bodies but have in fact proved to be new phenomena with other and new properties, differing from those of each separate, isolated constituent unit *per se* (see the papers delivered by physicists on this subject at the special session of the Communist Academy on the twenty-fifth anniversary of the publication of Lenin's *Materialism and Empirio-Criticism*).[219]

Our conception, I believe, comes closer to reflecting those structural principles on which the body of our social system is built. With us, unlike the bourgeois system, the fundamental point of departure is not the isolated unit, the single individual with his or her narrowly personal interests: a system which for selfish reasons only allows units to combine with others similar to themselves, by way of self-defence and aggression in those clashes with other, similar, but competing units that are equally egocentric and 'egotistical', clashes to which every individual unit within the bourgeois system is doomed. With us the basic cell, the prerequisite nucleus, is undoubtedly *the group of people* – not the 'human unit *per se*.' And when it *is* an individual human figure, then it is that figure regarded not as an enclosed unit but as a tiny fragment, a minute part of a certain collective group, which in its turn is a constituent element of a class.

Though this may be purely speculative when considering the individual human being, it is another matter when we come to the next step away from the individual. For the real point of departure, the module at the basis of our system, is the primary human collective, the principle of which reflects the idea and content of collective class solidarity precisely of the proletarian class, the working class, the only class in which the interests of the class are simultaneously and inseparably identical with the interests of each of its members. I believe that the basic, grassroots unit of Party organisation – the cell, not as the mere sum of its members but precisely as a Party *collective* –

fully reflects the collectivist conception of the way human beings should combine in a socialist state.* Here [in the USSR] we see this being put into effect, step by step, beginning with the combining of individual smallholdings into collective farms – which are significantly greater, both economically and socially, than the mere sum of their constituent farms – and continuing upwards to the federation of national republics into the totality of the Soviet Union, which politically, socially and economically is something completely different from the sum of the 'united states'. In America the federation is the outcome of a balance of compromise between the conflicting interests of its component parts, instead of a pooling of those parts into a joint, collective state interest, which, on socialist principles, even-handedly nourishes, develops and moves forward each collectively constituent republic, each of which is built to the same model, in the same spirit and on the same principles, without in any way limiting the scope of its own national development.

I believe that in our cinema the atomistic concept, i.e. one that is alien to us in both spirit and essence, is to be found in the narrative technique of certain films which set for themselves no function beyond the achievement of that objective. Indeed, the orthodox story-telling narrative is the most typical example of the atomistic piling up of fact on fact. Throughout this interminable 'large intestine' of facts strung out one after another, here and there signposts are put up, on which are written sententious reminders of the basic slogan that is supposed to run through a film as a whole. At necessary moments in the narrative one or another of the characters will utter some appropriate words of wisdom on the basic theme. In the same way, miles of film are used to spell out character-references for the various characters, from which judgments are made on their virtues and failings. And all this instead of making the slogan or theme emerge from the work's fundamental image; this should *arise* from the myriad particular images, which, like the fundamental image, should grow into a single image out of the dynamic combination of countless small links in a chain, instead of being lifelessly strung together on the boring thread of a sequential chronicle of events.

Thus, too, should emerge and grow the image of the chief proponent of the theme and content of a film, that collective of dramatic heroes, which is called upon to reflect the real-life heroes of our victorious socialist system.

---

*Compare this, for example, with the structure (though in principle they are not comparable) of the smallest party unit of the Italian Blackshirts or the German National Socialists. There, the unit is simply not understood as an organic collective; their party cells are organised on the model of a mechanistic combination of people into companies, half-companies, platoons and squads as understood by Prussian militarists or by the tsarist regime, i.e. purely 'atomistically'.

6 Pushkin the Montageur

'The Battle against the Pechenegs' and 'Poltava'[220]

We have already pointed out that montage is not, in essence, made up of *details* but of numerous general ideas about an object or phenomenon, ideas which by the law of *pars pro toto* arise *out of* details. Therefore what we have in a montage combination is not merely the sum of the constituent elements, not a static summary of the whole, but something significantly greater. It will not be the sum of, say, five details that form one whole; it will be five *wholes*, each taken from a different angle of vision and in a different aspect, all of which are interconnected. It will be, in dynamic form, what Galton's 'collective photographs' tried (though failed) to be in static form. (These attempted to create the 'typical features' of a group of faces by superimposing, one upon the other, the photographed faces of each member of that group. The result was a generalised set of features which did not correspond to any one of the constituent faces but emphasised the most frequent and striking features and relegated to the background those less frequent, less characteristic, random features of individual faces which were untypical of the group.)

Therefore an essential condition for composing a montage sequence will be that it contains not just *any detail* but details or elements capable by means of their *pars* of evoking a maximal perception of the *toto*. A detail correctly chosen according to this criterion permits enormous economy in the means of expression. This is truly an instance of how six thousand people can be fed with six small fishes![221] Six properly chosen details can produce the effect of an event on a grandiose scale.

A great master of this art is Pushkin in his battle scenes. In the acuteness of his choice of detail – detail of the kind described above – he is perhaps only surpassed by Leonardo da Vinci. The details of battle seem to be taken directly from those fragments.[222]

I shall cite here only two examples, one from 'Ruslan and Lyudmila', the other from 'Poltava'; one describes the fight against the Pechenegs, the other the battle against the Swedes.

Pushkin's technique of montage is very meticulous. His alternation of 'depth of shot' and 'shot dimension' is most carefully calculated and thought out. Furthermore, it is highly characteristic of Pushkin that these shots of differing length and scale are placed in *groups*. He does not employ an overall 'long shot' which he suddenly contrasts with a 'close-up' – a method of intercutting in which the two are *usually* incompatible, i.e. are incapable of being fused into one common perception. (This, by the way, is a mistake made very frequently by those who, lacking an organic comprehension of the nature of montage, tend to follow fashion or accepted ideas by cutting up scenes into pieces and sticking them together again.★)

As we have noted, not only does Pushkin place his various 'shot lengths' in groups; these are also invariably accompanied by an intensification of the action. At the moment when the foreground is occupied not so much by a description of the fighting as by the inherent drama of warlike action, when what Pushkin calls 'death and hell on every side' ('Poltava') comes to the fore, he will make use of a group of close-ups – and close-ups, what is more, of vivid unambiguity, while being extremely pure and typical of the action that occurs in them. Each is always a single example of what is being repeated a hundred times over in every corner of the field of battle.

Let us examine the first extract. It is 'the battle against the Pechenegs' from the sixth canto of 'Ruslan and Lyudmila'.

1. Advance! The battle now is joined;
2. As scenting death the horses prance
3. And swords begin to clash on shields;
4. Up flies a whistling cloud of arrows,
5. The valley floor is drenched with blood;
6. Now horsemen headlong charge the foe
7. And squadron meets with squadron 'midst the field.
8. Shoulder to shoulder, as though a solid wall,
9. Rank faces rank to thrust and slash;
10. A rider fights a man on foot;
11. There bolts away a frightened horse;
12. There battle-cries are heard, there others flee;
13. There falls a Russian, there a Pecheneg;
14. A heavy mace now fells this man,
15. While this one's by a slender arrow-shaft brought down;
16. Another's pinned beneath his shield
17. And crushed to death by maddened horses' hooves.

Line 1: 'The battle now is joined', a typical *title*.
Line 2: Typical treatment of the beginning of a sequence, by use of close-ups

---

★As a method of producing maximum shock through paradox, intercutting of this kind can, of course, be used – but in the appropriate place. The effect of such juxtaposition is always unexpected and induces a sharp jolt in perception. Sometimes this is necessary; but if so, it must be very much 'to the point'. Examples of it were used in the montage of the 'Odessa Steps' sequence, but with a strict awareness of their exceptional effect. The close-up of the dying mother is followed by an instant cut to an overall long shot of the massacre on the steps. Obviously it is this kind of 'shrieking' cut that leads so forcefully into the 'heartrending' scene of the baby carriage and so on.

showing some 'preliminary action'. Close-ups of prancing horses. This is, as it were, a *Vorschlag* to the rhythm and action of the picture itself.[223]

Line 3: The same thing in sound. Visually, 'swords . . . clash on shields' is a close-up. In sound it announced the basic tonality for the whole scene; it is, as it were, a 'close-up' of the timbre which will characterise the sound throughout the picture. The fighting, of course, has not yet begun; the sound is only the clink of metal made by the warriors beating their swords against their own shields.

Line 4: From one sound to another. The dull clank of metal gives way to the rising whistle of arrows flying *upward*. It is like a gauntlet thrown down, or an *answer* to the challenge of the previous clanking of metal. The 'cloud of arrows' is, of course, depicted in long shot.

Line 5: From sound to picture. Long shot, but closer, *from below*: the arrows strike home. 'The valley floor is drenched with blood'. The first blow is struck; the first blood is shed.

Line 6: Sharp reaction. Long shot of cavalry springing into action.

Line 7: Cavalry clashes head-on with the opposing cavalry charging towards it.

Line 8: The ranks close up.

Line 9 : Cut and thrust.

Lines 2 and 3; 4 and 5; 6, 7, 8 and 9 are all clearly defined groups that are internally closely welded together by subject matter and no less closely linked with each other by the logic of the action.

Taken together, lines 1 and 9 are, as it were, an introductory *general picture* of the battle (which is the function of long shot).

Lines 10 to 17 constitute eight close-ups. There is no point in listing and describing them separately; Pushkin has already done it. Let us merely observe that line 12 contains two long shots (one in sound, the other visual) which cut across the series of close-ups. They prevent, as it were, that group of close-ups from becoming isolated from the overall scene of fighting; they are a reminder that this group is an element of a whole, namely the battle. (This is another essential condition of montage; and it is also a typical cause of error, because it is often not observed. Very few films pass the test on this score!)

This series of close-ups is very remarkable for the following reason: it is not only a selection of details that are simultaneously taking place a hundred times over in every part of the field, as we mentioned above, e.g. 'There falls a Russian, there a Pecheneg'. The close-ups are also most remarkable not merely as details, but in the way these apparently chaotic, random elements of the fighting are actually welded together by a plot line. If we look carefully at lines 10 to 17, we shall see that they clearly function on two levels: they are simultaneously fragments illustrating the battle in general *and* a picture of one single encounter. In other words, these eight lines are so composed that they constitute, at one and the same time, a particular instance of fighting *and* a general pervading image of warfare as such. These lines, in fact, form an image which, while apparently depicting one episode, is in fact so all-embracing that it is a total, complete picture of the battle.

The beginning of the series of shots is in line 10: 'A rider fights a man on foot . . .'.

The series ends at lines 16–17: 'A third is pinned beneath his shield / And crushed to death by maddened horses' hooves . . .'.

Although the 'characters' in line 10 and lines 16–17 are evidently different, the section reads like the start and finish of a single action: foot-soldier fights horseman (line 10) . . . foot-soldier trampled to death by horse (lines 16–17). The two shots are not linked by unity of *characters* but by unity of *action*. The scene, of course, could *also* be played using *the same* characters; the fight would then have a stronger 'plot-value', but in essence nothing is changed.

Now let us examine what happens between these sections (i.e. in lines 11–15), what ensures the cohesion and unity of the lines enclosed between the first line (line 10) and the last two lines (lines 16–17), which are the first and last links in a single drama. The cohesion of them all, it transpires, is maintained by the two segments at either end.

It is quite obvious that lines 14 and 15 are simply the essential build-up to the final blow: to the man who falls and is crushed by the hooves of maddened horses. The first victim is 'felled' (line 14); the next is 'brought down' (line 15), the third 'crushed to death' (line 17). The unity of figuration in these three 'killings' is also maintained through their being internally joined by a play on the *degree* of force with which the men are killed: the first by a 'mace' (line 14), the second by an 'arrow' (line 15), the third by 'maddened horses' (line 17).

The relative force of these three weapons of death is very clear: the arrow is the lightest; the mace is heavy; the horses' hooves are heaviest of all. They are not, however, placed in straightforward order of rising magnitude, which would be: A arrow; B mace; C hooves. Instead they are disposed in a more expressive sequence: B middling (mace); A lightest (arrow); C heaviest (horse).

Indeed, if we were to illustrate the relative intervals by means of a graphic scheme, the result would be as follows (taking the mace as midway between the arrow and the horse):

1. A	B	C

In the first instance, which follows the sequence A–B–C, we would have the following set of intervals:

A	B
B	C

A–B and B–C. These intervals are short and are *equal in magnitude.*

2.

In the second instance, where the chosen sequence is A–C–B, the set of intervals would be

B	A
A	C

B–A and A–C; these intervals are *not equal*, and one of them, A–C, is the greatest possible, i.e. the distance from the first to the last element of the series in the sequence A–B–C. In the second series, the interval series B–A–C equals one-and-a-half times A–C. – the greatest of all!

If we illustrate graphically the relative effect of the different sets of intervals, the proposition becomes quite obvious (see Fig. 6.1).* Thus we see that lines 14, 15 and 17 are closely linked and that lines 14 and 15 act as a lead-in to the 'presentation' of the death of a foot-soldier under the horses' hooves (this foot-soldier could also, of course, be a man who has dismounted or fallen from his horse).

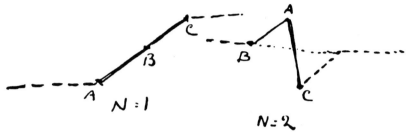

Fig. 6.1

Can a similar link also be extended to any of the other lines? Let us examine two analogous lines (lines 11 and 13) which are attached to the other end of the passage.

While in the examples analysed above we found an instance of lines directly linked by action, here we have a similar link by action but of a more complex (mediated) kind. Lines 13 and 11 are linked with line 10 in a way that is slightly different from the link with between lines 14–15 and line 17. lines 13 and 11 are, as it were, alternatives, prospects, prototypes of the possible outcomes of a fight between two participants.

Indeed, line 13 states the matter literally by *showing*: 'There falls a Russian, there a Pecheneg'; the line *illustrates* the fact that both have an equal chance

---

*The sequence B–A–C is the classic sequence of three consecutive points in indicating the phased progression of a movement. It illustrates, for instance, the basic condition for structuring a stage gesture so that it will 'read' more effectively: this prior condition is the so-called 'recoil' [*otkaz*: literally, 'refusal'] that should precede any movement. The concept of 'recoil' as a standard precondition for any expressive gesture was revived and popularised by V.E. Meyerhold, but in stage technique it has been known for a long time.[224] This principle is far more widely acceptable than might appear at first sight. Thus, where plot construction is concerned, I believe Edgar Allen Poe's formulation in his *Eureka* (1848) is absolutely relevant: 'In the construction of plot, for example, in fictitious literature, we should aim so to arrange the incidents that we shall not be able to determine of any one of them whether it depends on any other or upholds it.'

of death. But line 11 is more curious: it contains a clear indication, a 'foretelling' of the death of a horseman ('There bolts away a frightened horse' – obviously without a rider). But if we compare this 'foretelling' with the actual course of events we shall see that it is false: it is a *foot-soldier* who dies under the hooves of a horse! It is in this device that we detect yet another example of 'recoil', i.e. an intentional diversion away from the direction of the ultimate result or event, a wayward 'loop' in the plot, an artificial push towards a false suggestion of the outcome. It seems to be a little peep behind the curtain at what is going to happen, which is immediately followed by a completely 'neutral' statement (line 13), to the effect that the chances for both a Russian and a Pecheneg are absolutely equal! This is intended to add even greater emphasis to the blow delivered in lines 16–17. You think that the fate of the third man will be the *opposite* of what happens to the first (line 14) and the second (line 15). But it turns out that he – the third man – dies too, and that the hint given in line 11 was purposely meant to deceive you.

Line 12 is a typical montage 'reminder' of the overall scene, inserted into a series of close-ups. It is both an aural ('There battle-cries are heard') and a visual ('there others flee') reminder. This is one of those long shots that we should always remember to insert lest the series of close-ups lose their connecting links and become detached from the general ensemble of the scene.

It should further be noted that even within a group of what we have called close-ups (not in their dimensions but in their concentration on detail), Pushkin brings us closer and closer, in step with the heightening of the action. I refer to the five instances of 'there' (lines 11, 12 and 13), the two uses of 'this' (lines 14 and 15) and finally 'another' (line 16). It is quite obvious that this is aimed at bringing the spectator closer and drawing him into the action. 'There' is descriptive, depictive, narrative: at a distance; 'this' is personal, and in scenic terms closer. 'Another' is obviously slightly more distant than 'this' (lines 14, 15 and 16) so that line 17 with its weighty hooves can come crashing down on the man who is shown as being under the horses' feet in line 16. But those hooves (line 17) also round off and conclude the entire scene: we should not forget that the beginning of the scene (line 2) also starts with a close-up shot of horses!

As we have seen, the composition of these seventeen lines, looked at *only* from its illustrative or 'scenic' aspect, is arranged as a piece of montage with all the expressive finesse of a complete drama. It is this which creates the powerful effect exerted by what might seem to be a random combination of chance details; it is this, too, which dictates the choice of details and their sequence, and hence their remarkable effectiveness as montage.

The citation of this example once more affirms my position, which was last stated in the paper which I read to the All-Union Conference of Workers in Soviet Cinema, 8–13 January 1935:

I have divided [the recent past] into the following periods: the years 1924–9 are marked by strivings towards *type-casting* and *montage*. The next phase runs from 1929 to the end of 1934; this stage was most notable for an approach to the problems of *character* and *drama*. In fact, both 'character' and 'drama' are essentially the next step in development from the phenomena which figured embryonically in the earlier period as 'type-casting' and 'montage'. . . .

The 'molecular drama' created by the conflict between montage sequences grows into the full-scale conflict of passions between the participants in the drama.[225]

There this idea was formulated in terms appropriate to a description of the characteristics of various periods in the history of our cinema. But most important, of course, is the idea that the principle of dramatic construction should permeate the film as a whole, determining in equal degree both the interrelation between the acts of the drama and the smallest splice in the conflict of montage sequences (the 'molecular drama'). The quotation from 'Ruslan and Lyudmila' is, I think, a most vivid illustration of this idea.

Our second example is the famous passage describing the Battle of Poltava in 'Poltava':

1. A menacing horde,
2. The wind-borne cavalry advance
3. With clink of harness and of sword
4. And meet, their sabres slashing shoulder-high.
5. Flinging heap on heap of bodies,
6. From every side the iron cannon-balls
7. Between them ricochet and strike,
8. Throw up the dust and hiss in pools of blood.
9. Swede, Russian – alike they thrust and slash and cut.
10. The beat of drums, the cries, the clang of steel,
11. The cannon's thunder, hoofbeats, neighing, groans,
12. And death and hell are everywhere.

The scene is treated with much greater drama and tension than the battle with the Pechenegs in 'Ruslan and Lyudmila'. From the montage angle, too, we at once notice a quite different tempo and rhythm of montage cutting. It is not just a case of employing 'short montage'; here the stress of each shot is naturally concentrated not merely on one significant action, not merely on one significant *movement* but on a single *verb*, which in the literary arsenal corresponds to the *depiction* of a single movement in the shot.

In 'Ruslan and Lyudmila' we had one shot made up of two lines of verse (lines 16 and 17); four shots each of one line (lines 10, 11, 14 and 15); and four shots each of half a line of verse (lines 12 and 13).

In 'Poltava' a montage shot can be contained in as little as a quarter of a line, and one line can contain up to five scenes!

Line 6 – 1 shot
Line 7 – 2 shots
Line 8 – 2 shots
Line 9 – 5 shots
Line 10 – 3 shots
Line 11 – 4 shots

It is also interesting to compare the two passages by another criterion. The use of sound in the second passage significantly exceeds the quantity of sounds used in the first. One might dismiss this with a joke, saying that Pushkin too began in . . . the silent cinema ('Ruslan and Lyudmila', 1817–20), and moved on to sound films ('Poltava', 1828). A much more important observation, however, is this, namely that the number of sonic images in Pushkin's work (at least in a comparison of these two scenes) increases proportionately to the increase in the dramatic tension and the tempo of the action. One could say that along with the heightening of dramatic tension the means of depiction are transferred into sound as being the more intense medium of expression. This leads us towards a unified perception of pictures and sounds; it illustrates the merging of these 'opposing' spheres into one another, and thereby helps us to blaze a trail into the third part of our study, which will concern sound and picture and their interconnection.

We may observe exactly the same phenomenon in another composite art form: painting. Here too the same results can be achieved with a small number of figures – but correctly chosen. Here too what determines that choice is that they should not only be typical in themselves but that in combination they should set up a generalised image of the scene as a whole, of the action as a whole (I refer primarily to examples of dramatic narrative painting). This also serves to explain the phenomenon mentioned by the Chairman of the Committee for Artistic Affairs, Comrade Kerzhentsev, in one of his lectures at the House of Cinema (Winter, 1936–7).[226] The picture under discussion was Surikov's *The Morning of the Execution of the Streltsy*.[227] Comrade Kerzhentsev correctly drew attention to the fact that the effect of a mass execution was essentially achieved by the 'play' of the figures of the *streltsy* themselves. This effect, and the perception of an Execution with a capital E, derives of course from the concept of an image arising by montage out of two or three juxtaposed depictions: the idea that we have been discussing all the time. To give Surikov his due, it must be said that both the figures of the *streltsy* themselves and the individual attributes of behaviour with which the artist has endowed them are precisely such as to induce a perception of the collective image of the rebellious *streltsy* and the *streltsy* quarter of Moscow, which, lacking the necessary maturity to understand the political wisdom of Peter the Great's plan, had rebelled against him and supported the cause of backwardness and reaction.

The Iron Cannon-Balls

Let us stop for a moment to consider these remarkable lines:

Flinging heap on heap of bodies,
From every side the iron cannon-balls
Between them ricochet and strike,
Throw up the dust and hiss in pools of blood.

They have two noteworthy characteristics. If these lines are regarded as a sequence of shots, we discover the first peculiarity, namely the method of introducing an object or a human participant. In the given instance, the objects – iron cannon-balls – are simultaneously actors.

What is characteristic in the 'presentation' of these object-actors? It is that we are first given a picture of *what* is happening, and only afterwards is it revealed *who* is making it happen. First the action, then the actor: 1) 'Flinging heap on heap of bodies . . .'; and only then: 2) '. . . the iron cannon-balls'.

This becomes clearly evident as soon as we substitute actual depiction for the images of the action: obviously the first line is a shot (or rather a combination of several shots on the same theme), in which we see 'heap' falling on 'heap of bodies', but without being shown the reason why they are falling. And the reason – iron cannon-balls – is only revealed in the second series of shots, in a new montage phrase that begins with the words: 'From every side the iron cannon-balls'; this line must be read visually in such a way that there should be the same falling bodies, but with iron cannon-balls in the foreground, the centre of attention.

The third line gives us piles of bodies (i.e. falling men) and the cannon-balls in equal interaction: cannon-balls hitting human bodies. Roughly speaking, in the first line the people are in the foreground, the invisible cannon-balls are striking them from the distance (the people obviously have their backs to the camera) and the people collapse on to one another.

In the second line the cannon-balls are pouring into the foreground of the shot (clearly they are flying over the camera and landing in the scene of action). They bounce and hit people (long shot). 'Between them ricochet': medium shot of human figures with cannon-balls ricocheting between them and hitting them. 'And strike': typical close-up of a cannon-ball striking a man. In this line, Pushkin has allowed corresponding lengths of 'footage': 'Between them ricochet' [*mezh nimi prýgayut*] is six syllables, 'and strike' [*razyát*] is two syllables. In other words, the section that we read as medium shot has been allotted three times more footage than the section that read as a close-up, although both are on the same topic!

The next line ('Throw up the dust and hiss in pools of blood') characteristically introduces a new element by making play with the dimensions of the frame. Here there are two distinct shots: 'Throw up the dust and' [*prakh róyut i*] and 'hiss in pools of blood' [*v króvi shípyat*] of four syllables

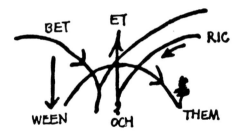

Fig. 6.2

each, i.e. both in footage and in action content these two shots are halfway between the medium shot and the big close-up of the previous line; if you count 'and strike' as a shot with a content of *one* action, then 'Throw up the dust' and 'hiss in pools of blood' must be seen as shots containing at least two actions each (for example 'Throw up the dust': (1) the cannon-ball hitting the ground and (2) the fountain of dust thrown up from the ground; 'hiss in pools of blood: (1) a puddle of blood, drops flying up as the cannon-ball hits it, the drops fall, and (2) the cannon-ball hissing in the pool of blood). 'Between them ricochet' is a medium shot with three accentuated movements and the reactive movements that result from them (Fig. 6.2).

It should not be thought that the number of movements in a shot is to be counted by the number of *words* in a phrase.

The number of movements is determined by our rhythmic perception of the passage, and whenever we want to find the visual equivalent of any line or phrase, the rhythmic factor is decisive. Let us try to listen to the visual pattern of the sound of the verse and derive from it the trajectories of the movements which it suggests. To me, the patterns suggested are as follows. 'Between them': the stress is not on the first syllable, therefore the movement is syncopated; '. . . tween': is like a short blow; 'them': unstressed, is an echo. The first ('. . . tween') is the hit, the second ('them') is the bounce.

I see the movement within the shot thus: the shot does not start with the movement, but earlier; 'Be . . .' dictates the motionless shot into which the cannon-ball lands – not simultaneously with the opening of the shot, but in syncopation (see Fig. 6.3).

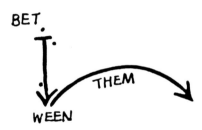

Fig. 6.3

Fig. 6.4

The sound of 'ricochet' – '*prýgayut*' – suggests to me a different pattern: '*Pry . . .*' is not a short upward flight in a straight line, but the flight of the cannon-ball into the frame in a curving trajectory; '. . . *ga* . . .' is a short upward bounce; '. . . *yut*' suggests to me a dull blow, flying into the frame in one trajectory and out in another, i.e. syncopation again: | $\bar{a}$ b′ | $\bar{c}$ |, in which 'a' and 'c' are pauses, intentionally introduced into the word by the director (see Fig. 6.4).

(N.B.: These diagrams are by no means diagrams for a *reading* of the verse; they are schemes for graphically *visualising* the action that is taking place within the verse. The two processes cannot coincide. The basic, motor impulse is transferred either into reading or into visualisation along separate, incompatible channels, unified only by the single motor image, which underlies both but does not link them (see Fig. 6.5).)

Fig. 6.5

If we now put the two diagrams ('Between them' and 'ricochet') together, we get the scheme of movement shown in Fig. 6.6 for the medium shot in question.

That more or less completes our analysis of the rhythm of this phrase. Let us now give due attention to its pictorial elements. 'Between them': the image of 'between' is most easily conveyed by two figures, between which there is necessarily a space. Obviously, therefore, two figures must be placed in the foreground of the shot. The two figures plus the three movements of the cannon-balls produce an excellent 'even-odd' combination, which is furthermore resolvable in different dimensions: the 'even' is resolved statically

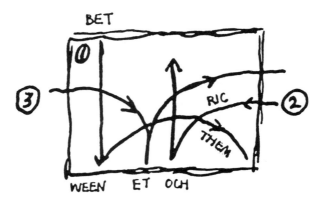

Fig. 6.6

(the two figures), the 'odd' dynamically (the three accents of movement).

By placing the two figures as in Fig. 6.7 the image of 'between' is only half-created, being in one plane only.

For the image of 'between' to resound in all its three-dimensionality, figures must also be placed at various planes in depth, in such a way that the plane of the curves shall pass between the planes of each of the figures. What is more, the plane of the cannon-balls' trajectory must be divided into three planes, with one plane for each movement.

Thus we acquire five planes of action for the medium shot required by this scene.

The question then arises: where shall we put them? The first layout, of course, which suggests itself is simple alternation: a = the planes of the figures, b = the planes of the trajectories, as in Fig. 6.8.

But would that be right? I think not, because this runs counter to the

Fig. 6.7

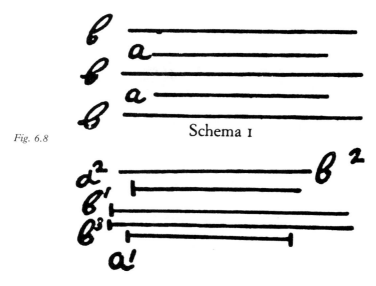

Fig. 6.8

Schema I

Fig. 6.9

indications for the 'between-them-ricochet' situation, bearing in mind that the *cannon-balls* are ricocheting between *men*. In Fig. 6.8 we have exactly the opposite picture: *men* between *cannon-balls*. This is, of course, a perfectly acceptable picture of a battle; if we had a situation in which men were, shall we say, 'advancing through a hurricane of cannon-shot', then Fig. 6.8 would be wholly satisfactory in conveying it visually. We have, however, been given a picture which is the reverse of that, and so the disposition must be of a different type, for example as shown in Fig. 6.9.

It does not have to be *exactly* like this; there can be as many variants as you like, but they must in equal measure fulfil the condition that the cannon-balls ricochet between people. Although in Fig. 6.9 this condition is observed by the fact that between a^1 and a^2 there are *two* planes b^1 and b^2, even the placing of b^2 beyond the limits of a^1 and a^2 does not contradict the requirements, because background figures will be placed beyond b^2.

In rough outline, therefore, the composition would be sketched as in Fig. 6.10. In this scheme it is unfortunate that trajectory number 2 is not connected with a figure (Phase II). This suggests the need for a solution which repeats certain characteristics of Phase I (the overall requirements of rhythm) and which furthermore *cuts across* the figure visually (the pictorial requirement): drawing the line of the cannon-ball's trajectory across the figure – 'crossing it out' – is an image of our perception of the way cannon-balls knock men out of the ranks. In addition, it is a *graphic* prefiguring of the theme of destruction by cannon-shot, which in the next close-up ('and strike') is depicted *factually*.

What are we to do? The answer is very simple. It is, after all, quite

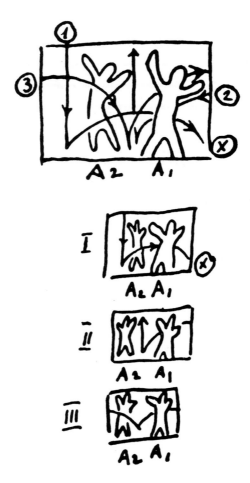

Fig. 6.10

unnatural for the figures to stand as though rooted to the spot and do nothing but wave their arms. Obviously Figure A1 will stagger sideways from the place where Cannon-Ball X strikes. It is entirely natural for the figure to move from Phase I into Phase II, i.e. from the right-hand to the left-hand edge of the frame. The maximum graphic emphasis, i.e. the maximal accentuation of the fact that the figure has not simply walked but has staggered, is provided, as always in such cases, by the very simple method of 'counter-movement' along another plane of depth, that is to say by means of simultaneously transferring Figure A2 from the left-hand into the right-hand corner. At the moment of the flight of Cannon-Ball 2, therefore, Phase II will appear as in Fig. 6.11.

For Phase III the figures could be returned to their previous places. But we do not have to do this. If the figures are returned, the left-hand curve of

Fig. 6.11

Trajectory 3 would become more effective, but there would also be confusion. On the other hand, if in Phase III we leave the figures where they were in Phase II, we gain in relation to . . . the next montage sequence ('and strike'). (Anything which may serve as a visual link *between one shot and another* is a most valuable compositional element *within* a shot.)

In fact, the next shot is obviously the cannon-shot *hitting* Figure A1 (bigger and closer to the spectator), after the balls have missed him three times. In order to sharpen the effect of the hit, it is natural to precede it with shots of people not being hit,[*] so that the hit then 'lands' harder and *strikes* with greater force.

From this point of view, the second variant of Phase III is more successful; it gives a sharper perception of the cannon-ball missing the man than does the first version of Phase III (where it visibly described an arc in front of Figure A1; in other words it did what we were trying to achieve with Figure A2 and for which we recomposed the whole phase).

It is *precisely* here that this would be out of place. The cannon-ball hitting was prefigured for Figure A1 in Phase I. (Phase II is a rhythmic repetition of the same subject with the pattern reversed in relation to Figure A2). Phase III (in the second variant) depicts an obvious *miss* by the cannon-ball, thereby

---

[*]Here we see a method that is the reverse of that used in the episode of Russia's battle with the Pechenegs. There, the lead-in to the finale – the man crushed to death by horses' hooves – was achieved by giving two particular instances of death (by mace and by arrow), followed by a man being overwhelmed by hooves. The 'false move' was given earlier (the riderless horse). Here, to emphasise the hit, the false move – the 'recoil' [*otkaz*], or opposing movement – is located in the immediate proximity.

creating an excellent counter-movement ('reculer pour mieux sauter') for the *hit quand même*, the hit by the cannon-ball which then occurs in close-up. Phase III, incidentally, quite distinctly prefigures the path which the cannon-ball will follow when it hits the figure in close-up.

Since the flight-path of Cannon-Ball 3 and the strike of the ball in close-up are *directly* linked by the narrative and are at the same time equal yet opposite to each other (as if one were preceded by a plus, the other by a minus sign), for the close-up it is natural to direct the flight of the cannon-ball along the same curve but in the reverse direction. This provides us with the diagram for the cannon-ball's line of flight in the close-up (see Fig. 6.12).

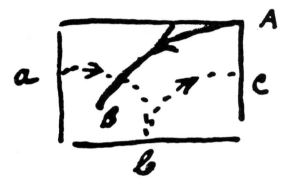

Fig. 6.12

Trajectory A–B follows the identical line but moves in exactly the opposite direction and is suitably magnified (doubled), since the altered depth of plane enlarges the dimensions. Thus the complete frame of the close-up will be constructed as in Fig. 6.13. Incidentally, of all the possible combinations this

Fig. 6.13

frame is, in my opinion, the most graphically vivid and therefore the most expressive of the subject matter: a hit. (The trajectory moves *diagonally*, i.e. along the *longest* possible line in the frame, the one whose dynamics make it most elementally expressive.)

We can move on further: 'Throw up the dust'. By now the outlines of this picture are becoming clearer. It is, in fact, a drama in two acts: 1) the cannon-ball ricochets from the body that it has struck, and 2) it buries itself in the dust. In other words, something like Fig. 6.14. It is right because the ricochet occurs spatially in the opposite direction to the hit: 'ab' and 'bc'. At 'c' the cannon-ball buries itself in sand. And here arises the problem of 'and' ('Throw up the dust *and* . . . hiss in pools of blood').

Fig. 6.14

In my first breakdown I allotted the 'and' to this frame. I think that is correct, because the pause on 'and' represents a sort of caesura of suspense for leading into a particularly impressive shot, which in the case of this whole passage is undoubtedly provided by the words 'hiss in pools of blood'. For this reason, 'and' requires the movement 'cd' – the ball rolling away out of the frame.

Thus in the two-phase movement that takes place in this frame the action at Point 'c' is, as it were, an off-beat twist which redirects the cannon-ball from direction 'bc' to 'cd'.

If we are to put the 'and' to good effect, namely to utilise it for a pause before flinging the final scene at the spectator, the way to do it here is very easy: to 'keep on playing' the cannon-ball when it is out of the frame. It is invisible – so of course it has to be 'kept playing' in sound. Is that legitimate? Absolutely, because in a moment the function of the cannon-ball will progress beyond all visual permutations into the next dimension – sound – when it hisses. In a moment it will be *both* visible *and* audible. Just now it was *visible but inaudible*. The transitional link will be *audibility* with *invisibility*.

What will that sound be?

The sound will be that of the cannon-ball landing in a pool of blood, invisible to the spectator but audible through the 'splash' of blood. That is, the cannon-ball rolls out of the frame from Point 'C' along Line 'cd' (corresponding to 'and'). The splash is audible out-of-frame (corresponding to the pause after 'and'). A new shot opens up. The fading of the *sound* of the splash will be revealed by *visual* 'ripples on the water', i.e. tremors on the surface of the blood, together with the sharp hissing sound of the hot cannon-ball, sticking half out of the pool of blood.

N.B. About the pause on 'and': pauses on 'and', 'but' or 'as though' are a typical cliché of 'provincial' reciters. Does our example fall into this kind of category (even though it is not so much concerned with declamation as with visual treatment)? Not at all, in my view, because our 'and' is unconnected with the scansion of the verse, whereas that is the very thing that would be typical of 'provincial-style' declamation. I have myself heard some veritable pearls of this kind of recitation, such as: 1) 'He was no more alive, *but* . . . dying', or 2) 'He opened wide prophetic eyes / *As though* . . . a frightened eaglet.'

In such instances the absurdity results from the fact that the scansion (the formal, mechanical stress) suggests the declamatory accent and the pause, and this purely mechanical stress is clothed in the garments of 'psychological' pseudo-significance.

In our example, the very reverse is the case. In the rhythmic structure of the text, the caesura falls *before* 'and', not *after* it, as we have placed it in our visual interpretation of the text.

The 'and' without a caesura might be treated as follows: in the penultimate shot, the cannon-ball would start rolling ('Throw up the dust . . .') and would roll into the last shot ('. . . hiss in pools of blood'). The caesura before 'and' would be shown thus; the cannon-ball hits Point 'c' and revolves upon it. The next shot is the pool of blood, and the cannon-ball rolls into it from out of frame.

Each of these solutions has, of course, its right to exist; and here it is not so much Pushkin's *structure* that plays a part as the *intonation* given by our interpretation. I think our interpretation is the least automatic and mechanical; this is, indeed, confirmed by its visual equivalent, which should of course be the most graphic, visually expressive and striking version possible.

(Let us note, by the way, that a montage break in a sentence can sometimes be read as a caesura: not always as a caesura in the structure of the text, but often as an interpretational caesura supplied by the reader, an interpretation that is a 'superstructure' on the poetry just as *mise en cadre* is a 'superstructure' in relation to *mise en scène*.) [. . . .]

If, however, we listen even more carefully to the sound of the verse, we shall inevitably feel the need not to disregard the original caesura in the text itself and the need to reflect it visually.

In what we have done, is there also a need for a corresponding element in the acting?

I think there is. In our example, the movement of the cannon-balls is *visually* quite well counterpointed by the movement of the human characters. It would also be a good idea if their respective moves could also be interwoven dramatically. Is there a justification for this and is the material for it present? Of course it is, and what is more it is material which, as they say, cries out to be used: not only the falling of cannon-balls but the falling of bodies. At the caesura after 'throw up the dust' and before 'and', there is an obvious need for a soundless fall, tracing in countervailing direction the line along which the cannon-ball bounces off the man's chest. The fall of the body, following the cannon-ball as it bounces away from it: *there* is the unstressed, or inter-stress, movement which the caesura requires at this point (Fig. 6.15).

This fall also provides the necessary physical impetus that causes the cannon-ball to roll away. The body has to fall *behind* the little hummock on which the cannon-ball comes to rest. The cannon-ball then starts to roll from the impetus of the fall; or to be absolutely precise, it jumps up slightly and rolls out of the frame. From then on everything occurs as we have decided above; during the pause and the splash, the legs remain in the frame, while the rest of the figure is behind the hummock (Fig. 6.16).

Fig. 6.15

Fig. 6.16

In general these two shots (the whole of this line of the verse) play the part of a special kind of caesura within this episode of the battle. 'Hiss in pools of blood' is like a sudden, visually arresting close-up: motionless in its visual aspect and all the more terrifying in its hissing sound. There is the noise and clatter that come before it, 'the beat of drums, the cries, the clang of steel' coming after it, while in between them there is this sudden, vivid detail of a faint sound in close-up, a detail which blots out the whole field of battle, just as sometimes a whisper right in your ear can conjure up a whole sea of chaotic sounds all around you.

Due to their position, these lines, as it happens, come within the area of the golden section of our extract.[228] In this same extract there is also a remarkable compositional echo between two passages, separated by four lines:

The first is:

'Mid fire, beneath a red-hot hail
Deflected by a living wall,
Above the fallen rank, a new, fresh rank
Fixes its bayonets. . . .

The second is familiar:

Flinging heap on heap of bodies,
From every side the iron cannon-balls. . . .

A similar echo is found at the beginning of the passage: 'a red-hot hail' and 'hiss in pools of blood'. The flight of the cannon-balls in the sky (like hail) before they reach the ground is, as it were, a visual summing-up of the whole passage. (For the sake of clarity in the sketches we have used foot-soldiers; cavalrymen would not have altered anything.)

We have been somewhat carried away by the details of our adaptation of this passage of verse; this is always entertaining when one is dealing with Pushkin. We should not, however, forget the two factors that we have been intending to discuss from the very beginning.

One of them is Pushkin's remarkable ability not only to combine picture and sound ('Swede, Russian – alike they thrust and slash and cut. / The beat of drums, the cries, the clang of steel . . .') in an amazing *rhythmic coincidence*, which replaces the *immediate* simultaneity of picture and sound as we have it on film and soundtrack in the cinema. But even more remarkable is Pushkin's ability to pass from picture into sound and from sound into picture, i.e. to introduce a theme by one set of means, develop it by means of another dimension and, when necessary, to crown the development by a new shift from dimension to dimension, from picture to sound. What is more, the move from depiction to sound occurs only when depiction has said and shown everything it can and the only thing left to do is transfer itself into sound.

This is precisely how the voice should naturally arise out of dramatic action and the communication of emotion. [. . . .]

In just this way the iron cannon-balls of 'Poltava', having exhausted all the visual possibilities, play the final note of the action as sound: they hiss. So, too, does Pushkin introduce the culminating episode of the battle and his incomparable description of Peter the Great:

And then, as from above inspired
Came forth the ringing voice of Peter:
'To the task, in Heaven's name!' And from the tent,
Surrounded by a swarm of favourites,
Comes Peter. . . .

The gradual way in which Peter is 'presented' is remarkable. First there is the voice, after it there is the crowd, with Peter in the midst of it but still invisible (like the cannon-balls in the first scene); only then is Peter revealed to us as such, or rather as 'the thunder of God itself03'.

The presentation itself is constructed by the same method: the text, the content of the words, are given last of all. At first we are told that the voice is inspired (from above) and 'ringing'. The visual appearance is *not* built up in a sequence such as: 'Peter comes out, surrounded by a swarm of favourites'; the vocal introduction is *not* made in a sequence such as: '"To the task, in Heaven's name!" came forth the ringing voice of Peter'. In both cases the sequence is the reverse: we are first made aware of *movement* and only after that is it revealed to us exactly who is moving. The first indication is that something is 'inspired' (abstract in the highest degree), then 'ringing' (more concrete), then 'the voice' (establishing that the sound is actually a voice); only then are we told that it is the voice of Peter (specific localisation), followed by the actual content of the words at the very end.

This is not, of course, dictated by 'the demands of rhythm'; we are dealing here with something considerably more profound. Rhythmically, the words could have been strung together in the alternative sequence. Here, the rhythm is not the point at all. I believe that altogether this manner of presenting phenomena, which is characteristic of so many instances in Pushkin's work, only provides futher support for the ideas which I put forward in my speech to the All-Union Cinema Conference in 1935. . . .[229]

Part Three
Sound-Film Montage

7 [Rhythm]

Broadly speaking, the image of what happens within a work of cinematic art has so far been outlined as clearly as it can be. Depiction is in the shot; the image is in montage. We have, however, also seen that internally the shot, if it aims to be artistically expressive, *must* unite both these principles. Montage has a dual function as the vehicle of both the depictive narrative and the rhythmically generalised image – again, provided that the montage relates to a work of art.

Here, perhaps, one further qualification should be made, for, on an equal footing with our interpretation of rhythm as given above, there also exist its *purely formal* definitions, such as the repetition of a certain combination or grouping at fixed and equal intervals of time: the alternative play between long and short, stressed and unstressed, etc. This kind of rhythm can also have its place in montage!

It is not, in this case, this kind of rhythm that I have been talking about; in this case it is first and foremost depiction, and furthermore depiction which does not absorb into itself a generalised image of the event which it is generalising. It is found in instances where a march is edited in march rhythm, a waltz in waltz rhythm. An example of transition into the other sort of rhythm would be 'metaphorical' montage, such as when a 'funeral' is edited as a 'waltz' or a 'waltz' as a 'funeral'. This occurs in cases where (as mentioned above in Part I) composition is used to give depiction another meaning. Finally there is the case of rhythmic generalisation of the inner content, where its scheme, its formula echoes only the internal progression of the content as it unfolds, fixing it by the alternation and length of the intervals of tension in the internal dynamics of the content. (But without the need to select an illustrative plot of *different* content, through which to make a comment on the *particular* content; we define this as a transferable metaphorical rhythm-diagram. An example of it is the 'waltz in funeral rhythm', as mentioned above).

However you look at it, montage has two inseparable functions: narrative, and rhythmic generalisation of the narrative. I spoke about this in detail in my lecture at the Sorbonne (Paris, February 1930).[230]

Taking these dual functions as the starting point, in my teaching programmes at VGIK and in articles written earlier, the types of montage are classified in two columns. In one of them are listed the various forms of the narrative (depictive) function of montage, in the other, the various forms through which the generalising, imagistic role of montage may proceed, these changing forms being understood as metamorphoses of the rhythmic principle, defined above as the ultimate limit to which generalisation can go without passing into abstraction.

Let us recall these lists, familiar to us since they were included in the programme of my 1935 course in film directing:[231]

Types of Montage Classified by Semantic Sequence
a) Montage parallel to the evolving course of the event (simple informational montage);
b) Montage parallel to the course of several sets of action ('parallel' montage);
c) Montage parallel to perception (montage of simple comparison);
d) Montage parallel to perception and meaning (image-forming montage);
e) Montage parallel to ideas (concept-forming montage). . . .

The above enumerates the potential forms of montage which arise from juxtaposition of the *narrative content* of separate pieces (of depiction).

The second column reads as follows:

Types of Montage Classified by Kinetic Sequence
a) metric;
b) rhythmic;
c) tonal (melodic);
d) overtonal;
e) intellectual, as a new quality in the development of overtonal montage towards significating overtones.

The above enumerates the forms of montage which arise from the process of juxtaposing these same pieces, i.e. it analyses the potential means whereby an idea can be realised not only in pictures within the pieces themselves but also through the various forms and processes of juxtaposition which also exist above and sometimes apart from the strictly narrative functions of montage, or rather the narrative functions of a heightened, generalising kind (i.e. rhythm as we understand it and as we have defined it above).

At this point it would perhaps be most pertinent also to mention that the transition from single set-up cinema to 'montage' cinema in itself also reflected the process which occurs at a certain stage in the development of any consciousness, namely the transition from *a reflection of phenomena themselves to a reflection of the relations between phenomena. In his excitement and enthusiasm at this achievement, some of the montage film-maker's extreme and excessive uses of the 'montage principle' as a process of relationships between phenomena have at times even hindered the depiction of those very phenomena!*

In my Sorbonne lecture, when I warmly welcomed the 'revelation of the sound film unto the multitude' (and in those days, whether or not to 'accept' the sound film was still a topic of discussion!), I said that this fact of the duality of its function was a fundamentally disruptive factor within montage. In the sound film I saw a way out of that internal contradiction between the two functions of montage. For the fact is that depiction and rhythm are inevitably in conflict in montage. The flexibility of rhythm sometimes demands microscopic 'cuts' (down to pieces of no more than two or three frames). The depictive function of a piece lies primarily in its being of adequate length, and the rhythmic construct is always dogged by a cautious concern not to lose the narrative and illustrative element, not to 'cut out' the depictive function of a piece. And as the narrative proceeds it must always be taking account of the rhythm: the narrative must not 'take over' so far as to lose the rhythmic link between the segments of the story as they are threaded together one after another. To release the montage segment from its time-bound rhythmic functions was one of the notably progressive factors which sound film introduced. I stress *time-bound* rhythmic functions, but it is quite obvious that here, in the dimension of length, lay the difficulty of which I am speaking. Whenever the viewing length of a segment is extended, the importance of visual rhythmicality of depiction increases even more, and that is why in this study we have devoted a whole section to the classic problem of shot-composition, a subject which *in itself* potentially contains the *entire theory* of the interconnection of picture and sound. For the rhythmic principle, to which we allotted the function of extreme generalisation (without breaking away into abstraction), is now in the sound film transferred away from the juxtaposition of montage segments into a new dimension – that of the 'sound contour' which *permeates* a series of segments, in exactly the way that the outlining physical, linear* contour did in the case of visual depiction of a [whole] picture or of a single shot, or the rhythmic 'progression' of a movement – by means of juxtaposed montage segments in the case of a 'montage' film-maker.

This establishes a completely indissoluble link unifying the conception of montage across all three qualitatively different stages.

This defines the status of sound not as an extraneous element thrusting itself into film-making but as something organic to cinema, as a further development of principles inherent in cinema's ability to create expressive images. This is made possible by the total image resulting from the double interpenetration of two different dimensions in a single expressive solution.

It is common knowledge that theatre, albeit very inadequately and clumsily, can to a certain extent serve as an apprenticeship to the audiovisual counterpoint of the sound film – in those cases where, as a matter of principle, the sound score in conjunction with the visual action are kept in the forefront of the director's attention and are consistently adhered to in practice. I myself

---

*Or the imaginary path that runs through the purposefully, specifically juxtaposed elements of depiction.

came to cinema with just this kind of background, derived from my personal experience in theatre.

In recalling that experience, even if only within the scope of the first big production that I undertook on my own, [Ostrovsky's] *Enough Simplicity for Every Wise Man* (1922–3),[232] we must look at the dual principle of its composition that ran through the entire production. Its stylistic premiss derived from a very simple starting point: the proposition that every action by an actor should expand in intensity to pass beyond the bounds of that activity itself. Roughly speaking, it meant that in registering 'astonishment' the actor should not limit himself to 'starting back'; starting back was insufficient: it had to be a backward somersault in the air. Such was the scale of movement prescribed by the impetuous young director.

In exactly the same way, the infuriated Mamayev, who is 'ready to hurl himself' at the caricatured portrait of himself done by his nephew Kurchayev, was made by the director to hurl himself physically at the portrait, and not only to hurl himself but to crash through it like a circus lion jumping through a hoop. Mamayeva's line 'it's enough to drive one up the pole' was instantly given concrete expression by having her thrust a long pole into a socket attached to Krutitsky's belt, whereupon she climbed up the pole and swung herself around from its top, doing the act known in circus jargon as 'the perch'. Metaphors were thus turned back into their original, primary, non-metaphoric, direct sense by carrying them out literally and thereby producing a comical, grotesque 'Aristophanic' effect. (The same method was used in farce in classical antiquity.)

Most amusing of all, I think, was the staging, on a similar level of metaphor, of the 'image' of Kurchayev the hussar. The idea of his nullity, his triteness, his banal conventionality was conveyed by having him played *simultaneously by three men*: all dressed alike, moving together and speaking his fatuous lines in chorus!

If at this point we recall the use of reversed metaphor in the examples quoted earlier – such as the staging of the scene with Vautrin – we shall discover that the method is exactly the same. But the *degree* of intensity with which it is applied produces different effects. If it is applied to an inadequate degree, the effort is dissipated into mere shapeless naturalism, whereas the physically *literal* representation of a metaphor gives a grotesquely comic effect. Here, if you like, there is in fact a direct congruence in method (although not in the scale of its application!) with that used by Ostrovsky himself: is there not metaphorical significance in the names that he gives to the chatterbox 'Gorodulin' ['Babbler'], or in 'Turusina' ['Mrs Twaddle'], his name for the superstitious old woman who believes any rubbish told her, and are not their images and behaviour on stage living incarnations of the metaphors contained in their surnames, expressed in character and action?

This principle, extended to the production as a whole, resulted in conventional theatrical form turning a backward somersault and landing up amid the conventions of the circus ring, and the production turned out to be a theatrical performance expressed in the idiom of the circus. Theatre-style depiction of emotion was expanded into the abstract style of circus movement. In the same way, Ostrovsky's drama of everyday characters suggested its own expansion into the interplay of the stylised, masked characters of the Italian *commedia dell'arte* and its great-great-grandchildren to be found in the modern circus ring. This was successful because Ostrovsky himself, working within the tradition of the Spanish and Italian theatre, had carried out the reverse process: he had personified the range of conventionalised, masked characters in the actual, everyday characteristics of a gallery of typical Muscovites of his own time – a theme in itself worthy of a dissertation by the 'Doctor of Bologna' (the conventionalised type of 'the scholar' in the *commedia dell'arte*). But its practical application evoked no less a gale of laughter and enjoyment than did the comic turns of the original masked characters.

Thus in this first change of treatment the generalised abstraction of the circus thrust its way through the visual objectivity of the theatre. This was the first example of 'two-level' performance in this production: from theatre 'downwards', to the circus. The second was from theatre 'upwards', to cinema; not only because the 'programmatic' arrangement of that production was restructured, away from the conventional succession of acts and scenes and into the type of composition known as the 'montage of attractions', which turned each episode of the play into a separate 'number' and gathered them into a unified 'montage' on the pattern of a music-hall programme. Not only for that reason but also because towards the end of the production the action itself was transferred on to film; and not only that, but to interaction between the actors in the ring and the same actors on the screen. The story of the theft of Glumov's diary was 'generalised' into a parody of a detective story with the aid of an appropriate sequence of film.[233] In those days we were all obsessed with *The Grey Shadow*, *The Secrets of New York*, *The House of Hate* and with Pearl White's cliff-hangers.[234] The depiction of the contents of the diary parodied a Pathé newsreel. In those days we were all fascinated by the newsreel and by Vertov's first issues of his *Cine-Pravda*.[235] But what was amusing about it was the fact that those contents themselves also generalised – in visual metaphors (literal and therefore comic) – the situations in the play about which the diary entries served as a confession. Glumov persuaded his uncle to teach him good sense: in the cinematic interpretation of this, Glumov was transformed by trick photography into an obedient ass, listening humbly to the uncle's admonitions. When talking to Krutitsky he figured as a militarist, and the film similarly turned him, by means of a dissolve, into a little cannon. The presence of Glumov's aunt, who allowed herself to take all sorts of 'liberties' with her 'little' nephew under the guise of family feelings, made this six-foot beanpole become a tiny baby in arms, also through the use of a dissolve. Thus the theatre took a leap into cinema, expanding metaphors to degrees of literalness unattainable in the theatre itself. And this culminated in the final stroke: when the audience called for me I did not come on stage to take any curtain-calls – instead I appeared on the screen, bowing like a peculiar version of the Pathé cockerel, with the shock of hair I affected in those days that was worthy of the Metro-Goldwyn-Mayer lion!

A long time ago Viktor Shklovsky, in his booklet entitled *Where Are They Now?*, wrote that there were no links between my *Enough Simplicity for Every Wise Man* and *The Battleship Potemkin*.[236]

It turned out, however, that there was a link between them. If the method in *Wise Man* was paradox and in *Potemkin* was realistic narrative, we can now see it as the way towards solving the most important, universal principles of composition, not only in cinema but far beyond its bounds, as we are here attempting to demonstrate and establish.

But let us return to our immediate, basic theme.

Such was our starting point in the 'preparatory school' of the theatre. From it I took the insights gained from treating the subject matter on two levels and in different dimensions, and, strange as it may seem, I found that in my first steps in cinema they (i.e. the different dimensions) could be applied too. We should bear in mind that I only gave full rein to such paradoxical treatment in my production of *Wise Man*. My subsequent work in the theatre was concerned with introducing and showing the same method of 'expanded metaphor' and 'generalised image' within the scope and degrees appropriate to realistic narrative. My film *The Strike*, however – although the chief attention was naturally concentrated on mastering the 'specifics' of cinema and on re-educating my thinking away from the theatrical to the cinematic – nevertheless contained what I might call the first experiment with sound in all my work in cinema.

It occurred in one scene in *The Strike*. Let us recall it. In its time it went down particularly well. As far as the overall plot was concerned, the scene, apart from introducing a certain lyrical note, was not especially significant, nor indeed was its use of trick photography either. Evidently, it was a case of an awareness – or a presentiment – that the problem I was setting myself here, a task which already went beyond the bounds of silent cinema, would one day be solved in its full scope. Moreover, this problem, which was formally solved by visual means alone, in juxtaposing these visual elements was already establishing their correct location for future purposes; it was also locating them correctly in accordance with the respective functions that were given to depiction on the one hand and, on the other, to what was – let us admit it – an attempt to convey sound by means of filming a visible object.

The scene was that of the 'accordion' in the first part of the film, which old film enthusiasts will perhaps recall. The scene showed how a 'mobile meeting' of the future strike committee was held, under the guise of an innocent evening's ramble through the countryside around the working-class district, with singing accompanied by an accordion. A few somewhat analogous scenes of such conspiratorial gatherings were also included in the first part of the film; they were not especially memorable. The following piece of trick photography, however, was used to rivet the spectators' attention to this particular scene as distinct from the others like it. In those days I was altogether fascinated by double exposure, and in particular by the double exposure of objects differing widely in scale. Perhaps this was a lingering sympathy for Cubism's use of multi-level space, which was to some extent why I transferred it to cinema. I now suspect, however, that this most likely was an interest, still in very vague form, in those multi-level and two-level functions which we no longer regard as trick photography but of which we are profoundly aware as being the two inseparably united levels on which every phenomenon reveals itself, and which are made up of: (1) a depiction of the phenomenon itself *through which* (2) a generalisation about its content also emerges as though by double exposure.

Thus the 'accordion' sequence contained one such element of double, two-level exposure, which stood in precisely the same cognitive relationship to the spectator as the one that we are expounding in this study. The sequence attracted attention, of course, because the method was not used for purely graphic purposes but as a means of conveying, through one exposure, a picture, and, through the second, a sound; through the realistic, objective long shot, a depiction of the event and the source of the sound; through the close-up, the idea of the sound itself, the sound of an accordion. The choice of close-up in the second exposure was the right one, and was very successful: a close-up is by its nature a self-contained abstraction, because it is cut off from other associations by the edge of the frame. Here the skill of Tisse[237] even extended this to making the accordion itself an abstraction: his photography pinpointed the closing up and opening out of a series of bright strips. This was the movement of the little metal bands which bind the edges of the accordion's bellows. As they alternately closed up and opened out, these strips swayed rhythmically across the centre of the picture, allowing us regular glimpses of the far distance, with the white patch of the pond at the end of the path along which the little group of singing workers was moving towards the camera. At the edge of the frame the distant view disappeared, allowing the keyboard of the accordion and the fingers moving over it to emerge sharply and solidly into the foreground. The rhythm of the moving metal strips corresponded to the walking rhythm of the approaching group, and the sound, conveyed by graphic means, embraced the whole landscape in song, thus embodying a generalisation of the entire scene.

Such was our preliminary attempt, in *The Strike*, to encompass the realm of sound. Excursions or 'trips' into sound were also to be found in my subsequent work in the silent cinema. In *October* they even figured in three different variants. These were achieved by visible objects being treated so as to suggest the way in which our hearing perceives them: the mobile machineguns which, as they were trundled along the flagstone floors of the Smolny Institute on the eve of the revolution, so disturbed the tender ears of the Mensheviks sitting behind the doors of their committee room; the visual interplay of different clocks striking the hours during the siege of the Winter Palace; the swaying of the glass chandeliers in the deserted palace, which conveyed the tinkling noise they made as they were caused to shudder by the gunfire outside on the Palace Square . . . and so on. These pictures were perceptually linked with the sound they made in reality.

Unlocalised, unreal sound was used metaphorically and led, through montage, to some complex baroque structures of aural association, e.g. by intercutting harps and balalaikas, in close-up, with the shots of Mensheviks and S.R.'s [Social Revolutionaries] speaking at the 2nd Congress of Soviets as they called upon the assembly to refrain from armed insurrection – at the time the Winter Palace had already, in fact, been taken by storm. Of course these visually clumsy devices were no more than an attempt, in the face of incredible difficulties, to convey by pictorial means what could easily have been done by having even the simplest soundtrack to give an ironic commentary, in sound, on the content of those speeches. Between these two extremes, however, there was one quite special example.

While the cruiser *Aurora* was firing her salvo, the Provisional Government was still holding an interminable, exhausting and pointless cabinet meeting inside the Winter Palace. A shot hits the palace; but, in the film, the members of the government do not immediately hear it. The sound of the shot rolls towards them through the thousand rooms of the Winter Palace (they are assumed to have taken refuge in its very depths). This effect was achieved (as the shell hit a corner of the palace with all the montage 'accents' necessary to 'perceive' the strike) by making it 'tear open' the next, dark, frame by means of an iris diaphragm opening rapidly from the centre. This revealed a deep-focus shot of a long space (the marble colonnade leading to the Jordan Staircase); then the iris diaphragm closed slightly more slowly, only to open again a fraction more slowly still, this time revealing another long room (the Malachite Room, I think) receding into the distance . . . and so on and so on. By opening and closing the iris diaphragm, revealing and then shutting out a sequence of length perspectives, and by gradually slowing down the tempo of the diaphragm and the montage length of each shot, I was able by visual means to convey the perception of a diminishing echo rolling deep into the palace through the endless suites of rooms.

The final diaphragm opened to reveal the last room, in which sat the petrified ministers. They shuddered: the echo had reached them.

It was almost a caricature of Homer, although an entirely appropriate one if we recall the 'Homeric' role ('Homeric' as in 'Homeric laughter') played by those ministers, the temporary masters of the land of Russia, a role which calls to mind those passages in Homer's epic of the Trojan War where the gods become involved as much as the mortals: 'The shout of the gods, reaching up to the heavens and penetrating to the underworld; a shout which shakes mountains, and the city, and the fleet, yet which remains unheard by men. For it was a shout so powerful that the puny organs of human hearing were incapable of perceiving it.' Thus wrote Lessing (in his twenty-seventh footnote to *Laocoön*), who regarded Homer's method as most apt.

The improbability, in realistic terms, of the Provisional Government hearing the *Aurora*'s salvo through a window giving on to the Neva only as an echo rumbling along a corridor is redeemed by its symbolic significance. For that group of 'rulers of Russia' suffered from an equal degree of 'aural blindness' towards the events that were rocking the country to its foundations in 1917. They only became aware of that process when it was too late: only when the actual, physical wave of the insurgent masses had rolled along those same corridors and reached the door of their little refuge among the palace's thousand rooms. In this sense, the echo of the *Aurora's* shot rushing through those rooms was, as it were, a forerunner of the human avalanche that overwhelmed the palace, sweeping aside 'all who opposed it' like the blizzard of history.

Such intense preoccupation with problems of form and with experiments in this area, however, inevitably had a fatal effect on the picture as a whole. Above all, insufficient attention to interpreting the great historical event that formed the centrepiece of that picture led to many errors of a political nature. But even though the formal experimentation in that picture was paid for so dearly, we must pay all the more attention to ensuring that the film-making experience we gained and those elements in it that were constructive should be preserved in the annals of the early development of that mastery later achieved by Soviet cinema. This also applies to *The Old and the New*. It is also, alas, equally true of the catastrophe with *Bezhin Meadow*.[238] The above-mentioned considerations oblige me, where necessary, to deal with the errors in my earlier work; at the same time, however, they also oblige me to face up to them and to take examples from the experience learned from them, in those instances where the examples themselves are not infected by errors in the interpretation of historical or current events.

The first serious step in realising the link between sound and picture, however, is not to be found in those other films of mine but in *Potemkin*. From the examples already cited it was clear that even in the silent cinema there was much that was conceived in audiovisual terms, and furthermore in the widest variety of ways of using sound: naturalistically or as crude metaphor (e.g. the harps and balalaika; in the same category, there was also the positive metaphor of the machine-gun blazing away, which was intercut with the fiery, insistent speech made by the Bolshevik orator as he routed the Menshevik and S.R. speakers at the Congress), and, finally, with considerable visual subtlety (the example of the 'echo' in the Winter Palace). Of course, I only really faced the problem of sound when I first had to deal with something that was not a question of 'arranging' sound – what I would call an aural 'cento' from various musical works in order to 'illustrate' a film – but when it was a case of music specially composed for a particular film. This happened with *Potemkin* in Berlin in 1926, when Edmund Meisel was commissioned to write a special score as an accompaniment to the film when it was shown in Europe and America.[239] I was in Berlin at the time and was able to give Meisel basic instructions concerning the sound as I had envisaged it. He succeeded in carrying out these ideas, not, unfortunately, in every detail, but in the main successfully.

Let us recall our definition of rhythm, which is in opposition to all the accepted, formal definitions of the term. We have seen how for us rhythm, at all stages of cinema's development, serves the same end by the same means: for us, rhythm has always been the ultimate means of generalising about a theme, as being the very image of the internal dynamics of its content.

This also occurred within a montage sequence (in the conditions of single set-up cinematography). There, in particular, it was the rhythm of the breaks in the pictorial contour which visually generalised both the content and the depictive element of a frame and of the outline of that depiction (we have demonstrated this, as applied to a series of adjacent frames, in Appendix No. . . .).[240] This function was also performed by the rhythm inherent in the relative disposition of the spatial masses of various objects, both mobile and static, within the picture or the shot. Finally, the same task was also given to rhythm when it was a question of building up a generalising image through the rhythmic use of gradations of light in depicting a scene (e.g. the mists in *Potemkin*, both in the gradations within individual shots and in combinations of them throughout the series of frames depicting the dawn).

Rhythm plays exactly the same role in an actor's performance. In the creation of a generalised image, rhythm is the next step after that initial metaphor of the gesture, which we have described above. We will not go into this in detail, as we are reserving the subject of acting skills for a separate study.[241] At this point, however, we can say that the rhythm of the actor's performance within the shot is the element which, more than any other, generalises the content of his actions.

Finally, and most obviously, it is through rhythm that the generalising function of montage itself is most powerfully expressed; without rhythm montage would simply be the 'shapeless' sum of a succession of 'facts'.

We have not limited ourselves to stating this as a thesis, but have traced, by research, the full potential inherent in rhythm itself. In doing so, we have touched on the subtler 'gradations' of the rhythmic principle. Thus, where montage is concerned, we have brought the melodic, tonal and overtonal principles, together with rhythm, into a single system.

Through visual overtones, we were able to establish that there could also be *physical* congruence between picture and sound through *sonic* overtones. Those were the first attempts to grope for congruence between the dimensions of picture and sound, the first steps towards finding links, psychological and semantic, that were more profound. (We will return to this in due course.) Here, however, the point to be stressed is that it is precisely rhythm which is the decisive principle enabling us to understand the organic, creative link between sound and picture, in such a way that it fits into our unitary conception of all the elements in all phases of cinematography.

It is not a matter of editing the film and composing the music in an *identical* rhythm. Nothing could be more mindless and simplistic.[242] I described to Meisel my requirements for the music as 'rhythm, rhythm and pure rhythm above all' – but by no means in the sense of rhythmic coincidence between sound and picture. What I wanted was that the rhythm of the music should function as a *mode of expressivity*. Meisel grasped this and realised it most fully in the fifth reel, where it was in fact most applicable, in the movement of the *Potemkin*'s engines as she steams to meet the squadron. I have already made detailed mention of *montage* rhythm as a means of raising *montage depiction into the category of a generalised image*. This was most completely achieved in the 'Odessa Steps': it was with this sequence that I illustrated my ideas in an earlier passage, and it was in this sequence, too, that the method could be most fully appreciated. The 'Odessa Steps' constituted the fourth reel of the film, and we naturally wanted to raise the expressive intensity of the film in the next, culminating reel. Rhythm, expressed through pictorial means, was used as a generalising medium in the fourth act of the drama. It remained to raise the rhythmic principle itself from one sphere to another, from one realm of application to another: thus the rhythm of the engines was raised beyond the realm of depiction into the realm of sound. This was so visually powerful and so generally convincing that it even, as later transpired, came to be recognised as a specific stage in the history of film music. Here, for example, is what Kurt London wrote about Meisel in his *Film Music*:

Next to him [Becce], the figure of Edmund Meisel, whose life was cut short all too prematurely, was and remains the most interesting of all. . . . His expressionistic style, turning first and foremost on rhythm, was many stages in advance of the films for which he composed. His musical accompaniment for the Russian film *Battleship Potemkin* marked him out as a pioneer in film music. . . . After that, he wasted his energy in useless musical experiments. *Berlin*, for instance, Ruttmann's documentary film, he ruined with his harsh atonalities. Later, shortly before the end of his brief career, he became a little more moderate. . . . Yet he remains as one of the strongest influences in film music.[243]

I think it will show Meisel's position with absolute clarity if I also add the passage that I have omitted from the above quotation:

And his first attempts in sound-films, after which death overtook him, showed that he died with the silent film, in a kind of common destiny: apparently it was only with difficulty and reluctance that he managed to submit to the laws of the sound-film.

At first sight these quotations may sound more like a contradiction than a clarification or an explanation! But that is not so; and the second flows logically from the first. Why was 'his Expressionist style, with its stress on rhythm . . . far ahead' of all the other films but not *Potemkin*? Because that stress on rhythm, above all, grew directly out of the demands made by the film itself and . . . by the director, not as *style* but as a *specific expressive mode*; exactly why and how it was done, we have tried to explain in earlier passages.

I am afraid that Meisel, fascinated by the effectiveness of that approach in *Potemkin* where it emerged as an imperative from the depths of the film itself, then went on to develop it mechanically into a method, a style, a 'school'. In those other examples of his musical scores, in which a similar treatment did *not* blend naturally with the films as an inevitable, organic, expressive element, then not only the effect but the whole method was bound to end in fiasco. But that is not all. The use of naked rhythm for its paradoxical effect in a sound-score proved to be very successful in the case of the specific requirements of *The Battleship Potemkin*, but it could not possibly become or remain a satisfactory method, an all-embracing panacea for the musical score of every other film. The unique factor in this case (especially when compared with Ruttmann's film *Berlin*) lies in the fact that in *Potemkin* the unadorned rhythm functioned as a generalising image, as the supreme mode of expressing the inner tension of an emotion that was integral to the plot of the film. It was not a generalisation of the rhythm of the ship's engines; it was a generalised image of the collective heartbeat of the battleship's crew, for which the engines themselves were a *visual* generalising image. Therein, no doubt, lies the secret of the one successful use of the 'rhythmic school' of film music in conjunction with a silent film. Even without recalling Ruttmann's *Berlin*, it is easy to imagine that in other instances 'the Expressionist style with its stress on rhythm' by no means functioned as the supreme mode of generalisation, but simply deafened the audience with its rhythmical drumming on every *superficial* pretext, seizing upon the external rhythm or the movement with which people, objects and events were depicted. In such cases, this atonality could provide nothing but an accompanying effect that was soulless, mechanistic and formal. But in sound film the failure of his work was even greater. Meisel got stuck in the rut of rhythm as such. Rhythm is what I would call the 'mime' element in music; in other words, it corresponds to the element of silent cinematography within the sound film. The sound film was a progression from man expressing himself in mime to man expressing his feelings by voice, words and tone.

The sonic aesthetics of the 'rhythmic school' should have progressed beyond the bounds of the purely mimetic principle of naked rhythm. Musical tone is equivalent to the stage of the movement of the whole body. It is a subtle stage of the same expressive movement which modulates the sounds of the voice, which in turn are also movements of human physical organs – the vocal cords, etc. – but movements of such high frequency and subtlety that they are not perceptible to our sight as movement but are perceptible as sounds to our hearing. Rhythm in music derives from those basic physical movements of work and dance which were the forerunners of what later became music proper. The voice, with its tones and modulations, was equally the forerunner of melody, and remains the source from which we draw the basic human emotional content of the melodic side of music. Naturally, with the transition to the significantly broader scope and subtle demands of the musical score of a sound film, the harsh atonality of the 'rhythmic school' was bound to sound like an archaic survival and an organically alien element. I believe it is along these lines that we must seek to understand what one might call the 'triumph and disaster' of the history of Edmund Meisel's contribution to film music. Thus it was *precisely in the area of rhythm*, through my collaboration with Meisel – who was unable, as a film composer, fully to realise himself in his most valuable function and unable to carry that function beyond atonality into the next phase of development – that the transition from the second to the third phase of cinematography was accomplished: namely in the sphere of rhythm and of the significance that we gave to it and to all its derivatives.

Now, in proceeding to the stage of sound-film montage, I want to stress one most important point above all: namely, that music in the broadest sense – including words, voice and sound in general* – is not something totally new which only came into cinema along with sound films, and that in the preceding stages of cinema we are right in discerning a kind of 'pre-music' in those characteristic elements of cinema that we have been investigating stage by stage. They have very specific artistic functions, and an analysis of these elements helps us to locate with precision the role of sound in talking pictures and to clarify its place within the synthetic composition which is the sound film.

Diderot wrote much of value about . . . *Kino*. Admittedly he was referring to the composer *Quinault*, who was not, however, a composer of film music.[244] These pronouncements were no doubt of great value to the composer Quinault. But in Diderot's *Third Dialogue*, in which he discusses musical drama, there is one passage that is also of value to sound cinema. At any rate it is a concrete example which will finally help us to demonstrate vividly exactly where the element of 'music' is to be found in the early stages of the cinema's development; also how the sound film and its concept of montage are directly derived from and linked with those foregoing periods.

Diderot describes how one of Clytemnestra's soliloquies from Racine's *Iphigénie* would sound if transferred to music in a musical drama:

Meanwhile, oh heavens – hapless mother that I am! –
My daughter, brow all garlanded with hateful wreaths,
Holds out her breast to knives her father has prepared!
Calchas is smeared with her blood. . . . Barbarians! Stop:
In her there flows the purest blood of Zeus himself.
I hear the thunder's roar; the earth begins to shake:
A god, a vengeful god gives warning of his wrath.

(Racine, *Iphigénie*, Act V, Scene 4)

---

*I insist on this turn of phrase rather than the formulation 'sound broadly understood both as word, as voice and as music' because we are not dealing here with an acoustic phenomenon (sound) and its various forms but with an emotional phenomenon in phonation that is artistically organised in various ways. It is in this sense that I bring them together under the term 'music'.

This is the extract from the soliloquy quoted by Diderot; and here is his idea of how the composer would express this material in sound:

He would make the thunder rumble, he would make the lightning flash; he would show me Clytemnestra threatening her daughter's executioners with the image of the god in whose name they are spilling that blood; in my imagination, already shaken by the pathos of the verse and the situation, that image would rise up with the utmost possible veracity and power. I no longer hear Iphigenia's mother: what I hear is the rumble of thunder, the earth shaking, the air vibrating with that terrifying roar.

(Diderot, *Troisième dialogue*)

Let us analyse this.

Thus, three things are shaking him: 1) the pathos of the situation; 2) the pathos of the poetry; and finally 3) the transposition into music, in which 'that image would rise up with the utmost possible veracity and power'.

Here we are given, as it were, the three phases in which the material is expressed in theatrical terms:

1) the situation (the raw material; the plot), the content of which is itself charged with pathos;
2) 'the poetry', that is to say its primary treatment by the compositional medium – in this case, literary;
3) its transposition into music, i.e. the transfer of the material that has already been poetically 'shaped' to the higher level of a new quality that has an even greater power and impact.

Furthermore, this latter aspect also has the special characteristic that in it he 'no longer hears Iphigenia's mother' but the roaring of the whole universe; in other words, the theme of Clytemnestra's anger and horror raised to the utmost level of generalisation. Indeed, the 'purpose' of the transposition into music is perceived as the desire also to convey, by depicting Clytemnestra's behaviour, a 'cosmic' generalisation (in this instance purely emotional in nature): Anger and Horror with capital letters; Anger and Horror through the anger and horror of Clytemnestra.

And *this* is the image which 'rises up with the utmost possible veracity and power'. As well as 'power', Diderot is right also to use 'veracity', i.e. realism in the highest sense of the word, and not simply 'truth to everyday life' – for it is a fundamental characteristic of realism that through the specific and the particular we descry the general, the universal. [. . . .][245]

I believe it will not be an empty *jeu d'esprit* or a merely formal analogy if we point out that in cinema we have had exactly the same way of treating our material and in three similar stages.

What is more, this occurs not only in cinema as a whole, which we have seen in its three phases – single set-up cinema; multiple set-up cinema; and sound cinema – which replicate Diderot's threefold division in all its fullness and perfection, but the same interrelationship also exists *within* each one of these three stages.

This is a fact. Let us examine, from this standpoint, everything that we have expounded about the first two stages of cinematic development: about single set-up cinematography and about multiple set-up cinematography (vulgarly called 'montage cinematography').

1) *Single set-up cinematography*

The first phase would be taken up by . . . the title. (For example: 'Barricades were thrown up throughout the city. . . .')

The second phase I would allot to the requirements of graphic composition, in which everything is made rhythmically congruent and spatially balanced. (For example: the composition of barricade No. 1.)

And the third phase I would locate in the graphic composition at the point where, apart from all that, it also becomes a generalised image of the fundamentals that underlie the graphic depiction. (For example: the composition of barricade No. 2. Paraphrasing Diderot and applying his words to *that* particular composition, we might say: 'I now not only see the barricade: what I see is the struggle, the attack, the clash of two forces.')

This type of composition would be, as it were, the transposition into static music, which conveys the same generalising effect that music does in the role that Diderot gives to it.

2) *Multiple set-up cinematography*

The first phase would belong to . . . a sequence shot from a single set-up. (For example, a long shot giving an information overview: 'Fighting on the barricades'.)

The second phase I would allocate to those logically consecutive montage sequences which reveal the course and development of the fighting at the barricades. Furthermore, these would show sequentially a series of strikingly well-planned and brilliantly acted episodes of the barricade fighting, the only aim of which would be to demonstrate it in comprehensive detail.

Finally, I see the third phase in the kind of montage editing in which the change of shots, their relative length and the particular scenes depicted in them all combine to create a dynamic perceptual image of the fighting; in other words, a dynamic visual music made up of the rhythm and tones (in the pictorial sense) of the successive sequences which, like a symphony on the same theme, underlie the depiction of events. (A 'mechanical' adjunct used for this purpose was the music accompanying silent films. The function of that music was either to provide the generalising image that was otherwise absent from a particular scene or, if it were present, to transpose precisely that image into sounds. The leap from there to the perception of sonic montage in sound film was easy and obvious.)

Let us now examine the first and second phases as they apply to the *sound film*.

1. The first is the 'voice-over' spoken by a narrator, which accompanies the successive shots with an explanation.

A distant cousin to the narrator is the synchronised soundtrack of realistic sounds (the door-bell which is seen and also heard to ring; the actor speaking; the bonfire which the spectator sees burning and hears crackling): this also is as much an aural commentary on the visual picture (or, if you like, it is a visual commentary on the aural event).

2. The second phase I would allot to the intelligible distribution of the audiovisual counterpoint within the audiopictorial *narrative* of the drama as a sequence of events; the skilful introduction into the action of plot-related music as a substitute for dialogue; the intelligible use of 'heightened tension', 'suspense' and so on, all of this being done in rhythmic sympathy with the composition as a whole, echoing the movement and pace of the drama. (For an example of this, see my treatment of episodes from *Anna Karenina*.[246])

3. Finally, the third phase. We can dwell on the third phase in greater detail, for the whole of Part Three of this book is devoted to it! Here, too, the situation is equally clear and distinct. It embraces: the function performed by the generalised compositional outline of the depictive element in the first stage of cinema; the function performed by the generalised image of an event which emerges from a group of montage sequences in the stage of so-called montage cinema; music must perform the same function of a generalised image in relation to the event visually depicted on the screen.

The reverse situation, of course, is entirely admissible: in that case the picture plays the role of generalised image in relation to the sound. Instances of this occur more rarely, which is a consequence of the essential nature of music and depiction respectively. The former is less concretely representational and objective but more suited to a generalising role, while the latter can only generalise with difficulty but on the other hand is much closer to material reality. Most effective of all is what happens in actual fact: the allocation of this role alternately to one medium and then to the other.

Thus if we adhere to our agreed classification – with only the proviso that we have just mentioned – we arrive at what would seem to be a single table applicable to all three phases of cinema.

Let us recall that the complete image arises from the fusion of depiction and generalised image; then, under the headings of 'depiction' and 'image', we can schematically distribute the cinema's modes of effect in the way that we have laid out.

Table I has been drawn up exactly as we might do it in relation to an actor and his part.[247] In the first column would be 'the personal qualities of Gordei Tortsov'; in the second would be 'typical characteristics of a Moscow merchant of Ostrovsky's time'. The mutual interpenetration of both would then create that inimitable total image, which is so fully provided in Ostrovsky's play as literary material, and which demands to be displayed with equal realism through the actor's feelings and performance. This table is compiled on exactly the same principles but applied to the cinema's different modes of effect and expressivity.

TABLE I

	Depictive principle	Generalised image
1. *Single set-up cinema and montage sequence*	Depiction of the object	Outline of the object (*or* the disposition of elements *or* the disposition of light over the elements, etc.)
2. *'Montage' cinema*	The shot	Montage
3. *Sound film*	The shot and montage	Sound (noise, voice, words, music)

The division and distribution are schematic, because both mixing and transposition are possible, enabling these functions to pass from one mode to another, but only if one condition is immutably observed: that these functions must be carried out in different dimensions and by different means. The fact that they belong to different categories of perception also requires that they be localised in expressive media that are materially different. (Failure to observe this condition leads to the visual confusion to be found, for instance, in Repin's portrait of Lev Tolstoy.[248])

One thing, however, is quite obvious: the identity of principle despite qualitative differences between particular films in all three phases.

Generalisation (1) was expressed by the *outline* of the depiction. Generalisation (2) was expressed by the *moving line* along which the montage sequences are combined (beyond the bounds of a single sequence and into the combination of sequences). Generalisation (3) is expressed beyond the bounds of the montage combination of sequences and into the *moving line of music* which runs through them.

It is interesting that in all three phases the very concept of movement itself undergoes qualitative shifts, and with each new phase enters into a new form of movement.

'Movement' in the first phase – the movement of the outline – is in essence a purely conventional concept: after all, the outline is static; it does not in fact move about. It is our eye that moves along the outline; and if we talk of the outline 'moving', this is actually no more than the reflected movement of our eye; we transfer to the outline the movement which it has forced our eye to make, and we conventionally attribute that process of movement to the outline.

The apparent movement of the outline is thus the *consequence* of a certain movement, but it is that apparent movement which has an expressive quality, not the act of movement itself. By creating the apparent movement, we also participate in it as if it had really taken place.

The second case is characterised by movement as such, in its most obvious and mechanically simple form: this is an instance of movement as locomotion. (As we know, Plekhanov, for instance, did not perceive of movement in any other way.[249])

The third case is interesting in that we are presented with the principle of movement in a new phase. In this instance we do not have movement as locomotion (melody moves differently from the movement of a grand piano being shifted by removal men), although, unlike the first phase, here it is a case of movement that is sequential in time. The actual movement has been transferred to a higher phase, into the realm of vibration. Later we shall see that this is true not only for sound and music, where it is inherently obvious due to the laws of physics; we shall see that the visual component of a film, as the new contribution to this phase, is joined to the first two forms of movement – which this phase by no means loses. What is much more striking, however, is the fact that the principle adduced in Table I is also strictly observed *within* each of these categories taken separately. We have already demonstrated this as being applicable *within* the graphic outline and *within* montage. It also holds good *within* the third stage.

Let us begin with words. Where words are concerned, the sentence is equivalent to the progression of a montage sequence through a series of frames. In a sentence, the depictive fragments – words – are combined into a meaning that embraces them all. This is obvious.* The cinema, however, is not simply concerned with the sentence as such but with the *spoken* sentence. It is also interesting that in relation to the sentence itself the *pronunciation* of a sentence, i.e. its tone, obeys exactly the same conditions that we have been discussing in such detail. For it is precisely *tone* which decisively adds the ultimate image, interpretation and generalised meaning to what is a collection of separate words joined into a sentence. Let us also recall the endless number of images which can be potentially created out of a spoken sentence thanks only to differences in the 'music' of its intonation.

There are many literary methods aimed solely at using intonation, which in accordance with an overall rhythm deploys the written words in unvarying repetition. An example of this kind of structure is:

> Riding, riding, riding to her,
> Riding to meet his beloved . . .

---

*It is also true in every detail, because the sentence can also string words together in two ways: using words, it can try to convey only a straight depiction of what is being described; or with the aid of its rhythm and structure it can try to convey a sense-perception of the object in question.

Nor should we forget the famous passage in Vasily Kamensky's 'Loco-motive Litany' ['*Parovoznaya obednya*']:

> We are sleepers, sleepers, sleepers
> Sleepers, sleepers, sleepers we . . .[250]

The first quotation reads exactly like the plan of a montage sequence, in which the first three 'ridings' are, as it were, like someone riding on three different levels from three different points which merge into an image of 'riding', which then in the second line conveys an image of the fact that it is a lover riding 'to her'. . . . Kamensky's 'Sleepers' seem to be filmed from a moving train, conveying their ever-accelerating tempo as they flash past.

This at once calls to mind another example from a related genre: the refrain from a traditional song that Paul Robeson used to sing, about a girl refusing a proposal of marriage from someone called John. Each verse ends with her refusal: 'Oh, no John, no John, no John, no.' This in turn links us with the genre of the popular song, especially French songs, in which the five or six verses invariably end with the same line. The whole half-spoken, half-sung art of the *diseuse* – in which Yvette Guilbert was undoubtedly unsurpassed – consisted in the skill of intonational phrasing and the nuances that were given to that unvarying refrain.[251] As an example, I will cite 'Les jeunes mariés' from Xanrof's *Chansons ironiques*.[252] It consists of a series of verses on the theme of the young bride and groom waking up the morning after their wedding night. Various images are invoked with a few strokes in each three-line couplet. One bride is distressed and weeps. Another says: 'Is that all?' A third says: 'It was more fun with my cousin', and so on and so forth. The fourth line of each couplet is invariably: 'Les jeunes mariés', and the whole art of performing the song is that the intonation given to that line should characterise each of the 'young brides', and should convey her 'image', together with the appropriate ironic wink to the audience.* At the level of irony, this is equivalent to what Bach does in his fugues on religious themes, where the inspiration is also a single line of text, e.g. 'Dies Irae' or 'Te Deum Laudamus'. The massive structures of these works of his are built on an endless variety of 'intonational' treatment, in this instance orchestral and choral. Thus intonation, as applied to the words of a text, plays the same role as outline in depiction or as the line followed through a series of montage sequences. At the same time, intonation also breaks down into onomatopoeic depiction;† the rhythm which generalises the appropriate emotion; and the

---

*For Yvette Guilbert's own comments on performing *chansons*, see her book: *L'Art de chanter une chanson* (Paris, 1928).

†in cases where the intonation is above all graphically descriptive, this may not even be done by onomatopoeia, as, for example, in cases where we want to convey an impression of great size and we pronounce the word *bolshoi* [big] as 'b-o-o-lsh-o-o-i', or of very small size by excessively dragging out the diphthong 'i-i-i' in the word 'tiny'. In onomatopoeic words or

meaning which is *conveyed* by a differentiated pronunciation of the same combination of words. Exactly the same process takes place in music.

What serves as the unifying link between these cases is the fact that the basic core of music – melody – is in itself the ultimate form of generalisation of the human use of intonation. We have already touched on this in passing. Let us now mention it at somewhat greater length. Again, it was Diderot who wrote about this generally known principle with unusual penetration.

The matter, however, does not end there; the most interesting thing about music is, of course, the fact that the movement of counterpoint within a piece of music also corresponds exactly to the phenomenon whereby the *visible*, *material* outline of the picture in a film-shot evolves into the *mental* 'path between sequences', the process that occurs when cinema moves on from the single set-up stage to multiple set-up (like a living organism evolving from the single-cell to the multicellular stage!). The juxtaposition of a number of melodic sequences also gives rise to a certain generalising 'line' that is not conveyed materially but which *emerges*, the line of harmony:

> The true contrapuntal style, in the form that Bach gave it to us, is characterised by a predominance of the melodic over the harmonic element. In this contrapuntal style, the separate melodic lines constitute the formative element, while the harmonic texture is, as it were, a *result* of the interweaving of the melodic voices. The harmonic texture is a consequence, a secondary phenomenon that accompanies the contrapuntal texture. In the network of interweaving voices, each one living a separate existence, the phantoms of passing harmonies are evoked, summoned up by the conjunction of several melodies.[253]

By tabulating (Table II) the characteristics that are found within each of the categories, we get an expanded version of Table I.

The same reservations apply to this as those that were made for the preceding table. In studying this table we should pay double attention to the chief, fundamental factor: namely, that the separation of the elements of depiction and generalisation is done here solely for purposes of research; also that the whole secret of the authenticity of a film, i.e. of its realistic form, consists of ensuring that *within the film* this separation should not occur, and that depiction and generalisation should mutually interpenetrate and form a unity. This also applies to those constituent parts of a film which have been distributed across various divisions of the table.

From all that has been said so far, we get a remarkable picture of the *three phases* in the history of montage, to say nothing of the fact that the very concept of montage has been raised up from the crude notion of 'cutting up

---

expressions this will be achieved by a particular over-emphasis of vocally descriptive characteristics in pronouncing the words.

and gluing together' to a very advanced conception of it as breaking down a phenomenon 'as such' and recombining it into something qualitatively new, into a view of an attitude towards a phenomenon that is a socially interpreted generalisation about it.[254]

TABLE II

	Depictive principle	*Generalised image*
Single set-up cinema	*Depiction of the object*	*Outline*
Outline	Pictorial outline of the object	Rhythm of the breaks in the outline
Montage cinema	*The shot*	*Montage*
Montage	The narrative element of montage	Rhythm of the montage
Sound Cinema	*Shot–montage*	*Sound*
Sound: Word–phrase	Objective content of word and phrase	Melody of the phrase
Melody	Melody of the phrase	Rhythm
Music	Sound–words, intonation of the human voice, musical melody	Intonation, musical melody, harmony arising from counterpoint of melodies
[Corresponding phenomenon in the area of expressive gesture]	Utilitarian content of the expressive gesture	Metaphor of the content of gesture
	The metaphor of gesture	Rhythm of gesture

First Phase. The picture does not move. The generalisation move rhythmically within the picture (conventionally) around the breaks in the contour of its outline.

Second Phase. The picture moves, both microscopically and macroscopically. The frames change and succeed one another within the shot. The shots change in the progression of montage sequences. The generalising thread is in the imaginary line that links these sequences.

Third Phase. The picture does not move. The generalisation proceeds rhythmically in the melody and harmony of the sound component that simultaneously runs through it.

In this study, all three phases have been described in terms of emphasising their characteristics to the utmost degree. In this 'pure' form they are particularly striking illustrations of the consecutive stages of a dialectical process of development. The third phase is, as it were, a return to the first. Then comes the break-up of the static unity of the first phase into the dynamics of montage sequences. The fragments of the break-up are extracted from this principle of dynamic unification, from which comes reunion into a new dynamic unity, in which the principles of both previous stages are, as it were, united: both the invariability and the dynamic variability. This is interesting both cognitively and theoretically.

It is quite obvious that, in practical terms, when speaking of immobility in the third phase this is not to be understood absolutely but relatively, i.e. in such a way that if it is entirely possible (and in practice, unfortunately, it happens all too often!) to have a lengthy, *unchanging* depictive sequence with a very complicated sound-score, it is equally possible for that score to be the counterpoint to a depiction that, as montage, is a highly complex structure.

These are the final considerations of a general nature that we wished to dwell on before plunging head-first into the midst of the third, audiovisual, stage of cinema: into the sound film, which has not only replaced the first two stages but has synthesised and absorbed the experience which they gained. That is also why we dwelt at such length on those first two stages. It has not only been an excursus into the history of cinematic form, it has also been an analysis of the most essential constituents of sound film. Unless one is thoroughly familiar with them, one cannot hope to make a sound film that is even literate, let alone well made![255]

8 'The Girl Like a Ray of Light'

Methodologically the matter is 'extremely simple': a single image has to carry the scene in both vision and sound. . . .

Problem: music is needed to accompany the girl's entrance.

But: it is impossible to write music to accompany the girl's entrance 'pure and simple', just as it is not possible to stage, much less to film, the girl's entrance 'pure and simple'.

Thus Stanislavsky's 'Method' quite rightly teaches that a person cannot enter through a door unless. . . .

But let the author of the 'Method' put it in his own words: 'Don't act "in general!"'

That is the general principle; here it is in more detailed exposition:

'Let us say that one of the persons of the play has to come into a room. . . . Can you walk into a room?' asked Tortsov.

'I can,' answered Vanya promptly.

'All right then, walk in. But let me assure you that you cannot do it until you know who you are, where you came from, what room you are entering, who lives in the house, and a mass of other given circumstances that must influence your action.'[256]

In quoting these principles, we ourselves are certainly not going to burst in through an 'open door', because *for us, essential though they are, they are still far from sufficient*.

They are sufficient for the actor and for his personal actions, but not for the 'setting' of his entry. Nothing has been said about the composer, the lighting expert or the set designer.

We need at least a hint of an image, the merest suggestion of a metaphor that will fill in the significance of the girl's entry, in order that all those dormant forces that go to make up the 'setting' may be brought into play and thus produce something that is more than a straightforward depiction of fact. And, most notably, that metaphor, that fleeting comparison, that verbal signpost should instantaneously and in equal degree serve as that generalising key through which all the *other* incompatible factors – the actor's performance, the cutting of the shot, the melodic structure, the distribution of the lighting tones, etc. – simultaneously come together into a whole.

You may make the most banal, trivial remark – though it must, of course, relate to the content, the plot, the meaning and the central idea of the given fragment of the piece as a whole. If you say, 'The girl burst into the stuffy atmosphere of the room like a ray of light', then everyone knows what they have to do, for even in that trivial remark there is a sufficiently concrete narrative element, *but also one that is sufficiently abstract and generalised* to be applicable to all facets of the production, at the same time without binding any one of them to its particular medium of application.

The theme of 'one element penetrating the realm of another that is opposed to it' is in equal degree a generalised objective for the composer, the lighting artist and the casting director, for the design of a set to express that idea and for the graphic composition of the shot that will sketch out the same idea on the flat surface of the screen. Indeed, it should even go as far as to express a generalised interpretation of the drama as a whole: the critic Dobrolyubov, after all, distilled the very image of Katerina in [Ostrovsky's play] *The Storm* into the title of his article on it: 'A Ray of Light in the Realm of Darkness'![257]

Thus, given a purely depictive shot in the visual medium, we should allocate the 'image' element to sound and we should not use it for 'depiction', which can only be achieved by imitative sound. On this point I cannot help recalling a funny incident from the era when the sound film still only existed as a 'silent film with musical accompaniment'. Even in those days, the problem we are discussing arose more than once, for example in 1925 at a session of the Anniversary Commission on the 1905 Revolution, when we were discussing the question of the music to accompany *Potemkin*. The late L. Sabaneyev protested furiously at being required to select (or write) music for that film. 'How am I supposed to illustrate . . . *maggots* in sound! It's something quite unworthy of music!' He failed to see the essential point: that it was neither the maggots nor the rotten meat that were important in themselves, but that quite apart from being a minor, factual, historical detail, they represented above all a symbolic image that would bring home to the audience the social oppression of the masses under tsarism! And surely *that* was a noble and most rewarding theme for any composer!

I also cannot resist recalling another amusing incident, this time from the making of the film *October*. What happened in this case was, as it were, the exact opposite of my first example; the only thing they have in common is an equal degree of absurdity! This one was a case of trying too hard for musical depiction, and confusing the purely formal side of music with its illustrative quality – an attempt carried to absurd lengths. You will recall that in that film, by a misuse of associational montage, Kerensky in the Winter Palace was intercut with shots of a gigantic, silver-gilt, mechanical peacock (which spreads its tail, flaps its wings and revolves on top of an enormous and elaborate clock – a present, I think, from Prince Potemkin to Catherine the Great). On seeing this gilded peacock, my zealous musical arranger (unlike Sabaneyev) immediately knew what was required: peering short-sightedly through his pince-nez and being unable to distinguish the exact breed of the bird, he at once proposed using the music from . . . *The Golden Cockerel*![258]

But even richer than this was his suggestion for the music to accompany the scene in which a dead horse dangles by its harness from the edge of one half of the Palace Bridge as the two bascules are raised to open it. 'A horse in the air . . . a horse in the air. . . . Let's use "The Ride of the Valkyries"'! It's a fact!

When choosing the methods to be used for creating a shot, here, as everywhere else, you are threatened on opposite sides by Scylla and Charybdis: Excess and Inadequacy, namely the excess or inadequacy of the *degree* to which generalisation can and should show through depiction. At the extreme of *inadequacy* lies flat-footed naturalism taken to an extent where music (and, what's more, music that in such a setting cannot even be *internally* synchronised with the action!) seems wholly out of place unless it is visually justified by the sight of a barrel-organ playing as the girl enters!

At its extreme, *excess* prevents the action from looking convincing at a realistic level: light and darkness, gloom and brightness play symbolically across the interior of a peasant cottage; the features of Pan and the Paschal lamb appear in the faces of two of the characters. . . . The reader will have already realised that I am citing some of my own excesses of generalisation from my failed film *Bezhin Meadow*.

The term 'show through' is, I think, the most correct formulation of what should happen. It excludes to an equal extent both 'imperceptibility' and 'obtrusiveness'.

Whereas in *Bezhin Meadow* we had occasional instances of one extreme (excess), the other extreme is to be found in many, many other films that we see screened. Therein lies the reason why hardly a single landscape that is shown with musical accompaniment in Soviet films is ever internally synchronised with the music. A happy exception to this still remains, I think, the shots of the Dnieper in Dovzhenko's *Ivan*.[259] And why? Because – probably empirically and not as a conscious device – both the director of that visual poem of filmed shots and the author of the song were unconsciously striving, each in his own medium, to recreate the incomparable flow of images of the Dnieper in Gogol's *The Terrible Vengeance* (the passage that begins 'Wonderful Dnieper . . .').[260]

I say 'empirically', because otherwise the absolute audiovisual failure (in the compositional sense) that occurs in an analogous passage in *Aerograd* could not have taken place.[261] In that, the running men, the landscape and the song of the Chukchis are completely unconnected by any kind of internal synchronicity and never succeed in blending into an audiovisual symphony.

This new principle of the third phase of cinematic development that we are studying echoes precisely the principles that applied to the first two phases.

In all three phases, the means of generalisation – i.e. those which extend beyond the immediate limits of the phase itself – prove to be creatively achieved through elements of another dimension, of a medium different from that of the basic narrative medium.

In the first phase it was the outlines of the depiction and the rhythmic congruence between these outlines, *as distinct from the depiction itself.*

In montage cinema, it was the generalised image of an object or a process which *was not present in the film itself* but which formed itself in the synthesising consciousness of the person perceiving it.

Finally in the phase of the most advanced form of cinematography, which we are now studying, we also find the same characteristic, but provided with a more perfect medium of expression; namely, an even subtler dimension (sound) and one which in addition has its own technical vehicle independent of the picture: the soundtrack. It is easier to grasp than the fleeting outline with which real objects are held on the surface of the screen. While it is recorded simultaneously with the picture, it is in the process of running the film through the projector that the soundtrack becomes more 'material' in terms of feet and inches than the elusive generalisation deriving from the mass of montage segments in a montage sequence. At the same time, however, the danger is all the greater of the soundtrack becoming 'self-sufficient' and not organically integrated with the picture (*vide* the example of the Chukchis running past in *Aerograd*).

Such is the interrelation of sound and picture in the system used in sound film.

We observe that it is precisely this interrelation which in the sound cinema occupies the same function that in so-called montage cinema was given to the process and *meaning* of a combination of phenomena out of a mass of montage segments.

On the other hand we have seen that in the preceding phase (single set-up cinema) this montage quality also existed embryonically in the interrelation between separate elements of the depiction, which had been, as it were, 'gathered up' and incorporated into the overall generalising plan.

We are therefore justified in saying that the basis of audiovisual montage lies in synchronised composition in the way that we understand it and have expounded it here.

In comparing the three phases again, we see that in the first phase montage had the quality of simultaneity. In the second it was sequential; and in the third ('a return, as it were, to the first') it is once more simultaneity, because in sound cinema it is perfectly possible to see the following type of sequence: a single ninety-metre shot shows the hunched, motionless figure of a woman while the music runs through the whole gamut of her inner struggles. This fully corresponds to the definition that we have given above.

But in sound film it is not only a case of simultaneity. This phase has also, as it were, absorbed the two preceding ones. It is also at the same time progressive and consecutive: the 'montage quality' (in the sense in which it applies to the second phase) has only in this particular 'immobile' case been transferred to another dimension: the 'forward movement' of sound. (N.B. Except where it is permissible, the visual component, edited according to all the principles of montage, should not be in any degree diminished or removed.)

Thus the basic key to mastering montage along with the other disciplines within sound film – a new degree of mastery of montage in the new stage of cinema – remains (along with all its previous depictive and narrative functions) the problem of mastering internal synchronicity, made up from the integrity of the sound (of the image) and the integrity of the picture (of the image) in the film as a whole – until, broadly speaking, the inner synchronicity of a 'piece of music' and a 'piece of photography' is achieved.

Now, on the basis of the foregoing, I wish to enunciate a fundamental thesis:

Solving the problem of audiovisual montage is solving the problem of . . . colour in cinema.

In other words only colour cinematography (and stereoscopic film, as a sub-theme of the visual aspect of the cinema of the future) is capable of fully solving the problem of genuine audiovisual synchronicity and consequently of the problem of montage in sound film.

9 On Colour

This is more obvious than it might seem at first sight. The crudest example of synchronisation that is not purely behavioural but is in some degree inherent would be the rhythmic correspondence between the on-screen action and the character of the music, with complete congruence at all levels. For example, a march tune plays and soldiers march in time to it, while it is also echoed in the rhythm of the montage. Or one may use the method of several complex but parallel rhythmic series, in which each element follows its own rhythmic line (one line for the music, another for the actors' movements, another for the cutting of the montage) based on a single, common rhythmic score.

However it is done, it will establish a single tempo in terms of movement in its simplest sense, namely locomotion. This, however, by no means exhausts the concept of movement: the concept of movement as 'locomotion *per se*' passes into the concept of movement as the locomotion (or oscillation) of particles. In the realm of sound, this progression takes rhythm into the next category: into a graphic representation of the oscillation of sonic particles, namely the interrelation between tones not only in terms of the time-frequency of the phenomenon, i.e. rhythmic terms, but also in terms of the periodicity of oscillation; that is to say, not only of the time-intervals between the appearance of identical pulses of energy, i.e. rhythm, but also in accordance with the intervals of oscillatory volume, i.e. tonality. In other words, when the melodic element is moving along the rhythmic skeleton.

What is there in visual depiction that can adequately replicate this second category of rhythm, the tonal structure of melody?

We will analyse this logically: obviously the *same* kind of factor exists in the visual dimension. We may define this factor thus: movement within depiction but in the absence of locomotion! It sounds almost absurd.

Let us, however, seek an example, limiting ourselves for the time being to the particular element of graphic depiction.

Let us take the line drawing.

The maximal approximation to our factor will be a figure that is totally immobile in terms of locomotion in space. The scope of movement is limited exclusively to movement within the lines themselves that constitute the figure.

They can wriggle like snakes, twist, contract and expand. But of course we have seen this somewhere! It seems we are not dealing with purely mathematical abstractions after all! I am referring to our old friend Walt Disney.

It is in his cows and horses that the lines depicting their necks expand

and contract. His are the peacocks whose tails wriggle and twist so elastically, in time not only to the rhythm but to the tonal picture of Offenbach's 'Barcarolle'.[262] It is the legs of his Mickey Mouse which shiver in imitation of the timbre of the instrument that is arousing our horror!

This is to be found in Walt Disney's work and *only* there. It is *there*, precisely *there*, that lies the great secret of Disney's power, a power which is inimitable, however much it may be copied. It is in this – his visual wit – that his imitators are invariably defeated; they are powerless to rise to his level in this dimension. For only Disney possesses the secret of making the *moving flow* of a line catch more than rhythm: he can make it catch the tonal progression of a melody.

But that is all very well for Disney in the medium of the animated cartoon: just you try and make a real pair of trousers produce a trembling, shivering line – a physically non-existent line – which can separate the shape of a leg from its background, or sing to a tune played on a saxophone, etc. So what can be done when you want to achieve that same ideal synchronicity when filming real things? The only available resource is the changing interplay of graphic shapes within the shot and in montage, the contrast of textures, and the play of light on shapes and textures.

In saying this, we have in fact almost reached the answer to our question: for the interplay of shapes and textures, and the play of light upon them, are also a transition from movement in the crude sense of locomotion to a higher stage of movement: to movement as the oscillation of light particles, with which shapes and surfaces play, as it were, a special form of ping-pong. If we then take one more step into the stage of yet more subtle forms of particle oscillation, we have entered the realm of . . . colour. For the differential oscillation of light particles is also the tonal gamut of difference of colour!

The approximation that has been *partially* achieved by animation (the remaining stage of what is still an incomplete correspondence between image and sound, and the arbitrary addition of a depictive role to the graphic outline, are what make the whole thing potentially funny: imagine, for a moment, the wave-like movement of two 'musically animated' lines which do not also depict the legs of a flamingo or the belly of a penguin, and there is nothing in the least funny about them) can only be fully realised in colour. And in that case, the filming of real objects will share all the advantages of the animated cartoon! Only the full gamut of colour is capable of combining totally with all the elements of melody, timbre and rhythm of that most perfect form of sound: in a word, music.

Here it is worth noting that Disney's astounding sensitivity to melody in his graphic line is, I think, developed in him to such a supra-normal degree that it makes him sound-blind where colour is concerned: colour in his works is an amorphous, extraneous element that plays no part in his amazing synchronous dance of lines and shapes, melody and rhythm.

Thus the problem of true synchronicity of sound and image – in other words the most basic problem of sound-film montage – can only be resolved by colour.

Having now defined this fundamental principle of audiovisual montage, we must immediately and firmly refute an erroneous view that is current among Western theorists: namely the idea that correspondence between sound and colour is absolute; that a timbre or a musical note corresponds absolutely to a particular shade of colour.

Even if this were to be physically established and proved (which it doubtless could be), it would be meaningless where art is concerned. Even a direct conjunction of this sort does not and never can exist in the arts, still less a rigid, absolute and once-for-all rule. For convergence between sound and colour can only take place through the visual image, i.e. through something psychologically specific but essentially changeable, subject as it is to the mutations imposed by its content and by the overall conceptual system. What is unique in an image and what can blend essentially with it are absolute only in the conditions of a *given* context, of a *given* iconography, of a *given* construct.

How can anyone look for absolute correspondence with a colour, when you are not dealing with a total abstraction but with the actual, objective reality, to say nothing of the emotional and intellectual reality, of an image! One only has to descend for a moment from the abstract to objective phenomena and one will see that there, too, colour assumes an endless multitude of forms and is bound up with a most complex set of phenomena.

Red! The colour of the revolutionary flag. And the colour of the ears of a liar caught *red*-handed. The colour of a boiled crayfish – and the colour of a 'crimson' sunset. The colour of cranberry juice – and the colour of warm human blood.

And some eccentrics claim to find a musical note that is the sole, absolute equivalent to a single colour which possesses such a multitude of objective links and subjective associations!

A meadow is green. The sea is green. And it is not the colour but the *content* of the one or the other that determines the theme music, not some mystical unity between the sound of the colour and the musical tone* of the colour green or a 'green' note!

Dealing as we are with an art form, we should not forget that not only the *green* of the sea or of a meadow, but the meadow itself and the ocean itself, as distinct from, say, a birch grove or a piece of snot (also green in colour),† are chosen by the author, by the author's emotions, with the sole

---

*Here I am not using the word 'mystical' in the hackneyed and outworn sense found in the set of clichés in the vocabulary of polemical argument. I have in mind those schools of aesthetics that are connected with certain genuinely mystical views and doctrines (e.g. 'the note *la* is "green"; so too is the noise of a mob'). Mysticism of this kind is, of course, nothing but the elevation into a system and a philosophy of the practices of the most primitive stage of human development, when a total factual and physical synaesthesia held sway. Even in these terms mystical teachings are profoundly regressive, and their doctrines cause our modern stage of development to revert to zero; they are profoundly reactionary in their very method.

†I apologise to the oceans and to my readers for making such a juxtaposition in a single breath, but anyone who has read Chapter Two of Joyce's *Ulysses* will inevitably have found a similar image linked to the word 'ocean'.

aim of thereby creating that absolutely precise visual image which encapsulates his perception of and emotional response to his subject-matter (naturally within the bounds imposed on him by the necessary demands of objective depiction).

In one instance the gamut of colour needed to create an image may be shot through with the yellow of sheaves of rye, the glinting curve of a scythe blade and the dazzling orb of the sun. In another it may be the matt yellow of a Chinaman's face; a row of old-gold bracelets; or the yellow marks on the back of a salamander. Can this multiplicity of shades of yellow really correspond to a single musical note or to a single chord? As much or as little, I would say, as does each of these two lists of examples, chosen entirely at random!

As it happens, this urge to find an absolute equivalence between colour and sound persistently rises to the surface of the human psyche; what is more, I can say without fear of contradiction that they invariably coincide with periods when mysticism is in the ascendant, i.e. at times that are marked by quite specific socio-economic factors. Apart from the Chinese whom we have already mentioned, and aside from the composer Scriabin whose searches in this field we all remember, let us recall just one of the most outstanding of Christian mystics, Meister Eckhart, who extended his quest even further in an 'olfactory' direction or, in plain language, to smell.[263]

Concerning the Romantics, let us quote Henry Lanz:

A.W. Schlegel (1767–1845) invents a whole series of colours correspond-ing to human vowels, and he attributes a special significance to every particular conjunction of the vowel-color. 'A' represents the light, clear red (*das licht-helle Rote*) and signifies Youth, Friendship and Radiance. 'I' stands for celestial blue, symbolising Love and Sincerity. 'O' is purple, 'U' stands for violet, and 'OO' is adorned in navy blue. This subjective vowel-symbolism was at the time very popular among the Romantics and Symbolists. Much eloquence was wasted on the question whether it ['A'] is really red or yellow.

Gaspar Poggel at a later date resumes the argument, and even the scholarly Grimm lends it a certain amount of favourable consideration. However arbitrary and subjective, this vowel-mysticism is an important element in the Romantic theory of rime [sic] and poetry.[264]

It is characteristic that even Schlegel's identification of sound (vowels) with colour was not created in the abstract. Even more amusing, therefore, is his attempt to fix these combinations, expressed as they are in terms of subjective imagery, as being linked *absolutely*. Herein, of course, lies the secret of the fact that no two seekers of such absolutes are ever able to agree with each other.

This method brings them close to another kind of quest: the search for the equivalent to a sound that corresponds exactly to a phenomenon, for which it serves as the initial letter of its meaning, a notion that has led to some curious treatises, e.g. Balmont's *Poetry as Magic* (1922), the not very convincing researches of Grammont, or the very capricious and at best poetically temperamental works of Khlebnikov, such as 'Zangezgi'.[265]

Contemporary researchers in search of an absolute audiovisual correspondence tend to argue their case with more recent examples from their Symbolist predecessors and do not invoke either Schlegel or Meister Eckhart. They usually quote the first line from Arthur Rimbaud's poem 'Voyelles' [Vowels]: 'A noir, E blanc, I rouge, U vert, O bleu'.

Compare these with Schlegel, and you will see to what extent all these quests are individual and arbitrary. More important than this, however, is the fact that with Rimbaud, too, these audiovisual congruences are once more profoundly conditioned by notions of imagery. The 'seekers' do not take the trouble to read and ponder the remaining thirteen lines of this little poem. For there we find that the idea is not only conditioned by imagery but by *very* individual forms of imagery. Incidentally, unlike Schlegel, Rimbaud confines himself to this one poem without elevating it into a theoretical or absolute canon; this function is assumed by his commentators and epigoni.

It remains for us to make only one more passing remark. Both Schlegel and Rimbaud, while interpreting the colour equivalents of this or that letter completely differently, agree on one thing: they both ascribe colour equivalents to . . . vowels (Rimbaud even introduces this into the title of his poem):

VOWELS

A black, E white, I red, U green, O blue: vowels,
One day I will tell your latent birth:
A – black and furry corset worn by glitt'ring flies
Which buzz around a piece of stinking carrion;

The deeps of shadow; pure white of mists and tents,
Proud glaciers, pallid kings and rippling parasols;
I – the purples of spat blood, of fair lips laughing,
In anger or in ecstasy of penitence;

U – whirlpools, emerald seas aswirl by hand divine,
The calm of pastures strewn with sheep, the furrowed calm
That's etched by alchemy upon great scholars' brows;

O – trumpet-call supreme, mysterious, shrill,
In silences alone traversed by worlds of angels:
O – Omega, the piercing shaft of violet from His Eyes![266]

This is yet another proof of the pitfalls that abound in the matter of fixing an image by audiovisual means, because in this respect [i.e. in their inherently subjective nature] they even clash with the only relatively authentic evidence for synaesthesia that we have.

In an absolutely normal person it is, of course, hard to find the full spectrum of synaesthetic capability. In poets and artists it is characteristically present to a very high degree, but even for the most sensitive painter the 'stridency' of a colour is very far from inducing actual aural distress, while the *'depth'* of a musical note only produces a *relative* spatial perception of physical depth. Indeed, one must pass beyond the limits of normality in order for the concept of the 'depth' of a note to become the physical perception of a completely real spatial picture and . . . a corresponding reaction to phenomena of colour.

Cases are certainly known to medical pathology in which a regressive type of patient is possessed of synaesthetic perceptions to such a degree that he cannot walk across a multicoloured carpet without stumbling. He perceives the polychrome patterns of the carpet as though they were actually at different depths or heights, and as he gauges the need to lift his foot in accordance with them he is inevitably caused to stumble by the disparity between the different heights to which he raises his feet and the absolutely smooth surface of the floor.

Whereas such cases are very rare in both the intensity and above all the permanence of the phenomenon, nevertheless we also know of cases of momentary and transitory conditions of the same kind which occur in quite normal circumstances. These include all instances in which for some reason the mind is shut off from its everyday functions, for example in cases of extreme mental absorption in some abstract problem. At such times, our behaviour is deprived of the control normally exerted by mediated experience. Behaviour becomes im-mediate, i.e. it is subjected to the factors characteristic of stages of development in which our conscious functions fail to correct and modify the im-mediate impressions produced by particular forms of behaviour. An example of this is the 'absent-minded professor' syndrome, in which mental concentration is extreme – but is not directed to phenomena of the person's immediate, everyday surroundings.

In such circumstances it is easy to fall into the 'clutches' of synaesthesia. I, for instance, have a vivid personal recollection of an instance when, in bright sunny weather, on the smooth asphalt outside the Telegraph Office in Myasnitskaya Street, I stumbled over the sharp, dark shadow cast by a street-lamp just as if the thing lying in front of me had been a log of wood or a steel rail. It happened at a moment of extreme mental absorption in some abstract problem.

I must repeat that in my own experience even such sporadic instances are rare. In pathological cases, moreover, it is somewhat difficult to obtain an exact description of what a patient experiences on the synaesthetic level, because the event is usually attended by accompanying phenomena which prevent him from giving a logical and coherent account of his perceptions in any detail.

I was therefore especially pleased when fate brought me into contact with a certain S. He is a quite unique example of someone who, while possessing all the completely developed faculties of a normal person, has also retained the full gamut of more primitive mechanisms of perception. Over many years professors Vygotsky and Luria have carried out comprehensive psychological observations and experiments on him, while in 1928 and 1933 I was able to have a series of interesting talks with him concerning synaesthesia, a faculty which he possessed to the full.[267]

Here I shall mention only one particularly curious piece of information which I obtained from my discussion with him on this subject.

The fact is that Comrade S perceived colour equivalents only with *consonants*. Vowels, on the other hand, produced for him various shades of intensity of *light*, but not of *colour*. In their sounds, vowels also seemed to him to represent a continuous flow; and be it noted that vowels do indeed have the attribute of flowing uninterruptedly one into another in an absolutely specific sequence (which, in terms of physics, follows a scale corresponding to the number of their oscillations). Dante, with his sensitive ear, aligned the vowels in a similar sequence in a curious passage of his *Convivio*. When this single, formless flow of sound encounters an obstacle (the lips, the teeth, etc.) it is, as it were, *broken up* by it, settles and materialises as distinct phonetic particles: consonants. This process is perceptually so close to what happens when a beam of white light strikes a prism and is *broken down* into the coloured rays of the spectrum that one is involuntarily inclined to believe in the synaesthetic description of consonants provided by S rather than those offered by Schlegel and Rimbaud!

At all events, our basic premiss remains in force: that for purposes of creating a work of art this unity of colour and sound, this inner synchronicity between them, is attainable – though only, of course, in and through an image and in the totality of the image that is formed by the combination of them.

This lack (or elusiveness?) of *absolute* correspondence of colour and sound in art is not a limitation. On the one hand, in a system that requires ever new images it is a perpetual stimulus to seek new forms of that fusion of sounds and colours; on the other hand, a fixed and once-for-all, absolute correspondence, i.e. a fixed and once-for-all scheme of mutually linked associations, would be profoundly inimical to the very nature of art. For one of the aims of art is to blaze new trails in our awareness of reality, to create *new chains of association* on the basis of utilising those which already exist. (In phases of greater 'rigour' in my thinking about the mechanism of such phenomena, I formulated this as 'the aim of creating new conditioned reflexes on the basis of existing unconditioned reflexes'; that was in 1923–4.*)

---

*This process is especially noteworthy in works whose artistic form gives them an inexorable effectiveness, enabling them to put forward ideas that are directly contrary to the views and sympathies of the audience, winning them over to those ideas against their will. This is a particular strength of the consciously propagandistic strain in Soviet cinema. With regard to *The Battleship Potemkin*, this psychological effect is well described by Lion Feuchtwanger in the chapter of his [novel] *Success* in which Otto Klenk, the former Minister of Justice of Bavaria, sees a showing in Berlin of the film *The Battleship Orloff*.

It is only a dull, sterile, feeble, parasitic art form that lives by exploiting the existing stock of associations and reflexes, without using them to create chains of new images which form themselves into new concepts.

Nomina sunt odiosa, but the plays performed in our theatres have included not a few examples of precisely this sort, and only since the spring of 1937 have they been conducting a determined fight against this 'parasitic' tendency in their own ranks.

Thus, even allowing that beyond the confines of subjective synaesthesia there *can* be absolute correspondence between colour and musical sound;

and assuming that it is present as a subconscious sub-text behind all attempts to find correspondence between colour and sound;

let us not forget that in its absolute form it can only be achieved, in lifeless abstraction, inside a physics laboratory, and not in the living organism of a work of art.

Let us also remember that this genuine, inner synchronicity is like the truth, of which Lenin wrote: 'The truth is a process. From a subjective idea man proceeds towards objective truth *through* "practice" (and technique).'[268]

We should therefore remember that in the progression of ever more perfect fusions of colour and sound, in the ever more perfect images that reflect the reality of our time,

we shall also draw nearer to an ever fuller representation of the absolute truth of our unique, socialist way of life.

On the question of colour, the aims of my article are very modest: I felt it important to establish *the place of colour on an equal footing with the other elements of montage* within film-making. We have identified it as the necessary and uniquely all-embracing precondition for achieving *total and genuine synchronicity between the sonic and the visual image, between sound and depiction as separate functions.*

At this point I should not miss the opportunity of pointing out that within the pictorial image itself – in this case a coloured image – the correspondence between sound and picture also uniquely replicates this interrelation in the form of a similar relationship between the *graphic* and the *chromatic* image. Within the pictorial image, colour stands in roughly the same relationship to the graphic outline as does music to the pictorial image as a whole.

Without laying down any absolute standards or giving a precise methodology of colour composition,★ I would just like to dwell for a moment on a few considerations and guidelines from areas where we might, perhaps, least expect to find useful material, at a time when everyone is turning to Shishkin, Semiradsky or Klever in search of the aesthetics of colour.[269] Those areas are . . . literature and . . . the black-and-white film.

The present edition cannot allow itself the luxury of coloured illustrations, but that does not matter; we can easily find illustrations of the problem of

---

★The methodology for this is included in a special section of my teaching course on direction.

colour in . . . literature. There are, after all, plenty of examples in literature of purely optical [three-dimensional] relief and multi-coloured [imagery].

An image of colour may come through in an author's writing not only by his verbal use of a palette of colours, not only by his choice of sounds, but from the actual prototype of what he is describing in words: the shimmering effect of light and colours which one occasionally senses through the 'canvas' of a verbal description can at times glow even more brightly than the same subject matter depicted, but less perfectly, on actual canvas (see, for example, Huysmans' descriptions of jewels 'glowing like flowers', or the _texture_ of descriptive passages in Oscar Wilde). *In the early stages* of the arts of painting and literature this synaesthesia is *so* vividly expressed that one can *only* elucidate certain turns of phrase and images by finding a corresponding visual depiction and deciphering its limitations and conventions; one then returns to the literary depiction in order fully to perceive and understand it. For instance, a description in Chinese lyric poetry may seem fantastic. If one admits its factual reality, then it will seem to be such, but one only has to understand it *optically* to perceive at once that here is a precise verbal description of the visual illusion of *two-dimensional* vision, to which we are thoroughly accustomed in ancient Chinese drawings and paintings. The visual perception has been directly transferred into verbal description (this example is taken from observations recorded in *The Chinese Eye*).[270]

I think Gogol wrote with no less an *immediacy* of colour perception, the only difference being that, unlike the Chinese primitive painter, with Gogol colour played not only a superficially depictive role; it was also integral to his total visual and aural conception of his subject matter.

His characters are so lively and many-sided and at the same time so strongly individualised that each of them 'comes through' with his own range of colours. This chromatic gamut is twofold, and, depending on the style and genre of the particular work, it emerges differently in the various characters. [Gogol's] realistic novel *Dead Souls* tends to use colour in character drawing in a straightforwardly pictorial way, whereas a tale of fantasy, such as *The Terrible Vengeance*, uses colour more as a generalising device, coming closer to a strictly chromatic image (at times almost to a symbol).

It is also notable that the very nature of the colouring changes with unusual flexibility in order thereby to reflect the mode in which one work is written as distinct from another. Whereas in *Dead Souls* the descriptive tone draws on intermediate colours (reality itself being rarely concerned with pure primary colours), and that tone is maintained through all the nuances of descriptive colouring, when we come to works whose subject matter is fantasy in which the characters appear not only as normal people but rather as more symbolic figures than those in his realistic stories, so the colouring changes from being intermediate and finely shaded to having broader chromatic tones, surpassing the expressive limits of intermediate colours and going over to a palette of pure primary colours. Pan Danilo is pure cobalt or Prussian blue. The magician is scarlet (*The Terrible Vengeance*). In a work which, as it were, combines the two (*Taras Bulba*), we see that the type of colouring changes flexibly from the depictive to the symbolic, sensitively reflecting the level on which, at any given moment, the narrative is being conducted.

There are places where Gogol's descriptive use of colour reaches such a degree of 'tangibility' that it is almost as much of a direct transference from the mental picture that was obviously in his mind's eye as was the example taken from Chinese painters. The optical equivalence is so strong that the descriptive colours begin to cast reflected tones on each other! (Pani Katerina, depending on whether the magician or Pan Danilo comes near to her.) In other words, the drama itself, the struggle between the characters, is not confined to the structure of the plot! It also 'shows through' in colour. The very clash of colours becomes an arena of the struggle and, echoing the drama, first one colour and then another 'captures' the characters. It is also curious to note that this battle waged in terms of the dynamics of colour relates not only to the fictional characters but also to the struggle that was going on inside the author who created them. The range of colours in Gogol's early works, blazing with the bright fullness of the spectrum of primary colours, undergoes a change in the later works written towards the end of his life, when he moves over to a palette containing more grey and black. 'He gets closer to the palette of the cinema', as I remarked to the late Andrei Bely,[271] whose researches into colour and statistics on Gogol's work I have used here. Whether or not Gogol was approaching the cinematic palette, we nevertheless see that the author himself – not only in terms of his moods, the stages of his social life or the themes of his works, but in the whole process of his growth and progression (and with Gogol we have every right to say: throughout the whole of his tragic life story) – also 'comes through' in the play of colours across the complete range of his works. If we were to make a film with a script based on Gogol's biography, surely this progression of the Gogolian palette through the whole course of his literary career would be the same range of colours that we would use in the composition of that film. The moving image in colour is no mere piece of frivolous amusement but a force capable of profound psychological revelation.

In the tragic sunset years of his life Gogol modified his palette to the greys of [monochrome] cinematic narrative. Our cinema is moving in the opposite direction: from the monkish asceticism of a narrow range of colours – black, grey and white – we are heading rapidly towards a full-blooded palette, a complete rainbow of colour.

It is generally true that, as in much else, where colour is concerned the Soviet cinema can learn a lot from its 'elder brother': literature. (As we have seen from an analysis of Gogol's literary technique, the deployment of colour and the dynamic use of colour 'leitmotivs', surprising as it may seem, can be learnt better from literature than from painting – which is, of course, the well-spring of the basic knowledge even though it by no means tells us everything about certain problems that are specific to films made in colour.)

So let us learn about colour from Gogol!

There is, of course, another source for the study of colour: the film-maker himself. Admittedly, as a source he is very limited, not only because the pre-colour range of tones available to him was so restricted, but chiefly because in this matter he is almost entirely confined to the single area of the silent cinema. With the coming of sound the problem of chiaroscuro in the 'look' of a film somehow melted away, as did many other problems that the cinema as an art form had managed to overcome.

I would say that a striking though highly skilful example of the 'medieval' use of colour in cinema may be noted in the work of Ernst Lubitsch, in the film he made of Wilde's *Lady Windermere's Fan*.[272] It is only partially cinematic, because it is an instance of draping the actors in colours (rather than a consistent application of the idiom of colour to the means and conditions of film-making), which was restricted, furthermore, to the characters alone.

Pudovkin's *The Mother* will bring us nearer to our theme.[273]

True, this film is more in the nature of a rough draft for the structural use of colour, which in large degree Pudovkin had not properly thought through, otherwise he would have undoubtedly brought it to perfection as a compositional device. The progressive 'advance' of colour would then have fallen into three phases, echoing the forward movement of the plot:

the black gloom of the first scenes (the father, the house, the arrest);

the grey shades of the middle section (the trial, prison, the revolt);

and finally the flood of white colour (the flow of ice as the frozen river breaks up during the demonstration).

Furthermore, all three thematic colour tones might have merged into a final 'coda' in the last scene: the black crowd of workers, the grey tones of the police and the victorious onrush of the white ice.

Unfortunately the third thematic colour – white – was not utilised in the overall colour composition and was never brought out photographically.

In my films, colour was used somewhat differently.

Whereas in Pudovkin's film we could discern the rudiments of dramatic plot movement reflected in the progression from colour to colour,* in my films the progression has usually been within the colour itself, in variations on a simple thematic colour.

Not for nothing is Pudovkin fond of Beethoven, while I am a follower and admirer of Bach.

The part played by colour progression (although white, grey and black are, in the final analysis, variations on a single tone, but admittedly with qualitative leaps) in my work extends over my *films as a whole*.

Thus *The Battleship Potemkin* keeps to the grey tones of the sea, the mists and the sides of the battleship. Within the film, the grey tone darkens in one direction to the black frock-coats and tunics of the officers and petty officers,

---

*Note that his subsequent films were made without recourse to colour effects.

to the black bowler hats of the people of Odessa, the outlines of the squadron of warships at night, and the night sky. In the other direction, it shifts towards the while sails of the flotilla of little sailing-boats, the seagulls and the sailors' white caps as they are thrown into the air. The basic theme, however, is expressed in tones of grey.

This grey tone was expanded and fixed at its extremities of black and white in my other films. The black dominates *October*, the white – *The Old and the New* [*The General Line*]. Oddly enough, these two pictures were shot simultaneously, alternating with each other; but it is even more curious that this disintegration of the basic chromatic integrity of *The Battleship Potemkin* also coincided with a disintegration of a different kind: the stylistic disintegration of the realistic idiom of *Potemkin*. In order not to repeat the painful process of describing that unfortunate stage in my career, I will simply quote what I myself wrote and published about it:

> At the outset of my career as a film-maker, in a dramatic (?) encounter with an episode in our country's great revolutionary past – in *The Battleship Potemkin* – I succeeded in faithfully reflecting reality in images on the level of [the public's] artistic demands at the time. It [the film] was created in the heat of a surge of emotion. And in those days that was enough. But our country is growing, the masses are growing up and the demands they make on art are growing. The artist's ardour must be reinforced by a firmly rooted Bolshevik outlook on the world. And this is the beginning of a painful journey. The transition from an emotional to a [politically] informed perception of reality does not come easily. Informed perception starts to function, but the [correct] world view has still not been formed. Hence the swings from side to side, from one extreme to another. In the turmoil of this process, the primal integrity of *Potemkin* breaks up into the one-sided extremes of *The Old and the New* and *October*. *October* was a swing in one direction – from concrete historical narrative to 'generalised' abstraction and thence to the inevitable formal experimentation and over-refinement. It fell to the lot of *The Old and the New* to be subjected to another extreme – the dense, naturalistic idiom of certain episodes, in which the integrity of the film as a whole foundered. The bull, the milk-separator, the waterfalls of milk blotted out the victorious advance of socialism in the countryside and the real, live people who were carrying it out.[274]

As we see from that, not only achievement but failures and mistakes are subject to one and the same set of rules that is common to all art forms!*

---

*And that set of rules is quite specific; one cannot help recalling what Eliot wrote about . . . Shakespeare's *Hamlet*: 'The only way of expressing emotion in the form of art is by finding an "objective"; in other words, a set of objects, a situation, a chain of events which shall be the formula of that *particular* emotion; such that when the external facts, which must terminate in sensory experience, are given, the emotion is immediately evoked.'[275]

I thought the realistic features of *Potemkin*, which had disintegrated into two extremes, would come together in a new synthesis in *Bezhin Meadow*. In the same article I wrote:

Having committed those mistakes and overcome them in practice, I stand once more on the path towards a new integrity. It will no longer be the integrity of a youthful surge of emotion, but an integrity fully armed with [politically] conscious ardour and the courage of maturity.

Unfortunately, that did not happen. The black and white colours in the film did not come together as a synthesis at all but were even more sharply separated: furthermore, they were fixed to the moral categories of 'good' and 'evil', which the excessively generalised characteristics of the pro- and anti-Soviet representatives of class forces in the countryside had grown into. The kulaks took on black colouring; white was reserved for the murdered boy. On a bright sunny day the blazing barn burned with black smoke – the kulaks' handiwork – while tones of white characterised everyone connected with the positive forces in the village who extinguished the fire: the ash-blond Stepok; the Komsomol member dressed in white; the white shirt of the political instructor and the white headscarves of the women; the white horses of the fire brigade; and, finally, the white pigeons rescued by Stepok against the background of a wall of black smoke.

Black was the night over *Bezhin Meadow* and like a white, other-worldly spectre the injured Stepok wandered through it to his death.

There were people who liked to see in this a materialisation of the line from Turgenev's 'Bezhin Meadow': 'The darkness did battle with the light.'[276]

I still think (as I have also stated in print on the subject) that this was due above all to the author's tendency to take generalisation to the point of abstraction* and to lose touch with concrete reality: it was by no means due to the screen's chromatic palette of black-white-grey.

If colour had been used, the matter would not have stood out so starkly, but probably that would only have been for the worse: I would not have been made so clearly aware of features that as a creative artist I should have eliminated!

In this sense, what happened with the film *Bezhin Meadow* was probably even more 'medieval', even more like a 'morality play', than the example I quoted from the work of Lubitsch, with which we began our citation of examples of the use of colour in . . . the black-and-white film.†

---

*Is this not a tribute paid to the Chinese and their culture, which helped me in so many ways to understand and analyse things, yet which at the same time, perhaps, infected me with something that is so characteristic in their art?

†As for my film *Que viva México!*, the situation there was quite special. In my mind's eye I invariably see it as a colour film, as a series of images in colour. The reason for this is very

How much further will the theme of the clash between black and white in my *œuvre* take me?

I hope that it may be a theme in which white and black take on the full-blooded forms of human beings, a theme that has long excited me, the theme of the racial problem, in which the 'whites' clash with the 'blacks', and where the 'black' will be played by that incomparable master of the screen, Paul Robeson![277] I also hope that it will be a black-and-white theme, yet composed in all the multicoloured diversity of the colours of real life. It is now up to our scientists and technicians.

As for all the achievements, exaggerations and failures in the area of colour made by our monochrome films, they were only possible thanks to the unique mastery of colour idiom that is possessed to perfection by the best of our cameramen, Tisse, Moskvin, Golovnya and others.[278] And that gives us the assurance that all the most subtle nuances of the internal synchronicity of depiction, colour and sound will be mastered by the skill of the makers of future Soviet sound films.

We should not forget that in the realm of sound we have composers no less brilliant, capable with equal finesse of translating a striking visual image on screen into the only possible corresponding images in music. Among their names are Shostakovich, Gavril Popov and others of that ilk.[279]

---

simple (I would say 'tragically' simple!): its shots have remained in my memory not as photographic pictures but as the very objects themselves as they were caught by the lens and as they actually appeared in front of the camera. The reason for this is that . . . *I never saw that work of mine on the screen.* Eighty per cent of it, and then not in full, I only ever saw briefly, once, in the form of 'rushes' in the laboratory, i.e. before it was edited and spliced together.

10 Unity in the Image

I believe we will be absolutely right in ascribing the meaning of this heading to the words of Goethe, which he himself left unelucidated in his *Farbenlehre*: 'Colour and sound do not admit of being directly compared together in any way, but both are referable to a universal formula.'[280]

I believe that this 'higher formula' may legitimately be interpreted as that intellectual-emotional image which both sound and colour are capable of expressing in equal measure, uniquely and independently.

For in these terms, an audiovisual combination whose constituent elements become commensurable through a single emotional image is not unprecedented.

Any comparison that assumes commensurability first and foremost can only fulfil this to the fullest and most striking degree when the comparison derives not from the objects themselves but from the syndrome of emotional and sensuous associations evoked by them, which thus serves both of them as a 'common language' and as the means whereby they can merge into a single image.

To take a particular example, a similar process in regard to verbal comparison (which also holds good for metaphors and images) has been well described by Hermann Cohen in his *Ästhetik des reinen Gefühls* [The Aesthetics of Pure Emotion]:*

How does an image arise? An example may serve to explain the process. In mythology all over the world the *Sun* is a hero [or man of great strength], e.g. *Hercules, Samson, Siegfried*. In the psalms the sun is identified with a heroic figure: 'His [the strong man's] going forth is from the end of heaven, and his circuit unto the ends of it . . .' (Psalm 19:6). At the same time the psalm also enables us to see how the simile derives from identity with the strong man; it is mediated through the simile of the *Bridegroom*: '[The sun] is as a bridegroom coming out of his chamber, and rejoiceth as a strong man to run a race' (Psalm 19:5). Here the *okeanos* becomes a bridal chamber, and this simile, too, has played its part,

---

*Despite all our disagreements in principle with the concepts of this follower of Kant, we may cite this passage, in which the phenomenon is correctly observed, although it is also taken out of a historical context and the author's very premises, in their subsequent development, are taken to conclusions which for us are entirely unacceptable.

through the bridegroom, in the progression to the anthropomorphic image of the heroic 'strong man'.

Verse 5 of the psalm allows us to see the process even more clearly: '. . . rejoiceth as a strong man . . .'. Rejoicing, or joy, is the final, decisive vehicle for the metamorphosis of identity into image. It is not the poetic transformation of the sun's 'circuit' into the 'race' that the 'strong man' is to 'run', nor the *okeanos* into the 'bridal chamber'; it is the 'rejoicing' that becomes the effective factor of comparison. 'Rejoicing' is the emotive word that links the sun-hero with the bridegroom; having effected this, it can now also establish the fact that although the sun may forfeit its identity with the strong man-hero, it yet becomes an image that enlarges to infinity the concept – henceforth a *poetic* concept – of the hero as signifying the sun.

We now understand the power of the *comparative particle*. It is not only a copula of superior degree, but at the same time an *entity* of extended degree. It establishes a new, unique association of units, which exist not only in semantic units but in their subjective links with *the emotions associated with denotative words*. . . .

The *denotative words* in poetry are at the same time words that connote emotion; sentences made from them are also emotive sentences. If we may perceive the *comparative particle* as an entity of extended degree, we must pursue this quality further still, in order to explain systematically how it is that through comparison poetry not only acquires its aesthetic uniqueness but *thereby becomes the common, fundamental linguistic element of all the arts* which make use of the device of *comparison*.[281]

Let us now take a look at the phenomenon of stereoscopy. Every pair of adjacent frames is, as it were, a reproduction on the plane of motion of what takes place in straightforward binocular vision with regard to spatial depth perception. In both cases, the basic factor is the juxtaposition of two non-identical views of the object: in the first, it is two *consecutive phases* of movement; in the second, the object is seen from two *viewpoints at an imperceptible distance from each other*. The results are: the fusion of the first two into an *image of movement*; and in the second case, the fusion of the two into an *image of depth and relief*. That is to say, in both cases there is a heightening of the dimensional category (both as depiction and as image).

Binocularity is the existence of *two* viewpoints that enable an object to be seen in relief. The same principle underlies the multi-viewpoint, sequential nature of montage, which also permits the object or event to be perceived, as it were, 'in relief'. Here the effect is one of many-sided, multi-faceted relief, i.e. not in the sense of obvious bulk but in a metaphorical sense that is nevertheless based on a very solid physical event.

This produces the very interesting situation in which the phenomenon of dynamic representation and the phenomenon of a sequentially changing viewpoint are further confirmed as proceeding from the same set of physical and mental premisses – whose prototype is the human being and the binocularity of his vision.

Such is the position in regard to a single object *per se* from the standpoint of seeing it in the fullness of its multi-faceted shape.

Thus binocular vision is a 'montage' of two 'shots' taken of a single object, i.e. one and the same object 'shot' from two viewpoints. It gives us 'relief' of a straightforward, non-metaphorical, immediate kind; in other words, stere-oscope. (Given that the relative location of these two viewpoints is in accordance with the angle of divergence of a normal pair of human eyes.)

If there is a greater divergence between these two viewpoints – both of angle and of the time of vision – there is a shift in the perception of the resultant image, which thereby forfeits its immediate *physical* relief in favour of a relief effect that is *metaphorical*. Take, for example, a view of the *front* and the *back* of a building. Shot from a single set-up, each of these views is flat, but a juxtaposition of the two, while it will not convey either of the sides stereoscopically, gives a 'relief' impression of the building that is 'mental'.

Finally, an increase in the number of viewpoints will give a total impression of the relief of the object.

In all three instances we have been concerned with only one object, although its outward aspects were multi-faceted – aspects, however, wholly contained within our perception of a single object.

What would happen if we were not dealing with one object, but if two *different* objects were presented to our imaginary binocular vision? I say 'imaginary' on purpose, because if we are to continue on a directly *experimental* route, an extremely serious counter-effect will arise: this is our highly developed capacity to differentiate, which never allows us simultaneously to discern fully the process of combination and fusion. Therefore if we are nevertheless to proceed along the path of experimentation, we must choose instances where the differentiating component of our attention is either artificially distracted or is absent for some reason. For our second example we have an abundance of material, because a child's mind is distinguished by precisely this characteristic: possessing a very intense capacity to unify, the child's ability to differentiate gives way to it. In children's drawings we can see some extremely interesting examples of this.

An eight-year-old girl is shown a hexagonal pyramid placed on top of a cylinder and asked to draw a picture of what she sees. What she draws is . . . a radiant star (Fig. 10.1). From the two objects she has created the image of a third, which incorporates the most striking and specific characteristics of each of the two! In this star, in fact, which resembles neither the pyramid nor the cylinder, she has seized upon the 'roundness' of the cylinder and the 'angularity' of the pyramid. (This example is taken from P. Werner's book where he quotes from Volkelt.[282])

But in the arts, too, we can be faced with exactly the same kind of task. It happens in cases when, for instance, one is required to express spatially several conflicting types of behaviour, each with its own quite specific traits,

Fig. 10.1

by means of movement within a stage- or film-set. This can be extremely difficult for would-be directors, because it obliges them to devise a spatial plot capable of synthesising two separate types of movement into one, just as an actor, at the moment when the character is experiencing conflicting emotions, has to find a single form of expression in which both kinds of feeling can be fused. In the academic year of 1928, when I was teaching in the then GIK, I set an exercise of this kind as part of my course on directing. I clearly remember one such problem, which was solved by one of the students after some fairly intense thought that was largely *sensuous* in nature. Although a synthesis of this kind, theoretically speaking, is entirely capable of being achieved by calculation, mathematics only comes into it, of course, at the stage of checking and proving after having worked it out and by the 'logic' of whether the *framework* of the solution has been devised correctly. The exercise, as I recall, was as follows: a sculptor completes the statue on which he has been working and in the excitement of admiring and inspecting it, he walks away from it step by step. (This walking away, or rather his excitement as he does it, conveyed by the kind of excitement that increases as a person walks away from something to get an ever fuller view of it, was needed here so that, all unawares and in the total grip of his emotion, he should bump into the other character in the scene who enters at that moment – his daughter – without noticing her.)

The student was called upon to sketch out a complete movement-plot that would correspond to the sculptor's state of mind. The path of his movements therefore had to fulfil two requirements: inspecting the statue and moving away from it. To this was added a third spatial factor: the limitations of the set.

The overall solution to the problem was as shown in Fig. 10.2; the student arrived at it purely intuitively, merely by imagining himself physically in the character's situation.

It is not difficult to 'substantiate' the choice of this line of movement, for the admiring inspection of the statue is expressed to the full by walking round it, i.e. by a circular path *around* the object. The *movement away* from it to get a better view is expressed to the full by the straight line from A to C (see Fig. 10.3). A combination of both motifs would have led logically to a series of concentric circles. Each circle in its relation to the previous circle, while providing the means of inspecting the statue, would simultaneously contribute to the motif of moving away from it.

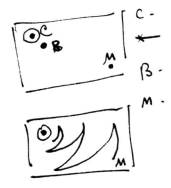

To describe a series of concentric circles in the course of a single uninterrupted movement can only be done, of course, by joining them up into a spiral (in this case a broadly expanding spiral –

Fig. 10.2

Fig. 10.4). But the limited size of the set did not permit the sculptor to describe a *complete* circle around the statue. The path of his movement would hit two of the walls of the set, and it is easy to see that if we also take account of this limitation, we are bound, in the end, to choose the path which the student found purely intuitively (Fig. 10.5).

In this way the actor is obliged to take the route ab1 and a1b2, i.e. not the long path that would be described if he were following a spiral but the shortest, flattened path between the same points, as it were avoiding the walls, being unable to walk through them, thereby still managing to carry out a

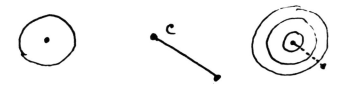

Fig. 10.3

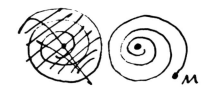

Fig. 10.4

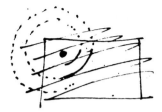 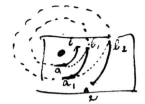

Fig. 10.5

logical pursuit of his objective: the spatial expression of the two inner motives underlying his performance. This path would be a spatial expression of the play of motivation taking place within the character's mind in the given situation. It is interesting that this solution has retained *not* the representation of a circle and a straight line but the principles behind them: 'encirclement' and 'moving away', i.e. the images of what would be contained in the actual representation of a circle and a straight line moving away. These images have been combined into something new that is designed to convey the desired objective in terms of expressive movement. This image may be 'read' through two . . . metaphors: (1) *the circle of his route* has expanded into a spiral; or (2) *the line of his route* has been twisted into a spiral. The spiral has absorbed into itself the two elements of *expansion* and *twisting*.

Thus, once again, from the juxtaposition of two given factors we have observed the emergence of a third: a new one which does not coincide with either of its two constituents and which introduces a new quality, a new connotative dimension, which incorporates not the original monosemantic elements but the new polysemantic dimension of its new meaning. And we come to the conclusion that not only is *das Urphänomen* of film (as the Germans would say) *movement*; that it not only contributes a new, enriched quality at a further stage of development, i.e. montage; but, as we have seen, an essential structural constituent is the deployment of metaphor, while the decisive element is its power to create images, all of which derive in equal degree from the same fundamental principle of *juxtaposition.*

This lends a particular harmony to the whole concept. It is interesting to note that even to construct a purely verbal metaphor, we will seek analogies and explicatory support in that same phenomenon of binocularity. For instance, in Karl Bühler's *Theory of Speech* we read:

Outside speech, in a great variety of representational techniques there are parallels, some distant, some close, to the linguistic technique of combining ideas in metaphor. Thus Galton, for instance, photographed several people in succession on the same area of a photographic plate, in order by a cunning exploitation of the technical characteristics of photography to achieve something that was otherwise only available as the product of psycho-physical 'arrangements' or from pictorial art, namely the picture of a *human type*. Even closer to the subject of our study is the well-known faculty of binocular vision – which projects one and the same object on two separate retinas, and which, under normal circumstances, is nevertheless perceived as a single object, simply and in greater relief than with each eye alone, since the minute difference between the two pictures (their horizontal separation) are utilised to produce the effect of sharper and more precise depth-perception. Much more important in binocular unification, however, is all the evidence pointing to instances in binocular unification where it *does not occur*. The 'Galton Picture' shows blurred outlines, whereas the binocular picture does not and fails equally to show what is being characterised metaphorically.[283]

In other words, what happens is not a summarising construct, but a truly *new entity*, with its own *new qualitative signification as an image*.

It thus transpires that colour (and stereoscopy) are not marginal 'enrichments of the means of film-making' but inalienable elements of the totality of an audiovisual art form (the sound film). No one has ever ascribed to the 'coming of colour' in cinematography the same revolutionary significance that was given to the 'coming of sound'. Its role has never been over-rated. Most people thought of it as did Chaplin, who said (in *Interciné*): 'Even if I regard the use of speech in film as incorrect from an aesthetic point of view, one must admit that words are directly expressive of thought. This cannot be said about colour.'[284] (I cannot agree with the first part of this statement.) Chaplin considered that colour film would not make nearly as much of a sensation as sound. Agreed. But this is partly because no one had ever given any thought to the fact that *colour is a structural element intrinsic to sound film*. In the event, it turns out to be just so, as we have attempted to show and substantiate.

But this does not mean that the organic entry of colour into the structure of sound film puts it in the category of just one more expressive device in the confetti-like shower of expressive devices! It is one of its intrinsic characteristics – and obliges one to speak in all seriousness of sound film in the future as a truly synthetic art form.

If painting, sculpture and architecture are now on the way to a fusion of the visual arts in [the design of] socialist housing and in the overall layout of the socialist city, then the arts which exist simultaneously in space and time, being both aural and visual, are with similar completeness and for the first time in history merging into the total spectacle that is the sound film of the era of socialism.

Of course, sound film itself as a complete entity may also merge with an even broader synthesis of all the arts in a unique 'montage' spectacle: this would unite the natural surroundings of the urban complex with the masses that have their being in the city and the individual protagonists of the drama taking place within it; with a sea of colour and light, music and radio; with theatre and sound film; with steamers on the Moscow-Volga Canal; and with squadrons of aircraft.

But the unrepeatability and uniqueness of such a spectacle is justified by its . . . unrepeatability and uniqueness.

Such spectacles, too, we will create.

But if we want an audiovisual spectacle in an *established* art form, capable of being distributed in innumerable copies to countless corners of the globe, i.e. an audiovisual spectacle which not only depicts the masses but is itself a genuinely *mass* medium (and not only on a national scale but internationally) in distribution and consumption – then it is indeed the sound film that is undoubtedly destined to become just such a medium and to remain as such for many years to come.

Past ages could not even dream of anything on such a scale, of such completeness and organic, inner cohesion combined with such popularity and accessibility to a mass audience.

In anticipation of certain turning-points in history, men have dreamed of creating something of this nature, and at the actual moment of those turning-points they sometimes partially succeeded in doing so, but they never achieved the result that will only be possible in the era of victorious socialism.

What then *was* achieved in the way of media synthesis by those forerunners of the sound film? At which happy moments were such dreams conceived? How were those dreams realised? And what, apart from its immediate, ephemeral effect, resulted from audiovisual synthesis in past ages?

I do not intend to discuss the problems of carnivals, solemn processions, triumphs or celebrations such as those held on the Champ de Mars during the French Revolution. In this study I shall restrict myself to those audiovisual spectacles which can be classified as 'productions' and not merely 'pageants' (a theatre performance belongs in the first of these categories, while a celebration such as a carnival is more properly classified as a 'pageant').

Throughout history, three approaches to the creation of an audiovisual production have been evident. They have coincided with the emergence and culmination of the ideological self-affirmation of new social forces, with the rise and attainment of power by new social classes. We are now seeing this inexorable process repeated in the case of the working class, which is coming close to the liquidation of classes as such. Although inevitably incomplete, by the same token the ideal of a synthesis of the arts invariably comes to the fore at turning-points in history similar to the present one. And vice versa: when the power of a class is declining and fading we observe not only the breakup of *the arts as a whole* into sharply differentiated compartments, but the process of decadence and disintegration also takes place within the various arts themselves.

In the most striking example of social decadence, namely the collapse of capitalist society in its highest stage (imperialism), that immediately precedes the attainment of power by the proletariat, this has been especially vivid and impressive. From the second half of the 19th century onward we have witnessed the unmistakable process of disintegration not only of the arts in general but of each separate branch of the arts. Photographic realism and a 'literary' narrative, for instance, crowded out everything else in the art of the late nineteenth-century Russian school of socially committed artists known as 'The Wanderers'. In their case, this was at least justified by the social message which it was their mission to convey, but this was not so with other trends, schools and 'isms'. Some concentrated on recording a momentary, fleeting impression, others on the optical relationship between colours, while a third group was concerned to catch movement and to convey a particular sense of dynamism. A fourth trend attempted to capture the perception of space, while still others strove to fix an otherwise inarticulate inner cry or *cri de coeur* in colour and sound. Another group was only interested in an interplay of the schematic forms underlying the structure of visible phenomena. It remained for others coming a little later to disregard every other aspect of the totality of a picture and to worship only surface textures – or to concentrate on instrumental timbre and rhythm to the exclusion of melody. The ultimate contribution of the Italians to the labyrinth of decadence was surely 'Tactilism' – painting intended to be perceived solely through the fingertips! Perhaps Stanislavsky was thinking of this when he said: 'Whereas the eyes are the mirror of the soul, the tips of the fingers are the eyes of the body . . .'[285]

It was, indeed, the loss of a wholeness of inner vision, alongside the loss of an integrated world-view, which was ultimately the cause of this disintegration [of the arts] into separate, dead fragments.

This is not the path to be taken by our flourishing [Soviet] art. For we are taking the opposite route – the direct route, that is, of vitality and progress, leaving behind both the disintegration of the arts which characterised past epochs and the over-analytical, fissiparous experimentation with forms, typical of the early post-Revolutionary years. We are now moving towards a full-blooded synthesis of the constituent elements of art and a synthesis of the arts themselves.

This is precisely the attitude that characterises periods in which classes are being formed, are emerging and flourishing.

So it was in *Renaissance* Italy.

So it was in the French Revolution and in the era that saw the *birth* of that ultimate [capitalist] form of class society which, after achieving its final form in 1848, was simultaneously destined to become the gravedigger of the whole class system.

We too are subject to the same laws of history, standing as we do at the cradle of an altogether new world and the birth of the forms specific to a universal, classless society, [which will come into existence] no matter how much the Fascist-minded remnants of the rest of the globe may resist it.*

---

*It is a curious fact that the rudiments of an audiovisual performance are to be found in *the celebration of the liturgy in the medieval church*: in its forms it is a combination of singing, of action, of the play of light and colour from stained-glass windows, of the mighty sounds of an organ, of passages from the holy scriptures, either read aloud or acted out as scenes, and accompanied by the aroma of incense – taken together, this undoubtedly possesses all the

It is also characteristic of all such cases of mankind's self-renewal, when new classes accede to power, that their art and culture begin precisely with the re-creation of ancient forms, as if through this 'second birth' they were re-living – even if only in images – the stage of their own initial conception, the physically unrepeatable era of the 'golden childhood of mankind' (Marx's term for the Greece of classical antiquity). Apart from the fact that this tendency is reflected in the very word 'Renaissance', it is to be found equally clearly in [Graeco-Roman] prototypes chosen for the art of the French Revolution – even to the extent of men like Babeuf adopting names such as 'Gracchus'.[286] Finally, in our own time and on an even wider basis socialist art is adopting not only the great Greek tradition in contemporary architecture, but everything in our cultural heritage worthy of being called classic, not merely on the strength of its antiquity but also for its qualitative perfection.

In practice, it is true, this aspiration often falls short of the ideal. Furthermore we tend to forget that, unlike other epochs in which a culture has flourished, we have less need than ever before to *reproduce the semblance* of classical styles, which were inevitably subject to the limitations imposed by historical circumstances; instead, we should learn from them the eternally valid principles which are common in equal degree to all phenomena that aspire to classical perfection. Fortunately our socialist registry offices – unlike the Parisian registry offices of the late 18th century! – have managed to avoid the mass-production of *Gracchus* Ivanovs, *Plutarch* Petrovs and Aristotle *Stepanovs*, or *Pericles* Rabinoviches! – although I have been personally fated to visit the 'Venus' collective farm in Turgenev's homeland in the former Tula Province. Unfortunately the designs for socialist [Soviet] cities often continue to abound in undigested, borrowed copies of the Parthenon, the Erechtheum or the Propylaea!

(They only lack their . . . *Plato* Kerzhentsev.)[287]

There have been three contributions to the concept and the formal structures of multi-media spectacle in the past:

Ancient Greek tragedy; opera, as it developed during the Renaissance; and music drama in the form in which Diderot longed to see it.

Each of these epochs aimed at solving the problems of multi-media

---

characteristics of a multi-media performance. We might describe it as a stage . . . in the rebirth to eternal life by water and by the spirit, which is indeed what Christianity claimed [it to be], together with the mystery of the Eucharist, in which ordinary bread and wine, tothe sound of appropriate choral music, are supposed to be 'transubstantiated' into the body and blood of a certain long-dead oriental 'preacher' (as Tolstoy put it). In spite of its insistence on upholding the diametrically opposed principle of *life-denial*, by its philosophical integrity and its international appeal as a single kingdom 'of the spirit' (it is in this sense that Engels writes of Christianity as the primary model for mankind's perception of the concept of supranational *unity*, so important for the future, though previously irreconcilably divided by incompatible differences of ritual and religious practice), it was thereby bound to give birth to the ideas and forms of that nucleus of a multi-media spectacle – the 'participatory' performance [of the liturgy] in churches, which soon expanded out of doors into the town squares as the 'mystery' plays.

performance in its own way, while striving for one thing: the organic fusion into one spectacle of acting, dance, music, singing and the visual dimension. Each epoch attempted to achieve it – and each of them inevitably paid for the attempt by concessions to convention or by failing to achieve completeness.

It is difficult for us to appreciate what ancient Greek tragedy was like – not in the sense of factual reconstruction but of the way in which the audience perceived it.

An expert on the Japanese Nō theatre, in trying to indicate an exact equivalent of this semi-religious form of drama, which is still performed in the age-old manner, once said that it reminded him of . . . an ancient Greek play!

It would be more apt to reverse the comparison: to use the surviving examples of traditional Japanese Nō plays, or the even more ancient Chinese theatre of Mei-Lan-Fan,[288] as a way of understanding the special characteristics of classical Greek drama. I was never in an ancient Greek theatre, but if one recalls Mei-Lan-Fan in one of the most archaic plays in his repertoire, or Sadanji in *Narukami*, or Syozyo in dance-drama, you come to the conclusion that the fundamental distinguishing feature of all these performances is one and the same, and that it consists of *the extreme conventionalisation of the imagery*. In conditions of almost total disregard of the 'dreary requirements of everyday reality', the creators of these styles have ascended into the realm of godlike, mythical treatment of general ideas. There, at that level of 'heightened reality', sound and visual representation are fused into one, and the plot – unreal both in content and in its existence in purely *stage* terms – is matched by the ecstatic, semi-religious acting of the performers. The masks or painting of the face reduce the actors' features to a set of conventional, hieroglyphic patterns, while the gestures – not so much movements as semi-ritualised conventional signals – are almost impossible to relate to their real-life origins . . . and so on.

All the evidence points to the fact that the *cothurnus* or buskins of the ancient Greek theatre, which made the actors taller than ordinary mortals, and the masks which concealed their real features, exerted a similar effect for the performance as a whole. Raising it to such a level of generalisation was achieved at the expense of *a total break with the realistic, representational aspect of drama*.

Thus in the Chinese theatre, for instance, the realistic dimension is completely absent from the staging of a drama. I have written elsewhere about the way in which the same ordinary, everyday props are used to signify many different things. A single, unchanging chair cannot, of course, serve to *depict* a mountain, a house or a bed; but it can function perfectly well as an accepted *image* for each of those things or for all three, and as such can be treated by the actors in the appropriate manner.

This idea will become quite clear if we compare it directly with 'normal', realistic theatre sets and props. The secret of acting with [non-realistic props] is not to depend on their deficient verisimilitude but to animate them through an image, produced in the spectator's mind by the way in which the actor behaves towards them – not only when it is not the real object but a representation of it (e.g. a doll representing a baby), but also when it is not a real thing at all. Only through the actor's behaviour towards it (augmented, too, by the attitude of *the character being played* to the usual manner of treating this object were it real) can the on-stage object acquire reality: its *image* will emerge through the conventions by which it is *represented*.

Let us emphasise that example by citing its exact opposite: by totally removing any trace of image-creation in the way the object is treated, we shall see that even a real object then ceases to be perceived as having its normal function – take, for example, the way a juggler treats the bottles with which he is juggling.

Thus the Chinese theatre – and evidently the ancient [Greek] theatre too – acquired the ability to generalise in their performances at the price of abstracting them from everyday reality.

I suggest that realism was banished to such a degree (it is also curious that, here again, both the Chinese and the ancient Greeks did it equally) that in order to restore realistic depiction to the stage (for which there is a deep-seated human need), an autonomous but parallel and strictly realistic genre of performance was created – comedy; it is comic precisely due to its exaggerated depiction of elements of real life. (*Exaggerated* rather than *generalised*, at least up to the time of Molière.) The elements of stylisation and realistic depiction varied in degree according to the difference in genre. The more the realistic element gained the upper hand within a given type of peformance, the more the original synthesis disintegrated, being unable (given the [technical] means available at the time) to combine narrative depiction with generalised ideas and a multiplicity of expressive elements.

The idea of the multi-media spectacle of classical antiquity was revived in the opera of the Renaissance era. Here, realistic depiction played a big part, but once again the representation of everyday reality was found to be incompatible with music, singing and dancing. The formalisation of the elements of [Japanese] 'Vampuki', which took place at least five or six centuries after the creation of the genre itself, was inevitable, although perhaps less noticeable over the full course of its history.

In order to avoid tedium and lack of verisimilitude, opera had to provide excuses for the singing and dancing (and sometimes the music too) in a manner quite as flat-footed as the method used in sound film: 'Why don't you sing something?' or 'Ah, here come the villagers – they are going to dance for the Count'. The 'play' part of an operatic plot could never manage to remain realistically plausible while at the same time being a combined music and dance spectacle.

At present we are witnessing an unprecedented renaissance not only of opera but of all genres of the arts. It is also noteworthy that in this process the creators of Soviet opera have immediately taken the right road: they have chosen their subject matter in such a way as radically to remove the causes of the inner contradictions between the elements of opera, as being one of the partial forms of a multi-media performance.

Where, though, can elements of all the arts be made to combine *naturally?* – in a work based on fantasy: [Glinka's] *Ruslan and Lyudmila.*[289]

But where else is this condition to be found, and where, furthermore, does it exist without being divorced from reality? In the everyday life of the Soviet peoples, in all its multi-ethnic diversity. Soviet opera, enriched by exposure to many different national cultures – Georgian, Uzbek, Kazakh, Ukrainian – is turning its attention to the creation of ethnic opera. This will be opera whose popular origins are themselves shot through and through with music and dance, where in real life a girl's longing will naturally find expression in song (and not in an *aria*, artificially given to some bourgeois lady to sing), while the hero, her lover, will captivate her with the dash and vigour of his dancing.

How immeasurably greater is the potential for a complete synthesis of the arts in cinema!

11 Tolstoy's 'Anna Karenina' – the Races

To illustrate what we understand by audiovisual counterpoint, we shall not take a musical example, which is difficult to describe, but a 'textual' one, which is much easier to demonstrate. In such a case, we shall be dealing with what technically is usually called a 'saturation' [*zakhlëst*].

Like most of the 'specific' features of cinema, this method, too, has its predecessors in art forms that are now closely related but were originally separated in time.

Let us take an example from literature.

Tolstoy. *Anna Karenina*, 'The Races'.

The adjutant-general was criticising horse-racing. Alexei Alexandrovich [Karenin] was objecting to his arguments and defending racing. Anna listened to his thin, steady voice, not missing a single word; every one of his words struck her as false and was physically painful to hear.

Before the start of the three-mile steeplechase she bent forward and, without lowering her eyes, watched Vronsky as he approached his horse and mounted, while at the same time hearing her husband's unceasing, repellent voice. She was suffering agonies of fear for Vronsky, but she was even more agonised by what seemed to her the incessant sound of her husband's thin voice with its familiar intonations.[290]

Without striving to be particularly sophisticated, the screen treatment, dictated by the nature of the extract itself, would look roughly as follows:

1. The adjutant-general and Karenin. Words of both.
2. Karenin separately. Karenin's words.
3. Anna watches. Karenin's words.
4. Vronsky approaches, mounts, etc. Karenin's words.
5. Anna. Karenin's words.
6. Karenin separately. Karenin's words.

Nos 1 and 2 are obviously descriptive and informative. The 'play' as such begins with No. 3. The actual content of what Karenin is saying, due to the conventions of literary prose, are given by Tolstoy later. We will introduce this where necessary.

As we see, Nos 3, 4, 5 and 6 are played over the text of what Karenin is saying.

Here the director has at his disposal two sets of expressive means: the text itself and the intonational treatment of that text. Furthermore, the text must be perceived as the next stage, after intonation, in heightening the expression, i.e. to begin with, expression must lie solely in the intonation of the spoken words. Then, increasingly, expression can also start spilling over into particular words. I stress this here, because an analogous change in the internal dynamics of the written text also occurs at this very point. The intensification of the intonational pattern, duplicating the intensification of the text, will also increase the effect (if that proves to be necessary).

'In horse-racing by cavalry officers, danger is a necessary condition.' These opening words of Karenin's provide an effective lead-in to a close-up of Anna. The content of what he is saying naturally seizes Anna's attention, as she is in any case alarmed and worried.

'If England can point to some brilliant cavalry actions in her military history, it is only thanks to the fact that historically she has developed this strength in both animals and men. Sport, in my opinion, has a great significance. . . .' A paragraph that undoubtedly fits the close-up of Anna. The tediousness, lack of colour and drawling rhythm are underlined by Tolstoy's ironic comment: 'Just as it is natural for a child to jump about, so it was natural to him to talk intelligently and well. So he spoke. . . .'

These words entirely fit Anna's reaction, given above: 'Anna listened to his thin, steady voice, not missing a single word; every one of his words struck her as false and was physically painful to hear.'

Further, if we are to follow Tolstoy exactly, it will be necessary to insert between Nos 3 and 4 an 'interpolation' showing the reaction of Princess Betsy Tverskaya. Obviously, this can be done best as a group, perhaps with Anna in the foreground and with Karenin, Betsy and the adjutant-general in the frame.

Continuing with Karenin's remarks:

'. . . Sport, in my opinion, has a great significance, and, as always, we only see what is most superficial in it.'

'Not so superficial,' said Princess Tverskaya. 'One officer, they say, broke two ribs.'

Alexei Alexandrovich smiled his usual smile, in which he only bared his teeth but nothing more.

'Let us agree, princess, that that is not something superficial. . . .'

Another close-up of Anna as Karenin continues, saying: '. . . but internal. But that's not the point. . . .'

(N.B. In outline and foreshortening, the close-up of Anna and her features in the foreground of the group must be close to each other, so that the transition from shot to shot occurs with the least possible jolt, in order not to disturb the drawling rhythm of Karenin's speech.)

The continuation of Karenin's remarks belongs with 'Vronsky as he approached his horse and mounted' (No. 4): '. . . Don't forget that the riders are army officers who have chosen to indulge in this activity, and you must agree that every calling has a reverse side to the medal. It is an integral part of an officer's duty. . . .'

These words are very appropriate at this point, because they contain, as it were, a premonition of disaster ('a reverse side to the medal'). Given that Vronsky is doing his best to put on a brave show as he mounts his horse (he, too, is nervous), this contrast with the text lends the necessary tension. Words and action complement each other by their divergence.

'A reverse side to the medal' which forms 'an integral part of an officer's duty' is again a remark that makes Anna listen to Karenin. It is the obvious point at which to show her again in close-up, listening. '. . . She was suffering agonies of fear for Vronsky, but she was even more agonised by what seemed to her the unceasing sound of her husband's thin voice with its familiar intonations. . . .'

The unpleasantness of her husband's intonations is increased by his even less pleasant choice of words, which could not have been better selected to echo Anna's rising feeling of distaste and anxiety. Karenin's voice obviously sounds louder and more emphatic, and he stresses the individual syllables more sharply.

'. . . Crude sports such as boxing or Spanish bullfighting are a sign of barbarism. But a sport requiring specialised skill is a sign of a developed culture. . . .'

Two inserts between Nos 5 and 6:

1. An exchange of remarks between Betsy and another lady, clearly in a group: Betsy, Anna ('without lowering her binoculars, she was staring at one point') and the other lady.
2. Remarks exchanged by 'a senior general' and Karenin. Medium shot.

> Alexei Alexandrovich rose, hastily but with dignity and bowed low to the passing officer. 'Aren't you riding in the race?' the general said jokingly to him. 'The race I have run is a harder one,' Alexei Alexandrovich answered respectfully. And although the reply meant nothing, the officer pretended that he had been given a clever answer by a clever man and that he fully understood *la pointe de la sauce*.

And back again to a full-length shot of Alexei Alexandrovich.

Here it is curious to note that the actor has to play this part of his lines as though 'saturated' by his own words.

The words are: 'There are two sides . . . – those of performer and spectator; and a fondness for these spectacles is the surest sign of a low level of culture in the spectators, I agree, but. . . .'

We are given some notable clues for the way he should act as he says these words:

Alexei Alexandrovich's particular loquacity at this juncture, which so irritated her, was only an expression of his inner alarm and unease. As an injured child jumps about and thereby moves his muscles in order to dull the pain, so Alexei Alexandrovich felt the need for mental movement in order to dull the thoughts about his wife, which, in her presence and in Vronsky's presence and with the constant repetition of the latter's name, were demanding [Karenin's] attention. And just as it was natural for a child to jump about, it was natural for him to talk intelligently and well. So he spoke. . . .

This can only be played in close-up to the sound of his own words. Thus in the course of this passage we have been faced with four kinds of impetus:

1. The usual combination of words, with play on the ways they are pronounced (No. 2).
2. The actor performing while hearing what someone else is saying (Nos 3 and 5 in differing degrees of intensity. No. 5 is also notable for a piece of 'triple' acting: i) Anna's basic state of mind; ii) her hearing is caught by words that are being spoken out of shot; iii) her eyes are fixed on out-of-shot action: on Vronsky).
3. Acting to an accompaniment inaudible to the actor but heard by the audience (No. 4).
4. Acting to the characters' own words, but which are spoken, as it were, 'separately'. Acting and dialogue each proceed along different registers.

We have so far sketched out this approximate treatment on a literary basis only, i.e. combining words and actions in accordance with the indications provided by the literary text: the rhythm of the dialogue; intensification of the verbal images (bullfighting, barbarism, boxing); the immediate drama of verbal associations (words capable of attracting Anna's attention); more complex interpretation of the juxtaposition of words and action: Vronsky mounts Frou-Frou and the 'prophetic' words about the reverse side of the medal, giving a premonition [of his fall]. (God forbid that the latter should sound like anything more than a throwaway hint and come across as intentional; nothing more crass can be imagined. But God forbid, too, that this passage should not reach the audience's 'registering' consciousness and thereby fail somehow to sneak into their vague perceptions [of the significance of the dialogue]; in that case, we should lose a very valuable 'tremolo' in the general picture of nervous tension and promonition of disaster.)

This, therefore, is the first stage: *the establishment of synchronicity*, whether at odds with or congruent with, but at least in a strictly established correlation between, the *content* of those *actions* and those *words* with which they will coincide in time.

The second stage involves an even more complex task: to establish synchronicity between the formal treatment of both the visual and the sonic elements.

In concrete terms: the actors playing Vronsky and Cord (Vronsky's trainer), the required number of 'extras', a thoroughbred horse in the role of Frou-Frou and the whole scene of Vronsky mounting Frou-Frou must be 'set', 'as though to music', to the words spoken by Karenin that have been chosen to accompany this scene.

We must find the rhythm, the slowing down and acceleration of the spoken words, the intervals between them, the points of accentuation, the hesitations, the pauses and the places where Karenin draws breath, through all of which his psychological condition and state of mind are expressed with the utmost clarity, using them simultaneously as the canvas, made up of sound and time, on which to lay the graphic construct of the scene in which Vronsky mounts Frou-Frou. We must suggest that elusive action that stresses the equally elusive association of ideas evoked by 'a reverse side of the medal'; that elusive element in Vronsky's bearing that fully reveals, by an emphatic or even overemphatic intonation of the words, what it is that is 'an integral part of an officer's duty', and so on and so on; those nuances of texture and lighting which will be synchronised – in purposeful congruence or divergence – with the timbre and melody of the accompanying voice (the comparison of 'design' with 'timbre' and of 'lighting' with 'melody' is not fortuitous; they are equivalents in their respective fields); that particular outline and linear flourish in the graphic composition of the frame that finds its equivalent in the rhythmic breakdown of the text and so on – in the immediate blending of organically synchronised events (a person is seen and speaks) with all the nuances of juxtaposition (see list) we must seek, find and establish that synaesthetic correspondence between sound and picture, between graphic image and sound image (are not the design and colour of Karenin's overcoat inseparable from the timbre of his voice?), the two inseparable aspects of creating the being and behaviour of the hero, the heroine, the scene, the whole work. [. . . .][291]

So . . . we have the interplay between people; the interplay of sounds, of music and voices; the interplay of mass and colour; the interplay of situations; the interplay of images and thoughts.

Such is the multiplicity of means of interplay in that synthesising spectacle, the sound film; a multiplicity born of man's social concern and strictly organised by man's social consciousness.

And the means of bringing together all these incompatible factors in the single, synthesising score of a sound film is: montage!

Such are the functions of montage, Montage with a capital letter, montage in our time!*

But what are we to do? Where are we to look for the principles governing *this* kind of montage? Where can we find firm ground in our search for ways to realise it in practical terms, without chasing after ready-made, cut-and-dried recipes, but seeking a permanent, inexhaustible source of inspiration for montage as the basis of structuring a work of art?

The blinkered fanatics who, like Diogenes, lantern in hand, seek *man* in art and in his name trample on the laws of art and the perfection of its forms, are wrong.

Man, human behaviour and human relationships are not only in the plot, not only in depiction: man is also ineradicably present in the fundamental principles and laws of artistic *structure*; it is as much a reflection of man, of human behaviour and relationships as is depiction. But he is equally present at the level of secondary generalisation, as we have been analysing it throughout our work, beginning with the depiction of a barricade and its outline that generalises the idea of it.

The same dual factors – depiction and generalising image – that we have pursued through all branches and subdivisions of cinema are to be found here too.

The principle that applies to each particular component part also applies to the entire system as a whole.

Depictive truth within a work of art lies in truth to life reflecting what is typical in man, in human behaviour and attitudes.

Structural truth in a work of art lies in reflecting the same thing in the principles of structure: *the very principles that are within man himself, within human behaviour and attitudes.*

And there lies the *ultimate* source of the ceaseless fertilisation not only of artistic images but of their sustaining principles and of their solutions – of the forms and methods of art.

Let us now adduce some examples of this principle as a whole before proceeding to its practical application to the problem of montage.

We will take two examples from the least representational of the arts, music† and architecture, and we will pursue the human element within their formal structures.

In our first example – music – Diderot once again offers us his co-operation, for it is to this very question that he dedicates a large section

---

*Here I deliberately distinguish this synthesising function of montage vis-à-vis all the elements of sound film from montage as a particular field among other methods of filmic effect (the actor, the shot, the sound image [*fonogramma*], etc.), thereby bearing in mind all three of its different stages, each of which is also simultaneously present in this highest stage of development of the sound film.

†We know that music which is directly illustrative is the least respected variety of music. In rare instances, almost requiring a *tour de force*, it reaches such incomparable heights of artistry as the depiction of the forest in Wagner's *Siegfried*. More often its illustrative character is given 'right of residence' in its lowest form – direct onomatopoeia. The fundamentally inorganic nature of this function makes it inevitably comic. This humorous element is sensibly exploited by a whole branch of music: by the onomatopoeic elements in jazz.

in the *Third Dialogue* with his 'Natural Son', from which we have already quoted.[292]

Here Diderot tackles the question with all the characteristic breadth of approach of which he was capable. Primarily, and fundamentally, he bases his position on the human element, but also allows the problem to expand into man's surrounding environment. He refers to the way in which it, too, can be realised in music. Historical limitations, however, inevitably oblige him to restrict himself in this matter to 'nature', without proceeding to the question of how musical forms can also reflect the social environment, i.e. human relations, not to mention the highest form of such relations – social relations. This task has fallen to the lot of Diderot's successors: our Marxist musicologists.

But let us now turn to the apparently least illustrative and imitative of the arts: to architecture.

The laws of architecture are steeped in 'the human principle' and the concept of human relationships, not only on grounds of rationality and the functional requirements of a dwelling (which is, as it were, the 'plot' in architecture!).

Its entire aesthetic is steeped in 'the human principle'.*

In earliest times it was soaked not only in 'the human principle' but in man's . . . blood – not metaphorically, but in the form of an actual human sacrifice that was performed beneath the intended foundations of a building about to be constructed.

Later, with the extraordinary degree of perfection attained by the Greeks, it was no longer the blood but the 'spirit' of man that permeated the building in every detail: the proportions replicate not so much – and this is the most curious feature of all – human physical proportions as the principles and characteristics of man's growth and development. It is, for instance, well known that the principle of the 'golden section', which plays such a decisive role in the proportions of Greek works of art, is none other than the formula for the growth of organic bodies in nature converted into a linear ratio.

These laws of organic growth and development are common to the growth and development of any element of organic nature. Therefore the works of Greek architecture were, through their proportions, purposely (or partly instinctively) incorporated into the natural order, and that is why more than any other architecture in the world, they produce such an extraordinary effect; an effect which, apart from anything else, is the same as that otherwise made upon us only by the phenomena of organic nature: the human body, a flower, or the surf on the seashore.

The dark years of the Middle Ages in turn reduce architecture from a

---

*The school of architecture that has sought to derive the *entire aesthetic* of construction from the characteristics and qualities of the building materials has briefly flourished and then suffered its thoroughly deserved eclipse in our lifetime. Its experimental contribution to one of the branches of that aesthetic is undeniable, but the all-embracing pretensions of that single factor are, of course, unfounded.

matter of 'principle' to narrow 'depictiveness', to symbolism and the crypto-gram. If the soaring vaults of Gothic architecture were a visual affirmation in stone of the urge to soar up to the unearthly realms of paradise (the only escape, it would seem, from the social hell of medieval life); if the transfor-mation of a mass of stone – standing, four-square and life-affirming, like a solid block on the firm soil, even in the waters that washed the islands of Elephantina (Egypt) – into the petrified lace of Gothic church walls was also an expression of that mystical urge to overcome and surmount reality; if in those cases the medieval view of the world was psychologically able to reflect its principles in the style and in the technology of architecture, then that architecture (admittedly not to the extent of the highest stages of its development mentioned above, but in its initial stages) displays examples of the most primitive kind of *encoded depiction.**

As an example of this, we may take the basic form, sanctioned by tradition, of a Christian church. Its fundamental shape is that of a cross, laid out in such a way that in the place where the head of the crucified Christ would be, there is the holiest place, the altar. The placing of the altar can in fact change depending on the particular epoch and confessional doctrine. In some cases the altar moves deeper into the chancel, in others it retains its position in the centre of the cruciform intersection of nave and transepts, a position that can astonish those who are more used to seeing it placed far back as in Orthodox churches, rather as the stage is positioned in a theatre.

The Renaissance . . . But we are not writing a history of proportion in architecture, so let us therefore touch on only one more example: the 'decadent' architecture of the style known as . . . art nouveau.[293]

Art nouveau, which coincided with the turn of the century, inevitably bore the marks of the trends of thought that produced it.

Belonging as it did to a period of social decay, it was doomed to lack its own self-affirming countenance (as was possessed, for example, by the 'Empire' style of the period that saw the *beginning* of imperialism). The style of such an epoch will inevitably be imitative. Marx revealed the causes of this phenomenon in the example of the age of Napoleon III. The object of imitation in that decadent epoch was not some other era but . . . nature! But what a distorted imitation! It is not the principle, not the functional charac-teristics of nature or natural phenomena that this architecture imitates but the outward appearances of the plant world and the human body, predominantly the female body. Iron is bent to imitate lianas; plasterwork is made to coil like lilies, and the shapes of windows try to imitate unevenly widening circles in water. Façades imitate the wing-span of dragonflies. Door-handles, forks, knives,

---

*This is all the stranger when placed alongside the commandment 'Thou shalt not make unto thyself any graven image.' The Jews were more consistent, reducing the Holy of Holies in the Temple of Jerusalem to 'nothing', an empty room: the dwelling-place and image of the invisible God. Similarly the Muslims in, for instance, Persian miniatures, while depicting relatively realistic 'landscapes', horsemen, and other people, show Mohammed in normal clothes and mounted on a horse but with a white blob instead of a face.

electric bells and lamp-bases writhe with figures of sinuous female bodies, among whose hair low-powered electric bulbs glow with a faint, mysterious light. Even uninhibited rococo was more chaste: the curves of its settees, armchairs and *bergères* at least imitated only the *lines* of the female figure!

This peculiar caricature-like 'biologism' in architecture was answered, several decades later, by a movement no less erroneous . . . 'physiologism'. This is how I like to characterise that naked functionalism in architectural aesthetics that was espoused by the followers of Le Corbusier:[294] a hypertrophy of functionality and the utilitarian principle.

It is as inhuman as art nouveau in its striving after the outward forms of nature. For the rationality of the structure of the skeleton, the reasonableness of the muscular system, of the nervous system or the network of blood-vessels, even the still more rational combination of all these, do not of themselves create the inspired wholeness of the living organism, the living man!

I confess that I used to be a great adherent of the architectural aesthetics of Le Corbusier and Gropius;[295] it was only direct contact with the fullness of life that opened my eyes to the fact that this architecture (chiefly in the distorted products of its epigones) lacked any reflection of the full-blooded joyousness of modern man, just as an anatomical atlas can never be a portrait in which a man can recognise himself, his thirst for life and his joy in a socialist existence.

I did not learn about this function of architecture from books, or from theoretical treatises, or from professors and architects; from none of these did I learn about the joyous expression of our humanity in our home, in our street, in the architectural ensemble of our town, or about the super-utilitarian character of our merely human needs. I heard about the need for an architect to incarnate *the joy of humankind* in the layout of his town and its buildings (and how much broader and superior is that need to the hitherto unsurpassed aesthetics and the principle of human proportions created by the Greeks*) from a remarkable man, a builder of socialism in one of the smallest regions of our vast Union: Betal Kalmykov,[296] when I discussed with him the creation of the socialist city of Nalchik that was to take the place of the previous town, hardly more than a large village. It was there, in fact, that I first gained a concrete perception of 'humanism' as a theme of architecture.†

But let us return from the realms of music and of music frozen in stone (architecture) to our final deductions concerning the montage of sound film.[297]

---

*Just as our socialist present is even more beautiful than the most beautiful of all previous epochs, the infancy of mankind: Greece!

†It is therefore a hundred times more disgraceful that the task of working for the joy of people who have thrown off the yoke of exploitation was not seized upon and used creatively by the architects. The brigade of architects that was invited to create the new Nalchik preferred (at least in the plan that I saw in 1933) to impose on the capital of Kabardino-Balkaria 'at its own expense' an architectural ensemble put together according to an extremely simple recipe. All that it required was a great deal of tracing-paper, an even greater amount of sheer cheek and many, many albums of architectural drawings. 'Palace of Culture?' – 'Give

'The human principle' as the source of a formative aesthetic of the cinema has never before presented itself in such fullness, and no wonder: never before has the cinema as a synthesising art form been presented with such enlarged demands and such a complex task; this necessity has never before been felt in such totality.

There have, however, been digressions and sideways leaps in that direction. They have grasped at . . . individual human sense organs, at particular human innards and limbs, hastily deducing from them an all-embracing aesthetic of cinematography. [. . . .][298]

There was 'Cine-Eye' and 'Radio-Ear', with an aesthetic [based on the idea] of eyes dazzled by the sight of socialism.[299] These were attacked by the 'Cine-Fist' (see my article of 1925, 'The Problem of the Materialist Approach to Form') and their aesthetic of landing a series of punches on the spectator's psyche ('bash 'em over the skull', etc.).[300]

All three of these were opposed by the 'Cine-Brain', who considered that a viewpoint was more important than merely seeing. (Montage of attractions as a montage of the spectator's brain cells.)

'Cine-Intellect' then emerged as the dynamic process in the functioning of that brain. This was rapidly opposed by the hotly emotional 'Cine-Heart' (to the accompaniment of a gramophone record of its precise contemporary, a certain song from a certain musical comedy).[301]

The excessive abstraction of this human '*flow* of thought and *flow* of consciousness' as the sole theme has reverted to a greater degree of humanness thanks to the 'inner monologue' as a source of method for *structuring* a film. The inner monologue also took as its starting-point a particular human manifestation – the structure of human speech – and what's more an *internal* manifestation![302]

All this was like gnawing at the problem of cinematic form from different sides, like a pack of dogs gnawing at the flanks of a wild boar at bay; and the more heated the attacks and assertions, the more one-sided became the views claiming to be of exhaustive and all-embracing significance.

In fact only now has the time arrived for everything to come together, for those keen eyes to return to their sockets and to penetrate contemporary reality with still greater keenness; for the ears to resume their place on either side of temples grown grey in battle; for the heart to beat with revolutionary fervour within the breast; for the intellect to think and to regulate the whole apparatus, so that all its parts may collaborate in not merely the progress but the rapid flow of consciousness and thought, sending out shattering blows by

---

'em a bit of Piranesi.' 'Palace of the Soviets?' – 'Copy the Palazzo Pitti. . . . Medicinal baths? Go on – how about the baths of Caracalla?' (provided the money holds out!). N.B. This retreat is not the way to draw on the architecture of the past. To ask the question 'What has all this to do with cinema?' is completely out of place. I leave the reader to think of analogies in cinema.

word, speech and action against those who have not yet submitted to the victory of socialism. Nothing that has been gained in past experience will be lost in making this synthesising art form work, but nor will anything slide out of the framework of its allotted place.*

Montage, as a method of bringing about the unity of all the multiform parts that go to make up a synthetic work of art on the pattern of a living original, must embrace the totality of man recreated in all his fullness.

But that pattern must not be a robot, mechanically (mechanistically!) assembled and screwed together, nor an artificial man with glass innards like the one at the Paris Universal Exhibition of 1937. Therefore montage – Montage with a capital M, not montage as one of the specialised branches of film-making (such as the actor, the shot or the sound) – must go and learn from the real, human prototype of what it is portraying. It must pattern itself on that prototype: the real, living, joyful and suffering, loving and hating, singing and dancing human originals, who bear children and retain remnants of their class origin: the cheerful and full-blooded man of emergent socialism and the man who is building socialism.

And I repeat: he must not only be present in the theme and the plot . . . but also in the fundamental principles that underlie the film's composition.

What does that mean in practice?

And how can it, without being a mere set of standard procedures and recipes, serve simultaneously as a permanent, fertile and inexhaustible source of the invention of ever new compositional ideas?

It was easy enough for Diderot.

He summed up eighteen centuries of musical culture plus that uncount-able phalanx of centuries that we count in backward sequence, starting from the so-called birth of Christ, at the end (or the beginning) of which lies its origin.

It was easy for him to identify, retrospectively, the courses and origins of music and the idea that the firm ground for deducing the laws of its aesthetics is expressive *man*, or more precisely – the *expressiveness* of man.

What is more, his chosen field – music – is a great deal more modest than the all-embracing audiovisual synthesis of the sound film!

How then are we – who have to make do with the mere forty-odd years of direct experience of cinema that preceded the phenomenon we are not concerned to summarise or analyse but to propel forward in an unprecedented forward movement – to create almost from zero a practical methodology, having to hand only the thread that links us to 'expressive man' as the source of the aesthetic principles of sound film?!

Even so, it is easier for us than for Diderot: ahead of us are as many centuries of the achievements of liberated mankind as there were centuries of human oppression behind him!

---

*That is why it is expedient to bring together the theoretical considerations proper to all the separate historical moments and stages in the broad totality of that synthesising art form, the sound film. No single element should be lost.

To be working on laying the foundations of an aesthetic of this synthesising art form, which liberated mankind is destined to create, is a most thrilling task.

What, therefore, is the most practical approach to the business of extracting from human expressiveness an inexhaustible flow of audiovisual scenarios, ever new, ever untried, ever vibrantly alive for each new theme?

It is both very simple and very complicated.

The foundation of the scenario, in which the theme is to be packaged, must consist of remarkably little: an urgent narrative that conveys the theme through the events of its content.

Is that all? Yes; so little yet so very much.

For what is an *urgent* narrative?

It is an idea that has been absorbed by all the expressive attributes of a human being and is embodied in them.

Watch a man who is urgently telling a story. He walks up and down the room. He cannot find the right words. For a while he utters only wordless sounds, which then turn into chaotic gesticulation. But even gestures are inadequate to express what he could not describe verbally. He paces back and forth. He wipes his brow. But his eyes begin to shine again; this time, however, he walks up and down with measured tread; words begin to fall into their right place in his narrative. Gestures and paces begin to alternate smoothly, but his excitement starts to rise again; the attitudes of his body say more than words. Suddenly his words begin to flow rhythmically. He is more and more in the grip of his narrative, he is not so much declaiming as almost singing. He circles around the room.

And with steely purposefulness all this is shot through with a single unifying thought, a unifying conception.

You must imagine your on-screen action as a representation of this excited man. And transfer the imagined episode into the structure of your scenario.

In the unbroken ebb and flow of genuine, inward emotion, the film scenario traces, as it were, the equivalent of one of Bach's four-part fugues.

As in a musical score, but in place of the 'voices' or 'instruments', the left-hand column on a sheet of graph-paper grows.

Along the top of the page runs the line of the text of an urgent narrative with, as a subtext, an undercurrent of emotions and ideas, which race along synchronously with the words. These and the emotions they evoke dictate how, in each phase of the action, the moods of the emotionally keyed-up protagonists are apportioned to the various 'instruments' of the orchestra.

TABLE III

1. Mise en scène			
2. Gesture			
3. Mime			
4. Intonation			

Certain verbal elements of the content are linked entirely to the *mise en scène* (1, 4); certain elements are linked to the gestures of a man when standing still (2, 3); others to mime only (3); others to wordless exclamation (4); still others embrace man in all his manifestations (1, 2, 3, 4).

In the action itself they overflow into one another, merge together and disperse again, carrying in themselves the fullness of the urgent, emotional flow of the theme. These manifestations of excited behaviour develop by stages. Intensity of experience forces thought to clothe itself in words. '*Wenn das Herz voll ist, dem geht der Mund über*' [His mouth floweth over whose heart is full], as one very fiery figure of the past said, none other than . . . Martin Luther, who threw inkwells at devils and translations of the Bible at popes. Exciting words express themselves through intonation. Intonation broadens into gesture and mime, while gesture and mimicry explode into the spatial displacement of their originator, into spatial behaviour, the prototype of performance. Organic in their links with one another, consequential in their stage-by-stage development, they are at the same time contrapuntal in their state of simultaneous co-presence.

So it is in the theatre. So it is in an actor's performance – in the theatre or, in equal degree, in the realm of a character's dramatic behaviour within the plot of a film. But I am not an actor. I am not even a *theatre* director. I am the director of that most remarkable of art forms, the sound film as a synthesis of the arts. So what am *I* to do? How am *I* to shout urgently about my theme, our theme? Where is *my* movement? Where are *my* sobs? Where are *my* gestures, *my* mime, *my* words?

My *mise en scène* is montage.

My gesture and mime are the composition of the action within the frame and the frame itself.

My intonation is the place of my soundtrack in the total audiovisual counterpoint.

A great poet of our epoch wrote of revolutionary creativity:

> The streets are our brushes,
> The squares – our palettes. . . .[303]

For the form of a work of art, in which I embody myself in order to present my theme, is like the way an actor transforms himself; the body of my work of art, its parts, limbs and organs are . . . the structure of my story, the rhythm of my dancing, the melody of my song, the metaphor of my cry, my treatment of the plot and the image of my perception of the whole: all these are the things with which I express – as an actor expresses with his arms and legs, his voice and the gleam in his eyes – that by which he and I, in our creative endeavours, are inwardly possessed.

Colour; rhythm; the actors' performance; the expression of the theme by a total, photographed performance, the soundtrack or the graphic image of a shot, a single sequence or a montage phrase made up of short, sharply cut shots, and soon – that is the range of instruments in my orchestra: one that has grown beyond all bounds, but which grew out of a tiny orchestra working from a score made up of wordless thought; words and intonations; mime and gesture, and finally – the flow of total performance that I have mentioned above.

The compositional scenario of the synthesising sound film, which grows out of, draws upon and listens keenly to the concept of the total performance: that is the basis of the montage of all those means and the range of their effect.

So now we have reached agreement on how and by what means the structural laws of a film can, on an equal footing with the plot, reflect the living human being! At first sight it is all absurdly simple. The principle is clear. To be able, however, to listen to oneself, to read one's own thoughts and to develop what one has read into a practical programme – the scenario of the piece as a whole – that is where the difficulties are boundless. And it is precisely on the methodology of how to do this that I have been working as a teacher for a number of years.[304] There is also another difficulty, the difficulty in the *culture of urgency*: to keep that excitement truthful and sincere all the way. For without the preconditions of love and hatred no work of art can come into being, either in form or in content; and in that prerequisite but *by no means exhaustive* culture of urgent emotion – needed in equal measure by both actor and director, although in different areas of application – lie one's greatest difficulties.

Stanislavsky's 'Method' went a long way towards dealing with this question of the 'culture of urgency', although not without a certain exaggeration, to the detriment of the study of other areas of creativity in the total work of art. That deviation was conscious and well-founded: 'Yes, I admit to an over-emphasis on the emotional aspect of artistic creativity and I do so with a purpose, because other approaches to art have too often forgotten about emotion.'[305]

And that is consistently maintained throughout Stanislavsky's book. No more than a few words, in fact, are devoted to the question of form, and then only in the most general terms: 'The aim of our art is not only to create "the life of a human spirit" in a role, but also to convey it outwardly in artistic form.'[306]

As to what that 'artistic form' consists of, there is not one word in the entire book.

But let us return to the question of reflecting living man in the formal structure of a work: it is at one and the same time the reflection of human behaviour and of human relationships, because it is not from real life but from the theatre . . . and by that I mean the anatomy theatre that man can emerge divorced (and even then only relatively!) from human behaviour, divorced from human social relationships.

But that sort of man is called a corpse!

For, as we have shown by visual demonstration, the affective element of my work, being the embodiment of my expressive emotional involvement with reality, is, after all, not involvement *per se* but a class involvement.

And in that unity of class consciousness and emotion, which dictates this whole 'bag of tricks' of affective and expressive devices, there is reflected the current phase in the chronicle of the struggle between the exploited and the exploiters, in which I am happy to have been both a witness and a fighter, a participant in the happiest of all those phases, the age that has brought that struggle to a victorious conclusion. And the secret of reflecting that *correctly* not only in the content but in the structural laws of a work of art is one and the same for both.

For it is this that removes the initial difficulty in the approach to the culture of emotionally urgent performance, providing it with a firm and indestructible premiss.

In defining it we may safely trust 'the frenzied Vissarion'.[307] What is needed to reveal this secret?

'For this one needs only to be a citizen, the offspring of one's society and one's times, to adopt its interests as one's own, to merge one's aspirations with those of the times' (Belinsky).

To be a citizen of the Land of the Soviets. To be the offspring of one's class, to be an active fighter for socialism. The rest will come by itself, will 'emerge' from a correctly ordered set of priorities. Witness the countless examples that I have adduced in dealing with each and every branch of our complicated trade. And that also applies to the conditions of our entire activity! Then the forms will fall into place on lines that are as strict and popularly accessible as the folk tale and the structure of a folk song.

Only by keeping strictly to the natural and organic qualities of the total expression of urgent emotion – our expressivity – shall we be masters of that reservoir which, when we are creating a scenario, prompts us as to when to use images and metaphysical language, when to break up the plot into short rapid montage fragments, when suddenly to see everything in colour, and when to pour out a whole hurricane of emotion in sound alone. Human expressivity is our one and only reliable support and the sole source that nourishes a mastery of form.

That is why in the course in which I taught film direction at VGIK I pedantically and in such detail (in defiance of the frenzied opposition of my carping critics) gave so much attention to the problem of human expressivity; in doing so I did not shrink from teaching – however much that might infuriate my opponents – not only a history of the theories of human expressivity but also the history of how the forms of expressivity evolved.

Without that we cannot understand all the knowledge concerning human creativity that has hitherto been gained.

And without that there is much that we will not understand about the inherent principles of art, that most sublime form of the social behaviour of expressive man.

Still less will we be able to master those hard creative tasks which, apart from ideas and subject matter, face us as we approach the expressive potential of that audiovisual synthesis: sound film.

12 Montage 1938[308]

There was a period in our cinema when montage was proclaimed as being 'everything'.[309] We are now coming to the end of a period when montage has been regarded as 'nothing'. Since we consider montage to be neither 'nothing' nor 'everything', we now think it necessary to recall that montage is as essential a component of film-making as all the other affective elements of cinematography. After the stormy polemics of 'pro-montage' and the counter-onslaughts of 'anti-montage', it is time to approach its problems afresh and with an open mind; and all the more so because the period of 'negation' of montage discredited even its most uncontroversial quality, the one aspect of montage which never should have invited attack in any form. The fact is that the makers of a number of films in recent years have so thoroughly 'parted company' with montage that they even forgot the basic aim and function, inseparable from its *cognitive* role, which every work of art sets for itself: *the function of providing a coherent, consistent exposition of the work's theme, plot, action and events,* and their progression both within each sequence and within the film as a whole. Not only the *affective* type of narrative but even the logically consistent, merely *coherent* narrative thread has in many cases been forfeited even in the works of some quite masterly film-makers and in the most varied cinematic genres. This does not, of course, call so much for criticism of these film-makers as for a campaign to reinstate the art of montage that so many of them have rejected, especially since our film industry is faced with the challenge of creating emotionally charged narrative that is not only *logically coherent* but *maximally affective.*

Montage is an invaluable aid to discharging this task.

Why do we edit film at all? Even the fiercest opponents of montage will agree that it is not because we do not have infinitely long strips of film at our disposal and, being doomed to a finite length of film, are forced from time to time to glue one piece of film to another.

The 'Leftist' proponents of montage have revealed a characteristic of this technique which goes to the other extreme. When playing with pieces of film they discovered one property of it that amazed them for a number of years. This property was that *any two sequences, when juxtaposed, inevitably combine into another concept which arises from that juxtaposition as something qualitatively new.*[310]

This is by no means a purely cinematic phenomenon, but one which inevitably accompanies the juxtaposition of two events, two facts, two objects.

We are almost automatically prone to draw a quite specific, conventional conclusion – a generalisation, in fact – whenever certain discrete objects are placed side by side before us. Take, for instance, a tomb in a graveyard. Put beside it a weeping woman in mourning and there can be few who will not conclude: 'a widow'. It is on precisely this sort of conventional deduction that the following little joke by Ambrose Bierce is based; it is from his *Fantastic Fables* and is called 'The Inconsolable Widow':

A woman in widow's weeds was sobbing upon a tombstone.

'Console yourself, madam', a sympathetic passer-by said to her. 'The mercy of heaven is infinite. Somewhere in the world there is another man beside your husband with whom you will be able to find happiness.'

'There was,' she sobbed in reply. 'Such a man did live, but alas . . . this is his grave.'[311]

The whole effect of this little story rests on the fact that a grave and a woman in mourning beside it will always, according to conventional deduction, lead to the conclusion that this is a widow mourning her husband whereas in fact the object of her grief was her lover!

This type of misunderstanding is also used in riddles. Here is an example from folklore: 'The crow was flying and the dog was sitting on its tail.' How can that be? We automatically juxtapose the two elements and merge them into *one*; in that case, the riddle reads as if the dog was sitting on the crow's tail. The riddle, however, relies on *both actions* being unrelated: the crow was flying, while the dog was sitting on its own tail.

There is thus nothing surprising in the fact that the spectator also draws a certain conclusion when faced with the juxtaposition of two pieces of glued-together film.

It is not for us to criticise facts, their uniqueness or universality, but the deductions and conclusions that are drawn from them, and to bring to these the necessary correctives.

What was the careless omission that we made when we first pointed out the unquestionable importance of the above-mentioned phenomenon for the understanding and mastery of montage?[312] What was correct and what was incorrect in our enthusiastic assertions made at that time?

It was and remains correct that the juxtaposition of two montage sequences resembles not so much their sum as their *product*. It resembles the product – as distinct from the sum – in that *the result of juxtaposition* always differs *qualitatively* (in dimension, or if you like in degree) from each constituent element taken separately. The woman (to return to our first example) is depicted; the woman's black dress is depicted, and both are capable of *objective representation*. 'Widow', however – the concept which arises from juxtaposition of the two depictions – is not capable of being objectively represented; it is a new perception, a new concept, a new image.

Wherein lay the 'exaggeration' in my earlier treatment of this incontestable phenomenon?

My error lay chiefly in the stress that I laid on the potential of juxtaposition, combined with insufficient stress on the *research* needed into the question of the *material* that went into the juxtaposition.

My critics did not fail to portray this as a lack of interest in the *content itself* of the sequences, thereby confusing my interest *as a researcher* in a particular aspect of the problem with the researcher's personal attitude to the reality depicted.[313]

I leave this to their consciences.

I think I was primarily obsessed by the fact that unrelated sequences, when juxtaposed by the will of the film editor – and often *despite* being unrelated – gave rise to a 'third something' and became related.[314] Thus I was captivated by the non-typical combinations that were possible in conditions of normal cinematic structuring and composition. Working primarily with examples of such [non-typical] material, it was natural to reflect above all on the possibilities inherent in juxtaposition. I gave less *analytical attention* to the content of the juxtaposed sequences themselves. That by itself, incidentally, would also have been insufficient: giving exclusive attention to the 'intra-frame' content has led in practice to the withering of montage, with all the attendant consequences.

To what, then, should we give most attention in order to make both extremes converge towards a golden mean?

We should address ourselves to the basic factor which determines in equal degree both the 'intra-frame' content and the compositional juxtaposition of those separate units of content; i.e. to the content of the *whole* to what is common to all such units, to the element which *unifies* them.

One extreme consisted in an excessive concentration on questions of the technique of unifying them (the methods of montage), the other in too great a concern with the elements to be unified (the content of the shots).

Instead, we should have given greater attention to the nature of that *unifying principle* itself: that very principle which in every film generates in equal degree both the content in each frame and the content that is revealed through *juxtaposition of those frames*.

For this, however, the researcher's interest ought not to have been directed towards those paradoxical instances in which the ultimate, common whole was not *intended* but arose unexpectedly. It should have been directed to cases where the sequences were not only related to each other, but where *the ultimate, common whole* was not only intended but itself determined both the elements themselves and the way they were juxtaposed. These would be examples of normal, accepted and universally accessible film-making. In them, that *whole* would arise in exactly the same way – as a 'third someting' – but the overall scheme of how both frame and montage were to be constituted – the content of both the one and the other – would be more obvious and more precise. And such instances are, of course, typical of film-making.

If montage is approached in this way, both the frames and their juxtaposition are found to be in their correct mutual relationship. What is more, the very nature of montage is not only congruent with the principles of film narrative but acts as one of the most consistent and suitable means of realistically conveying the film's content.

What then do we have, given this interpretation of montage? We have the fact that no montage sequence exists in isolation but is in the nature of a *partial depiction* of the single overall theme which in equal degree pervades all the sequences. The juxtaposition of other such partial details in a particular montage structure evokes in the spectator's perception that *common essence* which generated each separate element and binds them together into a *whole*, and specifically into that generalised *image* through which the author (and after him the spectator) has experienced the theme of the film in question.

If we *now* look at two consecutive sequences, we too will see their juxtaposition in a slightly different light, as follows:

Sequence A, made from elements of the film's theme, and Sequence B, put together from the same source, will, when juxtaposed, generate an image in which the content of the theme is most clearly embodied.

Expressed in the imperative mood, in more precise and more practical terms, this thesis will read as follows:

Depiction A and *Depiction B* must be so chosen from all the possible features inherent in the story that the *juxtaposition* of them – specifically the juxtaposition of *them*, not of any other elements – will evoke in the perceptions and emotions of the spectator the most exhaustive, total *image of the film's theme*.

So far in this discussion of montage we have introduced two terms: 'depiction' [*izobrazhenie*] and 'image' [*obraz*]. We should now describe precisely what we see as the difference between them.

Let us take an obvious example: a white circular disc of moderate dimensions with a smooth surface divided around its circumference into sixty equal segments. At every fifth segment a figure is placed in numerical sequence from one to twelve inclusive. At the centre of the circle is a spindle to which are attached two freely turning, narrow strips of metal which taper to a point at their unattached ends: the length of one of them is that of the radius of the circle, the other is slightly shorter. Let us suppose that the longer strip remains with its free end pointing to the figure 12, while the free end of the shorter strip points in turn to the figures 1, 2, 3 and so on up to 12 inclusive. This will be a series of sequential *geometric* depictions of the fact that the two metal strips stand in relation to each other at angles of, in turn, 30 degrees, 60 degrees, 90 degrees and so on up to 360 degrees inclusive.

If, however, this disc is provided with a mechanism which causes the metal strips to move around the circle at an even rate, then the geometric pattern on its surface acquires a special significance: it is not simply a *depiction* but is now an *image* of time.

This being so, the depiction and the image that it evokes in our perception are so thoroughly merged that quite special circumstances are needed in order to separate the geometric pattern of the hands on the clock-face from the concept of time. Yet this can happen to any of us, although admittedly in unusual circumstances.

Let us recall Vronsky after Anna Karenina has told him that she is pregnant. At the start of Chapter 24 of Part 2 of *Anna Karenina* we find just such an instance: 'When Vronsky looked at the clock on the Karenins' balcony, he was so disturbed and preoccupied with his thoughts that he saw the hands on the clock-face but could not tell what the time was.'[315]

The *image* of time, which the clock was creating, did not arise in his mind. All he could see was the geometric depiction represented by the face and hands of the clock.

Thus we see that, even in the simplest instance, when it is a case of telling the time its depiction alone on the clock-face is not enough. Seeing is insufficient: something has to happen to that depiction, it has to undergo some process in our mind. Only then will it cease to be perceived as a simple geometrical pattern and will instead be perceived as the image of 'something o'clock', as the time at which an event takes place. Tolstoy shows us what happens when this process does not occur.

What does this process consist of? A particular configuration of the hands on a clock-face summons up a swarm of ideas connected with the time of day that corresponds to a given numeral on the clock-face. Let it be, for example, the figure 5. In that case our imagination has been schooled, in response to that figure, to summon up mental pictures of all kinds of events which regularly occur at that hour. It may be supper, or the end of the working day, or the rush hour on the metro, or the bookshops closing, or the special light in those pre-twilight hours which is so characteristic of that time of day. . . . One way or another, it will be a whole series of pictures (depictions) of what happens at five o'clock.

The image of five o'clock is made up of all these different mental pictures.

The above is a description of that process in extended form, culminating in the stage at which we *interpret* the depiction of those figures which give rise to our images of the hours of the day and night. Then the laws of economy of psychic energy come into play. Within the process we have described, a certain 'compression' takes place: the intermediate links in the chain fall away, and there occurs an immediate, direct and instant connection between the figure and the perception of an image, the image of the 'time of day' that corresponds to that figure. From the example with Vronsky we saw how, under the influence of a powerful affect, that connection can be broken, and how depiction and image then become detached from each other.

We are interested in the *total* picture of how an image arises from a depiction as we have just described it. This 'mechanism' of image formation interests us because the way it functions in *real life* naturally serves as a prototype of the method used in art to create artistic images.

Let us therefore recall that, between the depiction of the time of day on a clock and our perception of an image of that time, there stretches a long associative chain of depictions of the separate aspects which characterise the given time of day. And let us repeat that a form of mental skill reduces that intermediate chain to a minimum and we perceive only the beginning and the end of that process.

But as soon as we are obliged, for one reason or another, to restore the associative chain between a certain depiction and the image which it should evoke in our minds, we must inevitably have recourse to a similar chain of intermediate depictions which coalesce into an image.

We shall begin by taking an example from everyday life which is quite close to those quoted above.

In New York the majority of streets do not have names; instead, they are indicated by numbers: 5th Avenue, 42nd Street and so on. For visitors this method of designating the streets can at first make it very difficult to remember them. We are used to streets having names, and this makes life much easier for us, because a name instantly evokes an image of the street, i.e. merely by pronouncing the appropriate name a specific cluster of perceptions arises along with the image.

I found it very difficult to remember the *images* of the streets of New York and consequently to know these streets. Streets given such neutral designations as '42nd Street' or '45th Street' simply did not evoke in me any images adding up to a perception of what they looked like. To help me in this, I had to memorise a set of objects which would come into my mind in response to the signal '42nd' as distinct from the signal '45th'. In my memory I accumulated theatres, cinemas, shops, buildings, etc., that were characteristic of each of the streets I needed to remember. This memorising process proceeded by distinct stages, of which I can single out two; in the first of them, my memory responded to the verbal designation '42nd Street' by recalling *with great difficulty* the entire sequence of features which characterised that street; but this did not evoke a real perception of the street, because the separate elements had not yet merged into a single image.

Only at the second stage did all these elements begin to fuse into a single, emerging image: at the mention of the street's number there arose *a whole swarm of separate elements of that street, though not as a chain but as a whole*, as a complete picture of the street, *as its total image*.

Not until that moment could it be said that I had really *remembered* the street. The image of that street came to life in my mind and senses in exactly the way that in the course of experiencing a work of art its elements gradually coalesce into a single, unforgettable total image.

In both cases – be it the process of recollection or the process of appreciating a work of art – it remains true that a unified experience enters our mind and emotions through the whole, and the whole does so through the *image*. This image enters our consciousness and through its *totality* every detail of it is also preserved in our memory *inseparably from the whole*. This may be an image in sound: some kind of rhythmic and melodic sound picture; or it may be a three-dimensional image, to which separate elements of the mnemonic series have contributed pictorially.

By one route or another, a set of ideas enters our mind, forming a complete image composed of the separate elements.

We have seen that in the process of remembering there are two essential stages; the first is that of the *formation* of an image; the second is the *result* of that first stage and its significance for memorisation. At the same time it is important for our memory to give as little attention as possible to the first stage and, bypassing the process of *formation* to arrive at the *result* as quickly as possible. This is what happens in life, unlike the process that occurs in art; for in proceeding from life into the realm of art we observe a distinct shifting of the stress. In arriving at the *result*, a work of art directs all the subtlety of its methods towards the *process*.

A work of art, understood dynamically, is also a process of forming images in the mind of the spectator.* Herein lies the peculiar quality of every genuinely vital work of art, which distinguishes it from a lifeless piece of work in which the spectator is presented with a depiction of the *results* of a certain past creative process instead of being drawn into a permanently occurring process.

This quality vindicates itself everywhere and always, with no matter what art form we may be concerned. In exactly the same way a vital performance by an actor is based on the fact that he is not depicting the imitated results of emotions but causes those emotions *to arise, to develop, to turn into others – in a word to live in front of the spectator.*

The image of a scene, an episode, a production, etc., does not, therefore, exist as a ready-made *datum* but must evolve, must unfold.

Similarly, in order to make a vivid impression, a character in a drama must take shape before the spectator in the course of the action and must not appear as some kind of mechanical doll endowed a priori with certain characteristics. In drama it is particularly important that the course of events on stage should not only build up the *idea* of a character but should also 'create' *the character itself.*

Consequently, in the method by which it creates images a work of art should reproduce the process through which new images are built up in the mind of a person *in real life.* We have just demonstrated this through the example of the New York streets. And we shall be right in expecting an artist, when faced with the task of expressing some image through the depiction of fact, to employ a method similar to that by which we 'familiarise ourselves' with the streets of New York.

We have cited an example of depiction on a clock-face and have

---

*Later we shall see that this same dynamic principle underlies all the vital images of such an apparently motionless and static art form as, for instance, painting.

discovered the process whereby the image of time arises from that depiction. And to create an image a work of art must have recourse to the analogous method of creating an associative chain of depictions.

Let us stay with our example of the clock.

In the case of Vronsky, the geometric pattern did not generate an image of the time of day. There are cases, however, where it is not important to perceive twelve o'clock midnight merely as a point in time but to experience midnight in all the associations and perceptions which the author wishes to evoke as part of his or her plot. It may be a time of tremulous anxiety while waiting for a midnight assignation; the time of a death at midnight; a fateful midnight escape; in other words, it may be far from the simple depiction of twelve o'clock at night *per se*. In that case the image of midnight as some kind of 'fateful' hour, charged with a special significance, must show through *a depiction of the twelve strokes of the clock*.

Let us illustrate this by an example; this time it comes from Maupassant's *Bel-Ami*, and is interesting because it involves *sound*. And it is even more interesting because its skilfully chosen narrative method, presented in the novel in the manner of an objective chronicler, is a pure example of montage.

The scene from *Bel-Ami* is the one in which Georges Duroy, who by now writes his name 'du Roy', is sitting in a cab waiting for Suzanne, who has agreed to elope with him at midnight.

Twelve o'clock midnight. Here least of all is this a moment in astronomical time, but it is above all a time at which everything (or at least a great deal) has been gambled on one card: 'It's over. All is ruined. She's not coming.'

This is how Maupassant engraves upon the reader's mind the image of that hour, its *significance*, as distinct from a straightforward description of the time of night:

> He left home at about eleven o'clock, wandered for a while, then took a cab to the Place de la Concorde, by the arcade of the Ministry of Marine.
>
> From time to time he lit a match and looked at his watch. Around twelve he was seized by feverish anxiety. Every minute he put his head out of the cab window to see whether she was coming.
>
> Somewhere far away a clock struck twelve, then again, nearer; then two other clocks struck at once, followed by another at a considerable distance. When the last stroke had died away, he thought: 'It's over. All is ruined. She's not coming.'
>
> He decided, however, to wait until morning. In such cases one must be patient.
>
> Soon he heard it strike a quarter past twelve, then the half-hour, then three-quarters and finally, all the clocks repeated the single stroke for one o'clock, just as they had earlier struck twelve.[316]

We see from this example that when Maupassant needed to impress on his readers' minds the *emotional significance* of midnight, he did not limit himself to simply letting the clocks strike twelve and then one o'clock. He made us experience this perception of midnight by having twelve o'clock struck in various places by several clocks. Combined together in our minds, these distinct sets of twelve strokes have merged into a general impression of midnight. *The separate depictions have fused into an image.* And this has been done strictly on montage principles.

This example can serve as a model of the subtlest montage structuring, in which 'twelve o'clock' is depicted in sound on three different planes: 'somewhere far away'; 'nearer'; 'at a considerable distance'. The striking of these clocks, heard at various distances, is like filming an object by shooting it in a number of dimensions and by a sequence of three different shots: 'long shot'; 'medium shot'; 'extra long shot'. What's more, the striking itself – the uncoordinated instances of bells striking on different notes – is by no means chosen as a naturalistic detail of Paris by night; by the use of these separate bells Maupassant is above all creating an image of 'midnight, the hour of decision', not simply informing us of the time.

If he had simply wanted to tell us the time of night, Maupassant would hardly have deployed such finesse in the writing of it. Equally, without the artistic use of montage technique in his description, he would never have achieved such a powerful emotional effect by such extremely simple means.

Talking of clocks and time, I cannot help recalling an example from my own work. In the Winter Palace, when we were filming *October* (1927), we came across a curious antique clock. The large central clock-face was surrounded by a circle made up of smaller dials, each one of which was marked by the name of a city; Paris, London, New York, and so on. Each of these dials showed the time in those cities, compared with the time in Moscow or St Petersburg (I forget which), which was indicated on the main clock-face. I remembered the appearance of that clock, and when in the film I wanted to stress with particular force the historic moment of victory and the establishment of Soviet rule, the clock prompted me to use a unique montage device: the hour at which the Provisional Government fell, shown by Petrograd time, was repeated by the entire series of smaller dials, on which that hour was displayed in the different times that applied to London, Paris, New York, etc. Thus that hour, unique in the history and fate of all nations, stood out through all the multiplicity of separate time-zones as though uniting and merging all the peoples of the world in the perception of that moment, the moment of victory of the working class. This idea was also picked up by the circular movement of the ring of smaller dials, a movement which, increasing in speed, added a further graphic dimension to the fusion of all the different indications of time into an awareness of that single historic hour. . . .

At this point I can clearly hear the question being put by my inevitable opponents: 'But what do you do in the case of a single, long, unbroken sequence in which the actor performs without any montage cuts? Isn't his performance impressive enough without those interruptions? Isn't the playing of a Cherkasov, an Okhlopkov, a Chirkov or a Sverdlin powerful enough by itself?'[317]

Do not imagine that this question will deal a death-blow to the concept of montage. The montage principle is infinitely broader in scope. It is wrong to assume that if an actor performs in a single sequence and the director doesn't cut that sequence into different depths of shot, then the structure of it is 'free of montage'. Not at all.

In this case, we must look for montage somewhere else, namely . . . *in the actor's performance itself.* The question of the extent to which the principles of his 'internal' technique are 'montage-governed' will be discussed later. For the moment it will suffice to allow one of the greatest actors of stage and screen, George Arliss, to have his say on this subject. In his autobiography he writes as follows:

I always used to think that for film one should act exaggeratedly, but I found that self-limitation is the most important thing for an actor to learn when moving from the theatre to cinema. On the screen, the art of self-limitation and merely hinting is something that can be learned most thoroughly by watching the acting of the inimitable Charlie Chaplin.[318]

Arliss contrasts self-limitation with overstressed depiction (exaggeration). He sees the degree of this self-limitation as one of reducing one's actions to hints. He rejects not only the exaggerated depiction of an action, but even the depiction of the whole action in its entirety. Instead of that he recommends the hint. But what is a 'hint', if not an element, what is a detail of an action, if not a 'close-up' of it, which when juxtaposed with others of the sort serves as the determinant of an entire sequence of action? And thus, according to Arliss, a carefully judged, integrated sequence of acting is none other than the juxtaposition of a series of suitably definitive close-ups which, in combination, create an image of the content of the performance as distinct from the mere depiction of that content. According to this view, an actor's playing can either produce a flat depiction or a genuine image, depending on the method with which the actor builds his performance. Even if the performance is shot from a single set-up, it will nevertheless – if all goes well – be a 'montage' performance in itself.

Of the examples given above one could say that the second one (*October*) is not, in fact, a normal example of montage, while the first (Maupassant) only illustrates the instance of a single object shot from different points and in varying depths of shot.

Let us quote another example, familiar to the film-maker yet at the same time one which does not deal with a single object but with the image of a whole vast phenomenon, and which is structured in exactly the same way.

This example will be the equivalent of a remarkable 'montage script'. In it, from a mass of particular details and depictions we shall observe the perceptible build-up of an image. The example is interesting in that it is not a finished work of literature but the notes made by a great master in which, for his own purposes, he wanted to fix the visions of 'The Deluge' which arose before his mind's eye.[319]

The 'montage script' of which I speak is Leonardo da Vinci's set of notes on how a deluge should be represented in painting. I have selected the following extract in particular because it contains an extraordinarily clear *audiovisual* picture of a great flood (which, coming from a painter, is unexpected) while at the same time being visually very striking.

Let it be seen how the dark and vaporous air is shaken by winds blowing from several quarters, winds laden with constant hail and rain and tossing in the air, now hither, now thither, a multitude of things together with innumerable leaves torn from the trees.

All around are venerable trees, torn up by their roots and battered by the fury of the wind.

We see great boulders, washed from mountainsides by floods and borne by them downhill to encumber the valleys.

Boiling and foaming, the swollen streams spill over and surge down to drown the plains and those who dwell there.

On the tops of many hills can be seen animals of a multitude of breeds gathered together, frightened and rendered tame in the company of fleeing men, women and children.

Across the flooded fields float tables, beds, boats and many a contrivance devised in the moment of peril and fear of death. Upon all these are women and men, howling and weeping children, maddened by the frenzy of the wind, whose violent gusts lash and shake the waters whereon there float the bodies of the drowned.

Upon every buoyant thing are clustered animals, no longer hostile to each other and standing together with other terrified creatures – wolves, foxes, snakes and other breeds, all escaping from death.

As the waters strike the sides of such floating rafts they fling against them the bodies of drowned creatures with violent blows which kill those in which there was still some spark of life.

Crowds of people are to be seen, weapons in hand, defending their little remaining patch of land against lions, wolves and other animals seeking safety there.

Ah, what horrible cries fill the dark air, rent by the fury of lightning and thunderbolts which hurl themselves at whatever may stand in their path and destroy it.

Ah, how many are those who stop their ears with their hands to shut out the terrible sounds made in the dark air by the roaring of the wind and rain, the rumbling of the sky and the death-dealing bolts of lightning!

Others cover their eyes, not with one hand alone but laying one hand on the other, the more fully to shut out the sight of this cruel scourging of the human race by an angry God.

Ah, the wailing!

For see – many people, demented by fear, hurl themselves from clifftops. The mighty limbs of great oaks, together with the people clinging to them, are hurled through the air, plucked up by the maddened wind.

Many are the boats, capsized and floating bottom-up – some still whole, some in fragments – and many are the people who struggle desperately from under them, with thrashing limbs that bear witness to the nearness of death.

Some there are who, having lost all hope of being saved, take their own lives, lacking the strength to bear such horror: some throw themselves from high cliffs, others strangle themselves with their own hands, still others seize their own children and . . . despatch them with a single blow.

Some, too, deal themselves mortal wounds with their own weapons, while others, falling to their knees, surrender themselves to the will of God.

Ah, how many mothers weep over their drowned children, still holding them, or raising their outstretched arms to heaven, and with voices wherein is blended every shade of lamentation they curse the wrath of God!

Some, clasping their hands with intertwined fingers, bite them until they draw blood and chew them, bodies doubled up with their great, unbearable pain.

We see herds of animals – horses, cattle, goats, sheep – surrounded by water, stranded on the tops of hills as though on islets, huddling against each other. Those in the middle clamber one over another in a bitter struggle to be the uppermost. Many are dying for lack of food.

Already birds have begun to perch on people and animals, finding no place that is not taken up by other living creatures.

Already hunger – death's weapon – has taken the lives of many animals, while many dead beasts, their corpses disturbed by the raging of the elements, rise from the watery depths to the surface and, bloated like balloons filled with air, they strike one against another and rebound from the collision to lie across the bodies of those newly dead.

And above all the wailing and cursing is the sky, full of dark clouds rent asunder by the jagged paths of heaven's deadly arrows that flash out now here, now there, from the depths of gloom.[320]

This description was not cast in the form of a poem or a literary draft. Péladan – who published the French translation of Leonardo da Vinci's *Treatise on Painting* – sees in it an unrealised project for a picture, which would have been an unsurpassed 'masterpiece of landscape and the elemental clash of the forces of nature'.[321] Nevertheless these notes are not chaotic and are laid out on principles more appropriate to the arts that are extensive in *time* rather than in space.

Without going into a detailed examination of the structure of this remarkable 'montage script', let us turn our attention to the fact that the description follows a quite definite pattern of movement. What is more, the *course of this movement* is by no means fortuitous. The movement follows a definite order, and then in a similarly strict *reverse order* it returns to the same phenomena with which it began. Beginning with a description of the sky, the picture concludes with another description of the sky. In the centre is a group of people and their sufferings; the progression of the scene from the sky to people and from people back to the sky passes through a group of animals. The most powerful details ('close-ups') are found in the middle, where the description culminates (the clasped hands with interlocked fingers bitten until they bleed, and so on). The typical elements of montage composition stand out absolutely clearly.

The 'intra-frame' content of the separate scenes is heightened by the growing intensity of the action.

Let us examine what we might call the 'animal theme': the animals flee to safety; the flood carries the animals away; the animals drown; the animals fight the people; the animals fight each other; the corpses of drowned animals float to the surface. Or the gradual disappearance of *terra firma* from under the feet of humans, animals and birds alike, culminating in the point at which the birds are forced to perch on people and animals, being unable to find a single unoccupied piece of land or tree. This part of Leonardo da Vinci's notes reminds us yet again that the disposition of detail on the single, flat surface of a picture is also composed on the assumption of a strict path of movement followed by the eyes from one partial scene to another. Here, of course, this movement is less clearly laid down than in film, where the eye *cannot* see the sequence of details in any order other than that created by the montage editor.

There is no doubt, however, that by using a sequential description Leonardo da Vinci was pursuing an aim that was not merely to enumerate details but also to trace the trajectory of the eye's future movement across the surface of a canvas. Here we see a brilliant example of how, in the apparently static, simultaneous 'co-presence' of details in a motionless picture, the artist has applied exactly the same technique of selection that is used in montage, the same strict sequence in the juxtaposition of details that is also used in 'time-extensive' arts.

Montage has a realistic significance provided that the separate sequences, when juxtaposed, give rise to a common element, a synthesis of the theme, i.e. an image which embodies the theme.

Moving from that definition to the actual creative process, we shall see that the process occurs in the following manner: a certain image hovers in front of the author's inward eye, an image which for him is an emotional embodiment of the theme of this work. He is then faced with the task of turning that image into two or three *partial depictions*, which in combination and juxtaposition will evoke in the mind and emotions of their perceiver precisely that initial generalised image which the author saw with his mind's eye.

I am talking of both the image of the work as a whole and the image of a separate scene. With equal justification, and in the same sense, one may talk of the image created by an actor.

The actor is faced with exactly the same task: in two, three, or four character traits or actions, to express the basic elements which, in juxtaposition, will create the total image conceived by the author, the director and the actor himself.

What is remarkable about this method? Above all, its dynamism: the very fact that the desired image is not something *ready-made* but *has to arise or be born from something else*. The image conceived by author, director and actor, and fixed by them in the separate depictive elements, will finally come into being anew in the perceptions of the spectator.

Gorky described this very picturesquely in a letter to another author, Konstantin Fedin:

> You say you are worried by the question: 'How should I write?' For twenty-five years I have been observing how that question torments people. . . . Yes, yes, it is a serious question. I was worried by it too, it still worries me and will do so to the end of my days; but to me the answer to the question should be put like this: one must write in such a way that a character, whoever he may be, should arise from the pages of a story with the same force of physical perception of his existence, with the same conviction about his *half-imaginary* reality with which I see and perceive him. That is how I understand it, that is the secret of the matter.[322]

Montage helps to solve this problem. The strength of montage lies in the fact that it involves the spectator's emotions and reason. The spectator is forced to follow the same creative path that the author followed when creating the image. The spectator does not only see the depicted elements of the work; he also experiences the dynamic process of the emergence and formation of the image in the same way that the author experienced it. This is obviously as close as it is possible to get to conveying visually the fullness of the author's thought and intention, to conveying them 'with the same force of physical perception' with which they faced the author in his moments of creative vision.

This is a suitable point at which to recall how Marx defined the process of true research:

> Not only the results of research but the route leading to them should be a truthful one. The investigation of the truth must itself be truthful; truthful research is the truth dissected, the separated limbs of which are reunited in the result.[323]

The strength of the montage method lies also in the fact that the spectator is drawn into a creative act of a kind in which his individual nature is not only not enslaved to the individuality of the author but is deployed to the full by a fusion with the author's purpose, in the way that the individual nature of a great actor is fused with the individuality of a great playwright in the creation of a classic stage interpretation. In fact, every spectator in his own way – from his past experience; from the depths of his imagination; from the web of his mental associations; from the given preconditions of his character, temperament and social origin – creates an image according to those precisely chosen depictions suggested to him by the author, and which lead inexorably to understanding and experiencing the theme of the work. This is the same image that has been conceived by the author, but that image will also have been simultaneously brought into being by a creative act on the part of the spectator.

What, it might seem, can be clearer and more exact than the almost scientific notes on the details of 'The Deluge' as they pass before us in Leonardo da Vinci's 'montage script'? At the same time, no matter how personal and individual are the ultimate images evoked in different readers' minds, the author's enumeration and juxtaposition of the details is common to them all. Those 'evoked' images are thus as alike and as different as are the roles of Hamlet or Lear played by different actors in different countries, at different eras and in different theatres.

Maupassant offers each reader the same montage-like construct in his account of the clocks striking. He knows that what this structuring will evoke in people's perceptions is *not* information about the time of night but an awareness of the emotional meaning of that particular midnight. Each reader/ spectator hears the same striking of the clocks; but each will create his own image, his own conception of that midnight and its significance. All these conceptions are, as images, individual and different, yet at the same time they are thematically identical. And each reader's/spectator's image of that midnight is simultaneously the author's image and – equally – *his own* image, which is alive and 'intimate'.

The image conceived by the author has become flesh of the flesh of the spectator's image . . . which was created by me, the spectator. Thus the process is creative not only for the author, but also for me, the spectator, in whose mind it has also taken shape.

Earlier, we were talking about the exciting, affective type of narrative as distinct from the objective, logical statement of facts.

An *objective statement* would not be a *montage* construct, as are all the examples quoted above: an objective statement would be Leonardo da Vinci's description but made without regard to those differential planes that he deploys in order to induce a calculated trajectory for the eye to follow across the surface of a future painting. It would be the motionless dial of a clock marking the hour of the overthrow of the Provisional Government in the film *October*. In Maupassant's story it would be a brief piece of information stating that twelve o'clock had struck. In other words, these would be documentary statements that have not been raised by means of art to the level where they make a truly thrilling emotional impact. Cinematically speaking, they would all be *simple depictions shot from a single set-up*. But in the form that they have been cast by the artists who created them, they are images, brought to life by *montage-structuring*.

So now we can say that it is precisely the *montage* principle, as distinct from the *depictive* principle, which forces the spectator himself to *create*, and thereby releases that great force of latent creative excitement★ within the spectator which distinguishes an emotional work from the informational logic of a plain exposition of events.

At the same time we also discover that the montage principle as used in cinema is only a partial instance of the application of *the general principle of montage*, a principle which, properly understood, goes far beyond the limited business of gluing bits of film together. [. . . .] In the above passage, we purposely equated *the creativity of the spectator with the creativity of the actor*. For it is precisely here that a meeting occurs between montage and what might seem to be something most unlikely: the actor's *inner* technique and the forms of that *internal process* through which the actor creates authentic emotion which will make his actions on stage or screen truthful and convincing.

A number of systems and doctrines have been devised to master the problems of acting technique, or rather they can be reduced to two or three systems and their various offshoots. These offshoots differ not only in terminology and nomenclature but chiefly in what their proponents regard as the key points of acting technique; consequently they also differ in the stress they lay on these points. Sometimes one school or another almost completely ignores a whole link in the psychological sequence of creating an image. Sometimes, on the other hand, it will bring to the forefront a link in that process that is not *decisive*. Even within such a monolith as the Moscow Art Theatre method there are some independent variants in interpretation, despite the fact that its fundamental premises are shared in common.[325]

I do not intend to go into the nuances of substantive or terminological differences in the various methods of working with actors. I shall only dwell on those principles of 'internal' technique which inevitably form part of an actor's method in instances where his acting really achieves results, i.e. when it grips an audience. Any actor can, in the final analysis, deduce these principles from what is happening inside him, provided he can stop the process for a moment and look into himself. Furthermore, an *actor's* technique and a *director's* technique in this area of their craft are indistinguishable, to the extent that a director is, in some degree, himself an actor. From having observed that 'actor *manqué*' in myself when directing, I shall use a specific example to describe the particular 'internal' technique that interests us here. I should stress that I am least of all concerned with saying anything *new* in *this* regard.

Let us assume that I have to play the part of a man the morning after

---

★It is quite obvious that a theme *as such* is also capable of exciting us, regardless of the form in which it is presented. A short newspaper report about a Republican victory at Guadalajara excites us more than does the use of artistic means to bring an inherently exciting theme or plot to its maximum level of impact.[324] This being so, it is also quite obvious that at this level montage as such is by no means an exhaustive technique, though a very powerful one.

the night in which he has gambled away at cards a large sum of money belonging to public funds. We will suppose that the scene is full of twists and turns: these might include a conversation with his unsuspecting wife; a scene with his daughter who looks searchingly at her father, having noticed something odd in his behaviour; and a scene where he is waiting fearfully for the telephone call that will summon the embezzler to account for the money, and so on. We shall so arrange it that a whole series of such scenes gradually induces the embezzler to try and shoot himself, and that the actor will have to play the last part of the scene in which he realises that there is only one way out – suicide; and how, without his looking down, his hand begins almost automatically to fumble through the drawers of his desk in search of his revolver. . . .

I don't think there can be a single intelligent actor nowadays who in that scene would start to 'act the emotions' of the man contemplating suicide. Instead of straining to think of what actions to perform here, he would approach it differently. He would make the appropriate mood and actions *take over*. And that emotional state, the feelings and the suffering, would immediately 'show through' in the emotionally correct and convincing movements, actions and behaviour. *This is the way to find the essential elements* of correct acting, correct in the sense that it reflects emotions and perceptions that are genuinely experienced.

The next stage of work consists of composing the performance by developing these elements, refining them by eliminating what is incidental and haphazard, and bringing the essentials to a peak of expressivity. That is the *next* stage. But what interests us at the moment is the *preceding* stage of that process: that part of it in which the actor is *taken over* by the emotion. How is that achieved and 'how is it done'? We have already said we will not strain ourselves to *depict* the emotion. Instead, we will follow a course that is well known and used almost universally.

It consists of making our imagination picture a series of realistic scenes or situations appropriate to our theme. Taken together, these imagined scenes will evoke in us the emotions, perceptions and painful feelings that we are seeking. The subject matter of these scenes pictured by the imagination will, of course, differ according to the nature and temperament of the character whom the actor happens to be playing at the time.

Let us suppose that a typical character trait of our embezzler is a terror of public opinion. In that case his main source of fear will be not so much his own pangs of conscience, a sense of guilt or the likely hardships of a prison sentence, but a horror of what people will say, for example. That being so, the man in this situation will chiefly imagine the awful consequences of his embezzlement in *those* terms. For it is precisely those consequences that will bring the man to the level of desperation which induces him to take the fateful step.

This is exactly what happens in real life. The fear aroused by an awareness of criminal liability induces a feverish evocation of mental pictures of the consequences. And the sum total of such pictures will play on the emotions and heighten them even more, bringing the embezzler to the utmost degree of horror and despair.

On stage in the theatre, the actor, by an absolutely identical process, will start to bring himself to the same state of mind. The only difference is that he is consciously forcing his imagination to picture the same consequences that in real life the imagination would evoke of its own accord.

It is no part of my task here to describe how one induces one's imagination to do this in a fictional or invented situation. I shall describe the process from the moment when the imagination actually starts picturing the scenes called for by the situation. The actor will not have to make himself feel and experience the foreseeable consequences: the emotion and the suffering, as well as the actions which flow from them, will arise unprompted, brought to life by the scenes that his imagination has pictured. The visible emotions will be called forth by the scenes themselves, their combination and juxtaposition. In seeking ways to ensure that the required emotion is evoked, I picture to myself a multitude of situations and scenes in which the same common theme will figure.

As an example, let us select from that multitude the first two situations that come to mind. Without analysing them, we will try and write them down exactly as they now pass before my mind's eye: 'I am a criminal in the eyes of my erstwhile friends and acquaintances. People shun me. I have been ostracised by them', and so on. In order to feel all this emotionally, I will, as has been said, picture to myself specific situations, real-life scenes of what awaits me. Let the first scene be in the courtroom during the trial of my case. Let the second one be my return to normal life after serving my prison sentence.

We will try to describe as vividly and realistically as possible the numerous fragments of the overall situation which our imagination instantly conjures up before us. For each actor this will take place in accordance with his own individual fantasy. Here I shall record the first thoughts that came into my mind when I set *myself* this particular exercise.

The courtroom. My case is being heard. I am in the dock. The public gallery is full of people who know me. I catch sight of my neighbour, who is watching me. We have lived next door to each other for thirty years. He notices that I have caught his eye. With feigned vagueness, his glance slides away from me; pretending to be bored, he looks out of the window. . . . Over there is another member of the public: the woman who lives on the floor above mine. Meeting my gaze, she looks nervously down, while still continuing to watch me out of the corner of her eye. My usual partner at billiards turns his back on me with a deliberate movement. . . . And over there the fat proprietor of the billiard-hall and his wife are staring insolently at me, glassy-eyed. . . . I fidget uncomfortably and look down at my feet. Now I cannot see anyone, but all around me I hear the hiss of voices, whispering censure. . . . The words of the verdict of guilty fall on me, blow by blow. . . .

With equal success I imagine to myself the other scene, that of my return from prison.

The crash of the prison gates closing behind me as I am let out. . . . The startled look of a maid, who stops cleaning a window in the next-door house as I walk along my street. . . . A new name on the door-plate of my old apartment. . . . The floorboards of the landing have been repainted, there is a new mat in front of the door. . . . The neighbour's door opens. . . . Some new people, unknown to me, peer out from behind the door with suspicion and curiosity. Some children are huddled beside them: they are instinctively frightened by the sight of me. The old porter, his nose protruding from his lop-sided spectacles, stares up disapprovingly from below through the stairwell; he remembers me from the old days. . . . Three or four yellowing letters addressed to me, which came before my disgrace was common knowledge. . . . A few coins clink in my pocket. . . . And then the doors of my previous acquaintances are shut in my face. . . . Diffidently, my legs start to take me up the staircase to my erstwhile friend, but before I have climbed two steps, they turn back. . . . The hastily turned-up collar of a passer-by who has recognised me . . . and so on.

That is approximately how an honest transcription of the ideas swarming and flashing through my mind might look when, as director or actor, I would attempt to achieve an emotional grasp of the proposed situation.

Having mentally put myself in the first situation and mentally lived through the second one; having then done the same thing with two or three analogous situations differing slightly in content, I gradually arrive at an authentic perception of what awaits me, and from there I achieve a feeling of the hopelessness and tragedy of the situation I am now in. The cumulative details of the first (courtroom) scene given rise to one shade of that feeling; the details of the second scene produce another nuance of the same emotion. One shade of feeling combines with the other, and from three or four such variants there emerges the total image of hopelessness, inseparable from the keen emotional pain caused by the sense of hopelessness itself.

Thus without straining to 'act out' the emotion as such, one succeeds in evoking it through the selection and juxtaposition of consciously chosen details and situations.

For the purpose of this exercise it does not matter at all whether or not my description of the process corresponds in all its nuances to any of the existing schools of acting technique. What does matter is that a stage similar to the one I have described inevitably occurs in the progression towards the *creation and intensification* of emotion, be it in real life or in the technique of the creative process. The smallest degree of self-observation will suffice to convince us of this, whether in the circumstances of artistic creation or of real life.

At the same time it is important that creative techniques should reproduce the process exactly as it occurs in life, when it is applied to the special conditions in which art places us.

It is, of course, quite obvious that we are not dealing here with a total system of acting technique, but only with one of the links in its chain. Here, for instance, we have made no mention of the imagination itself and the technique of 'heating it up', or of the process whereby our imagination succeeds in picturing the required scenes to our mind's eye. Lack of space prevents us from examining these links in the chain, although to analyse them would confirm in no less a degree that our propositions are correct. For the time being, however, we shall limit ourselves to what we have so far discussed; we should firmly bear in mind, however, that the process we have been analysing is of no less importance in acting technique than is . . . montage in the film-maker's battery of expressive devices. That is no less than the truth.

But . . . in what way, if you please, does our example drawn from acting technique differ, either practically or theoretically, from what we discovered in the earlier passage to be the very essence of cinematic montage? While the field of application may be different, the essence of the method is the same.

In acting, it is a question of how to make authentic emotion and suffering manifest themselves in an actor.

In cinema, it is a matter of how to evoke the required image in the emotions of the spectator.

In both cases, static elements – either given or invented – and their juxtaposition give rise *dynamically* to an emotion or an image.

As we have seen, none of this differs in principle from what cinematic montage does: we see the same vivid actualisation of an emotion in key details, together with the feedback effect of juxtaposing details that have already evoked the emotion itself.

As for the nature of those 'visions' that constitute what passes in front of the actor's 'inward eye', they are visually (or aurally) identical with the specific features that distinguish film-shots. It was no accident that in the above passages we called these 'visions' fragments, in the sense of separate pictures, taken not as a whole but only in their key details. For if we analyse that almost automatic sequence of our 'visions', which we tried to record with the photographic precision of a psychological document, we shall see that these 'scenes' themselves are as consistently cinematic as are the different shot-depths, the different dimensions and the different 'cuts' in montage sequences.

In fact, a prime example of one shot is the man turning his back, i.e. an obvious 'cut' from his figure as a whole. The two heads with staring eyes – as distinct from the lowered eyelashes through which my female neighbour surreptitiously watches me out of the corner of her eye – make an obvious difference in shot dimension. Elsewhere, the new name-plate on the door and the three envelopes are obvious 'close-ups'. Or in another sequence: the aural long shot of the people whispering in the public gallery, as distinct from the close-up sound of a few coins clinking in my pocket, and so on and so forth. The 'lens' of the mind's eye also uses different depths of shot: close-up or long shot; it functions, in fact, exactly as does the lens of a cine-camera, which firmly cuts off the components of a shot with the edges of the frame. One only has to put a number on each of the fragmentary scenes in my quoted examples to get a typical montage sequence.

Thus we have revealed the secret of how montage scripts are composed in reality: they are constructed to achieve a genuine grip on the emotions, not just as a stupefying, random scatter of close-ups, medium shots and long shots!

The basic justification for the method remains true for both areas [the shot content and the work as a whole]. Having laid out the theme in a number of key depictions, the task is then to combine these depictions in order to evoke *the basic image of the theme*. The process of evoking this image in the perceiver's mind is inseparable from experiencing its thematic content. Equally inseparable from this emotional experience is the job of the director when he draws up his montage script. For only this process is capable of suggesting to him those key depictions which will illuminate the thematic image in the perception of the spectator.

Herein lies the secret of the emotional nature of the narrative (as distinct from the objective reporting of fact) which we discussed at the beginning, and which is quite as typical of an actor's performance as of the film-maker's montage work.

Similarly, it is also in the greatest works of literature that we can be sure of finding a similar swarm of depictions, ruthlessly selected and reduced to the utterly laconic choice of two or three details.

Let us take Pushkin's epic poem 'Poltava', and in particular the episode of Kochubei's execution. In this scene, the theme of 'the end of Kochubei' is expressed with particular intensity through the image of 'the end of Kochubei's execution'. The image of the end of the execution itself arises and grows out of a juxtaposition of the 'documentary' depiction of three details which conclude the execution:

> 'Too late', a witness said to them
> And pointed to the field. For there
> The men were taking down the fateful scaffold,
> A priest in sombre vestments was at prayer,
> Into a cart two burly Cossacks
> Were lifting up the oaken box.[326]

It would be hard to find a more powerful choice of details to convey the perception of an image of death in all its horror than this, the finale of the execution scene.

The fact that it is precisely an emotional impact that is achieved by the method under discussion is confirmed by some curious examples. Let us take another scene from 'Poltava', in which Pushkin magically makes the image of a nocturnal escape arise before the reader in all its vividness and emotional quality:

For no one knew quite when and how
She did escape. A fisherman
That night did hear the sound of hooves,
Some cossacks' talk, a woman's whisper. . . .[327]

Three sequences: 1) the sound of hooves; 2) cossacks' talk; 3) a woman's whisper.

Once again three objective depictions (in sound!) combine into a unifying image conveyed in emotional terms, quite unlike the way these three facts would be perceived if they were given to us with no connections between them. This method is used with the sole aim of evoking the required emotional experience in the reader. And specifically *experience*, because in the line above the author has already given us the straightforward information that Maria got away ('She did escape. A fisherman . . .'). Having told us that she escaped, the author immediately wants the reader to *feel* what this was like; and for that he at once turns to montage, using three details of the night time escape through which we may experience it emotionally.

To the three sound pictures he then adds a fourth. The effect is of putting a full-stop to the account. For this fourth picture he chooses one from another dimension: he does not give it in sound but in a graphic, three-dimensional 'close-up': 'Next day eight horse-shoe traces / Were seen upon the meadows' dew. . . .'

Thus Pushkin uses 'montage' when he creates the image of a scene. But he is quite as much of a 'montage-editor' when he is dealing with human images, with the graphic delineation of his *dramatis personae*. In this area Pushkin achieves a staggering degree of verisimilitude in his word-portraits, with an astonishingly skilful combination of different viewpoints (i.e. 'set-ups') and different elements (i.e. depictions, sharpened by being cut off by the edge of the frame). The people that arise from the pages of Pushkin's poems are so perceptible as to be positively tangible.

But in cases where there are a lot of 'sequences' Pushkin goes even further in his use of montage. The rhythm set up by the alternation between long sentences and very short sentences also gives his image a dynamic dimension. The rhythm, as it were, represents the temperament of the person depicted, gives a sense of movement to that character's actions.

Finally, there is also much to be learned from Pushkin about the right sequence in which to reveal the features and personality traits of a character. The best example of this is the description of Peter the Great's appearance in 'Poltava'. Let us recall it:

I   And then, inspired as from on high,
II   Came forth the ringing voice of Peter:
III   'God speed! To battle!' From the tent,
IV   Surrounded by his favourite henchmen,
V   The tsar comes out. His piercing eyes

VI	Are shining. Grim his countenance;
VII	His movements quick. Magnificent
VIII	His person, like the wrath of God.
IX	He strides. His horse is brought to him.
X	Though calm, yet fiery is the faithful steed:
XI	He sniffs the fateful powder-smoke
XII	And trembles. Wild eyes rolling,
XIII	He gallops 'mid the dust of battle
XIV	And bears with pride his mighty rider.[328]

We have numbered the lines. Now let us rewrite this passage as if it were a montage script, numbering the separate 'shots' as given to us by Pushkin.

1. And then, inspired as from on high, came forth the ringing voice of Peter: 'God speed! To battle!'
2. From the tent, surrounded by his favourite henchmen,
3. The tsar comes out.
4. His piercing eyes are shining.
5. Grim his countenance;
6. His movements quick.
7. Magnificent his person,
8. Like the wrath of God.
9. He strides.
10. His horse is brought to him.
11. Though calm, yet fiery is the faithful steed;
12. He sniffs the fateful powder-smoke and trembles.
13. Wild eyes rolling,
14. He gallops 'mid the dust of battle, and bears with pride his mighty rider.

The number of *lines* and the number of '*shots*' have proved to be *identical*: fourteen of each. Yet despite this, the breakdown by lines and the breakdown by 'shots' hardly coincide at all; in all fourteen instances it only occurs twice: Line VIII = Shot 8; and Line X = Shot 11. What is more, the amount of wordage that goes to make up a 'shot' varies from two whole lines (Shot 1 and Shot 14) down to two words (Shot 9).

This is highly instructive for those who work in film, and in sound film above all. Let us see how Peter is 'introduced' in montage terms.

1, 2 and 3: a magnificent example of the *significant* presentation of a character. Here there are three quite clear steps or stages in his appearance:

1. Peter has not yet been shown to us, but is first announced only in sound (by his voice);
2. Peter has come out of the tent, but is not yet visible. All that we see is the crowd of his favourites coming out of the tent with him;
3. Finally, in the third shot it becomes clear that Peter himself is coming out of the tent.

Further: the shining eyes as the most striking detail of his features (4). After that, the whole face (5). Only then are we shown his whole figure (probably down to knee-height) in order to stress how quick and abrupt his movements are. The rhythm and characteristics of the way he moves are here expressed by the effect of 'impetuousness' produced through the clash of short sentences. His figure is not shown at full length until the seventh shot, and not even literally but colourfully (allusively): 'Magnificent his person'. In the next frame that generalised description is strengthened by a specific simile: 'Like the wrath of God'. Thus it is only in the eighth shot that Peter is revealed in all his physical power. That eighth shot evidently shows Peter in his full height, composed with all the means of pictorial expressivity available in a frame, including the appropriate arrangement of a crown of clouds in the sky above him; the tent; the people around him and at his feet. And after that broad 'easel-painting' type of shot the poet immediately takes us back into the realm of movement and action with just two words: 'He strides' (9). It would be hard to find a more exact, economical way of impressing on us (after his glinting eyes in Shot 4) Peter's second most striking feature: his stride. That brief, laconic 'He strides' wholly conveys a perception of Peter's huge, elemental, energetic walk, which makes it hard for his suite to keep up with him. Peter's stride was caught with equal mastery by the artist Valentin Serov in his famous picture of Peter overseeing the building of St Petersburg.[329]

I believe the sequence and content of the shots of Peter's appearance that we have derived from the text is correct, precisely in the form that we have set it out above. First, this kind of 'presentation' of his character is altogether characteristic of Pushkin's manner. To take just one other brilliant example, there is his 'presentation' of the ballerina Istomina in *Eugene Onegin*. Second, the order itself of Pushkin's words represents quite precisely the *sequence of seeing* those elements which in the final analysis add up to the image of the character in question and 'reveal' it graphically.

2 and 3 would be structured quite differently if instead of 'From the tent, surrounded by his favourite henchmen, / The tsar comes out . . .', the text had read: 'The tsar, surrounded by his favourite henchmen, / Comes out of the tent. . . .'

The impression of his entry, beginning with Peter but not leading up to Peter, would be completely different. Pushkin's version is an example of expressivity achieved by way of montage and by purely montage means. In every such instance there will be a different expressive structure, and on each occasion that expressive structure prescribes and preordains that 'only possible order' of 'the only possible words' of which Lev Tolstoy wrote in his essay *What is Art?*

The sound and the words uttered by Peter in (1) are structured equally purposefully. The text does *not* say:

'God speed! To battle!' –
Came forth the voice of Peter,

> Ringing, and as from above inspired. . . .

It says:

> And then, as from above inspired,
> Came forth the ringing voice of Peter:
> 'God speed! To battle!'

To convey the expressiveness of that exclamation, we would have to reveal first *the fact of it being inspired*; then its ringing, sonorous character; then we would have to *recognise it* as specifically the voice of Peter; and only then, finally, do we make out what Peter's inspired, ringing voice *is actually saying* ('God speed! To battle!'). Obviously, when 'staging' a fragment of this kind the first three priorities would be met by some phrase preceding the exclamation and coming from inside the tent, in which the words themselves would be indistinguishable, but in which the inspiration and the ringing sonority would already be heard, from which we could then recognise the characteristic voice of Peter.

As we can see, all this has enormous significance when it comes to enriching the expressive means available to cinema.

It also serves as an example of the complexities of audiovisual editing. One might think that this is an area in which it is impossible to find an 'illustrated textbook', and that the only way of acquiring the necessary experience is to study the ways in which music and action are combined in opera or ballet! Pushkin, however, teaches us what to do so that separate visual shots do not coincide mechanically with the structural articulation of the music.

For that moment we will dwell only on a very simple example: on the non-coincidence of the rhythmic articulation (in this case, not of music but of the lines of verse) with the ends, beginnings and duration of the separate 'shots' or visual episodes. Very roughly, the layout would look something like this.

Music	I	II	III	IV	V	VI	VII	VIII	IX	X	XI	XII	XIII	XIV
Depiction		1		2		3	4	5	6	7	8	9	10	11	12	13	14

The upper row indicates the fourteen lines of verse, the lower row shows the fourteen 'shots' which the passage contains.

The whole diagram demonstrates how the 'shots' are disposed in relation to the verses.

It is quite clear from this diagram how subtle is the contrapuntal pattern of audiovisual articulation that Pushkin deploys in order to achieve his remarkable results in a passage of such diverse content. With the exception of 'VIII – 8' and 'X – 11', in none of the twelve others do we find a single instance of complete concordance between the lines of verse and the corresponding visual depictions.

Furthermore, depiction and verse coincide precisely in extent and sequence only once, namely VIII and 8. This is not by chance. This concordance in the articulation of both depiction and verse marks the most significant 'shot' within the montage composition. It really is unique of its kind: it is in this, the eighth episode, that the features of Peter are revealed and displayed in their totality. It is in this verse, too, that there is the only illustrative simile ('He is like the wrath of God'). Clearly, Pushkin makes the articulation of both depiction and verse coincide in order to emphasise the moment of most striking effect. An experienced montage editor – the true author of audiovisual integration – would have proceeded in the same way.

In poetry, the carry-over of a descriptive sentence from one line to the next is known by the French term *enjambement*.

> When the articulation of metre and syntax do not coincide, the poet uses a so-called *enjambement*. . . . The most characteristic feature of *enjambement* is the presence within a verse of a *syntactical pause* that is more significant than the pause at the beginning or end of a verse.[331]

Zhirmunsky also makes mention of a use of this type of structure which has a certain relevance to audiovisual matching:

> Every non-concordance between syntactical and metrical articulation is an artistically calculated dissonance that is resolved at the point where, after a series of such discordances, a syntactical pause finally coincides with the end of a rhythmic series.[332]

This can be clearly seen in a particularly striking example from the poetry of Yakov Polonsky,[333] which Yuri Tynyanov cites in his *Problems of Poetic Language*:

> For look, behind us, still intact,
> Is that same mountain hut where
> Half a century ago I longingly
> Did gaze upon my heart's beloved.[334]

Let us recall that metrical articulation which does not coincide with syntactical articulation replicates, as it were, the non-coincidence between *words and metrical feet*, the latter phenomenon occurring much more widely than do instances of *enjambement*. 'Usually the lengths of words do not correspond to the lengths of metrical feet. In the past, theorists of Russian versification saw this as one of the conditions for poetic euphony'.[335]

Here, it is the *exception*, not the rule, for the two to coincide; indeed, when they do coincide it is for special and unexpected effects, for instance in passages of Konstantin Balmont's poetry.[336]

Pushkin is a particularly rich source of *enjambement* in Russian poetry.

In English poetry it is to be found in Shakespeare and Milton, in the eighteenth-century poet James Thomson, and in Keats and Shelley. Of the French poets, considerable use of *enjambement* is made by André Chénier and Victor Hugo.[337] By reading examples of their work, and by analysing the *compositional motivation and expressive effects* in each case where it is used, we shall greatly enrich ourselves in the experience needed for the audiovisual juxtaposition of image and sound in montage.

Normally a poem is printed on the page in strophic form, i.e. in verses made up of fixed sets of lines divided according to a regular metrical scheme. But in [modern Russian] poetry we have a proponent of a different style of layout: Mayakovsky. In his 'chopped line' the articulation does not correspond to the limits of a line of verse but to the limits of [cinematic] 'frames'.

Mayakovsky does not divide his verse by lines –

> The void. Fly, you,
> Cutting into the stars . . .

but by 'frames':

> The void . . .
>   Fly, you,
>   Cutting into the stars. . . .

In doing so, Mayakovsky chops up the line in the way that an experienced montage editor would do it, arranging a typical scene of confrontation (between 'the stars' and 'the poet Yesenin'[338]). First one, then the other. Then a clash between them:

1. *The void* (if one were to shoot this 'frame', then it would have to be shot in such a way as to stress the void while at the same time enabling the presence of the stars to be felt).
2. *Fly, you* [i.e. Yesenin].
3. Only in this *third* shot would the content of the first and second frames be shown in a confrontation.

Equally subtle *enjambements* are to be found in the verse of the playwright Griboyedov.[339] His satirical comedy *Woe from Wit* abounds with them. For example (from Act I):

> LISA. Well, of course, he also should have
> Wealth enough to live, to be able to give balls;
> Take, for instance, Colonel Skalozub:
> A well-lined purse, and aims to be a general . . .

or (from Act II):

> CHATSKY. You seem a little low in spirits;

Pray tell me, why is that
Was my coming here untimely?
Has Sophia Pavlovna perhaps
Some cause to be unhappy?

For a montage editor, however, *Woe from Wit* is even more interesting in another respect. This interest arises when one begins to compare the author's manuscript with the various published editions of the play. The fact is that later editions differ from the earlier ones not only in variant wording but primarily in the *altered punctuation*, although the same words have been preserved and in the same order. In many cases the later editions have diverged from the *author's original* punctuation, and a return to the punctuation of the early editions proves to be extremely instructive from a montage angle.

Nowadays, a tradition has been established of typesetting the text – and hence of reading it – in a style of which the following is an example:

Oh when will the Creator save us
From all their hats, caps, pins and hat-pins,
Their bookshops and their pastrycooks . . .

whereas in his original version Griboyedov punctuated this passage as follows:

Oh when will the Creator save us
From all their hats! caps! pins!! and hat-pins!!!
Their bookshops and their pastrycooks!!!

It is obvious that, spoken aloud, the delivery of the two versions must be quite different. But that is not all: as soon as we try to imagine this catalogue of items as images in visual frames, we see at once that [in the more modern punctuation] this enumeration requires Griboyedov's list of hats, caps, pins and hat-pins to be shown in a single medium shot, in which all these objects are depicted *together*; whereas in Griboyedov's original version each of these articles of the female *toilette* is, as it were, allotted *its own close-up* and the listing of them should be done by a series of separate shots in the manner of *montage*.

Most characteristic of this passage are the double and triple exclamation marks. They tell us that the shots move successively towards close-up, a heightening of emphasis which, when the lines are read aloud, is achieved by rising volume and intonational stress, but which in filming would be expressed by the progressively enlarging dimensions of the objects themselves.

To talk of changing the dimensions of the *visible* objects in this list is entirely legitimate. It is unaffected by the fact that here we are not dealing with Pushkin's *descriptive* material, as in the example we were discussing earlier. As for the above-quoted lines spoken by the character Famusov in *Woe from Wit*, they are not a description of a scene, nor is the author deploying a sequence of details through which he wants us gradually to perceive, for instance, Peter the Great in 'Poltava'. Here we are concerned with a *list*, spoken by an indignant character in a play. But is there any difference between these two types of writing? Of course not!

After all, for the actor to rant away with genuine fury about all these hats, hat-pins, caps and pins when delivering this tirade, he must sense them as being all around him – he must see them! In doing so, he may see them in a single cluster (medium shot), but he can also see them piling up in the form of a rapid 'montage' sequence made up of each object separately, and what is more, in increasing close-up, as suggested by the double and triple exclamation marks. And this discussion of how to see the objects in the list – in a single shot or in a montage sequence – is no mere idle *jeu d'esprit*: this or that way of seeing these objects in one's mind's eye will also evoke this or that degree of intensification in the delivery. This intensification will not be 'put on' but will correspond naturally to the degree of intensity with which the actor's imagination conjures up the objects in his mind's eye.

It becomes vividly clear from this passage how much more powerful and expressive is a montage construct than one built on the 'single viewpoint', as given in the later editions of the play's script.

It is a curious fact that there are a great many such examples in Griboyedov's work. Furthermore, the distinguishing feature of the earlier version is that it always results in breaking the picture down from a single 'medium shot' to a series of 'close-ups' *and not vice versa*.

In the following example the style of punctuation that became traditional in later editions is incorrect:

> To complete the miracle
> The floor did open up and from it you,
> Pale as death. . . .

What Griboyedov wrote was this:

> To complete the miracle
> The floor did open up and from it you,
> Pale! As death!

His original punctuation is even more unexpected and remarkable in a line whose reading has become a cliché, such as this one: 'And they'll see you as one who's a dangerous dreamer.'

Griboyedov, it transpires, wrote it differently: 'They'll see you as a dreamer! And a dangerous one!'

In both cases we are dealing with a purely montage phenomenon. Instead of the trite picture evoked by the phrase 'pale as death', the author's version conjures up two images of increasing power: 1) 'pale!' and 2) 'as death!' Exactly the same comparison applies to the second quotation, too, where once again the idea is intensified from 'shot' to 'shot'.

As we see, the period of Griboyedov and Pushkin made considerable and pointed use of the montage principle. Without having recourse to splitting up the line *à la montage*, as Mayakovsky does, Griboyedov, for instance, with his instinctive awareness of the montage principle has much in common with our greatest modern poet.

It is amusing that those responsible for distorting Griboyedov have gone backwards from what Mayakovsky does in successive variants or reworkings of his poems – which he always does along the lines of montage. This is the case, for example, with a passage from his poem 'After the Fashion of Heine', two stages of his work on which have been preserved. The first draft reads as follows:

> You are the basest, meanest of men,
> She walked on and on, cursing . . .

while the final text is:

> 'You are the basest,
> The meanest of men',
> She walked
> And walked
> And walked on, cursing. . . .

(I quote from V.V. Trenin's *In the Workshop of Mayakovsky's Verse* [*V masterskoi stikha Mayakovskogo*].)

In the first draft there are at the most two shots; in the second there are clearly five: a 'close-up' in the second line as compared with the first line, followed by a build-up by repetition of the same theme in the third, fourth and fifth lines.

As we see, Mayakovsky's artistry is very striking in its use of the montage principle. Even in this respect, however, it is actually more interesting to look at Pushkin, because he belongs to an era when the idea 'montage' as such had not yet been formulated. Mayakovsky, on the other hand, belongs wholly to the period when montage thinking and montage principles were widely represented in all art forms connected with literature: theatre, cinema, photomontage, etc. Therefore the more pointed, more interesting and, I believe, the more instructive examples of strict, realistic montage writing are to be found in the works of our classic *heritage*, in which the interaction with related art forms either existed to a much lesser degree or was completely absent (there was obviously no interaction with cinema, for example).

Thus whether it be in visual, auditory or audiovisual combinations, whether in creating an image or a situation or in the 'magical' conjuring up of a character, whether with Pushkin or Mayakovsky, the same montage method is equally present everywhere.

What conclusion is to be drawn from all that has been said in the foregoing?

The conclusion is that there is no contradiction between the method used in writing poetry; the method used *within himself* by an actor when performing

it; the method by which the actor structures his performance within the shot
. . . and the method by which his actions and the treatment of his surrounding
and environment (i.e. the total content of a motion picture) are made to shine
and sparkle with iridescence in the hands of a director who uses montage in
the narrative and the structuring of a film as a whole. For they are all equally
based on the vitalising characteristics and innate features common to every
human being, just as they are common to every humane and vital art form.

For it would seem that in whatever polar circles each art form may have
moved, they could not and cannot avoid meeting up in the ultimate kinship
and unity of the montage method as we now perceive it.

The principles of this method oblige us, with greater urgency than ever,
to face the fact that, together with a study of dramatic literature and acting
technique, skilled practitioners of cinematic art must master all the subtleties
of the creative use of montage.

13 Vertical Montage[340]

I

In the article entitled 'Montage 1938', we gave the following final definition of the nature of montage: 'Sequence A, made from elements of the film's theme, and Sequence B, put together from the same source, will, when juxtaposed, generate an image in which the content of the theme is most clearly embodied'; that is to say:

> *Depiction A* and *Depiction B* must be so chosen from all the possible features inherent in the story that the *juxtaposition* of them – specifically the juxtaposition of *them,* not of any other elements – will evoke in the perceptions and emotions of the spectator the most exhaustive, total *image of the film's theme.*[341]

In that formulation we avoided defining to which *qualitative* category A or B might belong, and whether they might both belong to the same dimensional category or to different ones.

It was not by chance that we wrote: 'from all the possible features inherent in the story', because, since it is the one preconceived, generalising image arising from them that is decisive, the fact that those separate component features may belong to different modes of expression is not of primary importance.

Moreover, nearly all the examples [quoted in the previous chapter, 'Montage 1938'] from Leonardo da Vinci to Pushkin and Mayakovsky actually rely on the expressive media being of the most diverse kinds.

In Leonardo's 'The Deluge', some purely graphic (i.e. visual) elements, elements of human behaviour (i.e. dramatic acting), elements of noise, rumbling, crashing and screaming (i.e. in sound) are all in equal degree combined into a single, ultimate, generalising image of the idea of a deluge.

Thus we see that the change from silent-film montage to audiovisual montage changes nothing *in principle.*

While our conception of montage embraces both silent-film montage and the montage of sound film, this by no means implies that the actual practice of audiovisual montage does not face us with new tasks, new difficulties, and techniques that are to a greater extent entirely new.

On the contrary, it does so.

For that reason we must analyse the very nature of the audiovisual phenomenon in the greatest possible detail. Above all, the question arises of where to look for the sources of direct experience from which to gain a mastery of the technique.

As always, an inexhaustible storehouse of experience is and will always be . . . people; the observation of human behaviour will always be decisive: in particular, in this instance, the observation of how people perceive reality and how they take it in by creating for themselves an adequate image of it.

Later, we shall see that in matters strictly confined to shot composition, too, the human being and the interaction between his *gesture and intonation* when they are generated by a single emotion will prove to be the determining prototype for shaping audiovisual structures which also, and in equal degree, derive from a single determining image. But of that, as the saying goes, more later. For the moment, the following proposition will suffice for our purposes: that in order to make the correct choice of precisely those montage elements from which will arise precisely *the* image in which we perceive this or that phenomenon, the best method of all is keen self-observation, clear awareness of exactly those elements of reality from which that image is, in fact, built up within our own minds.

In doing so, the best way of all is to catch and keep one's first, i.e. *most immediate*, perception, for it is precisely this which will always be sharpest, freshest and liveliest, compounded of impressions *drawn from the greatest number of sensory sources*. Therefore when dealing with material drawn from the classics, the best method must also be not to operate with finished works but with those sketches, drafts or notes in which the artist attempts to record the whole gamut of his first, most vivid and immediate impressions. It is because of this, after all, that a sketch or a draft version often has more vitality than the finished canvas (e.g. Ivanov's *Christ Appearing to the Multitude* and the sketches for it, and in particular Ivanov's compositional drafts for other pictures that were never realised).[342]

We should not forget that Leonardo's 'Deluge' is also a 'draft', if not drawn from nature then at any rate a *sketch in the form of notes*, which feverishly attempts to record all the features and visual impressions of a 'deluge' which passed before Leonardo's inner eye. It is this, in fact, which gave rise to such an abundance of elements in that description which are not only depictive and graphic but auditory and dramatic.

For the sake of emphasis, however, let us take another example of a sketch 'from nature', which has preserved all the 'shimmer' of an immediate, first impression.

It is a footnote to the entry for 18 December 1867 in the *Journal* of the brothers Goncourt:

A description of an *Athletic Arena*. . . . I found it in a notebook intended for use in connection with our future novels (*romans futurs*) which were, alas, never written.

At both ends of the hall, in deep shadow, can be seen the glitter from the buttons and sword-hilts of policemen.

The gleaming limbs of the wrestlers as they stride into the bright light of the ring. The challenging stare of their eyes. The slap of palms on flesh as they grapple. The sweat, smelling of wild animals. The pallor of their faces, merging with the ash-blond shade of their moustaches. Their bodies, glowing pink in the places where they have taken blows. Backs, from which the sweat runs as though from two gutters. The movements of the two figures as they struggle back and forth on their knees or pirouette on their heads, etc. etc.[343]

A familiar picture: a combination of extremely sharp-focus 'close-ups', from whose juxtaposition arises an unusually vivid image of a wrestling ring, etc., etc. But what is particularly remarkable in this passage? It is the fact that in no more than a few lines of description all the different angles – the 'montage elements' – relate to literally almost the whole range of human sensory perceptions:

1. *Tactile* (the feel of sweat streaming down wet backs).
2. *Olfactory* (the smell of sweat, like the reek of wild animals).
3. *Visual*:
   a) *Light and Shade* (deep shadow and the glistening limbs of the wrestlers as they stride into the bright light; the policemen's buttons and sword-hilts glittering out of the darkness).
   b) *Colour* (pale faces, ash-blond moustaches, bodies turning pink under blows).
4. *Auditory* (the slap of hands on bodies).
5. *Mobility* (the wrestlers' movements on their knees, or pirouetting on their heads).
6. *Emotional-'Dramatic'* (challenging glances, etc.).

One could adduce countless other examples, but all of them illustrate with varying degrees of specific detail the proposition stated above, namely:

that there is no difference in principle between purely visual montage and montage that embraces different areas of sensory perception, in particular the visual image and the auditory image, for the purpose of creating a single, generalising audiovisual image.

As a principle, this was already understood when Pudovkin, Alexandrov and I signed our joint 'Statement' on sound film as early as 1929.[344]

Principles are all very well, but the chief purpose of this study is to find practical ways to approach this new form of montage.

Our searches in this direction are closely linked with my film *Alexander Nevsky*. And the new form of montage, which remains inseparable from that picture in my memory, I shall call: *vertical montage*.

Where does that name come from and what is the reason for using it?

Everyone is familiar with the appearance of an orchestral score. There are a certain number of staves on the page, each stave being allotted to the part for one particular instrument. Each part develops in a forward movement along the horizontal. No less important and decisive a factor, however, is the vertical: the musical interaction between the various elements of the orchestra in every given bar. Thus the advancing movement of the *vertical*, which permeates the entire orchestra and moves horizontally, creates the complex harmonic movement of the orchestra as a whole.

In making the transition from this image of the page of a musical score to an audiovisual score, we would have to say that in this new stage a further line is, as it were, added to the purely musical score. This is the sequential progression of a line moving from one visual frame to the next, which in its own way corresponds graphically to the movement of the music and vice versa (cf. Figs 13.1 and 13.2 on p. 333).

We could equally well draw a similar picture if we were not starting from the example of a musical score but from the montage structure of a silent film. In that case, one might take from the silent film an example of *polyphonic* montage, i.e. a kind in which sequence after sequence is not simply linked by a single factor – movement, lighting, stages of the plot, etc. – but one in which the *simultaneous movement* of a number of motifs advances through a succession of sequences, each motif having its own rate of compositional progression, while being at the same time inseparable from the overall compositional progression as a whole.[345]

The montage of the religious procession from the film *The Old and the New* may serve as an example of this kind.

In that episode we see a whole skein of separate motifs which unfold simultaneously yet independently right through the sequence of frames, of which the following are some examples:

1) *The motif of 'heat'*, progressing, growing all the time, from sequence to sequence.

2) *The motif of successive close-ups*, increasing in purely graphic intensity.

3) *The motif of the mounting intoxication of religious fanaticism*, i.e. the *histrionic content* of the close-ups.

4) *The motif of female 'voices'* – the faces of the peasant women singing and carrying icons.

5) *The motif of male 'voices'* – the faces of the peasant men singing and carrying icons.

6) *The motif of a rising tempo* of movement by the people 'diving' under the icons. This counter-flow of people passing through the procession from the opposite direction imparted movement to the chief contrasting theme, a movement which, in the shots themselves and by way of montage intercutting, becomes enmeshed with the primary theme, i.e. the theme of people carrying the icons, crosses and religious banners.

7) *The general theme of 'grovelling'*, which unites both streams of people in a common progression of sequences 'from the sky to the dust', i.e. from the crosses and the tops of the banner-staffs in the sky to the people prostrate in the dust and ashes as they senselessly beat their foreheads against the dry earth.

This theme was actually adumbrated in a separate, prior sequence, which gave as it were the keynote of what follows: the sweeping panoramic shot of the bell-tower, from the cross at the top, gleaming bright in the sky, down to the door of the church whence the procession is starting out, etc., etc.

The overall procession of the montage advanced uninterrupted, weaving all these diverse themes and motifs into a single, cumulative movement. Furthermore, apart from the *general direction* of that movement as a whole, each montage sequence also took strict account of all the vagaries of movement *within each separate motif.*

Sometimes a sequence would embrace almost all of the motifs, sometimes one or two, pausing to include others; sometimes, with one theme, a sequence would take a necessary step backwards in order the more vividly to dash two steps forward, while the other themes continued to progress at a steady pace, and so on. Throughout, each montage sequence had to be checked against not just *one* criterion but against *a whole set of criteria* before it could be decided whether that sequence was suitable as a 'neighbour' for some other sequence.

A sequence that was satisfactory as regards the *degree of intensity of the heat*, for instance, might prove to be unacceptable because it included the wrong *choir of 'voices'*. The *size* of a face might be satisfactory, but the actor's *degree of expressiveness* dictated that the sequence should be somewhere else, and so on. No one should be surprised at the complexity of this work: almost the same kind of thing has to be done, after all, when orchestrating even the most modest piece of music. In our case, of course, the complexity is greater in the sense that filmed material is much less flexible, and it is precisely *in this respect* that if offers almost no opportunities for permutation.

On the other hand, we should bear in mind that both the polyphonic structure itself and its separate strands are woven into the *final shape* not only according to a plan sketched out in advance but also in response to what is suggested by the *complete set of filmed sequences.*

With similar dogged persistence, we also achieved exactly the same kind of 'fusion', though it was further complicated (and perhaps simplified?) by the 'line' of the soundtrack, in *Alexander Nevsky*, and especially in the scene of the charge of the Teutonic knights. Here, compositional elements such as *the tonality of the sky – cloudy and cloudless –* the mounting *tempo* of the charge, the *direction* of the charge, the *sequence* of intercutting between the Russians and the German knights, between close-ups of faces and *long shots*, the *tonality* of the music, its themes, its tempos, its rhythm and so on, all made the job no less difficult and complex. Many, many were the hours spent on co-ordinating all these elements into a *single organic* whole.

In this case, of course, the task was helped by the fact that, apart from certain particular features of it, polyphonic structure basically works by creating an *overall perception of a sequence as a whole*. It forms, as it were, the 'physiognomy' of a sequence, summarising all its separate elements into a *general perception of the sequence*. I wrote about this quality of polyphonic montage and its significance for sound film (which then lay in the future) in connection with the first screening of *The Old and the New* in 1929.[347]

This *general perception* is of decisive significance for combining pictures with music, because it is directly linked to a *perception of the image* of both the music and what is depicted. While one must retain this perception of the whole as the determinant, the combinations themselves, however, require constant correctives in accordance with the separate, inherent features of the elements that make them up.

For a diagram of what happens in *vertical montage*, this characteristic allows the process to be represented in the form of two lines. In doing this, we must bear in mind that each of the lines is *made up of its own multi-vocal score*, and that, this being so, the search for correspondences between them must be regarded as part and parcel of the similar correspondences for the combined, overall 'imagistic' resonance of both visual depiction and music.

Fig. 13.2 shows precisely the new, extra 'vertical' factor of mutual correspondence which comes into play from the moment that sequences are joined in audiovisual montage.

Where the montage structure of the *pictorial element* is concerned, we now have not only the familiar 'sideways annexation' [*pristroika*] of sequence to sequence on the horizontal plane, but also an 'upward superstructure' on the vertical plane above each depictive sequence, in the form of a new sequence *in another dimension*: the *sound* sequence, i.e. a sequence whose link with the depiction is not subsequent but simultaneous.

It is interesting to note that here, too, an audiovisual combination does not differ *in principle* either from purely musical combinations or from visual combinations in silent-film montage.

For in silent-film montage (leaving music out of account) its effect is basically not created by the fact that the sequences are successive in time but by their *simultaneity*, because the impression made by the following sequence is *superimposed* on the impression created by the previous one. The device of 'double exposure' in trick photography gave materialised expression, as it were, to the basic phenomenon of the way we perceive cinematography. This phenomenon is identical both in the fairly advanced stage of silent-film montage and at the cinema's most elementary stage of creating the illusion of movement: *motionless* pictures of an object shot in a series of different positions from frame to frame *superimpose themselves one upon the other* and create the illusion of movement. We now see that a similar superimposition of one upon another also takes place at the *very highest stage* of montage, audiovisual montage, and that here, too, the image of 'double exposure' is as characteristic in principle as it is for all other phenomena of cinematography.

In the early days of silent film, therefore, when I wanted to convey the effect of the sound of music, it was natural that I had recourse to precisely this technical device:

> In *The Strike* (1924) there are attempts to achieve this. In that film there was a small scene in which the strikers get together to make plans under cover of an innocent outing to the accompaniment of accordion music.
>
> It ended with a sequence in which we attempted to convey the perception of that sound by purely visual means.
>
> In this case the substitute for what in future were to be two parallel strips on the film-stock – the picture and the soundtrack – was the use of double exposure. One exposure showed the white expanse of a pond, disappearing into the far distance at the foot of a hill. From it, moving towards the camera, came the group of revellers with an accordion. In the second exposure, framing the landscape with their rhythmic move-ment, were spread a row of gleaming strips – the spotlit bellows of a huge accordion, shot so as to cover the whole screen. By their movement and by the interplay of their relative positions, as seen from several different angles, they gave a complete impression of the movement of the melody, which in turn echoed [the movement] of the entire scene. . . .[348]

Fig. 13.1 shows the system of compositional linkage in silent film; Fig. 13.2 shows that in sound film. It is specifically a scheme of linkage, because montage itself, of course, gives the impression of being something like a *broad, developing thematic progression* which moves forward through an analogous scheme of separate montage linkages.

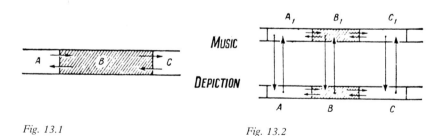

Fig. 13.1   Fig. 13.2

The basic difficulties lie in discovering the essence of this new form of *linkage along the vertical plane.* For the structure of the compositional linkage along the line $A_1 - B_1 - C_1$ is familiar enough in music; while the laws of compositional movement along the line $A - B - C$ have been exhaustively investigated in the practice of editing silent film.

Now, the new problem faced by the sound film is going to be to find a way of joining $A - A_1$; $A_1 - B_1 - C_1$; $B - B_1$; $C - C_1$, and so on, which will effect the complex audiovisual progression of the theme through such a complex system of combinations as e.g. $A - A_1 - B_1 - B - C - C_1$, and so on, and in their most varied combinations.

Thus the problem here is to find the key to the hitherto unknown vertical linkages of $A - A_1$, $B - B_1$, etc., which we must learn to be able to combine and separate as naturally as the trained musical ear does it with the series A_1, B_1 . . . and so on, or as the eye trained in visual montage does with the series A, B and so on.

From here on, the essential problem becomes that of finding what makes *picture and sound* compatible, and of finding, for this purpose, the relevant indices, units of measurement, techniques and methodology. This will be primarily a matter of finding an *inner synchronicity between picture and music* that is as sharply perceptible to us as it already is in our perception of examples of outward synchronicity (we have already learned to be keenly aware of the slightest failure of synchronisation between lip movements and the spoken word!).[349]

This perception, however, will be far removed from that inner synchronicity that exists between a boot and the creak that it makes; it must aspire to 'that "mysterious" inner synchronicity' in which the visual principle merges wholly with the tonal.

The connecting link between sound and vision, the *lingua franca* of synchronicity is, of course, movement. Plekhanov has said that in the final analysis all phenomena are reducible to movement. It is movement that will reveal to us all the deeper layers of synchronicity that we shall subsequently identify. It is movement, too, that will also reveal to our senses the *meaning* of an associative combination and its *methodology*. We shall follow a route from outward and visible things to things inward and less immediate.

The role of movement in synchronicity is quite obvious. All the same, let us examine the following series of examples.

The series begins with the type of synchronicity which, in essence, lies outside the limits of artistic treatment: *inherent* synchronicity, i.e. the natural sound of the object or phenomenon to be filmed (a croaking frog, the sobbing chord of a broken harp, the click of cab wheels on a cobbled street).

In our subject, art actually begins from the moment when the combination of sound and picture does not simply *reproduce* a connection existing in nature but *establishes* a connection demanded by the expressive requirements of the work in question.

In its most rudimentary forms this will be done by subordinating both spheres [aural and visual] to one and the same rhythm, a rhythm corresponding to the content of the scene. This will be the simplest, the most accessible, the most frequently encountered example of audiovisual montage, when the pictorial sequences are cut and glued together in accord with the rhythm of the music running parallel to them on the soundtrack. Here it is immaterial whether there is movement within the shot or whether the shots are motionless. In the first case one only needs to ensure that the intra-shot movement should be in the appropriate rhythms.

Clearly, even at this rather lowly stage of synchronicity it is also possible to achieve some very precise, interesting and expressive effects.

Starting from this very simple example of a straight 'metrical' concordance of stress accents – a kind of 'rhythmic declamation' – it is then possible to move on to any number of combinations of syncopated rhythms and of purely rhythmic counterpoint through the formal play of non-coincident stress accents, lengths and frequency of repetitions, etc.

But what will be the next step after this second example of externally impelled synchronicity? Obviously it will be a synchronicity in the visual medium which is capable of imparting not only a rhythmic movement but a *melodic movement*.

Henry Lanz, in his book *The Physical Basis of Rime* (1931), is correct when he says of melody: 'Strictly speaking, we do not "hear" melody at all. We are either capable or incapable of following it, by which is meant our ability or inability to combine a series of sounds into a certain unity of a higher order.'[350]

In all the multiplicity of visual means of expression there must be those which by their movement are able to echo not only the rhythm but also the moving *line* of a melody. We can already guess what those means may be, but because a large separate section will later be devoted to this particular question, here we will merely make a passing suggestion that, basically, this will be . . . the 'linear' element in the visual medium.

We shall now turn our attention to the next category of movement.

That 'unity of a higher order', into which we are capable of combining the *separate sounds* of a series of notes, is quite clearly determined for us by a line which links the notes as it moves forward. But the tonal *intervals* between those notes are also characterised by movement, this time by movement of the next category: not movement as locomotion but *oscillatory movement*, whose various characteristics we perceive as sounds of different pitch and key.

What is the pictorial element which here, too, can echo this 'movement' of sounds? Obviously it is that element which is also based on oscillatory movement (admittedly in a different band of physical wavelengths), the element that is also characterised by the same designation . . . 'tone'; in the visual medium it is colour. (Pitch, roughly speaking, will obviously correspond to the play of *light*, while the visual equivalent of the key in music is *colour tone*.)

Let us stop for a moment and take stock. We have established that synchronicity can be 'inherent', metrical, rhythmic, melodic and tonal.[351]

Furthermore an audiovisual combination can satisfy by its synchronicity in all these modes (this only occurs extremely rarely) or it can be built on a synchronisation within any of them, without, nevertheless, concealing a general discord between the media of sound and picture. This latter is found very frequently. When it occurs, we say that the pictures are 'one thing' and the music 'another'; the sound and picture elements each run independently without fusing into an organic whole. At the same time, we should bear in mind that we are far from regarding synchronicity as necessarily implying absolute, literal concordance between sound and picture; any interplay of the coincidence and non-coincidence of 'movement' is entirely possible, but in either case the combination should nevertheless be *structurally purposeful*. It is equally obvious that, depending on the expressive aims of the work, any one of the aspects of synchronicity can be the 'leading' feature of the structure. For some scenes the basic affective factor may be rhythm, for others tonality, and so on.

But let us return to the possible variants, or rather the various modes of synchronicity.

We have seen that these variants wholly correspond to those of silent-film montage which we identified earlier (in 1928–9) and which I subsequently also included in my general course for teaching film direction.[352]

(There was a time when certain comrades might have regarded my 'nomenclature' as excessive pedantry or an arbitrary game of playing with analogies. Yet even then we were pointing out the importance of this matter for something that lay in the future: the sound film. Nowadays we have discovered it vividly and tangibly through the practical business of audiovisual editing.)

That series of variants also included 'overtonal' montage. We mentioned this kind of synchronicity earlier, when citing the case of *The Old and the New*. And within this (perhaps not quite precise) designation we should maybe include the 'total', polyphonic, reciprocal 'sensory' resonance of the sequence (musical and pictorial) *as wholes*. This totality is the sensory factor which most immediately synthesises the principal image of the sequence.

Here we have reached the chief, fundamental factor that creates the *ultimate inner synchronicity, the image and the meaning of the sequences.*

With this the circle, as it were, is completed. For this formula concerning the *meaning* of a sequence also unites the *most straightforward method of linking the sequences* – the so-called simple 'thematic selection' made according to the logic of the plot – with *the highest form of all*, when that combination of sequences is the means of disclosing the meaning, when the *basic image of the theme* really *emerges* through a combination of sequences charged with *the ideas that make up the content of the work.*

This principle is, of course, the starting point and foundation for a whole series of others. For each 'variant' of synchronicity within an overall organic whole is no more than the embodiment of the basic image within that variant's specifically demarcated areas.

Let us start our enquiries in the area of colour. And not only because the problem of colour is nowadays the most topical and intriguing problem for our cinema, but fundamentally because it is in the area of colour that a question of principle has been sharply posed and is now being resolved: the question of the absolute and relative concordance of *picture and sound to each other* and of the two together *to specific human emotions*. This has a cardinal significance for the principle that underlies the audiovisual image. The *methodology* of the process itself can be most clearly and best displayed in the area of *melodic synchronisation*, which is most conveniently adapted to graphic analysis and to printed reproduction in monochrome (this will form the subject matter of further essays).

So let us address ourselves in the first instance to the question of concordance between music and colour, which for convenience I shall call 'chromophonic'.

To demolish the contradictions between picture and sound, between the visible world and the audible world! To create a unity and a harmonic concordance between them! What a fascinating undertaking! The Greeks, Diderot, Wagner, Scriabin – who has not dreamed of it? Who has not tried his hand at the task? But our review of those dreams will not begin with such figures as these.

We shall conduct the review as a way of working out a methodology of fusing sound and picture by looking at some of its salient features. So let us begin examining the form in which the dream of amalgamating sight and sound has for so long inspired mankind. In this, the lion's share of attention has been given to the realm of colour.

We shall take the first example from the not-too-distant past; it is no further back in time than the turn of the 18th and 19th centuries, but it is very striking. First to speak shall be Karl von Eckartshausen, author of a book entitled *The Key to Nature's Secrets* (by 1791 the German original had already gone into a second edition). On pp. 295–9 of the Russian edition he writes:

I have long been engaged in research into the harmony of all sensory impressions. In order to make this clearer and more perceptible, I improved upon the machine for rendering music visible, invented by Pastor Kastell, and brought it to a condition that made it possible to produce upon it chords composed of colours in precisely the same fashion that chords are made up from musical notes. Here is a description of this machine. I ordered the manufacture of a number of small cylinders of glass, equal in size and of half an inch in diameter; I then filled them with liquids of different hues in accordance with the theory of colours, and I disposed these small glasses as if they were the strings of a clavichord, distributing the tints of colour in accord with the division of musical notes. Behind these glasses I placed a number of brass valves, which enabled each glass to be concealed from view. I so connected these valves with wire that when the keys of the clavichord were struck the valves were raised and the colours revealed. As the note dies away when the finger leaves the key, so the colour fades as soon as one removes one's finger, for the valves, by their own weight, fall down at once and shut out the glasses from sight.

I illuminated this clavichord from behind with tall candles. The beauty of the colours which appeared is indescribable; it surpassed that o the most precious jewels. It is equally impossible to express the delightful effects perceived by the eye on observing the different chords of colour.

The Theory of Ocular Music

Just as musical notes should correspond to the words written by the author of a melodrama, so also should colours accord with words. The better to understand this, I will cite in example a song which I set to the music of colours and which I accompany upon my ocular clavichord. It is as follows:

1. *Words*: 'A homeless little orphan child'
   Music: A doleful melody on the flute.
   Colours: Olive-green, mingled with pink and white.

2. *Words*: 'Walking through a meadow filled with flowers'
   Music: A cheerful tune on a rising scale.
   Colours: Green, mingled with violet and pale yellow.

3. *Words*: 'Sang plaintively, like a robin redbreast.'
   Music: Gentle notes, in quick succession, growing louder, then softer.
   Colours: Dark blue with scarlet and yellowish-greenish.

4. *Words*: 'God heard the little orphan's song,'
   Music: Dignified, majestic, powerful.
   Colours: Light blue, red and green shot with yellow and purple, changing to bright green and pale yellow.

5. *Words*: 'The bright sun came out from behind the hills'
   Music: Majestic bass notes, middle notes, gently rising!
   Colours: Bright yellow, mingled with pink, changing to green and bright yellow.

6. *Words*: 'And sent a sunbeam down upon a violet.'
   Music: Low, gently falling notes.
   Colours: Violet, mingled with different shades of green.

This is enough to show that colours can also express the emotions of the soul.[353]

As this example is probably little known, we shall turn next to one which, on the contrary, is among the most popular: Rimbaud's famous sonnet on colours entitled 'Voyelles' [Vowels], which for so long has thrilled people with its scheme of correspondences between colours and sounds:

VOWELS

A black, E white, I red, U green, O blue: vowels,
One day I will tell your latent birth:
A – black and furry corset worn by glitt'ring flies
Which buzz around a piece of stinking carrion;

The deeps of shadow; pure white of mists and tents,
Proud glaciers, pallid kings and rippling parasols;
I – the purples of spat blood, of fair lips laughing,
In anger or in ecstasy of penitence;

U – whirlpools, emerald seas aswirl by hand divine,
The calm of pastures strewn with sheep, the furrowed calm
That's etched by alchemy upon great scholars' brows;

O – trumpet-call supreme, mysterious, shrill,
In silences alone traversed by worlds and angels:
O – Omega, the piercing shaft of violet from His Eyes![354]

Rimbaud is very close in time to René Ghil, who also drew up tables of
vowel-colour correspondence, although the two diverge considerably:

ou, où, iou, oui:	from black to reddish-brown.
o, ô, io, oi:	red.
a, à, ai:	vermilion.
eu, eù, ueu, eui:	from pink to pale gold.
u, û, iu, ui:	gold
e, è, é, ei:	from white to azure flecked with gold.
ie, ié, iè, i, i:	azure.[355]

After Helmholtz[356] had published the findings of his experiments on the
correspondence between vocal and instrumental sounds, Ghil 'expanded' his
tables, adding to them consonants and the timbres of instruments, together
with a whole catalogue of emotions, ideas and concepts which allegedly
corresponded to them.

In his book on romanticism (*Das Wesen der Romantik* [The Essence of
Romanticism], 1921), Max Deutschbein considers 'the synthesis of different
classes of emotion' to be one of the distinguishing features in the writing of
the Romantics.

In complete accord with this view, we find a similar table of correspondences between vowels and colours compiled by August-Wilhelm Schlegel
(1767–1845); I quote again from Henry Lanz: '"A" corresponds to a pale,
bright red (*das rote, licht-helle A*) and denotes youth, friendship and radiance,
"I" corresponds to sky-blue, symbolising love and sincerity. "O" corresponds
to purple, "Y" to violet and "U" to ultramarine.'[357]

Another Romantic of a later period – Lafcadio Hearn, a man with a
profound and subtle knowledge of Japan – also gives considerable attention
to this question in his *Japanese Letters*;[358] he does not, however, try to make
such a 'classification', and indeed he condemns any attempt to move away
from immediacy and towards systematisation (in his criticism of a book by
Symonds entitled *In the Key of Blue*, contained in a letter dated 14 June
1893).[359]

Yet four days later he writes to his friend Basil Hall Chamberlain: 'You were a true artist in your last letter. Your manner of describing colours in musical terms (the "deep bass" of a certain shade of green, etc.) thrilled me.'

In a letter of a few days earlier, however, he lets loose a passionate tirade on this subject:

> If you allow ugliness in words, you must at the same time also admit to the beauty of their physiognomy. To me words have colour, shape, character; they have faces, posture, gestures; they have moods and eccentricities; they have nuances, tones, individualities.

Later, attacking editors of magazines who object to his style and manner of writing, he writes that they are, of course, right when they insist:

> The readers do not feel about words at all as you do. They do not want to know that you imagine the letter 'A' as pale pink, the letter 'E' as pale blue. They do not want to know that in your perception the letters 'KH' placed together have a beard and wear a turban, that an initial 'X' is an elderly Greek covered in wrinkles, and so on.

But in response, Hearn immediately rounds on his critics:

> Because they cannot see the colours of words, the shadings of words, the mysterious, transparent movement of words; because they cannot hear the whispering of words, the rustling made by processions of words, the fluting and drumming of words; because they cannot perceive the sullenness of words, the sobbing of words, the rebellion of words; because they are insensitive to the phosphorescence of words, the softness and hardness of words, their dryness or juiciness, the alternation of gold, silver, brass and copper in words, should we therefore abandon the attempt to make them listen, to make them see, to make them feel words?

In another passage he talks of the inconstancy of words: 'I said long ago that words are like those little lizards that are able to change their colouring according to their surroundings.'

Hearn did not acquire such refined sensitivity by chance. In part it was a result of his being short-sighted, which particularly sharpened these aspects of his perceptions. It was, of course, chiefly due to the fact that he had lived in Japan, where the capacity to detect audiovisual correspondences has been developed with particular finesse. (In 1929 I wrote a detailed article, entitled 'An Unexpected Juncture', on the problem of audiovisual correspondences, with reference to sound film and the Japanese tradition.[360])

Lafcadio Hearn has taken us to the Orient, where, in Chinese teaching, audiovisual correspondences are not only present but are indeed laid down in a specific canon. Here, too, they are subject to the principles of Yin and Yang, which pervade the entire system of Chinese philosophy. The correspondences themselves are structured as follows:

1) Fire – South – Morals – Summer – Red – *Ji* (the note 'D') – bitter.
2) Water – North – Wisdom – Winter – Black – *Yü* (the note 'E') – salty.
3) Tree – East – Love – Spring – Blue (or Green) – *Guo* (the note 'B') – sour.
4) Metal – West – Justice – Autumn – White – *Shang* (the note 'A') – spicy.[361]

Quite as interesting as the correspondence between individual sounds and colours is an analogous reflection of the *stylistic aspirations* of particular 'eras' *in both the structuring of music and the structuring of painting.*

The late René Guilleré wrote interestingly about this in an article entitled 'Il n'y a plus de perspectives':

> In the past, aesthetics rested on a merging of [structural] elements. In music – on a line of unbroken melody which pervaded the chords of the harmony; in literature – on joining together the elements of a sentence with conjunctions and linking phrases; in painting – on a seamless structural design which ordered the parts into a whole.
>
> Modern aesthetics is based instead on the separation of elements, which contrast with each other: the repetition of the same element is only a reinforcement, to lend greater intensity to the contrast.[362]

Here it should be noted, in parenthesis, that *repetition* can serve two aims in equal degree.

On the one hand, repetition can promote the creation of an organic whole; on the other, it can also serve as a means towards that heightening of intensity which Guilleré has in mind. We do not need to go far to find examples. Both cases can be demonstrated from two films.

For the first case, a repetition of this kind is the word 'Brothers!' in *The Battleship Potemkin*: it is first used in the scene on the quarterdeck, when the men of the firing squad disobey the order to shoot; it is used a second time when the people on shore link up with the battleship's crew by coming out to them in the flotilla of sailing-boats; the third time, in the form of the signal 'Brothers!', when the approaching squadron refuses to fire on the battleship.

For the second case, there is an example in *Alexander Nevsky*, where instead of repeating *four* identical bars of music, as written in the score, I put in *twelve* of them, i.e. a triple repetition. This occurs in that sequence of the film in which the peasant militia cuts its way from the rear into the dense wedge formation of the Teutonic knights. This unfailingly produces a sense of heightened tension, and the effect of the music is invariably accompanied by thunderous applause.

But let us continue with what Guilleré has to say:

> The form of jazz, if one analyses the elements of the music and the methods of its composition, is a typical expression of this new aesthetic. . . .

Its basic components are syncopation of the music and assertion of the rhythm. As a result, the smoothly curving lines of melody, its convoluted phrases shaped like curls (typical of Massenet), its slow arabesques, all have been thrown out. The rhythm is assertive, sharp and angular. Its structure is harsh; it is firm; it is constructive. It strives for solid form. Jazz creates blocks of sound, block-like phrases. Classical music was built up of planes (not of blocks) – planes disposed on different storeys, laid on top of another; horizontal and vertical planes, which created an architecture of noble proportions: palaces with terraces, colonnades, staircases of monumental design, long vistas. In jazz, everything is brought into the foreground. This is an important principle. It applies equally to pictures, to stage sets, to film, to poetry: a total rejection of conventional perspective, with its single fixed viewpoint and its converging lines.

Painters paint and writers write using several different perspectives, aiming for a complex synthesis of angles of vision, which in a single picture may incorporate some which approach the subject from below, others which approach it from above.

Previously, perspective gave us a geometrical perception of things as they would be seen by one ideal eye. Our modern perspective presents us with things as we see them with two eyes, as if groping for them. We no longer create perspective from an acute angle, of which the two lines meet at the horizon. We widen that angle, we straighten out its lines. And we pull the picture towards us, at us, into ourselves. . . . We are co-participants in it. Therefore we are not afraid to use close-ups as in film: to depict the human figure out of its natural proportions, as it appears to us when it is fifty centimetres away from our eyes; we are not afraid of a metaphor that leaps out of a poem, not afraid of the sound of a trombone bursting out of the orchestra in an aggressive lunge.

In the old perspective, the planes receded like the wings of a stage set as though forming a tube or a funnel through which to reveal in the distance the colonnade of a palace or a monumental staircase. Similarly in [classical] music, the receding 'wings' represented by the double basses, the cellos, the violins – on successive planes one after another, like the half-landings of a staircase – led us up and away to terraces from whence was revealed, like a sunset, the triumph of the brass instruments. Equally, in literature the setting of the plot was gradually revealed, laid out like an avenue, tree by tree; and people were described on the same principle, starting with the colour of their hair. . . .

In modern perspective there are no gradations, no half-landings, no avenues. People form part of the surroundings, the surroundings emerge through people. Both are functions of each other.

In a word, in our new perspective there is no longer any perspective. The shape and size of things are no longer created by means of perspective . . . it is differences of intensity, the relative richness of the colouring which create the shapes and sizes. In music, shape or bulk are no longer produced by receding planes but by a foreground of sounds which recede. Shape is created by the totality of sounds. There are no longer any large sound canvases which support the whole in the manner of stage backdrops. In jazz everything is mass. There is no longer an accompaniment and a voice, like a figure against a background. Every element contributes equally. No longer is there a solo instrument against an orchestral background; as each instrument performs its solo, it participates in the whole. Nor is there an impressionistic dismemberment of the orchestra, according to which the first and second violins, for example, play the same theme but a few intervals apart, in order to lend greater richness to the sound.

In jazz each one plays for himself within the ensemble. The same rule applies to painting: the background itself must be an equal, integral part of the whole.

This passage interests us above all as a picture of the complete equivalence between musical and visual structures, in this case not only in painting but also in architecture, since the argument is chiefly about concepts of space and volume. It would, however, be enough to look at a series of Cubist paintings for the similarity between what happens in those pictures and what happens in jazz to be quite as evident.

Equally evident is the correspondence of both kinds of music to architectural landscapes: of pre-jazz music to classical architecture, and of jazz to a modern cityscape.

In fact, the parks and terraces of Versailles, Roman town planning and Roman villas seem like 'prototypes' for the structure of classical music.

Modern urban layout, on the other hand, especially the nighttime streetscape of a big city, also looks like the visual equivalent of jazz, above all in that basic feature which Guilleré singled out, namely its lack of perspective.

At night, perspective and the perception of real distance are destroyed by a sea of coloured, illuminated advertisements. Far and near, small (in the *foreground*) and big (in the *background*), flashing on and off, moving and revolving, popping up and disappearing, they ultimately nullify all perception of real space, and at certain moments they seem like a drawing made up of coloured dotted lines or strips flickering over a single flat surface, the black velvet of the night sky. People once imagined the stars to be like this: little glowing nailheads hammered into the vault of heaven!

What is more, the headlights of speeding cars and buses, the light reflected from railway tracks and from patches of wet asphalt, together with the upside-down reflections in puddles which destroy our perception of which way is 'up' and which 'down': all these contribute to forming a similar mirage of light under our feet; and as we make our way through this double world of neon advertisements, they seem not to be on a single plane but a system of stage 'flats' hanging in the air, past which rush the lighted streams of nighttime traffic. There is one starry sky above and one starry sky below: a world, in fact, just as it was imagined by the characters in Gogol's *The Terrible Vengeance*, as they sailed down the Dnieper between the real star-studded heaven above and its reflection in the water.

That is an approximate eyewitness impression of the streets of New York in the hours of darkness, though it can be confirmed equally well from many fantastic photographs of other cities at night.

The passage [from Guilleré] quoted above is, however, even more interesting in the degree to which it not only relates music and painting to each other, but both of them, taken together, to the very *image of the era and to the cast of mind* of the people historically connected with that era. Is not Guilleré's whole picture typical of it, beginning with that very 'absence of perspective', which seems to be a reflection of the historic dead end of bourgeois society, which in imperialism has reached the highest stage of capitalism, up to and including that image of the jazz band in which 'everyone plays for himself' and each one tries to thrust himself forward out of that *non-organic* whole, out of that ensemble of independent units, each pursuing his own aims, fettered to each other only by the *iron necessity* of a common rhythm?

It is in fact interesting that all the features which Guilleré lists have already been encountered at different times in the history of the arts. At all past stages the arts have striven *for a single wholeness and a higher unity*; it is only in the era of imperialism triumphant and of the beginning of decadence in the arts that *centripetal* movement reverses into one that is *centrifugal*, which flings aside all such tendencies towards unity, tendencies incompatible with the dominance of all-pervasive individualism. Let us recall Nietzsche:

> What is it that characterises every period of decadence in literature? It is that the *whole* is no longer imbued with life. The word becomes sovereign and leaps out of the sentence; the sentence thrusts itself forward and obscures the meaning of the page; the page takes on a life independent of the whole – the whole no longer *is* whole. . . . The whole, indeed, is no longer alive: it is simply a collection of parts, calculated, artificial.
>
> (Friedrich Nietzsche, *Der Fall Wagner*, 1888, p.28)

The fundamental, typical sign of decadence lies precisely in that, and not in particular details. Do not ancient Egyptian bas-reliefs dispense with perspective? When Dürer and Leonardo da Vinci find it necessary, do they not use multiple perspectives deriving from several different viewpoints? (In Leonardo da Vinci's *Last Supper*, for instance, the objects on the table are shown in a perspective derived from a different viewpoint from that on which the perspective of the rest of the room is based.) And in Van Eyck's portrait of the Arnolfini couple there are no less than three perspectives derived from different viewpoints. In that particular case this device was probably used unwittingly by the artist, but what a quite special charm is given to this picture by the *tension* between contrasting impressions of depth!

Does not Chinese landscape painting dispense with drawing the specta-tor's eye into the picture, and instead does it not spread the angle of vision laterally, making the mountains and waterfalls move towards us?

Do not Japanese wood-engravings use *super-large* close-ups and ex-pressive disproportion in the feature of those *super-large* faces?

Some people may object that this is not really a question of the tendency of the art of previous eras to strive towards unity, but simply of . . . their narrower and less forceful *application* of this or that feature, compared with the way it has been applied in an era of decadence.

Where in the past, for instance, can there be found such a degree of simultaneity as in the quoted examples of 'complex synthesis' in the depiction of objects shown simultaneously from above and below? In the mixture of vertical and horizontal planes?

One need only look, however, at the drawing of the layout of the seventeenth-century palace of Kolomenskoye to be convinced that it repre-sents a projection that is simultaneously both *vertical and horizontal!*[363]

In 'simultaneous' theatre sets, for example the sets designed by Yakulov 'in the spirit of the traditions of Cubism', geographically separate scenes of action intersect with each other, interiors overlap with exteriors. These sets astonished theatregoers in the immediate post-Revolutionary period of the theatre (e.g. the designs for Shakespeare's *Measure for Measure* at the Model Theatre).[364] Yet they have absolutely exact prototypes in the technique of stage design of the 16th and 17th centuries. In those days the theatres in [Russian] schools and seminaries used scenery in which the sets for different scenes cut across each other, showing simultaneously, for instance, a desert and a palace; a hermit's cave, the tsar's throne and the tsarina's bedchamber; an abandoned tomb and the expanse of heaven!

What's more, there are even prototypes for such 'astounding' phenomena as, for instance, the portraits by Yuri Annenkov, in one of which, on the cheek of a portrait head of the theatre director Nikolai Petrov, the artist has drawn the middle part of his features, but turned so as to show them . . . full face![365] There is a seventeenth-century copper engraving which shows St John of the Cross looking sideways and downwards at the crucifixion. And there, intruding on that depiction, *the same crucifixion is repeated*, scrupulously drawn in a perspective view from half-way up (i.e. from the saint's point of view had he actually witnessed the crucifixion!).

But if that is not enough, then let us turn to . . . El Greco.[366] In his work, there is an example in which the artist's viewpoint leaps madly backwards and forwards, putting on to a single canvas details of a town taken not only from different viewpoints but from different streets, alleyways and squares! Furthermore, this was done with the artist's absolute conviction that he was doing the right thing, so much so that he described it in detail on a special little panel painted into the townscape, probably to avoid any misunderstand-ings, because to people who knew that city his picture must have seemed as much a piece of 'artistic Leftism' as Annenkov's portraits or Burlyuk's simultaneous [multi-angle] drawings.[367]

The picture in question is a general view of the city of Toledo, known by the title of *A View and Plan of the City of Toledo*. It was painted between 1604 and 1614 and is in the Toledo Museum.

In it, a general view of Toledo is depicted from a distance of about a kilometre to the east. On the right-hand side is painted a young man, holding an unrolled plan of the city. On this plan El Greco instructed his son to write the words which are of particular interest to us at this point:

> I was obliged to depict the hospital of Don Juan de Tavera on a small scale, like a little model; otherwise it would have concealed the city's de Vizagra gates, and its dome would have risen high above the city. That is why it had to be placed here, as a model, and turned around, too, because I prefer to show the main façade rather than the other (rear) aspect of it – besides, it can be seen from the plan where the hospital is situated in relation to the city.

What difference does this make? The *real correlation of dimensions* has been changed, and a part of the city has been shown as facing *one* way, while a particular detail of it is shown *from exactly the opposite direction*!

It is this which makes me include El Greco among the forebears of . . . film montage. If in this instance he is a slightly eccentric forerunner of . . . the newsreel film, and his re-montage is more *informational* than anything else, in another of his views of Toledo (the famous *Storm over Toledo*, painted at around the same time), he performs a no less radical *montage distortion* of the real landscape, but in this case as a function of that *emotional* hurricane which makes the picture so remarkable.

El Greco has, however, brought us back to our basic theme, because as it happens his painting has, strangely enough, an exact musical equivalent in one of the varieties of Spanish folk music. Thus El Greco also has affinities with the problem of chromophonic montage, because he must have known that music, and what he does in painting is very close in spirit to what characterises so-called 'cante hondo'.[368]

The resemblance and affinity of these two art forms (naturally, devoid of any cinematic considerations) has been noted by Legendre and Hartmann in their authoritative monograph on El Greco.

They begin by quoting the evidence of José Martinez that El Greco often invited musicians to his house. Martinez disapproved of this as 'excessive extravagance'; but we may assume that this close link between music and his activity as a painter must have influenced the artist's work as he was temperamentally inclined to a fondness for music.

Legendre and Hartmann state it quite plainly: 'We like to believe that El Greco loved "cante hondo", and we shall show to what degree his pictures constitute the equivalent in painting to what "cante hondo" is in music!'

Later, they describe the special characteristics of the melodies of 'cante hondo', quoting from a booklet published by Manuel de Falla in 1922.[369]

This composer-author recalls the three historical factors which influenced Spanish music: the fact that the Spanish Church adopted the Byzantine chant; the Arab occupation; and the immigration of gypsies. Within this combination he stresses the connection between 'cante hondo' and oriental melody:

> In both cases enharmonics are used, i.e. the division or sub-division into smaller intervals than in the accepted [European] scale of notes; the melody line is not divided into bars; its compass rarely extends beyond a major sixth, but that sixth is not made up of nine semitones, as is the case in our equal-temperament [diatonic] scale, since the enharmonic scale considerably increases the number of notes available to the singer; the use of the same note is repeated with the insistence of an incantation and is often accompanied by a rising or falling appoggiatura. Thus although the melody of gypsy music is rich in ornamentation, as in primitive oriental melody, these additions only come into play at certain moments, as though stressing an increase or outburst of feeling evoked by the emotional content of the words.

Similar comments apply to performance:

> The chief thing that surprises a foreigner on first hearing 'cante hondo' is the unusual simplicity of the singer and the guitarist accompanying him; there is no theatricality, no artificiality, no special costume: the performers wear everyday clothes. Their faces are impassive, their looks sometimes seem to lack all conscious awareness and are devoid of expression.
>
> But under that layer of cooled lava there seethes a suppressed fire. At the climactic moment of emotional expression (whose theme has first been sketched out in a few trivial words), there suddenly wells up from breast to throat such a powerful surge of passion that it seems as if the singer's vocal cords may break at any moment, and in modulations as tense and extended as a long death agony the singer pours out the upsurge of his passion until the audience can restrain itself no longer and bursts into shouts of rapture.

And now back to El Greco; the subject is the same picture:

> Out of the monochrome surroundings – where the 'intervals' of colouring are differentiated into the minutest tonal subdivisions and the basic modulations are endlessly interwoven with each other – like flashes, like explosions, like zigzags come the sudden outbursts of colour which are so shocking to colourless and mediocre minds. We hear the 'cante hondo'

of painting – the combined expression of the Orient and of Spain; of the East penetrating the West.[370]

Although other scholars who have written on El Greco (Maurice Barrès, Meier-Graefe, Carrière, Willumsen, *et al.*) never refer to music, they nevertheless describe the painterly effects of El Greco's canvases *in almost exactly the same words*. Anyone who has been lucky enough to see those paintings for themselves can confirm such comments from first-hand experience!

Although not systematised, similar ideas were expressed by Rimsky-Korsakov:

During the course of the evening the talk again turned to tonality, and Rimsky repeated that for him personally sharp keys evoked impressions of *colours*, whereas *flat keys* conjured up moods or an impression of different degrees of heat; and that the alternation of C sharp minor with D flat major in the 'Egypt' scene from his opera *Mlada* was no coincidence, but that on the contrary he had purposely used it in order to convey *a sense of heat*, just as red colours always suggest the notion of *heat*, whereas *blues and violets* are associated with *cold and darkness*. Perhaps that is why – said Korsakov – Wagner's brilliant prelude to *Das Rheingold* makes such a grim impression on me, precisely because of the strange key (E flat major) chosen for that particular piece. I, for instance, would certainly have transposed that *Vorspiel* into E major.[371]

Here we may recall in passing Whistler's 'symphonies' in paint: *Harmony in Blue and Yellow*; *Nocturne in Blue and Silver*; *Nocturne in Blue and Gold*; his *Symphonies in White* Nos 1–4, dated between 1862 and 1867.[372]

Correlations between sound and colour are found even in the thinking of such a little-respected figure as the Swiss artist Böcklin.[373] Max Schlesinger writes:

For [Böcklin], who was – as Floerke tells us – constantly reflecting on the mystery of colour, all colours possessed the power of speech, and he, in a reverse process, translated everything that he perceived into the language of colour. . . . To him, the sound of a trumpet always evoked the colour of cinnabar red.

As we see, this tendency is universal, and consequently there is every justification for the demand made by Novalis: 'One should never contemplate works of the visual arts without the accompaniment of music; nor should one listen to music except in the surroundings of rooms appropriately decorated.'[374]

As for a carefully detailed 'alphabet of colours', on this point one must unfortunately agree with a man whom I otherwise profoundly despise for his crass vulgarity, François Coppet, when he writes:

Foolish is our jolly Rimbaud,
Telling us in sonnet free
That the letters E, O, I show
France's flag in colours three.[375]

Nevertheless, this matter must be investigated, because the question of similar absolute correspondences still exercises people's minds, and even the minds of American film-makers. Thus a few years ago I happened to read a very thoughtful argument in an American magazine to the effect that the sound of a piccolo directly corresponds to . . . the colour yellow!

But let that yellow (or not yellow) colour which allegedly pervades the sound of the piccolo serve as a transition – not in rarefied abstraction but in the actual process of artistic creation – to the way in which the artist handles colour.

This will be the subject of our next section.

II

In the foregoing section on vertical montage we dwelt in some detail on the question of seeking 'absolute' correspondences between sound and colour. In order to throw some light on this, let us examine another question closely connected with it, namely the question of absolute correspondences between certain *emotions* and certain colours.

For the sake of variety, we will pursue this theme not so much through pronouncements on the theory of the subject as through the actual emotional effects of what artists do by their use of colour.

For convenience, we will keep all our examples within the same 'key' of colour, and having for this purpose chosen the colour yellow, we shall use these examples to paint something in the nature of a 'rhapsody in yellow'.

Let us begin our examples by taking an extreme case. We can talk about an 'inner resonance', about the 'inner harmony of line, shape and colours'. In doing so, we clearly imply that it is in harmony *with* something, and that the perception of that inner harmony points to a certain *meaning*, vague perhaps, but nevertheless directed towards something that is in the final analysis concrete and which is striving to be expressed in colour, light, line and shape.

There exists a point of view, however, which regards this formulation of ours as allowing insufficient 'freedom' to our perceptions. In opposition to our ideas, the supporters of the latter viewpoint postulate an equally vague 'inner resonance' (*der innere Klang*) that is 'absolutely free', which is not *a means* but *an end in itself*; that this 'inner resonance' is in itself the ultimate achievement, the end result.

In those terms, that 'freedom' is above all freedom from . . . common sense, which is, *entre nous*, the only freedom that is *absolutely* attainable in the conditions of bourgeois society.

A product of the decay of that society at its highest, imperialist, level of development is Kandinsky, the apostle of such an ideal [of 'absolute freedom'] and author of the work from which we shall quote a passage as the first in our 'yellow rhapsody' of examples.[376]

I quote from the collection of essays entitled *Der blaue Reiter* [The Blue Rider], published in Munich, which played such a big part in the theoretical and programmatic underpinning of the so-called 'left-wing trends' in art.[377]

Serving as a supplementary colour to the 'Blue Rider' on the cover of that book, there is a 'stage composition' (*Bühnenkomposition*) by Kandinsky called . . . 'The Yellow Sound' (*Der gelbe Klang*).

This 'Yellow Sound' is a programme for staging the author's vague perceptions of the interplay of colours understood as music, of the interplay of music understood as colours, of the interplay of people . . . not understood at all.

In such confusion and vagueness, one always senses something that is always very hard to submit to definition – a core of mysticism. Here it is even given a religious tinge, which culminates in the sixth scene:

A dull blue background. . . .

In the middle of it is a yellow and blue Giant with an indistinct white face and big, round, black eyes. . . .

He slowly raises his hands past his torso – palms downward – and as he does so he grows upward. . . .

At the moment when he has reached the full height of the stage and his figure begins to resemble a cross, the scene suddenly becomes quite dark. The music is expressive and resembles what is happening on the stage.

(p. 131)

It is impossible to convey the lack of specific content in the work as a whole in view of the absence of both specificity and . . . content. We will therefore quote only a few examples of the author's feelings about the interplay of 'yellow sounds':

Second Scene

A blue mist gradually gives way to a harsh white light. As far to the back of the stage as possible there is a large, completely round, bright yellow hill.

The background is violet, fairly light in tone.

The music is harsh and stormy. Towards the end, individual notes have been swallowed up in the tempestuous sound of the whole orchestra. Suddenly there is absolute silence. Pause. . . .

The background becomes a dirty brown. The hill turns to dirty green, and in the very middle of the hill a vague black spot materialises which shows up now distinctly, now obscurely. Each time the spot changes shape, the bright white light is dulled, modulating by sharp gradations to grey. On the left side of the hill there suddenly appears a large white flower. From a distance it looks like a big curved cucumber and grows brighter and brighter. The stem of the flower is long and thin. Only one long, narrow leaf grows sideways out of the stem. Long pause. . . .

Then, *in total silence*, the flower begins slowly to sway from right to left. After a while the leaf starts to do the same thing, but not in time with the flower. Later still, both are swaying but in quite different tempi. The flower shudders and stiffens. The music continues to play. At that moment a group of people enters from stage left; they are wearing long, bright, shapeless garments (one is all blue, another red, a third one is green, and so on – the only missing colour is yellow). The people are holding large white flowers of the same shape as the yellow flower. . . . They speak in many voices and declaim. . . .

Suddenly the whole scene loses all clarity of outline and is plunged into a dull red colour. . . .

Then the total darkness gives way to a bright blue light. . . .

Everything turns grey (all colours disappear!) Only the yellow flower shines more brightly than ever!

Gradually the orchestra enters and drowns out the voices. The music becomes restless, leaping from fortissimo to pianissimo. . . .

The yellow flower shudders convulsively. Then it suddenly disappears. Equally suddenly, all the white flowers turn yellow. . . .

At the end, all the flowers are apparently suffused with blood. The people throw them away and, bunching together, they run up to the forestage. . . . Sudden darkness falls.

Third Scene

At the back of the stage are two reddish-brown cliffs; one of them is sharply pointed, the other rounded and larger than the first cliff. The backdrop is black. Between the cliffs stand the Giants (the characters from the first scene); they whisper silently to each other, first in pairs, then bringing all their heads close together, but with their bodies remaining motionless. In rapid succession they are picked out by beams of light (blue, red, violet, green – changing several times). Then all the beams meet in the middle and merge with each other. Everything is still. The Giants are barely visible. Suddenly all colours vanish. For a moment all is black. Then a pale yellow light spreads over the stage, increasing greatly in intensity until th whole stage is coloured a bright lemon-yellow. As the intensity of light grows, the music fades and then everything starts to darken (this movement recalls a snail withdrawing into its shell).

During this double movement there should be nothing on stage except light.

(pp. 123–5)

And so on and so forth.

The aim of this method – an attempt to show only the abstract 'inner resonances', free of all 'extraneous' subject matter – is obvious.

The method *consciously strives to separate the elements of form and content*: everything objective or thematic is removed, leaving only that which in a *normal work* belongs to the marginal aspects of form. (See Kandinsky's 'programmatic' statements in the same publication.)

It is hard to deny that while such compositions are unclear and confused, they do have a *vaguely disturbing* effect. But . . . that is all.

Paul Gauguin deals in similar 'inner resonances'. In his manuscript *Choses diverses*, there is the following extract headed 'The Genesis of a Picture':

Manao Tupapau – A Spirit of the Dead Awakens
A young Kanak girl is lying on her stomach, showing one side of her face distorted by fear. She is resting on a couch on which are spread a blue *pareo* and a yellow sheet, painted in bright chrome yellow. The violet-purple background is spattered with flowers like electric sparks; beside the couch stands a somewhat strange figure.

Being fascinated by form and movement, in painting them I had no other concern than to depict a naked body. It is no more than a study of a naked body, somewhat immodest, but nonetheless I wanted to create from it a chaste picture, conveying the spirit of the Kanak people, its character and traditions.

Throughout his life a Kanak is intimately connected with his *pareo*; I therefore use it as the bed-covering. The sheet, of a material made from tree-bark, should be yellow, because that colour arouses in the spectator a foreboding of something unexpected, and because it creates an impression of lamp-light; this absolves me from the need to introduce a real lamp. I need a slightly frightening background. The colour violet is entirely suitable for this.

That is the musical side of the picture, shown in heightened tones.

What can a young Kanak girl be doing, naked on a bed, in this somewhat brazen attitude? Preparing for love? That is entirely in character, but it is immodest, and I do not want that. Sleeping? That would imply that the act of love had just finished, and that, too, is immodest. I see only fear. But what kind of fear? Naturally not the fear of Susanna, surprised by the elders; that fear does not exist in Oceania.

The '*tupapau*' (a spirit of the dead) is intended for this purpose. It induces constant fear in the Kanaks. They always light a fire at night. No one walks out of doors when there is no moon; if a lantern is available, they will go out in groups.

Having hit on the idea of the *tupapau*, I adopt it wholeheartedly and make it the fundamental theme of the picture. The motif of the naked body becomes secondary.

What sort of ghost could appear to a Kanak girl? She has never been to the theatre, she does not read novels, so when she thinks of a dead person she necessarily thinks of someone she has already seen. My ghost may be only a little old woman. Her hand is stretched out as though to seize her prey.

It was the need for decoration that prompted me to strew the background with flowers. These are the flowers of the *tupapau*, and they glow as a sign that the ghost is interested in you. This is a Tahitian belief.

The title '*Manao tupapau*' has two meanings: it can mean 'she is thinking about a ghost' or 'a ghost is thinking about her'.

Let us sum up. The musical side: a wavy horizontal line, the combination of orange and blue joined to their derivatives – shades of yellow and violet – and illuminated by greenish sparks. The literary side: the soul of a living woman, drawn to a spirit of the dead. Night and day.

This description of the origins of a picture is written for those who always want to know 'why' and 'because'. Otherwise it is simply a study of a naked body in Oceania.[378]

Here is everything we need. Both the 'musical side of the picture, shown in heightened tones' and the psychological analysis of colours: the 'frightening' violet, and the yellow, which interests us, as being the colour which awakens in the spectator 'a foreboding of something unexpected'.

And this is what another artist, Yuri Bondi,[379] writes about the colour yellow in connection with a production in 1912 of August Strindberg's *The Guilty are Innocent*:

In this production of Strindberg's play there was an attempt to make the set designs and costumes into immediate participants in the play's action.

To this end, every detail of the set had to express something (i.e. had to play a specific role). In many cases, for instance, direct use was made of the capacity of certain colours to exert a particular effect on the spectator. There were also certain leitmotifs, expressed in colours, which revealed a deeper symbolic link between separate moments in the play's action. Thus, beginning with Scene Three, the colour yellow is gradually introduced. It first appears when Maurice and Henriette are sitting in the 'Auberge des Adrets'; the general colour of the whole scene is black; the big stained-glass window has just been hung with black material; a candelabrum with three candles is on the table. Maurice takes off the tie and gloves given to him by Jeanne. The colour yellow appears for the first time. Yellow becomes the motif of Maurice's 'original sin' (in this he is inevitably linked with Jeanne and Adolf).

In Scene Five, after Adolf's exit, when Maurice and Henriette become aware of their crime, a lot of yellow flowers are brought on to the stage. In Scene Seven, Maurice and Henriette are sitting (with anguished expressions) on a bench in an avenue of the Jardin du Luxembourg. Here the whole sky is bright yellow, and the interlaced knots of bare branches, the bench and the figures of Maurice and

Henriette stand out against it in silhouette. . . . It should be said that in general the play was treated on a mystical level.

Here Bondi puts forward the idea of 'the capacity of certain colours to exert a particular effect on the spectator,' making a connection between the colour yellow and sin, the effect of this colour on the psyche. . . . And he speaks of mysticism. . . .

Let us recall in passing that yellow is imbued with similar associations, if not necessarily 'sinful' then still fateful and deadening in, for example, the poetry of Anna Akhmatova: 'The lifeless heat of a yellow chandelier', she writes in her poem 'The White Flock' (1914).[380] Given similar attributes, the colour yellow is also found in poems of different periods in her collection published in 1940:

> This is a song of a final meeting.
> I looked at the darkened house.
> In one bedroom alone were candles burning
> With a yellow, indifferent light.[381]

> A circle of yellow from the lamp . . .
> I hear a rustling.
> Why did you go away?
> I do not understand.[382]

> The faded flag above the customs-house,
> The yellow murk above the city:
> My heart contracts with weariness;
> It hurts me to draw breath . . .[383]

> I cry aloud as though in pain
> From the enigma of your love,
> I'm yellow now, half-paralysed,
> Can scarcely drag my feet along.[384]

But in order to make yellow quite 'terrible' let us quote another example.

There can be few writers who have felt colouring as keenly as did Gogol, and few writers of a later age who felt Gogol as keenly as did Andrei Bely.[385]

In his exhaustive study of Gogol, *Gogol's Mastery* (1934), Bely analyses in detail the transformations in Gogol's chromatic palette throughout the whole of his literary career. And what do we find? The biggest percentage increase is shown in the upward curve of his use of the colour yellow from his early, cheerful *Evenings on a Farm near Dikanka* and *Taras Bulba* to the sinister catastrophe of Volume Two of *Dead Souls*.

In the first group (the first two works named above) the average use of the colour yellow is only 3.5 per cent.

In the second group (the novellas and comedies) it is already 8.5 per cent. The third group (Volume One of *Dead Souls*) has 10.3 per cent. Finally, the second volume of *Dead Souls* shows no less than 12.8 per cent. The corresponding figures for green, the colour closest in frequency to yellow, give the following: 8.6 per cent; 7.7 per cent; 9.6 per cent; and 21.6 per cent. Taken together, the two colours thus constitute more than *a third* of Gogol's entire palette!

On the other hand, of almost equal frequency, strangely enough, is the 12.8 per cent allotted to . . . gold. For, as Bely rightly says:

> The gold of Volume Two is not the gold of tableware vessels, of gilded or brass helmets but the gold of church crosses, marking his increased leanings towards Orthodoxy; here the 'golden' sound of church bells contrasts with the 'scarlet resonance' of Cossack finery; the second volume of *Dead Souls* is sharply differentiated from the spectrum used in *Evenings on a Farm near Dikanka* by a reduction in red and an increase in yellow and gold.
>
> (p. 158)

The 'fateful' connotation of the colour yellow is all the more terrible if we recall that precisely the same gamut of colours dominates in another work that belongs, tragically, to the sunset phase in the life of another artist, in Rembrandt's self-portrait painted at the age of sixty-five.

In order to avoid any accusation of bias in my exposition of this subject, here I shall not quote my own description of the colouring of this picture but will give it in Allen's words from his article on the relationship between aesthetics and psychology: 'The colours here are dark and dim, the brightest being in the centre. There the combination is of dirty green and yellowish-grey, mixed with pale brown; all around everything is almost black.'

This gamut of yellow dissolving into dirty green and pale brown is set off even more sharply by contrast with the bottom part of the picture: 'Only from below are the red tones visible; also muted and overshadowed, thanks to the thickness of the layer of paint and its relatively high chromatic intensity, these tones nevertheless create a clearly expressed contrast to everything else.'[386]

(Here, by the way, I cannot help mentioning the talentless way in which the figure of Rembrandt was presented in the film *Rembrandt*, made by Charles Laughton and Alexander Korda.[387] Although Laughton was accurately costumed and correctly made up, the film gave not the remotest hint of the relation between the *light* and the tragic palette that characterises Rembrandt's *choice of colours* in that self-portrait!) In this instance, I think, it is even more obvious that the colour yellow and probably much of what is ascribed to it owes its reputation partly to the characteristics of its immediate neighbour in the spectrum, green. For green is equally closely associated both with the typical attributes of life – the rippling green of foliage, leaves themselves, and 'greenery' in general – and with the marks of death and decay; mould, slime, the tinge of a corpse's features.

One may pile up as many examples as one likes, but these are already enough to make one ask cautiously: is there really not something fateful and ill-omened in the very nature of the colour yellow? Does this not lie deeper than conventional symbolism and similar customary or chance associations?

For an answer to that question, the best place to look is *a history of the origins of the symbolic connotations of colours*, and to learn from it. One can read all about this subject in the very thorough work of Frédéric Portal, a book published as long ago as 1837 and reprinted in 1938.[388]

Here is what another expert on this question has to say about the 'symbolic connotation' of our chosen colour yellow, but also, most importantly, about the origins of its associations with the ideas of *perfidy, treachery and sin*:

> Christian religious symbolism identified the soul's fusion with God with gold and the colour yellow, yet it also linked them with its opposite – apostasy.
>
> Extrapolated from the sphere of religion into everyday usage, gold and yellow came to signify connubial love – and simultaneously its opposite: adultery, which breaks the bond of marriage.
>
> To the Greeks, the golden apple was the emblem of love and harmony – and simultaneously of its opposite: discord, and all the misfortunes that it brings in its train.
>
> The judgment of Paris is a clear illustration of this. Equally so is the legend of Atalanta stopping to pick up the three golden apples of the Hesperides, as a result of which she is beaten in a race and becomes the prize of the winner.[389]

One characteristic bears witness to the truly ancient origins of these beliefs about colour, namely *the ambivalence* of the connotations ascribed to them. This is due to the fact that in early stages of human cultural development *one and the same concept, symbol or word can simultaneously connote two mutually exclusive opposites*.

In the case of the colour yellow, this is simultaneously 'loving wedlock' and 'adultery'.

In one of the lectures given by the late Academician Marr,[390] which I happened to attend, he cited as an example of this the [Russian] root-syllable *-kon-*, which is simultaneously identified with the concepts of 'end' [*konets*] and . . . beginning [is-*kon*-i]. The same thing may be found in Hebrew, where *kaddish* signifies both 'sacred' and 'unclean' . . . etc., etc. Another instance is even to be found in the passage from Gauguin quoted above, in which he tells us that the phrase *'Manao tupapau'* can mean two things at once: '*she* is thinking *about a ghost*' and '*a ghost* is thinking *about her*'.

Still keeping within the area of the connotations of yellow and gold, we may also note that in accordance with the same law of ambivalence, gold as a symbol of *supreme value* can simultaneously serve as a favourite metaphor to connote . . . filth, in the common parlance not only of Europe but of Russia in, for instance, the term 'gold miner' to denote people of a certain profession.

Thus we see that the first, 'positive' way in which we interpret the brightness of gold or yellow is somehow founded in *direct sensory perception*, and that it is quite naturally linked with certain fairly obvious associations (the sun, gold itself, the stars).

Even Picasso, for instance, writes about the colour yellow in precisely such associative terms: 'There are artists who turn the sun into a yellow spot, but there are others, who, thanks to their artistic skill and wisdom, turn a yellow spot into the sun.'

And as though speaking for all artists of the latter kind, Van Gogh writes in his *Letters*:

> Instead of conveying exactly what I see before me, I treat colour arbitrarily. This is because above all I want to achieve the utmost in expressivity. . . . . Imagine that I am painting the portrait of an artist of my acquaintance. . . . Let us say that he is fair-haired. . . . At first, I will paint him as he is, in the most realistic way, but that is only a beginning. At this stage, the picture is by no means finished. I am only just beginning my arbitrary use of colour: I exaggerate the blondness of his hair, using such colours as orange, chrome yellow, matt lemon-yellow. Instead of the banal wall of the room behind his head, I paint infinity; I make a plain background out of the richest shade of blue that my palette is capable of producing. And thus, by means of this simple juxtaposition, a brightly lit blond head set against a blue background begins to glow mysteriously like a star in the dark depths of the ether.

In the first case, the strongly positive, major-key principle of the colour yellow links it with *the sun* (Picasso); in the second case, *with a star* (Van Gogh).

Let us take one more example of yellow gold, also in the form of blond hair, in this case the ash-blond hair of the poet himself. Yesenin writes:

Don't curse me! That's the way it is!
I'm not the one to haggle over words.
My golden head's grown heavy,
Slumped back. . . .[391]

A sudden bump . . . and from the sledge I'm flung into a snowdrift.
Awake, I see: what's this?! In place of troika swift. . . .
I'm lying bandaged in a bed, in hospital.
Instead of horses, now the jolting of the road
Is me, my sodden bandage beating the hard bed.
The hands upon the clock face, moustache-like, point to ten to two.
The sleepy nurses, bending over me, lean down
And hoarsely whisper: 'Ah, my golden-headed lad,
It is yourself you've poisoned with a bitter venom.'[392]

> No longer does betrayal cause me pain,
> Nor does an easy conquest please me any more –
> That golden hay which grew on my young head
> Is changing colour now to dullest grey.[393]

It is curious that despite the obvious major-key associations of gold in general, here it is three times linked to minor-key themes: lassitude; illness; fading powers. In this case, though, it is not surprising, and it is unconnected with any ambivalence.

For the country-bred Yesenin, gold was associated with the sense of fading through its direct connection with autumn.

THE LOVE OF A HOOLIGAN

> That bright autumnal gold,
> That mop of ash-blond hair –
> It once was my salvation,
> Restless scapegrace that I am.[394]

> I've no regrets, complaints or tears;
> All passions fade, as morning mists from apple-blossom.
> The gold of autumn's now upon me,
> I never shall be young again.[395]

By extrapolating from these thoughts, yellow becomes the colour of a corpse, a skeleton, decay:

THE SONG OF WHEAT

> Uncounted are the years our fields have known
> The morning shimmer of hot August days.
> The sickled wheat lies bound in sheaves,
> Each sheaf laid out in death, a yellow corpse.[396]

And, in another poem:

> Torment me not with coolness or with shade
> And ask me not how old I am in years;
> I'm past my prime, declining fast,
> And withered is my soul, a yellow skeleton.[397]

Or again:

> The loss of love? I fear it not;
> I find delight in other joys.
> For nothing more is left to me
> But yellowing decay and damp.[398]

Finally, yellow becomes generalised as the colour of sadness:

> Once more they're drinking here, they fight and weep
> To the sad and yellow strains of an accordion.[399]

It is not my intention to draw any generalising conclusions about Yesenin's poetry as a whole. All nine examples have been taken from a single collection of his verse – *Sergei Yesenin. Poems 1920–1924*, published by Krug [The Circle].

Let us, however, continue to follow the twists and turns in the connotations of the colour yellow.

Here it must be said that despite such individual instances as those in Yesenin's poetry, a 'negative' interpretation of yellow does not have such an immediately sensory basis as does its 'positive' interpretation, and stems chiefly from being the opposite of the latter.

'The Middle Ages', writes Portal, 'automatically retained those traditions concerning the colour yellow.'

It is interesting, however, that a single shade [of yellow], which in antiquity expressed *both opposites at once*, in the Middle Ages was 'rationalised' and was transferred to the difference between two shades, each of which signified *only one of the two opposites*: 'The Moors distinguished between the opposing symbols, as belonging to two different shades of the colour yellow. Golden yellow signified "wisdom" and "good advice,' while pale yellow symbolised treachery and deceit.'

Even more interesting was the interpretation given by the learned rabbis of medieval Spain:

> The rabbis considered that the forbidden fruit of the tree of knowledge of good and evil was . . . the lemon, contrasting its pale yellow colour and sharp taste with the golden colour and sweetness of the orange – that 'golden apple', according to its Latin designation.

In various forms, that distinction has persisted: 'In heraldry, gold signifies love, constancy and wisdom, while yellow stands for the opposites of those qualities: inconstancy, envy and adultery.'

Hence the French custom of smearing yellow paint on the doors of a traitor's house (under François I, Charles de Bourbon was subjected to this for his treachery). In Spain, the official costume of an executioner had to consist of two colours: yellow and red, of which the yellow signified the treason committed by the convicted man and the red stood for retribution – and so on and so forth.

Such are the 'mystical' sources from which the Symbolists claimed to draw the 'external' connotations of colours and the immutability of their influence on the psyche of anyone perceiving them.

Even so, how tenacious traditions are in this matter! An example of how they have survived is to be found in *argot*, that endlessly lively, witty, graphic Parisian slang. Let us open one of the many glossaries of Parisian *argot* at the word *jaune* (yellow):

> Yellow is the colour of cuckolded husbands. For example, the expression: 'His wife covered him in yellow from head to foot' (*Sa femme le passait en jaune de la tête aux pieds*) means that his wife deceived him. 'A yellow ball' (*un bal jaune*) is a ball of cuckolds.

But there is more. The meaning of treachery is applied more widely: 'c) "To be yellow" = to belong to an anti-socialist trade union.'[400]

This latter connotation is even used in our [Russian] everyday speech. We talk about 'yellow trade unions' and 'the Second, or Yellow, International'. By tradition, as it were, we have kept yellow as the colour of treachery to signify traitors to the working class!

Cousins of Parisian *argot* are the 'cant' or 'slang' of England and America, which treat yellow in exactly the same way. According to *A New Canting Dictionary* published in England in 1725, 'yellow signifies jealousy'. 'He wears yellow breeches' or 'yellow stockings' meant 'He is jealous'.[401]

In American slang, yellow signifies cowardice: 'He is yellow = He is a coward. To become yellow = To be afraid. Yellow-livered = Cowardly. A yellow streak = Unreliability', etc., etc.

These examples are taken from Maurice H. Weesen, *A Dictionary of American Slang*, 1936.

The same use of yellow can be found in American screenplays, as for example in *Transatlantic Merry-go-Round*,[402] a United Artists film with Joseph March and Gerry Conn, in which there is this conversation between the detective McKinney and Ned, who is suspected of murder:

NED   [*excitedly*]. I'm glad he's dead. Yes, I've thought of killing him myself, but I didn't.
McKINNEY Why didn't you?
NED   Because I was yellow, I guess.

Finally, on both sides of the Atlantic yellow signifies something false or faked, e.g. 'yellow stuff = false gold'.[403]

There, too, yellow also indicates venality, for example in the universally used expression 'the yellow press'.

The most interesting aspect, however, of this 'symbolic interpretation' of the colour yellow is the fact that, essentially, it is not yellow as a colour that has determined it.

In antiquity, as we have shown above, this kind of interpretation arose as an automatic opposite to the 'positive resonance' of yellow through its association with the sun. In the Middle Ages, however, this negative 'reputation' was formed primarily from the sum of its *'associative' and not of its narrowly chromatic features.* 'Paleness' as opposed to 'glitter' for the Arabs; 'pallor' instead of 'brightness' for the rabbis. And for the latter, it was primarily determined by associations of taste: the 'treacherous' sour flavour of the lemon as opposed to the sweetness of the orange!

Interestingly enough, this detail has also persisted in *argot*: there is a popular French expression . . . *le rire jaune* ('yellow laughter'). Balzac, in a booklet he published in 1846: *Paris marié – philosophie de la vie conjugale* [Married Paris. The Philosophy of Conjugal Life], entitles the third chapter 'Des risettes jaunes'. Pierre Mac Orlan called one of his novels *Le Rire jaune*. This expression is also listed in *Parisismen*, the *argot* dictionary quoted above. What does it mean?

In Russian its precise equivalent would be *kislaya ulybka* ['a sour smile']. German has the same expression: *Ein saueres Lächeln*. It is interesting that the French use a metaphor derived from *colour*, the Russians and the Germans both traditionally use a metaphor of *taste*. Perhaps the lemon favoured by the Spanish rabbis helps to explain this apparent divergence!

The tradition of giving *two* connotations to the colour yellow according to its associative characteristics was even upheld by Goethe. When he applied it to objects, he linked them through various factors of their outward appearance; psychologically, however, with a new pair of concepts: 'noble' [*edel*] and 'ignoble' [*unedel*], in which we detect not only the element of physical characteristics but of social and class motives!

In the section headed 'The Sensory and Moral Effects of Colour' of his *Farbenlehre* [Theory of Colours] we read the following:

Yellow

765. This is the colour closest to light. . . .

766. In its highest degree of purity it is always of a luminous nature and is distinguished by clarity, cheerfulness, tender charm.

767. In that degree, it is pleasant as adornment or furnishing – be it a dress, a curtain, a wallpaper. Gold in its absolutely unmixed state offers us, especially when glitter is also added to it, a new and sublime conception of that colour; just as undiluted yellow in shining silk or satin, produces an impression of luxury and nobility. . . .

770. If in its pure and luminous state this colour is pleasant, delights us and stands out at full strength in its brightness and nobility, it is on the other hand extremely sensitive and can produce a very unpleasant effect if it is soiled or in some degree inclined towards the negative. The colour of sulphur, therefore, verging on green, contains an element of something unpleasant.

771. Thus an unpleasant effect is produced when a yellow colouring is given to impure or ignoble surfaces, such as cheap cloth or felt, etc., where the colour is unable to manifest itself in its full force. An insignificant or inconspicuous movement can turn the splendid impression of fire or gold into a sense of disgust, and the colour of honour and

joy turns into the colour of shame, revulsion and displeasure. Hence, perhaps, the yellow hats worn by indigent debtors, and even the so-called colour of cuckolds, which is, in fact, nothing but a dirty yellow.

Let us stop here for a moment and briefly add to all this some data about the colour green, the nearest neighbour to yellow. Here the picture is the same. If the positive interpretation of this colour wholly coincides with the primary image that we suggested above, its sinister connotations, too, are not based on direct association but on that same ambivalence.

In the primary interpretation it is a symbol of life, rebirth, spring, hope. In this the Christian, Chinese and Muslim beliefs all agree. According to Islamic belief, Mohammed was always accompanied at the most important and fateful moments in his life by 'angels in green turbans', and a *green flag* became *the standard of the Prophet.*

At the same time, a series of opposing interpretations have also evolved. The colour of hope simultaneously represents hopelessness and despair; in the ancient Greek theatre, the colour of sea-green had a sinister connotation in certain circumstances. That particular shade of green is close to blue, and it is interesting that in the Japanese theatre, where the significance of colours is inextricably linked with certain characters, it is blue that is always given to the sinister figures.

Masaru Kobayashi, the author of a detailed study of 'Kumadori', the make-up and colouring of characters in the Kabuki theatre, wrote to me in a letter of 31 October 1931: 'Kumadori basically uses red and blue. Red is seen as warm and attractive. Blue is the opposite. Blue is the colour of villains and – where supernatural beings are concerned – of ghosts and demons.'

Let us for a moment also return to what Portal wrote about green:

Being the colour of spiritual rebirth and wisdom, at the same time it also signifies moral decadence and insanity. The Swedish theosophist Sweden-borg[405] describes as green the eyes of madmen being tormented in hell. One of the stained-glass windows of Chartres Cathedral shows the temptation of Christ; in it Satan has a green skin and enormous green eyes. . . . In symbolism, the eye denotes the intellect. A person may direct it towards good or evil. Satan and Minerva – representing insanity and wisdom – are both depicted with green eyes.[406]

These are the data. In abstracting the colour green from the green of coloured objects or yellow from objects which happen to be yellow, by elevating these colours into an 'eternal greenness' or into the 'symbolically yellow', a symbolist of that kind resembles the madman of whom Diderot wrote in a letter to Mlle Volland:

A single physical attribute can bring an infinite variety of things to your mind. Take a colour, yellow for instance. Gold is yellow, silk is yellow, marigolds are yellow, bile is yellow, light is yellow, straw is yellow, and heaven knows how many other threads are attached to this yellow one! Madness, dreaming, and the disorder of conversation consist in going from one subject to another by way of a common attribute. The madman does not notice that he is changing subjects. He grasps a piece of shining yellow straw and shouts that he is holding the sun.[407]

That madman is an ultra-Formalist: he sees only the *shape* of the stem and the *yellowness* of its colour; he sees only *line* and *colour*, but he ascribes exclusive significance to the colour and the line, divorced from the *real nature of the object as such.* In this he resembles his ancestor of antiquity, of the ages when people believed in magic; then, too, an exclusive significance was ascribed to the colour yellow *per se.*

Working on that principle, the ancient Hindus, for instance, would use the following method to cure . . . jaundice:

The essence of the magical operation consisted in driving the yellow colour out of the patient and into creatures or objects that were naturally yellow, such as the sun. The other aspect of the method was to dose the patient with something red, transferred from some healthy, full-blooded source, such as a red bull.

Incantations designed to 'banish the jaundice to the sun', etc., were devised on the same principle. Similar curative powers were also ascribed to a certain yellow-coloured species of jackdaw, especially to its large, golden-yellow eyes. It was thought that if a patient stared hard into its eyes and the bird responded by staring back, then that person would be cured: the sickness would be transferred to the bird 'like unto a stream, flowing thither together with the [patient's] glance' (Plutarch). Pliny the Elder also mentions the same bird, and furthermore he ascribes the same property to a certain yellow stone, similar in shade to the colouring of the patient's face. In Greece to this day jaundice is called 'the golden sickness', and its cure is allegedly assisted by a gold amulet or ring, etc., etc. (For details of this belief see Sir James Frazer, *The Golden Bough*.[408])

We should not fall into the erroneous beliefs held either by the madman or the Hindu magician, who saw the great power of the sun or the evil power of the disease in their golden colour alone.

By ascribing such independent and self-sufficient meanings to the colour itself;

by separating the colour *from the concrete phenomenon which actually provides it with the accompanying set of conceptions and associations;*

by seeking absolute correspondence between colour and sound, between colours and emotions;

by abstracting the specificity of a colour as part of a system of supposedly 'perpetually valid' effects produced by colours *per se* –

we will get nowhere, or worse still, we will arrive at the conclusions reached by the French Symbolists of the second half of the 19th century, which Gorky wrote about at the time:

'We should' – they have said – 'link each letter with a certain perception: A – with cold; O – with anguish; U – with fear, and so on. Then we should give those letters colours, as Rimbaud has already done, next give them sounds and generally enliven them so as to make each letter a little living organism. Having done that, we may then begin to combine them into words.'[409]

The drivel that can result from such a method of playing with absolute correspondences is obvious. (Gorky also exposed this in one of his novels, when he had his character Klim Samgin [in *The Life of Klim Samgin*] babble about 'lilac-coloured words'.)

If, however, we take a closer look at the examples of 'tables of absolute correspondence' cited in the preceding article, we shall see that almost invariably their compilers are not in fact talking about the 'absolute' correspondences which they claim to be establishing but about the *images* which they *personally* associate with this or that colour. And it is because of the dissimilarity of all those images that different authors ascribe such a variety of 'meanings' or 'connotations' to one and the same colour.

Rimbaud begins very firmly with a table of absolute correspondences: 'A black, E white . . .' and so on. In the second line, however, he says, 'One day I'll tell the secret story of your birth'. He then proceeds to reveal the 'secret', and not only the secret of how his own *personal* sound associations were formed, but the very principle on which *anyone* may establish correspondences of a similar kind. As a result of his personal experiences and his emotional make-up, Rimbaud associates each vowel with a particular set of images in which a certain colour predominates. And it is not just the colour red ('I red') but: 'I – the purples of spat blood, of fair lips laughing, / In anger or in ecstasy of penitence.' And not just green, but: 'the furrowed calm / That's etched by alchemy upon great scholars' brows.' (Let us recall that for Lafcadio Hearn, a figure similar to Rimbaud's alchemist: 'an elderly Greek, covered in wrinkles' is evoked by a capital 'X', etc., etc.)

Here, colour is no more than a stimulant on the level of a conditioned reflex, which leads to the perception and recall of the entire complex of which it once formed part.

It is generally held that Rimbaud's 'Voyelles' was written under the influence of his memories of a children's 'ABC' primer. Such primers, as we know, are often illustrated with big letters accompanied by a pictorial list of objects or animals whose names begin with that letter, and the poem was most probably composed on such a model. Rimbaud provides similar 'little pictures', which for him are associated with the letter in question. These pictures being differently coloured, certain colours have thus become associated with certain vowels.

Exactly the same process occurs in the minds of the other authors we have quoted.

In general, this 'psychological' interpretation of colours *per se* is a very tricky business. Such interpretation could turn out to be equally fallacious if it should also claim to have 'social' connotations.

How tempting it is, for instance, to see in the washed-out colours of the clothes worn by French aristocrats of the late 18th century and in their powdered wigs an apparent reflection of the 'fading away of vital powers from the upper strata of society, which are about to be superseded by the middling strata and the third estate'. How expressively this idea might seem to be confirmed by the pallid range of gentle (i.e. effete!) shades of colour used in aristocratic costume! In fact, of course, the matter was much more mundane: the initial source of that pale range of colours was . . . the powder which dropped from their powdered white wigs on to the bright colours of their clothes. Hence the notion of the 'paleness' of the range of colours; but then the idea took a 'utilitarian' turn: pallid shades became something like a protective colouring – on the lines of using khaki for army uniforms – upon which the white powder would no longer look out of place or untidy, but simply . . . unnoticeable.

Red and white have long been traditionally regarded as opposites (as in the Wars of the Roses); later this became associated with the espousal of opposing political aims (similar to the concepts of 'left-wing' and 'right-wing' in parliamentary systems). As long ago as the time of the French Revolution, the émigrés and legitimists were the 'Whites'. Red (the favourite colour of Karl Marx and Emile Zola) is usually connected with revolution, though here there have been moments when even this equivalence was 'temporarily disturbed'. Thus towards the end of the French Revolution the surviving members of the aristocracy, i.e. the most fervent representatives of reaction, started the fashion of wearing . . . *red* kerchiefs and scarves. This was the period when the same people adopted a characteristic hair-style, distantly reminiscent of the cropped hair favoured by the Roman emperor Titus, and therefore dubbed 'à la Titus'. It had no 'genetic' connection with Titus at all, apart from the coincidence of its outward resemblance. In fact, it was a symbol of an intransigent counter-revolutionary vendetta, because it reproduced the cropping of the hair which bared the nape of the neck of aristocrats condemned to the guillotine. Hence, too, the red kerchiefs, in memory of the cloths used to mop up the blood of the victims of the guillotine, creating a gruesome kind of relic which shrieked for vengeance on the Revolution.

In the same way, the rest of the spectrum of colours which have gone in and out of fashion has almost always been linked with a *story*, i.e. with a particular episode which linked a colour with a certain association of ideas.

It is worth recalling that in the epoch preceding the [French] Revolution, a particular shade of brown became fashionable at the time of the birth of one of the last Louis, a colour whose name leaves no doubt as to its origin:

caca Dauphin ('Dauphin's shit'). Also well known is the colour that was given the name of *caca d'oie* ('goose-shit'). Equally expressive is the name of the colour 'puce' (from the French *une puce* = a flea). When Marie Antoinette was alive, the fashion that persisted for a time among the aristocracy of wearing scarlet and yellow had little to do with the costume of the Spanish executioner (see above). This combination of colours was called *Cardinal sur la paille* ('Cardinal on the straw') and was intended as a protest against the imprisonment in the Bastille of Cardinal de Rohan in connection with the famous case of 'the queen's necklace'.[410]

These and similar examples, which could be accumulated *ad infinitum*, rest on exactly the same 'anecdotal' basis as do the reasons which make the majority of the above-quoted authors produce their 'special' interpretations of the significance of colours; in our examples, the interpretations are only more obvious and better known thanks to our awareness of the anecdotes which gave rise to them!

On the basis of everything we have recounted, is it possible to deny completely the existence of any correspondences between emotions, timbres, sounds and colours? Correspondences that are common, if not to all mankind, then at least to certain groups of people?

Of course not, even on purely statistical grounds; to say nothing of the special statistical literature on this subject. We can again quote Gorky. In the article cited above in which he discusses Rimbaud's sonnet, Gorky writes:

> It is strange and incomprehensible, but if one recalls that in 1885, according to the research carried out by a famous oculist, 526 of the students of Oxford University ascribed colours to sounds and, in reverse, equated sounds with colours – including the unanimous assertion that the colour brown sounded like a trombone, and green sounded like a hunting-horn – it may well be that Rimbaud's sonnet does indeed have a certain psychological basis.

It is quite obvious that for people in a purely 'psychiatric' condition these phenomena will be even more heightened and marked. Within those limits, the same may also be said about the connection between colours and particular feelings.

Binet's experiments established that impressions which reach the brain via the sensory nerves exert a considerable influence on the nature and strength of the stimuli transmitted by the brain to the motor nerves. Certain sensory impressions have a debilitating or retarding effect on movement (the effects are classified as 'depressive' or 'prohibitory'), while others, on the contrary, add strength, speed and vitality to movement (these effects are called 'dynamic' or 'motive'). Since movement or the stimulation of force is always connected with a sense of pleasure, every living creature strives towards dynamic sensory impressions and, *per contra*, tries to avoid impressions which retard or weaken. The colour red is found to be extremely stimulating. In describing an experiment with a female hysteric suffering from lack of sensation in one half of her body, Binet writes:

> When we put a dynamometer into the insensible hand of Emilie C., the hand was able to exert a pressure of 12 kilograms. We then only had to show her a red circle and immediately the kilogram-equivalent of the unconscious pressure from that hand was doubled.[411]

> Just as the colour red stimulates to activity, so by contrast violet restrains and weakens it.[412]

It is no mere chance that in some cultures violet is exclusively the colour of mourning. 'The sight of that colour has a depressive effect, and the feeling of sadness evoked by it corresponds to the sadness of a depressed spirit', etc. (I quote from Max Nordau, *Fin de Siècle*, Book I.[413])

Goethe ascribes similar qualities to red. Certain considerations make him divide colours into 'active' and 'passive' ('plus' and 'minus'). Linked with this is the popular division of colour tones into the 'hot' and 'cold'. Thus in his pamphlet addressed to the popes of the post-Raphaelite era, William Blake (1757–1827) exclaims: 'Hire idiots to paint cold light and warm shadows.'

If all these data are perhaps still far from sufficient to form a convincing scientific theorem, nevertheless art has used them for a long time and fairly unerringly. Even despite the fact that a normal person reacts less intensely than did Mlle Emilie C. to the sight of red, artists are well aware of the effects produced by their palette. Nor is it by chance that in order to produce the positive hurricane of movement in his [paintings of] peasant women the artist Filipp Malyavin drenches his canvas in a riot of *bright red!*[414]

Once again Goethe has something relevant to say about this. He divides the colour red into three gradations: red, red-yellow and yellow-red. Of course, he ascribes to the colour yellow-red – i.e. the colour that we would call 'tangerine' – the following properties of exerting psychic effect:

> 775. Here the active principle attains its highest energy, and it is no wonder that energetic, healthy and uneducated people find a special pleasure in this colour. A leaning towards it has been observed everywhere among savage peoples. And when children, left to themselves, busy themselves with painting, they do not spare the colours of cinnabar and red lead.

> 776. When you stare at a yellow-red surface, it truly seems as though the colour is penetrating into your eyes. . . .

> Yellow-red material makes animals uneasy and furious. I have also known educated people who cannot tolerate it when, on a dull day, they encounter a person wearing a crimson coat.

As for the subject of our study – the correspondences not only between sounds and emotions, but among each group – I have personally come across a number of curious facts apart from those to be found in scientific or semi-scientific books.

This source is perhaps not quite 'canonical', but is on the other hand very direct and quite logically convincing.

I refer to a certain acquaintance of mine, Comrade S, to whom I was introduced by the late Professor Vygotsky and Professor Luria.[415] Comrade S, unable to find any other application for his unique gifts, worked for several years in the variety theatre, astonishing the public with his feats of memory. Comrade S's unique gifts were due to the fact that, while being a person of absolutely normal development, he had also retained into mature age all the characteristics of primal mental activity which other people lose as they develop intellectually and evolve towards normal, logical patterns of thought. Above all, these characteristics include an unlimited capacity to *remember*, including the ability to visualise in concrete form *the subjects of conversations* (that early form of mental activity characterised by an accumulation of *single facts retained in the memory* normally dies out in parallel with the development of our capacity to *generalise*).

Thus *after a single hearing* Comrade S could remember *any* number of figures or random lists of words. He could then, from memory, 'read them back' from beginning to end; from end to beginning; at intervals of one, two or three; in numerical sequence forwards or backwards, and so on. What is more, if he were to meet you a year or eighteen months later, he could repeat the exercise in the identical sequences and equally unerringly. He could not only reproduce any previous conversation in every detail, but also all the tests of memory to which he had ever been subjected (and the 'lists' sometimes included several hundreds of words!). He also had the 'eidetic' gift, i.e. the ability, not analytically but automatically and precisely, to reproduce any drawing, however complicated (this capability normally begins to be lost as one acquires the capacity *to interpret the relationship between the parts* of a drawing or picture and to relate consciously to the things depicted in them).

I repeat: in this particular case, these characteristics and abilities were retained alongside all the completely normal features of a fully developed mind and intellect.

More than anyone else, of course, Comrade S also possessed the gift of *synaesthesia*, examples of which we have, in part, cited above, and which consists of the ability *to see sounds as colours and to hear colours as sounds*. I had more than one opportunity to talk to him on this subject, and most interesting of all – for which I can personally vouch – is the fact that he does not see *vowels* as being *coloured* but only as *gradations of light*. *Colour only enters with consonants*. To me, this picture sounds much more convincing than all those lists we quoted earlier.

It may be said that purely physical correspondences between sonic and chromatic oscillations undoubtedly exist.

But it can also be said, equally categorically, that *such facts, expressible in terms of pure physics, have very little in common with art.*

If an absolute correspondence between colour and [musical] tone does exist – and it probably does – then even the application of such 'absolute' correspondences would, at best, lead our film-makers to the same eccentric results as those achieved by a goldsmith described by Giovanni da Udine:

> A goldsmith of my acquaintance – very intelligent, highly educated, but obviously with little artistic gift – made it his aim to produce at all costs objects that were *original*: devoid of creative inventiveness, he decided that all natural forms were beautiful (which, by the way, is completely untrue): in his work he therefore limited himself to the exact reproduction of the curves and lines which result from various natural phenomena when they are analysed mechanically in a physics laboratory. Thus he would take as his model the curves of light produced on a screen by the use of tuning forks with mirrors attached to their ends and vibrating in planes perpendicular to one another (a device used in physics to study the relative complexity of musical intervals). He would copy, for instance on a belt-buckle, the curves formed by [the vibrations of] two notes an octave apart, and naturally no one could convince him that although the consonance of octaves in music comprises a very simple chord, the belt-buckle that he had invented could not evoke visually the same impression as that produced by an octave. Or he would make a brooch by cutting out, in gold, the characteristic curve produced by the notes of two tuning forks separated by the interval of a ninth, and he was quite convinced that he had created in a solid medium something equivalent to what Debussy had introduced into music.[416]

In art it is not *absolute* correspondences that are decisive, but those which result in *willed images* that are dictated by the *graphic system* of the work in question.

This problem cannot and never will be solved by drawing up an immutable table of colour symbolism, but *the emotional interpretation and the efficacy of colour will always arise within the actual making of the chromatic imagery of a work, in the process itself of forming that imagery, in the vital movement of the work as a whole.*

Even in a *black-and-white* film, a single colour tone can not only represent a *wholly specific* graphic 'valeur' within a particular film, but at the same time can also be one that is completely *different*, depending on the graphic interpretation that *has been ascribed to that tone by the general graphic system of other, different films.*

It is sufficient to compare the thematic use of black and white in two films, *The Old and the New* and *Alexander Nevsky.* In the former, black was associated with everything reactionary, criminal and backward, while white represented joy, life, new forms of agricultural practice. In the latter, along with the cloaks of the Teutonic knights, white was chosen to symbolise the themes of cruelty, villainy and death (this greatly surprised people abroad and was commented on by the foreign press); the colour black, reflecting the costume of the Russian troops, stood for a positive theme: heroism and patriotism.

I cited an example of the *graphic relativity of colour* a long time ago, when I was analysing the question of the *relativity of the montage image in general*:

In fact, even if we have a *series* of montage shots:

    1) a grey-haired old man,
    2) a grey-haired old woman,
    3) a white horse,
    4) a snow-covered roof,

it is far from clear whether this series works on 'old age' or 'whiteness'.

This series might continue for a very long time before we finally come upon the signpost shot that immediately 'christens' the whole series with a particular 'sign'.

That is why it is better to place this kind of indicator as near as possible to the beginning (in 'orthodox' construction). Sometimes it is even necessary to do this . . . with an intertitle.[417]

This means that *we do not submit ourselves to any 'immanent laws' of absolute 'connotations' and relationships between colours and sounds, or to any 'absolute' correspondences between them and specific emotions, but that we prescribe to colours and sounds the task of serving the purposes and emotions that we find necessary.*

Of course, a 'conventional' interpretation can function as a stimulus, and even a very effective one, when structuring the colour imagery of a drama. The guiding principle, however, should not be the 'general idea' of absolute correspondence, but the consistency within the work of a particular tonal-chromatic key, which in the course of the piece as a whole prescribes the image structure of the entire work in strict concordance with its subject matter and the idea behind it.

III

In the first section of our discussion of vertical montage we wrote that combining sound and pictures complicates montage by the need to solve a quite new compositional problem. This problem lies in finding *a key to the congruence* between a *musical* sequence and a *pictorial* sequence; congruence of a kind that will allow us to *combine 'vertically', i.e. simultaneously*, the progression of each phrase of music in parallel with the progression of the graphic units of depiction, the shots; and this must be done within conditions that must be quite as strictly observed as those within which we *combine pictures 'horizontally', i.e. sequentially*, shot by shot in silent montage or phrase by phrase in the development of a theme in music. We have analysed this problem in terms of the general principles of correspondence between visual and auditory phenomena, and we have analysed the problems of the relationship of visual and auditory phenomena to particular emotions.

For this purpose we also dealt with the question of correspondence between music and colour, and here we came to the conclusion that the presence of 'absolute' equivalents between sound and colour – if they exist in nature – do not play a decisive role in a work of art, although they can sometimes be useful in an 'auxiliary' capacity.

Here, the decisive role is played by the *graphic structure* of the work, which does not so much *make use* of existent or non-existent correspondences as *establish* graphically those correspondences which *the idea and the theme of the given work* prescribe for its graphic structure.

Now let us leave *general principles* and turn to the *actual methods* by which correspondences between depiction and music are set up. These methods will be the same for all cases; it does not matter whether the composer writes music to fit random sequences or sequences that have already been edited into either a trial or a final montage, or whether the job is done in reverse and the director edits the filmed material to fit a particular piece of music that has already been written and recorded on the soundtrack.

It should be said that in *Alexander Nevsky* literally every possible permutation of these methods is to be found. There are scenes in which the pictures were edited in accordance with music pre-recorded on the sound-track. There are scenes where the music was entirely written to fit a fully completed visual montage; and there are scenes in which every available intermediate method was used. Finally, there are also some cases that have become almost legendary, such as, for instance, the scene with the pipes and tabors played by the Russian troops: I was totally unable to explain in detail to Sergei Prokofiev exactly what I wanted to 'see' in sound for that scene. Finally, losing my temper, I ordered up a selection of the appropriate property instruments (i.e. soundless ones) and made the actors visually 'play' on them what I wanted; I filmed them doing this, showed it to Prokofiev and . . . almost instantly he produced for me an exact 'musical equivalent' of the visual image of those pipers and drummers which I had shown him.

The same happened with the horns of the Teutonic knights. Similarly, in a number of instances pre-recorded pieces of music sometimes prompted us to find graphically expressive solutions which neither he nor I had foreseen. Many of these coincided so well with the 'inner resonance' linking music and pictures that they now seem to have been the most carefully 'pre-arranged' combinations (for instance, the scene in which Vaska and Gavrila Olexich embrace each other in farewell, which was quite unexpectedly set against the complex musical theme of the galloping knights, and so on).

All of this goes to confirm the fact that the 'method' I am describing was tested on the film 'all ways out', i.e. through the use of every possible manner of application.

What is the method of creating audiovisual combinations?

The naïve view of this question is to search for adequacy between the depictive elements of the music and the pictures themselves.

This approach is simple-minded and pointless, and will inevitably lead to the kind of embarrassment described by Pyotr Pavlenko in his novel *In the East*:

'What is that?' she asked.

'My ideas about music. I once tried to reduce all the music I heard to a system, in an attempt to understand the logic of music before understanding the music itself. I made friends with an old man, a cinema pianist, an ex-colonel of the Guards. "What does that music signify?" "Bravery," the old man would say. "Why bravery?" I would ask. He shrugged his shoulders. "C major, A flat major, F flat major are firm, decisive, noble," he explained to me. I started to visit the old man before the film showings began, gave him cigarettes from my rations – I don't smoke – and I would ask him how to understand music. . . .

'On old sweet-wrappers he wrote down for me the titles of the works he used to play and the corresponding emotions they conjured up. We can read them in this notebook of mine and have a good laugh at them.' . . .

She read the following:

'We Walk to the Bright Aragva': the maidens' song from Rubinstein's 'The Demon' = *sadness*.

Schumann. Opus 12, No. 2 = *emotional fervour*.

Offenbach. Barcarolle from *The Tales of Hoffmann* = *love*.[418]

Tchaikovsky. Overture to *The Queen of Spades* = *illness*.

She closed the notebook.

'I can't go on,' she said. 'I'm ashamed of you.'

He blushed, but did not give in.

'You see, I wrote and wrote, listened and noted down what he said, compared and checked. One day the old man was inspired, and played something great, joyous, invigorating – and I guessed that this signified: rapture. He finished playing and tossed me a note. The piece turned out to be Saint-Saëns' *Danse Macabre* – a theme of fear and horror. And I realised three things: firstly, that my colonel didn't understand a damn' thing about music; secondly, that he was as daft as a brush. . . .'[419]

Definitions like those given in this passage are not only absurd in themselves, but when expressed in those terms, i.e. *in a narrowly 'pictorial' interpretation of music*, they will also inevitably lead to the most crass forms of visual illustration, if this sort of thing is what is needed: 'love' – a couple embrace; 'illness' – an old woman with a hot-water bottle on her stomach.

And if Offenbach's 'Barcarolle' is supposed to accompany a series of views of Venice, and the Overture to *The Queen of Spades* to go with panoramas of St Petersburg, what then? In those cases, neither the 'picture' of two lovers nor the 'picture' of an old woman are of any use at all.

On the other hand, however, the 'ebb and flow' with which the waters of the Venetian scene might be suggested, the interplay of *receding and approaching* reflections of lamps on canals, and any other appropriate scenes, none of those would seem to be copying what is 'depicted' in this music, but would have arisen in response to an *awareness of the inner movement* of the barcarolle.

There can be any number of such 'partial' visual responses to the pulse of the barcarolle; they will all echo it and the same perception will underlie all of them, up to and including Walt Disney's visualisation of it, a work of genius which depicts . . . a peacock, the iridescence of its tail shimmering 'in time' to the music as the peacock looks at its reflection mirrored in a pond, seeing in it an exactly similar peacock with an iridescent tail, only upside-down.

The ebb and flow, the waves, the reflections and iridescence with which Venetian scenes might be shown to this music have also been used in Disney's conception, and in the same relationship to the music: the tail and its reflection 'ebb and flow' as the tail approaches or moves away from the surface of the pond, as the tail itself waves and shimmers, and so on.

Here the most important thing is that this treatment by no means contradicts . . . the 'love' theme of the barcarolle. It is merely that in this case, instead of a 'depiction' of two lovers, a characteristic feature of lovers' behaviour has been taken, namely the way they alternately come close to each other and then move away again. Furthermore, this has not been used merely pictorially but as *the basis of the total composition*, which pervades both Disney's animated drawings and the movement of the music (I have written about this compositional principle in my article 'On the Structure of Things'[420]).

J.S. Bach, incidentally, uses exactly the same method of structuring his music in his attempts to convey, with the means available to him, the basic movement that characterises a theme. In his book on J.S. Bach, Albert Schweitzer cites countless musical quotations to illustrate this, even including the curious instance that occurs in his Cantata No. 121, 'Christum wir sollen loben schon' ('Let us now praise'): the author of the text writes at one point 'The infant leaped for joy in His mother's womb', and here the music represents . . . a prolonged convulsive movement![421]

In their narrowly 'pictorial' aspects, music and pictures really are not congruent. If it is at all possible to speak of any genuine, profound correspondence and congruence between them, it can only be a correspondence between fundamental elements of the *movement* of music and pictures, i.e. between compositional and structural elements, because 'pictorial' correspondences between one and the other, indeed the very 'pictures' in musical 'depiction' as such, are mostly perceived differently by every individual and are so subjective in nature that they cannot be made to fit into any strict methodological 'scheme'. The passage quoted above bears eloquent witness to this.

For our purposes, it is only possible to talk about what is really 'commensurable', *i.e. about movement*, which is fundamental both to a passage of music and to the structural imperatives of a pictorial sequence. This being so, an understanding of the laws of structure, of the process and rhythms by which both music and visual depiction come into being and develop, will give us the only firm foundation for establishing a unity between them.

This is not only because movement, understood in this way, is capable of being 'materialised' through the specific features of *any* art form, but chiefly because a structural law such as this is above all the first step towards expressing a theme through the image and form of a work, regardless of which medium is used to express it.

That, quite obviously, is how the matter stands in theory. But how is it to be achieved in practice?

In practice, the way to achieve it is even clearer and simpler; and the practice is based on the following.

Any of us may say that a particular piece of music is 'transparent'; that another piece 'leaps around'; that a third has 'strict, clear lines'; another has 'blurred outlines'. This is because when we listen to music most of us 'visualise' certain graphic images; these may be vague or clear, objective or abstract, but in one way or another they respond – or correspond – to that music *as we perceive it.*

In rare cases, what is visualised is neither objective nor mobile but an 'abstract' notion, such as that recorded in someone's recollections of the French composer Charles Gounod: one day at a concert where Gounod was listening to Bach he suddenly said thoughtfully: 'I think there is something octagonal about this music.'

This remark will sound less unexpected if we realise that Gounod's father was a distinguished painter and that his mother was a talented musician. As a child he was exposed to strong impressions of the two arts practised by his parents, which – as he writes in his memoirs – gave him almost equal chances of mastering either painting or music.

Incidentally, this capacity to visualise geometric images is probably not, after all, such a rarity. Tolstoy, for instance, makes Natasha Rostov's imagination visualise a notably complex subject – an entire human being – as a geometric figure: Natasha imagines Pierre Bezukhov as a 'blue square'.[422]

Another great realist – Dickens – sometimes sees the figures of his characters 'geometrically', and on occasions it is precisely through this geometrism that he reveals his characters in their full depth. Let us recall Mr Gradgrind in *Hard Times*, that man of chapter and verse, of figures, and facts, facts, facts:

> The scene of action was a classroom with a plain, bare, monotonous vaulted ceiling, and the *square* finger of the speaker added weight to his words as he stressed each maxim with a tap on the teacher's sleeve. The speaker's upright stance, his *rectangular* clothes, *rectangular* legs, *rectangular* shoulders – everything, down to the cravat which encircled his throat

in a tight knot like one of those obstinate facts which he literally personified, all contributed to that weight: 'In this life we need only facts, sir, nothing but facts. . . .'

(Book I, Chapter 1)

It is shown particular clearly by the fact that each of us – with more or less precision and, of course, with any number of individual variations – is capable of 'depicting', with a movement of our hand, the impression which a certain detail of a piece of music makes on us.

Exactly the same thing also occurs in poetry, where the rhythm and scansion shape themselves in the poet's mind above all as images of movement. . . .[423]

This has been expressed best of all from the poet's personal viewpoint, of course, by Pushkin in the famous ironic sixth stanza of his poem 'The Little House at Kolomna':

> I must confess that in pentameters
> Caesura's best put in the second foot.
> If not, the verse will either jolt or bump,
> And though I'm lying on this well-sprung couch,
> I feel I'm being flung from side to side,
> O'er frozen ploughland, in a peasant's cart.

And it is in the works of Pushkin that we shall, of course, also find the finest examples of the transposition of natural movement into verse.

The breaking of a wave. The Russian language has no word which contains the whole picture of the curving rise and crashing fall of a breaking wave. German is more fortunate: it has the composite word *Wellenschlag*, which exactly conveys that dynamic picture. Somewhere (I think it is in *The Three Musketeers*) Dumas *père* bemoans the fact that the French language is forced to write 'the sound of water hitting a surface', and lacks that brief and expressive English word 'splash'.

On the other hand, there can scarcely be another literature that can show examples of such brilliant transpositions of the dynamics of a breaking wave into the rhythm of verse than those which Pushkin created in six lines of his poem 'The Bronze Horseman' [which describes the flood that inundated St Petersburg in 1824]. After the famous couplet:

> And, Triton-like, the city swam
> Waist-high in flooding waters wild

the passage in question reads thus:

> Besieged! Assaulted! Angry waves,
> Like thieves, break panes. Loose boats adrift
> Smash windows with their swinging sterns.
> Amid the foam float broken troughs,
> Remains of cottages, planks, roofs,

> The goods by prudent merchants stored . . .[424]

and so on until:

> They float along the streets!
> The people . . .*

From all that has been said above there is one very simple deduction to be drawn about the methodology of making audiovisual combinations; it is:

to be able to grasp the movement of a given piece of music and take the 'trace' of that movement, i.e. its line or shape, as the basis of a pictorial composition which should correspond to that music.

This applies to those cases where the graphic composition is structured to fit the music (the most obvious example of this is in the movement and the *scenery designs* for a ballet).

For cases where there is an existing series of filmed shots which all have equal rights'† as to the position they will occupy but are different in composition, then these will be fitted to the music in accordance with the above-stated principle.

The same thing has to be done by the composer, when he is faced with an edited episode or scene: he has to understand the montage movement in the whole system of montage sequences, as well as the intra-shot movement. He must then take these as the structural basis of his musical images.

For music – the 'gesture' which underlies both sound and picture – is not something abstract and unrelated to the theme, but is the most generalised expressive embodiment of the image through which the theme is articulated.

'Striving upwards', 'spreading', 'fragmented', 'well-balanced', 'stumbling', 'smoothly deployed', 'flexible', 'zigzagging': these are some of the epithets applicable to movement in the simplest abstract and generalised cases. But, as we shall see in our example, any one of these qualities can also encompass not only a dynamic element but also a whole set of essential connotations which characterise the image seeking to be given form. Sometimes the primary embodiment of the future image will be a *tune*. But that does not alter anything, because a tune is *a movement of the voice* deriving from the same kind of *emotive movement* that is a vital factor in delineating the image graphically.

That is precisely why it is as easy to depict a tune visually by gesture as it is by the movement of the music itself, which is based on the vocal intonation, gesture and movement of the person performing it. This question

---

*In another place I will give an exact 'reconstruction' of the flow, breaking and ebb of a wave in this passage.

†They have 'equal rights' in the sense that as far as the plot is concerned they can be placed in any sequence. Just such are the twelve shots of the 'scene of waiting' which we analyse below. From the standpoint of plot and narrative, all these shots could have been put in *any order*. Their eventual sequence (which was, as we shall see, quite strictly justified) was composed on purely expressive and emotional grounds.

will be dealt with in greater detail elsewhere.

Here it only remains to make a qualification concerning the fact that *pure linearity*, i.e. a narrowly 'graphic' structuring of the composition, is *only one of many ways* of establishing the nature of movement.

The 'line', i.e. the path of movement, in the different circumstances that pertain to various forms of the graphic arts, can also be structured by means that are not only purely linear. Movement can be structured with equal success, for instance, by means of progression through a sequence of shades of light or the colour structure of a picture, or it may be revealed by the successive interplay of mass and space.

With Rembrandt, a 'line of movement' of this kind would be produced by the movement in the varying density of his glimmering chiaroscuro.

Delacroix would have perceived it in the way the eye slides over piled-up masses of shapes. It is, after all, in his *Journals* that we find comments on Leonardo da Vinci's sketches, which thrilled him because he finds in them a renaissance of what he calls 'le système antique du dessin par boules' [the method of drawing by means of balls (i.e. masses) used in antiquity].[425]

This induced Balzac, whose ideas were very close to Delacroix's theories, to state through the mouths of artists in his novels that the human body 'cannot be reduced to lines', and that, strictly speaking, 'Il n'y a pas de lignes dans la nature, où tout est plein' [there are no lines in nature, where everything is filled (i.e. rounded)].[426]

One might oppose this with the furious philippic composed by that enthusiast for 'outline', William Blake (1757–1827), with its pathetic exclamation: 'O dear Mother Outline! O wisdom most sage!' and his bitter polemic against Sir Joshua Reynolds, who allegedly lacked sufficient respect for the rigorous demands of outline.

In spite of all this, it is quite obvious that the dispute here is not about *the fact of movement* within the work itself but merely about the *means of embodying* that movement which are characteristic of different artists.

With Dürer, movement might be said to be expressed *through the alteration of the mathematically precise formulae that he used for the proportions of his figures*. In just the same way with, let's say, Michelangelo, the rhythm of his works would break out in his dynamic modelling of twisting and swelling clusters of muscles, reproducing not only the attitudes and movements of the sculpted figures but above all the movement of the artist's own fiery emotions.*

With Piranesi a no less temperamental kind of movement would be traceable through the thrusting lines and the alternation of . . . 'countermasses', the gaps between the arches and vaults of his 'Prisons'; these interweave their

---

*Let us recall what Gogol wrote about him: 'Michelangelo, for whom the body served only to show the strength of the soul, its suffering, its shrieks of protest, its dark underside – in whose work realistic depiction is destroyed, the outline of a man acquires gigantic proportions because it only serves as clothing for an idea, as an emblem; in which was represented not a man but only – his passions. . . .'[427]

line of movement with flights of endless stairs, whose *linear fugue* cuts across the structure of a *spatial fugue*.

Van Gogh embodies the same thing in the frenzied linear curve . . . of his running brushstrokes, as though thereby welding together the movement of a line and a brilliant explosion of colour. In this he was doing in his own way the same thing that Cézanne, in a different individual mode, had in mind when he wrote: 'Le dessin et la couleur ne sont pas distincts' [Drawing and colour are not distinct], and so on.

What's more, any artist of the nineteenth-century Russian Wanderers school was aware of a similar 'line'. In their work that line is not created from graphic, but . . . from purely 'acted' or narrative elements. Such pictures as Makovsky's *The Failure of the Bank* and Perov's *Nikita Pustosvyat* are structured in that way.[428]

At the same time we must bear in mind that where cinema is concerned, looking for 'correspondences' between picture and music is far from being confined to one of these 'lines' or to a combination of several of them. Not only are the elements of form common to all, but the same imperative also governs the cinema's selection of *people and their looks, objects, behaviour, actions and whole episodes* from all the equally available possibilities in a given situation.

Thus in the days when film was still silent we used to talk about the 'orchestration' of type-cast faces (for instance, in the rising curve of grief as conveyed by close-ups in the scene of 'mourning for Vakulinchuk' [in *The Battleship Potemkin*] etc.).

In sound film, too, there can be what I have called 'played action' [*igrovoe deistvie*], e.g. the *farewell embrace* of Vaska and Gavrilo Olexich in *Alexander Nevsky*, coinciding with *precisely* that passage in the music; but the close-ups of the knights' helmets cannot appear before that particular moment in the attack where they *are* cut in, because it is only at that point that the music begins to represent what has so far been impossible to express in the long shots and medium shots of the attack, and which requires rhythmic percussion, galloping close-ups, etc.

Along with all this we cannot deny the fact that the *most striking* and immediate feature that will be the first to seize our attention will be, of course, an example of coincidence between *a movement of the music and a graphic or linear movement* in the graphic composition of a shot, because the shape-outline-line element is in itself the most precise expression of the concept of movement.

Let us, however, turn our attention to the actual subject of our analysis and, using one passage from the film *Alexander Nevsky*, let us try to show how and why a certain set of shots placed in a particular sequence and cut to those specific lengths was linked to a certain piece of music in just *that way* and *not otherwise*.

We shall take this opportunity to reveal the 'secret' of the sequence of those *vertical correspondences*, which link the music step by step with the shots through the *mediation of a single gesture* that is fundamental to the movement of both the music and the pictures.

This example is curious, in so far as in this instance the music was written to fit a fully completed sequence of visual montage. The graphic movement of the theme in this episode was brilliantly grasped by the composer – to such a degree that the musical movement was also grasped by the director in the next scene of the attack, in which the pictorial sequence was 'attached' to music that had been written in advance.

The method of establishing an organic link through movement was the same in both cases, and therefore the order in which we set about establishing the audiovisual combinations made no difference to the method.

The audiovisual aspect of *Alexander Nevsky* achieved its most integrated fusion in the scenes of 'the battle on the ice', and in particular in 'the charge of the knights' and in the episode in which the knights form their 'defensive square'. This is largely due to the fact that of all the scenes in *Alexander Nevsky* the attack was one of the most impressive and memorable. The method of creating audiovisual combinations is the same throughout all the scenes in the film. For purposes of analysis, therefore, we shall choose the kind of scene that is easiest to convey on the printed page, namely one in which the whole sequence was composed of *still* shots; in other word, those which can be most conveniently reproduced here. It was easy to find a sequence of this type; furthermore, it is one of those which was most strictly composed in accordance with the demands of the [audiovisual] medium.

The sequence comprises the twelve shots of that 'dawn, full of anxious expectation', which preceded the start of the attack, after a night of anxiety, the eve of the 'battle on the ice'. The narrative content of these twelve shots is all one: on the shore of the frozen Lake Peipus, Alexander on top of Raven Rock and the Russian troops at its foot are staring into the distance and waiting for the enemy to advance.

The columns shown on the diagram (see insert) demonstrate the sequence of shots and music through which this particular situation was expressed. (The reasons why the pictures and the bars of music were juxtaposed in precisely this way will become clear in the process of analysis: it is connected with the essential inner articulation of music and pictures.)

Imagine that these twelve shots and seventeen bars of music are unrolling in front of us, and try to remember, as though they were our first impressions, which of these audiovisual combinations seized our attention most strongly.

The first and most impressive is the combination of shot III and shot IV. Here we must not consider the impact made by the pictures alone, but the total *audiovisual impression* made by the juxtaposition of these two shots combined with the music that accompanies the passage of these pictures across the screen. The music which corresponds to shots III and IV is in bars 5, 6, 7 and 8.

That this is the most impressive audiovisual pair is easily proved if we play the corresponding four bars of music alone. This was confirmed when analysing this extract in an auditorium, for example in the student auditorium of the State Institute of Cinematography, where I discussed the scene in question.

Let us take those four bars and try to describe in the air, with our hand, the line of movement dictated to us by the movement of the music.

The first chord is perceived as something like a point of 'take-off'.

The following five crochets, in a rising series, are naturally read as the gradations of a line of rising tension. Therefore we will draw it not just as a line rising straight upwards but a slightly arching curve.

We will draw this in Fig. 13.3 as the curve 'a–b'. In the given context, the next chord (at the start of bar 7) with its preceding sharply accented

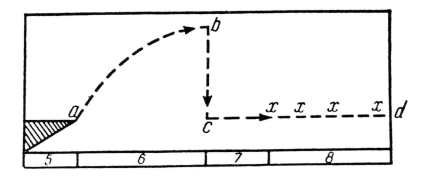

Fig. 13.3

semiquaver, produces on one the impression of a sharp fall, shown on the figure as 'b–c'.*

The next phrase, of one note repeated four times between quaver rests, is naturally interpreted as a *horizontal line*, on which the quavers themselves are represented by the accented points shown as 'xxxx' on the line 'cmd'. This, too, we will draw on the figure and put that diagram of the musical movement 'a–b–c–d' under the corresponding passage in the musical score.

Now imagine *a diagram of our eye movements* along the main lines of shots III and IV which 'respond' to that music. Let us repeat this by a movement of our hand. This will give us the following diagram, the *gesture* representing the movement inherent in the linear composition of these two shots (Fig. 13.4).

The line 'a–b' moves *upwards in a rising 'arc'*: that 'arc' is traced by the outline of the dark clouds hanging above the lower, brighter part of the sky.

The line 'b–c' is the eye dropping sharply downward, from the upper edge of shot III almost to the bottom edge of shot IV, the maximum possible

---

*In terms of melody, the perception of 'falling' is produced by the drop from B to G sharp.

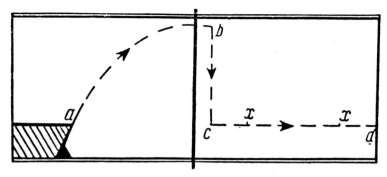

Fig. 13.4

distance that the eye can move vertically downward.

The traverse from 'c' to 'd' – *along a flat horizontal line*, a movement which neither rises nor falls – is twice interrupted by the points of the flags which stand out above the horizontal outline of the troops.

Now let us compare the two diagrams. What does this show? That the two patterns of movement are identical, i.e. *the movement of the music and the movement of the eye over the lines of the graphic composition coincide.*

In other words, *the same gesture, common to both, is the basis of both the musical and the graphic structures.*

Apart from that, I think the gesture was also correctly devised to correspond to the emotional movement. The rising tremolo passage for the cellos in the key of C minor at this point clearly reflects the rising nervous tension and the growing intentness with which we watch [the scene in shot III]. The first chord in bar 7 makes us, as it were, tear our gaze away from it. The succession of quavers on one note then draws, as it were, the motionless horizontal line of the troops: the line of these troops is spread across the whole front, creating a feeling which, after the single shot V, again starts to grow into a similar feeling of tension in shot VI, and so on.

It is noteworthy that shot IV, corresponding to bars 7 and 8, has two little flags in it, while the music has four quavers. The eye, as it were, passes twice across the two flags and the line [of troops] appears twice as wide as it is actually seen in the shot. Moving from left to right, the eye 'registers' the quavers as flags, and the two of them lead our perception out of the frame to the right, where our imagination pictures a continuation of the line of troops.

The primary reason why precisely these two shots grip our attention is now clear: the graphic elements of movement and the movement of the music coincide totally, and, what is more, with the utmost clarity.

Let us proceed further, however, and try to work out what are the 'secondary' reasons why the shots hold our attention. A second 'viewing' of the shots before us will then fix our attention on shots I, VI–VII and IX–X.

If we examine the music for these latter shots, we shall see that in structure they are identical with the music for shot III. (Altogether the whole musical score for this scene consists of two successive two-bar phrases, 'A' and 'B', which alternate in a particular fashion. The only difference is that while belonging *structurally* to the same phrase 'A', they are in different keys: for shots I and III the phrases are in C minor, and for shots VI–VII and IX–X the key changes to C sharp. The narrative significance of this key shift will be indicated below, in the analysis of shot V.)

Thus for shots I, VI–VII and IX–X the music will have exactly the same pattern of movement as for shot III (see Fig. 13.3).

But let us look at the shots themselves. Do we again find in them the same pattern of linear composition, in which a single movement 'welded' shots III and IV together, along with their music (bars 5, 6, 7 and 8)?

No.

Yet the sense of audiovisual unity is just as strong.

Why is this so?

The fact is that the pattern of movement [in shots III and IV] can be expressed *not only* through the line 'a–b–c', but also *by using any other means* of graphic expression. Having mentioned this in the introductory section, we are now dealing with just such a case.

Let us follow this through all three new examples – shots I, VI–VII and IX–X.

I. Photography alone cannot convey the full perception of shot I, because this shot *arises out of darkness*: at first a shadowy group of men emerges from the left with a banner; then the sky gradually lightens, and we can discern a few patches of ragged cloud.

As we see, the movement within this shot is almost identical with the movement that we drew for shot III. The only difference is that this is not a linear movement but one caused by the gradual brightening of the shot, i.e. the movement of a growing intensity of light. Accordingly that 'starting point' 'a', which in shot III corresponded to the initial chord, is here the *darkest* patch, which at moments shows up prominently as the 'floor' or 'bottom line' of darkness from which the 'countdown' of the shot's gradual brightening begins. Here the 'arching' effect takes shape as a sequence of frames, in which each frame is brighter than the previous one. The *arching* is expressed by the curve of the shot's gradual brightening. As the whole shot emerges from darkness, the darkest (central) patch of sky will emerge first of all, then the brightest (upper) patch, then the mottled fleecy clouds to right and left in the transition to the overall bright tone of the sky.

We see that here, too, the same curve of movement has been observed even in detail, though its medium is *not the outline* of the graphic composition but *the tonality of light*. Thus shot I repeats the same basic curving *gesture*, but in this case *tonally*.

II. Now let us examine the next couple of shots, VI–VII. We shall take them together as a pair, because whereas two bars of the music's phrase A in shot I are given wholly to *one picture*, in this instance phrase A1 (identical to phrase A but in a new key) is given to almost *two whole shots*: shots VI and VII. (See the overall table of correspondences between pictures and bars of music.)

Let us test this through our perception of the music.

On the left-hand side of shot VI stand four soldiers with shields and with pikes held upright. Behind and to the left of them can be seen the edge of a cliff. On the right, the ranks of troops stretch into the distance.

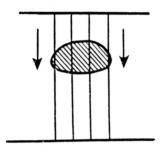

I do not know how it affects other people, but the subjective effect on me of the first chord of bar 10 is always to produce the impression of a ponderous mass of sound which is, as it were, sliding down the line of pikes from the top (see Fig. 13.5).

(It was due to precisely this perception that I put *this* shot in *this* place in the montage.)

Fig. 13.5

Behind this group of four pikemen is the line of troops, receding towards the distant right-hand edge of the frame. The biggest 'step' will be the move from shot VI as a whole to . . . shot VII, which continues the line of troops in the same left-to-right direction into the distance. Here the soldiers are shown in a slightly closer shot, but the overall 'stepped' movement into the distance continues the same movement as in shot VI. What is more, this shot also contains one other very abrupt 'step': the white space of completely empty horizon in the right-hand quarter of shot VII. That space breaks the line of troops and continues the movement into a new area: the line of the horizon, at which the heavens touch the frozen surface of Lake Peipus.

Let us make a schematic drawing of that basic movement by 'steps' through the two shots.

Here the troops are drawn up, as it were, in *echelons*, numbered 1, 2, 3 and 4 and curving from left to right into the distance; this starts with the four figures functioning as the *initial plane*, which coincides with the plane of the screen and from which the *movement into the distance* begins. If we now imagine a line joining those echelons, we get a certain curve 'a, 1, 2, 3, 4'. What sort of a curve is this? If we look at it carefully, we shall see that it turns out to be the same curve as our 'arch', but this time not disposed along the *vertical plane*, as in the case of shot III, but laid out *horizontally* in perspective leading into the distance.

This curve has exactly the same kind of *initial plane* 'a' (also echeloned), made up of the four figures standing side by side. Furthermore, even though the boundaries of the echelons are not very clearly noticeable, the division into phases is delineated by four verticals; the figures of three soldiers in shot VII (x, y, z) and . . . the line dividing shot VI from shot VII.

What is there in the music that corresponds to the piece of the horizon in shot VII?

Note that the music of phrase A1 is insufficient for the full length of shots VI and VII, and that shot VII includes the beginning of phrase B1 – to be precise, seven-eighths of bar 12.

What are those seven-eighths of a bar?

They are, it turns out, exactly the same chord preceded by a strongly accented semiquaver which in shot III corresponded to a sharp fall in the vertical plane at the transition from shot III to shot IV.

In those shots, all movement took place vertically, and the abrupt break in the music was interpreted as a fall (from the *upper* right-hand corner of shot III to the *lower* left-hand corner of shot IV. Here (in shots VI–VII) it is deployed along the horizontal, deep into the shot. And as a graphic equivalent to that abrupt break in the music, we should assume at this point a similar sharp graphic shock, though not from the top downward but . . . by means of a sudden glance into the far distance. *Just such a shock is the 'jump' in shot VII from the line of troops . . . to the line of the horizon.* Therefore this is again a 'maximum break', for in a landscape the horizon is the ultimate in distance!

We are thus fully justified in saying that the visual equivalent of the musical 'jump' between bar 11 and the first seven-eighths of bar 12 will be that stretch of the horizon in the right-hand quarter of shot VII. We might also add that this purely psychological audiovisual combination fully conveys the perceptions of the [Russians], whose attention is fixed on the distant horizon, whence they are awaiting the enemy's attack.

Thus we see that two structurally identical pieces of music – the effect of the 'jump' at the beginning of bar 7 and of bar 12 – are echoed graphically in both cases in a completely analogous way by a *visual break*. But in the first case it is a break *on the vertical plane and at the transition from shot III to shot IV*, while in the second case it occurs on the horizontal plane and within shot VII at the point 'M' (see Fig. 13.6).

But that is not all. In the case of shot III our 'arching line' was located on *one plane*. In shots VI and VII it is deployed in depth, leading into the

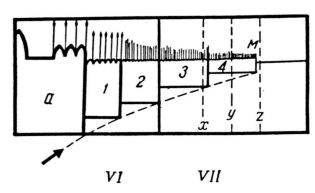

Fig. 13.6

distance, i.e. *spatially*. This line is formed by the system of echelons which repeat the upward movement of the scale of notes as they extend backwards from the plane of the screen (echelon 'a') deep into screen space.

Thus in shots VI and VII we can observe yet another aspect of the correspondence between music and picture, achieved on the same pattern, through the same gesture: in this case it is a *spatial correspondence*.

Let us now draw this new variant of the correspondence of movement between music and picture on the diagram. To complete the picture we will also finish the musical phrase 'B' (by adding the remaining one-and-a-quarter bars). In the music, therefore, this gives us a complete replay of the accompaniment to shots III–IV. As far as the pictures are concerned, this obliges us to add shot VIII, the end of which coincides with the end of bar 13, i.e. with the end of phrase B1.

So let us at the same time take a look at shot VIII.

Graphically it is, as it were, divided into three parts. For the first time in all eight shots, a *close-up* (Vasilisa in her helmet) comes strikingly to the forefront of our attention. It only takes us part of the shot, leaving the rest to the line of troops, drawn up in similar fashion to that in the preceding shots. Shot VIII thus serves a kind of transitional function. On the one hand it completes graphically the motif of shots VI–VIII. (We should not forget that along with the fact of it *receding* into the distance, shot VII is, in its dimensions, an enlargement in relation to the preceding shot VI, so preparing the ground for shot VIII to move into close-up.) The organic linkage between these three shots (VI–VII–VIII) as a single whole is also demonstrated by the fact that musically they are firmly held together by the phrases A1–B1. This is clear from the fact that the *extreme* limits of those four bars – 10, 11, 12 and 13 – coincide with the edges of shots VI and VIII, whereas within them the bar-line between bars 10 and 11 does not coincide with the graphic articulation, nor does the division between shots VII and VIII coincide with their articulation with bars 11 and 12. (See insert of these three shots and the corresponding music.)

In shot VIII, the phase of medium shots of the line of troops that runs through shots VI, VII and VIII comes to an end, and the phase of close-ups in shots VIII-IX-X begins.

Similarly, the phase of *Alexander Nevsky standing on top of the cliff* runs through shots I, II and III, after which begins the phase of *long shots of the troops at the foot of the cliff*. The depiction did not move into the latter phase by *transition within one shot*, but by *transition through montage*. After shot III the next – 'troops' – phase entered the sequence through the long shot in IV, after which 'Nevsky on the cliff' appeared again, also in long shot, in V.

This *substantive* transition from 'Nevsky' to 'troops' was marked by a *substantive* shift in the music: the change of key from C minor to C sharp minor.

A less major transition, this time not from *theme* (Nevsky) to *theme* (troops), but *within one theme* – from the medium shots of the troops to the close-ups – is not achieved by the *montage linking as used in III–IV–V–VI, but within shot VIII.* (See reverse side of the insert.)

Here it is achieved by means of *two-level composition*; the new theme (close-ups) emerges into the forefront, and the 'fading' theme (the long shots of the front line) moves into the background. Apart from this, it should be mentioned that the 'fading' of the previous theme is also expressed by shooting the line of troops out of focus; they thus act as a background to the close-up of Vasilisa.

Vasilisa introduces the close-ups of Ignat and Savka in shots IX and X, which together with the subsequent two shots XI and XII provide the next *new graphic interpretation* of our previous pattern of gesture.

But of that more later.

Now let us analyse shot VIII, in order that we may draw up the necessary diagram of the three shots VI–VII–VIII.

Shot VIII is clearly made up of three parts.

The first is the close-up of Vasilisa's face. To the right is a long line of troops, out of focus but with the sun glinting on their helmets. In the left-hand section of the front line is a banner, which separates Vasilisa's head from the left-hand edge of the frame.

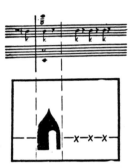

Fig. 13.7

Now let us look at the corresponding music. That complete picture (shot VIII) is allotted one-and-a-quarter bars: the last quarter of bar 12 and the whole of bar 13. In that passage of music there are quite clearly three elements, of which the middle one stands out: the chord at the start of bar 13. This chord quite distinctly reflects the 'shock' of the impression produced at this point by the first close-up.

Starting from the middle of the bar is a row of four quavers, interrupted by quaver rests. And where previously that horizontal progression on one note was echoed in shot IV by the [enemy] flag, so here the three quavers are echoed by . . . the flashes of sunlight glinting on the soldiers' helmets (shown in Fig. 13.7 by 'X, X, X'). The left-hand border of the shot seems to have no 'corresponding' music. But . . . we have forgotten the quaver left over from bar 12,

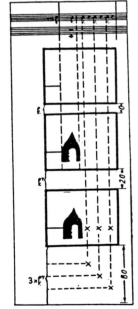

Fig. 13.8

which comes 'to the left' of the first chord, in bar 13: it is that quaver which is 'responsible' for the segment of space to the left of Vasilisa's head.

On the basis of what we have said, shot VIII and its parallel passage of music can be represented as in Fig. 13.7.

At this point it is quite natural to ask: wait a moment, how can you equate a line of music with a picture?! After all, the left-hand side of one and the left-hand side of the other denote quite different things.

A *still* picture exists *spatially*, i.e. *in simultaneity*, and neither its sides nor its centre relates to *a sequence of events in time*. On the musical stave, however, *the passage of time* is precisely what we do have; there, the left-hand side denotes *'before'*, and the right-hand side *'after'*.

All these considerations would be relevant if the separate elements *in the shot were to appear sequentially*, i.e. as shown in Fig. 13.8. Indeed, at first sight this objection sounds thoroughly reasonable and well-grounded; we have, however, omitted one extremely important fact, namely that it is by no means the case that *the whole of a still picture* enters the spectator's perception *all at once* (except in those cases where the composition has been purposely calculated to produce just that effect).

The art of graphic composition consists in leading the spectator's attention along exactly the path and in exactly the sequence that the artist wants the spectator's eye to move over the surface of the picture (or, in the case of a film, over the surface of the screen).

It is worth noting that at an earlier stage of painting, when the concept of 'the path of the eye' was difficult to separate from the physical image . . . of an actual path, artists used to put into their pictures . . . *a literal depiction of a path*, along which the events were located in accordance with the desired sequence in which the spectator was meant to perceive them. This device was above all used to indicate the temporal sequence of various scenes which in those days used to be depicted on one canvas, even though they actually took place at different times. The scenes which the spectator was meant to see in the desired sequence were located at the appropriate points along a path painted for that purpose. Thus, for instance, in the painting by Dirck Bouts, *The Dream of Elijah in the Wilderness*, Elijah is asleep in the foreground and a path winds towards the background, while Elijah himself is also depicted walking along that path. In Domenico Ghirlandaio's *Adoration of the Shepherds*, the foreground is taken up with the actual scene around the baby, while a path meanders from the background to the foreground, with the Three Wise Men moving along it: thus a path links events which were no less than thirteen days apart in time (24 December to 6 January)!

In exactly the same way, the Flemish painter Hans Memling locates his seven days of Passiontide in different streets of one city.

Later, when similar leaps in time were no longer painted on the plane surface of one picture, the physically depicted path, as one of the means of predetermining the sequential path for the eye when contemplating a picture, also disappeared. *A literal path* became *the path of the eye*, thus moving from the sphere of *depiction* into the sphere of composition.

A classic example of this is Ivanov's *Christ Appearing to the Multitude*, in which the composition moves along a twisting curve, which has as its focal point the figure which in size is the smallest and thematically the most important: the approaching figure of Christ. In a manner essential to the artist's purpose, this curve leads the spectator's attention over the surface of the picture to precisely that figure in the distance.

The most varied means can be used for this purpose, although they all share one characteristic: the picture usually contains something which initially catches the eye; from there, our attention will then move along the path desired by the artist. That path may be traced either by a line of movement in the graphic composition, or as a path along a gradation of colour tones, or even via the grouping and interplay of figures in the picture (a good example of this, undertaken with just this aim in view, is Rodin's deciphering of the figures in Watteau's *L'Embarquement pour Cythère*; see Paul Gsell's book on Rodin.[430]

Are we entitled to say of our shots that they, too, contain a similar path of the eye's movement, determined in a particular way?

Not only can we answer this in the affirmative, but we can also add that this movement goes specifically from *left to right*, furthermore that it is absolutely *identical* for all *twelve shots*, and is by its nature in *total correspondence* with the *movement in the music*.

Throughout the whole sequence the music has two types of phrase: 'A' and 'B'.

'A' is structured according to Fig. 13.9.

'B' is structured according to Fig. 13.10.

First comes a chord, and then, against the background of its resonance, there is either the 'arching' rise of a scale* or a single note repeated in *horizontal* progression.

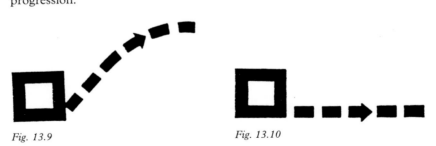

Fig. 13.9   *Fig. 13.10*

All the shots are structured graphically on exactly the same lines (except for shots IV and XII, which do not function independently but as continuations of the movement in the preceding shots). In all of them the left-hand

---

*For example, in shot III this will be the rising scale of C minor played tremolando by the cellos.

portion of the shot contains the darkest, heaviest, most solid graphic equivalent of a weighty 'chord', which immediately seizes our attention.

In shots I, II and III these are the black figures placed on top of the heavy mass of the cliff. They seize our attention not only because they are black, but because they are the only living beings in those frames.

In shot VI there are the four pikemen in the foreground.

In shot VII there is the mass of troops, etc.

In all these shots, the element to which one gives one's attention secondarily is spread out to the right: something light, airy, which makes the eye follow it as it moves.

In shot III, the upward-arching line of cloud.

In shots VI–VII, the troops 'echeloned' into the distance.

In shot V, the strips of sky being 'washed away' to the right.

Thus for the succession of graphic shots, too, the left-hand side denotes 'before' and the right-hand side denotes 'after', because the eye quite definitely moves from left to right across each shot, even though they are *still* pictures.

Dividing the composition of the shots vertically enables us to allot to each of them its share of music which fits the separate graphic elements and the 'entry' of new ones. This was the perceptual basis on which the shots were assembled and the precise audiovisual correspondences and combinations were achieved. The painstaking analysis and the indication of correspondences which we are doing now are, of course, only possible *ex post facto*, but it does at least demonstrate just how structurally important is that compositional 'intuition' which assembles an audiovisual construct by 'feel' and 'touch'.

Thus shot by shot the eye is trained to read a picture from left to right.

But that is not all: this horizontal reading of each separate shot, always in the same direction – from left to right – is so effective in training the eye to read horizontally *altogether* that all the shots are also *psychologically* lined up one after the other as though *in a series along the horizontal*, always in the same *left-to-right direction*.

And this enables us not only to articulate each separate shot in vertically divided time segments but also to *line up shot to shot on the horizontal* and to structure the progression of the music in parallel with them.

Let us take advantage of this fact and draw a single joint diagram of the three successive shots VI–VII–VIII (see insert), the movement of the music which blends with them and the progression of that common graphic gesture that is fundamental to the movement of both. This gesture is the same as that which moves through the combined shots III and IV. It is interesting that here it was not achieved through *two* shots but *three*, and that the effect of 'falling' is located inside shot VII and not at the point of transition from shot to shot, as happened in shots III–IV.★

On this basis, after adding another set of pictures, we can proceed to draw up an overall graphic diagram for all twelve shots. Comparing the diagram for shots VI–VII–VIII with that for III–IV, we shall see in that instance how much more complicated the structuring of 'variations' based on the same initial movement-gesture can be.

Earlier in this article we pointed out that the movement from left to right, repeated in each shot, provides the psychological prerequisite for aligning the shots themselves along the horizontal, and for their movement in the same left-to-right sequence. This, in part, is the reason why we have been able to lay out the sequence of our shots horizontally in the diagram.

At the same time, however, we must take account of a much more important factor, and one that is of a different order, namely that the psychological effect produced by these shots (apart from shots IV and XII, of which more below) as they relentlessly hurtle from left to right, is subsumed under the generalising image of our attention moving from somewhere on the left to somewhere on the right.

This is also stressed by the 'message' that is signalled by the acting: the fact that all the actors are looking in the same direction, as in shots I, II, III, V, VI, VII, VIII, IX and X.

The close-up figure in shot IX is looking to the left, but this only emphasises the other characters' general concentration on looking to the right. Shot IX stresses this within the interplay of the 'triad' formed by the three close-ups – shots VIII, IX and X – where it occupies the *middle* position and lasts for the shortest length of time (three-quarters of a bar of music, as against one-and-an-eighth and one-and-a-quarter bars allotted to shots VIII and X respectively). Instead of a monotonous series (see Fig. 13.11), his turn to the left makes for a more disturbing series (see Fig. 13.12), in which the third close-up in shot X gives extra stress to the direction of the actor's gaze because it has swung round through 180 degrees, instead of the inexpressive effect that would have resulted from all three of them looking the same way.

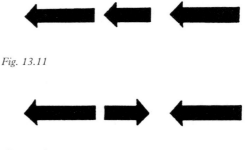

Fig. 13.11

Fig. 13.12

★The fact that the bars of music are shown in the diagram as being of different lengths (e.g. bars 10 and 12) is of no significance. The same is true of the discrepancies of time-scale within the shots (e.g. when seven-eighths of a minute is so drawn that it looks much longer than a whole minute, etc.). These are caused by purely graphic considerations in the layout of the diagram.

In certain cases Pushkin, too, uses this type of construction. In his long poem 'Ruslan and Lyudmila' he gives details of the ways in which three men are killed in the battle against the Pechenegs: one is struck down by an arrow, another by a mace and the third is trampled to death by a horse.

The sequence 'arrow-mace-horse' would represent a straightforward rise [in the degree of violence].

Pushkin proceeds differently. He does not deploy the 'massiveness' of the blow along a simple rising line, but with a 'deviation' in the middle link, namely: *not* 'arrow-mace-horse', *but* 'mace-arrow-horse'.

> A heavy mace has felled this one;
> That one's laid low by lightweight arrow;
> While yet a third, trapped 'neath his shield,
> Is trampled by a maddened horse . . .
> ('Ruslan and Lyudmila', Canto VI, Stanza 12)[431]

Thus the continual movement of the eye scanning the picture systematically from left to right throughout all the shots adds up to a single generalising image of something located on the left of each picture but 'instinctively' straining towards a point somewhere to the right.

But . . . precisely this perception is achieved by this whole set of twelve shots: Nevsky on the cliff-top, the troops at the foot of the cliff, the general sense of expectation, everything is directed to the right, into the distance, to a point somewhere across the lake, whence the as yet invisible enemy will appear.

So far, at this stage of the scene, the enemy is only represented through the expectancy of the Russian army.

There follow three empty shots of the snow-covered frozen surface of the lake.

Then in the middle of the third shot, the enemy will appear 'in a new guise': the booming sound of his horns. The end of the sounding of the horns will overlay a shot depicting Alexander Nevsky's group. This gives the impression that the sound 'came from afar' (i.e. through the series of empty shots of the lake) and 'reached' Nevsky (i.e. because it overlays a shot of the Russians).

The sound enters in the *middle* of a shot of the empty, frozen lake, and by this means the sound is perceived as coming from the middle of the picture, from straight ahead. Thence (because they are facing the enemy) the group of Russians also hears the sound as if coming from head-on.

Soon afterwards the charge of the enemy cavalry will start, gradually growing out of the line of the horizon, of which, at first, it seems to be a part. (Long before this, the theme of a head-on charge is prepared for us in advance by shots IV and XII, which both look towards the enemy line; and *that* is the basic compositional reason for including them, apart from the fact that they are an absolutely precise graphic equivalent of the music at those points.)

We now need to make one most essential qualification of everything that has been said hitherto.

It is obvious that the method of 'reading' the shots horizontally and 'lining them up' in our perception one after another along the horizontal is not always used. As we have shown, its use here derives wholly from the need to evoke a particular image through this scene, an image based on the need to direct our attention from the left to the right-hand side of the screen.

Both the pictures and the music, together with their complete synchronisation, are equally effective in creating this image. (The music, too, is structured as a rightward movement, starting from the heavy chords which make up the 'left-hand' side of each phrase. To realise the importance of this, one only has to imagine for a moment what it would be like if those chords were on the 'right-hand side' of the musical phrases, i.e. if the phrases *ended* with chords: in that case, the sensation of 'flying' across the surface of Lake Peipus would be lacking!)

If it were done otherwise, in order to achieve a *different image*, the composition of the shots would be designed to 'train' the eye into a completely different graphic 'reading'. The aim would not be to accustom the eye to align the shots sideways-on, but might, for instance, make the eye *layer* the shots one upon the other. This induces a perception of our attention being drawn into the depth, or of pictures rushing towards the spectator.

Let us, for example, imagine a sequence of four close-ups of different people, each one placed strictly centre-frame. The eye will naturally not perceive them according to Example I, but in the manner shown in Example II (see Fig. 13.13), i.e. not as moving past the eye from left to right but as a movement away from the eye in the sequence 1, 2, 3, 4 or towards the eye in the sequence 4, 3, 2, 1.

We mentioned a variant of Example II when we were discussing the sound of the horns and the consequent change to looking straight ahead into the distance in the scene which immediately follows the episode we have been analysing.

After all, a shot of the type of shot XII, in which the sound of the horn is first heard, is perfectly likely to be read 'by inertia' from left to right instead of in depth (Fig. 13.14). Two factors, however, assist in switching our

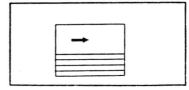

Fig. 13.13   Fig. 13.14

attention into the depth of this shot. First, the sound, which is timed to burst forth in the middle of the shot: by spatial analogy, our perception involuntarily places it in the centre of the shot. Second, the graduated progression of grey-white strips of snow which is moving 'upwards' and 'backwards' in the lower part of the shot. (See Fig. 13.15.)

Fig. 13.15

This kind of 'staircase' leads our attention upwards, but since this upward movement simultaneously draws our eye to the line of the horizon, it therefore 'reads' psychologically as a spatial movement towards the horizon, i.e. into the distance, in exactly the way that we require. This effect is increased by the fact that the next shot is almost the same but with the line of the horizon placed even lower: the increased space taken up by the sky induces our eye to perceive the distance as ever greater. Subsequently, this conditional movement of the eye – prompted first by means of the approaching sound, then by the galloping cavalry – is finally given material form at the moment of the charge.

It is equally easy to train the eye by a system of placing points, lines or movements in such a way that they 'read' vertically, etc., etc.

We now have to make some further brief comments on shots IX–X and XI–XII. As already indicated above, shots IX–X are accompanied by phrase A1 (the same as phrase A but in a different key). To this we may add that shots XI and XII are accompanied in exactly the same way by phrase B1.

Unlike shots III–IV, in which the two bars of the phrases A1–B1 are given one picture each, here each of the bars of phrases A1–B1 are given two pictures.

Let us see whether shots IX–X–XI–XII repeat the same gestural pattern of movement that we had in shots III–IV, and if so what is new about the way it is done. The first three-quarters of the first bar (bar 14) are taken up with the introductory chord, the 'starting point', as we have called it. And the picture which echoes it seems like an enlargement of the first three-quarters of shot VI: a close-up of a bearded man (Ignat) against a dense background of pikes – reminiscent of the four pikemen in shot VI – while the remaining five crochets are allotted to shot X. Compared with shot IX, shot X has almost no pikes (there are eight times more of them in shot IX): this has the same 'lightening' effect as do the 'echelons' of the right-hand side of shot VI compared with its left-hand side. It is curious to note, however, that the blobs which formed an 'arch' are also present in this shot; and what is more in a quite unexpected way, namely in the form of blobs of vapour exhaled from people's mouths as they breathe heavily and irregularly. The main element, however, which represents our 'arch' here is, of course, the mounting tension conveyed by the acting, with its growing depiction of nervous excitement.

Thus we find here a new factor in the embodiment of our 'gesture': the psychological, acting factor, which works through the rising intensity of emotion. This embodiment, however, may also be regarded as three-dimensional, for in the transition from shot X to shot XI, as with the 'fall' between shots III and IV, we have a no less sharp jump from the full-face close-up of a young man turned towards the camera (Savka), back to a long shot of small figures with their backs to the camera and looking into the distance. Here this 'jump' is expressed not only by a 'fall' in scale but also by the figures being turned around.

These two shots X and XI are analogous to the right and left sides of a previous single shot, shot VII. Each of the halves of shot VII is here represented by a whole shot of similar resonance. Naturally they are represented in X and XI in richer and weightier form (compare VII and XI, or the section of horizon in VII with the total empty space of shot XII).

For the rest, however, they perform an absolutely similar function. Curiously enough, an echo of the little flags in shot IV or the sunglints in shot VIII also figures in shot XII: here, those elements are conveyed in the vertical by means of the white strips dividing the grey strips on the surface of the snow.

Thus we see that a single type of gesture, which establishes synchronicity between the inner movements of music and pictures, is conveyed graphically by all the following variants:

tonal (shot I);
linear (shot III);
spatial (by the echeloned troops in VI and VII);
acting and volume (by the actors' behaviour in shots IX and X;
by the graphic use of volume in the transition from shots X to XI).

The impression of anxious expectation of the enemy's attack was produced by equally diverse methods: this vague, general and unspoken sense was evoked by light in shot I; by line in shot III; by the setting and grouping in shots VI and VII; and finally, directly through the actors' straightforward depiction of mounting tension in shots VIII–IX–X.

It only remains to make a few qualifying remarks about shot V, which so far has not been dealt with. During the course of our analysis, this shot has already been referred to as 'transitional'. Thematically this is so: it is the transition from Nevsky on the cliff to the troops at the foot of the cliff.

Musically, too, it marks a transition from one key to another, which is entirely justified by the narrative. Finally, it is equally justified in graphic terms. This is the only shot within the whole episode in which we have a reversed example of what we have called 'the arch': it is on the left-hand side of the shot instead of on the right; it does not serve as an outline for the light side of the shot but for the heavy side; and it does not move upwards but downwards, in complete concordance with the music, where this is expressed in a falling scale on the bass clarinet against the background of a chord played tremolando by the violins.

Despite all that, however, the shot cannot be wholly detached from the general picture; it cannot stand out in complete contrast to the rest, because its thematic content (Nevsky on top of the cliff) is linked by a unity with the thematic content of the following shots (the Russian troops at the foot of the cliff).

It would be a different matter if some antagonistic theme were to figure in this shot, a theme connected, for example, with the hostile knights. In that case, a sharp intercut, a conscious break in the overall fabric would be not only 'desirable' but imperative. In just that way later in the film the theme of the enemy breaks in as a sharp sound (see description above). Further on, this 'clash' between the themes of the two opponents is intercut like a duel between colliding shots. At first it proceeds like a clash of montage sequences that differ sharply in composition and structure: the white knights versus the black-clad Russian troops; the motionless Russians versus the galloping knights; the lively, open, emotionally expressive faces of the Russians versus the rigid iron masks of the knights' helmets, and so on.

The idea of hostile forces is first conveyed as a confrontation between montage sequences composed in contrasting ways. This is how the first, introductory phase of the battle is presented: a battle being fought, as yet, without physical contact between the armies, but nevertheless a battle that can already be felt, resounding through the clash of the graphic elements of the costumes designed for the two opposing armies.

Nothing of this sort, of course, occurs between shot V and the others shots. And it should be stressed that despite the fact that the attributes of shot V are the opposite of all those in the other shots, it nevertheless does not stand out excessively and does not disrupt the unity of the whole.

How was this achieved?

Clearly not by the characteristics of the shot itself, which, as we have seen, differs in its features from all the others.

What is it that nevertheless 'welds' it firmly into their midst?

Obviously the reason for this must be sought outside the shot itself.

If we look at the whole sequence of shots displayed on the diagram when it is unfolded, we will quickly discover that there are two shots which, although in lesser degree, trace out the reversed curve of the 'arch' that characterises the falling line of the black cliff in shot V.

The two shots in question are located on different sides of V, i.e. one of them precedes it in time, the other follows it.

In other words, one of these shots is a graphic preparation for the appearance of shot V; the other 'cancels it out'.

Both shots function, as it were, as 'shock-absorbers' to the appearance and disappearance of shot V, without which it would be too abrupt.

Furthermore, both shots are separated from shot V by an equal distance (i.e. by the number of intermediate shots located between them and shot V).

The two in question are: shot II and shot VIII.

In fact, if we trace on them the basic directional line of their main graphic masses, we shall see that these lines coincide with the outline of the cliff in shot V (see Fig. 13.16).

Unlike what happens in shot V, in shots II and VIII that line is not *physically* delineated as such, but it functions as the *structural line* along which the principal graphic masses of both shots II and VIII are erected.

Apart from these basic means of 'welding' shot V to the rest, there are also some curious 'ties' between this shot and those alongside it.

It is linked to shot IV . . . by the flag on the cliff, which echoes, as it were, the flags on the [enemy's] front line in shot IV; and the final musical accent given to those flags actually coincides with the appearance of the flag in shot V.

Shot V is linked to shot VI by the fact that on the extreme left-hand edge of shot VI we can see the black outline of the base of the cliff which dominates shot V.

II   *VIII*

Fig. 13.16

The foot of the cliff is important here, not only for reasons of graphic composition, but also as a piece of purely topographical information: it tells us that the troops actually are drawn up at the foot of Raven Rock. The failure to supply what might seem 'trivial' bits of information such as this is found,

every listener or reader when you give them an insight into the compositional imperatives of structuring films: 'Did you know all that *in advance*? Did you really have all that in mind before you *started*? Had you really worked all that out *beforehand*?'

Questions like this usually reveal the questioner's total ignorance of how the creative process actually works. It is a mistake to imagine that the creative process consists of laying down a set of inviolable compositional rules which define a priori all the subtleties of construction, and is brought to a conclusion by simply putting all the pieces together in the director's allegedly 'cast-iron' preconceived scenario. That is not at all what happens, or at best it only happens to a certain extent, and especially not in scenes and episodes that are 'symphonic' in character, in which the shots are linked by the dynamic development of some broad emotional theme rather than by a thin ribbon of plot, whose stages can only be laid out in a certain sequence prescribed by the practical logic of real life.

Closely connected with this is another fact, namely that when you are actually at work on the job you do not *formulate* all those 'hows' and 'whys' which dictate this or that sequence, the choice of this or that 'correspondence'. At such times, the choices one makes and the grounds for making them are not translated into *logical evaluation*, as happens in a *post hoc* analysis of the kind we have been conducting, but into *immediate action*.

One does not express one's ideas as logical deductions; one embodies them in camera shots and creative editing.

One cannot help recalling Oscar Wilde, who said that an artist's ideas are never born 'naked', later to be clothed in marble, paint or sound. The artist thinks directly in terms of the interaction between his media and his materials. His thinking is translated into immediate action, formulated not by formulas but by form. (I beg my readers' forgiveness for that alliteration, but it does express so very well the interconnection between all three.)

Naturally, even in such 'immediacy' the necessary ground-rules, justification and motivation for *precisely that* and *not another* disposition pass through one's mind (sometimes even burst out in speech!), *but one's mind does not linger in order to express such motifs in full*; it hastens on to *make the idea into reality*. The work of deciphering those 'motivations' will be one of the pleasures of post-analysis, which is sometimes conducted many years after the 'frenzy' of the creative 'act', that creative 'act' of which Wagner wrote in the heat of his surge of creativity in 1853, when he refused to contribute to a journal of musical theory that had been founded by his friends: 'When you act, you do not explain.'[432]

This does not mean, however, that the fruits of the 'creative act' are any the less subject to strict rules and principles, as we have tried to show in our analysis of the material we have chosen.

Notes

Eisenstein's own notes are placed at the end of the relevant page. In these end notes he is referred to as E.

1. The attempt under the leadership of Boris Z. Shumyatsky (1886–1938) to create a Soviet cinema that was both ideologically acceptable to the authorities and accessible to, and popular with, the mass audience led to an emphasis on clear narrative plot-line and vivid characterisation (with the 1934 film by the Vasiliev 'brothers', *Chapayev*, as the model), to the detriment of concepts like montage, which were criticised for making the most famous films of the 1920s, and especially those of E, 'unintelligible to the millions'. See also E's opening remarks in 'Montage 1938', p. 296. See also notes 120 and 309.
2. Presumably a reference to E's essay 'On the Structure of Things' ('O stroenii veshchei'), written in 1939 and available in English in H. Marshall (trans.), *Nonindifferent Nature* (Cambridge, 1987), pp. 3–37.
3. This is partly a reference to the damaging effects on the arts of the doctrine of Socialist Realism adopted at the first Congress of Soviet Writers in August 1934 and partly also to the failure of Soviet sound cinema in that context to develop the non-naturalistic and non-narrative techniques advocated by E and others in, for instance, the 'Statement on Sound', vol. 1, pp. 113–14.
4. Konstantin S. Stanislavsky (1863–1938), co-founder in 1898 of the Moscow Art Theatre, was the leading exponent of both the theory and practice of psychological realism and naturalism on stage. In the 1920s E frequently criticised what he regarded as the sterility of Stanislavsky's 'Method' but by the mid-1930s he was prepared to recognise the continuities between that and his own theoretical and practical platform.
5. Stanislavsky's *An Actor Prepares* was first published in English in New York in an abridged version in 1936, two years before the publication of the fuller original Russian version, *Rabota aktëra nad soboi*, in the USSR. Hence E, writing in 1937, quotes from the English-language edition published in the United States. Irritatingly, the page numbers are somewhat different in the British edition, published in London, also in 1936. References in these notes to the Russian text are to *Sobranie sochinenii* [Collected Works], vol. 2 (Moscow, 1954). Where possible, references are also given to both the American and British editions. However, the published English translation is at best a rather loose version of the Russian: where there is an exact equivalent, this translation is used; where there is no exact equivalent, translations in this volume are by Michael Glenny from the Russian text and a comparative reference to the relevant passage in the published versions is indicated by 'cf.'. In subsequent notes the following abbreviations will be used: R (Russian); US (American); GB (British).
6. A reference to E's early association with Vsevolod E. Meyerhold (1874–1940), the radically innovatory theatre director whom he once described as his 'spiritual father'. The reference here is circumspect because at the time E was writing

Meyerhold was already in disfavour, even though Stanislavsky (whose naturalism Meyerhold emphatically rebelled against) had done his best to protect him. After Stanislavsky's death in 1938, Meyerhold's long record of experimentation left him exposed. He was arrested in 1939 and his wife, the actress Zinaida Raikh, was found brutally murdered. Meyerhold was tried and shot in prison on 2 February 1940. It was E who secretly preserved Meyerhold's archive through the Second World War. See R. Leach, *Vsevolod Meyerhold* (Cambridge, 1989), p. 29; and K. Rudnitskii, 'Krushenie teatra', *Ogonëk*, no. 22, May 1988, pp. 10–14.

7. See below, 'On Colour', pp. 254–67.
8. Vol. 1, pp. 138–50.
9. E left a note inserted into the original draft:

> I have defined the 'overtone' as the summation, or rather the *general* emotional 'resonance' that derives from the sequence. It is general in that it arises from both content and structure; from both the style of playing (by the actor) and the play of linear elements; from the emotional associations of form and the interplay of the forms themselves, etc., etc.
>
> I established the feasibility of the montage editing of sequences on the basis of individual component factors (e.g. movement, light, etc.). This interpretation of 'overtone' also fits in with the examples that are analysed here: it is an *emotional generalisation* about all the elements in a sequence (a definition which differs from the concept of 'overtone' in musical terminology).
>
> When it is simultaneously an idea which has not yet assumed any other form of expression, the overtone begins to sound like an overall image of the sequence. One further step – and we read it as the 'meaning' of the sequence. We should not forget this – but it is more dangerous to remember *only* this! Here the highest point coincides with . . . the lowest: *montage* based only on the parameter of 'meaning' – i.e. based only on the plot or the event content of the sequence and without taking into account the complex of all the other elements and their sum total – has nothing in common with a real work of art, however great may be the contribution of the on-screen events that are lined up on this parameter alone. The result is as senseless as films that are edited by disregarding meaning for the sake of all the other elements!

See also 'The Fourth Dimension in Cinema', vol. 1, pp. 181–94, and 'Vertical Montage', in this volume, pp. 327–99.

10. 'The Middle of Three' ('Srednyaya iz trëkh'), written in September 1934 and published in *Sovetskoe kino*, no. 11/12, November/December 1934, is translated as 'Through Theater to Cinema' in *Film Form, Essays in Film Theory* (J. Leyda ed. and trans.) (New York, 1949 and London, 1951), pp. 3–17. E's speech to the All-Union Conference of Workers in Soviet Cinema, held in January 1935, will be included in vol. 3 of the present edition.
11. E is paraphrasing the first chapter, 'General', from F. Engels, *Anti-Dühring* (Moscow, 1954), pp. 17–43.
12. *Que viva México!* was E's unfinished Mexican film project, dating from 1931–2. The American socialist and millionaire writer and politician, Upton Sinclair, had originally agreed to fund the film but withdrew financial support when no end-result appeared to be in sight. The project collapsed amid bitter recriminations and wild allegations, and E returned to the USSR in May 1932. E always maintained that he had been promised that the filmed material would be shipped to Moscow so that he could edit it. This was never done. Variants of the film and of episodes within it were produced in the West, for example Sol Lesser's *Thunder Over Mexico* (1933) and *Death Day* and *Eisenstein in Mexico* (both 1934). E's later biographer, Marie Seton, reassembled more of the footage in a manner faithful to his original concept and script in *Time in the Sun* (1939), but by then much

of the material had been mutilated beyond repair. See H.M. Geduld and R. Gottesman (eds), *The Making and Unmaking of 'Que Viva México!'* (London and Bloomington, Ind., 1970), pp. 309–11.

13. By the period of 'single set-up cinematography' E means the years 1896 to 1915–16 when films, particularly in Russia, were characterised by prolonged and static shots, against which the notion of the primacy of montage was at least in part a reaction.

14. Balzac himself wrote the play *Vautrin* in 1840, based on the character from his novel *Père Goriot*, published in 1834.

15. For a more detailed account of this exercise, see the first chapter, 'Directorial Solution', in V. Nizhny, *Lessons with Eisenstein* (New York, 1969), pp. 3–18, edited and translated by I. Montagu and J. Leyda from: V. Nizhnii, *Na urokakh rezhissury u Eizenshteina* (Moscow, 1958), pp. 13–30. GTK (1925–30), GIK (1930–4) and VGIK (since 1934) are the various abbreviations by which the State Film School in Moscow has been known. E lectured there from the late 1920s; in October 1932 he was put in charge of the Direction Department and in January 1937 he was made Professor.

16. A reference to E's comments on the Acropolis in 'Montage and Architecture'; see pp. 59–81.

17. Alexander N. Ostrovsky (1823–86), Russian playwright. E staged a reworked version of his *Enough Simplicity for Every Wise Man* for Proletkult in 1923. This quotation is from his *Zapiska o teatral'nykh shkolakh* [Note on Theatrical Schools].

18. Mark M. Antokolsky (1842–1902), Russian sculptor whose best-known work is probably the statue of Beethoven outside the composer's birthplace in Bonn. E is referring to the ninety-fifth anniversary of his birth.

19. R.L. Binyon, *Painting in the Far East* (3rd edn, London, 1923), p. 10.

20. Ibid.

21. Chiang Yee, *The Chinese Eye. An Interpretation of Chinese Painting* (London, 1935) pp. 98–9.

22. F. Burger, *Cézanne und Hodler. Einführung in die Probleme der Malerei der Gegenwart* [Cézanne and Hodler. Introduction to the Problems of Contemporary Art] (5th edn, 2 vols, Munich, 1923), vol. 1, p. 166.

23. Ibid.

24. Vishnu, the all-pervading presence, one of the central gods of the Hindu pantheon.

25. D. Diderot, 'Lettre sur les aveugles à l'usage de ceux qui voient' [A Letter on the Blind Intended for Those Who Can See] (R. Niklaus ed.) (Geneva, 1951), pp. 31–2.

26. The quotation is from the the the 'Third Song' of the poem 'Poltava' (1823) by the Russian poet, Alexander S. Pushkin (1799–1837), which focuses on the confrontation between Peter the Great and the Ukrainian hetman Mazeppa. See also n. 220 below.

27. These are the last words of Chekhov's play *The Cherry Orchard* and are spoken by the aged family retainer, Firs, who is left behind alone in the deserted house after all the other characters have left for ever.

28. Johann Jacob Engel (1741–1802), whose work was entitled *Ideen zu einer Mimik* [Towards a Theory of Mimicry] (2 vols, Berlin, 1785–6).

29. Marietta S. Shaginyan (1888–1982), the Soviet novelist and critic. Her *Besedy ob iskusstve* [Conversations on Art] were also written in 1937.

30. Charles-Maurice Talleyrand (1754–1838), French politician and diplomat, renowned for his command of foreign policy under five successive regimes and whose name became a byword for subtlety and ambiguity in the language of diplomacy.

31. This translation by Michael Glenny. Cf. A.S. Pushkin, 'The Captain's Daughter', in *The Queen of Spades and Other Stories* (trans. R. Edmonds) (Harmondsworth, 1962), pp. 201–2.

32. Lion Feuchtwanger (1884–1958), German dramatist and novelist. *Jew Süss* was first published in 1925 (English translation, London, 1926).
33. Quoted in Georges Duthuit, *Chinese Mysticism and Modern Painting* (Paris and London, 1936).
34. The French painter Paul Gauguin (1848–1903), who left Europe for the island of Tahiti in the Pacific, is here compared by E to the Swiss-French philosopher Jean-Jacques Rousseau (1712–78) and his belief in the noble savage and man's need to return to nature.
35. For further discussion of the Acropolis, see 'Montage and Architecture', below, pp. 000–000.
36. Søren Kierkegaard (1813–55), Danish philosopher. This extract is from his *The Concept of Irony with Constant Reference to Socrates* (London, 1966), pp. 56–7, first published in Copenhagen in 1841.
37. Stanislavsky, *An Actor Prepares*; R pp. 336–7; US pp. 257–8; GB pp. 272–3.
38. See n. 12.
39. The reference is to Sol Lesser's *Thunder Over Mexico*; see n. 12.
40. Fernando Cortés (1485–1547) was the leader of the expeditions that conquered Mexico for Spain.
41. A *haciendado* is the owner of a landed estate or hacienda.
42. An *avasallada* is a woman who has been reduced to the status of a vassal or serf.
43. Cuauhtemoc was the last king of the Aztecs, who surrendered to Cortés and was tortured on his orders.
44. José Guadalupe Posada (1851–1913), Mexican graphic artist and creator of numerous popular calendars, broadsheets and political cartoons.
45. Gogol's *The Government Inspector* [*Revizor*] was first published in 1836. *The Dénouement of 'The Government Inspector'* was an alternative ending written in 1846 for a benefit performance for the poor. See N.V. Gogol, *Polnoe sobranie sochinenii* [Complete Collected Works], vol. 4 (Moscow, 1951), pp. 121–33.
46. *Bezhin Meadow* (USSR, 1935–7) was the unfinished film about collectivisation that E started between the failure of *Que viva México!* and the success of *Alexander Nevsky*. E was dogged by illness and political problems and filming was finally stopped by Shumyatsky in March 1937 and E forced to publish an apologia, 'The Mistakes of *Bezhin Meadow*' [*Oshibki fil'ma Bezhin lug*], to be included in vol. 3 of the present edition.
47. Chkalov, Baidukov and Belyakov were three pilots who were made Heroes of the Soviet Union for their long-distance non-stop polar flights. In June 1936 they flew 9,374 km from Moscow to Kamchatka and in June 1937 they flew from Moscow to Vancouver over the North Pole, a distance of 8,504 km, in 63 hours 16 minutes. Vodopyanov was another Soviet pilot who in 1934 had helped to rescue the crew of the Soviet ship *Chelyuskin*, trapped in the polar ice; he too was made a Hero of the Soviet Union.
48. *Conversations of Goethe with Eckermann* (J. Oxenford trans.) (London and New York, 1930), p. 152; this conversation is dated 17 January 1827.
49. The reference is to the campaign leading to the fall of Bilbao, the centre of Basque resistance during the Spanish Civil War, to Franco's forces on 19 June 1937.
50. See above, pp. 3–4.
51. For other discussions of *The Battleship Potemkin*, see vol. 1, especially pp. 67–70, 74–6, 169–74 and 290–5.
52. The references are to episodes in *The General Line, The Battleship Potemkin* and *Bezhin Meadow* respectively.
53. L. Tolstoy, *War and Peace* (trans. C. Garnett) (New York, 1956), p. 728.
54. Ibid., pp. 568–9.
55. The score by Edmund Meisel for *The Battleship Potemkin* certainly underlines this point. See also pp. 235–9 and note 239.

56. *Lady Windermere's Fan* (USA, 1925) was filmed by Ernst Lubitsch from the play by Oscar Wilde. *Becky Sharp* (USA, 1934/5) was directed by Rouben Mamoulian. The scene to which E refers is that of the Battle of Waterloo, one of the first attempts to use colour expressively in cinema.
57. Lacuna in the original text.
58. See vol. 1, pp. 138–50.
59. See '"Eh!" On the Purity of Film Language', vol. 1, pp. 285–95.
60. Lacuna in the original text.
61. This drawing has not been traced.
62. Kolomenskoye, now in the south-eastern suburbs of Moscow, became the summer residence of the Grand Princes of Muscovy in 1532. The wooden palace referred to here was begun in 1667 but was destroyed on the orders of Catherine the Great. Kolomenskoye is now an open-air museum of Russian architecture.
63. This painting has not been traced.
64. David D. Burlyuk (1882–1967), Russian artist, poet and critic, one of the founding fathers of Futurism, emigrated in 1918.
65. Robert Delaunay (1885–1941), French painter particularly interested in the relationships between colour and movement. See also p. 120.
66. The reference is to the French architect and engineer, Auguste Choisy (1841–1909), whose *Histoire de l'architecture* (1899) was illustrated with axonometric projections of the buildings he was discussing.
67. The Black Hundreds were the anti-Semitic terrorist groups who led the pogroms against the Jews in pre-Revolutionary Russia.
68. Maria N. Yermolova (1853–1928) was the leading Russian tragic actress of her generation, best known for her performances in the plays of Ostrovsky and in the title roles of such classics as Lessing's *Emilia Galotti*, Schiller's *Maria Stuart* and Racine's *Phèdre*. Valentin A. Serov (1865–1911), Russian painter, member of the Wanderers (see below, n. 71), did a series of portraits of figures from the artistic world, including Rimsky-Korsakov, Chaliapin, Gorky and Rubinstein. His portrait of Yermolova discussed here was painted in 1905. See also n. 329.
69. Ivan A. Aksionov (1884-1935), Russian theatre critic and historian, specialist in Elizabethan drama.
70. K.S. Stanislavsky, *Moya zhizn' v iskusstve* (Moscow, 1962; reprint of 2nd edn, 1928), pp. 70–1. The abridged English translation by J.J. Robbins (C. Stanislavski, *My Life in Art* (Harmondsworth, 1967), does not include this passage in ch. 8, 'Russian Dramatic Schools'.
71. Paul Signac (1863–1935), French neo-Impressionist landscape painter. The Wanderers were a group of naturalist painters, including Repin (see below, n. 76), who rebelled against the Imperial Academy of Arts in 1870. Their paintings were characterised by a realism imbued with an element of social criticism. They were committed to showing their works as widely as possible through touring exhibitions; hence their name *Peredvizhniki*, the Wanderers, or Itinerants.
72. See E's own analysis of this sequence in 'The Dramaturgy of Film Form', vol. 1, pp. 172–4.
73. Honoré Daumier (1808–79), French caricaturist and lithographer. Jacopo Tintoretto (1518–94), Venetian painter.
74. For this and the three subsequent quotations, see n. 70.
75. Lacuna in the text.
76. For Serov, see n. 68. Ilya Ye Repin (1844–1930), Russian painter associated with the Wanderers.
77. Chekhov's short story *Svidanie khotya i ne sostoyalos'*, *no . . .* [Although the Meeting Never Took Place . . .] was written in 1882.
78. Lacuna in the text.
79. In his unfinished manuscript for the book 'Direction' [Rezhissura]. The first

published use of the term was in '"Eh!" On the Purity of Film Language', vol. 1, p. 290.

80. The Constructivists in Soviet Russia included Tatlin, Rodchenko, Gabo and Pevsner. They espoused a non-objective socially useful production art that differed radically from the Russian Realist tradition exemplified by the Wanderers.

81. Igor E. Grabar (1871–1960), Russian neo-Impressionist painter and art historian. His two-volume work on Repin was published in Moscow in 1937. This quotation is from vol. 2, p. 151.

82. Ibid., vol. 2, p. 78. Vasili I. Surikov (1848–1916), Russian painter associated with the Wanderers. Two of his most famous paintings, *Menshikov at Beryozova* (1883), discussed below, and *The Boyarina Morozova* (1887), hang in the Tretyakov Gallery.

83. E is here referring to his draft article 'El Greco y el cine' [El Greco and Cinema], not included in the present edition. A French translation is available: F. Albera (ed.), *S.M. Eisenstein, Cinématisme: Peinture et cinéma* (Brussels, 1980), pp. 15–104.

84. The manuscript breaks off at this point half-way down the page. The text that follows begins on a new page.

85. See above, n. 82.

86. Alexander A. Ivanov (1806–58), painted *Christ Appearing to the Multitude*, for which he produced over three hundred preparatory sketches, between 1833 and 1857. It is also in the Tretyakov Gallery collection.

87. N.E. Radlov, *Ot Repina do Grigor'eva* [From Repin to Grigoriev] (Moscow, 1923).

88. E is here referring to the 1920s. Cf. n. 1.

89. E is referring to a painting by Giacomo Balla (1871–1958), who was closely associated with Italian Futurism. He makes a similar reference in 'The Dramaturgy of Film Form', but there the painting has six legs! See vol. 1, p. 165.

90. Lucian (*c.* AD 120–80) was a Greek satirist characterised by Engels as 'the Voltaire of classical antiquity'. Proteus, in Greek mythology, was a herdsman who lived in a cave and had the ability to change himself into any shape he chose in order to avoid capture.

91. The description comes from Ch. 2, 'The Storm', in *Boyhood*; see L.V. Tolstoy, *Childhood, Boyhood, Youth* (Harmondsworth, 1964), p. 114.

92. See above, n. 73.

93. A reference to the lithograph by Daumier entitled *Ratapoil Offering His Arm to Mme La République*, from his series 'L'Actualité', published in the newspaper *Charivari* on 25 September 1851. 'Ratapoil' figured in many of Daumier's political cartoons and personified the negative characteristics that Daumier identified with the supporters of Bonapartism.

94. Hans Memling (*c.* 1430–94), German-born painter of the Flemish school.

95. In his book *L'Art* (conversations edited by Paul Gsell) (Paris, 1912), when analysing the disposition of the figures in the painting *L'Embarquement pour Cythère* by Antoine Watteau (1684–1721), Auguste Rodin points out how they are intended to depict the complex development of the action in time.

96. S. Freud, *Moses and Monotheism* (London, 1939). There follows a lacuna in the text.

97. Guillaume-Benjamin-Arnaud Duchenne (1806–75), French neurologist and author of *Mécanisme de la physionomie humaine ou Analyse électro-physiologique de l'expression des passions* [The Mechanism of Human Physiognomy or the Electro-Physiological Analysis of the Expression of the Passions] (Paris, 1876). E also referred to Duchenne's work in 'The Montage of Film Attractions' in 1924. See vol. 1, pp. 51 and 306 n. 16.

98. E also discussed the form of the Japanese *tanka* in 'An Unexpected Juncture' in 1928, vol. 1, pp. 120–1, and 'Beyond the Shot' in 1929, vol. 1, pp. 139–41. 'The

Lay of Igor's Host' [Slovo o polku Igoreve], generally considered to be the greatest work of Russian literature before Pushkin, is an anonymous heroic poem, written *c.* 1185, about the contemporary campaign of the Russian Prince Igor against the Turkic Polovtsians from the steppes.

99. John Phoenix was the pen-name of the American humorist George H. Derby (1823–61).

100. *The Great Train Robbery*, directed by the American Edwin S. Porter in 1903, was the first film in which dramatic use of close-ups and changes in focal length was made during the editing of the film.

101. E discussed this sequence in 'The Dramaturgy of Film Form' in 1929. See vol. 1, pp. 175, 179–80.

102. J. Cocteau, *Portraits-souvenirs 1900–1914* (Paris, 1935), pp. 100–2.

103. Alexander N. Scriabin (also Skryabin) (1871–1915), Russian pianist and composer, whose 'Poem of Fire' (also known as 'Prometheus'), written in 1913, had a line in its score for a lighting keyboard to control the play of colour on a screen to accompany the music. E also referred to Scriabin in 'The Fourth Dimension in Cinema' in 1929; see vol. 1, pp. 183, 186, 187.

104. Leonid L. Sabaneyev (1881–1968), Russian composer and musicologist, author of *Skryabin* (Moscow, 1923). This quotation is from pp. 93–4.

105. A. Gleizes and J. Metzinger, *Du Cubisme* [On Cubism] (Paris, 1912).

106. Gino Severini (1886–1966), Italian painter, whose book *Du cubisme au classicisme. Esthétique du compas et du nombre* was first published in Paris in 1921 and in Russian translation in Moscow in 1923. The Russian title of G.V. Shaposhnikov's brochure is *Estetika chisla i tsirkulya*. The first quotation is from Shaposhnikov; the second from the Russian translation of Severini. E gives the source of both as p. 25, but this has not proved possible to check.

107. Kazusika Hokusai (1760–1849), Japanese painter and engraver particularly noted for his views of Mount Fuji. See also 'The Dynamic Square' (1930), vol. 1, pp. 211–12.

108. See n. 65.

109. Baudelaire's line, 'Je haïs le mouvement qui déplace les lignes', comes from the section of *Les Fleurs du mal* entitled 'La Beauté'. The whole poem is given a prose translation in F. Scarfe (ed.), *Baudelaire* (Harmondsworth, 1964), pp. 26–7.

110. 'Eidetics': the ability of the human brain to retain the image of an object after that object has passed out of the observer's field of vision. Cinema depends on this ability to create the illusion of the moving image.

111. See above, p. 116.

112. See above, pp. 24–6.

113. Reference to the manifesto issued by Nicholas II on 17 October 1905, in which he granted Russia civil rights entrenched in law and a parliament, or Duma, indirectly elected on a property-based franchise, while he retained sole prerogative over executive power; hence E's reference to 'treachery and mendacity'. Mstislav V. Dobuzhinsky (1875–1957), Russian painter, graphic artist and set designer.

114. On 9 January 1905 a peaceful march led by Father Gapon to the Winter Palace in St Petersburg was fired on by soldiers and many of the demonstrators were killed. The event has become known as 'Bloody Sunday'.

115. *Mastera sovremennoi gravyury i grafiki* (Moscow, 1928), p. 34.

116. Viktor B. Shklovsky (1893–1985) was a Russian writer, critic, literary theorist and scriptwriter; Vladislav F. Khodasevich (1886–1939) was a Russian poet who emigrated to France in 1922. His *Poeticheskoe khozyaistvo Pushkina* [Pushkin's Poetic Method] was published in 1937; his biography of Pushkin was incomplete at the time of his death.

117. These are the closing lines of Gogol's play.

118. Ivan M. Moskvin (1874–1946), a distinguished Russian actor, one of the founding

members of the Moscow Art Theatre, who first played the part of the mayor in *The Government Inspector* in 1921.

119. The titles of two songs popular in pre-Revolutionary Russia, the second being an answer to the first.

120. *Chapayev* (USSR, 1934) was directed by the so-called 'brothers': Georgi N. Vasiliev (1899–1946) and Sergei D. Vasiliev (1900–59). E discussed the film in 'At Last!', vol. 1, pp. 296–300. See also n. 1.

121. Gavrik is the affectionate diminutive form of the first name of Gavril N. Popov (1904–72), the Soviet composer who wrote the scores for a number of films, including *Chapayev* and *Bezhin Meadow*.

122. See n. 46.

123. See vol. 1, pp. 138–50.

124. Lacuna in the text.

125. For 'The Middle of Three', see n. 10. The text of the Yale lecture has not been preserved.

126. See 'The Montage of Film Attractions', vol. 1, pp. 39–58.

127. Stanislavsky, *An Actor Prepares*; R p. 157; US pp. 110–11; GB p. 117.

128. Sabaneyev, *Skryabin*, p. 66.

129. I. Lapshin, *Zavetnye dumy Skryabina* [The Intimate Thoughts of Scriabin] (Petrograd, 1922), pp. 37–8.

130. See n. 15.

131. See n. 71.

132. These paintings are all in the Tretyakov Gallery, Moscow; see n. 82. E also discussed *The Boyarina Morozova* in the section entitled 'Organic Unity and Pathos' in Marshall (trans.), *Nonindifferent Nature*, pp. 23–4, 26.

133. Lacuna in the text.

134. Stanislavsky, *An Actor Prepares*; see n. 5; R p. 226; US p. 166; GB p. 176.

135. Ibid., R p. 355; no exact English equivalent: cf. US p. 271 and GB p. 286.

136. Ibid., R p. 347; US p. 264; GB p. 280.

137. Ibid., R p. 355; US p. 266; GB p. 281.

138. Ibid., R p. 364; US p. 276; GB p. 292.

139. Ibid. E has reversed the order of these last two quotations.

140. Ibid., R p. 365; US p. 277; GB p. 293.

141. Ibid., R p. 51; US p. 38; GB p. 41.

142. Ibid., R p. 62; US p. 48; GB p. 51.

143. Ibid., R p. 63; US p. 49; GB p. 52.

144. Ibid., US p. 136; GB p. 144. There is no exact equivalent in the Russian version but cf. R p. 196.

145. Ibid., R p. 200; US p. 136; GB pp. 144–5.

146. Ibid., R p. 201; US p. 137; GB p. 145.

147. Ibid. This follows on from the previous quotation.

148. Ibid., R p. 201; cf. US pp. 137–8; GB pp. 145–6.

149. US and GB ibid.

150. The section 'The Exercises of Stanislavsky and Loyola', which is assumed to belong at this point, has been omitted from this edition for reasons of space.

151. Walt Whitman (1819–92), American poet.

152. E is using the Russian translation made by Konstantin Balmont in 1911.

153. For Repin, see n. 76.

154. See n. 17.

155. *The End of St Petersburg (Konets Sankt-Peterburga)* (USSR, 1927), directed by Vsevolod I. Pudovkin.

156. *Aerograd* (USSR, 1935), directed by Alexander P. Dovzhenko.

157. *The Youth of Maxim (Yunost' Maksima)* (USSR, 1934), directed by Grigori M. Kozintsev and Leonid Z. Trauberg.

158. The da Vinci text referred to by E, 'The Deluge', is missing from the manuscript. See also pp. 203, 305–10 and n. 222 below.

159. *The Old and the New (Staroe i novoe)* (USSR, 1929) was the release title for E's first film about collectivisation, which he began in 1926 as *The General Line (General'naya liniya)* and broke off to make *October* for the tenth anniversary of the 1917 Revolution. By the time the film was completed, the Party's general line on agriculture had changed and the film therefore had to be released under a different title.

160. In the manuscript at this point there is a remark in E's hand: 'Etude with *Brand*'. The quotation, however, is missing. The Soviet editors have therefore included an extract from Stanislavsky's *An Actor Prepares* (R pp. 164–5; GB p. 125) consisting of the spontaneous 'wants' expressed by the actors during a rehearsal of Henrik Ibsen's *Brand*:

'I wish to remember my dead child.'
'I wish to be near him, to communicate with him.'
'I wish to care for, to caress, to tend him.'
'I wish to bring him back! I wish to follow him! I wish to feel him near me! I wish to see him with his toys! I wish to call him back from the grave! I wish to bring back the past! I wish to forget the present, to drown my sorrow.'

Louder than anyone I heard Maria cry: 'I wish to be so close to him that we can never be separated!'

161. Lacuna in the text.

162. See the discussion of ideograms in vol. 1, especially pp. 120–1, 138–50.

163. Lessing, *Laocoön*, ch. XVII. The Virgil quotations are from *The Georgics*, ch. III, ll. 51–9, 79–81.

164. Thomas A. Edison (1847–1931), American who invented the phonograph, the incandescent electric lamp, and the kinetoscope (predecessor to the cinematograph). Auguste (1861–1954) and Louis (1864–1948) Lumière, who invented and first exploited the cinematograph.

165. See above, n. 95.

166. Giuseppe Mazzuoli (1644–1725), sculptor who specialised in funeral monuments. Anne Claude de Tubières-Grimoard, Comte de Caylus (1692–1765), was Watteau's patron.

167. The Pointillistes, such as Seurat and Signac, believed that brighter optical mixtures could be achieved by the use of separate blobs of primary colours.

168. See above, p. 103.

169. Lessing, *Laocoön*, ch. 6. Cardinal Jacques Sadolet (Jacopo Sadoleto) (1477–1547), classical scholar and poet. The Latin poem in question was addressed to a statue of Laocoön and is entitled 'De Laocoontis Statua Jacobi Sadoletis Carmen'.

170. Stéphane Mallarmé (1842–98), French Symbolist poet.

171. Georges Bonneau's book, *Le Symbolisme dans la poésie française contemporaine* [Symbolism in Contemporary French Poetry] was published in Paris in 1930.

172. See above, pp. 37–8.

173. B. Lifshits, *Frantsuzskie liricheskie poety XIX i XX vekov* [French Lyric Poets of the 19th and 20th Centuries] (Moscow, 1937), p. 208.

174. In French in the original.

175. Mayakovsky, 'To Sergei Yesenin'; see below, p. 322 and n. 338. Mayakovsky wrote this poem after Yesenin's suicide.

176. Andrei Bely (pseudonym of Boris N. Bugayev) (1880–1934), Russian writer and, in the pre-Revolutionary period, one of the leading figures in Russian Symbolism. His book *Masterstvo Gogolya* [Gogol's Mastery] was published in Moscow in 1934. Vlas M. Doroshevich (1864–1922), Russian journalist and theatre critic.

177. Balzac's *Louis Lambert* dates from 1832.

178. E used similar imagery of Chronos/Saturn devouring his own children in 'Imitation as Mastery', written in 1929.

179. The Spanish Civil War was still raging in 1937.

180. F. Engels, 'Bruno Bauer and Early Christianity', in *Marx and Engels on Religion* (Moscow, 1957).

181. A. Winterstein, *Der Ursprung der Tragödie. Ein psychoanalytischer Beitrag zur Geschichte des griechischen Theaters* [The Origin of Tragedy. A Psychoanalytical Essay on the History of Greek Theatre] (Leipzig, 1925), pp. 159–61.

182. From the first edition of Gogol's *Collected Works* published by Brockhaus-Efron, vol. 1, p. 370.

183. Teofilo Folengo (1496–1544) was an Italian poet who invented verse in macaronics, a combination of Italian and Latin. His masterpiece is generally regarded as *Baldus* in twenty volumes. Clément Marot (1496–1544) was a French Court poet and translator who is generally credited with having written the first sonnet in the French language.

184. Isaac D'Israeli, the father of Benjamin, first published his *Amenities of Literature* in three volumes in London in 1841.

185. *The Ellery Queen Omnibus* (London, 1934).

186. L. Lalanne, *Curiosités littéraires* (Paris, 1857).

187. François Rabelais, *Pantagruel*, ch. V. Cf. 'Pantagruel Will be Born', vol. 1, pp. 246–9.

188. Esfir I. Shub (1894–1959), compilation film-maker and editor. *The Fall of the Romanov Dynasty (Padenie dinastii Romanovykh)* was made by her from old newsreel footage in 1927 for the tenth anniversary of the October Revolution.

189. These translations are from Virgil, *Eclogues. Georgics. Aeneid. The Minor Poems* (H.R. Fairclough trans.) (2 vols, Loeb Classical Library, Cambridge, Mass., and London, 1928). The last reference, to A 1/241 is incorrect and is a misquotation of A 1/237: 'Quae te, genitor, sententia vertit?' [What thought, father, has turned thee?]

190. Max Ernst (1891–1976), German-French Surrealist painter and collage artist, associated with Dada. John Heartfield (1891–1968), German artist, founder of Dada and pioneer of photomontage. Alexander M. Rodchenko (1891–1956), Russian Constructivist artist and designer.

191. The first two are characters in Griboyedov's works; the second two from Gogol.

192. Here E intended to quote a passage from *L'Echarpe rouge* [The Red Scarf], one of Maurice Leblanc's 'Arsène Lupin' books, but the passage is missing from the manuscript.

193. *Chapayev*, directed by the Vasiliev 'brothers' in 1934; *The Baltic Deputy (Deputat Baltiki)*, directed by Iosif Kheifits and Natan Zarkhi in 1936; *Peter the First (Petr Pervyi)*, directed by Vladimir Petrov in two parts in 1937/8; *Suvorov*, directed by Pudovkin and Mikhail Doller in 1941; E's own *Alexander Nevsky* was released in December 1938.

194. *The Story of Louis Pasteur* (USA, 1936), directed by William Dieterle for Warner Bros; *Viva Villa!* (USA, 1934), directed by Jack Conway for MGM.

195. See n. 69.

196. J. Webster, *The White Devil*, in *Three Jacobean Tragedies* (ed. C. Salgado) (Harmondsworth, 1985), pp. 174–5.

197. C. Spurgeon, *Shakespeare's Imagery and What It Tells Us* (Cambridge, 1935), p. 216.

198. Ibid., p. 257.

199. Ibid., pp. 49–50.

200. A.C. Bradley, *Shakespearian Tragedy* (London, 1904).

201. Spurgeon, *Shakespeare's Imagery*, pp. 18–19.

202. Ibid., pp. 87–8.

203. J. Frazer, *The Golden Bough*, part V *Spirits of the Corn and of the Wild*, vol. II, ch. 9 'Ancient Deities of Vegetation as Animals', para. 1 'Dionysus, the Goat and the Bull' (3rd edn, London, 1912), p. 1.

204. Spurgeon, *Shakespeare's Imagery*, p. 347.

205. Here E refers to the horticultural associations of the name of 'Plantagenet', which derives from the Latin *planta genista*, meaning the shrub 'broom'.

206. The 1936 Soviet Constitution was supposed to mark the country's transition from the dictatorship of the proletariat to a socialist society. Stalin described the Constitution as 'the most democratic' in the world; it survived until replaced under Brezhnev's rule in 1977.

207. F. Schiller, *On the Aesthetic Education of Man, in a Series of Letters* (E.M. Wilkinson and L.A. Willoughby ed. and trans.) (Oxford, 1967). The quotation is from the first paragraph of the Second Letter, p. 7.

208. When E met Joyce in Paris on 30 November 1929 he listened to a recording of the author reading from his 'Work in Progress', which was to be published as *Finnegan's Wake* in 1939. *Ulysses* had been published in Paris in 1922. See also vol. 1, pp. 96, 226, 235.

209. Cf. the discussion of Zola in vol. 1, pp. 95, 226, 288–9.

210. S. Zweig, 'Anmerkungen zum *Ulysses*', *Neue Rundschau*, October 1928.

211. L. Feuchtwanger, *Erfolg. Drei Jahre Geschichte einer Provinz* [Success. Three Years' History of a Province] (Berlin, 1930); translated as *Success* (London, 1930).

212. *Pravda*, 7 June 1936.

213. *Gil Blas* (named after the picaresque satire by Le Sage, 1715) was a left-of-centre French daily newspaper, published from 1879 to 1914. Maupassant was one of the contributors. *L'Histoire comique de Francion*, one of the first French novels, was written between 1623 and 1633 by Charles Sorel (1582–1674).

214. From the foreword to the Russian translation of Lessing's *Laocoön* (Moscow, 1934).

215. Vol. 1, pp. 138–50.

216. Lev V. Kuleshov (1899–1970), Russian film director and theorist who first developed the notion of montage, although his interpretation of its proper function differed from that of E and led to polemics, especially in the 1930s. The quotation is from his *Iskusstvo kino* [The Art of Cinema] (Moscow, 1929), p. 100; in English in R. Levaco (ed. and trans.), *Kuleshov on Film: Writings of Lev Kuleshov* (Berkeley, 1974), p. 91.

217. This remark, more or less meaningless in translation, is a pun on the fact that the Russian verb used by Kuleshov for 'lay out' [*vyladyvat*'] can also mean 'castrate' in vernacular usage.

218. E is here citing a line from the Russian version of the 'Internationale'. The equivalent line in the English version is: 'The last fight let us face.'

219. Lenin's *Materialism and Empirio-Criticism* was written between February and October 1908 and first published in Moscow in May 1909; the anniversary meeting would therefore have been held in May 1934.

220. The subheading of this section refers to passages from two of Pushkin's long narrative poems, both of which describe battle scenes. The 'Battle against the Pechenegs' is an episode from Canto 6 of 'Ruslan and Lyudmila' (1820) and, although entirely imaginary in detail, it is based on historical fact: the incursions into Kievan Russia in the 9th and 10th centuries AD by marauding nomadic tribes from Asia. 'Poltava' (1823) is based more firmly on recorded history: Peter the Great's decisive defeat of the invading Swedish army under Karl XII at the Battle of Poltava in the Ukraine in 1708. See n. 26 above.

221. A misrecollection of the New Testament account of the 'feeding of the five thousand' where the food available is recorded as having been 'five barley loaves and two small fishes' (John 6: 5–14).

222. The passage in question, referring to da Vinci's 'Deluge', is missing from the original manuscript at this point. Cf. n. 158 above and pp. 150–2 and 305–10.

223. *Vorschlag*: German musical term indicating a melodic ornament or flourish that precedes the principal note.

224. E devoted a series of lectures at VGIK, as well as a chapter in his book 'Direction' to the 'recoil movement' (a term borrowed from Meyerhold), which he defined as follows: 'The movement which, when intending to move in one direction, you first make, partially or wholly, in the opposite direction; in stage practice the prior movement is called the "recoil".'

225. The transcript of E's speech is included in the published version of the Conference proceedings, *Za bol'shoe kinoiskusstvo* [For a Great Cinema Art] (Moscow, 1935), pp. 24 ff. This quotation is from p. 28. It will be included in vol. 3 of the present edition. Cf. n. 10.

226. Platon M. Kerzhentsev (1881–1940), Soviet journalist, diplomat and historian, who was a leading member of the Proletkult in the 1920s. E's acrimonious split with Proletkult over the authorship of the script for *The Strike* cannot have endeared them to one another. The correspondence is translated in J. Leyda (ed.), *Eisenstein 2: A Premature Celebration of Eisenstein's Centenary* (Calcutta, 1985), pp. 1–8. From 1933 to 1936 Kerzhentsev was Chairman of the All-Union Radio Committee; from 1936 to 1938 Chairman of the Committee for the Arts of the Council of People's Commissars of the USSR, and thus in a powerful position to influence E's career for better or for worse.

227. For Surikov, see n. 82. The picture cited here is an imaginary reconstruction of the moments preceding the mass execution of soldiers of the regiments of *streltsy* (literally: 'archers' but by the early 18th century armed with flintlock guns) who had mutinied against Peter the Great. Painted in realistic style, the canvas is peopled with large numbers of dramatically expressive figures, ranging from Peter the Great to the condemned men and their wives and children.

228. The 'golden section' is the term used in aesthetics to describe the division of a whole into two unequal parts, whereby the greater part stands in the same relation to the lesser part as does the whole to the greater.

229. See n. 225 above.

230. 'The Principles of the New Russian Cinema', vol. 1, pp. 195–202.

231. First published in *Iskusstvo kino*, no. 4, April 1936, pp. 51–8; this quotation is from p. 57. Reprinted in vol. 2 of the Russian *Izbrannye proizvedeniya v shesti tomakh* [Selected Works in Six Volumes), Moscow, 1964–71, pp. 131–55; this quotation is on pp. 149–50. In the original the order of the examples here cited by E is reversed. Cf. n. 352 below.

232. See vol. 1, especially pp. 33–8.

233. E inserted the short film *Glumov's Diary* into his production of the Ostrovsky play in an exercise that was by no means unique in Russian theatre practice at the time.

234. These are the Russian release titles for three films starring the American actress Pearl White (1889–1938): *The Grey Shadow* is *Shadowed* (1914); *The Secrets of New York* is *The Exploits of Elaine* (1915); *The House of Hate* was also the original title (1919).

235. Dziga Vertov (pseudonym of Denis A. Kaufman). (1896–1954) was the leading documentary film-maker and theorist of Soviet cinema and the founder of the Cine-Eyes group, which produced the *Cine-Pravda (Kinopravda)* newsreels between 1922 and 1924.

236. V.B. Shklovskii, *Ikh nastoyashchee* (Moscow, 1927), p. 69.

237. Eduard K. Tisse (1897–1961) was the cameraman of Latvian origin who worked on all E's films.

238. E is referring to the decision in March 1937 by Boris Shumyatsky to stop production of this film. See n. 46.

239. Edmund Meisel (1874–1930), Austrian-born violinist in the Berlin Philharmonic Orchestra, composer for the Deutsches Theatre under Max Reinhardt and for Prometheus-Film; he wrote music for the German release versions of both *Potemkin* and *October* and for Walter Ruttmann's *Berlin. Symphony of a Great City (Berlin. Sinfonie einer Großstadt)* (Germany, 1929).

240. E intended to use his article '"Eh!" On the Purity of Film Language' (vol. 1, pp. 285–95) as an appendix to the current volume.

241. This was a central concern of E's lecture course at VGIK, which formed the basis for his unfinished book 'Direction'.

242. See the 'Statement on Sound', vol. 1, pp. 113–14.

243. K. London, *Film Music* (London, 1936), pp. 93–4.

244. The reference is presumably not to a composer, but to Philippe Quinault (1635–88), French poet and playwright.

245. Lacuna in the original text.

246. See below, pp. 281–96.

247. See also 'The Girl Like a Ray of Light', below, pp. 249–53.

248. See above, pp. 93–105.

249. See especially *The Development of the Monist View of History* (1895) and 'A Critique of Our Critics' (1899) in G.V. Plekhanov, *Selected Philosophical Works in Five Volumes* (3rd edn, Moscow, 1974–81), vols 1 and 2.

250. Vasili V. Kamensky (1884–1961), one of the leaders of Russian Futurism before the Revolution.

251. Yvette Guilbert (1867–1948), French cabaret singer. E recalls his meeting with her in Paris in 1929 in *Immoral Memories. An Autobiography* (H. Marshall trans.) (London, 1985), pp. 127–30, where he describes her as 'the lady in the black gloves'. Guilbert recorded her own reminiscences in: *La Chanson de ma vie* [The Song of My Life] (Paris, 1927) and *L'Art de chanter une chanson* [The Art of Singing a Song] (Paris, 1928).

252. Xanrof, the pseudonym of Léon Fourneau (1867–1953), a leading French humorist, singer and composer, who wrote many of Yvette Guilbert's songs and the French libretto for Oskar Straus's operetta *Ein Walzertraum* (1907).

253. Sabaneyev, *Skryabin*, p. 97.

254. At this point in the text there is a note: 'Quote "Beyond the Shot"' (vol. 1, pp. 138–50).

255. The manuscript breaks off at this point. Judging from the note E made in 1937, the bulk of the analysis for this third part of his work on montage went into 'Vertical Montage' (see below, pp. 327–99) and *Nonindifferent Nature*.

256. Stanislavsky, *An Actor Prepares*, US p. 287; GB p. 304; not in the Russian version.

257. Nikolai A. Dobrolyubov (1836–61), Russian literary critic and revolutionary journalist. The article 'Luch sveta v tsarstve temnoty' ('A Ray of Light in the Realm of Darkness') was written in 1860 and is translated in N.A. Dobrolyubov, *Selected Philosophical Essays* (Moscow, 1956), pp. 548–635.

258. *The Golden Cockerel* was the last opera by Nikolai Rimsky-Korsakov (1844–1908), first performed posthumously in 1909.

259. *Ivan* was the first sound film directed by the Ukrainian film-maker Alexander P. Dovzhenko (1894–1956) in 1932.

260. See vol. 1, p. 288.

261. The film *Aerograd*, set in the Soviet Far East, was made by Dovzhenko in 1935. The Chukchis are the local ethnic group depicted in the film.

262. 'Barcarolle' describes the rhythm of a Venetian boat song, ostensibly imitating the motion of a gondola. This rhythm was used most famously by Jacques Offenbach (1819–1880) in his opera *Les Contes d'Hoffmann (The Tales of Hoffmann)*, which Disney used for the soundtrack of his 'Silly Symphony', *Birds of a Feather* (USA, 1931). See also J. Leyda (ed.), *Eisenstein on Disney* (Calcutta, 1986).

263. Meister Eckhart (*c.* 1260–*c.* 1327), German Dominican mystic.
264. H. Lanz, *The Physical Basis of Rime* (Stanford, Cal., 1931), pp. 167–8.
265. Konstantin D. Balmont (1867–1942) was a Russian Symbolist poet and translator, whose *Poeziya kak volshebstvo* [Poetry as Magic] was published in 1922. Grammont is presumably a reference to the works of Maurice Grammont which include: *Le Vers français* [French Verse] (Paris, 1904) and *Petit traité de versification française* [Small Treatise on French Versification] (Paris, 1908). Velimir (pseudonym of Viktor V.) Khlebnikov (1896–1934) was a Russian poet who experimented with 'trans-sense' language and sound. Mayakovsky called him a 'master of verse'.
266. Translation by Michael Glenny. Cf. A. Rimbaud, *Complete Works, Selected Letters* (trans. W. Fowlie) (Chicago, 1966), pp. 120–1.
267. Lev S. Vygotsky (1896–1934) and Alexander R. Luria (1902–77) were both leading Russian psychologists. Luria was a friend of E; see also vol. 1, p. 141.
268. V.I. Lenin, *Philosophical Notebooks* (Moscow, 1933), p. 193.
269. Ivan I. Shishkin (1832–98), Russian painter of the Wanderers group known particularly for his forest landscapes. Genrikh I. Semiradsky (Henryk Siemiradzki) (1843–1902), Polish–Russian academic painter. Yuli Yu. Klever (1850–1924), Russian landscape painter.
270. See above, n. 21.
271. See n. 176.
272. Ernst Lubitsch (1892–1947), German-born theatre and cinema actor who became one of Hollywood's most accomplished film directors. He made *Lady Windermere's Fan* in 1925. See n. 56.
273. Vsevolod I. Pudovkin (1893–1953), Soviet film director, actor and scriptwriter. His first feature film, *The Mother* (*Mat'*) was released in 1926.
274. 'Pro sebya i vslukh' [About Myself and Talking Aloud], *Kino*, 6 May 1936.
275. T.S. Eliot, *The Sacred Wood* (London, 1920), p. 100.
276. Turgenev's 'Bezhin Meadow' was the eighth story in his collection entitled *A Huntsman's Tales* and provided the inspiration for E's film of the same name.
277. Paul Robeson (1898–1976), the black American singer and actor, was to have starred in E's unrealised film 'The Black Consul', based on the Haitian Revolution. He went to Moscow to discuss the project after E's return from Mexico in 1932.
278. For Tisse, see above n. 237. Andrei N. Moskvin (1901–61) was associated with the FEKS group and worked with E on *Ivan the Terrible*. Anatoli D. Golovnya (1900–82) worked first with the Kuleshov collective and then with Pudovkin.
279. Dmitri D. Shostakovich (1906–75) wrote numerous film scores, including *New Babylon* (1929), *The Maxim Trilogy* (1934–7) and *A Great Citizen* (1937–9). For Popov, see above, n. 121.
280. J.W. von Goethe, *Farbenlehre*, translated as *Goethe's Colour Theory* (R. Mattaei ed., H. Aach ed. and trans.) (London, 1971), p. 166.
281. In German in the original, quoted from H. Cohen, *Ästhetik des reinen Gefühls* [Aesthetics of Pure Feeling] (Berlin, 1912), pp. 369–72.
282. P. Werner, *Einführung in die Entwicklungspsychologie* [Introduction to Developmental Psychology], p. 93.
283. K. Bühler, *Sprachtheorie. Die Darstellungsfunktion der Sprache* [Theory of Speech. The Representational Function of Language] (Jena, 1934), p. 345.
284. Not traced.
285. Stanislavsky, *An Actor Prepares*, US, p. 198; GB p. 210.
286. Gracchus refers to Gracchus Babeuf, pseudonym of Francis Noël (1760–97), French utopian communist and leader of the 'Conspiracy of Equals' in 1796.
287. See above, n. 226.
288. Mei-Lan-Fan (1894–1961) was a Chinese classical actor whom E met in Moscow in 1935. Itakawa Sadanji (1880–1940), director, actor and dramatist with the Japanese Kabuki theatre, who visited the USSR in 1928 and met E; see vol. 1,

p. 128. Syozyo was an actor with the same company.

289. *Ruslan and Lyudmila*, based on the poem by Pushkin, was composed by Mikhail I. Glinka (1804–57) and first performed in 1842.

290. L. Tolstoy, *Anna Karenina* (trans. R. Edmonds) (Harmondsworth, 1954). This scene is from Part 2, ch. 28, which in this edition falls on pp. 225–8.

291. Lacuna in the text.

292. See above, pp. 239–41.

293. A style associated with E's father, the city architect of Riga.

294. Le Corbusier, pseudonym of Charles Jeanneret (1887–1965), Swiss-born architect and pioneer of modernism.

295. Walter Gropius (1883–1969), German architect and director of the Bauhaus.

296. Betal E. Kalmykov (1893–1940), First Secretary of the Regional Committee of the Soviet Communist Party in Kabardino-Balkaria at the time.

297. The remark that 'Architecture is frozen music' derives from *Conversations of Goethe with Eckermann* (London, 1930), p. 303. E used the same metaphor in 'The Dramaturgy of Film Form' in 1929; see vol. 1, p. 163.

298. Lacuna in the text.

299. Vertov developed the notion of the 'Radio-Ear' as a sound complement to the 'Cine-Eye' as early as 1923. See: A. Michelson (ed.), *Kino-Eye, The Writings of Dziga Vertov* (trans. K. O'Brien) (Berkeley, 1984), p. 18; R. Taylor and I. Christie (eds), *The Film Factory, Russian and Soviet Cinema in Documents, 1896–1939* (London and Cambridge, Mass., 1988), p. 93.

300. See vol. 1, pp. 59–64.

301. E is here referring to the theory of intellectual cinema that he expounded in his 1929 article 'Perspectives'; see vol. 1, pp. 151–60. The reference to 'a certain song from a certain musical comedy' alludes to the film *The Happy Guys (Vesëlye rebyata)*, directed by his close friend Grigori Alexandrov and released in 1934.

302. Cf. 'Pantagruel Will Be Born', vol. 1, pp. 246–9.

303. The quotation is from the poem 'An Order to the Army of the Arts', written in 1918 by Vladimir V. Mayakovsky (1883–1930).

304. The reference is to the unfinished project 'Direction' (*Rezhissura*).

305. Stanislavsky, *An Actor Prepares*, US p. 233; GB p. 248. No exact equivalent in the Russian version.

306. Ibid., US and GB p. 15. No exact equivalent in the Russian version.

307. The nickname of the distinguished radical literary critic Vissarion G. Belinsky (1811–48).

308. This article was written between March and May 1938 and first published in *Iskusstvo kino* [The Art of Cinema], no. 1, January 1939, pp. 37–49. Much of it was translated as 'Word and Image' in J. Leyda (ed. and trans.), *The Film Sense* (New York, 1942), pp. 3–65. Four versions of the Russian survive in the archives (TsGALI, 1923/1/1180 – 6); this translation is based on the fourth, which was first reproduced in L.V. Kuleshov, *Osnovy kinorezhissury* [The Foundations of Film Direction] (Moscow, 1941), pp. 310–33.

309. E is referring to the period following the First Party Conference on Cinema in March 1928 which called for a cinema that was 'intelligible to the millions' and the subsequent 'proletarianisation' campaign to purge Soviet cinema of its 'Formalist' avant-garde, in the course of which montage was identified, by Boris Shumyatsky among others, as the principal obstacle to that intelligibility. See also n. 1 and p. 3.

310. E is being somewhat inconsistent here in distancing himself by characterising as 'Leftist' the views which he himself put forward in 'The Dramaturgy of Film Form' (see vol. 1, pp. 161–80) and which he appears still to hold in the present essay.

311. A. Bierce, 'The Inconsolable Widow', in *Fantastic Fables* (1925), reproduced in

The Collected Works of Ambrose Bierce (New York, 1966), p. 311.

312. E is here referring to his articles 'Béla Forgets the Scissors' (1926), vol. 1, pp. 77–81; 'Beyond the Shot' and 'Perspectives' (both 1929), vol. 1, pp. 138–60.

313. Cf. 'Perspectives', vol. 1, pp. 151–60.

314. E is here referring to the experiments conducted by Kuleshov (see n. 216) in which he demonstrated that the meaning of an individual shot could be altered by its context. Cf. 'The Fourth Dimension in Cinema', vol. 1, pp. 181–94.

315. Tolstoy, *Anna Karenina*, part 2, ch. 24. This translation is by Michael Glenny. Cf. p. 209 of the edition previously cited.

316. G. de Maupassant, *Bel-Ami*, part 2, ch. 9.

317. Nikolai K. Cherkasov (1903–66) played the title roles in both *Alexander Nevsky* and *Ivan the Terrible*. Nikolai P. Okhlopkov (1900–67) appeared in *Men and Jobs* (1932), *Lenin in October* (1937), *Alexander Nevsky* (1938) and *Lenin in 1918* (1938) among others. Boris P. Chirkov (1901–82) is best known for his title role in *The Maxim Trilogy* (1935–9). Lev. N. Sverdlin's (1901–69) films included *By the Deep Blue Sea* (1936) and *Volochayevsk Days* (1938).

318. G. Arliss, *Up the Years from Bloomsbury* (New York, 1927), p. 289.

319. Cf. pp. 150–2, 203 above.

320. A.L. Volynsky, *Leonardo da Vinci* (Moscow, 1900), Appendix V, pp. 624–6.

321. Footnote by Joséphin Péladan to his French translation of Leonardo da Vinci's *Treatise on Painting: Traité de la peinture* (Paris, 1910), p. 181.

322. Konstantin A. Fedin (1892–1977), Russian writer, member of the Serapion Brotherhood of 'fellow-travellers' in the 1920s. Quoted from *Literaturnaya gazeta*, 26 March 1938.

323. Marx's 'Observations on the Latest Prussian Censorship Instruction', quoted from the Russian edition of the *Works* of Marx and Engels, vol. 1, p. 113.

324. The Republican forces in the Spanish Civil War won a resounding victory over Franco at Guadalajara in March 1937.

325. E is here using the Moscow Art Theatre as a synonym for Stanislavsky.

326. Pushkin, 'Poltava'; from the end of the 'Second Song'.

327. Ibid., from the beginning of the 'First Song'.

328. Ibid.

329. Peter the Great was seven feet tall with legs to match. The painting by Serov (see n. 68) dates from 1907 and hangs in the Tretyakov Gallery in Moscow.

330. *Eugene Onegin*, ch. 1, stanza 20.

331. Viktor M. Zhirmunsky (1891–1971), Russian philologist. The quotation is from *Vvedenie v metriku. Teoriya stikha* [Introduction to Poetic Metre. The Theory of Verse] (Leningrad, 1925), pp. 173–4.

332. Ibid., p. 178.

333. In the version of this piece that appears in Leyda (ed. and trans.), *The Film Sense*, the translator has, with E's permission, chosen examples from English verse to make E's points. We have adhered to the original Russian text in this version. Yakov P. Polonsky (1819–98), Russian poet.

334. Yuri N. Tynyanov (1894–1943), Soviet writer and critic; the quotation is from *Problemy stikhotvornogo yazyka* [Problems of Poetic Language] (Leningrad, 1924), p. 65.

335. Zhirmunsky, *Vvedenie v metriku*, p. 168.

336. See n. 265. Balmont achieves an atmospheric effect by using both alliteration and short, mostly two-syllable words, whose syllabic stress and length correspond to metrical feet.

337. James Thomson (1700–48), English poet who wrote the words for 'Rule Britannia!'. André Chénier (1762–94), French poet and publicist who was guillotined for his political activities and became the subject of the opera *Andrea Chénier* by Umberto Giordano.

338. Sergei A. Yesenin (1895–1925), Russian 'peasant poet', who was married to Isadora Duncan and committed suicide. Mayakovsky addressed this poem 'To Sergei Yesenin'. See also pp. 357–9 and n. 175.

339. Alexander S. Griboyedov (1794–1829), founding father of Russian drama, whose most famous comedy *Woe from Wit*, written in 1824, is generally accepted as the first Russian classic.

340. Written in July and August 1940 and first published in *Iskusstvo kino*, no. 9, September 1940, pp. 16–25; no. 1, January 1941, pp. 29–38. Translated as 'Synchronization of Senses', 'Colour and Meaning' and 'Form and Content: Practice', Parts 2, 3 and 4 of Leyda (ed. and trans.), *The Film Sense*, pp. 69–216.

341. See above, p. 299.

342. See n. 86.

343. The journal of the brothers Edmond (1822–96) and Jules (1830–70) Goncourt covers the period from 1850 to 1870.

344. See vol. 1, pp. 113–14.

345. See also 'The Fourth Dimension in Cinema', vol. 1, pp. 181–94.

346. The reliance on this technique prolonged the process of film-making and was a contributing factor to the problems E experienced with *Que viva México* and *Bezhin Meadow*.

347. See 'The Fourth Dimension in Cinema', vol. 1, pp. 181–94.

348. 'Ne tsvetnoe, a tsvetovoe' [Not Coloured, but of Colour'], *Kino*, no. 24, May 1940. See also above, pp. 232–3.

349. See the discussion of the search for a common denominator for sound and image in: 'An Unexpected Juncture', 'Beyond the Shot' and 'The Fourth Dimension in Cinema', vol. 1, pp. 115–22, 138–50, 185–6.

350. Lanz, *The Physical Basis of Rime*, p. 271.

351. See 'The Fourth Dimension in Cinema', vol. 1, pp. 181–94.

352. 'Programma prepodavaniya teorii i praktiki kinorezhissury' [A Programme for Teaching the Theory and Practice of Direction], *Iskusstvo kino*, no. 4, April 1936, p. 57. Cf. n. 231 above. E is referring to the Third Course (5th semester), Part 2 'The Special Elements of Film Production', Section B 'Special Section', Paragraph 3 'Montage', which reads as follows:

> Types of montage in their kinetic order:
> (a) metric;
> (b) rhythmic;
> (c) tonal (melodic);
> (d) overtonal;
> (e) intellectual, as a new quality in the line of development of the overtonal towards semantic overtones.
> The stage-by-stage dependence of the separate types of montage and their contrapuntal co-presence.

353. Karl von Eckartshausen (1752–1803), author of *Aufschlüsse zur Magie aus geprüften Erfahrungen über verborgene philosophische Wissenschaften und verdeckte Geheimnisse der Natur* [Explanations of Magic from Proven Experiments on Concealed Philosophical Knowledge and the Hidden Secrets of Nature] (2nd edn, Munich, 1791), vol. 1, pp. 336–9. The Russian translation *Klyuch k tainstvam natury* [The Key to Nature's Secrets] was published in St Petersburg in 1804.

354. See n. 266.

355. René Ghil, pseudonym of Belgian-born French poet, René Gilbert (1862–1925). In his *Traité du verbe* [Treatise on the Verb] (1886) he tried to put into practice the system of correlation between sound and colour that had been suggested by Rimbaud. This quotation is from *En méthode à l'œuvre* [An approach to the work], first published in 1891; *Œuvres complètes* [Complete Works] (Paris, 1938), vol. 3, p. 239.

356. Hermann von Helmholtz (1821–94), German specialist in the physiology of sight and hearing. E is referring to his *Die Lehre von den Tonempfindungen* [The Theory of Sound Perceptions].

357. Lanz, *The Physical Basis of Rime*, pp. 167–8.

358. Lafcadio Hearn, English writer and author of numerous books on Japan and the Far East. Basil Hall Chamberlain also wrote of Japan: with W.B. Mason, he wrote *A Handbook for Travellers in Japan (including Formosa)* (London, 1891). The correspondence between Hearn and Chamberlain is partially reproduced in *More Letters from Basil Hall Chamberlain to Lafcadio Hearn* (Tokyo, 1937). The reference here is to *The Japanese Letters of Lafcadio Hearn* (E. Bisland ed.) (London, 1910).

359. J.A. Symonds, *In the Key of Blue* (London, 1893).

360. See 'An Unexpected Juncture' and 'Beyond the Shot', vol. 1, pp. 115–22, 138–50.

361. *Herbst und Frühling des Lü-Bu-We* [The Autumn and Spring of Lu-Bu-Wei] (Jena, 1926), pp. 463–4.

362. R. Guilleré, 'Il n'y a plus de perspectives' [No More Perspectives], *Cahier bleu*, no. 4, 1933.

363. See n. 62.

364. Georgi B. Yakulov (1884–1928), painter and stage designer. His sets for *Measure for Measure* date from 1919.

365. Yuri P. Annenkov (1890–1974), Russian painter and set designer, associated with Nikolai N. Evreinov (1879–1953); designed the sets for the latter's re-enactment of *The Storming of the Winter Palace* (1920); emigrated in 1924.

366. El Greco [the Greek] was the pseudonym of the painter Domenikos Theotoko-poulos (1541–1614).

367. See n. 64.

368. 'Cante hondo' (literally, deep song) is a form of popular Spanish song with a repetitive note structure and unusual cadences.

369. Manuel de Falla (1876–1946), the Spanish composer, published this booklet to accompany the festival of 'cante hondo' that he organised in Granada in 1922: *El 'Cante Jondo'. (Canto primitivo andaluz)* ['Canto Hondo'. (Primitive Andalusian Song)].

370. M. Legendre and A. Hartmann, *Domenico Theotocopouli dit El Greco* [Domenico Theotokopoulos, Known as El Greco] (Paris, 1937), pp. 16, 26, 27. The other references are to: A.M. Barrès, *Greco, ou le secret de Tolède* (Greco or the Secret of Toledo) (Paris, 1912); A.J. Meier-Graefe, *The Spanish Journey* (London, 1926); J.F. Willumsen, *La Jeunesse du peintre El Greco. Essai sur la transformation de l'artiste byzantin en peintre européen* [The Youth of the Painter El Greco. An Essay on the Transformation of a Byzantine Artist into a European Painter] (2 vols, Paris, 1927). The other reference is probably to the work of Moriz Carrière, although no single work has been identified.

371. V.V. Yastrebtsev, *Moi vospominaniya o N.A. Rimskom-Korsakove* [My Reminis-cences of N.A. Rimsky-Korsakov] (Petrograd, 1917), vol. 1, pp. 104–5; entry for 8 April 1893. Rimsky-Korsakov's 'magic opera-ballet' *Mlada* was first performed in 1892.

372. James McNeill Whistler (1834–1903), American artist, who gave many of his landscapes musical titles to emphasise his rejection of the dominance of the subject in Victorian painting.

373. Arnold Böcklin (1827–1901) was a Swiss landscape painter. The quotation is from M. Schlesinger, *Geschichte des Symbols. Ein Versuch* [The History of Symbol. An Essay] (Berlin, 1912), p. 376. Schlesinger is referring to: G. Floerke, *Zehn Jahre mit Böcklin* [Ten Years with Böcklin] (Munich, 1901).

374. Friedrich Novalis (1772–1801), German Romantic poet.

375. François Coppet (1842–1908), 'Ballade', cited in R. Etiemble, 'Le sonnet des voyelles' [The Sonnet of Vowels], *Revue de littérature comparée*, April-June 1939.

376. Wassily Kandinsky (1866–1944), Russian-born abstract artist, one of the founders of 'Der blaue Reiter' group in Munich in 1911.
377. *Der blaue Reiter* [The Blue Rider] (Munich, 1912).
378. P. Gauguin, 'Notes éparses. Genèse d'un tableau' [Rough Notes. The Genesis of a Picture], cited in J. de Rotonchamp, *Paul Gauguin, 1848–1903* (Paris, 1903). E is quoting from the German edition (Weimar, 1906), pp. 218–20.
379. Yuri M. Bondi (1889–1926), Russian theatre designer and director who worked with Meyerhold on this production in 1912.
380. Anna A. Akhmatova (pseudonym of Anna Gorenko) (1888–1966), Russian poet. The references that follow are from the *Biblioteka poeta* edition: V.M. Zhirmunskii (ed.), *Anna Akhmatova. Stikhotvoreniya i poemy* [Anna Akhmatova. Verses and Poems] (Leningrad, 1976). The first quotation is the second line of the second stanza of the poem beginning 'Podoshla' [She approached] (p. 99), written in 1914 and forming part of the *Belaya staya* [White Flock] cycle, first published in Petrograd in 1917.
381. The last stanza of the poem 'Pesnya poslednei vstrechi' [A Song of a Final Meeting], p. 30. Both this and the next poem cited were written in February 1911 and form part of the cycle known as *Vecher* [Evening], Akhmatova's first book of poems published in St Petersburg in 1912.
382. The second stanza of the poem beginning 'Dver' poluotkryta' [The Door Is Half-Open], p. 29. Also translated in A. Akhmatova, *Selected Poems* (R. McKane trans.) (Harmondsworth, 1969), p. 19.
383. The opening stanza ('Vizhu vytsvetshii flag nad tamozhnei') of a poem (p. 71) written in the autumn of 1913 and forming part of the third section of the cycle entitled *Chëtki* [Rosary], first published in St Petersburg in 1914.
384. The opening stanza ('Ot lyubvi tvoei zagadochnoy') of the third poem (p. 152) in the cycle *Chërnyi son* [Black Dream], written in July 1918 and first published separately in the same year.
385. See above, n. 176.
386. Not traced.
387. *Rembrandt* (Great Britain, 1937), directed by Alexander Korda.
388. F. Portal, *Des couleurs symboliques dans l'antiquité, le moyen-âge et les temps modernes* [Symbolic Colours in Antiquity, the Middle Ages and the Present Day] (Paris, 1938).
389. G.F. Creuzer, *Symbolik und Mythologie der altern Völker* [The Symbolism and Mythology of Ancient Peoples] (Leipzig and Darmstadt, 1810–23). E is here quoting from the French translation, *Religions de l'antiquité* [Religions of Antiquity] (4 vols, Paris, 1825–51), vol. 2, p. 660.
390. Nikolai Ya. Marr (1864–1934), Russian Orientalist and philologist.
391. See n. 338. The references that follow are from: S. Yesenin, *Sobranie sochinenii v pyati tomakh* [Collected Works in Five Volumes], vol. 2 (Moscow, 1961). The first quotation is the opening stanza ('Ne rugaites'!') of a poem written in 1922 and first published in 1923; p. 117.
392. The penultimate stanzas from a poem beginning 'Gody molodye s zabubënnoi slavoi' [Youthful years of dissolute renown], written and published in 1924; ibid., p. 154.
393. The fourth stanza of a poem beginning 'Ya ustalym takim eschë ne byl' [I wasn't yet as tired], probably written in 1923 and first published in 1924; ibid., p. 151.
394. The second stanza of a poem beginning 'Dorogaya, syadem ryadom' [Let's sit together, dear], written and published in 1923; ibid., p. 139.
395. The opening stanza of a poem written and published in 1922; ibid., p. 113.
396. The second stanza of the poem 'Pesn' o khlebe' [Song about Bread], written and published in 1921; ibid., p. 105.
397. The opening stanza of a poem probably written in 1923 and published the following year; ibid., p. 143.

398. The third stanza of a poem beginning 'Mne grustno na tebya smotret' [Looking at you makes me sad], probably written in 1923; ibid., p. 141.

399. The opening lines of a poem written and published in 1923; ibid., p. 123.

400. C. Villette, *'Parisismen': Alphabetisch geordnete Sammlung der eigenartigen Ausdrücke des Pariser Argot* [Parisisms: An Alphabetically Arranged Collection of the Peculiar Expressions in Parisian Argot] (1912), p. 210.

401. E. Partridge, *A Dictionary of Slang and Unconventional English* (London, 1937).

402. *Transatlantic Merry-go-Round* (USA, 1934), directed by Ben Stoloff.

403. H. Baumann, *Londinismen – Slang und Cant. Alphabetisch geordnete Sammlung der eigenartigen Ausdruckweisen der Londoner Volkssprache* [Londonisms – Slang and Cant. An Alphabetically Arranged Collection of the Peculiar Expressions in London Colloquial Language] (Berlin, 1887).

404. Pierre Mac Orlan, pseudonym of Pierre Dumarchais (1882–1970), French writer of adventure stories with a legendary or epic character.

405. Emanuel Swedenborg (1688–1772), Swedish naturalist, mystic and philosopher who argued that the Bible was the immediate word of God.

406. Portal, *Des couleurs symboliques* [Symbolic Colours], p. 132.

407. The correspondence between Denis Diderot (1713–84) and Sophie Volland lasted many years and covered a wide range of topics. This quotation is from a letter dated 20 October 1760. See *Diderot's Letters to Sophie Volland* (P. France ed. and trans.) (London, 1972), pp. 85–6.

408. The reference is to Part One of *The Golden Bough* entitled *The Magic Art and the Evolution of Kings*, vol. 1, ch. 3, 'Sympathetic Magic', section 2, 'Homeopathic or Imitative Magic', the subsection on homeopathic treatment of jaundice.

409. M. Gorky, 'Pol' Verlen i dekadenty' [Paul Verlaine and the Decadents], *Samarskaya gazeta*, nos 81, 85, 1896.

410. Cardinal Edouard de Rohan (1734–1803) was the anti-hero of the Affair of the Diamond Necklace in 1785. Hoping to regain favour at Court, he allowed himself to be duped into purchasing for 1,600,000 livres a necklace for Queen Marie-Antoinette, without her authority and without funds of his own. He was imprisoned in the Bastille and tried for fraud. Although acquitted, he was exiled in disgrace from the Court, thus becoming a martyr in the eyes of the Queen's enemies and the critics of royal absolutism. The Affair of the Diamond Necklace came to symbolise the corruption and decadence of the ancien régime.

411. Alfred Binet (1857–1912), psychologist and physiologist regarded as the father of French experimental psychology. The quotation is from his 'Recherches sur les altérations de la conscience chez les hystériques' [Research on Changes in Consciousness among Hysterics], *Revue philosophique*, Paris, 1889.

412. Charles Féré (1852–1907), French doctor who specialised in nervous diseases. The quotation is from 'Sensation et mouvement' [Feeling and Movement], *Revue philosophique*, 1886.

413. Max Nordau (1849–1923), German writer. The quotation is from *Degeneration* [*Entartung*] (London, 1898), Book 1, 'Fin-de-siècle', ch. 2, 'The Symptoms', p. 29. Both the previous references to Binet and Féré come from footnotes in *Degeneration*, pp. 28–9.

414. Filipp A. Malyavin (1869–1939), Russian painter who specialised in portraits of brightly clad peasant women. E is referring to the picture *The Whirlwind*, which hangs in the Tretyakov Gallery in Moscow.

415. See n. 267.

416. Giovanni da Udine (1487–1564) (Italian painter who collaborated with Raphael), *L'Art et le geste* [Art and Gesture] (Paris, 1910), p. 60 of the Russian translation.

417. 'The Fourth Dimension in Cinema', vol. 1, p. 182.

418. Cf. n. 262 above.

419. Pyotr A. Pavlenko (1899–1951), Russian writer and co-author of the script for

Alexander Nevsky. His novel *Na vostoke* [In the East] was published in 1936 and filmed as *Na dal'nem vostoke* [In the Far East] in 1937. This translation is by Michael Glenny. The whole novel has been translated by Stephen Garry, *Red Planes Fly East* (New York, 1938); cf. pp. 256–7.

420. See Marshall (trans.) *Nonindifferent Nature*, pp. 3–37.

421. A Schweitzer, *J.S. Bach* (London, 1911), vol. 2, ch. 23, 'The Musical Language of the Cantatas'. The reference is to the very end of the section on 'Pictorial Themes', 1923 edn, p. 86.

422. L. Tolstoy, *War and Peace*, book 6, ch. 13.

423. At this point in the manuscript there follows a text containing examples from the works of the Russian fabulist Ivan Krylov and from Lion Feuchtwanger's novel *The False Nero*. This text was not included in the final redaction.

424. Cf. J. Fennell (ed.), *Pushkin* (Harmondsworth, 1964), p. 242.

425. In French in the original.

426. In French in the original.

427. E is referring to Gogol's article 'Poslednii den' Pompei (Kartina Bryulova)' [The Last Day of Pompeii (Bryulov's Picture)], *Polnoe sobranie sochinenii* [Complete Collected Works], vol. 8 (Moscow, 1952), p. 111.

428. Both Vladimir Ye. Makovsky (1846–1920) and Vasili G. Perov (1833–1882) were members of the Wanderers group and both paintings date from 1881 and hang in the Tretyakov Gallery.

429. See n. 86.

430. See n. 95.

431. At this point in Eisenstein's MS there follows a passage on 'the presentation of the three elements' in Japanese aesthetics, with quotations from a number of sources; this passage was not included in the final redaction.

432. *Correspondence of Wagner and Liszt* (New York, 1897), vol. 1, letter dated 16 August 1853.

Index

This index covers the main text and important references in the endnotes, but not the Introduction. The examples that Eisenstein chooses to illustrate his theoretical arguments are grouped together under 'Eisenstein, examples'. Elsewhere, as in the endnotes, Eisenstein is referred to as E. Film titles are followed by the name of the director.